CUSTOM TEXTBOOK
ORGANISATIONS AND MANAGEMENT
ULMS151

ORGANISATIONS AND MANAGEMENT

ULMS151

Compiled for

DANE ANDERTON
GARY BROWN
CLAIRE MCKENZIE

palgrave
macmillan

First published 2013 by
PALGRAVE MACMILLAN

Palgrave Macmillan in the UK is an imprint of Macmillan Publishers Limited, registered in England, company number 785998, of Houndmills, Basingstoke, Hampshire RG21 6XS.

Palgrave Macmillan in the US is a division of St Martin's Press LLC, 175 Fifth Avenue, New York, NY 10010.

Palgrave Macmillan is the global academic imprint of the above companies and has companies and representatives throughout the world.

Palgrave® and Macmillan® are registered trademarks in the United States, the United Kingdom, Europe and other countries.

ISBN 978–1–137–39579–5

This book is printed on paper suitable for recycling and made from fully managed and sustained forest sources. Logging, pulping and manufacturing processes are expected to conform to the environmental regulations of the country of origin.

A catalogue record for this book is available from the British Library.

A catalog record for this book is available from the Library of Congress.

Typeset by MPS Limited, Chennai, India.

CONTENTS

LIST OF FIGURES

LIST OF TABLES

SOURCES

This custom publication has been compiled for use in the **University of Liverpool.** The chapters included are reproduced from the following works:

Chapter 1 from **JEANNE GODFREY:** *HOW TO USE YOUR READING IN YOUR ESSAYS 2ND EDITION* © JEANNE GODFREY 2009, 2013

Chapter 2 from **JOHN BRATTON, PETER SAWCHUK, CAROLYN FORSHAW, MILITZA CALLINAN AND MARTIN CORBETT:** *WORK AND ORGANIZATIONAL BEHAVIOUR 2ND EDITION* © JOHN BRATTON 2007, 2010

Chapter 3 from **MIKE NOON, PAUL BLYTON AND KEVIN MORRELL:** *THE REALITIES OF WORK 4TH EDITION* © MIKE NOON, PAUL BLYTON AND KEVIN MORRELL 1997, 2002, 2007, 2013

Chapter 4 from **JOHN BRATTON, PETER SAWCHUK, CAROLYN FORSHAW, MILITZA CALLINAN AND MARTIN CORBETT:** *WORK AND ORGANIZATIONAL BEHAVIOUR 2ND EDITION* © JOHN BRATTON 2007, 2010

Chapter 5 from **PAUL THOMPSON AND DAVID MCHUGH:** *WORK ORGANISATIONS 4TH EDITION* © PAUL THOMPSON AND DAVID MCHUGH 1990, 1995, 2002, 2009

Chapter 6 from **JOHN BRATTON, PETER SAWCHUK, CAROLYN FORSHAW, MILITZA CALLINAN AND MARTIN CORBETT:** *WORK AND ORGANIZATIONAL BEHAVIOUR 2ND EDITION* © JOHN BRATTON 2007, 2010

Chapter 7 from **JOHN BRATTON, PETER SAWCHUK, CAROLYN FORSHAW, MILITZA CALLINAN AND MARTIN CORBETT:** *WORK AND ORGANIZATIONAL BEHAVIOUR 2ND EDITION* © JOHN BRATTON 2007, 2010

Chapter 8 from **ALISON PULLEN, NIC BEECH AND DAVID SIMS:** *EXPLORING IDENTITY* © TONY WATSON 2007

Chapter 9 from **STEPHEN LINSTEAD, LIZ FULOP AND SIMON LILLEY:** *MANAGING AND ORGANIZATION 2ND EDITION* © STEPHEN LINSTEAD 2004, 2009

Chapter 10 from **PAUL BURNS:** *ENTREPRENEURSHIP AND SMALL BUSINESS 3RD EDITION* © PAUL BURNS 2001, 2007, 2011

INTRODUCTION

This custom textbook is the result of collaboration with academic publisher *Palgrave Macmillan*. Its purpose is to help you navigate the rough, often unpredictable terrain of organisations. You will find that key terms such as *management*, *organisation*, *employee* and *sector* are understood and analysed in many contrasting ways in the academic literature, not least because the people occupying workplace environments have contrasting experiences of them. How we talk about these things also reflects our own particular position at work. For example, managers often describe organisations in ways that contrast employee perspectives, emphasising the profit imperative or when attempting to garner support for their arguments. It might be supposed, therefore, that managers themselves share similar perspectives to other managers, but close analysis actually reveals considerable variation in views among this group. We make this point at the outset to encourage you to acknowledge and explore the complexity of organisations and as a prelude to investigating, querying and, ultimately, critiquing all that you read. This is necessary because, although organisational leaders and management gurus often offer them to us, there are no ready-made, indisputable answers to the major questions about organisations and their managements. Aspects of psychology, political undercurrents and cultural norms, among other things, conspire to give organisations their particular look and feel. They are also changeable and dynamic systems with their own ecology, never settling in one place or reaching an endpoint. Thus, whilst it is understandable that individuals seek wide-ranging explanations for organisational behaviour, we have yet to come up with an all-encompassing, irrefutable theory of it.

We want the text and the ideas within to travel with you beyond ULMS151. Subsequent management-related modules examine many of the themes we address, and so the chapters should prove valuable resources as you progress. Many of the arguments will be unfamiliar at this early stage, as will some of the terminology used. Please do not recoil at the prospect of reading and deciphering the digest of academic discourse. The underpinning ideas relate directly to personal experiences in contemporary workplaces and, therefore, are much more familiar and easier to grasp than it may appear initially. This will be true of many other aspects of your academic study. Take up the challenge and persevere!

CHAPTER OVERVIEW

The first chapter (**Chapter 1**) provides a step-by-step guide to conducting scholarship to degree-level standard. It provides succinct guidance on writing academically, undertaking good quality literature reviews and analysing academic material in detail. The first of the specific subject content chapters (**Chapter 2**) introduces foundational ideas on the nature of work and organisation. How we frame our perspectives on contemporary organisations is historically located and can be traced to arguments by influential thinkers like Emile Durkheim, Max Weber and Karl Marx. This chapter provides an overview of the 'big ideas' generated by these figures and relates them to the theories of work and management to be discussed in greater detail during the module.

The remaining chapters follow a linear structure, taking as their starting point the development of scientific management in the early 20th century. Based on experiments by engineer F.W. Taylor, scientific management precipitated the development of modern corporations by emphasising the need for efficiency and predictability in work processes to speed up production and address 'systematic soldiering' among workers (**Chapter 3**). The same chapter explains how the Ford Motor Company, under the leadership of Henry Ford, advocated the ethos of scientific management. Believing in the need for maximum efficiency, Ford incorporated division of labour, work specialisation and standardised tasks into many aspects of car production. However, it also extended Taylor's principles by implementing the moving, mechanical *assembly line* whereby constituent components of motor vehicles were transported to workers at a pace decided by management – a keystone development in *mass production*. The previous approach, *craft production*, saw skilled assemblers build vehicles at a speed largely determined by them. Although profound in its impact on contemporary organisations, this approach was criticised for offering employees simple (or *atomised*) repetitive tasks that gave them little scope for intellectual or social engagement.

As organisations accumulated increased resources and sought to expand in size, bureaucratic mechanisms became increasingly important. **Chapter 4** explains the value of bureaucracy in providing a sense of order within organisations, establishing and enforcing agreed routines for carrying out operations. Yet, and as we hear regularly in political discourse, what aids effective decision-making, allowing orderliness, can lead to dysfunction and cause confusion. The existence of 'too much paperwork', 'red tape', 'too many bureaucrats', is said to slow decision-making and put a strain on much-needed resources – that is, bureaucracy both enables and constrains. Ergo, it is argued that other forms of organisational design should be introduced to accommodate the many demands of a post-modern age. The rationality associated with scientific management, Fordism and bureaucracy is often juxtaposed with human relations theory (**Chapter 5**). Based on the work of Elton Mayo and colleagues, human relations theory was presented as alternative to rational techniques placing greater emphasis on the social dimensions of work as a means of achieving maximum utilisation of (particularly human) resources. This formulation established a correlation between 'informal' behaviour, productivity and profitability, rejected the image of worker as 'economic animal' and favoured instead one of worker as 'social man'.

This takes us tidily to **Chapter 6** on the social nature of work. Perceiving organisations as social and cultural entities opened up new trajectories for management thought. As greater consideration was given to informal aspects of work, organisations explored group work and self-managed teams as mechanisms for addressing industrial problems. Drawing parallels with human relations theory, the philosophy here was that appropriately composed teams can achieve more together than apart – an assumption that continues to underpin many gradations of contemporary management practice (**Chapter 7**). More recently, and retaining the interest in informal dimensions of work, organisations have been investigating employee identity as a vehicle for achieving their aims (**Chapter 8**). In basic terms, how we perceive ourselves and how others perceive us has been shown to have a considerable bearing on our level of engagement at work. Being viewed as a 'cog in a machine', for instance, may undermine self-esteem and induce compliance rather than fulsome commitment to work practice. In contrast, 'valued assets' making an important contribution to organisational success may be more willing to exert effort during work time. Whatever policy initiative or strategy we strive to implement in organisations, workplace cultures will also have a bearing on their success or failure. This was recognised in the early 1980s when financially successful multi-national organisations were said to benefit from 'strong' corporate cultures (**Chapter 9**), leading managers and academics to show widespread interest in culture management with some believing that culture could be managed from above and others suggesting that organisational cultures are unpredictable and difficult to manage.

Another significant development, and one that informs popular cultural representations of management, is the entrepreneurial ethos in organisations. **Chapter 10** explores entrepreneurship in smaller organisations and the benefits of entrepreneurial thinking. Moving our focus from the larger entities is important because small- and medium-sized enterprises are integral to economic development but, just as significantly, larger organisations have sought to emulate their smaller counterparts' capacity for flexibility, ingenuity and creativity. If we compare contemporary views on organisation and management with those expressed by theorists such as F.W. Taylor, Elton Mayo and Henri Fayol, there is much less concern with capturing the undiluted essence of fixed or stable organisations and greater recognition of their flexibility as living, growing and changing phenomena. This has considerable implications for how we think about and practise work and management and raises questions such as 'Does greater fluidity increase insecurity and community fragmentation?'

The shift in emphasis towards social, cultural and entrepreneurial dimensions of organisation does not mean that rational approaches have been jettisoned. Heavy bureaucracy and the increased use of technology at work in some settings have led others to conclude that close surveillance of employees is the hallmark of work processes in the 21st century (**Chapter 11**). Managers are encouraged to adopt employee and customer-monitoring systems such that overt and covert surveillance techniques are an increasingly significant component of the management toolkit.

Whilst there is linearity to the structure of the chapters, we do not mean to imply that developments in organisation and management are quite so smooth. Scientific management was subject to sustained critique but it remains with us, informing many aspects of organisation in current times, as even the most progressive, humanistic organisations retain principles such as standardisation, task fragmentation and division of labour. Similarly, whilst the configuration may have changed, moving assembly line technologies persist in factory-based manufacturing.

USING THE BOOK

We stress that organisations are intricate entities and, as such, no theoretical or practical argument can explain entirely their actions. Likewise, the chapters in this custom text do not cover all aspects of the learning necessary to understanding them. You should also be aware that lecture material does not follow verbatim the content of the chapters, if for no other reason than to maintain your interest. Lectures cover a wider range of themes, some of which may be added on an ad hoc basis, providing enhanced detail and using illustrative examples of organisational practice to aid your learning. Hence, we dip in and out of the book, drawing from relevant aspects when necessary but, sometimes, not referring to the book at all. We would ask, therefore, that you regard each chapter as a platform upon which to build knowledge rather than as endpoints to learning. This means that you need to read beyond the text and any supplementary materials we provide, engaging in additional, self-directed study. There are many resources available to assist you here, including the supply of hard copies of books and journals in the library, as well as electronic journals, e-books, trade publications and government reports (online via the library catalogue). It is also very valuable to reflect continually on your personal experience, relating this to the ideas encountered.

We hope you really enjoy both the custom text and the ULMS151 module!
Dane Anderton
Gary Brown
Claire McKenzie

Chapter

1

HOW TO USE READING IN YOUR ESSAYS

INTRODUCTION TO THIS CHAPTER: KEY POINTS FOR READING AT UNIVERSITY

The types of books and articles you read at university will probably be different from those you used at school or college. Why and how you read at university will also be different, requiring more independence from you in deciding what to read, higher levels of concentration and more questioning of the material. Finally, the way in which reading is used in academic essays makes this type of writing quite different from work you may have done up to now.

This chapter gives you:

o important information and strategies to take you through the process of reading and of using this reading in your essays in the form of quotation, paraphrase or summary;

o real academic articles, real student writing and an excellent short student essay to demonstrate each stage of the process; short practice exercises on all of the points covered.

It is best to go through each section of this chapter in order, but you can also read and reread different sections as and when you need.

Five key points to remember about reading

o A common reason why students struggle with reading at university is simply that they do not give enough time to it, and so don't enjoy it because of the stress of trying to fit too much reading into too little time. Reading and thinking is where most of your learning and creativity will happen, so take it seriously and make reading a priority in your time management schedule.

o Identify your purpose for reading a book or article and decide what it is you want to learn from it, and then be flexible in how you read, matching your reading method to your reading purpose. You may need to read some articles from start to finish, but for other texts you may only need to scan briefly or read just one particular paragraph in detail.

o Try to engage with the material rather than just reading the words on the page. This means being (or becoming) interested in what you are reading, and thinking about what the author is doing and trying to say. This will greatly improve your understanding and will further increase your interest in the subject.

o Some of the books and articles you need to read may seem complex, formal and difficult to understand at first. Everyone approaches reading in a slightly different way and it may take a little time to build up your 'reading muscles' and to discover what works best for you. Start by reading short articles or short sections before tackling longer ones; as with everything else, you will improve with practice. Bear in mind that most people need to re-read complex texts, and that the struggle to understand is a normal part of taking in new information.

o Reading will also help improve your writing skills by increasing your knowledge of new words and your awareness of how to structure a piece of written work. Bear in mind however, that not everything you read will be well written.

1.1   HOW DO YOU DECIDE WHAT TO READ?

It seems obvious that for a good essay you need good sources, but what exactly *is* a 'good' source? When looking for sources, don't be tempted to just type your essay title straight into an online search engine in the hope that something useful will come up. Knowing what types of sources are suitable for university work, and spending some time thinking about what information you need before you start searching, will save you a great deal of time and will result in a much better piece of work. This section gives you the key steps and information you need for finding the best sources for your essay.

FIVE STEPS FOR DECIDING WHAT TO READ

Step 1   Think: what question do you want to answer?

Do some thinking before you start searching for sources. Check that you really understand the title of your essay. For example, does the title ask you to develop an argument, give your opinion, give examples, or some of these things together? Does it ask for definitions, information on a process, advantages and disadvantages or for different views on an issue?

Rewrite the title in your own words - this will really help you to understand it. For example, the business ethics essay title could be rewritten as: 'Give a brief overview of what business ethics is and then argue that business ethics either is or is not important, giving your reasons for your view'.

Step 2   Think: what do you already know about the topic and what ideas do you already have?

Think (and perhaps write down) what you already know and think about the essay question. For the business ethics essay, you would ask yourself what *you* think business ethics is and whether *you* think it is important. You will probably also have already have done some reading and discussion on the essay topic during your course, so think about what you have already read that is relevant.

Step 3   Think: what types of source will you need?

Make notes on any suggested reading and other instructions about sources your tutor has given you. Think about what types of sources you will need to answer your essay title.

For example, which of the following will you need?

- an introductory textbook to give you some initial ideas;
- chapters in more advanced textbooks;
- important major works on the topic;
- original data from experiments or other research;
- recent academic journal articles on new developments or ideas on the topic;
- non-expert or public opinion on the issue.

For the business ethics essay, after thinking about the essay title, the student decided to look in some current academic textbooks for definitions of business ethics. He also read some relevant journal articles and reports by key authors for their views on the importance of business ethics, and he also decided to look at some company websites to find out what businesses themselves say about business ethics.

Step 4   Do a first search

Decide how good you want your essay to be and how much time and effort you are willing to give to finding appropriate sources. Then use your thoughts on the types of sources you need to start searching. Looking for sources is called a literature search, and it is a vital part of academic research. As you search, keep checking that your sources are relevant, specific and reliable (see below).

Content pages and chapter headings of books and journal article abstracts can help you to decide whether a source is relevant. Reading the introduction and conclusion of a book chapter or journal article is also a quick way of finding out whether a source will be useful. The reference list at the end of one book or article may provide you with details of further useful sources.

It is important at this stage to write down the precise details of each source you think you might use (author, date, title, journal/publisher) and also where and how you found it. You may not think this is important but you will be surprised how useful this information is, and remember that for academic work, *who* wrote something is as important as what they wrote about.

Is it better to use the library or to do your own online search?

With so much material available online, some students don't go near their university library until the end of their second year or later. This is a real shame because your library can help you with some of the very problems that arise from information overload. Don't make the mistake of thinking that the internet is just like a big online library - it isn't!

Searching for sources using the university library

Advantages

- Material has already been pre-selected by lecturers and library staff for its importance, relevance, reliability and academic quality.
- The intranet and library catalogue material (again, chosen by your tutors/library) are more likely to be reliable than material from the internet.
- Library staff are there to help you with selecting and finding texts.
- Has an online catalogue system that contains all its resources. Will also give you free access to other academic online databases.
- You can use the 'sort' facility of the library catalogue to put sources in order of publication.
- Has primary printed material and back copies of journals, newspapers and magazines that are not available online.
- Has specialist dictionaries, study guides and material written by your university not available online (e.g. advice on how to reference your work).
- Provides a quiet and comfortable environment in which to study, away from distractions.
- Has free Wi-Fi connection and use of DVDs
- Has free use of magazines and newspapers, dictionaries, encyclopaedias and other print material.
- Will probably have agreement with other libraries.

Disadvantages

○ The copies of a book or article may be out on loan (but you can reserve them!).

Searching for sources using the internet

Advantages

○ A huge number of sources are available.
○ 24 hour access every day of the year (although your library may also be open 24 hours a day).

Disadvantages

○ Search engines will often return a large number of returns and false matches, and so it can be hard to find the most relevant source.
○ It is sometimes difficult to find out who wrote something and whether the source is reliable and peer-reviewed.
○ A significant number of academic sources are not yet available online.
○ You often have to pay for downloads of complete books or articles.

Step 5   Think, sort and select your sources for detailed reading

When you have done your first search for sources, think again about what you will want to say in your essay and what you think your conclusion might be. This may change as you read more, but by now you should have some idea of how you want to answer the essay title.

You might need to do some general background reading on a topic, but most essay titles will ask for something specific, so try not to waste time by reading sources that are on the correct general topic but that are not specific enough. For the business ethics essay, you would not want to spend time reading about general business topics or about the meaning or history of ethics; you would need to focus specifically on *business* ethics. Even when you had found a book on business ethics, you would not need to read it all, just the chapters or sections which described what business ethics is and whether/why it is important.

Select your sources for more detailed reading and ask yourself the following questions about each source.

○ What type of source is it and who wrote it?
○ Is it relevant and specific to my essay?
○ Is it a reliable and academic source?
○ Why exactly am I going to read it?
○ Will it probably support my conclusion or give an opposing viewpoint?
○ Will I probably use it as an important piece of information or only as a minor source?

WHAT IS A RELIABLE SOURCE?

At university you are expected to make sure that your sources are reliable - that you can trust what they say. This usually means knowing who wrote something and that they are an authority on their topic. Reliable sources are usually those that have a named author, as this ensures that you reader knows who is accountable for the information given. Anonymous sources are much more likely to be of poor quality and/or contain incorrect information.

Up-to-date information will probably be more reliable than older information, so check when your source was written. You may want to read older sources that are key texts or to build up your knowledge, but for most topics you will also need current sources. Always check online sources to see when they were last updated and whether any links are active.

A reliable source is also one that gives information that is as accurate and complete as possible, rather than giving only the information that suits the author's purpose. Business and political organisations for example, may present information in a biased way. However, you need to think about what 'reliable' means for the type of information you need. If your essay is about public opinion in the media, then newspapers and television programmes would be a reliable source for this particular type of information. Equally, if you are writing about the views of different political organisations, their leaflets and websites would provide reliable information on what these views are, even though such information may not be balanced or reliable in the general sense of the word.

Are abstracts, reviews and summaries reliable sources?

These are all useful in different ways to give you a general idea of a text, but are not reliable sources in themselves as they do not give enough detail.

Article abstracts

Written by the author. Abstracts give an outline of the argument but not always the conclusion. You will not be able to evaluate the evidence, argument or conclusion of the article fully just by reading the abstract.

Summaries of a book or article

Could be written by the author or by someone else. A summary does not provide enough detail for you to be able to evaluate the evidence or argument of the source.

Article or book reviews

Always written by someone else. If the review has been written by an expert, it may give you useful information about the context of the source and other published work in the field. However, reviews are of no use for detailed information and may often be the biased, personal opinion of the reviewer.

Introduction and conclusion of a book or article

Written by the author. Reading just the introduction and conclusion of a source will give you a good idea of the main points and argument, but are not enough for you to evaluate the evidence or argument of the whole article, section or book.

Primary and secondary sources

Try to find the original (primary) source of information where possible, as something that is reported second or third hand may not be accurate and will be relatively unreliable. If you want data on the results of an experiment, try to read the original report rather than use an article that discusses the experiment second-hand (this is called a secondary source). Similarly, if you want to write about what an expert has said, read the actual book or article they have written rather than an article by another author who discusses what the expert has said. In reality, it will not always be possible or necessary to use only primary sources, but your tutor will usually expect you to read the key primary sources on a topic.

For the business ethics essay, the student found some primary material about companies from their websites. The textbooks and articles he used were partly primary material but they also discussed the previous work of other experts and so also acted as secondary sources of the material they used. Several of the articles mentioned a key text written by Albert Carr in 1968, so the student made sure that he found and read this primary source.

WHAT IS AN ACADEMIC SOURCE?

For most university assignments you will need to use information from sources that are not only reliable but are also regarded as academic. Academic sources are those written by authorities on a topic and which have usually been peer-reviewed. The peer-review process is when the book or article is sent by the publisher to other experts for checking and discussion before being published. Peer-reviewed sources are reliable, and are called academic (or reputable or authoritative) sources because they have been written by people who have attained a high standard of knowledge and research in their subject. Reliable and academic sources always have a named author or organisation. The academic community relies on knowing who wrote what, so that academics in a particular field can question, discuss and work with each other to build knowledge and develop ideas.

Non-academic sources

Below is a list of source types which are not academic and should not normally be used as sources for university essays:

- encyclopedias (including Wikipedia, which is an online encylopedia);
- college-level textbooks;
- newspapers (including long articles in quality papers such as *The Times* or *The Guardian*);
- magazines (including quality magazines such as *The Economist, Newsweek* and *New Scientist*);
- news or TV Channel websites (e.g. the BBC News);
- trade publications and company websites;
- publications and websites of charities, campaign or pressure groups;
- student theses or essays;
- pamphlets and brochures;
- blogs and wikis.

CHECKING THAT YOUR SOURCES ARE ACADEMIC

Books and journals on the library shelves and on your reading lists will usually be reliable and academic. However, you may want to find other sources, and you will need to make the effort to check that these are also reliable and academic. Books have normally gone through a peer-review process and so are usually reliable. Journals described as an academic journal, a peer-reviewed journal or a scholarly journal will be reliable and academic.

Check your online sources

Take particular care when you are using online sources. Your tutor will suggest suitable places to search online but it is your responsibility to check that your sources are reliable and academic. Wikipedia may be useful for some initial definitions and to give you links to other sources, but you should not use it as an actual source in your essay. This is because Wikipedia is a type of encyclopedia and is therefore only a basic summary and a secondary source. It is also anonymous and is not peer-reviewed and is therefore not reliable and not academic.

Words that should warn you that an online article is probably not academic are: *magazine, digest, personals, news, press release, correspondent, journalist, special report, company, classified, personals and advertisement.* However, don't be fooled into thinking that an online article is reliable and academic just because it is well-written and has an author's name, includes statistics and has in-text references. Even words such as *journal, research or volume/issue number, Society or Research Centre* are being increasingly used by unreliable and non-academic sources and websites. You need to check that the article is in fact from a peer-reviewed journal.

Check your online databases

Some online databases contain only peer-reviewed academic journals, but some of them (even one which describes itself as a 'research database') also contain newspapers, magazines and trade publications. Read the description of the database before you go into it - what does it say it contains? You may be able to google a database and get a description of its publications from the 'home' or 'about us' page.

Remember - always check whether an article is academically reliable, even if you have found it through a database.

Check your web search engines

Search engines such as Google, Yahoo and Bing are not usually appropriate or helpful when searching for academic sources. Google Scholar is better, as it contains only literature related to academic work, but you still need to be careful, as not all of this literature is peer-reviewed material - Google Scholar also includes some magazines and student theses.

Where to check a website

If you are not sure about the reliability of an online website, article, database or search engine, try to find its homepage and look under sections such as 'about us' 'contact us' 'editorial board' 'board of directors' 'information for authors' 'submission process' 'sponsors' 'funders' and 'partners'. These sections will give you information about who runs and supports the website, and whether its articles are peer-reviewed.

Practice 1 | would you use these sources?

Read the descriptions below of ten potential sources for five different essay titles. Do you think these sources are not reliable, reliable but not academic, or reliable *and* academic?

Sources for an essay on government support for people with disabilities

1 An article written in July 2006 in an online magazine called 'Mobility Now'. It has news, information and stories and is a magazine for people with disabilities. It is published by a leading charity organisation for people with disabilities.

Sources for an essay on youth crime

2 A recent online article on ASBOs written by Jane Smith, Home Correspondent. The URL is the online business section of a national quality newspaper.

Sources for an essay on recent developments in stem cell research

3 An online article on stem cells, published jointly by three authors in 2009. The article has a date, volume and issue number. The article on a website called 'Stem Cells'. This seems to be the title of the journal and at the bottom of the page there is a publisher: Beta Res Press. In the 'information for authors' section, the website tells authors how to track the progress of their article as it goes through the peer-review process.

4 Three different online science publications with similar titles that all look like magazines. They all have news sections, advertisements and jobs sections. They all have issue numbers and two of them also have volume numbers.

4a The first one has an 'about us' page that describes how its correspondents get their information by contacting leading scientists, reading scientific journals and websites and attending conferences.

4b The second magazine has the name of an organisation at the top of its website. On its 'about' page it describes the magazine as its journal, and states that it is a peer-reviewed general science journal. Another page states that its board of directors consists of university academics.

4c The third publication has no 'about us' information. Wikipedia describes the magazine as 'a well-respected publication despite not being peer-reviewed'.

Sources for an essay on developments in animal cloning

5 An article from a printed booklet titled 'Animal Cloning' published in 1999. There is a series of booklets, each with a volume and issue number. Each booklet contains a collection of short articles and newspaper and magazine clippings which give a simple introduction to issues and public debate on a scientific topic.

Sources for an essay on business ethics

6 A well-written report (which starts with an executive summary) on business ethics in companies. The website is run by an organisation called SEB - Social Ethics in Business. On the 'about' page, the organisation describes itself as part of a network of business organisations that focus on corporate responsibility. Its funders and partners are large national and international business foundations and development agencies.

7 An online article titled 'Business Ethics Guidelines'. The website address is 'Harold Jones International Company'.

8 An online article about McDonald's on a website called 'Centre for Management Research'. There is no 'about us' page but there is a homepage stating that the centre is involved in business research, management consulting and the development of case studies and training materials.

9 An online article on business ethics found on the website of the 'Centre for Business Ethics' of a university. On the centre's homepage it states that it helps businesses and the community, and offers workshops, conferences and lectures. It also states that the centre publishes its own *Journal of Ethics*.

10 An online article about a drinks company's activities in India. The article has no author but is well written and says 'for immediate release' at the top of the page. The website is titled as a 'Resource Centre'. The 'home /about us' page states that the centre has evolved from networks and discussions by activists, and describes itself as a platform for movements to publicise their demands and apply pressure to governments.

(The articles and websites are fictitious but are closely based on real examples).

1.2 HOW DO YOU UNDERSTAND AND QUESTION WHAT YOU READ?

When you sit down to read a book, chapter or article (we can call all of these *texts*) you should usually already know what type of text it is, who wrote it, that it is reliable and academic, and that it is relevant and specific to your essay question, so you will probably already have some idea about its content. The next step is to sit down and actually read it. This may sound straightforward, but the two most common reasons for students getting low marks for their essays are firstly, not reading carefully enough and/or not properly understanding the main point of the text, and secondly, not questioning what they read.

To use your sources effectively you need to really understand each text, and to read it with some questions in mind. This section gives you advice, examples and practice for doing so.

FIVE STEPS TO UNDERSTANDING AND QUESTIONING WHAT YOU READ

Step 1   Think: why are you reading?

Before you start reading a text, ask yourself *why* you are going to read it and what type of information you are looking for. For example;

- Are you looking for the answers to specific questions (e.g., what business ethics is or whether it is important)?
- Are you looking for general information on a point that you don't know much about and that will help you develop your own ideas and argument?
- Are you just looking for just a few basic facts, or do you need to read in detail so that you can follow the author's argument?
- Are you looking for evidence and examples as support for what you want to argue in your essay?
- Are you looking for points which you will then argue against?
- Look at who wrote the text and at the title and sub-titles, and make some predictions about what the text might say. It doesn't matter if your predictions turn out to be wrong - the important thing is to get engaged and interested in what you are going to read.

Step 2   Match your reading method to your reading purpose

In reality there simply isn't enough time to read everything from cover to cover, and you probably wouldn't want to anyway. We read different things in different ways, and you should apply the same principle to your academic reading – matching the *way* you read something to *why* you are reading it.

Three different ways to read

Scanning – looking over material quite quickly in order to pick out specific information
You might scan when you are browsing a database for texts on a specific topic, or you might scan a text for specific information. You might also scan when you are looking back over material to check something.

Gist reading – reading something fairly quickly in order to get the general idea
You might do this by reading just the headings, introduction and conclusion, or you might read for gist by going over the whole text fairly quickly. You might want to read for gist in order to decide whether to reject a text or to go back and read it in more detail. Reading for gist is also sometimes called 'skimming' or 'reading for breadth'.

Close reading – reading something in detail
You may want to read something in detail for several different reasons: as background reading; as a 'way in' to a new and difficult topic; to make sure you understand discussions of data, or to clearly understand the detail or argument. Close reading is also called 'reading for depth'.

It is important to remember that scanning or reading for gist is *not* a substitute for close reading. You will need to do a lot of detailed reading for academic work and the whole point of only scanning or gist reading some texts is to give you enough time for careful and close reading of the more important ones. You need, therefore, to develop the skill of recognising when it is appropriate to scan, when to read for gist and when to do close, careful and reflective reading.

Remember also to stay flexible about which reading method to use. You will often need to use combinations of methods, not just across different texts but also within a single text – zooming in and out. You might, for example, first quickly read over a whole text for gist, then read a section of it in detail, read some bits you find difficult again *very* carefully, and finally go back and scan the text for anything you think you may have missed.

You might also decide to change your reading approach as you read. After reading a quarter or a third of the text, ask yourself 'Is it giving me what I want? Am I learning and thinking as I read? Do I understand what I'm reading?' If the answer to these questions is no, then stop and think about why this is. It may be that you dived straight in with close reading and that it would be better to zoom out and get the general feel of the text first before going back to the detail. It may be that you need to find an easier text as a way in to the topic, or it may be that the material is not as relevant as you thought and that you should stop and move on to something else.

Step 3   Read actively

Read with your questions in mind. If you are only looking for one or two facts, you can just quickly scan the text for this information. Usually however, you will want to read in more detail. It may be better *not* to write anything down at this stage. Read the first section of the text (or all of a short text) and try to identify:

- what the key message of the text is;
- which parts of the text are main points, which are more minor points and which parts are examples of the points made;
- which parts of the text are facts, which are description and which are the author's opinion.

Try to identify what the author is trying to do overall. For example, are they giving information, putting forward an idea or theory, arguing and trying to persuade you of something, or a combination of these things? Finally, explain to yourself what the main point of the text is in your own words.

Step 4   Read, ask questions and evaluate

Read the text again and this time, question, evaluate and locate what the author says, using the prompts below (you can do this either in your head or on paper).

Question what the author says

o What assumptions does the author make?
o Do you think these assumptions are correct?
o Are the stages of the argument clear and logical?
o Does the conclusion follow from the evidence given?
o How does the author's argument and position fit in with what you already know?

Evaluate what the author says

o Are you persuaded by what the author says? Why/why not?
o If someone asked your opinion of the author's viewpoint, what would you say?
o Stand back and give the text an overall evaluation:
   what is the author's general way of thinking and position on the issue?
   what are they trying to do and how well do they do it?
   why do you think people would read this text, and do *you* think it is worth reading?
   how you think your background, experiences and viewpoint have affected what you think about the text?
o How has the text developed, modified or perhaps completely changed your thinking and therefore your argument?
o How will you use what the author says in your argument?

Step 5   Locate the author, other authors and yourself in the subject area

Locate the author in the subject area

o Find out who the author is and who they work for (Internet search engines are useful for this).
o Does the author's argument belong to a particular school of thought (e.g. behaviourism, Marxism, feminism)?
o How is the author's argument different or similar to other experts on the subject?

Locate other authors and yourself in the subject area

After reflecting on the specific text you have read, relate it to the other material you have read on the topic. As you do more reading, try to build up a mental picture of the 'location' of different authors.

o How do different texts you have read on the subject differ and how are they similar?
o Where does each author sit in the subject?
o Which authors agree with each other and which disagree?
o Are there any authors who have a unique position?

Think about where you now sit in the subject area, and which authors are closest to your own current position.

OPINION, CRITICAL ANALYSIS AND ARGUMENT

Students often think (or are told) that they should not give their opinions in an essay. It is true that you should not just give your personal opinion about something based only on your feelings. However, you *are* expected to give your opinion on an issue or essay question, provided that you have arrived at it through clear reasoning. Your reasons should be supported by evidence, and you should come to a conclusion that is persuasive because it follows logically from your reasoning and evidence. This sequence is called an argument. Arguing in academic study does not mean that you have to argue *against* something; an argument in the academic sense means a logical, structured and evidenced answer or conclusion to an issue or question.

As part of your argument, you will need to state whether you agree or disagree with the sources you discuss, and you won't be able to do this unless you have analysed (broken down), questioned, evaluated and located them, as shown above. The analysis involved in this process is sometimes called 'critical analysis', and the whole process is part of what is called a 'critical thinking approach'. As with the word *argument*, critical thinking in the academic sense does not mean that you can only say negative things about a text; indeed, you might want to be very positive about it. Critically analysing a text just means that you have asked yourself questions about what it says and formed your own views on it, based on clear reasoning rather than just personal experience or opinion.

Looking at an example of questioning, evaluating and locating a text

Below are three short sections from a long article the student read for his business ethics essay. Read the extracts to give you some idea of the authors' argument, and then look at the student's informal notes showing his thoughts from his critical analysis of the whole article.

A Model of Business Ethics

If one searches the literature, it appears that in the thirty years that business ethics has been a discipline in its own right a model of business ethics has not been proffered. This paper attempts to address this gap in the literature by proposing a model of business ethics that the authors hope will stimulate debate. This model is one that is predicated on the tenets of developed countries operating within a capitalist paradigm.

. . .

Socially responsible managers do the right thing because it is the right thing to do. It is the correct action to take and an action that society expects. Executives should "act ethically not out of fear of being caught when doing wrong. Rather, they should embrace ethical behaviour in business because of the freedom, self-confirmation, and success that it brings" (Thomas et al., 2004, p. 64).

. . . it is important to see business ethics as a highly dynamic and continuous process without an end. A process, however, that is predicated on the interrelationship between business and society where each one is interdependent and responsible together for the outcomes. Hoffman and Moore (1982) suggest that the pre-eminence of business ethics is because of a perceived failing, by the general community, of business to act for the general good of the society. They, therefore, suggest that the mutual obligations of business to the community and the community to business need to be restated.

Extracts from: Svensson, G. and Wood, G. (2008) 'A model of business ethics' *Journal of Business Ethics*, 77, pp. 303–322.

The student's thoughts on the Svensson and Wood article

Questioning

The authors look at businesses operating in a developed world, capitalist context. Presumably there are lots of businesses outside these types of context - how do they behave? Svensson and Wood also seem to assume that individuals and society always expect businesses to behave well and to trust them - I don't think they do. S and W also assume that there are socially responsible managers who want to do what is right - this might not be a correct assumption and they don't give any examples as evidence of this.

Evaluating

It's a good persuasive argument - seems to be well researched and expert. The article is very clear, well-structured and has detailed points. Their conclusion is supported by evidence, although this is mainly by reference to other authors - I will need to read a couple of these primary sources for myself.

Svensson and Wood argue strongly and clearly that business and society influence each other and, are dependent on each other, and have a responsibility to each other to behave ethically. However, they seem to ignore the fact that not everyone thinks we should trust businesses or that organisations should be responsible to society, and their argument seems to be based on some unproven assumptions. Also, S and W leave out some other simple models of business ethics I've read about and they don't use real business examples for some of their points - they only make references to primary sources that have the examples.

Still, I think that this article is solid enough to use as one of my main sources as evidence for what I think my conclusion will probably be, which is that businesses need to have good ethics and that business ethics is important both to businesses and to society. If anything, reading the article has developed my ideas by making me even more convinced that business ethics is crucial to us all in the wider social context.

Locating

Generally, this article fits in with what I think about the importance of business ethics. The article puts forward a theoretical model which they say has not been done before and that it is therefore doing something new, i.e. filling a gap in theory. They expect other academics to argue or disagree with their model of business ethics.

Svensson and Wood take a similar position to that of Esty, Collins, Shaw and Barry, and on the opposite side to Freidman, Wolf and Carr. I think that this article is an important one on the issue because it is relatively recent and seems to bring together in a detailed and persuasive way, what a lot of the other articles from the last 10 years have said.

Practice 2 | how would you question, evaluate and locate this article?

Below are sections from another article (the 1968 article by Albert Carr) the student used for his business ethics essay. Read the sections and then try to question, evaluate and locate the sections. You won't be able to evaluate and locate the article fully, but you should be able to do some critical analysis even without any specific business knowledge.

There is no one correct answer to this exercise, but you can compare your thoughts with those on p. 125.

Is business bluffing ethical?

We can learn a good deal about the nature of business by comparing it with poker. Poker's own brand of ethics is different from the ethical ideals of civilized human relationships as the game calls for distrust of the other fellow . . .

That most businessmen are not indifferent to ethics in their private lives, everyone will agree. My point is that in their office lives they cease to be private citizens; they become game players who must be guided by a somewhat different set of ethical standards . . .

The illusion that business can afford to be guided by ethics as conceived in private life is often fostered by speeches and articles containing such phrases as, 'It pays to be ethical', or, 'Sound ethics is good for business'.

Actually this is not an ethical position at all; it is a self-serving calculation in disguise. The speaker is really saying that in the long run a company can make more money if it does not antagonize competitors, suppliers, employees, and customers by squeezing them too hard. He is saying that overly sharp policies reduce ultimate gains. This is true, but it has nothing to do with ethics.

To be a winner, a man must play to win. This does not mean that he must be ruthless, cruel, harsh, or treacherous. On the contrary, the better his reputation for integrity, honesty, and decency, the better his chances of victory will be in the long run. But from time to time every businessman, like every poker player, is offered a choice between certain loss or bluffing within the legal rules of the game. If he is not resigned to losing, if he wants to rise in his company and industry, then in such a crisis he will bluff- and bluff hard.

Whatever the form of the bluff, it is an integral part of the game, and the executive who does not master its techniques is not likely to accumulate much money or power.

Adapted extracts from: Carr, A. Z. (1968) 'Is business bluffing ethical?' *Harvard Business Review*, 46(1), pp. 143–153.

1.3 WHAT SHOULD YOU WRITE DOWN?

WHY BOTHER MAKING NOTES?

The mental and physical process of making notes helps you to understand, think and reflect on what you have read. Making notes also helps you to formulate your own thoughts and ideas, making connections in your mind with other pieces of knowledge. If you don't make notes and just go straight from the text to writing your assignment, you will be bypassing key elements in the critical thinking process, and you will find it harder to develop your own independent understanding of the text. Importantly, making notes also helps you to start using your own words, which is essential for when you come to writing your essay. In summary, making notes helps you to control and exploit your sources rather than letting your sources control your essay.[1]

In addition, making notes (rather than just highlighting or cutting and pasting) will also:

- help you concentrate;
- keep you motivated by tracking and signalling progress;
- help you remember information more easily;
- give you your own unique record of the text;
- save you time when you come to write your assignment.

For all these reasons, students who make notes on their reading usually get better marks than those who go straight from reading a text to writing their essay. However, for your notes to be really effective, they need to be purposeful, clear, meaningful and of real use to you in the essay writing stage. This section gives you some advice, examples and practice to help you write effective notes.

TOP TIPS FOR MAKING NOTES

Read first, note later

Try reading the text first without making any notes and then summarise it in your mind or out loud.

Go easy on the highlighter

If you do want to mark the text at a first reading, just pick out the most relevant sections by putting a line down alongside them, using a pencil rather than a high-lighter. Remember, though, that you probably won't really get a clear idea of the main points of a text until you have got to the end, and that if you highlight as you read for the first time, you will be stuck with it. A better use of the highlighter might be to use it on your own notes to bring out and emphasise important information.

Do more than just annotate

Annotating a text is fine, but try also to write notes that are separate from the text. Online note-making software usually only allows you to make short annotations on or around the text and so again, also make your own notes either on a separate e-document or on paper.

Explain your reactions to yourself

It's good to react to the text but don't just put !! or ? in the margin - write out your thoughts in full.

FIVE STEPS FOR MAKING NOTES

Step 1   Have a clear purpose and *make* notes rather than *take* notes

To be effective, your notes need to be purposeful and meaningful. A clear purpose is just as important for note-making as it is for reading - your notes should address the questions you want answered. Think also about the function you want your notes to fulfil. Do you want your notes to:

- extract all the essential points and arguments;
- contain only information on a specific theme;
- focus only on information that addresses your own angle or question;
- clarify the way the points relate to each other and see how the ideas are organised;
- re-organise or connect the text information in a new way?

Remember that you should *make* notes, not *take* notes. Unless you are trying to learn something by heart, there isn't much point in copying down lots of individual sentences or chunks from the text; this usually means that you are on auto-pilot rather than actively reading and thinking. Try to build up the confidence to read and think first and then make notes in your own words that address your own questions. Copy down phrases only if they are really special and powerful.

Step 2   Write down the reference details

You should already have written down the author, title and publication date of each source (called the reference or bibliographic details) when you found them. For books this should include the publishing company and where it was published. These days we are all used to getting information from the media and websites without knowing where it came from. However, in academic study, knowing exactly who wrote something and where the text can be found is vital, as the authors, in a way, own the knowledge or ideas they have communicated in writing (referred to as 'intellectual property').

Write down the bibliographic information fully and accurately, and be careful not to change the case (upper to lower or vice versa) or punctuation of book or article titles. You should also write down where and how you found the source. This will save you time if you need to go back to check a source, and will help you find new sources in the future.

Below is an example of the student's research record (also called a research log) for the article by Albert Carr. The student found the article by using an e-database on 20 November 2012.

Reference details:
Albert Z. Carr. 1968. 'Is business bluffing ethical?' Harvard Business Review. Vol. 46 Issue 1. pages 143-153.

Comments and search notes:
HBR is a peer-reviewed acad. journal.
Got ref. from list at back of Crane and Matten 2010.
Found it on 20/11/12 in Infolinx - Business Source Complete - Business Resources - Titles - HBR.

Step 3   Make notes on your reading

People make notes in different ways; diagrams, flow charts, bullet points or index cards. You may want to make notes on only parts of the text, on one particular aspect of the text, or on the whole text, depending on why you are reading it. Some people prefer to make notes on paper and others make notes online. Whatever method you use to take notes, you should always:

- note down the reference details, page numbers (particularly for quotations) and the date on which you make your notes;
- read carefully and make accurate notes - don't accidentally change the meaning of the text.

Common student mistakes include:

- not noticing comparatives or superlatives such as *the best / greatest / worst / one of*;
- being inaccurate about the strength, degree or extent of the author's view: for example, if the text says business ethics is *fairly* important, your notes should not report the text as saying that business ethics is *very* important;
- overlooking the words *not* or *no* - if you don't notice these words you may end up with an interpretation that is the opposite of what the text says;
- being imprecise about who says what - if the text paraphrases or quotes *another* author, make sure your notes record this;
- not being precise enough in describing data from graphs, diagrams and tables.
- Make clear in your notes which ideas are major points, which are only examples of these major points, and which are more minor points of information.
- Don't make your notes too brief *or* too detailed.
  If your notes are too brief, the meaning will be unclear and you won't understand them in a month's or year's time. If your notes are too detailed then it probably means you are copying from the text too much - making notes does not mean copying whole sections from the text.
- Try to use some of your own words and abbreviations.
  You may be worried about changing the meaning of the text accidentally, of 'moving away' from it, or feel that you can't put things into your own words as well as the original. However, you don't have to use *all* your own words, and using some of your own words will help you to start the paraphrasing process. Remember that confidence in using your own words in your notes will increase with practice.
- Have a system that allows you to distinguish between:
  - exact words from the text (quotations);
  - *most* of the same words from the text (close paraphrase);
  - your *own* words to describe ideas in the text (paraphrase);
  - your own ideas or comments.
  You must record these differences carefully so that when you use your notes in your essay you do not accidentally claim source words or ideas as your own. You can use different highlight colours, separate columns, and/or quotation marks for differentiating between quotation, paraphrase and your own comments.

Step 4   Review and rework your notes

Look again at your assignment title and check the focus and relevance of your notes. Familiarise yourself with them and start to put them to work. Ways of doing this include:

- reworking your notes using a different format - linear to pattern or vice versa;
- reorganising your notes around your assignment question title, adding comments and identifying any knowledge gaps;

○ reorganising your notes around your own unique question or angle to help develop your own written voice;

○ using your notes to write an annotated bibliography.

Step 5   Write a short reflection

Research has shown that students who look back over their notes to check for clarity and meaning and who reflect on them are more successful learners than those who don't. When you have finished making your notes, use them, together with your critical analysis of the text, to write a short reflection. This can be informal and so take any form you find helpful. However, it is a good idea to write in your own words and in full sentences and to use quotation marks for exact phrases from the original text. The reflection should include a short summary of what you have learnt. If the text has a diagram or table, try to summarise what it shows in one sentence.

Writing a short reflection from your notes will consolidate your reading, thinking and questioning, and will maximise the effectiveness of the whole process. It will help you to restate information and ideas from your sources in your own words, and will enable you to further develop your own ideas. Finally, it will help you relate what you have read to what you already know, and will enable you to see how and where you want to use your sources in your essay.

LOOKING AT AN EXAMPLE OF SOME NOTES

Below are the student's notes from the sections of the Svensson and Wood article on p. 13.

	Svensson, G. and Wood, G. (2008) 'A model of business ethics' *Journal of Business Ethics*, 77, pp. 303-322. Notes written on 1/12/2012.
p. 310 true? no model?	In 30 yrs. of BE as a subject, no model of BE - S + W want to fill this gap in BE theory, for debate.
p. 310	'Socially responsible managers do the right thing because it is the right thing to do'.
does it? - don't think so.	Soc. expects the correct action. (CP)
p.319 (conclusion)	Mangs. should want to be ethical because it brings freedom and success. (S + W citing Thomas et al. 2004).
p. 319 main point	BE-'...dynamic and continuous process...' - 'interrelationship between businesses and society...' - each responsible for the other.
good point re.	BE becoming impt. because people feel that buss. do <u>not</u>
importance of BE	behave ethically .·. the 'mutual obligations need to be restated' (cited from Hoffman and Moore 1982).

Comments on the notes

○ The student's notes are brief, but detailed enough to be meaningful. If the first line of the notes had been *'In 30 yrs. no model - S + W want to fill this gap'* this would have been too brief, and when reading these notes at a later stage the student would have been asking himself: '30 years of what?' 'A model of what?' 'What type of gap do they want to fill?'

○ Notice how the student has a clear system for recording which parts of the notes are quotation, close paraphrase or paraphrase, and which are his own thoughts.

Firstly, he has put phrases and key words taken from the text in quotation marks and has been careful to write down quotes accurately, using three dots to indicate when a quotation is not a whole sentence. Secondly, he has used the letters 'CP' (close paraphrase) to indicate when he has used *mostly* the same words as the text. This is important, as he would need to put such sections much more into his own words if he wanted to use them in his essay (see p. 39). Thirdly, he has used the margin for page numbers and for his own comments and ideas.

○ The student has noted when Svensson and Wood have quoted other authors (Thomas et al. and then Hoffman and Moore). This is vital in order to avoid accidentally attributing the ideas of these other authors to Svensson and Wood in his essay.

○ You can see that in making notes the student has naturally started the process of using his own words.

Looking at an example of a short reflection

Below is a short reflection on the Svensson and Wood article that the student wrote after reading and critically analysing the text, making notes and then re-reading them. You will notice that by now he is using mostly his own words and style of expression.

The authors propose and describe their own model of business ethics, which centres around a 'dynamic and continuous process' between business and society. They argue persuasively that business and society influence each other, are dependent on each other and have a responsibility to each other. Importantly, they stress that the ethical standards of society are also those of business and that therefore business ethics is important.

   Their model assumes that individuals and society always expect businesses to behave well and that we should be able to trust them. They also assume that good managers exist who are socially responsible. I think that these assumptions may be true some of the time but not all of the time. However, their model is well researched and comprehensive, and is supported by a great deal of other research in the field, and their idea of an 'interrelationship between business and society' accords with the ideas of Esty, Collins and Shaw and Barry. I agree with Svensson and Wood that the way businesses behave does affect society and vice versa, and I will use their article as a key source to support my argument that business ethics is important.

Practice 3 | make notes and write a reflection

Before you can come up with a clearer system for making meaningful notes you need to be aware of how you normally *do* take notes. To do this, read and make notes on the extracts from the article by Carr on pp. 22 and 23 (or use a short text of your own if you prefer). Read your notes a week later and compare them with the original text. Check your notes for the following:

○ Is the meaning of what you have written clear?
○ Can you distinguish between major and minor points?
○ Can you distinguish clearly between exact words from the text, mixtures of your own and the author's words, your own words for the author's ideas, and your own ideas?

If anything is unclear, how could you improve the way you make notes so that you really would be able to use them accurately and effectively in an essay?

   After you have reviewed and improved your notes, use them together with your critical analysis of the text to write a short reflection.

1.4 WHY AND HOW SHOULD YOU QUOTE?

Quotations are phrases or sentences taken from a source unchanged. Below are the last few sentences from the business ethics essay with the quotation the student used given in blue.

> Most importantly, I have shown that businesses are part of society and that they should therefore adhere to the same moral principles, and I have used the 2008 financial collapse as an example of what can happen to society when businesses act unethically. As Trevino and Nelson (2010) state: 'Ethics is not just about the connection we have to other beings - we are all connected; rather, it's about the quality of that connection' (p. 32). I have shown that this is as true in the business context as in any other.

REASONS TO QUOTE

Quotations can be a powerful tool when writing an essay but only if you use them sparingly and for the right reasons. Quotations are useful for helping you:

- give a definition;
- state a fact or idea which the author has expressed in a unique and powerful way;
- establish or summarise an author's argument or position;
- provide a powerful and interesting start or end to your essay.

REASONS NOT TO QUOTE

Don't quote someone just because:

- you think that putting quotations in your essay will make it look academic and will impress your tutor;
- some of the articles you have read used lots of quotations so you think your essay should too;
- you have written half of your essay and haven't used any quotations yet, so you think you should put some in;
- you haven't given enough time to reading critically and making notes, so it seems much easier to cut and paste some quotations into your essay rather than putting things into your own words.

HOW MANY QUOTATIONS SHOULD YOU USE?

A mistake students often make is to use too many quotations, as most of the time you should restate sources using your own words (for example, only about 4% of the business ethics essay is made up of quotation).

The number of quotations you decide to use will depend on your subject discipline and assignment type, but whatever your topic, you should always ask yourself *why* you are quoting, not how much. You should use quotations only if you think the phrase is particularly interesting or expressed in a powerful and/or unique way.

Indeed, an essay may not have *any* quotations but still be a very successful piece of work because the student has expressed her sources effectively using her own words.

Indeed, using too many quotations, for example for more than a quarter of your essay, is a type of plagiarism even if you put in all the correct in-essay references and quotation marks. This is because you can't really claim that your essay is your own work if a significant proportion of it consists of other people's exact words.

DON'T OVERUSE QUOTATION MARKS FOR INDIVIDUAL WORDS

If a specialised term is now a normal part of the language of your discipline, you probably don't need to make it stand out by putting quotation marks around it. If you want to refer to a specialised term coined by a specific author, you can often use italics rather than quotation marks (you can check with your tutor how they want you to mark out special terminology). For example: The term *anomie* refers to a condition of malaise or mild depression.

If you want to refer to a word as a word, you can use quotation marks or italics. For example: People overuse the word 'progress'. *OR* People overuse the word *progress*.

If you want to show that you disagree with how a word has been used, don't just put it in quotation marks and leave it at that; it is often better to put the word in normal font and explain why you disagree with how it has been used. For example: People talk a great deal about 'progress'. ✗

People talk a great deal about progress without really thinking about what it really means. ✓

LOOKING AT EXAMPLES OF QUOTATIONS USED EFFECTIVELY

Below are three slightly adapted extracts from the business ethics essay that contain quotations (given in blue, with their in-essay reference in red). Read the extracts and for each extract, think about why the student decided to use the quotation.

1 Shaw and Barry (2007) define business ethics as 'the study of what constitutes right and wrong (or good and bad) human conduct in a business context' (p. 25). Another definition describes business ethics as the 'principles and standards that guide behaviour in the world of business' (Ferrell et al. 2002, p. 6).
2 Others, such as Wolf, share the view that businesses do not need to be ethical, and Prindl and Prodham (1994) suggest that 'Finance as practised in the professions and in industry is seen as a value-neutral positive discipline promoting efficiency without regard to the social consequences which follow from its products' (p. 3).
3 My first proposition is that businesses actually *need* to behave in an ethical manner. This idea is expressed succinctly by Collins (1994) when he states that 'good ethics is synonymous with good management' (p. 2).

COMMENTS ON THE QUOTATIONS

The student decided to quote in extract 1 to give examples of different academic definitions of business ethics. In extract 2, the student quoted Prindl and Prodham because he felt that they expressed in a succinct and powerful way the fact that many people in the business world do not feel the need to take an ethical approach.

In extract 3 the student uses the quotation to support the main point of his essay, that business ethics is central to business. He also felt that the statement was a very clear and powerful summary by Collins of this idea.

Note that in all three extracts, the student introduces the quotation so that the reader understands why it is being used. In other parts of his essay, the student quotes two individual words, *bluffing* and *dysfunctional* because he felt that these were key words used by the respective authors.

FOUR STEPS FOR USING QUOTATIONS PROPERLY

Step 1   Make effective notes

Being able to use quotations effectively is a result of the whole process of selecting and reading with questions in mind, critically evaluating, making meaningful notes, and reflecting on your reading. If you follow this process, you should be able to make good choices in what to quote.

Step 2   Ask yourself why

Before you put a quotation into your essay, ask yourself *why* you are putting it in. Is it special enough? Is it really relevant to your point? Would it not be better to put it into your own words?

Step 3   Give the context and make a comment

When you have written your first draft, separate out each quotation and its surrounding sentences from the rest of your essay. Read each quotation and surrounding sentences slowly and carefully. Make sure you have not taken the quotation out of context and/or misrepresented the author. It is important to show that you understand why the author said what they did before you agree or disagree with them.

Always introduce your quotation clearly and always comment on it, showing clearly how it is relevant to your own point.

Step 4   Be accurate and give an in-essay reference

Once you are sure that your quotation is worth putting in, check that you have quoted accurately, that you have used quotation marks *and* an in-essay reference, and that you have used the correct grammar and punctuation before, during and after the quotation.

FOUR COMMON MISTAKES STUDENTS MAKE WITH THE CONTENT OF QUOTATIONS

The four most common and serious mistakes students make with what they quote are:
- using a quotation that is not special enough and where they should, therefore, have used their own words. This includes common facts or knowledge, which don't usually need to be quoted;
- using a quotation that does not directly support their own point;
- not introducing or showing clearly why they have used the quotation;
- using a reporting verb (e.g. *states*, *shows*, *suggests*, *points out*, *claims*) that is not correct for the context and function of the quotation (see section B1).

Practice 4 | **would you use these quotations?**

Below are some quotations from several student essays on bioscience topics. Read them and identify which of the above mistakes the students have made.

1 Kzanty (2004) states that 'Organs such as the heart, liver, small bowel, pancreas and lungs are used for transplants' (p.11).

2 Logan (1999) states that 'The second world war ended in 1945' (p.111).

3 The main benefit of organ transplant is that it saves lives. As stated by Smith (2005), 'heart transplantation can save lives, but the procedure carries serious risks and complications and a high mortality rate' (p. 12).

4 Improvements in transplantation have made it possible for animal organs to be used. This is beneficial, as patients are not forced to wait for transplants. As stated by Kline (2005): 'advances in genetic techniques mean that there is less chance of animal organs being rejected by the human immune system' (p. 53).

5 Transplantation carries the risk of being attacked by the immune system and the patient is therefore at risk or organ failure again. As stated by Smith (2005): 'Everyone reported common side effects which included diarrhoea, edemas, fatigue and ulcers' (p. 5).

THREE COMMON MISTAKES STUDENTS MAKE WITH IN-ESSAY REFERENCES FOR QUOTATIONS

The three most common serious mistakes students make when referencing quotations are:

○ **Not using both quotation marks *and* an in-essay reference**

Some students make the mistake of using quotation marks but not an in-essay reference because they think that using quotation marks and a reference in the bibliography at the end of the essay are enough. Other students make the mistake of giving an in-essay reference but not using quotation marks because they think that the in-essay reference is enough. In academic writing, however, giving an in-essay reference and no quotation marks always indicates that you are expressing an idea from a source *in your own words*. Therefore, quoting without using quotation marks is plagiarism (claiming someone else's words or ideas as your own) even if you have given an in-essay reference. The only time you do not use quotation marks is for longer quotations (more than three sentences) in which case indentation is used instead of quotation marks.

Look again at essay extracts 1-3 on p. 21 and notice how the student uses both quotation marks *and* an in-essay reference with each quotation.

○ **Giving only an in-essay reference for a primary source that was read in a secondary text**

You must make clear in your essay which book or article you have actually read. In the essay extract below (one that was not used in the final essay) the student correctly uses the phrase *cited in* to show that he did not actually read the Hoffman and Moore article, but read a quotation from their work in the article by Svensson and Wood. It would be poor scholarship, and a misrepresentation of what you have read, to give only the reference for Hoffman and Moore.

> Hoffman and Moore (1982) suggest that the public feels that businesses fail to behave in a socially acceptable manner and that 'the mutual obligations of business to the community and the community to business need to be restated' (Hoffman and Moore 1982, cited in Svensson and Wood 2008).

○ **Putting parentheses (round brackets) in the wrong place**

Look again at the extract from the business ethics essay below. Notice that for the first quotation, because the student uses Shaw and Barry as part of the introductory sentence, he uses parentheses only for the year of publication and for the page number. For the second quotation however, the student does not use the authors

Ferrell et al. as part of his sentence, so both the names and year of publication date are in parentheses at the end of the quotation.

> Shaw and Barry (2007) define it as 'the study of what constitutes right and wrong (or good and bad) human conduct in a business context' (p. 25). Another definition describes business ethics as the 'principles and standards that guide behaviour in the world of business' (Ferrell et al. 2002, p. 6).

Practice 5 | are these quotations referenced properly?

Below are four incorrect versions of the first part of essay extract 1 on p. 21. Look at these altered versions and identify what the mistakes are in how the quotations have been referenced.

1 Business ethics is the study of what constitutes right and wrong (or good and bad) human conduct in a business context.

2 Shaw and Barry (2007) define business ethics as the study of what constitutes right and wrong (or good and bad) human conduct in a business context (p. 25).

3 Business ethics is 'the study of what constitutes right and wrong (or good and bad) human conduct in a business context'.

4 (Shaw and Barry 2007) define business ethics as 'the study of what constitutes right and wrong (or good and bad) human conduct in a business context'.

FOUR COMMON MISTAKES STUDENTS MAKE WITH STRUCTURE, GRAMMAR OR PUNCTUATION WHEN USING QUOTATIONS

It's important not to accidentally misrepresent an author because of the way you structure or integrate a quotation into your writing. The most common mistakes students make with this are:

- **Changing words or other elements in the quotation**

  You must not change any words or spellings or do anything that leads to a misrepresentation of the quotation. If there is a mistake or non-standard usage in the quotation, you can choose to add *sic* in square brackets immediately after the item to inform your reader that it is not your mistake. *Sic* is the abbreviated form of the Latin phrase *sic erat scriptum* meaning 'thus was it written'. For example: The guidelines state that 'staff should discuss all problems with there [sic] manager'.

- If you need to add a word of your own to make the quotation fit with your surrounding sentence or to clarify its meaning, use a square bracket to show that you have added something that was not in the original text. For example: Emille (2002) states that 'they [the public] only hear what they want to hear' (p. 10). The one change you are allowed to make without using square brackets is to change the first letter of a quotation from upper to lower case, so that your quotation integrates smoothly into the rest of your sentence. If you want to leave out part of a quotation, use an ellipsis (three dots with a space in between each one) to indicate that you have done so. As an example, below is an extract from the article by Albert Carr followed by a quotation used in a student essay. In the quotation, the student has used an ellipsis and has also changed the first letter of the quotation from 'T' to 't' so that it fits in with her sentence. Extract:

  > The illusion that business can afford to be guided by ethics as conceived in private life is often fostered by speeches and articles containing such phrases as, 'It pays to be ethical,' or, 'Sound ethics is good for business'. Actually this is not an ethical position at all; it is a self-serving calculation in disguise.

  Quotation from the extract:

  > Carr (1968) states that 'the illusion that business can afford to be guided by ethics . . . is a self-serving calculation in disguise'.

You do not usually need to use an ellipsis to show that you have missed out the *start* of the sentence in a quotation, as long as this does not lead to a misrepresentation of what the author is saying; if it does then do use ellipsis to start the quotation. Note that the use of the ellipsis varies slightly between different referencing styles, so check your referencing guide.

○ **Putting in an extra *he / she / it /they* or topic word before a quotation**
If you use the author's name as the subject of your introductory sentence, you should not use also a subject pronoun such as he or it. Equally, if you use the topic word (e.g. 'business ethics') in your introductory sentence, you should not repeat it in the quotation.

○ **Using the wrong punctuation in front of a quotation**
Use a colon if you use a complete phrase (called an independent clause) to introduce a quotation. For instance: Carr's central maxim is very clear: 'To be a winner a man must play to win' (p. 153).

> Carr makes the following statement: 'To be a winner a man must play to win' (p. 153).

Use a comma if you use an introductory, incomplete phrase to introduce a quotation. For instance: As Tomalin (2010) states, 'Pepys was . . . mapping a recognizably modern world' (p. 148).

> According to Brandon (2008), 'History is a record of relationships' (p. 151).

Don't use any punctuation if you integrate your quotation smoothly into the rest of your sentence. For instance:

> This idea is expressed succinctly by Collins (1994) when he states that 'good ethics is synonymous with good management' (p. 2).

○ **Putting punctuation marks in the wrong place at the end of a quotation**
Don't worry too much about making small mistakes with the punctuation of quotations but do try to develop correct use over time. Keep question marks and other punctuation from the original text inside the quotation marks. The exception to this is the full-stop; for the author/date in-essay reference style you should put the full-stop at the very end, after the page number brackets.

Practice 6 | is the grammar and punctuation of these quotations correct?

Below is one of the extracts from the business ethics essay followed by four incorrect versions. Identify the mistakes in each incorrect version.

Correct essay extract

My first proposition is that businesses actually *need* to behave in an ethical manner. This idea is expressed succinctly by Collins (1994) when he states that 'good ethics is synonymous with good management' (p. 2).

Incorrect versions

1 My first proposition is that businesses actually *need* to behave in an ethical manner. This idea is expressed succinctly by Collins (1994) when he states that 'good business ethics is synonymous with good management' (p. 2).

2 My first proposition is that businesses actually *need* to behave in an ethical manner. This idea is expressed succinctly by Collins (1994) when he states that 'good ethics is good management' (p. 2).

3 My first proposition is that businesses actually *need* to behave in an ethical manner. This idea is expressed succinctly by Collins (1994) when talking about good ethics that 'good ethics is synonymous with good management' (p. 2).

4 My first proposition is that businesses actually *need* to behave in an ethical manner. This idea is expressed succinctly by Collins (1994) when he states that 'good ethics is synonymous with good management.' (p. 2)

1.5 WHY AND HOW SHOULD YOU PARAPHRASE?

Paraphrasing is when you express one specific idea or piece of information from a short section of source text, using your own words and style. Being able to paraphrase well is central to academic writing, and is also an ability employers look for in graduates. This section gives you essential points on paraphrasing, takes you through some examples of good and poor paraphrasing, and gives you a short practice exercise to help you acquire this complex skill.

WHY PARAPHRASE?

Restating what you have read in your own way allows you to:

- go through a mental process that helps you to understand and think about what you have read in a more independent way;
- express the information and ideas from sources in your own style of thinking and writing so that you can integrate them smoothly into your argument and essay;
- restate information and ideas from sources in a way that best supports your own argument;
- show your tutor that you have understood what you have read and how you have used it to develop your knowledge and ideas;
- express information and ideas from complicated texts more clearly and simply;
- restate information and ideas from your sources that are not special enough to quote.

LOOKING AT EXAMPLES OF GOOD PARAPHRASING

Below are two extracts from a book the student read for his business ethics essay. Each extract is followed by the section in his essay where he introduces his own point and then paraphrases from the source (in blue). Read and compare the source extracts with the paraphrases in the essay extracts.

Source extract 1

> . . . amazon.com currently stocks more than 14,000 books related to business ethics and corporate responsibility, whilst a Google search on 'business ethics' returns more than 4 million hits at the time of writing. . . . One annual UK survey, for instance, estimates the country's 'ethical market' (i.e. consumer spending on ethical products and services) to be worth something like £35bn annually (The Co-operative Bank 2008).
>
> Extract from: Crane, A. and Matten D. (2010) *Business Ethics*. p. 14.

Essay extract 1

> Over the past couple of decades, the ethical credentials of businesses appear to have become an explicit factor in consumer choice. . . . The UK ethical market is valued at over 30 billion euros per year, and there are currently over 14,000 books and 4 million web entries related to business ethics (The Co-operative Bank 2008, cited in Crane and Matten, 2010).

Source extract 2

. . . there is indeed considerable overlap between ethics and the law. In fact, the law is essentially and institutionalisation or codification of ethics into specific social rules, regulations, and proscriptions. Nevertheless, the two are not equivalent. . . . The law might be said to be a definition of the minimum acceptable standards of behaviour. However, many morally contestable issues, whether in business of elsewhere, are not explicitly covered by the law. . . . In one sense then, business ethics can be said to begin where the law ends. Business ethics is primarily concerned with those issues not covered by the law, or where there is no definite consensus on whether something is right or wrong.

Extracts from: Crane, A. and Matten, D. (2010) *Business Ethics*. pp. 5 and 7.

Essay extract 2

It is important to emphasise here that business ethics is not synonymous with legality. There is some overlap between law and ethics, but legislation usually only regulates the lowest level of acceptable behaviour (Crane and Matten 2010). In addition, as Trevino and Nelson (2010) point out, the law is limited in what it can do to prevent unacceptable actions, because legislation follows rather than precedes trends in behaviour. Business ethics then, as Crane and Matten state, is mainly concerned with areas of conduct that are *not* specifically covered by law and that are therefore open to different interpretations, a fact that means a particular behaviour may be legal albeit viewed as unethical.

Comments on the paraphrases

Notice how the student has not just replaced individual words in his paraphrases. His paraphrases are a complete rewriting of the source, based on his independent understanding of the texts, and written from his notes in his own style so that they make sense to him. His paraphrases are less complex than the original and he has changed the order of the information.

In essay extract 2 the student has emphasised the fact that ethics is not the same thing as the law. He has emphasised this difference because in this part of his essay he is defining and describing what business ethics is, and so wants to point out the differences between business ethics, the law and morality.

Notice that both paraphrases are shorter than the original. A paraphrase can be as long and as detailed as the original text but will often be shorter because the points are condensed and/or the language and sentence structure is simpler. Paraphrase 1 is shorter than the original extract because the student has used this paraphrase in his essay introduction as just a brief example of the importance of business ethics.

Paraphrase 2 is also shorter than the original extract because although the student has included all the points from the original source, he has used simpler language and condensed the ideas in his own way.

Five key points for paraphrasing

1 Check that your paraphrase clearly supports the point *you* are making

Don't let your paraphrases take control of your essay. Decide what point you want to make and then check that your paraphrase is relevant. Make sure that you comment on the paraphrase, showing how it supports your point. Check that you have reported the source information accurately and that you have used reporting verbs (e.g. *show, suggest, claim*) in such a way as to give the emphasis which best supports your argument (see section B1).

2 Write your paraphrase from your notes and reflection, not straight from the original text

If you have approached your reading in a similar way to that suggested in sections A1, A2 and A3, you will already be well on the way to writing good paraphrases. Using your own words will be much easier if you have gone through the process of making good notes and writing a reflection on your reading. Remember that your paraphrase should be your own understanding and rewriting of short sections of a source, not a translation straight from the text.

3 Use your own words and writing style

When you paraphrase you must use your own words as far as possible - around 90% of the wording should be your own. The rules of academic writing do not allow you to change only a few words or even half of the words from the original text, as this would be plagiarism. You must either change nothing and use the source as a quotation, or rewrite the source as a paraphrase, using about 90% of your own words. The pattern and structure of your sentences should also be your own as far as possible.

Keeping words from the original text

There will be some words or short phrases you can't change; in the example paraphrases these words are *business ethics, ethical market, law and behaviour.* You do not need to put quotation marks around such commonly used words. However, if you are keeping a word from the source that the author has used in a unique or special way, or if the word is a new term coined by the author, you should use it as a one-word quotation and put quotation marks around it. Always check that you have not accidentally used the same words or sentence patterns as the original text unless absolutely necessary.

You should also try to rephrase statistics. For example, *one fifth* can also be expressed as *20%*, and *more than double* can be expressed as *over twice as many / much.* It may not always be possible or make sense to rephrase numbers and statistics but you should do this if you can.

4 Always use an in-essay reference

Using in-essay references with your paraphrases is essential, not optional. In academic writing, if something is not referenced, it is assumed to be both your own words *and* your own idea. You must therefore *always* give in-essay references when paraphrasing, because the ideas and information you have restated are not yours, even though you have used your own words. Not giving an in-essay reference for paraphrases is the most common cause of of accidental student plagiarism.

Giving in-essay references is also an important way of getting marks. Your in-essay references will show your tutor that you have done some reading and that you have understood it. In-essay references also show your tutor (and yourself) how your reading has helped you to develop your own ideas.

5 Use reference reminder phrases

Giving an in-essay reference at the start of your paraphrase will often not be enough. In essay extracts 1 and 2 above, the student gives an in-essay reference at the end of the first sentence of each paraphrase. This is enough for these paraphrases because they are only one sentence long. If a paraphrase is more than one sentence long, however, you will probably need to use what I call a 'reference reminder phrase'.

Below is an example of another section from the business ethics essay in which the student paraphrases from Carr. The student has used the reference reminder phrase *he suggests that* to make clear that the ideas in the second sentence are also those of Carr. If this phrase were deleted from the essay extract, the tutor might assume that the idea in the second sentence was that of the student.

Carr (1968) uses the analogy of a poker game to argue that a successful businessman needs to play by the rules of the industry and that these include 'bluffing' as an acceptable form of behaviour. He suggests that what is, in effect, lying is merely part of legitimate business strategy, and that business rules do not need to take account of personal or social principles.

If you don't use reference reminder phrases, it may become unclear in your essay which of your sentences express your own ideas and which ones express the ideas of other authors. This lack of clarity could lead you to plagiarise accidentally because as stated above, it is always assumed in academic writing that anything that is not referenced is your own comment or idea.

HOW MUCH OF YOUR ESSAY SHOULD CONSIST OF PARAPHRASES?

This will depend on how many sources you use, your subject and on your assignment title and type. If you are conducting your own experiment or research, you may not be using many sources and therefore not paraphrasing. However, most types of under-graduate essay will consist of many short paraphrases from different sources. If you look at some academic journal articles in your subject you will see that some of them have about 50% of their content in the form of paraphrase (from lots of different sources and therefore with lots of different in-essay references). The business ethics essay has about 50% of its word count as paraphrase, but is still original because of the student's choice of sources and how he has used and evaluated them. However, try not to end up with lots of short paraphrases that are merely strung together by individual phrases or sentences of your own. If you find yourself doing this, go back and do some more thinking about what your argument is. Then try to emphasise your own argument more in your writing, summarise your sources more, and give more of your own evaluations and comments on sources to show how they support your points.

FOUR COMMON MISTAKES STUDENTS MAKE WHEN PARAPHRASING

○ **Not showing clearly where a paraphrase begins and ends**
Student essays often do not show clearly enough which sentences are their own words and ideas and which sentences are paraphrases of sources. For example, if you only give one in-essay reference in brackets at the end of a long paragraph, it probably won't be clear which sentences in that paragraph are paraphrase and which sentences are your own points. As discussed in the key points above, you must use both in-essay references and reference reminder phrases.
○ **Not making enough changes from the original source**
Students sometimes use just a few of their own words to sew together unchanged sentences or phrases from a source or from several different sources. Even if you give the relevant in-essay references, this type of 'sewing' is plagiarism because most of the words and style are not your own.
○ **Changing individual words but keeping the same sentence pattern as the original**
This might happen if you don't make notes and reflect on your reading but just try to 'translate' word by word from the text straight into your essay. Even if you change all the words, your paraphrase will still have the same style and pattern of the original text and this is therefore still a type of plagiarism.
○ **Accidentally changing the meaning of the original text**
This might happen if you have not read and understood the text carefully enough, not thought critically about it or have not made clear notes. Make sure you under-stand from the text what is fact and what is opinion and pay particular attention to small but important words such as *no, not* or *not as* and comparatives such as *faster*. For example, saying that smoking cannabis is *not as* damaging as smoking cigarettes is very different from saying that smoking cannabis is not damaging.

LOOKING AT SOME EXAMPLES OF POOR PARAPHRASING

Below is a short extract from a journal article that looks at whether mobile phones are a health risk.

The extract is followed by three unacceptable paraphrases which all try to use this article to support the view that mobile phones do not damage health. Read the extract and then the unacceptable paraphrases. Finally, read the comments and the example of a good paraphrase of the article extract.

Source extract

So far there is no clear evidence from health studies of a relation between mobile phone use and mortality or morbidity. Indeed, tantalising findings in humans include a speeding up of reaction time during exposure, particularly during behavioural tasks calling for attention and electrical brain activity changes during cognitive processes. It is not clear, however, whether these findings have any positive implications for health.

Adapted from: Maier, M., Blakemore, C. and Koivisto, M. (2000)
'The health hazards of mobile phones' *British Medical Journal*,
320(7245), pp. 1288–1289.

Unacceptable paraphrases

1 Maier et al. (2000) show that there is no clear evidence from health studies of a relation between mobile phone use and mortality or morbidity. They state that in fact, tantalising findings in humans include a speeding up of reaction time during exposure, particularly during behavioural tasks calling for attention and changes in brain electricity during cognitive processes. It is not clear, however, whether these findings have any positive implications for health.

2 Some studies point to interesting results which suggest that while using a phone, the user has quicker reaction times to some behavioural tasks (Maier et al. 2000). In fact, there are interesting findings in humans that show a speeding up of reaction time during exposure, particularly during behavioural tasks calling for attention and changes in brain electricity during cognitive processes. It is unclear whether these findings have any positive implications for health.

3 Maier et al. (2000) show that up to now there is not any strong proof from studies on disease, of a link between the use of mobile phones and death or disease. In fact, interesting results in humans include a faster time of reaction during use, especially while doing practical tasks that need concentration and brain electricity change during the thought process. It is unclear whether these results imply any health benefits (ibid.)

et al. = and the other authors.
ibid. = from the same source as previously mentioned.

COMMENTS ON THE UNACCEPTABLE PARAPHRASES

Paraphrase 1

The student has correctly used an in-essay reference and the reference reminder phrase *They state that*. However, the only changes she has made from the source it to put in these references, take off the first two words and reword the phrase 'electrical brain activity changes'. Everything else is copied word for word from the source without any use of quotation marks. This is plagiarism.

Paraphrase 2

The student has used an in-essay reference and has also made some significant changes in wording. However, there are two problems with this paraphrase. The first is that there are still several long phrases which are unchanged from the original source (underlined below). This could be seen as plagiarism. Secondly, there is no reference reminder phrase and so the reader is not sure whether the information in the second sentence comes from Maier et al. or from the student. By the time the reader gets to the third sentence, it could easily be assumed that the point expressed in this sentence is that of the student and this could therefore be seen as plagiarism. To summarise, this paraphrase contains plagiarism on two counts; lack of adequate referencing and phrases copied from the original source.

Paraphrase 2 with phrases from the source underlined:

Some studies point to interesting results which suggest that while using a phone, the user has quicker reaction times to some behavioural tasks (Maier et al. 2000). In fact, there are interesting findings in humans that show a speeding up of reaction time during exposure, particularly during behavioural tasks calling for attention and changes in brain electricity during cognitive processes. It is unclear whether these findings have any positive implications for health.

Paraphrase 3

The student has used nearly all her own words and has used two in-essay references. However, she has merely translated the original word by word as she goes along. The student has been too dependent on her source and instead of making and using notes, has gone straight from reading the article to writing her paraphrase. The result is a paraphrase that has exactly the same 'pattern' as the original. This does not show a clear understanding of the original or control of her source and is a type of plagiarism.

An example of a good paraphrase of the extract

Studies point to interesting results suggesting that mobile phone users experience quicker reaction times to tasks which require both changes in electrical brain activity and concentration (Maier et al. 2000). Although it has not been shown that that this effect represents an actual benefit to health, there has equally been no data from any disease studies to suggest that mobile phones actually damage health in any way (ibid.).

Practice 7 | what do you think of these paraphrases?

Below is a short extract from a different article on the issue of mobile phones and health risks. Underneath the extracts are four unacceptable paraphrases. Read the extract and then the paraphrases and identify what is wrong with each one. Two examples of good paraphrases are given on p. 128, one using author/date referencing and the other numeric referencing.

Source extract

Mobile phones provide an interesting example of a source risk to health which may be largely non-existent but which cannot be totally dismissed. Such risks, when possibly serious and with long-term consequences, are typically dealt with by appeal to the so-called precautionary principle but, of course, precaution comes at a price.
Cox, D.R. (2003) 'Communication of risk: health hazards from mobile phones' *Journal of the Royal Statistical Society: Series A (Statistics in Society)*, 166(2), pp. 214–246.

Unacceptable paraphrases

1 Advising caution in the use of mobile phones is an example of a typical approach to the fear of a possible health risk which may be of a serious nature. Such an approach may have negative consequences, but is taken because although there may in fact be no health risk, this has not yet been proven.

2 Cox (2003) suggests that advising caution in the use of mobile phones is an example of a typical approach to the fear of a possible health risk which may be of a serious nature. Such an approach may have negative consequences, but is taken because although there may in fact be no health risk, this has not yet been proven.

3 Advising caution in the use of mobile phones is an example of a typical approach to the fear of a possible health risk which may be of a serious nature. Such an approach may have negative consequences but is taken because although there may in fact be no health risk, this has not yet been proven (Cox 2003).

4 Mobile phones provide an interesting example of a source risk to health which may be largely non-existent but which cannot be totally dismissed (Cox 2003). So far there is no clear evidence from health studies of a relation between mobile phone use and mortality or morbidity.

Practice 8 | write your own paraphrase

Paraphrase the source extract below.

Source extract

The National Radiological Protection Board said that more than 50 million mobile phones are used in the UK today, a number that has doubled since 2000. The mobile phone industry has contended that no research has shown that mobile phone use is hazardous to the health of the public.

Adapted from: Telecommunications Reports (2005) 'U.K. finds "No hard evidence" of cellphone health risk' 71(2), pp. 19–20.

1.6 WHY AND HOW SHOULD YOU SUMMARISE?

Summarising a source is when you express its main points in your own way, using your own words. Both paraphrasing and summarising sources require you to use your own words and in-essay references, but while a paraphrase expresses *all* the information contained in a specific part of a text, a summary gives only the *main* points from a much larger section or from the whole text. Summarising is a complex skill and one that is central to academic writing and that you will need both at university and in your future career. This section gives you key points and steps for summarising, looks at common problems, and gives examples of good and poor summarising.

WHY SUMMARISE?

Summarising is a key element in writing essays and other types of assignment, and is important for the same reasons for paraphrasing (see p. 26). However, a summary can be an even more powerful writing tool than a paraphrase because it allows you to show that you have understood the key point of a text and that you can express this clearly in your own way. Summarising therefore allows you great control over your use of sources.

There are two main reasons for giving a summary of a source in your essay:

- to give evidence and support for your own argument;
- to give an overview of different authors who support a particular position.

An overview is commonly given near the beginning of an essay, although you can give a brief overview of the literature at any stage in your essay when you are setting the scene for a specific point in your argument. Giving a summary of the position of key authors (see p. 34) shows that you understand where they locate themselves in the subject.

HOW LONG SHOULD A SUMMARY BE?

The length and level of detail of your summary will depend on what you want it to do in your essay. A summary that includes all the main points of a text may be up to a third as long as the original text. Often however, you will want to give a very brief summary of only a few sentences or even just one phrase that expresses the key point of the text.

LOOKING AT SOME EXAMPLES OF SUMMARIES

Below are two separate extracts you will recognise from the business ethics essay. Read each extract and think about why and how the student has briefly summarised his sources in the essay (the summaries are in blue) and then read the comments on each extract.

Essay extract 1

Opponents of the concept of ethics in business include those who claim that making a profit is the only responsibility a business has to society (Friedman

1970, cited in Fisher and Lovell 2003). Others such as Wolf (2008) share this view, and Prindl and Prodham (1994) suggest that 'Finance as practised in the professions and in industry is seen as a value-neutral positive discipline, promoting efficiency without regard to the social consequences which follow from its products' (p. 3). Carr (1968) uses the analogy of a poker game to argue that a successful businessman needs to play by the rules of the industry and that these include 'bluffing' as an acceptable form of behaviour. He suggests that what is, in effect, lying is merely part of legitimate business strategy and that business rules do not need to take account of personal or social principles.

Essay extract 2

My first proposition is that businesses actually *need* to behave in an ethical manner. This idea is expressed succinctly by Collins (1994) when he states that 'good ethics is synonymous with good management' (p. 2). Collins states that if managers only concern themselves with profit, they will become 'dysfunctional'. This is because any business is made up of people: employees, customers and other stakeholders. He states that if businesses do not operate with a degree of trust, co-operation and consideration both inside the organisation and externally, they will in fact be putting constraints on profitability. This idea of the interdependence of any business organisation is also supported by Shaw and Barry (2007), Green (1994), Fritzsche (2005) and Svensson and Wood (2008).

Comments on the extracts

In essay extract 1, the student summarises the view of Friedman in one sentence and then summarises the position of Wolf in only three words by stating that Wolf shares the same view. The student then uses a key quotation as a type of summary to state the position of Prindl and Prodham. The extract ends with a one-sentence summary of Carr's position. The extract gives an effective overview of key authors who oppose the idea that business ethics are important.

In essay extract 2, the student first establishes his own point by using a key quotation which also acts as a summary of Collins' position. He then explains Collins' view in a bit more detail by giving a two-sentence summary. In the final sentence of the extract the student summarises the main point of four other articles and six authors in a phrase of only 13 words: 'This idea of the interdependence of any business organisation is also supported by...' By doing all of this, the student shows that he understands the key point of all of these texts and also emphasises that these authors all hold a similar position on the issue.

Five points to remember when summarising

○ Express only the main point or points in the text.

○ Give an objective and balanced summary of these points and do not include your own opinion or comments.

○ As with paraphrasing, your summary should be your own expression, style and words as far as possible. It is not acceptable to change only a few words of the original text or to sew together key sentences copied from the text.

○ As with paraphrasing, you must always give in-essay references with your summary, because the ideas and information you have restated are not yours, even though the way you have expressed them is. Summarising without giving an in-essay reference is a form of plagiarism.

○ As with paraphrasing, if your summary is more than one sentence long, check whether you need to use reference reminder phrases to make clear that the later sentences are still points from your source.

FIVE STEPS FOR WRITING GOOD SUMMARIES

Step 1   Identify how the source text is organised

Writing a good summary starts with your reading. Make sure that you understand how the text is structured. Read the title, sub-headings, introduction and conclusion of the text to help you identify the key points. Identify which parts of the text are main points and which are examples of these points or more minor points.

Step 2   Understand, make clear notes and critically reflect on your reading

If you have approached your reading in a similar way to the steps given in section A1, A2 and A3, you will already be well on the way to writing a good summary. If you have written a critical reflection on what you have read it probably already includes a summary of the text.

Step 3   Summarise what the text is about in one or two sentences

A really useful exercise is to use your notes to write a very short summary of only one or two sentences. Doing this helps you to clarify in your mind what the main point of the text is. If you need to, you can then write a longer, more detailed summary that includes all the main points.

Step 4   Think about why and how you want to use the summary

Before you put your summary into your essay, ask yourself how it fits into your essay plan and argument. Make sure you show clearly how your summary supports your own point.

Step 5   Check that you have used your own words and style, in-essay references, and reference reminder phrases

As with paraphrasing, check that you have written your summary using your own words as far as possible and that you have used adequate in-essay referencing.

SIX COMMON MISTAKES STUDENTS MAKE WHEN SUMMARISING:

- accidently changing the meaning of the original text;
- giving too much detail and putting in minor points, examples or definitions from the text, rather than just the main points;
- adding their own opinion or comments;
- not making enough changes in words and style from the original source;
- not making clear where the summary begins and ends (i.e. not using clear in-essay references and reference reminder phrases);
- giving the primary source as the in-essay reference when they have only read the secondary source.

Practice 9 | what's wrong with these summaries?

Below is a short text. Read it and make your own notes. Use your notes to write first a one-sentence summary of the text, then a summary of three or four sentences. After you have written your own summaries, read the five unacceptable summaries and identify what is wrong with them. Finally, read the comments on the unacceptable summaries and then look at the good summaries.

A study on links between emotion regulation, job satisfaction and intentions to quit

Emotion regulation is the conscious and unconscious efforts people make to increase, maintain or decrease their emotions and is manifested by changes in facial expression and by changes in vocal and body signals. People often regulate their emotions at work. An example of emotion suppression is when a worker tries to hide anger they might be feeling towards a colleague or manager. Emotion amplification on the other hand, is when one pretends to be happier than one actually is. For example, an insurance or telephone salesperson may amplify their display of positive emotion to customers in order to increase their level of sales and quality of service.

Cote and Morgan (2002) conducted a study that looks at the relationship between emotion regulation, job satisfaction and intention to quit one's job. They collected two sets of data from 111 workers. The participants gave informed consent and were asked to complete two questionnaires on how they felt they had regulated their emotions at work and their feelings about their job. There was a time interval of four weeks between the two questionnaires to allow enough time for changes in emotion regulation but also to have a short enough period to maintain the retention of the participants.

Cote and Morgan showed from their data that the amplification of pleasant emotions happened more frequently than the suppression of unpleasant emotions. Importantly, they also found a strong correlation between emotion regulation and job satisfaction and intention to quit. They demonstrated that, as they predicted, the suppression of unpleasant emotions leads to a decrease in job satisfaction and therefore an increase in intention to quit. Their findings also suggest that an increase in the amplification of pleasant emotions will increase job satisfaction, because it increases positive social interaction and more positive responses from colleagues and customers.

Although their experiment showed that emotion regulation affects job satisfaction, there was no strong evidence to suggest a reverse correlation i.e. that job satisfaction and intention to quit influence emotional regulation.

Source: Robinson, J. (2011) 'A study on links between emotion regulation, job satisfaction and intentions to quit' *Business Reports that Matter*(3) p. 41.

Unacceptable summaries

1 Emotion regulation is the conscious and unconscious efforts people make to increase, maintain or decrease their emotions. Cote and Morgan (2002) have conducted a study that looks at the relationship between emotion regulation, job satisfaction and intention to quit one's job. Cote and Morgan showed from their data that the amplification of pleasant emotions happened more frequently than the suppression of unpleasant emotions. Importantly, they also found a strong correlation between emotion regulation and job satisfaction and intention to quit.

2 A study has shown a strong link between emotion regulation and job satisfaction and intention to quit (Cote and Morgan 2002, cited in Robinson, 2011). An example of emotion regulation is when someone attempts to hide the anger they feel towards their boss or when they pretend to be happier than they really are during a work meeting or when dealing with customers. Cote and Morgan tested 111 workers by asking them to complete two questionnaires at an interval of four weeks. They found and that workers exaggerate positive emotions more than they hide negative feelings. The findings also showed that suppressing negative feelings leads to lower job satisfaction and that amplifying positive feelings leads to better work relationships and therefore higher job satisfaction.

3 Robinson (2011) describes a study conducted by Cote and Morgan, in which they obtained data on emotion regulation from 111 workers. The findings suggest that workers exaggerate positive emotions more than they hide negative feelings and that there is strong evidence that how you feel about your job influences how you regulate your emotions at work.

4 A study has shown a strong link between emotion regulation and job satisfaction and intention to quit (Cote and Morgan 2002, cited in Robinson, 2011) and that workers exaggerate positive emotions more than they hide negative feelings. This might be because workers are worried that if they show their negative feelings, they might not get promoted, or worse, that they may lose their job. The findings also showed that suppressing negative feelings leads to a decrease in job satisfaction and a corresponding increase in wanting to leave, and that amplifying positive feelings leads to more positive interaction at work and therefore more job satisfaction.

Comments on the unacceptable summaries

Summary 1 consists of four key sentences copied word for word from the original text. This is therefore plagiarism. In addition to this, the student has only given an in-essay reference for Cote and Morgan, which implies that they have read the primary Cote and Morgan article, when in fact they have only read the Robinson text. This is a misrepresentation of both Cote and Morgan and of what the student has read.

The first and the last two sentences of summary 2 are good, with correct in-essay references. However, in the middle of the summary the student has included different examples of what emotion regulation is and also details of the method of the study, neither of which should be in a summary.

Summary 3 starts with a correct in-essay reference, and the summary is written in the student's own words and style, which is good. However, the last point in the summary is not correct - the study showed that emotion regulation can influence how you feel about your job but that there was *no* evidence that job satisfaction affects emotion regulation.

Summary 4 starts and ends well, with a clear statement of the key point and correct in-essay references. However, the second sentence is the student's own idea of why workers might hide negative feelings, and this should not be part of the summary. Any comments or opinion by the student on the results of the Cote and Morgan study should come after the summary rather than within it.

An example of an acceptable one-sentence summary

A study has shown a strong link between regulating emotions at work and job satisfaction levels, and therefore intention to quit (Cote and Morgan 2002, cited in Robinson 2011).

An example of an acceptable three-sentence summary

A study has shown that people exaggerate positive emotions more than they hide negative feelings when at work (Cote and Morgan 2002, cited in Robinson 2011). Cote and Morgan established a strong link between regulating emotions, job satisfaction and intention to quit. They found that suppressing negative feelings leads to lower levels of job satisfaction, and that amplifying positive feelings leads to better relationships at work and therefore more job satisfaction. However, they found no evidence of job satisfaction level affecting how people regulate their emotions at work.

Practice 10 | write a summary

Read and make notes on the informative source text below. From your notes, write a one-sentence summary and then a two- or three-sentence summary. Each summary should include an in-essay reference and reference reminder phrase.

Source text

Sport in the UK: the role of the DCMS
The Department for Culture, Media and Sport (DCMS) is responsible for delivering Government policy on sport, from supporting the performance and preparation of elite individual performers and teams to increasing sporting opportunities at all levels, but especially for the young, to encourage long-lasting participation.

DCMS recognizes that success in sport by UK representatives at the elite level, such as athletes at the Olympics or football teams in European competition, can enhance the reputation of the country and make large numbers of people feel proud. To that end, it provides funding where it will make a difference, such as through the Talented Athlete Scholarship Scheme, and political support where that is more suitable, such as to the Football Association's attempts to be awarded the right to host the 2018 FIFA World Cup in England.

DCMS also supports opportunities to participate in sport in schools and communities, regardless of the level of performance. Among DCMS' targets are that by 2008, 85% of 5-16-year-olds will be taking physical education and other school sports for a minimum of two hours per week, and that by 2012 all children will have the opportunity of at least four hours of weekly sport (DCMS 2008).

Widening participation will help to identify the next generation of potential elite performers at an early stage, but DCMS also has other less obvious goals in mind. They claim that continued participation in sport from an early age will lead to a more active population and that this will help to address the problem of increasing levels and frequency of obesity and so reduce the risk of coronary heart disease, stroke, type 2 diabetes and certain types of cancer. Clearly, the benefits of sport to the nation are not simply about medal tables and championships.

Source: Dobson, C. (2010) *Sport and the Nation*.

1.7 PUTTING IT ALL TOGETHER IN YOUR ESSAY

The final section of this chapter reviews the process of using sources and looks at how to integrate quotation, paraphrase and summary into an essay paragraph. It also gives you some final comments and advice on avoiding plagiarism, and a practice exercise to help you become more aware of integrating sources into your writing. Throughout this chapter we have used extracts from the business ethics essay as examples of how to use sources, and below is a another colour-coded extract from the essay as a final example. Notice the paragraph's sequence of black - blue - black, representing the pattern of student point, sources used as support, and follow-up student comment.

Essay extract

My third and final reason for stating that business ethics is important is as a tool for analysis, research, study and education. As shown above, the power of organisations is increasing both nationally and globally, and the decisions business people make can have far-reaching effects. Despite this fact, managers surprisingly often have no specific training in ethics. I would argue that events such as the 2008 crash outlined above demonstrate that such training is needed, and that business ethics as a field of education and training within organisations is vital. — Student point

The study of business ethics is also important because it provides an informed framework and source of criteria through which business behaviour can be analysed and evaluated by legal bodies and other groups in society. — Student point

As Crouch (2011) states when discussing the political and financial power of multinational corporations, civic society now has a crucial role in analysing how these businesses behave and in criticising them and voicing concerns. — Source used as support

Even if particular behaviour is legal at the time of an event, analysis of the activity and an explicit discussion on its impact in terms of agreed ethical standards can lead to modified or even new legislation. — Student point

REVIEWING THE WHOLE PROCESS FROM READING SOURCES TO WRITING THE ESSAY

To get an overview of how the whole process works, look at Table 1.1, which summarises each stage in the use of a very short section of the Svensson and Wood article, with the relevant page numbers so that you can go back and review each stage in full if you wish. This is followed by Table 1.2, which gives a list of the page numbers for each stage in the use of the article by Albert Carr (note that we did not look at a short reflection for the Carr article, so there is no reference to one in Table 1.2).

Table 1.1 – Stages in the use of the Svensson and Wood article

Stage 1: Reading the article. Page 21
. . . it is important to see business ethics as a highly dynamic and continuous process without an end. A process, however, that is predicated on the interrelationship between business and society where each one is interdependent and responsible together for the outcomes.
Extract from: Svensson, G. and Wood, G. (2008) 'A Model of Business Ethics'
Journal of Business Ethics, 77, pp. 303–322.

Stage 2: Critically analysing the article as you read. Pages 21–22
Svensson and Wood argue strongly and clearly that business and society influence each other and are dependent on each other and have a responsibility to each other to behave ethically. However, they seem to ignore the fact that . . . Still, I think that this article is solid enough to use as one of my main sources as evidence for what I think my conclusion will probably be, which is that businesses need to have good ethics and that business ethics is important both to businesses and to society.

Stage 3: Making notes on the article. Page 28
p.319.
A main point
BE-'. . . dynamic and continuous process . . .' – 'interrelationship between businesses and society . . .' – each responsible for the other.

Stage 4: Writing a critical reflection of the article. Page 29
The authors propose and describe their own model of business ethics, which centres around a 'dynamic and continuous process' between business and society. They argue persuasively that business and society influence each other, are dependent on each other and have a responsibility to each other.

Stage 5: Using the article in the business ethics essay. Appendix 3, Page 146
On a more theoretical level, Svensson and Wood (2008) offer a model that shows how business and society are mutually dependent, and that both are responsible for the consequences and effects of the other as part of a dynamic two-way process.

Table 1.2 – Stages in the use of the Carr article

Stage 1	Article extract. pp. 22–23
Stage 2	Critical analysis. Appendix 1, pp. 125–126
Stage 3	Notes. Appendix 1, pp. 126–127
Stage 5	Paraphrase in essay. Appendix 3, p. 145

TIME MANAGEMENT FOR EACH STAGE OF THE PROCESS OF USING YOUR READING IN YOUR ESSAYS

Figure 1.1 summarises each stage of the process, and gives the approximate minimum times needed if you were searching online and using four journal articles. The precise time you will need will of course vary but it's useful to have some rough guidelines, particularly as one reason students get poor marks for their work is simply because they have not given enough time to each part of the process.

AVOIDING ACCIDENTAL PLAGIARISM

Common causes of both purposeful and accidental plagiarism are:

- not giving enough time to reading and understanding texts;
- not taking notes or writing a reflection;

- not understanding what counts as plagiarism in writing;
- lack of ability or confidence in restating something using your own words;
- not wanting to highlight the fact that you have used lots of sources;
- not giving clear in-text referencing;
- writing an essay that consists almost entirely of sources (even if they are all correctly referenced).

This Part has taken you through key steps and practice exercises that address each of the issues listed above. This Part have hopefully helped you to understand what plagiarism is, and given you the knowledge and confidence to use your sources properly and effectively. Plagiarising will not do anything to help you learn and will not help you gain the skills you need for your future career. Even if your goal at university is only to get good marks, plagiarising is still a waste of time because it almost always results in poor-quality work. It is in fact easier, more enjoyable, and a better strategy for getting good marks, to do the work needed to produce your own essay.

A useful metaphor: building a house

When thinking about originality and avoiding plagiarism, you might find it helpful to think of the essay writing process in terms of designing and building a house (the house is your essay and the materials and fittings are your sources).

The first thing you would need to do is to be clear about the purpose of the house; why you were building it and what requirements you wanted it to meet. Even if you had been given the basic design and requirements of the house (the essay title), you would still need to think about exactly how to meet the specifications of the design.

The materials for building the house (your sources) would need to be well researched, reliable and right for the job. The different materials and fittings you would use would mainly be ones that someone else had produced, but the house would be original to you because of your design features, which materials and fittings you had decided to use and how you had decided to use them. You would also keep receipts and manufacturer's details (a research log) in case of any problems and for use on future building projects.

When you had finished your house and were showing people round (anyone who reads your essay) they would be interested in who had designed and made various fittings such as the windows or kitchen units. You would hopefully be proud to answer their questions honestly. No-one would expect you to have made the kitchen units or windows yourself (and it would be obvious to anyone with any building experience that you had not done so). What *would* be important would be showing your intelligence and skill in finding and selecting the right materials, understanding how they worked, and using them effectively in your own way to build your own house that meets the design brief.

Eight Key points to remember about using your reading in your essays

- Your tutors want to see that you have been able to discriminate between different sources and select the most relevant ones.
- It is essential that you become really familiar with what you read so that you have a clear and independent understanding of it. Your tutors also want to see that you have been able to use and integrate your sources appropriately in your essay.
- You should read with a purpose in mind, but also be prepared to modify or change your viewpoint as a result of how your thinking develops as you read.

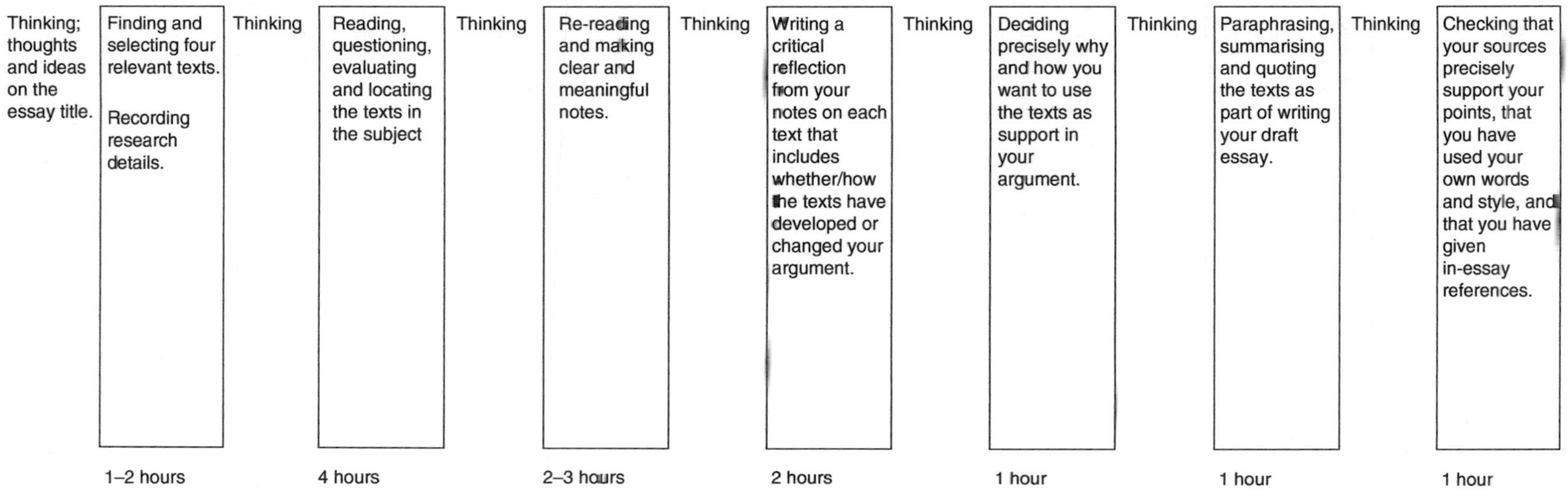

Thinking; thoughts and ideas on the essay title.

Thinking → Finding and selecting four relevant texts. Recording research details. — 1–2 hours

Thinking → Reading, questioning, evaluating and locating the texts in the subject — 4 hours

Thinking → Re-reading and making clear and meaningful notes. — 2–3 hours

Thinking → Writing a critical reflection from your notes on each text that includes whether/how the texts have developed or changed your argument. — 2 hours

Thinking → Deciding precisely why and how you want to use the texts as support in your argument. — 1 hour

Thinking → Paraphrasing, summarising and quoting the texts as part of writing your draft essay. — 1 hour

Thinking → Checking that your sources precisely support your points, that you have used your own words and style, and that you have given in-essay references. — 1 hour

Figure 1.1 – Time management for using your reading in your essay

○ Get the best marks possible for your work by always giving in-essay references so that your tutor can distinguish your ideas from those of your sources. Referencing all your sources also makes your work more credible and therefore more persuasive.

○ An effective use of quotation, paraphrase and summary will enable you to control your sources and make them work for you in your essay.

○ Never use a source without commenting on it in some way.

○ Everyone approaches writing differently, and there is not one correct way to write an essay. It is important that you care about your writing and that you feel it is your own individual piece of work. Even if you use lots of sources, as long as you reference them, your essay will still be original because of which sources you have used, how you have analysed and evaluated them and how you have used them to support your argument and your individual answer to the assignment question.

○ Skills and confidence and in quoting, paraphrasing and summarising will come with practice.

Practice 11 | what do you think of the way these students have used this source in their essay?

Below are three paragraphs from three separate essays addressing the title: 'In what ways might personality affect job satisfaction?'

All three students have used the Robinson text on p. 36. Re-read the Robinson text and then read the three essay paragraphs to decide what the problem is in each case, then read the comments on each paragraph.

Finally, look at the example of a good paragraph in which the student has used their notes and reflection on the text as a basis for integrating the source information into their essay.

Unacceptable essay paragraphs

1 There does seem to be a link between personality and job satisfaction, although there are different views on how strong this link is. One interesting study on emotion regulation has demonstrated that there is a strong link between how we regulate our emotions at work and how satisfied we are with our jobs (Cote and Morgan 2002, cited in Robinson 2011). Their data showed that the amplification of pleasant emotions happened more frequently than the suppression of unpleasant emotions. Importantly, they also found a strong correlation between emotion regulation and job satisfaction and intention to quit. These finding would suggest that if you are good at regulating your emotions and particularly if you are able to be (or at least pretend to be) positive, you are likely to have a higher level of job satisfaction than someone who cannot or does not want to amplify positive emotions. Although emotion regulation is not synonymous with personality, it seems likely that personality type is linked to emotion regulation and therefore to job satisfaction.

2 There does seem to be a link between personality and job satisfaction, although there are different views on how strong this link is. A study has shown that there is a strong link between how we regulate our emotions at work and how satisfied we are with our jobs. Workers exaggerate positive emotions more than they hide negative feelings. In addition, suppressing negative emotions leads to less job satisfaction and amplifying positive emotions leads to better social interaction at work and therefore more job satisfaction. If you are good at regulating your emotions and particularly if you are able to be (or at least pretend to be) positive, you are likely to have a higher level of job satisfaction than someone who cannot or does not want to amplify positive emotions. Although emotion regulation is not synonymous with personality, it seems likely that personality type is linked to emotion regulation and therefore to job satisfaction (Cote and Morgan 2002, cited in Robinson 2011).

3 Cote and Morgan claim that there is a strong link between emotion regulation and job satisfaction and intention to quit (Cote and Morgan 2002, cited in Robinson 2011). The findings showed that workers exaggerate positive emotions more than they hide negative feelings. Cote and Morgan also found that suppressing negative emotions leads to less job satisfaction and that amplifying positive emotions leads to better social interaction at work and therefore more job satisfaction.

Comments on the unacceptable essay paragraphs

1 This paragraph starts well, with the student introducing her own point that there is a link between personality and job satisfaction. She then starts to paraphrase the Robinson article and gives a correct in-essay reference. However, the third and fourth sentences are copied word for word from the Robinson text without any quotation marks; this is plagiarism. The paragraph ends well with the student's own comments.

2 The student starts well by introducing her own point. She continues by summarising the Robinson text in her own words, which is good. However, she does not give any in-essay references or reference reminder phrases; this is plagiarism. After her summary she continues with her own comments on the implications of the study. At the end of the last sentence she gives an in-essay reference, even though this last sentence is her own point, not that of Cote and Morgan - this means that the student is misrepresenting the source and in addition is not getting credit for her own idea. When reading this paragraph, the tutor would not be able to see clearly which points were those of the student and which those of the source.

3 This paragraph contains only the summary of the Robinson text. There are in-essay references but there is no introduction or conclusion by the student and we therefore have no idea what point the student is trying to make. This is an example of the sources controlling the essay -the student has merely found sources she thinks might be relevant and put them in, without introducing them or thinking about what point she wants them to support in her essay.

EXAMPLE OF AN ACCEPTABLE ESSAY PARAGRAPH USING THE ROBINSON TEXT

There does seem to be a link between personality and job satisfaction, although there are different views on how strong this link is. [Student point]

One interesting study on emotion regulation has demonstrated that there is a strong link between how we regulate our emotions at work, and how satisfied we are with our jobs (Cote and Morgan 2002, cited in Robinson 2011). The findings showed that workers exaggerate positive emotions more than they hide negative feelings. Cote and Morgan also found that suppressing negative feelings leads to less job satisfaction, and that amplifying positive ones leads to better social interaction at work and therefore higher job satisfaction. [Summary of source used as evidence and support]

These findings would suggest that if you are good at regulating your emotions (and particularly if you are able to be, or at least pretend to be positive) you are likely to have a higher level of job satisfaction than someone who cannot or does not want to amplify their positive emotions. The fact that if you suppress negative feelings you will have lower job satisfaction, suggests that if you are someone who can express negative feelings in a constructive way at work in order to find a solution to the problem, you will probably have higher job satisfaction than someone who hides negative emotions without trying to resolve them. [Student's ideas on the implications of the findings]

Although emotion regulation is not synonymous with personality, it seems likely that personality type is linked to emotion regulation and therefore to job satisfaction. [Conclusion of student's point.]

APPENDIX 1

Glossary

Abstract a summary (usually of about 100 words) of an article, report or book, which includes the main argument or problem, the procedures, results and conclusion. Abstracts are always written by the authors of the source and are normally used by readers to decide whether they want to read the whole text.

Academic/scholarly journal a journal which contains reliable, peer-reviewed articles of good quality.

Academic source a book, article or other type of text which has been peer-reviewed and/or is written by experts in the subject.

Argument a sequence of reasons to support a particular theory or point of view.

Bibliographic details the full details of a source, given at the end of a written text.

Citation information on who wrote something, given within the piece of writing. *Citation* is also sometimes used to mean a quotation.

Close paraphrase when most of the words of the original source are used with only small changes. Close paraphrase should only be used when taking notes.

Critical analysis/thought the process of identifying the argument of a text and then questioning and evaluating it to decide whether it is based on correct assumptions, logical reasoning and sound evidence.

Digest a brief summary of one source or a compilation of summaries of many different sources on a particular topic. It can be written by the authors themselves or by a third party.

Draft a rough version of an essay or other piece of written work, which is changed and improved to produce the finished piece.

et al. abbreviation of the latin *et alii* meaning 'and others'. Used for in-essay referencing when a source has more than two authors.

Evaluation, to evaluate to reflect on and assess the information and argument of something.

Extract a section of text.

ibid. from the latin *ibidem* meaning 'in the same place'. Used as an in-essay reference to indicate that the source is exactly the same as the one previously given.

i.e. from the latin *id est*, meaning 'that is'. In writing, *i.e.* is used to mean 'that is to say' or 'in other words'. Be careful not to confuse *i.e.* with *e.g.* With *i.e.* you must restate the complete idea or complete set of items. With *e.g.* you only give one or two examples of the set.

Literature review summarising and comparing the key authors and sources on a particular topic or issue.

Literature search the process of looking for, finding and selecting relevant material and sources.

Paraphrase, to paraphrase re-expressing all the information and ideas from a section of text in your own words and style.

Peer-review the system by which articles are checked for quality and accuracy by relevant academic experts before being published.

Plagiarism, to plagiarise presenting someone else's ideas, information, wording or style (or any combination of these) as your own, even if it is only a single sentence. Plagiarism also includes claiming that work done jointly with other students is solely your own work (this is called 'collusion'). Plagiarism can occur accidentally due to poor writing and referencing, or on purpose to gain a particular advantage or benefit.

Primary source the first, original source of information or ideas, for example the original report written by the person who conducted an experiment or the original article or book written by an author.

Quotation, to quote a phrase, sentence or section of a source given in your writing, word for word, without any changes in wording from the original text.

Research any type of organised search, study, investigation or work that is done in order to develop ideas and knowledge.

Scan to look at or read something quickly in order to identify key points or to assess whether something is relevant for more detailed reading.

School of thought a way of thinking, set of beliefs, or accepted theory or approach, e.g. behaviourism, socialism, Marxism, feminism.

Secondary source a source which writes about, discusses or uses a previously written primary source.

Text a word used to describe any type of written document when focusing on the content rather than the type of document.

APPENDIX 2

Answers to practice execises

1.1   How do you decide what to read?

Practice 1

1. Reliable information for general issues on disability but may be biased. Not an academic source.
2. Not reliable and not an academic source.
3. Reliable and an academic source but 2002 is quite old for such a topic, which decreases the reliability of the information.

4. a. Reliable for some ideas on issues but may be biased and inaccurate. Not an academic source.
    b. Reliable and an academic source.
    c. Quite reliable but not an academic source.
5. Reliable for introducing main issues but not an academic source. Also the booklet is quite old for this topic and this further decreases how reliable the source is for information on animal cloning.
6. Probably reliable as information from businesses but not an academic source. You would also need to check when the website was updated.
7. Not reliable and not an academic source.
8. Reliable as information from businesses but not an academic source.
9. Reliable for general discussion and ideas but not peer-reviewed and therefore not academically reliable. You should find and use articles from the centre's 'Journal of Ethics' for academic sources.
10. Not reliable and will be biased, as it seems to be written by a pressure group. Not an academic source.

1.2   How do you understand and question what you read?

Practice 2

Questioning

Carr assumes that businessmen are ethical in their private lives – this may not be true. He also assumes that all businesses operate in the same way, that they all have ethical standards separate from private ones and that you always have to choose between losing and lying. This may not be true – there may be other options or other types of business models.

Evaluating

His style is quite persuasive – I instinctively feel he is partly right – but he is very cynical and over-simplifies. He gives no evidence for his views and doesn't try to be objective or look at opposing evidence. His argument isn't very well ordered as it is continuous opinion rather than a developed argument. I agree with Carr that some people feel they do need to lie in business but not that this is always the case or that business ethics are totally separate from social norms – particularly nowadays? I will use Carr as a key source to show an expert who opposes the idea of business ethics and I will then criticise his argument by giving opposing evidence from Svensson and Wood.

Locating

Carr's article seems to have been radical and important at the time (1968) because a lot of other texts still refer to it. In terms of business ethics he is definitely in the 'no' camp. His article is very dated now and things have moved on since then – now there is more legislation on regulation of corporate behaviour, corporate transparency and accountability and more emphasis on ethics and sustainability.

1.3   What should you write down?

Practice 3
Example notes

	Carr, A. Z. (1968) 'Is business bluffing ethical?' *Harvard Business Review*, 46 (1), pp. 143–153. Notes written on 16/2/2009
p. 145 main point.	Ethics of bus. are like the rules of poker (distrust) – diff. from 'civilised human relationships'.
p. 145 (bottom) Not true?	Most busmn. are ethical in private lives, but at work they stop being 'private citizens' + follow the *different*. ethical rules of bus.
p. 148	The image that bus. gives of using ethics from private life e.g."'Sound ethics is good for business"' is only a self-serving + profit making deception, not a true ethical position.
p.153 (Conclusion) Not true now/all (lying) choose betwn. losing and 'bluffing' businesses? – other choices?	'To be a winner, a man must play to win'. Busmn will sometimes have to like poker. To succeed he will have to 'bluff hard'.
2nd main point	'Bluffing' is 'integral' to business.

NB 'Sound ethics is good for business' is a quotation by Carr in the original text. The student has made this clear in his notes by using double and then also single quotation marks to show that Carr is quoting someone else.

1.4   Why and how should you quote?

Practice 4

1   This quotation is not special in what it says or how it is expressed. The student should have given this information in their own words as far as possible, for example: *Kzanty (2004) states that organs such as the lungs, pancreas and heart are used in transplantation.*

2   This information is common fact and knowledge so can be given in the essay without attribution to the author.

3   The quotation partially contradicts the student's point that transplants save lives.

4   The quotation is about the student's first point (improvements in transplantation techniques using animal organs), not about the point that is immediately in front of the quotation, that patients do not have to wait for transplants.

5   The quotation is not introduced clearly – it does not explain which trial or study is referred to or who 'everyone' is.

Practice 5

1   There are no quotation marks and no in-essay reference. This is plagiarism.

2   There is an in-essay reference but no quotation marks. This is plagiarism.

3   There are quotation marks but no in-essay reference. This might be seen as plagiarism.

4   There are quotation marks and an in-essay reference, but the authors' names should not be in brackets and the page number is missing. The page number must be included for quotations if you use the author/year system of referencing.

Practice 6

1   The student has added the word 'business' to the original wording. She should either take this word out or put it in square brackets, e.g. [business].

2   The student has taken out the words 'synonymous with' from the original text. She should use ... to show this, for example: *This is that 'good ethics is ... good management' (p. 2).*

3   The topic words 'good ethics' are used twice, once in the introductory sentence and again in the quotation. They should be used in one or the other but not both, for example: *This is that good ethical behaviour 'is synonymous with good management' (p. 2),* or *This is that 'good ethics is synonymous with good management' (p. 2).*

4   The full-stop at the end of the quotation is inside the quotation marks. It should come outside the quotation marks after the page number brackets, for example: *This is that 'good ethics is synonymous with good management' (p. 2).*

Correct version of the extract using a numeric system of referencing

Secondly, an even stronger argument for the view that good ethics in business do in fact exist, is that given by Collins and by other prominent experts on the subject. This is that 'good ethics is synonymous with good management' (1).

WORKS CITED

1.   J. W. Collins. 'Is business ethics an oxymoron?' *Business Horizons* 1994; 37 (5): 1–8.

1.5   Why and how should you use your own words?

Practice 7

1   The paraphrase itself is good as it is written in the student's own words. However, there are no in-essay references and so this counts as plagiarism.

2 The paraphrase is rewritten in the student's own words and has an initial in-essay reference. However, there is no reference reminder phrase in the second sentence and so it is not clear whether this sentence is an idea from the student or from the source. This could be seen as plagiarism.

3 There is only one in-essay reference, given at the end of the paragraph. It is therefore not clear whether the first sentence is the student's idea or an idea from the source – this could be seen as plagiarism. It is much better to integrate a reference into the first sentence of a paraphrase and then to use reference reminder phrases.

4 This paraphrase consists of one sentence copied from Cox and a second sentence copied from the Maier, Blakemore and Koivisto text. The sentences have been stitched together without the use of quotation marks and without adequate referencing. This is plagiarism.

Example of an acceptable paraphrase of the Cox extract

Using the author/year style of in-essay referencing:

> Cox (2003) suggests that advising caution in the use of mobile phones is an example of a typical approach to the fear of a possible health risk which may be of a serious nature. He states that such an approach may have negative consequences, but is taken because although there may in fact be no health risk, this has not yet been proven.

Using the numeric style of in-essay referencing:

> Cox (1) suggests that advising caution in the use of mobile phones is an example of a typical approach to the fear of a possible health risk which may be of a serious nature. He states that such an approach may have negative consequences, but is taken because although there may in fact be no health risk, this has not yet been proven.

WORKS CITED

1. D. R. Cox, 'Communication of risk: health hazards from mobile phones'. *Journal of the Royal Statistical Society: Series A (Statistics in Society)* 2003; 166 (2): 214–246.

1.6 Why and how should you summarise?

Practice 8

Example of a good personal reflection on the Robinson text

Robinson states that Côté and Morgan's study shows a strong link between regulating emotions at work and job satisfaction and intentions to quit.

Robinson doesn't go into great detail about the Côté and Morgan study, so I would need to read the original text to really do a critical analysis of it and find out whether the experiment has any flaws. However, just from reading Robinson's summary of the study, it seems to me to be an important experiment – the only one I have found so far on emotion regulation. I think that the idea of regulating emotions at work and the effects this has on how someone feels about their job is very interesting.

Thinking about the essay title, I think that Côté and Morgan's findings imply that if you have a personality that is good at regulating your emotions and particularly that if you are able to be (or at least pretend to be) positive, then you are likely to have a higher level of job satisfaction than someone who can't or doesn't want to amplify positive emotions.

The findings also show that if you suppress negative emotions, you will have less job satisfaction. I think that this shows that if you are someone who can express negative feelings in a constructive way at work in order to find a solution to the problem, then you will probably have more job satisfaction than someone who just always hides negative emotions without trying to do anything about them.

<table>
<tr><td>Chapter
2</td><td></td></tr>
</table>

STUDYING WORK & ORGANIZATIONS

CHAPTER OUTLINE

- Introduction
- Classical approaches to studying work
- Contemporary theories of work organizations
- The value of theory about contemporary organizational behaviour
- Summary and end-of-chapter features
- Chapter case study 1: Butting out smoking in Russia
- Chapter case study 2: Research at Aeroprecision AB

CHAPTER OBJECTIVES

After completing this chapter, you should be able to:

- explain the classical approaches to studying work through the ideas of Marx, Durkheim and Weber
- explain contemporary theories of work organizations and the importance of theory to understanding work and behaviour in the workplace

INTRODUCTION

This chapter examines classical and contemporary approaches to studying work and work organizations. We begin by considering the classical social theories about paid work through the ideas of Marx, Weber and Durkheim. These can be described as classical partly because they had their roots in European industrialization and culture – from about 1800 through to the early 1900s – and also because, in their response to industrial capitalism, the early social theorists set out a series of themes, concepts, assumptions, problems and ideas that continue to exercise an enormous influence over contemporary organizational theory. As others have pointed out, both the perspectives of analysis that are clearly set out in the works of the classical theorists, and the characteristic focuses of those traditions, continue to dominate study of the sociology of work.[1-3]

Over the last three decades not only have organizations fundamentally changed how they organize work, but new approaches and concepts have also been developed for studying work organizations. In the 1970s, the orthodox consensus on organization theory focused on 'functionalism', which emphasized consensus and coherence rather than asymmetrical power relations and conflict.[4] The key concept is that of the organization as a 'system' that functions effectively if it achieves explicit goals, which are formally defined through 'rational' decision making. Alternative theoretical approaches have since challenged the supremacy of functionalism.

A multitude of contemporary theories of formal organizations exist, so we cannot hope to do justice to the complexities of such a wide-ranging debate. We therefore seek here to highlight the major distinguishing themes related to work and organizations. Drawing on the work of Keith Grint,[5] we review 12 competing theoretical perspectives or 'conversations' in organization theory: the technical, human relations, neo-human relations, systems thinking, contingency, cultures, learning, control, feminist, social action, political and postmodernist perspectives.

CLASSICAL APPROACHES TO STUDYING WORK

Marx, Durkheim and Weber each analysed the new work forms, but also placed their analysis within a wider discourse on modern society and social change. While Karl Marx focused on social fragmentation, conflict and social change, Emile Durkheim concerned himself with social fragmentation and the nature of order, and Max Weber developed his theory of rationality and bureaucracy.

Plate 1 – Karl Marx.
Source: Marxists Internet Archive

Karl Marx (1818–83)

stop reflect
Do contemporary organizational behaviour theorists have anything to learn from the classical sociologists such as Marx, Durkheim and Weber?

Marx believed that industrialization was a necessary stage for the eventual triumph of human potential, but that the mainspring of this social formation was capitalism, and not industrialism as such. It is only capitalism that carries within it the seeds of its own destruction. For Marx, the human species is different from all other animal species, not because of its consciousness, but because it alone produces its own means of subsistence.

Marx's argument is that what distinguishes humans from other animals is that our labour creates something in reality that previously existed only in our imagination:

> We presuppose labour in a form that stamps it as exclusively human ... But what distinguishes the worst architect from the best bees is this, that the architect raises his structure in imagination before he erects it in reality. At the end of every labour process we get a result that existed in the *imagination* of the labourer at its commencement. He not only effects a change of form in the material on which he works, but he also realizes a purpose.
>
> (ref 6, p. 178, emphasis added)

objectification: Karl Marx's term to describe the action of human labour on resources to produce a commodity, which under the control of the capitalist remains divorced from and opposed to the direct producer

Marx calls this process whereby humans create external objects from their internal thoughts **objectification**. This labour does not just transform raw materials or nature; it also transforms humans, including human nature, people's needs and their consciousness. We can begin to understand Marx's concept of objectification by thinking of the creative activity of an artist. The artist's labour is a representation of the imagination of the artist: 'the art work is an objectification of the artist'.[7] In addition, through the labour process, the artist's ideas of the object change, or the experience, may prompt a new vision or creativity that needs objectification. Labour, for Marx, provides the means through which humans can realize their true human powers and potential. By transforming raw materials, we transform ourselves, and we also transform society. Thus, according to Marx, the transformation of the individual through work and the transformation of society are inseparable.

Marx's discussion of work under capitalism focuses on the nature of employment relationships. Under capitalism, the aim is to buy labour at sufficiently low rates to make a profit. Marx is careful to distinguish between 'labour' and 'labour power'. Human labour is the actual physical or mental activity incorporated in the body of the worker. Labour power, on the other hand, refers to the *potential* of labour to add use value to raw materials or commodities. This labour power is bought by the capitalist at a value less than the value it creates. In purchasing the worker's potential or capacity to labour and add use values to materials, at a wage level less than the value created by the worker's labour, the capitalist is able to make a profit.

We can begin to appreciate the significance of Marx's use of the term 'labour power' when we think of it as a promise: it is therefore indeterminate, and there may be a gap between the potential or promise of labour and the actual labour. This distinction between 'labour' and 'labour power' allowed Marx to locate the precise mechanism that creates profit in capitalist societies. It also gives rise to the creation of two classes that are potentially, if not always in practice, in conflict with each other.

surplus value: the portion of the working day during which workers produce value that is appropriated by the capitalist

Capitalism involves the work relationship between the buyers and sellers of labour power. Marx's concept of **surplus value** is rooted in this social relationship. Surplus value is the value remaining when the worker's daily costs of subsistence have been subtracted from the value that she or he produces for the capitalist. As such, it is unpaid and 'goes to the heart of the exploitation of the worker'.[8]

In the workplace, the primacy of profit and conflict relationships gives rise to three broad necessary features of activity and change. Each of these involves substantial shifts in the work performed. Most significant is the need for the capitalist to centralize the labour power that is purchased, and to discipline the interior of the factory, by organizing space, time and the behaviour of workers whose commitment is unreliable. The aim is to close or minimize the gap between potential labour power and actual labour power. For Marx, the accumulation of profit is inevitably and irrevocably mediated by managerial control strategies. It is the inevitable outcome of capitalism: 'The directing motive, the end and aim of capitalist production, is to extract the greatest possible amount of surplus-value, and consequently to exploit labour-power to the fullest possible extent' (ref. 6, p. 331).

division of labour: the allocation of work tasks to various groups or categories of employee

The second broad plane of activity changing the nature of work is the **division of labour**. To increase control and surplus value for the capitalist, extensive division of labour takes place within the factory. According to Marx, 'Division of labour within the workshop implies the undisputed authority of the capitalist over men that are but parts of a mechanism that belong to him' (ref. 6, p. 356). As an example, Marx described the manufacture of horse carriages. In pre-capitalist production, the manufacture of carriages involved the simple cooperation of various trades: coach construction, ironwork, upholstery and wheelwright work. Each of these trades was regulated by guilds in order to maintain their specialization and control over these operations. In capitalist production, simple cooperation gives way to what Marx described as 'complex cooperation', as individual trades lose their specialized skills, and workers perform operations that are disconnected and isolated from one another, and carried out alongside each other. According to Marx and his colleague Engels, this mode of production also creates a hierarchy of managers and supervisors:

> Modern industry has converted the little workshop of the patriarchal master into the great factory of the industrial capitalist. Masses of labourers, crowded into the factory, are organized like soldiers. As privates of the industrial army they are placed under the command of a perfect hierarchy of officers [managers] and sergeants [supervisors].
>
> (ref. 9, p. 227)

Marx examined the impact of technological change on employment relationships. He argued that machinery is used by the capitalist to increase surplus labour by cheapening labour, to deskill workers and thus make it easier to recruit, control and discipline workers. Machinery, he argued, led to the progressive reduction of skills:

> On the automatic plan skilled labour gets progressively superseded. The effect of improvements in machinery [results] in substituting one description of human labour for another, the less skilled for the more skilled, juvenile for adult, female for male, [and] causes a fresh disturbance in the rate of wages.
>
> (ref. 6, p. 433)

Machinery allows the capitalist to transfer the knowledge and skill in production from the worker to reliable agents of capital – that is, managers. Marx described the process like this: 'Intelligence in production expands in one direction, because it vanishes in many others. What is lost by the detail labourers, is concentrated in the capital that employs them' (ref. 6, p. 361). Machinery also increases the capitalist's control over workers' work activities. In what Marx referred to as the despotism of the factory, machinery sets the pace of work and embodies powerful mechanisms of control: 'the technical subordination of the workman to the uniform motion of the instruments of labour [machinery] ... gave rise to a barrack discipline'. He continued: 'To devise and administer a successful code of factory discipline, suited to the necessities of factory diligence, was the Herculean enterprise, the noble achievement of Arkwright!' (ref. 6, pp. 423–4).

These characteristics of work in industrial capitalism have two major consequences: the **alienation** of the workers, and conflict resulting ultimately in social change. Whereas objectification embodies the worker's creativity, work under capitalism is devoid of the producer's own potential creativity and sensuousness. Because workers' labour is not their own, it no longer transforms them. Hence, the unique quality of human beings – their ability to control the forces of nature and produce their own means of existence, to realize their full creative capacity through work – is stultified by capitalism.

> **alienation:** a feeling of powerlessness and estrangement from other people and from oneself

Drawing on the 1807 work by Georg Hegel, *The Phenomenology of Mind*, Marx developed the theory of alienation. In essence, alienation ruptures the fundamental connection that human beings have to the self-defining aspect of their labouring activity.[8] Marx broke down the formulation of alienation into four conceptually discrete but related spheres. First, workers are alienated (or separated) from the product of their labour. The product – its design, quality, quantity and how it is marketed and disposed of – is not determined by those whose labour is responsible for its manufacture.

Second, workers are alienated from productive activity. Marx emphasized the tendency for machinery to deskill work:

> Owing to the extensive use of machinery and to division of labour, the work of the proletarians has lost all individual character, and, consequently, all charm for the workman. He becomes an appendage of the machine, and it is only the most simple, most monotonous, and most easily acquired knack, that is required of him.
>
> (ref. 9, p. 227)

Thus, work offers no intrinsic satisfaction. Workers only work for the money; workers only work because they have to. Marx called this the 'cash nexus'. Accordingly, work takes on an instrumental meaning: it is regarded simply as a means to an end.

The third type of alienation discussed by Marx is alienation from the human species. Marx contended that self-estrangement develops because of the 'cash nexus'. In order to be clear on Marx's meaning, we need to know that Marx believed that people were essentially creative and that individuals expressed creativity through their work. Work, according to Marx, is the medium for self-expression and self-development. It is through work that people should be able to shape themselves and their communities in accordance with their own needs, interests and values. Under alienating conditions, however, work becomes not a social activity that personifies life, but simply a means for physical survival: people become detached from their true selves.

The fourth type of alienation discussed by Marx is alienation from fellow human beings and from the community. This results when the sole purpose of life is competition and all social relations are transformed into economic relations. Workers and managers are alienated from each other. This economic relationship – between those who are controlled and the controllers – is an antagonistic one. And this asymmetry of social relationships in the workplace creates the foundation for a class structure that necessitates sharp differences in power, income and life chances.

Marx's analysis of the social organization of work underscores the fact that people express themselves through their work, and in so far as their labour is merely a commodity to be paid for with a wage, they are alienated. Although Marx did not explicitly focus on the analysis of emotion in the workplace, he did acknowledge that the way in which industrial work was organized and managed did provoke in workers feelings of numbness, anger and resentment. Alienation is characteristic of a certain kind of organization of work – industrial capitalism – that is predicated on a set of socioeconomic conditions. In short, then, capitalism destroys the pleasure associated with labour, the distinctively human capacity to shape and reshape the world.

The second major consequence of work in capitalism, that relations between capitalists and workers are in constant conflict, is the engine of social change. Impelled by its internal **contradictions**, the reverberation of work under capitalism helps the development of **class consciousness** among the workers or proletariat. The defining features of work – deskilling, intensification of work, constant pressure to lower the wages allocated to labour – encourage the development of **class conflict**. Marx and Engels explain the logic whereby capitalism develops and then destroys itself. In their search for profits, capitalists closely control and discipline workers.[9]

Capitalism creates new contradictions, such as the concentration of workers into factories. As workers are concentrated under one roof, they become aware of their common exploitation and circumstances. As a result, over time, workers begin to resist capitalist controls, initially as individuals, and then collectively as groups. Gradually, the workers become organized, through trade unions, and increasingly they become more combative and engage the ruling class in wider social struggles, which Marx believed would culminate in replacing the rule of the **bourgeoisie** and ridding society of capitalism: 'What the bourgeoisie therefore produces above all, is its own gravediggers. Its fall and the victory of the **proletariat** are equally inevitable.'[9] Thus, those selling their labour power, the workers, are exposed to such exploitation and degradation that they begin to oppose capitalists, in order to replace the system.

Marx provides a sophisticated theory of capitalism, with the working class as the embodiment of good, but his concentration on the extraction of surplus value in the labour process inhibits him from considering managerial and government strategies that serve to develop consent and cooperation. The capitalist mode of production is not characterized solely by the conflict between employer and labour: it is also marked by competition between organizations and economies. To put it another way, profits are realized by gaining a competitive advantage, and the need to gain workers' cooperation undermines the contradictory laws that promote constant conflict and crises. Thus, Marx systematically underestimates the possibility that management may need to organize on the basis of consent as well as coercion.

The reconceptualization of management as necessarily engaged in consent building also suggests that Marx's zero-sum theory of power is insufficient. Critics argue that although the interests of labour and capital do not coincide, the assumption that they are irreconcilably and utterly antagonistic is misleading. Therefore, the inadequacy of Marx's account lies at the level of analysis. Marx emphasized the irreconcilable interests of social classes at the societal level, and this obscures the very real way in which, in the workplace, the interests of employers and employees may be very closely intertwined.

Despite the strong criticisms of Marx's analysis of work on capitalism, his impact on the sociology of work is immense. His illumination of the politics of work and organizations – the relationship between work and the distribution of interests and power in the society outside the workplace, and the relationships of power and managerial strategies inside the workplace – still informs contemporary analyses of work and employment relations, as we shall see later in this chapter.

contradictions:
contradictions are said to occur within social systems when the various principles that underlie these social arrangements conflict with each other

class consciousness:
Karl Marx's term for awareness of a common identity based on a person's position in the means of production

class conflict: a term for the struggle between the capitalist class and the working class

bourgeoisie (or capitalist class): Karl Marx's term for the class comprising those who own and control the means of production

proletariat (or working class): Karl Marx's term for those who must sell their labour because they have no other means of earning a livelihood

weblink
Go to the following websites for more information on Marx: http://plato.stanford.edu/entries/marx; www.anu.edu.au/polsci/marx/classics/manifesto.html; www.marxists.org

Plate 2 – Emile Durkheim.
Source: Wikipedia

Emile Durkheim (1858–1917)

Emile Durkheim's contribution to our understanding of work is essentially derived from his book *The Division of Labor in Society*,[10] and its discussion of the relationship between individuals and society, and the conditions for social cohesion. Durkheim was preoccupied with the issue of **social solidarity** and unity during a time when France was subject to the profound revolutionary changes that created modern society. The popular belief of the time was that the collapse of social life was imminent, in response to the expansion of the division of labour, ever-increasing industrialization and **urbanization**, and the declining significance of traditional moral beliefs. This was described as the transition from *Gemeinschaft* or 'community' forms of society, to *Gesellschaft* or 'social' forms, representing mere 'associations' where social solidarity was disintegrating. Durkheim suggested that such fears were not just exaggerated, but actually wrong. His thesis held that heightened feelings of group solidarity and order were being reconstructed in a different form. Durkheim's position was that the interdependence resulting from the progressive differentiation and specialization of labour gave rise to a new form of social solidarity, which is the bond that unites individuals when there is no normative consensus.

Durkheim's prime question was, if pre-industrial societies were held together by shared understandings, ideas, norms and values, what holds a complex industrial society together? He believed that the increasing division of labour has enormous implications for the structure of society. In pre-industrial society,

social solidarity: the state of having shared beliefs and values among members of a social group, along with intense and frequent interaction among group members

urbanization: the process by which an increasing proportion of a population lives in cities rather than in rural areas

mechanical solidarity:
a term to describe the
social cohesion that
exists in pre-industrial
societies, in which there
is a minimal division of
labour and people feel
united by shared values
and common
social bonds

organic solidarity:
a term for the social
cohesion that exists in
industrial (and perhaps
post-industrial) societies,
in which people perform
very specialized tasks
and feel united by their
mutual dependence

social solidarity is derived from people's similarities and the rather suffocating effects of uniformity of experience and thought. Such societies are held together through the collective consciousness at the direct expense of individuality: 'individual personality is absorbed into the collective personality', as Durkheim put it (ref. 10, p. 85). He called this form of social unity **mechanical solidarity**. In contrast, the increasing division of labour causes a diminution of collective consciousness, and 'this leaves much more room for the free play of our imitative' (ref. 10, p. 85).

Complex industrial societies, with new work forms based on functional specialization, are held together by relations of exchange and people's reciprocal need for the services of many others. This symmetry of life Durkheim called **organic solidarity**. He believed that in societies whose solidarity is organic, individuals are linked increasingly to each other rather than to society as a whole. The totality of the nature of these social links compels individuals to remain in contact with one another, which in turn binds them to one another and to society. Thus, each of us becomes aware of our dependence on others and of the new cultural norms that shape and restrain our actions.

For Durkheim, only the division of labour could furnish social solidarity and ethical individualism: 'Since the division of labour becomes the source of social solidarity, it becomes, at the same time, the foundation of moral order' (ref. 10, p. 333). In summary, he argued that there was no necessary correlation between increased division of labour and decreasing solidarity. On the contrary, it was a source not of disorder and conflict, but of order and social solidarity. The nature of moral solidarity in industrial society has not disappeared, but changed.

Of course, Durkheim was not oblivious to the reality of industrialization in Western Europe, which might have been argued to show the opposite. Not least, there were intense class conflicts and widespread labour strikes in France, often led by radical workers known as revolutionary syndicalists, in unions organized in the *Confédération Générale du Travail*. Durkheim explained the existence of instability and social fragmentation by analysing what he called 'abnormal' forms of the division of labour. These abnormal forms occur when the development of the division of labour is obstructed and distorted by various factors. He identified these as the anomie division of labour, the forced division of labour and the mismanagement of operations.

anomie: a state condition
in which social control
becomes ineffective as
a result of the loss of
shared values and a sense
of purpose in society

The first abnormal effects can arise because of the 'anomie' condition of the division of labour. The word **anomie** comes from the Greek *anomia*, meaning 'without law'. For Durkheim, anomie results from a condition in which social norms and/ or moral norms are confused or simply absent. Generally, Durkheim believed that anomie results from widespread business failure, or when there is rapid and uneven economic development that has expanded ahead of the necessary developments in social regulation. In such circumstances, he suggests, breaches occur in the social solidarity existing between specialized occupations, causing tensions in social relationships and eroding social cohesion.

Durkheim also considered anomie as another 'pathology' of industrialization, but believed that such deviant behaviour could be 'cured' through the proper level of regulation. He argued that occupational associations centred within civil society are the most effective means of regulating anomie in modern society. Such collective institutions provide moral authority, which dominates the life of their members. They are also a method by which individualistic egotism can be subordinated harmoniously to the general interest.

Durkheim explained the importance of occupational groups like this: 'wherever a group is formed, a moral discipline is also formed.' He continued:

> A group is not only a moral authority regulating the life of its members, but also a source of life *sui generis*. From it there arises warmth that quickens or gives fresh life to each individual, which makes him disposed to empathise, causing selfishness to melt away.
>
> (ref. 10, p. 111)

Durkheim also warned that the mere construction of consensually grounded goals without any associated provision of opportunities to achieve such goals would extend the form of social 'pathology' under which anomie prevailed.

The second factor causing abnormal development, according to Durkheim, is the 'forced division of labour' (ref. 10, p. 310). He emphasized that the division of labour is frequently not 'spontaneous' because of class and inherited privilege that operate to limit life chances. Durkheim, then, is considered to be a supporter of meritocracy. The normal division of labour would occur if social inequalities mirrored what Durkheim took to be personal inequalities:

> The division of labour only produces solidarity if it is spontaneous, and to the degree that it is spontaneous. But spontaneity must mean not simply the absence of any deliberate, formal type of violence, but of anything that may hamper, even indirectly, the free unfolding of the social force each individual contains within himself ... In short, labour only divides up spontaneously if society is constituted in such a way that social inequalities express precisely natural inequalities.
>
> (ref. 10, pp. 313–14)

Thus, Durkheim's 'normal' division of labour is a 'perfect meritocracy' produced by the eradication of personal inheritance.[1,5] For the division of labour to engender solidarity, society must allocate functions based on ability, not class or hereditary tendencies, so that 'The sole cause then determining how labour is divided up is the diversity of abilities' (ref. 10, p. 313).

The third factor responsible for an 'abnormal' development of the division of labour is mismanagement of functions in society. Durkheim believed that when functions are faltering or are badly coordinated with one another, individuals are unaware of their mutual dependence, and this lessens social solidarity. Thus, if work is insufficient, as a result of mismanagement and organization, Durkheim argues that solidarity 'is itself naturally not only less than perfect, but may even be more or less completely missing' (ref. 10, p. 326).

In addition, if class-based social inequalities are imposed on groups, this not only forces the division of labour, but also undermines social linkages. It means that individuals are mismatched to their functions, and that linkages between individuals are disrupted, and this creates inequitable forms of exchange. In the absence of restraint from a centralized authority (either the state or the government), there is disequilibrium, which leads to instability and conflict. For Durkheim, most of the pathologies of the new industrial order were attributed to the prevalence of anomie.

In sum, while Marx's critique was directed at capitalism, Durkheim's critique was aimed not at the essence of capitalism, but at industrialism. Whereas Marx is against the fragmentation of work and for the reintegration of skills, Durkheim is for the expansion of specialization in line with individuals' 'natural' abilities. Although the concepts of alienation and anomie lead to significantly different analysis and political results, and are different too in their assumptions about human nature, the two concepts have been compared by sociologists. For Marx, alienation results from certain kinds of social control; on the other hand, according to Durkheim, anomie results from the absence of social control. While Marx's solution to the crisis of capitalism is dependent on the state or government, Durkheim argued that centralized government was too far removed from the everyday experience of people to play this role. He believed that mediating organizations would form the primary mode of social organization. For Durkheim, the crisis of modern society is a moral one, caused by a lack of social unity. The solution is therefore achieved by socially regulated institutions coupled with an ever-widening division of labour. He believed this would facilitate the development of individual potential and create a future Utopia. The process of social change was to be evolutionary, not revolutionary.

In this chapter, we cannot provide a thorough critique of Durkheim's theory of the relationship between the increasing differentiation and specialization of labour, and transformative social change. However, we must critically assess some of his assumptions, for example those about 'natural' inequalities. He regarded men as more intelligent than women, and industrial workers as more intelligent than farmers. Durkheim also assumed that the gender-based domestic division of labour was a good example of the social harmony generated when social inequalities were allowed to mirror 'natural' inequalities. His assumptions about gender relations provoked the beginnings of a critique of patriarchy.[5]

weblink
Go to the following website for more information on Durkheim: www.epistemelinks.com/Main/Philosophers.aspx?PhilCode=Durk

Max Weber (1864–1920)

Max Weber's work is broad and wide-ranging, and has been much misrepresented. It is often assumed to be a dialogue with the ghost of Marx, but that does not do justice to it. Weber wrote on a wide range of topics including art, architecture and music; he examined the role of ideology in social change; and he explored the emergence and nature of modernity. His contribution to the study of work and work organizations has been extensive. The main contributions he made are: first, his theory concerning the rise of capitalism; second, his arguments concerning rationality, the nature of bureaucracy and authority; third, his theory of social class and inequality; and fourth, his methodology and theory of knowledge.

Plate 3 – Max Weber.
Source: Wikipedia

The rise of capitalism and rationalization

Weber's interpretation of the rise of capitalism in the West is presented in his best-known work, *The Protestant Ethic and the 'Spirit' of Capitalism* (written in 1905),[11] which links the rise of modern capitalism to Protestant (or, more precisely, Calvinist) religious beliefs and practices. Briefly, he argued that a new attitude to work and the pursuit of wealth was linked to the rise of Calvinism. In this attitude, work became a means of demonstrating godliness, and Weber saw this cultural shift as being associated with the rise of 'rational' capitalism itself.

According to Weber, while Catholics believed they could secure their place in heaven through (among other things) 'good works' on behalf of the poor or by performing acts of faith on earth, Calvinism developed a set of beliefs around the concept of predestination, which broke the hold of tradition. It was believed by followers of Calvin that it was already decided by God ('predestined') whether they would go to heaven (as one of the 'elect') or hell after their death. They had no means of knowing their ultimate destination, and also no means of altering it. This uncertainty led Calvinists to search for signs from God, since naturally they were anxious to be among the elect. Wealth was taken as a manifestation that they were one of God's elect, and this encouraged followers of Calvin to apply themselves rationally to acquiring wealth. They did this through their ascetic lifestyles and hard work.

The distinctive features of 'rational capitalism' that Weber identified – limits on consumption, especially luxury consumption, and a tendency to reinvest profits in order to systematically accumulate more wealth – had a clear similarity to the Calvinist lifestyle. Although Weber did not believe that Calvinism was the cause of the rise of industrial capitalism, he did believe that capitalism in part grew from Calvinism. Contrary to Marx, Weber argued that the development of rational capitalism could not be explained through wholly material and structural forces; the rise of modern Western society was embedded in the process of rationalization.

Rationalization

rationality: the process by which traditional methods of social organization, characterized by informality and spontaneity, are gradually replaced by efficiently administered formal rules and procedures – bureaucracy

Central to Weber's analysis of the rise of capitalism and new organizational forms is this concept of rationalization. But what did he mean by this term? Weber's use of **rationality** is complex and multifaceted. He used the term to describe the overall historical process 'by which nature, society and individual action are increasingly mastered by an orientation to planning, technical procedure and rational action' (ref. 8, p. 218). For Weber, all societies exhibit rationality, in that all people can explain the basis of their behaviour, but only in the West does a particular type of rationality, based on capitalization, bureaucracy and calculation, become dominant. The essence of the concept consisted of three facets: secularization, calculability and rational action.

Rationality means the decline of magical interpretations and explanations of the world. Scientific models of nature and human behaviour are good examples of this type of rationalization, which involves calculating maximum results at minimum cost. It means the replacement of 'traditional' action by 'rational' action. Rationalization depends on two types of activity: strategies of human action, and modification of the means and ends of action in the pursuit of goals. Rather than doing things for emotional reasons, people do things because they calculate that the benefits will outweigh the cost, or because they assess the action as being the most efficient way to achieve their goals. Human actions are also guided by the use of rational decision making in pursuit of unlimited profit. Rules are obeyed because they appear to be built upon rational principles and common sense. In the business sphere, for example, technical and managerial rules are obeyed because they result in efficiency and profits.

Rationalization is different from rationality. Rationalization, the principal process of modernity, refers to the overall process by which reality is increasingly mastered by calculation and rational action, while rationality refers to the capacity of human action to be subject to calculation about means and ends.

Four types of rationality have been identified in Weber's work: practical, theoretical, formal and substantive:

- *Practical rationality* assumes that there are no external mystical causes affecting the outcome of human actions, and sees reality in terms of what is given.
- *Theoretical or technical rationality* involves a cognitive effort to master the world through causality, logical deduction and induction. This type of rationality allows individuals to understand the 'meaning of life' by means of abstract concepts and conceptual reasoning.
- *Formal rationality* refers to the accurate calculation procedures that go into decisions, to ensure consistency of outcome and efficiency in attaining goals.
- *Substantive rationality* refers to the degree to which human action is guided or shaped by a value system, regardless of the outcome of the action. Accordingly, 'Where formal rationality involves a practical orientation of action regarding outcomes, substantive rationality involves an orientation to values' (ref. 8, p. 222).

Although these four different rationalization processes can complement each other, they can also conflict. For example, the pursuit of efficiency and productivity by calculating the 'best' means to achieve a given end (formal rationality) sometimes conflicts with ethical behaviour (substantive rationality). When examined through a substantive lens, formal rationality is often irrational. In his book, *The McDonaldization of Society*,[12] George Ritzer makes a strong case that formal rationality, embodied in standardized fast-food products, undermines values of social responsibility and individualism in the pursuit of efficiency. In the early twenty-first century, rationalization shapes the subjective experiences of peoples as they understand and evaluate climate change and global warming in terms of non-sustainable growth, profit maximization and **corporate social responsibility**.

corporate social responsibility: an organization's moral obligation to its stakeholders

Bureaucracy

bureaucratization: a tendency towards a formal organization with a hierarchy of authority, a clear division of labour and an emphasis on written rules

According to Weber, **bureaucratization** is an inescapable development of modern society. Weber's analysis of the development of capitalism was similar to that of Marx, in that he believed that the rise of capitalism had been marked by the centralization of production, by increased specialization and mechanization, by the progressive loss by workers of the means of production, and by an increase in the function and growth of management. With centralized production, all human activity gives way to a more systematic, rational and extensive use of resources, including labour, which is facilitated by calculable techniques such as accounting. Weber's contention was that 'Where capitalist acquisition is rationally pursued, the corresponding action is oriented towards the calculation of capital. In other words, such action takes place within a planned utilization of material or personal output' (ref. 11, p. 359).

According to Weber, bureaucracies are goal-oriented organizations, administered by qualified specialists, and designed according to rational principles in order to efficiently attain the stated goals. He saw the development of bureaucracy as involving the exorcism of emotional or 'irrational' personal elements such as hate, love or sentiment. In his *Economy and Society*, written in 1921, Weber explained that 'Bureaucracy ... is fully developed in the private economy only in the most advanced institutions of capitalism' (ref. 13, p. 956). He also noted that as the complexity of modern society increases, bureaucracies grow. He defined the bureaucratic 'ideal type' by these characteristics: business is continually conducted, there are stipulated rules, individual spheres of competence are structured in a hierarchy, offices (that is, positions at work) are not owned, selection and promotion is through proven ability, and rewards are commensurate with people's qualifications, ability and performance.

formalization: the degree to which organizations standardize behaviour through rules, procedures, formal training and related mechanisms

Two core ideas underscore Weber's concept of bureaucracy: formal rationality and **formalized** decision making. Formal rationality operates on the principles of expert knowledge and calculability, whereas formalized decision making operates on the basis of set procedures. This means that decisions can be judged as correct or otherwise by reference to a body of rules.

It would, however, be a misrepresentation of Weber to assume that he was an avid supporter of bureaucracy. Weber was not unaware of the dysfunctions of any over-formalized work form. Bureaucracy removes workers from the decision-making process. It consists of rational and established rules, and restricts individual activity. As a result, it can resemble an 'iron cage and it can mean that organizational behaviour becomes less and less regulated by ethical principles, as these are replaced by technical means and ends' (ref. 8, p. 297). Weber's argument is that because bureaucratic work forms remove workers, including white-collar and managerial staff, from ownership of the means of production, there is a loss of democracy in the workplace, and a panoply of managerial control measures are then necessary to keep the workers in line.[13]

Types of authority

All systems of work require a minimum of 'voluntary compliance' and some mechanism of coordination and control over the activity. This compliance, which is defined as 'an interest in obedience' (ref. 13, p. 212) of the subordinate controlled (such as a worker) to the dominant controller (such as a manager), is based on the ulterior motives of the subordinate, which are governed by custom and a material calculation of advantage, as well as her or his perception of the employment relationship.

power: a term defined in multiple ways, involving cultural values, authority, influence and coercion as well as control over the distribution of symbolic and material resources. At its broadest, power is defined as a social system that imparts patterned meaning

Weber's analysis of authority relations provides another insight into the changing structure of work systems. Weber used the terms 'domination' and 'authority' interchangeably in *Economy and Society*. Both derive from the German term *Herrschaft*, which points to leadership, and his theory of domination does have direct relevance to theories of organizational leadership. However, Weber did make a distinction between power and domination. He defined **power** as the ability to impose one's will on others in a given situation, even when the others resist. Domination, or authority, is the right of a controller to issue commands to others and expect them to be obeyed. Underscoring Weber's study of authority is his concern for 'legitimacy'. Essentially, he was interested in knowing on what basis subordinates actively acknowledge the validity of authority figures in an established order, and give obedience to them, and on what basis men and women claim authority over others.

Subordinates and the controlled obey dominant controllers by custom and for material advantage and reward, but a belief in legitimacy is also a prerequisite. Weber pointed out that each authority system varies 'According to the kind of legitimacy which is claimed, the type of obedience, the kind of administrative staff developed to guarantee it, and the mode of exercising authority' (ref. 13, p. 213). He then went on to propose three types of legitimate authority: traditional, rational-legal and

Plate 4 – Rational-legal authority is derived from the rationality of the authority. For example, car drivers usually obey police officers imposing traffic laws (like this one in Paris) because their actions appear to make sense, not because police officers have some inherited authority or are charismatic.
Source: Nick Tutton

charismatic. All types of authority, however, require a managerial system characterized by efficiency and continuity.

Traditional authority is based on the sanctity of tradition and the legitimacy of those exercising authority under such regimes. It is usually acquired through inheritance: this, for example, is the kind of authority held by kings and queens in monarchies. Compliance rests on a framework of obligations that binds followers to leaders by personal loyalties.

Rational-legal authority is derived from the rationality of the authority. For example, car drivers usually obey traffic laws because they appear to make sense, and not because police officers have some inherited authority or are charismatic.

Charismatic authority refers to an attribute or exceptional quality possessed by an individual. In charismatic domination, the leader's claim to legitimacy originates from his or her followers' belief that the leader is to be obeyed because of his or her extraordinary attributes or powers of inspiration and communication.

Weber's typology of authority is important in understanding why individuals behave as they do in the workplace. He was one of the earliest social theorists who saw domination as being characteristic of the relationship between leaders and followers, rather than an attribute of the leader alone.

Social class, inequality and types of class struggle

Authority is equated to possessing power, and difference in the degree of power is one factor that gives rise to differentiated social classes. Weber's description of social class was similar to Marx's, in that he defined a social class by property ownership and by market relations. He stated that:

> a class is a number of people having in common a specific causal component of their life chances. This component is represented exclusively by economic interests in the possession of goods and opportunities for income, under the conditions of the commodity or labour markets.
>
> (ref. 13, p. 927)

However, whereas Marx had proposed that individuals carry forward their class interests by virtue of dominant economic forces, Weber argued that the 'mere differentiation of property classes is not "dynamic", that is, it need not result in class struggles and revolutions' (ref. 13, p. 303). He argued instead that the complex and multidimensional nature of social stratification in modern society necessarily inhibits the acquisition of the degree of class consciousness that is necessary for a revolution to occur.

In this argument, people who experience inequality and who have a degree of political consciousness are much more likely to form into rational associations (such as trade unions and social democratic political parties) that would thrust them to the forefront of political activity, than they are to start a revolution. Under these conditions, there are no class interests as such, only the 'average interests' of individuals in similar economic situations, and therefore the class struggle and revolution predicted by Marx are extremely unlikely to happen. Instead, the nature of class conflict changes in a modern society in two fundamental ways. First, there is a shift from direct confrontation between the owners of capital and workers to mediated pay disputes, and second, conflicts between social classes are resolved through the courts and legal means.

Weber's methodology

Between 1902 and 1903, Weber wrote two papers that were central to shaping his views about the nature of doing research in the social sciences, and which continue to influence contemporary inquiry into work and behaviour in the workplace. Let us look at two concepts he developed: ideal types and *Verstehen*.

ideal type: an abstract model that describes the recurring characteristics of some phenomenon

The **ideal type** is one of Weber's best-known contributions to contemporary organizational theory. At its most basic level, an ideal type is a theoretical abstraction constructed by a social scientist, who draws out important characteristics and simultaneously suppresses less important characteristics. It can be viewed as a measuring rod or yardstick whose function is to compare **empirical** reality with preconceived notions of a reality. Weber put it like this: 'It functions in formulating terminology, classifications, and hypotheses, in working out concrete causal explanation of individual events' (ref. 13, p. 21). As a methodological construction, ideal types are neither ideal nor typical. That is, they are not ideal in any evaluative sense, nor are they typical because they do not represent any norm. They merely approximate reality. To put it differently, ideal types are heuristic devices (teaching aids) that are used to study slices of reality and enable us to compare empirical forms. Organizational theorists refer for example to an 'ideal type of bureaucracy' or 'ideal flexibility'.

empiricism: an approach to the study of social reality that suggests that only knowledge gained through experience and the senses is acceptable

Verstehen: a method of understanding human behaviour by situating it in the context of an individual's or actor's meaning

The second concept, **Verstehen**. Weber believed that social scientists must look at the actions of individuals and examine the meanings attached to these behaviours. His approach to understanding human behaviour suggests that observational language is never theoretically independent of the way in which the observer sees a phenomenon and the questions he or she asks about the action. As a consequence, an individual researcher's interpretation of human activity is an inherent aspect of knowledge about organizational behaviour. Weber's 'interpretative' methodology is based on *Verstehen*, meaning 'human understanding'. Human subjects, in contrast to the objects studied in the natural sciences, always rely on their 'understanding' of each other's behaviour and on the 'meanings' they assign to what they and others do.

This interpretive approach to studying reality is best illustrated by distinguishing between someone walking in a park as a pleasurable leisure experience, and someone walking in a park in an aimless way to kill time because he or she is unemployed and bored. The outer behaviour is exactly the same, but the inner state of the two people is different. It is difficult for a researcher to understand and explain the fundamental distinction between the inner states of the employed and unemployed (in this case) just by observing their outer states, or behaviour. We need an interpretive understanding in order to give a convincing analysis of what is seen.

weblink

Go to this website for more information on Weber: www.marxists.org/reference/archive/weber

Weber's theories have been challenged. For instance, it is argued that the earliest examples of rational capitalism are not restricted to Calvinist or even Protestant nations. Some Calvinist countries, such as Scotland, failed to 'take off' as capitalist industrialized nations, and some Catholic nations, such as Belgium, were among the market leaders.

As our review of the theories of work moves from the classical sociological theories of the 'big three' – Marx, Durkheim and Weber – to contemporary perspectives on work organizations, we will be better equipped to see how these classical theories continue to inform contemporary theories of work, organizational design and managerial behaviour.

stop reflect

Can you think of any workplace studies that have based their findings on data gathered through observing people in the workplace? How should the interpretative method affect your evaluation of the studies?

CONTEMPORARY THEORIES OF WORK ORGANIZATIONS

Organizational studies constitute a discipline in itself, with a plethora of alternative theoretical perspectives. In recent years, different theoretical approaches to studying work and organizations have forced organizational theorists to re-examine and be more reflexive about organizational 'knowledge'. With these changes, as Clegg and Hardy put it, 'Gone is the certainty about what organizations are; gone, too, is the certainty about how they should be studied' (ref. 4, p. 3). In this chapter, we cannot hope to do justice to the complexities of the bewildering variety of perspectives, and we shall therefore seek to highlight what Clegg and Hardy call the major 'conversations' in organizational studies.

How we represent these conversations always involves a choice concerning what theories we wish to represent and how we represent them. To help, we have drawn a schema of organizational theories. The competing theories are plotted along two interlocking axes: the horizontal critical–managerial axis, and the vertical positivist–interpretivist axis (Figure 2.1).

The *critical–managerial axis* represents the political left–right continuum. At one extreme, the managerial pole positions those perspectives which are essentially concerned with issues of organizational efficiency and performance. Thus, researchers adopting this approach have tended to develop theoretical frameworks and generate empirical data aimed at understanding organizational structures, work arrangements and social processes that can improve labour productivity and organizational effectiveness, or can help solve people-related 'problems' in the workplace. This particular framework is often viewed as mainstream thinking in organizational behaviour texts. At the other extreme, the critical pole, lie critical explanations of work and organizational behaviour that have traditionally been concerned with

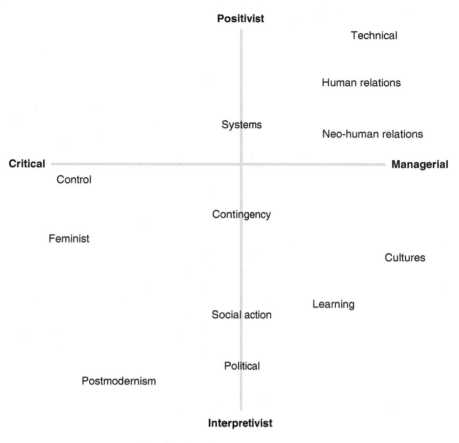

Figure 2.1 – Contemporary theories of work organizations

issues of exploitation and the alienating effects of dividing and routinizing paid work. Researchers adopting this perspective tend to conceptualize organizational structures and management behaviour as control mechanisms that function to fulfil economic imperatives.

The *positivist–interpretivist axis* affirms the importance of epistemological considerations when conducting research: what is (or should be) regarded as acceptable knowledge in organizational behaviour theory. The axis distinguishes between the doctrines of 'positivism' and 'interpretivism'. The positivist epistemological position is generally taken to involve the application of natural science research methods to the study of work organizations. It puts emphasis on the scientific and technical way in which organizational activities can be studied and assessed (using goals, efficiency ratios, rational decision making, productivity measures and so on). In contrast, the interpretivist position maintains that human behaviour is not fully controllable, and therefore a research strategy for organizational behaviour must respect the differences between people and inanimate objects. For interpretivists, the role of the social scientist is to grasp the subjective meaning of behaviour or social action. Researchers focus on the indeterminate and contingent nature of social reality, the unintended consequences of human action and the influence of interpretation.

Where these 12 conversations or theories are plotted on the 'map' is clearly a matter of interpretation and subject to dispute; here the map's function is to act as a heuristic device.

Technical

The 'technical' approach to studying work organizations is most closely associated with the work of Frederick Winslow Taylor (1865–1915). Taylor, an engineer at an American steel mill, experimented with work arrangements to improve labour productivity. Taylor's work configuration rests upon the principle of the technical and social divisions of mental and manual labour. The technical division of labour generally refers to how a complex task is broken down into component parts. Adam Smith's classic observations on pin manufacturing[14] give us one of the first discussions of this in relation to potential increases in labour productivity.

The social division of labour refers to issues of which individuals occupy specific positions in the technical division of labour, how, why and for how long. In addition, **scientific management**, or Taylorism (as it became known), involved the following five principles: maximum job fragmentation, the separation of planning and doing, the separation of direct and indirect labour, minimum skill requirements and minimum material handling. These five job design principles gave to management 'the collective concept of control' (ref. 15, p. 97).

Other important theorists contributing to this organization studies genre were Henry Gantt (1861–1919), a protégé of Taylor, who designed the Gantt chart, a straight-line chart to display and measure planned and completed work as time elapsed, Frank Gilbreth (1868–1924), who helped to improve labour productivity through the pioneering use of time and motion techniques, and Henry Ford (1863–1947), who perfected the application of the principles of scientific management to assembly-line production, an approach others would later call 'Fordism'. For most of the twentieth century, the essential principles of Taylorism and Fordism represented a 'common-sense' management strategy in North America and Western Europe.[16–18]

Human relations

Disenchantment with the technical approach to work and organizational design led to the development of the **human relations** school of thought. Data gathered at the Hawthorne plant of the Western Electric Companies – subsequently known as the Hawthorne studies – suggested a positive association between labour productivity and management style. The phenomenon can be explained like this: 'The determinants of working behaviour are sought in the structure and culture of the group, which is spontaneously formed by the interaction of individuals working together' (ref. 19, p. 99).

Elton Mayo is most closely associated with the Hawthorne studies. Another pioneering management theorist, Mary Parker Follett, is associated with the early human relations management movement. She contended that traditional authority as an act of subordination was offensive to an individual's emotions, and therefore could not serve as a good foundation for cooperative relations in the workplace. Instead, Follett proposed an authority function, whereby the individual has authority over her or his own job area.[15]

The Hawthorne studies have been criticized at both the technical and the political level. Technically, it has been contended that the researchers used a 'rudimentary' research design and that their analysis of the data was faulty. At a political level, charges of managerial bias, insularity from wider socioeconomic factors, a neglect of workers' organization (that is, trade unions) and organizational conflict were effectively levelled against the researchers. The critique included the charge that human relations theorists conceptualized the 'normal' state of the work organization in

scientific management: this involves systematically partitioning work into its smallest elements and standardizing tasks to achieve maximum efficiency

weblink
Go to the following websites for more information on Taylorism and Fordism: http://kapitalism101.wordpress.com/frederick-taylor-the-biggest-bastard-ever; www.nationmaster.com/encyclopedia/Taylorism; www.nosweat.org.uk; www.nationmaster.com/encyclopedia/Fordism

human relations: a school of management thought that emphasizes the importance of social processes in the organization

'romantic' and harmonious terms, and neglected workplace conflict because of their pro-management bias.[20,21]

Despite the criticisms, the Hawthorne studies provided the impetus for a new 'common-sense' management strategy sometimes known as 'neo-human relations', which revisited Mayo's work. The human relations school focused on a paternalistic style of management, emphasizing workers' social needs as the key to harmonious relations and better performance, albeit narrowly conceived. Prominent contributors to human relations theory were Abraham Maslow (1908–70), with his idea of 'self-actualization' needs, and Douglas McGregor (1906–64), with his Theory X and Theory Y approach to work motivation. These contributions to organizational studies promoted five principles of 'good' work design: closure, whereby the scope of the job includes all the tasks to complete a product or process; task variety, whereby the worker learns a wider range of skills to increase job flexibility; self-regulation, allowing workers to assume responsibility for scheduling their work and quality control; social interaction to allow cooperation and reflectivity; and continuous work-based learning.[22]

Systems theory

Systems theory has played, and continues to play, an influential part in attempts to analyse and explain work organizations. Systems theory involves providing holistic explanations for social phenomena, with a tendency to 'treat societies or social wholes as having characteristics similar to those of organic matter or organisms'.[23] It shows the relationships and interactions between elements, and these in turn are claimed to explain the behaviour of the whole. The notion of 'system' is associated with 'functionalism' and the work of Talcott Parsons (1902–79). Parsons used a systems model that was designed to demonstrate how formal organizations carry out a necessary set of functions to ensure survival.[24] The Parsonian model was also adopted by Dunlop to explain rule-bound behaviour among all major actors within the industrial relations system: unions, management and government.[25] Peter Senge's elaboration of systems thinking provides insight into 'personal mastery', team learning and 'shared vision'.[26] A systems perspective is also used to examine the multidimensional and changing nature of the work context.[27]

Figure 2.2 shows a systems model, with a set of interrelated and interdependent parts configured in a manner that produces a unified whole. That is, any working system takes inputs, transforms them and produces some output. Systems may be classified as either 'closed' or 'open' to their environment. Work organizations are said to be **open systems** in that they acquire inputs from the environment (such as materials, energy, people and finance), transform them into services or products, and discharge outputs in the form of services, products and sometimes pollutants to the external environment.

The open-system model emphasizes that management action is not separate from the world but is connected to the wider context. That is, 'The existing internal structure, strategy, and success of an organization is heavily influenced by environmental forces in which it operates and with which it interacts and competes' (ref. 28, p. 209). However, it is too simple to regard the influence of context as only a one-way flow. Systems thinking is closely linked to the Weberian notion of the paradox of consequences in organizational life. A systems approach can illustrate how managerial behaviour and actions designed to advance a goal or solve a problem have unintended consequences that undermine or exacerbate the problem.[5]

This kind of systems or functionalist thinking highlights the apparent functions of different work organizations. But the system has its critics. Detractors emphasize

stop reflect
What contemporary jobs tend to incorporate neo-human relations principles into job design, and what kind of jobs seem to be imbued with neo-Taylorism?

open systems:
organizations that take their sustenance from the environment, and in turn affect that environment through their output

stop reflect
Can you think of an example from your own work experience of the paradox of consequences? What did management do, and what was the unintended outcome(s)?

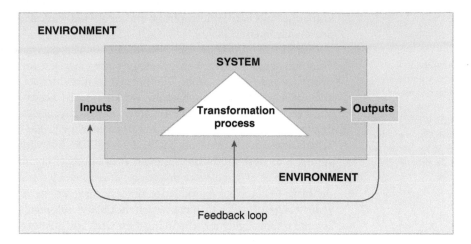

Figure 2.2 – An open system

that systems analysis reifies organizations: in other words, it treats a concept as if it were a real thing. To assert that organizations make decisions implies that organizations have an existence beyond their human members, but it can be argued that this is not so: organizations are merely legal constructs. So when we talk of organizations 'making decisions', we really mean that some or all of the dominant controllers of an organization make the decisions.

Second, systems theory suggests a greater degree of stability and order in organizations than might actually exist across time. Third, systems theories tend to downplay the significance of historical developments to explain contemporary organizational phenomena. And finally, the essential thrust of functionalism or systems analysis is towards consensus. It is inherently deterministic: it 'is not only technocratic in its denial of conflicting ideologies and material interests but also deterministic in its pursuit of the correct prediction of behaviour through an analysis of organizational rules' (ref. 5, pp. 132–3).

Contingency theory

Contingency theory focuses on the three-way relationship between structure, contingency and outcomes, and has proved to be one of the most influential of all organizational theories. Contingency, as it applies to work organizations, means that the effectiveness of a particular strategy, structure or managerial style depends on the presence or absence of other factors or forces. Accordingly, there are no absolutely 'one best' strategies, structures or styles. Instead, whether an action is 'best' must be gauged relative to the context, the circumstances or the other factors.

The most noted contingency research was conducted over 40 years ago.[29–32] Joan Woodward, for example, found that there was no best way of organizing production, but that a particular organizational design and managerial style of behaviour was most appropriate for each technological situation (for example, worker-oriented production as found in car assembly compared with process production as found in a chemical plant). She reported that organizations differed not only in the general character of their structure and technology, but also in such detailed respects as managerial behaviour, methods of intermanagement communication, and interactions. In some organizations studied, 'it was not always easy to distinguish between those who gave and those who took orders' (ref. 30, p. 27).

The British writers Burns and Stalker suggested that organizational structures and managerial behaviours differed according to a range of environments differentiated by their degree of predictability and stability. Management styles would tend to be different in what they called 'mechanistic' or 'organic' systems. The American researchers Lawrence and Lorsch developed contingency analysis, by showing the importance of establishing integrative mechanisms to counter the centrifugal forces that differentiate and fragment managers and non-managers alike.

For dominant controllers of work organizations, the appeal of a contingency perspective is in part because the 'if–then' formula represents an explicit fracture with the simpler 'one best way' approach, while offering persuasive normative guidelines for what organizational leaders should do to sustain organizational performance. Where the contingency approach is most vulnerable to criticism is in its construction of independent variables, and this is why it is positioned close to the determinist line. The various studies argue that although some degree of contingency exists, in so far as controllers can choose between different forms of organizational structure, only those who choose the most 'appropriate' structure are likely to be successful. Others have noted the role of 'environmental determinism', and the removal of contingency by specifying the external conditions under which success can be determined: 'environments are not only given determinate power ... but they are literally reified through the language of environments acting on passive organizations' (ref. 33, p. 63).

Culture theory

The notion of applying 'cultural' thinking to organizational studies is derived from Durkheimian concerns for organizational solidarity through ideological consensus, and from Max Weber's pronouncements in *The Protestant Ethic* on the connections between a distinctive 'cultural phenomenon' and Western capitalist modernity. Organizational culture refers to artefacts, the shared beliefs and values and core assumptions that exist in an organization. Typically, the approach tends to be normative: that is, it is intended to explain not so much what the contemporary culture of an organization is, but what it should be. Thus, it may well persuade managers to act as if the preferred cultural attributes already existed, so the acting out of a cultural myth becomes the organizational reality.[34] A less manipulative approach to the significance of organizational cultures is provided by Gareth Morgan.[35] According to Morgan, culture is shared property and has a language and symbolism that can be decoded.

Morgan believes that how we define, understand and conceptualize organizations depends on our images or mental models of the essential shape, artefacts and features of organizations. He has argued that most definitions and theories of work organizations can be associated with a particular organizational metaphor. The most common metaphors view organizations as cultures, organisms, an iron cage, machines, networks or learning systems. These metaphors are embedded in various theories of organizational behaviour.

Charles Handy has suggested that 'role cultures', which are typically found in large bureaucracies, exude rationality, specialization, routines and rule following.[36] Generally speaking, he suggests that the larger an organization, the more expensive its technology, and the more routine its environment, the more likely it will be to adopt a role culture.

The cultural perspective converges with popular human resource management models, which highlight the importance of 'contextual relations' and organizational 'climate' to generate employee commitment.[37,38] Although the use of metaphor has entered popular culture, we need to be aware of the common error of treating metaphors as literal descriptions of social reality (for early literature on this, see ref. 39).

Learning theories

weblink
Go to the following website for more information on **organizational learning**: www.fieldbook.com

organizational learning: the knowledge management process in which organizations acquire, share and use knowledge to succeed

The learning organization and 'workplace learning' are two popular, and relatively new, metaphors in organizational studies. A learning organization is one that 'facilitates the learning of all its members and continually transforms itself'.[34] Proponents of management and workplace learning equate the learning organization with organizational economic success.[40] Typically, the learning organization approach is interpretive, because it is more closely related to the concept of organizational culture than to something tangible. The focus in a learning organization is on creating an environment that fosters learning through strategies that promote a 'growth-oriented workplace'.[22,41,42] A learning organization is normally understood as one that is 'good' at learning because of the types of activity it employs. Learning organizations are understood as places where individuals can be 'creative' and where people 'learn how to learn together'.

Critical insight

Learning organizations and organizational learning

For a critical review and evaluation of the literature on learning organizations and organizational learning, *Workplace Learning: A Critical Introduction,* by John Bratton, Jean Helms Mills and Peter Sawchuk.[22] A review of this literature is also given by Thomas Garavan in his article 'The learning organization: a review and evaluation'.[42]

Social action theory

The most influential contributions to social action theory were those of Silverman.[43] He provided a powerful critique of the reification embodied in systems thinking, and advocated a view of organizations as the product of individuals pursuing their own ends with the available means. He argued that social reality did not just happen, but had to be made to happen. The implication of this was that, through social interaction, people could modify and possibly even transform social meanings, and therefore any explanation of human activity had to take into account the meanings that those involved assigned to their actions. For example, whether a failure to obey a manager's instruction is a sign of worker insubordination or militancy, or caused by the beginnings of deafness, depends not on what managers or researchers observe to happen, but on what the worker involved means by her or his behaviour. This approach drew from Weber's work on the methodology and theory of knowledge action.

The social action approach involves examining six interrelated areas:

- the nature of the role system and pattern of interaction that has developed in the organization
- the nature of involvement of 'ideal-typical' actors and the characteristic hierarchy of ends they pursue

⊙ the actors' present definitions of their situation within the organization, and their expectations of the likely behaviour of others

⊙ the typical actions of different actors, and the meaning they attach to their actions

⊙ the nature and source of the intended and unintended consequences of action

⊙ any changes in the involvement and ends of the actors and in the role system.[44]

This method of analysing workplace behaviour is influenced by the work of George Herbert Mead (1863–1931) and symbolic interactionism. The approach assumes that human beings act towards things on the basis of subject meanings, and these meanings are the product of social interaction in human society. Organizational study, therefore, involves notions of 'symbolic meaning' and 'sense making' so that individuals can make sense of what they do. Critics have stressed that the micro-level approach of symbolic interactionism does not give sufficient attention to the 'big picture' and the inherent conflict of interest between the key actors representing capital and labour.

Political theory

The political approach to understanding work organizations characterizes the workplace as a purposive miniature society, with politics pervading all managerial work. By politics we mean the power relationships between managers and relevant others, and in turn the capacity of an individual manager to influence others who are in a state of dependence. It refers to those social processes which are not part of a manager's formal role, but which influence (perhaps not directly) the distribution of resources for the purpose of promoting personal objectives.

OB in focus

Developing organizational learning in the UK National Health Service

Learning has been identified as a central concern for a modernized British National Health Service (NHS). Continuing professional development has an important role to play in improving learning, but there is also a need to pay more attention to collective (organizational) learning. Such learning is concerned with the way organizations build and organize knowledge.

The recent emphasis within the NHS has been on the codification of individual and collective knowledge – for example, in guidelines and National Service Frameworks. This needs to be balanced by more personalized knowledge management strategies, especially when dealing with innovative services that rely on tacit knowledge to solve problems. Having robust systems for storing and communicating knowledge is only one part of the challenge. It is also important to consider how such knowledge gets used, and how routines become established in organizations to structure the way in which knowledge is deployed.

In many organizations, these routines favour the adaptive use of knowledge, which helps organizations to achieve incremental improvements in existing practice. However, the development of organizational learning in the NHS needs to move beyond adaptive (single-loop) learning, to foster skills in generative (double-loop) learning and meta-learning. Such learning leads to a redefinition of the organization's goals, norms, policies, procedures or even structures. However, moving the NHS in this direction will require attention to the cultural values and structural mechanisms that facilitate organizational learning.

Source: Sandra M. Nutley and Huw T. O. Davies (ref. 45, p. 35).

Politics in organizations is simply a fact of life. However, as others have observed, the political quality of the management practice is 'denied' or 'trivialized' in many studies of work organizations. And although individual managers might privately question the moral value and integrity of their actions, 'Caught in the maelstrom of capitalist organization, managers are pressured to emulate and reward all kinds of manipulative and destructive behaviours' (ref. 46, p. 39). This perspective on studying organizations offers an approach that examines individual managers as 'knowledgeable human agents' functioning within a dynamic arena where both organizational resources and outcomes can be substantially shaped by their actions. It also reinforces the theoretical and practical importance attached to building alliances and networks of cooperative relationships among organizational members. These negotiating processes shape, and in turn are shaped by, organizational dynamics.

An early study of management adopting a political perspective was undertaken by Dalton in 1959.[47] Building on work by Fox,[48] Graeme Salaman pronounced the political approach most clearly. Power relations that reflect the social inequality prevailing in the wider society determine the structure of work organizations. Organizations are not independent bodies but are embedded into a wider (again political) environment. Furthermore, notions of identity and the part played by organizational life in the construction of both individual and group identity are important.

The political perspective has also drawn attention to the role of strategic choice in shaping organizational structures and management behaviour.[49-52] The strategic choice approach emphasizes the importance of the political power of dominant coalitions and ideological commitments in explaining variations in managerial policies and behaviour, and ultimately explaining variations in managerial effectiveness and organizational outcomes. The political perspective has been criticized for failing to offer little or no explanation of the asymmetrical nature of power, which is the essence of the 'radical' control perspective on management.

Control theories

At the critical pole of the managerial–critical continuum lie the 'control' theories. Much of this work has its roots in Marx's analysis of capitalism. This approach to work and management has come to be associated with the seminal work of Harry Braverman.[16] Organizational theorists approaching the study of work and organizations from this perspective stress the inherent source of tension in organizations arising from technological rationality.[20,53-58] A related focus is the **labour process** approach, which conceptualizes organizational managers as controlling agents who serve the economic imperatives imposed by capitalist market relations. Managerial control is thus *the* central focus of management activity. According to this perspective, organizational structures and employment strategies are instruments and techniques to control the labour process in order to secure high levels of labour productivity and corresponding levels of profitability.

The control perspective views work organizations as hierarchical structures in which workers are deskilled by scientific management techniques and new technology. Managerial behaviour is characterized primarily as control relations: 'organizations are structures of inequality and control'.[17] Such an approach recognizes the existence of inconsistent organizational designs and management practices, and these paradoxical tendencies provide the source of further management strategies that attempt to eradicate the tensions caused by them. The most important of these paradoxes is considered to be the simultaneous desire for control over workers, and cooperation and commitment from them.

The control perspective has also attracted much criticism from both critical and mainstream management theorists. For example, critiques of the deskilling and control thesis draw attention to moderating factors such as markets, worker resistance and batch size.[59-61]

labour process: the process whereby labour is applied to materials and technology to produce goods and services that can be sold in the market as commodities. The term is typically applied to the distinctive labour processes of capitalism in which owners/managers design, control and monitor work tasks so as to maximize the extraction of surplus value from the labour activity of workers

Feminist theory

Until relatively recently, studying the workplace using a 'feminist' approach had not been a major topic of inquiry. The organizational discourse is still, in the main, a masculine endeavour to illuminate organizational behaviour. For radical feminists, science is not sexless: on the contrary, 'the attributes of science are the attributes of males' (ref. 62, p. 207). Research about work organizations tends to be both andro-centric (focused on males) and ethnocentric (focused on the white Anglo-Saxon culture). One interpretation is that it has focused on the management agenda, and up to now this has consisted largely of 'important' white men in one field (academia) talking to, reflecting on and writing about 'important' white men in another field (organizations).[63]

Work and Society: Benign control and precarious work

Sociologist Derek Layder argues that interpersonal control in its many forms is the 'bedrock' on which all social institutions (including work organizations) rest. Central to his argument is a distinction between benign and more problematic and exploitative forms of control. Layder (2004) suggests that we are accustomed to thinking about control in negative ways. The typical image of control portrays a stronger person dominating a weaker person. In Layder's view, this negative image of control is only part of the larger domain of control – and we have failed to conceptualize fully the more benign forms of control that lie at the heart of everyday interactions. As he puts it:

> The common thread in all control is that it is aimed at securing the compliance of the target ... Benignity in control is reflected in its attempt to take the interests of others at least partly into account. By contrast, in domination the interests of the more powerful person are overriding. Also benign control is inherently partial and open-ended ... the control remains benign only as long as a broadly equal reciprocity is maintained, where each party has an opportunity to 'have their say' and 'get their way'. (p. 60)

Layder's comments on the informal face-to-face interactions that form the basis of all social life offer us a useful vantage point on the social nature of work. In fact, we could use his continuum (benign control at one end and domination at the other end) to think about and describe the nature of control in any given work organization. Especially worthwhile would be exercises that enabled managers and employees to participate in discussions about the qualities that distinguish benign informal social control from domination. Such exercises are valuable not just for their contribution to team building, trust and a sense of security among workers, but also because they prepare employees to participate in the processes of collaborative problem solving that are essential to effective organizations.

It is important, however, to place the idea of benign control in a larger context. Layder is right to stress that academic interpretations of control have focused on its negative forms and features and that, consequently, a theoretical account of benign control has not received sufficient attention. But there is perhaps good reason for this: if we look at work from a historical and comparative perspective, we find no shortage of examples of workers whose working lives have been characterized by coercion and domination.

The history of the employment contract is itself very telling. Mac Neil (2002) notes that the employment contract has roots in the master–servant relationship. Although there is evidence that, throughout the twentieth century, Western industrialized nations have moved away from the idea of a master–servant relationship towards a workplace where benign control has triumphed over coercion and domination, there is also, sadly, evidence of the opposite. Kalleberg (2009) reminds us of the immense variability of employment relations, even in the developed world. Some employment relations are characterized by respect, security reasonable pay and other indications of quality. Yet among large segments of the workforce, there is a trend towards 'precarious work' and an overall reduction in the quality of working life. (Kalleberg cites as a cause of this trend employer efforts to 'obtain greater flexibility to meet growing competition' (p. 12).).

What are the implications of the trend towards precarious work for the forms of social control identified by Layder? As work becomes more precarious, will the balance between benign and more problematic forms of control be tilted towards the problematic end of the continuum? Will historical forms of employment relations reappear, causing workers to once again occupy 'the subservient status of the servant' (Mac Neil, 2002, p. 174)? These questions are best answered by focusing on particular cases.

stop!   Consider the following definition: '"precarious work" ... [is] employment that is uncertain, unpredictable, and risky from the point of view of the worker' (Kalleberg, p. 2). Now, reflect on the following questions:

- What kinds of organization are likely to generate precarious work for their employees?
- Are some workers more likely than others to experience the negative effects of precarious work?
- Will the workers subjected to precarious work inevitably experience problematic forms of social control?
- What can be done to reduce the likelihood that problematic control will trump benign control in organizations employing large numbers of precarious workers?

Sources and further information:

Kalleberg, A. (2009) 'Precarious work, insecure workers: employment relations in transition', *American Sociological Review*, **74**, pp. 1–22.

Layder, D. (2004) *Emotion in Social Life: The Lost Heart of Society*, London: Sage.

Mac Neil, M. (2002). 'Governing employment', pp. 171–87 in M. Mac Neil, N. Sargent and P. Swan (eds), *Law, Regulation and Governance*, Dons Mills, ON: Oxford University Press.

Note: This feature was written by David MacLennan, Assistant Professor at Thompson Rivers University, BC, Canada

Theoretically, one of the most important consequences of gender analysis in organizational studies is its power to question research findings that segregate organizational behaviour from the larger structure of social and historical life. Accordingly, much of the recent work most directly related to the feminist approach requires us to look at the interface between social context and work. It is argued that this shapes and reshapes the employment relationship. We need to look at gender divisions in the labour market, patriarchal power, issues of sexuality and inequality in society and at work, and the interface between home and work (the 'dual-role' syndrome). More importantly, however, incorporating gender development into the study of organizational studies will represent the life experience of both men and women in a more comprehensive and inclusive way.

Postmodernism

postmodernism: the sociological approach that attempts to explain social life in modern societies that are characterized by post-industrialization, consumerism and global communications

A new focus for organization theory is **postmodernism**. While traditional writings on organization theory tend to view work organizations as fine examples of human rationality, postmodernists such as Michel Foucault regard organizations as more akin to defensive reactions against inherently destabilizing forces.[5,64] The postmodernist perspective has its roots in the French intellectual tradition of post-structuralism, an approach to knowledge that puts the consideration of 'reflexivity' and how language is used at the centre of the study of all aspects of human activity. Thus, postmodern perspectives question attempts to 'know' or 'discover' the genuine order of things (what is known as representation). Researchers must possess the ability to be critical of their own intellectual assumptions (that is, exercise reflexivity).

This approach plays down the notion of a disinterested observer, and instead stresses the way in which people's notion of who and what they are – their agency, in other words – is shaped by the discourses that surround them. This is known as decentering the subject. Postmodernists also believe that researchers are materially involved in constructing the world they observe through language (by writing about it). Thus, where modernists perceive history as a grand narrative of human activity, rationality and progress, postmodernists reject the grand narrative and the notion of progressive intent. Clegg and Hardy frame the postmodern approach this way: 'They are histories, not history. Any pattern that is constituted can only be a series of assumptions framed in and by a historical context' (ref. 4, p. 2).

Michel Foucault's relevance to organizational theory lies in several related spheres.[65,66] First, he argues that contemporary management controls human behaviour neither by consensus nor by coercion, but rather by systems of surveillance and human relations management techniques. Second, he suggests that although an organization is 'constructed by power', its members do not 'have' power. Power is not the property of any individual or group. While modernists see the direction of power flowing downwards against subordinates, and its essence as negative, Foucault argues that power should be configured as a relationship between subjects. It has 'capillary' qualities that enable it to be exercised *within* the social body, rather than *above* it' (ref. 67, p. 39). Third, with the ever-increasing expansion of electronic surveillance in the workplace, Foucault offers his own image of an 'iron cage' in the form of the extended panopticon – hidden surveillance.

Postmodernism is a useful way to study work organizations. In particular, the notion of power as a 'web' within which managers and non-managers are held has much to offer. However, some critics, for example Martin Parker, have described postmodern epistemology as a reactionary intellectual trend, which amounts to a 'fatal distraction' from engagement in a rigorous analysis of organizational changes located within late modernity.[68]

THE VALUE OF THEORY ABOUT CONTEMPORARY ORGANIZATIONAL BEHAVIOUR

In this chapter, we have reviewed the main themes and arguments of both classical and contemporary theories of work. As we explained, the classical theories are derived from the works of Karl Marx, Emile Durkheim and Max Weber, and are an intellectual response to the transformation of society caused by industrial capitalism. A legitimate question for students of organizational behaviour is, 'Why bother studying sociological classics – three "dead white men"?' We believe that an understanding of the classical accounts of work is important because, as others have also argued, the epistemological, theoretical and methodological difficulties that were identified and debated by Marx, Durkheim and Weber remain central to the conduct of contemporary research on organizational behaviour.[2,69–73] Those of us who study contemporary work organizations are informed by the 'canonical' writers and constantly return to them for ideas and inspiration.

In terms of understanding what goes on in the workplace, theory cannot be separated from management practice. It is used both to defend existing management practices and to validate new ways of organizing work, or *doing*. The nature of the employment relationship is clearly an issue of central importance to understanding human behaviour in work organizations. The classical sociologists developed a body of work that, directly or by inference, provides an account of the relations between employers and employees.

For Marx, conflict is structured into the employment relationship and is, for most of the time, asymmetrical. That is, the power of the employer or agent (manager) typically exceeds that of the workers. Durkheim's work influenced how theorists have studied organizations, and he reminds us that there are multiple ways in which society imposes itself upon us and shapes our behaviour.

A number of Weber's concepts also continue to have much relevance in the early twenty-first century. For example, his concept of charismatic domination is prominent in contemporary leadership theories. In addition, Weber's concepts of bureaucracy and rationalization have been applied to the fast-food sector, and have exposed the irrationality associated with the paradigm of McDonaldization. Weber's interpretive method, and in particular the researcher's capacity to assign different meanings to shared reality, gives a postmodern ring to his theory.

Finally, classical theories enter the contemporary debates on work organization and management practices by reinforcing the message that understanding the nature of the employment relationship necessarily involves considering organizational culture, societal values and norms as well as national institutions. It is through these that individuals acquire a self-identity and the mental, physical and social skills that shape their behaviour both outside and inside the work organization.

SUMMARY

○ The three founders of the sociology of work all continue to have their contemporary adherents and detractors.

○ Marx's fascination with class, conflict and the labour process formed the basis for the most popular new approach throughout much of industrial sociology, from the late 1960s to the 1980s. It spawned a complete school of thought in the labour process tradition, but its limitations became more evident as the approach attempted to explain all manner of social phenomena directly through the prism of class.

○ Durkheim's moral concerns continue to pervade the market economy, and make predictions about human actions that are based on amoral, economically rational behaviour less than convincing. Perhaps where Durkheim has been most vigorously criticized has been in relation to the allegedly cohering effects of an extended division of labour. The mainstream of managerial theories does not support Durkheim on this point: dependency does not generate mutual solidarity.

○ Weber's theories of rationalization and bureaucracy have never been far from the minds of those analysing the trend towards larger and larger organizations, and the recent movement towards more flexible work organization patterns. Again, however, Weber's over-rationalized approach underestimated the significance of destabilizing and sectional forces within work organizations.

○ This chapter has reviewed 12 theoretical approaches or conversations on organizational studies: the technical, human relations, neo-human relations, systems thinking, contingency, cultures, learning, control, feminist, social action, political and postmodernist approaches. It has adopted a particular form of differentiating between the various theories through an organizational grid based on two axes: managerial–critical and determinist–interpretative. This is a heuristic way of structuring the various possibilities.

KEY CONCEPTS

alienation
androcentrism

anomie
ideal type
labour power
paradox of consequences
rationality
strategic choice

KEY VOCAB CHECKLIST FOR ESL STUDENTS

- Alienation
- Anomie
- Bourgeoisie
- Class conflict
- Class consciousness
- Contingency theory
- Contradiction, contradict
- Corporate social responsibility
- Division of labour
- Empiricism, empirical
- Formalization, formal, formalize
- Human relations
- Ideal type
- Input
- Labour process
- Mechanical solidarity
- Objectification, objectify
- Open systems
- Organic solidarity
- Organizational learning
- Output
- Postmodernism
- Power
- Proletariat
- Rationalization, rationality, rational, rationalize
- Scientific management
- Social solidarity
- Surplus value
- Survey
- Urbanization
- *Verstehen*

REVIEW QUESTIONS

1 To what extent has the decline of Communism undermined the utility of Marx's ideas?
2 Why was Weber so pessimistic about work when Durkheim and Marx were so optimistic?
3 Do we need theory to explain the way organizations work?

4 What is the relevance of Weber's concept of *Verstehen* for organizational behaviour researchers?

5 What is meant by open systems, contingency theory and social action theory? Why is it important to understand each of them?

6 What is meant by the suggestion that theory cannot be separated from management practice?

RESEARCH QUESTIONS

1 Form a study group of three to five people. Having read a review of the classical sociological theorists and contemporary approaches to studying work and organizations, is the role of the academics in organizational behaviour to unmask inequality in organizational life or to be detached? Is it possible for organizational behaviour researchers to be value-free and objective in their research? If a researcher adopted a feminist perspective, how would this guide his or her research?

2 Obtain a copy of Stephen Ackroyd and others' (2006) *The Oxford Handbook of Work and Organization* and read pages 2–8. To what extent are this textbook – *Work and Organizational Behaviour* – and the topics selected for study a product of its times? If you had to do some organizational behaviour research, what would your topic be and what factors would influence your choice?

3 Retrieve and read Christine Coupland and others' (2008) article, 'Saying it with feeling: analyzing speakable emotions' (see Further reading, below). What does the term 'constructionism' mean? How does Marx's analysis of capitalist employer–employee relations help us to understand that how people talk about emotional experiences in the workplace is bound up in relations of power?

FURTHER READING

Bratton, J., Denham, D. and Deutschmann, L. (2009) *Capitalism and Classical Sociological Theory*, Toronto: University of Toronto Press.

Coupland, C., Brown, A. D., Daniels, K. and Humphreys, M. (2008) 'Saying it with feeling: analyzing speakable emotions', *Human Relations*, **61**(3), pp. 327–53.

Heracleous, L. and Jacob, C. D. (2008) 'Understanding organizations through embodied metaphors', *Organization Studies*, **29**(1), pp. 45–78.

Jaffee, D. (2001) *Organization Theory: Tension and Change*, Boston, MA: McGraw-Hill, Chapters 1 and 2.

Manning, P. K. (2008) 'Goffman on organizations', *Organization Studies*, **29**(5), pp. 677–99.

Parker, M. (2000) 'The sociology of organizations and the organization of sociology: some reflections on the making of a division of labour', *Sociological Review*, **4**(1), pp. 124–46.

Reed, M. (1999) 'Organizational theorizing: a historically contested terrain', pp. 25–50 in S. R. Clegg and C. Hardy (eds), *Studying Organization: Theory and Method*, London: Sage.

Rowlinson, M. (2004) 'Challenging the foundations of organization theory', *Work, Employment and Society*, **18**(3), pp. 607–20.

Swingewood, A. (2000) *A Short History of Sociological Thought*, New York: St Martin's Press, Chapters 2, 3 and 4.

Tsoukas, H. (1992) 'Postmodernism, reflexive rationalism and organizational studies: a reply to Martin Parker', *Organizational Studies*, **13**(4), pp. 643–9.

Chapter case study 1

Butting out smoking in Russia

Setting

With the collapse of the Soviet Union, the privatization of Russia's tobacco industry began. In the new Russia, tobacco advertising is unavoidable. Smoking is promoted on half of all billboards in Moscow and on three-quarters of the plastic bags in the country. As a result of tobacco companies promoting smoking as part of a 'Western lifestyle' and striving to capitalize on the public's new disposable income, smoking rates have doubled. Russia is now the fourth heaviest smoking country in the world, with one in four boys under the age of 10 and 60 per cent of men over the age of 15 classified as smokers. While most of the Western world is experiencing a decrease in smoking rates, the number of Russian smokers continues to climb.

The government has proposed legislation banning smoking in workplaces and other public places, such as on aircraft, trains and municipal transport as well as in schools, hospitals, cultural institutions and government buildings. The legislation also requires specially designated smoking areas to be set up, and for restaurants and cafes to set up no-smoking areas. The changes will affect not only Russian companies, but also international firms looking to invest in the expanding privatization of the economy. The emerging middle class has produced a potential market of 150 million consumers that lures companies from all over the world hoping to tap into the vast natural resources, advanced technology and skilled workers that Russia has to offer.

The problem

Kendles & Smith is a global British pharmaceutical, medical devices and consumer packaged goods manufacturer, with 150 subsidiary companies operating in over 32 countries. It recently opened a new operation in Moscow as part of a strategy to make its mark on the new prosperous Russian economy.

The management at Kendles & Smith were versed in Russian history and understood that worker attitudes and behaviours had been shaped by 70 years of Communist dictatorship, a centrally planned economic system, and government bureaucracy that had ruled the people's lives. Like most international firms, management at Kendles & Smith found Russian workers to be cooperative and compliant, but not risk takers. Many of the supervisors hired from the local labour pool lacked confidence and drive. Although they followed corporate policies strictly, the employees in turn expected the new company to take care of them and their families.

With the UK having one of the lowest smoking rates in Europe, the management at Kendles & Smith were surprised at the number of the employees who were smokers – almost 65 per cent. As a company with a focus on health products, one of its first goals was to develop a voluntary tobacco reduction programme, including counselling and nicotine cessation aids, to improve the health of its new staff. Unfortunately, only a small group of workers took advantage of the programme in its first year, and the majority of these were supervisors.

The next step was to implement a smoking ban in the Russian operations. Although it was made clear to all employees that the company president wanted to see the worksites smoke-free, regardless of the government's legislation, only the supervisors were to be given an opportunity to express their positions on the matter. Jonathan Williams, one of the UK managers assigned to the Moscow operation, was given the task of doing the research. There were over 100 supervisors, and Jonathan was given only a short time-frame within which to present his findings. Although Jonathan was free to speak to the supervisors, the company president stressed that he really just wanted to know whether or not the majority of the supervisors favoured the ban.

As Jonathan had not conducted workplace research before, he felt overwhelmed when he began reading about the various methods that could be used. He wanted the rich qualitative information that in-person interviews could give, but he thought that taking a more quantitative approach, such as using a questionnaire, would provide the anonymity that the supervisors might need to be honest with their answers.

Tasks

As Jonathan, ask yourself the following questions:

1 What would be the disadvantages of using a questionnaire in this case?
2 What might be missed by gathering only the supervisors' opinions?
3 What qualities do the Russian workers exhibit that could influence the research results? Why?

Further reading

Allan, G. and Skinner, C. (eds) (1991) *Handbook for Research Students in the Social Sciences*, London: Falmer Press.

Bryman, J. (ed.) (1988) *Doing Research in Organizations*, London: Routledge.

Elenkov, D. (1998) 'Can American management concepts work in Russia?', *California Management Review*, **40**(4), pp. 133–56.

Oppenheim, A. N. (1992) *Questionnaire Design, Interviewing and Attitude Measurement*, London: Pinter.

Visit http://pre.ethics.gc.ca/eng/policy-politique/tcps-eptc/readtcps-lireeptc for an example of a research ethics policy.

Note

This case study was written by Lori Rilkoff, MSc, CHRP, Senior Human Resources Manager at the City of Kamloops, and lecturer in HRM at Thompson Rivers University, BC, Canada. Data on smoking in Russia were taken from http://news.bbc.co.uk/2/hi/health/7209551.stm; www.scientificblogging.com/news_releases/russian_women_exercise_post_soviet_free_will_by_smoking_a_lot_more

Chapter case study 2

Research at Aeroprecision AB

Visit www.palgrave.com/business/brattinob2e to view this case study

WEB-BASED ASSIGNMENT

How are we to make sense of the competing assortment of theoretical approaches to organizational behaviour? We address this question here with reference to the classical accounts of sociology and contemporary approaches to studying formal organizations. Our collective experience in teaching and researching aspects of organizational behaviour has made it clear that the contemporary student of organizational behaviour cannot understand the discipline without an appreciation of the works of Marx, Weber and Durkheim. In their own way, each addressed the following two fundamental questions:

- What is the source of societal and organizational conflict?
- What is the relationship between consciousness (the 'self' or 'inside') and society or social structure (the 'outside')?

On an individual basis, or working in a small group, visit the following websites and write a brief summary of how Marx, Weber and Durkheim have fundamentally shaped the modern debate about work and organizations:

- http://plato.stanford.edu/entries/marx
- www.epistemelinks.com/Main/Philosophers.aspx?PhilCode=Durk
- www.marxists.org/reference/archive/weber

OB IN FILM

The film *Roger & Me* (1989), directed by Michael Moore, is a documentary about the closure of General Motors' car plant at Flint, Michigan, which resulted in the loss of 30,000 jobs. The film provides insight into corporate restructuring and US deindustrialization, and details the attempts of the film maker to conduct a face-to-face interview with General Motors Chief Executive Officer Roger Smith. The film also raises questions about values, politics and the practical considerations of doing organizational behaviour research.

Values reflect the personal beliefs of a researcher. Gaining access to organizations, particularly to top managers, is a political process. Access is usually mediated by gate-keepers concerned not only about what the organization can gain from the research, but also about the researcher's motives.

Watch the documentary, and consider these questions:

⊚ Can organizational behaviour researchers be value-free and objective in their research?

⊚ Who are the gatekeepers in *Roger & Me?* How can gatekeepers influence how the inquiry will take place?

Practical considerations refer to issues about how to carry out organizational behaviour research: for example, choices of research design or method need to be dovetailed with specific research questions.

⊚ What alternative methods could a researcher use to investigate the closure of General Motors' factory at Flint?

REFERENCES

1. Salaman, G. (1981) *Class and the Corporation*, London: Fontana.
2. Turner, B. S. (1999) *Classical Sociology*, London: Sage.
3. Hurst, C. (2005) *Living Theory*, Boston, MA: Pearson.
4. Clegg, S. and Hardy, C. (1999) *Studying Organization: Theory and Method*, Thousand Oaks, CA: Sage.
5. Grint, K. (1998) *The Sociology of Work* (2nd edn), Cambridge: Polity Press.
6. Marx, K. (1867/1970) *Capital: A Critique of Political Economy*, Volume 1, London: Lawrence & Wishart.
7. Ritzer, G. and Goodman, D. J. (2004) *Classical Social Theory* (4th edn), New York: McGraw-Hill.
8. Morrison, K. (1995) *Marx, Durkheim, Weber*, London: Sage.
9. Marx, K. and Engels, F. (1848/1967) *The Communist Manifesto*, London: Penguin.
10. Durkheim, E. (1893/1997) *The Division of Labor in Society*, New York: Free Press.
11. Weber, M. (1905/2002) *The Protestant Ethic and the 'Spirit' of Capitalism*, London: Penguin.
12. Ritzer, G. (2000) *The McDonaldization of Society*, Thousand Oaks, CA: Pine Forge Press.
13. Weber, M. (1922/1968) *Economy and Society*, New York: Bedminster.
14. Smith, A. (1776/1982) *The Wealth of Nations*, Harmondsworth: Penguin.
15. George, C. S. (1972) *The History of Management Thought* (2nd edn), Englewood Cliffs, NJ: Prentice-Hall.
16. Braverman, H. (1974) *Labor and Monopoly Capitalism: The Degradation of Work in the Twentieth Century*, New York: Monthly Review Press.
17. Littler, C. R. and Salaman, G. (1984) *Class at Work: The Design, Allocation and Control of Jobs*, London: Batsford.
18. Thompson, P. and McHugh, D. (2006) *Work Organizations: A Critical Introduction* (4th edn), Basingstoke: Palgrave.
19. Mouzelis, N. (1967) *Organization and Bureaucracy*, London: Routledge & Kegan Paul.
20. Clegg, S. and Dunkerley, D. (1980) *Organization, Class and Control*, London: Routledge & Kegan Paul.
21. Thompson, P. (1989) *The Nature of Work* (2nd edn), London: Macmillan.

22. Bratton, J., Helms Mills, J. and Sawchuk, P. (2004) *Workplace Learning: A Critical Introduction*, Toronto: Garamond.
23. Cohen, P. S. (1968) *Modern Social Theory*, London: Heinemann.
24. Parsons, T. (1960) *Structure and Process in Modern Societies*, Chicago: Free Press.
25. Dunlop, J. T. (1958) *Industrial Relations System*, New York: Holt.
26. Senge, P. (1990) *The Fifth Discipline*, New York: Doubleday.
27. Scott, R. W. (2003) *Organizations: Rational, Natural, and Open Systems*, Upper Saddle River, NJ: Prentice-Hall.
28. Jaffee, D. (2001) *Organization Theory: Tension and Change*, Boston, MA: McGraw-Hill.
29. Woodward, J. (1958) *Management and Technology*. Problems of Progress in Industry No. 5, London: HMSO.
30. Woodward, J. (1965) *Industrial Organizations: Theory and Practice*, London: Oxford University Press.
31. Burns, T. and Stalker, G. M. (1961) *The Management of Innovation*, London: Tavistock.
32. Lawrence, P. R. and Lorsch, J. W. (1967) *Organisation and Environment: Managing Differentiation and Integration*, Cambridge, MA: Harvard University Press.
33. Thompson, P. and McHugh, D. (2009) *Work Organizations: A Critical Introduction* (4th edn), Basingstoke: Palgrave.
34. Lopez, J. (2003) *Society and its Metaphors: Language, Social Theory and Social Structure*, London: Continuum.
35. Morgan, G. (1997) *Images of Organization* (2nd edn), Thousand Oaks, CA: Sage.
36. Handy, C. (1985) *Understanding Organizations*, London: Penguin.
37. Rigney, F. (2001) *The Metaphorical Society: An Invitation to Social Theory*, Lanham, MD: Rowman & Littlefield.
38. Crow, G. (2005) *The Art of Sociological Argument*, Basingstoke: Palgrave.
39. Etzioni, A. (1988) *The Moral Dimension*, New York: Free Press.
40. Pedler, M., Boydell, T. and Burgoyne, J. (1988) *The Learning Company Project Report*, Sheffield: Employment Department.
41. Fenwick, T. (1998) 'Questioning the concept of the learning organization', pp. 140–52 in S. Scott, B. Spencer and A. Thomas (eds), *Learning for Life*, Toronto: Thompson Educational.
42. Garavan, T. (1997) 'The learning organization: a review and evaluation', *Learning Organization*, **4**(1), pp. 18–29.
43. Silverman, D. (1970) *The Theory of Organizations*, London: Heinemann.
44. Brown, R. K. (1992) *Understanding Industrial Organizations*, London: Routledge.
45. Nutley, S. M. and Davies, H. T. O. (2001) 'Developing organizational learning in the NHS', *Medical Education*, **35**(1), Wiley-Blackwell, p. 35.
46. Alvesson, M. and Willmott, H. (1996) *Making Sense of Management: A Critical Introduction*, London: Sage.
47. Dalton, M. (1959) *Men Who Manage*, New York: McGraw-Hill.
48. Fox, A. (1971) *The Sociology of Work in Industry*, London: Collier Macmillan.
49. Child, J. (1972) 'Organizational structure, environment and performance: the role of strategic choice', *Sociology*, **6**(1), pp. 331–50.
50. Pettigrew, A. (1973) *The Politics of Organizational Decision-Making*, London: Tavistock.
51. Kotter, J. P. (1979) *Power in Management*, New York: Amocom.
52. Kochan, T. E., Katz, H. and McKersie, R. (1986) *The Transformation of American Industrial Relations*, New York: Basic Books.
53. Alvesson, M. (1987) *Organization Theory: Technocratic Consciousness*, Berlin: De Gruyter.
54. Alvesson, M. and Willmott, H. (eds) (1992) *Critical Management Studies*, London: Sage.
55. Habermas, J. (1970) *Towards a Rational Society*, London: Heinemann.
56. Habermas, J. (1971) *Knowledge and Human Interests*, London: Heinemann
57. Marcuse, H. (1964) *One Dimensional Man*, Boston, MA: Beacon.
58. Marcuse, H. (1969) *An Essay on Liberation*, Boston, MA: Beacon.

59. Kelly, J. (1985) 'Management's redesign of work: labour process, labour markets and product markets', in D. Knights, H. Willmott and D. Collinson (eds), *Job Redesign: Critical Perspectives on the Labour Process*, Aldershot: Gower.

60. Wood, S. (ed.) (1982) *The Transformation of Work?*, London: Unwin Hyman.

61. Bratton, J. (1992) *Japanization at Work*, Basingstoke: Macmillan.

62. Sydie, R. A. (1994) *Natural Women, Cultured Men*, Vancouver: UBC Press.

63. Townley, B. (1994) *Reframing Human Resource Management: Power, Ethics and the Subject of Work*, London: Sage.

64. Hassard, J. and Parker, M. (eds) (1993) *Postmodernism and Organizations*, London: Sage.

65. Foucault, M. (1977) *Discipline and Punish: The Birth of the Prison*, New York: Pantheon.

66. Foucault, M. (1979) *The History of Sexuality*, Harmondsworth: Penguin.

67. Sheridan, A. (1980) *Michel Foucault: The Will to Power*, London: Tavistock.

68. Parker, M. (1993) 'Life after Jean-Francois', pp. 204–12 in J. Hassard and M. Parker (eds), *Postmodernism and Organizations*, London: Sage.

69. Ray, L. J. (1999) *Theorizing Classical Sociology*, Buckingham: Open University Press.

70. Craib, I. (1997) *Classical Social Theory*, Oxford: Oxford University Press.

71. Delaney, T. (2004) *Classical Social Theory: Investigation and Application*, Upper Saddle River, NJ: Pearson/Prentice-Hall.

72. Smart, B. (2003) *Economy, Culture and Society*, Buckingham: Open University Press.

73. Goodwin, G. A. and Scimecca, J. A. (2006) *Classical Social Theory*, Belmont, CA: Thomson.

Chapter
3

WORK ROUTINES & SKILL CHANGE

CHAPTER AIM

To explain the dominant forms of work organisation and explore competing theories of skill change.

KEY CONCEPTS

- Taylorism
- Fordism
- deskilling
- labour process
- upskilling
- human capital
- offshoring
- flexible specialisation
- polarisation of skills
- compensatory theory of skill
- automating and informating
- range of work
- discretion in work
- work organisation paradigms

LEARNING OUTCOMES

After reading and understanding the material in this chapter you will be able to:
1 Describe the main features of Taylorism and assess their relevance to contemporary work.
2 Describe the methods and application of Fordism.
3 Explain the theory behind the deskilling thesis.
4 Outline and evaluate the main criticisms of the deskilling thesis.
5 Explain the theory behind the upskilling thesis.
6 Outline and evaluate the main criticisms of the upskilling thesis.
7 Describe alternative approaches to examining skill change.
8 Use the work categorisation framework to analyse jobs.
9 Explain the relationship between skill change and work organisation paradigms.

INTRODUCTION

This chapter addresses a puzzle that has occupied the minds of researchers and theorists for decades: whether the fundamental shifts that have been occurring in the nature of work are causing people to experience either deskilling and degrading, or upskilling and enrichment, in their working lives. We have previously noted some of the structural changes occurring in patterns of employment, but here we assess the impact of these broader employment dynamics by focusing on the nature of work tasks.

To explore these issues, the chapter is divided into five sections. The first examines two dominant traditions in work organisation – Taylorism and Fordism – using contemporary examples to illustrate the central principles of each. This provides the basis for the next three sections, each of which examines a different perspective on how work is changing: the deskilling thesis, the upskilling antithesis and the attempts to synthesise these contrasting approaches. The fifth section of the chapter develops a conceptual framework to integrate the analysis.

DOMINANT TRADITIONS OF WORK ORGANISATION – TAYLORISM AND FORDISM

Routine work in the service sector – burgers and Taylor

Imagine the scene: you are visiting a city for the first time. It is lunchtime and you are feeling hungry, you do not have much money to spend on food, and you only have 30 minutes before your train leaves. As you look along the busy, unfamiliar street you recognise a sign in the distance: a large yellow letter 'M'. A sense of relief overwhelms you as you head for the home of American pulp cuisine, McDonald's. Any uncertainty and anxiety has been replaced by the predictability of the McDonald's experience: no matter where you are, you will get the standard-tasting burger, covered with the same relish, lodged in the same bun, served in the same packaging for consumption in the familiar decor of the restaurant.

Consistency is McDonald's strong selling point – if you are one of the company's 50 million daily customers, you will know exactly what you are going to get when you order your Big Mac and large fries, in any one of McDonald's 31,000 outlets in 119 countries. Of course, to guarantee such a standardised product, the work processes as well as the food have all been standardised. So leaving aside the issue of the product itself, how can we characterise and understand work at organisations such as McDonald's?

If we use a metaphor, we can describe McDonald's as a well-maintained machine in almost every aspect of its operations, from the customer interface to the centralised planning and financial control (Morgan, 1986). Employees at McDonald's (or 'crew members' as they are called) are treated as components of this machine. Each receives simple training to perform a number of tasks, which require little judgement and leave limited room for discretion. Crew members are given precise instructions on what to say, what to do and how to do it. They are the necessary 'living' labour joining the precisely timed computer-controlled equipment that cooks the burgers, fries the potatoes, dispenses the drinks, heats the pies, records the order and calculates the customer's change:

> Much of the food prepared at McDonald's arrives at the restaurant pre-formed, pre-cut, pre-sliced and pre-prepared, often by non-human technologies. This serves to drastically limit what employees need to do .... McDonald's has developed a variety of machines to control its employees. When a worker must decide when a glass is full and the soft-drink dispenser needs to be shut

off, there is always the risk that the worker may be distracted and allow the glass to overflow. Thus a sensor has been developed that automatically shuts off the soft-drink dispenser when the glass is full.

(Ritzer, 1993: 105–6)

This logic of automation is extended to all the processes, with the consequence that the employees push buttons, respond to beeps and buzzers and repeat stock phrases to customers like subjects in a bizarre Pavlovian experiment. The dehumanising effects can often be seen in the glazed expressions of the young people who serve you. But the most poignant, if not ironic, aspect of all this is that one of the world's most successful multinational corporations at the beginning of the twenty-first century relies on labour management techniques that were developed at the beginning of the twentieth century. Indeed, the pioneer of 'scientific management', F. W. Taylor, would have certainly recognised and endorsed the principles upon which McDonald's is organised.

3.1 | Exercise

McJobs are good for some people

Some young people are well suited to boring jobs. That was one of the conclusions reached by Gould (2010) in a study of McDonald's restaurants across Australia. In an interesting piece of research, Gould distributed a questionnaire to managers and crew members in 50 restaurants with the approval of the McDonald's corporation. Responses were received from 812 crew members and 102 managers (the total Australian McDonald's workforce is about 55,000, based in 733 outlets). The findings confirmed that the work is organised around Tayloristic principles: 'crew overwhelmingly perceive their duties as comprised of a limited range of non-complex tasks which, by implication, should be done in a prescribed way' (Gould, 2010: 799). However, Gould argues that this has less of a negative effect on employees than often assumed by McDonald's critics (e.g. Leidner 1993, Royle 2000 and Schlosser 2002). The benefits of working at McDonald's include job security, the possibility of a career and flexible working hours.

Most notable, Gould's survey data leads him to conclude that it is important to take a person-specific perspective on fast food work – so looking at individual differences to explain attitudes to the work. In particular, there seems to be an age-related effect:

Compared with their older peers, crew work may be more suitable and offer greater benefits to younger teenagers who mostly appear relatively content. As they get older, crew indicate that they find the work easier and more repetitive and, in these respects, less attractive. Such trends are statistically significant. Older crew are also more inclined to assert their rights at work, a tendency which may be less compatible with a fast-food work environment.

(Gould, 2010: 797)

Gould concludes that those who are satisfied with working at McDonald's are not in the minority and have not been indoctrinated. They work there because they are not looking for a complex job and the flexibility suits their lifestyles.

1 What issues do Gould's findings raise about how we should consider routine jobs?
2 What else would you need to know in order to evaluate these findings thoroughly?

F. W. TAYLOR'S GUIDING PRINCIPLES

The ideas of Taylor have been well documented elsewhere (see, for example, Kelly, 1982; Littler, 1982; Rose, 1988), so it is only necessary here to restate the central principles to see how closely aligned the contemporary work processes at McDonald's are to concepts that were originally published in 1911. Efficiency was Taylor's guiding obsession. His own work experience as an engineer led him to believe there was an optimum way of performing any job: the 'one best way'. It was the task of management to discover this through the application of rigorous scientific testing, which involved breaking all activities down into their smallest components and systematically analysing each step. No activity was too complex or too mundane to be subjected to this scientific analysis, argued Taylor (see Extract 3.1).

Applying scientific management

Taylor illustrates his theory with the example of managing pig-iron handling and shovelling.

> Probably the most important element in the science of shoveling is this: There must be some shovel load at which a first-class shoveler will do his biggest day's work. What is that load? ... Under scientific management the answer to this question is not a matter of anyone's opinion; it is a question for accurate, careful, scientific investigation. Under the old system you would call in a first-rate shoveler and say, 'See here, Pat, how much ought you to take on at one shovel load?' And if a couple of fellows agreed, you would say that's about the right load and let it go at that. But under scientific management absolutely every element in the work of every man in your establishment, sooner or later, becomes the subject of exact, precise, scientific investigation and knowledge to replace the old, 'I believe so,' and 'I guess so.' Every motion, every small fact becomes the subject of careful, scientific investigation.
>
> (ibid: 51–2)

> Now one of the very first requirements for a man who is fit to handle pig iron as a regular occupation is that he shall be so stupid and so phlegmatic that he more nearly resembles in his mental make-up the ox than any other type. The man who is mentally alert and intelligent is for this reason entirely unsuited to what would, for him, be the grinding monotony of work of this character. Therefore the workman who is best suited to handling pig iron is unable to understand the real science of doing this class of work. He is so stupid that the word 'percentage' has no meaning to him, and he must consequently be trained by a man more intelligent than himself into the habit of working in accordance with the laws of this science before he can be successful.
>
> (Taylor, ibid: 59)

Having discovered the 'one best way' of performing a task, management's responsibility was to allocate tasks to employees, attempting to fit the right person to each job. The employee should have the requisite skills, acquired through systematic training, to complete the task at hand, and no more than those required by the job.

Emerging from Taylor's principles of organising the work process is a distinctive managerial ideology in which four themes dominate:

- *Division of labour*: this involves the separation of manual work (the doing) from mental work (the thinking). By removing from the employee any discretion over the organisation and execution of work, managers are able to secure control over the method and pace of working. As we shall see, this can have important consequences for determining the skill definition of a work activity.
- *Planning*: managers play an important role in planning each activity to ensure that it is in line with business objectives. In pursuit of these objectives, employees are to be used dispassionately, along with capital equipment and raw materials, in the search for greater efficiency, productivity and profitability. As a consequence, rigorous selection and training of people (to instil required behaviours) become a critical management function.
- *Surveillance*: based on the assumption that people cannot be trusted to perform their jobs diligently, there needs to be control through close supervision and monitoring of all work activities. Hierarchies of authority are constructed giving legitimacy to surveillance and simultaneously constructing a 'division of management' (Littler, 1982: 53).
- *Performance-related pay*: Taylor's deeply entrenched belief was that people were essentially instrumental, and so money could be used as a powerful motivator providing it was linked directly to the productivity of the individual: a linkage achieved by piece-rate payment systems.

While the logic of Taylorism is impeccable, the conditions of work it produces are often dehumanising and bleak: a set of highly segmented work activities, with no opportunity for employees to use their discretion and a system of close supervision to monitor their work performance. However, the practice of Taylorism has not necessarily followed the theory as closely as its original protagonist would have wished, leading some commentators (notably Edwards, 1979; Palmer, 1975) to argue that Taylor's influence has been overstated because the practical impact of his ideas was limited – not least because of the collective resistance exerted by employees through trade unions.

Certainly, in Taylor's own lifetime the diffusion of the principles of scientific management was modest. Many managers remained unconvinced about the possibility of planning and measuring activities sufficiently accurately to enable the 'science' to work. There were also competing ideas about the nature of job design from the human relations movement (starting with the famous Hawthorne experiments in the 1920s) which brought out the importance of the social factors at work and challenged the economic assumptions underlying Taylor's theory of work design (Schein, 1965).

Notwithstanding these reservations, Taylor's ideas have made (and continue to make) a crucial impact on the thinking about job design and the division of labour. Indeed, as Littler (1982) argues, we must be cautious of assuming a linear progression of management theory where each set of ideas neatly supersedes the previous ones. The persistence of Taylorist principles in contemporary organisations is testimony to the resilience of Taylorism (e.g. see the discussions by Bain, Watson, Mulvey, Taylor and Gall, 2002; Jones, 2000; Nyland, 1995). Of particular importance is the way that service sector organisations such as McDonald's can use features of 'classic' Taylorism in a similar way to the manufacturing industry. Indeed, we might ask whether shovelling chips into a cardboard carton is the twenty-first century equivalent of shovelling pig iron into a furnace, which Taylor studied a century earlier.

The widespread effects of Tayloristic division of labour in the expanding service sector was noted by Ritzer (1993). He contends that McDonald's represents the archetypal rational organisation in search of four goals: efficiency, calculability, predictability and control. McDonald's is a contemporary symbol of a relentless process of rationalisation, where the employee is simply treated as a factor of production. Ritzer's thesis (rather pessimistically) is that both theoretically and empirically this constitutes a general process of 'McDonaldisation' which extends beyond work into the culture of society (Ritzer, 1998). His conclusion suggests there is an inevitable tendency towards a dehumanisation of work – a theme that echoes the work of the deskilling theorists, whose ideas are explored after considering a second key actor in the design of jobs in the twentieth century.

3.2 | Exercise

What do you think?

Taylor was obsessed with finding the ultimate solution to the problem of organising work. He believed that by analysing and measuring work activities it was possible to find the optimum method of performing every task. In effect, he was suggesting that by careful, scientific, logical analysis, using his guiding principles, managers can find the best way of managing.

1   What is your opinion about Taylor's theory? What are your reasons for agreeing or disagreeing with him?
2   Why do some organisations follow his methods, whilst others reject them?
3   Consider your own work experiences. Would you describe the work as Tayloristic? If not, does it have elements that reflect Taylor's principles of work organisation?
4   Are some jobs impossible to Taylorise? Use examples to explain why/why not.

Routine work on the assembly line – chickens and Ford

If asked to visualise an assembly line, many people would probably have an image of a car plant, with a steady procession of partly finished vehicles passing groups of workers (or robots) who are rapidly attaching windscreens, wheels, spraying paint and so on. This has been the stereotypical image of assembly line work, not least because its innovative form was originally developed and exploited by the Ford Motor Company – an issue that we return to below.

Let us imagine a different contemporary work setting. You are in a massive room dominated by the sound of humming and churning machinery, though you can occasionally hear the voices of an all-women workforce. The room is cool and the air heavy with the smell of blood. Overhead, weaving around the factory is a conveyor from which hooks are suspended; hanging from each hook is the carcass of a dead bird. It is a chicken factory, made up of a variety of 'assembly lines' that convert live birds into the packets of meat displayed in supermarkets.

The work is Tayloristic in the sense it is segmented into simple, repetitive operations. For example, 'packing' involves four distinct tasks each performed by different employees: inserting the giblets (internal organs) and tucking the legs in, bagging the chicken, weighing it and securing the top of the bag. Not only are these and similar tasks around the factory simple and repetitive, but the pace of the work is also relentless. This is vividly portrayed by an employee carrying out 'inspection' in such a chicken factory, interviewed for a television programme, 'Dangerous Lives':

Employee:	The line was coming round with about four and a half thousand birds an hour and you used to have to check the chickens for livers, hearts or anything, by putting your hand in the backside of a chicken, feeling around and then bringing anything out, dropping it in the bin, and then going on to the next. Used to be, sort of, every other chicken.
Interviewer:	You were doing two chickens at a time?
Employee:	Yes, both hands in chickens together. You hadn't got time to wipe your nose or do anything really.
Interviewer:	Did that line ever stop?
Employee:	Only if they had a breakdown, you know, a pin went in the line, or there was a breakdown or anything.
Interviewer:	So you were doing over 2000 chickens an hour?
Employee:	Yes.
Interviewer:	14,000 chickens a day?
Employee:	Yes.
Interviewer:	What did you think about that?
Employee:	Hard work. Real hard work!

Similar experiences of unremitting 'hard work' have been found by researchers studying the harsh realities of factory life in different industries: for example, Pollert (1981) in the tobacco industry, Westwood (1984) in hosiery (legwear), Cavendish (1982) in motor components, Beynon (1973) and Linhart (1981) in cars and Delbridge (1998) in auto components and consumer electronics. The experiences of employees are explored in closer detail, but for now, the emphasis is on the work organisation principles which give rise to the assembly line.

Henry Ford's methods

The name most commonly associated with the development of the assembly line is Henry Ford. His unique contribution was in adapting Taylorist principles to a factory setting geared to the mass production of standardised products. Ford established a production method benchmark against which assembly line work has since been assessed, and the term 'Fordist' has come to be used to describe the combination of linear work sequencing, the interdependence of tasks, a moving assembly line, the use and refinement of dedicated machinery and specialised machine tools (for a detailed discussion, see Meyer, 1981). It has been argued that Fordism is distinguishable from Taylorism because it is a form of work organisation specifically designed for efficient mass production (Wood, 1989).

The success of Ford as mass *production* can only be fully appreciated if seen as part of a system of industrial organisation that also sought to create, perpetuate and satisfy mass *consumption*. The development of mass markets provided the demand for large numbers of rapidly produced standardised products. This was shown best by the output at the Highland Park factory which rose from 13,941 Model-T Fords in 1909 to 585,400 by 1916 (Williams, Haslam and Williams, 1992: 550). This volume of mass production was only possible because of the development of capital equipment capable of producing on a large scale, and the creation of an efficient electricity supply to drive the machinery. In other words, mass production, mass consumption, technological innovation and segmented work organisation were ingredients in Ford's recipe for success. Consequently, as Littler (1985) has argued, Fordism came to be the preferred form of organising work for mass production. It was adopted by Ford's main competitor in the United States, General Motors, and then by Ford's European rivals – Austin, Morris and Citroen. Fordism also transferred to other, newer industries such as electrical engineering and chemicals.

A widely accepted view is that Fordism is synonymous with mass production, rigidity and standardisation, and that the impact of the ideas pioneered by Ford has been widespread. However, there are some voices of dissent. Williams and colleagues (1987, 1992) argue that Fordism has become a stereotype, distorted over time by British and US academics who are keen to attribute failing industrial performance to the persistence of an outdated form of production. In a detailed analysis of Ford's production operations at Highland Park (1909–19), Williams et al (1992) reveal a picture of greater flexibility and less standardisation of the product than most texts on the subject would suggest. Overall, however, such findings do little to dispel the picture of an authoritarian work regime with closely monitored, machine-paced, short-cycle and unremitting tasks.

As the chicken factory example illustrates, Fordist principles persist in contemporary work settings, and these are not restricted to factory work. One can argue that his assembly line can be found in other work settings (see Extract 3.2). McDonald's shows Fordist elements in terms of its mass production of standardised products for mass consumption. Similarly, the supermarket in general, and checkout operations in particular, embody a Fordist approach to retailing: the customer's items pass along the conveyor and are swept across the barcode reader by an operator who carries out a series of repetitive actions. The flow-line, the dedicated machinery and the segmented work tasks are evidence of Fordist principles of work organisation. Similarly the chicken, as an object for consumption, is typically reared through (Ford-like) battery farming, slaughtered and processed in a Fordist factory, and sold through a Fordist retail outlet (the supermarket) or even consumed as chicken pieces in a Fordist restaurant.

3.2 | Extract

The white-collar assembly line?

Researchers undertaking an extensive study of call centres in Scotland have come to the conclusion that although not all call centres are identical, the majority of them can justifiably be seen as 'white-collar factories' because employees are subjected to Tayloristic management techniques and the type of routinised, repetitive work normally associated with the assembly line (Taylor and Bain, 1999; Taylor, Hyman, Mulvey and Bain, 2002). The following is a quote from their study:

> The typical call centre operator is young, female and works in a large, open plan office or fabricated building…. Although, probably full-time, she is increasingly likely to be a part-time permanent employee, working complex shift patterns which correspond to the peaks of customer demand. Promotion prospects and career advancement are limited so that the attraction of better pay and conditions in another call centre may prove irresistible. In all probability, work consists of an uninterrupted and endless sequence of similar conversations with customers she never meets. She has to concentrate hard on what is being said, jump from page to page on a screen, making sure that the details entered are accurate and that she has said the right things in a pleasant manner. The conversation ends and as she tidies up the loose ends there is another voice in her headset. The pressure is intense because she knows her work is being measured, her speech monitored, and it often leaves her mentally, physically and emotionally exhausted…. There is no question that the integration of telephone and computer technologies, which defines the call centre, has produced new developments in the Taylorisation of white-collar work.
>
> (Taylor and Bain, 1999: 115)

An alternative perspective is taken by Korczynski, Shire, Frenkel and Tam (1996) in their detailed analysis of three call centres (two in Australia and one in Japan). They argue that while the customer service representatives have routine aspects to their work, it is misleading to equate their jobs with the sort of routine work typically found in factories. This is because service work relies on the extensive use of social skills when dealing with customers, which can provide a source of creativity for employees. In short, they are cautious not to equate service work with routinisation or deskilling, yet also suggest that there is little evidence of substantial upskilling taking place, even though there were some opportunities for it to occur in their case study companies.

TO SUM UP

The significance of Taylor, Ford and mass production for the way work has been organised is profound. These principles and methods changed the work process by introducing greater amounts of rigidity and regulation, which in turn had important consequences for the skill content of jobs. In particular, this raises the question of whether work, in general, is becoming less or more skilled. The evaluation of the different attempts to answer this question begins with the deskilling thesis.

THESIS – THE DESKILLING OF WORK

The year 1974 saw the publication of one of the most influential books concerned with the study of work: Braverman's *Labor and Monopoly Capital*. Braverman's thesis is that there is an inevitable tendency towards degradation and deskilling of work as capitalists search for profits in increasingly competitive economic environments. His contribution to the study of work must not be underestimated. Although his thesis has since been subjected to a great deal of criticism, in the 1970s, it injected adrenaline into the tired discipline of industrial sociology, and it continues to have an impact on how work is analysed. Indeed the book was republished in 1998. The discussion below explains the central argument of this 'deskilling thesis' and identifies the main criticisms.

Braverman's argument

At the risk of oversimplifying, Braverman's argument is this. Managers perpetually seek to control the process by which a workforce's labour power (its ability to work) is directed towards the production of commodities (goods and services) that can be sold for a profit. The control of this labour process is essential because profit is accumulated through two stages: first, through the extraction of the surplus value of labour (the price of a commodity has to be greater than the costs incurred in its production); and second, through the realisation of that value when the commodities are actually sold. These two stages are frequently referred to as 'valorisation' (a process where value is realised). In other words, managers seek to control the way work is organised, the pace of work and the duration of work, because these affect profitability. Control of labour is the link between the purchase of labour power and valorisation. In Braverman's analysis the managerial obsession with labour control is the key to understanding capitalism, and it leads managers to seek ways of reducing the discretion exercised by the workforce in performing their jobs. In order to exert their own control over the workforce and limit the control and influence of employees, managers pursue a general strategy of deskilling which, according to Braverman, can be identified in two forms: organisational and technological.

Organisational deskilling

Organisational deskilling is embedded in the Tayloristic principle of the separation of the conception and execution of work. The conceptual tasks (the more challenging and interesting parts of the job, such as planning, diagnosing problems and developing new working methods) are transferred to technical and managerial staff, while the execution of the work (often the mundane, less-challenging part of the job) remains in the hands of shopfloor workers. Theoretically, this process allows managers to limit the discretion of the shopfloor workers and to secure a monopoly over technical knowledge about the work. This can be used to exercise greater direct control over the activities of the workforce:

> A necessary consequence of the separation of conception and execution is that the labor process is now divided between separate sites and separate bodies of workers. In one location, the physical processes of production are executed. In another are concentrated the design, planning, calculation and record-keeping…. The physical processes of production are now carried out more or less blindly, not only by the workers who perform them, but often by lower ranks of supervisory employees as well. The production units operate like a hand, watched, corrected, and controlled by a distant brain.
>
> (Braverman, 1974: 124–5)

Technological deskilling

Technological deskilling occurs when automation is used to transfer discretion and autonomy from the shopfloor to the office (from blue-collar to white-collar workers) and to eliminate the need for some direct labour. Braverman focuses on the example of the operation of machines by numerical control (NC) – the latest technology at the time he was writing and before the invention of the microchip – which allowed the planning and programming of the machines to be undertaken away from the shopfloor by technical staff, who prepared punched paper tapes that contained the information for the machine to run automatically. Prior to NC, the machinists would use their own judgement and discretion to set and operate the machines, but they were subsequently left only with the relatively simple tasks of loading and switching the machines. In other words, a technological development (NC – and then later on computer numerical control) allowed the separation of task conception from task execution. This sort of new technology does not inevitably lead to a deskilling of work, but Braverman argues that managers selectively use automation to this end, in order to secure their central objective of exerting control over labour. He writes:

> In reality, machinery embraces a host of possibilities, many of which are systematically thwarted, rather than developed, by capital. An automatic system of machinery opens up the possibility of the true control over a highly productive factory by a relatively small corps of workers, providing these workers attain the level of mastery over the machinery offered by engineering knowledge, and providing they then share out among themselves the routines of the operation, from the most technically advanced to the most routine…. [But such a possibility] is frustrated by the capitalist effort to reconstitute and even deepen the division of labor in all its worst aspects, despite the fact that this division of labor becomes more archaic with every passing day…. The 'progress' of capitalism seems only to deepen the gulf between workers and machine and to subordinate the worker ever more decisively to the yoke of the machine…. The chief advantage of the industrial assembly-line is the control it affords over the pace of labor, and as such it is supremely useful to owners and managers whose interests are at loggerheads with those of their workers.
>
> (Braverman, 1974: 230–2)

There have been plenty of writers willing to comment on Braverman's work. McLoughlin and Clark (1994) divide these into 'sympathisers' and 'agnostics' (see Table 3.1). If you want to explore the issues in more detail, a good starting point is Thompson (1989) followed by the chapters in the edited collection by Knights and Willmott (1990). There is also a thorough and persuasive defence of the value of Braverman's thesis by Tinker (2002), who particularly takes to task the more recent postmodern criticisms of Braverman's analysis of the labour process (e.g. O'Doherty and Willmott, 2001). The main criticisms of and revisions to Braverman's thesis are summarised in the next section, but before reading this, attempt Exercise 3.3.

Table 3.1 – The key critics of Braverman's thesis

Sympathisers Accept the general approach but offer some refinement	Agnostics Acknowledge some value in the approach, but consider it inadequate
Friedman, 1977a,b, 1990	Littler, 1982
Burawoy, 1979	Wood, 1982
Edwards, 1979	Littler and Salaman, 1982
Zimbalist, 1979	Knights, Willmott and Collinson, 1985
Armstrong, 1988	Knights and Willmott, 1986, 1990
Rose, 1988	Watson, 1986
Thompson, 1989	

Source: Based on McLoughlin and Clark (1994).

3.3 | Exercise

What do you think?

Interview someone who has been employed in the same organisation for about ten years and ask them about the changes they have experienced. The interview need not be long, but you should structure it in such a way to ensure that you find out about the type of changes introduced and the effect they have had on work.

You must then use this information to assess whether this helps to substantiate or refute Braverman's deskilling thesis and produce a written or verbal report. Remember there were two components to Braverman's argument, organisational deskilling and technological deskilling, so your interview should be designed in such a way as to elicit information on both these aspects of change. Your report should make explicit reference to these.

Six common criticisms of the deskilling thesis

Criticism 1: the deskilling thesis ignores alternative management strategies

Friedman (1977a, 1977b, 1990) argues that it is false to assume a single trend towards deskilling, since this fails to acknowledge the occasions when it is in the interest of managers to leave some discretion in the hands of employees. He calls this a strategy of 'responsible autonomy' and contrasts it with the 'direct control' which Braverman described. Friedman had in mind job enrichment and quality circles, but a contemporary expression of responsible autonomy is the notion of 'empowerment', whereby individual employees are expected to take responsibility for their own actions and initiate improvements in the way they work for the benefit of the organisation as a whole. Under responsible autonomy, employees are not deskilled but management continue to control the labour process. Thus, the argument here is that there is a wider choice in the mechanisms employed by management for the accumulation of capital than Braverman suggests.

Criticism 2: the deskilling thesis overstates management's objective of controlling labour

The control of the labour process is not an end in itself, but a means to achieve profit. To concentrate solely on labour control objectives ignores the importance of valorisation:

> It is not simply the *extraction* of surplus value in the labour process which is problematic for capital, but the *realisation* of that surplus through the sale of commodities in markets .... In other words we need to consider the *full circuit* of industrial capital as the starting point for analyses of changes in the division of labour: purchase of labour power; extraction of surplus value within the labour process; realisation of surplus value within product markets. There is no sound theoretical reason for privileging one moment in this circuit – the labour-capital relation within the labour process – if our objective is to account for changes (or variations) in the division of labour.
>
> (Kelly, 1985: 32, emphasis in original)

Moreover, the assumption that labour issues (rather than, for example, product development, marketing or investment) are the central concern of management during strategy formation is highly questionable (Purcell, 1989, 1995). Thus, as Littler and Salaman (1982: 257) contend, the process of capital accumulation acts beyond the labour process:

> The firm is primarily a capital fund with a legal corporate personality, linked to a production process .... While the production process results in a flow of

income to the firm, this does not preclude alternative sources playing a major role or even a predominant one e.g. currency speculation, cumulative acquisition and asset stripping, commodity speculation, and credit manipulation of various kinds.

Child (1972, 1984, 1985) has highlighted the importance of political manoeuvring by managers in an organisation who, as key decision makers, are making 'strategic choices' that reflect their own values and vested interests. The argument here is that internal politics have a greater impact on deciding how work is organised, and on skill requirements, than Braverman implies. The logic of capitalist accumulation may remain the overarching tendency, but this can be mitigated by managers at all levels who are defending their vested interests.

As a consequence, the criticism is that Braverman's thesis underestimates the diversity and complexity of management objectives. The assumption that there is a single shared objective by management – that of labour control – ignores the plurality of interests within management and the diverse, and sometimes competing, objectives (Batstone, Gourlay, Levie and Moore, 1987; Buchanan, 1986; Buchanan and Boddy, 1983; Child, 1985). For example, in research into technological change in the UK provincial newspaper industry undertaken by one of the authors (Noon, 1994), it was found that when managers were questioned about the objectives for introducing new technology, they stressed different reasons which seemed to reflect their own functional responsibilities. In other words, the objective of increased control over labour was not the primary focus for most managers. Instead, they said technological change provided new opportunities in terms of product quality, product development, production control, efficiency and flexibility, together with a reduction in labour cost. This suggests that while labour control objectives may be relevant, they must be placed within the context of broader business objectives. As Armstrong (1989, 1995) argues, the pervasive influence of management accountants at board level in UK companies tends to lead to more strategic thinking based on financial concerns rather than human resource matters.

Criticism 3: the deskilling thesis treats labour as passive

Employees have not been very compliant and have resisted change towards deskilling through both trade union collective action and individual action. Indeed, Edwards (1979) argues that management has sought more sophisticated forms of control as a direct response to (and as a way to suppress) worker resistance. He argues there has been a shifting reliance from the 'simple control' typified by the methods of direct supervision that Taylor advocated, to the 'technical control' of the mechanised assembly line (and more recent developments in computer technology) and the 'bureaucratic control' of workplace rules, procedures and a regulated internal labour market.

Criticism 4: the deskilling thesis understates the degree of consent and accommodation by employees

The work of Burawoy (1979) stands as an important counterpoint to Braverman in that it explores the extent to which the workforce consents to its own subordination. In part, this contrasts also with the previous criticism because it suggests that, rather than challenging management control of the labour process, the workforce may develop an informal culture that offers alternative definitions of the work situation and provides the opportunity for meaningful activity. The labour process is thereby redefined as a type of game through which the employees can derive satisfaction (e.g. by beating the clock, outwitting the supervisor or manipulating the rules). These games act as powerful means of social regulation (self-control) among the work groups and obscure the exploitative nature of the labour process. In so doing, they unwittingly provide alternative additional sources of control for management. Such a brief summary hardly does justice to the subtleties of Burawoy's work.

Criticism 5: the deskilling thesis ignores gender

Beechey (1982) has argued that several problems emerge from the gender-blind nature of Braverman's argument. First, he fails to appreciate the importance of women's distinct role as domestic labourers because of his 'conceptual isolation of the family from the labour process and of both the family and the labour process from an analysis of the capitalist mode of production as a whole' (Beechey, 1982: 71). Second, his discussion of the pre-industrial family can be criticised for romanticising the past and ignoring the existence of patriarchal structures. Third, his concept of skill fails to explore gender dimensions where it was noted that the social construction of skill is particularly important in creating 'gendered jobs', resulting in the undervaluation of women's labour power and skills.

Criticism 6: the deskilling thesis overlooks skill transfer possibilities

The failure of Braverman to recognise that deskilling in one area of work may be compensated by upskilling in another is most forcefully argued by Penn (1983, 1990), whose ideas are examined in some detail later. However, it might be argued that this constitutes one of the most unfair criticisms of Braverman. As Armstrong (1988) points out, Braverman explicitly recognised that change would occur unevenly across industries, and that in some instances new skills and technical specialities might be temporarily created within the workforce.

A defence of Braverman's thesis

A persuasive defence of Braverman comes from Armstrong, who argues that:

> any sensitive reading of his work should reveal that Braverman actually regarded the deskilling tendencies of technical change as a system-wide dynamic or 'law of motion' in capitalist economies which could, temporarily and locally, be interrupted or reversed by a variety of factors, many of which have been rediscovered by his critics as supposed refutations.
>
> (Armstrong, 1988: 157)

This is an important point because, like all meta-theory (i.e. theory about theory), Braverman's thesis will never be able to explain all contingencies, yet this does not necessarily mean its analytical insight is worthless. Indeed, as Armstrong suggests, many of the 'critics' are in practice offering revisions and amendments to the theory, rather than rejecting it.

Another defender of Braverman, Spencer (2000), suggests that the constant revisions and modifications to Braverman's original ideas by subsequent labour process theorists (academic commentators and researchers) show they have lost sight of the subversive intent of Braverman's original text and have become obsessed with the social relations of the workplace, rather than the broader critique of capitalism. In short, Spencer laments the way that Braverman's ideas have been brought into the mainstream, and now run the risk of aiding rather than tormenting capitalism.

Braverman has also been defended against the attacks from academics of a post-modern leaning by Tinker (2002), who suggests that such attacks are deficient for a host of reasons, which he elaborates in detail. One of his main arguments is that the political aims and impact of Braverman's work are under-appreciated (not least the wide reading of the text by non-academics), and that postmodernist analysis:

> is blind to the social and historical specificity of Braverman's political task; exposing 'skill upgrading via education' as an ideology that obfuscates economic decline, recession and deindustrialization.
>
> (Tinker, 2002: 251)

He is also scathing about the philosophical position of postmodernists, which leaves them resorting to philosophies of indecision and able to offer only frivolous, condescending and politically timorous advice to working people (ibid: 273). In contrast, for Tinker, the abiding value of Braverman's analysis is that 'It debunks academic dogmas of management, popular nostrums about skill upgrading via education, and the tacit promises to restore a "golden past" (ibid: 274).

While some commentators (e.g. Lewis, 1995) remain unconvinced by defenders of Braverman, a re-reading of the original text reveals that Braverman had a less deterministic approach than is frequently attributed to him. Therefore, the deskilling thesis needs to be seen as an overall tendency, rather than a universal law applying in all cases:

> Braverman does *not* propound a universal law of deskilling. What he *does* claim is that there exists a general tendency for deskilling to occur in capitalist economies which will become actual where products and processes make this possible and where its effects are not masked by initiatives aimed at changing technology for other reasons.
>
> (Armstrong, 1988: 147, emphasis in original)

If Braverman's thesis is to be countered, it should be challenged on comparable terms: rather than a tendency towards deskilling, there is an opposite trend towards upskilling occurring within capitalist economies. It is to this antithesis that the discussion now turns.

ANTITHESIS – THE UPSKILLING OF WORK

Whereas the deskilling thesis drew from Marxist economic theory and the crisis of capitalism in industrial societies, the upskilling thesis tends to be based on the economics of human capital theory concerning a supposedly new stage of capitalism: the post-industrial society. Human capital theorists (Becker, 1964; Fuchs, 1968) suggest that, increasingly, firms are investing in their workforces through greater training provision, thus shifting the emphasis to 'human capital' as a central means of accumulating profit. One argument for this is that rapid advances in technology require a more educated, better-trained workforce in order to cope with the increasing complexity of work tasks (Blauner, 1964; Kerr, Dunlop, Harbison and Myers, 1960). In turn, this is linked to an ever-reducing demand for manual/physical labour as Western capitalist economies undergo a structural shift away from manufacturing towards service sector activities (Fuchs, 1968).

This shift in the economic base of advanced industrial societies is considered by commentators such as Daniel Bell to signal a fundamental transformation to the post-industrial society, in which theoretical knowledge becomes 'the axis around which new technology, economic growth and the stratification of society will be organized' (Bell, 1973: 112). In other words, the upskilling thesis suggests that the general tendency is towards more complex work requiring higher levels of skill. As a consequence, the shift in the pattern of work organisation will not be towards degradation (as Braverman suggested) but to an enrichment of work. Extract 3.3 provides survey evidence about upskilling patterns in Europe.

The upskilling thesis found expression in Piore and Sabel's (1984) concept of 'flexible specialisation'. They argue that the crisis of accumulation under capitalism is leading to an important shift away from Fordism towards more craft-based, flexible, innovation-led and customer-focused work organisation. So, just as the move from traditional craft production to mass production was 'the first industrial divide', the move from mass production to flexible specialisation is described by Piore and Sabel as 'the second industrial divide'.

The new emphasis is on flexible production systems, which can meet the demands for customised products in increasingly diversified markets. In particular, developments in microelectronic technology allow for more flexibility in the use of capital equipment: machinery no longer needs to be dedicated to specific tasks but can be reprogrammed to perform a variety of tasks. Traditional production methods typically involve long set-up times for the machinery, which mean large production runs are necessary to recover the cost; short production runs for small batches are an inefficient use of the equipment. In contrast, computerised machinery requires shorter set-up times, enabling greater diversity of (small batch) production without incurring the inefficiencies. In other words, economies of scale now have to be considered alongside economies of scope. This is important because customers are supposed to be increasingly discerning and wanting a greater variety of goods which allow them to express their individual identity (Sabel, 1982). Economies of scope become a necessity in a dynamic, competitive market where customers want variety and choice. Computerised production and information-processing capabilities provide the technological infrastructure and (according to the upskilling thesis) bring a demand for highly qualified rather than deskilled labour.

Coupled with this are changes in work organisation that mean employees are expected to work in different ways. Principal among these is teamworking, which is seen as a move away from the individualised, segmented work processes to flexible teams of employees who are multiskilled and take greater responsibility for their work through increased task discretion (control over the work methods, time and quality). It is argued that working in this fashion requires employees to develop and use a wide range of skills. In particular this has been associated with various supposedly post-Fordist production techniques in manufacturing, such as lean production (Womack, Jones and Roos, 1990) and business process re-engineering (Hammer and Champy, 1993).

3.3 | Extract

Skill change in Europe

Gallie (2005) assessed the impact of skill change in 15 EU countries by analysing the results of two surveys of employees – one conducted in 1996, the other in 2001. Skill change was measured by asking people whether or not their jobs have become more skilled, evaluating the amount of training received, and assessing the extent to which employees considered they had control over their work (the first two are measures of complexity, the third is a measure of discretion).

Among Gallie's findings are the following:

o The dominant trend is upskilling.
o The pace of upskilling slowed down after the mid-1990s.

○ Women are less likely than men to have experienced increases in skill.

○ The decline in the pace of upskilling has affected women and men in similar ways.

○ The reduction in the pace of upskilling is evident in 12 of the 15 countries in Europe surveyed.

○ The decline in the pace of upskilling is statistically significant only in Finland, Germany, Great Britain, Greece, Ireland, the Netherlands and Spain.

One particular aspect of skill that showed clear evidence of decline was job control (the measure of discretion). Employees were asked questions about whether they have a say in what happens in their jobs. Gallie found the following:

○ There is a significant decline in job control between the two periods.

○ Women were typically in jobs with lower opportunities for control than men in both 1996 and 2001, but the decline in job control was similar for both sexes.

○ Job control scores declined in nine of the 15 countries, although the trend reached statistical significance in only seven countries: Belgium, France, Great Britain, Italy, the Netherlands, Spain and Sweden.

○ Only in Denmark was there evidence of an increase in control over jobs.

Source: Summarised from Gallie (2005).

Five criticisms of the upskilling thesis

Criticism 1: the upskilling thesis falsely assumes that the growth of the service sector will create skilled jobs

The growth of the service sector and the increasing importance of considering the customer can give the impression that all white-collar workers are now engaged with handling customer interactions, and that the traditional routinised factory work associated with manufacturing has given way to more varied, expressive forms of work involving customer interaction. It is certainly the case that customer-facing work involves the use of skills that require the management of emotions, but much of the new service work is as monotonous and dull as work on an assembly line.

Korczynski (2004) analysed the work of back-office staff in an insurance company and two banks in Australia. He found that work tended to be routinised with little scope for discretion in how the tasks were performed (particularly in the case of the insurance company). This was reinforced through performance-monitoring systems which set targets (e.g. processing a set number of applications per day) and measured work quality. There was no customer interaction, staff were not required to have (or learn) customer-oriented skills, and on a day-to-day basis they referred to customers in an impersonal way. Echoing the findings of earlier case studies (Crompton and Jones, 1984; Sturdy, 1992), the conclusion Korczynski drew is that back-office work in financial services resembles the formalised, routinised and regulated processes consistent with traditional bureaucratic forms of work organisation. This makes back-office, service work very similar to Fordist production work.

Front-line service work – where the majority of the working day involves dealing with customers either face to face or over the phone – tends to be organised in ways that are slightly less rigid, because of the variation in customer interaction requiring social skills and elements of emotional labour. Even so, front-line service employees are typically faced with a huge amount of routine and repetitive activity. (See Extract 3.2 for two perspectives on call centre workers.) Korczynski (2002) uses the term 'customer-oriented bureaucracy' to suggest that the essential features of bureaucracy are present (e.g. hierarchies, rules and procedures) but that the customer is cared for in the process:

> The concept of the customer-oriented bureaucracy captures the requirement for the organisation to be both formally rational, to respond to competitive

pressures to appeal to customers' wishes for efficiency, and to be formally irrational, to enchant, responding to the customers' desire for pleasure, particularly through the perpetuation of the enchanting myth of customer sovereignty [the myth that the customer is 'King' or always right].

(Korczynski, 2002: 64)

This means employees have to work within clearly defined rules and follow procedures and protocols, while ensuring that customers feel satisfied about the service they are receiving and gain the impression that they are in control (the myth of customer sovereignty). This may require employees to use a range of skills to manage their own emotions and those of the customers.

Criticism 2: the upskilling thesis overstates the extent to which advanced technology requires higher skill levels

The upskilling thesis is as vulnerable as the deskilling thesis to the criticism that there are numerous managerial objectives which reflect vested interests and politics – so the design of work will be based on these just as much as 'technical' decisions about skill requirements. In the 1980s, research revealed that managers could choose to implement technology in different ways that have variable skill consequences for employees. In their study of United Biscuits, Buchanan and Boddy (1983) show that even within one company there can be a mixture of skill changes associated with the introduction of advanced technology which makes any generalisation about upskilling or deskilling difficult to substantiate. Similarly, Sorge, Hartman, Warner and Nicholas (1983) reveal how computer numerical control (CNC) technology was used by British managers to deskill shopfloor workers and turn them into mere machine minders. In contrast, in Germany, the same technology was implemented in such a way as to integrate the (skilled) programming into the work of the operators, and in doing so enhancing their skill (also relevant here is Zuboff's (1988) dual impact theory of technology, which is discussed later in this chapter).

Criticism 3: the upskilling thesis overstates the extent of change

Generally, theorists who support the upskilling thesis, and those who support flexible specialisation in particular, assume a radical break with Fordism is taking place. However, this understates the resilience of mass production for mass markets. For example, the almost insatiable demand for consumer electronics has typically been met by the supply of goods manufactured using production systems that are labour intensive and low skilled (see, for example, Delbridge, Turnbull and Wilkinson, 1992; Sewell and Wilkinson, 1992a). Similarly, the flexible specialisation thesis overstates the extent to which small batch production will create upskilled and multiskilled workers. As Pollert (1991) and Smith (1989) point out, small batch production can and has adopted low-skilled, short-cycle assembly line techniques. So the criticism here is that the upskilling thesis relies on a false dichotomy between mass and craft production (see, for example, Hyman, 1991; Williams, Cutler, Williams and Haslam, 1987; Wood, 1989).

Criticism 4: the upskilling thesis overstates the skill-enhancing impact of new working methods

Employees have not experienced an enhancement of their skills through teamworking to the extent that the upskilling thesis suggests. In an analysis of survey data covering the period from 1996 to 2001, Gallie, Felstead and Green (2004) found that teamworking in the UK was on the increase, but this was accompanied by a decline in task discretion (measured by asking people how much influence they had over how hard they worked, what tasks they did, how they did the tasks and quality standards). This means that although an increasing proportion of the workforce is working in teams, these are not the semi-autonomous teams envisaged by the upskilling thesis.

A survey of ten European countries (Benders, Huijen and Pekruhl, 2001) revealed that forms of team or group working existed in 24 per cent of the workplaces. However, in the majority of these only a minority of core employees were covered, or else the groups had a very restricted range of decision-making rights (mainly concerning the regulation of day-to-day tasks, such as scheduling the work and improving the work processes). Issues such as controlling absence or organising job rotation were least likely to be delegated, and in only 4 per cent of organisations were the majority of core workers in what might be described as semi-autonomous teams. There was also notable variation between countries, with organisations in Sweden and the Netherlands being the most likely to have work groups and also the most likely to have groups who possessed real decision-making authority. Italy and Ireland were the countries with organisations least likely to have adopted group working. The authors of this European survey purposely used the term 'group working' rather than 'teamworking', because they argue it more accurately captures the range of forms or working arrangements – only some of which require upskilling.

Other studies confirm that the term 'teamworking' can mean a variety of things (Procter and Mueller, 2000). In the case of service sector work, it has been shown that 'team' often signifies nothing more than a group of workers who share one supervisor (Frenkel, Korczynski, Shire and Tam, 1999); as such, teamworking cannot be equated with upskilling.

Case studies can be useful in revealing how changes, such as increased flexibility and teamworking, do not result in enhancing skills so much as increase the volume of work at the same skill level. For example, commenting on the impact of multiskilling in a case study of a bank, Grimshaw, Beynon, Rubery and Ward (2002: 105) note that 'multi-skilling was introduced with limited employee discretion over how to vary and control and the timing and division of tasks …. Expansion in the range of job content was associated with increased pressure and a strong loss of autonomy'. Equally, in their case study of a telecommunications call centre these authors found that team-working did not involve multiskilling or job rotation but was a form of teambuilding based on social activities during work time, representing an attempt by managers to break the monotony of the routinised work of employees.

Criticism 5: the upskilling thesis needs to be put into a global perspective

With the rise of the multinational organisation, it is no longer sufficient to consider change simply in a national context. The reduction in demand for low-skilled work in one country might be accompanied by increased demand in another country. As a result, it becomes problematic to try to interpret a fall in the demand for low-skilled labour in one national context as a sign of general upskilling. It may indicate a global redistribution of demand for skills, reflecting the mobility of capital in the search for lower labour costs and the pursuit of greater profitability.

A good illustration of this point is the tendency for large organisations in advanced capitalist economies to outsource parts of their customer services and back-office data processing to countries where labour is considerably cheaper. Typically,

Australian companies are outsourcing to India and Indonesia, UK companies to India, US companies to the Philippines and Costa Rica and French companies to Morocco. This process, known as 'offshoring', means that when customers make an inquiry to their bank, insurance company, phone company or rail network they are likely to find themselves talking to an employee in a call centre in another country. Service sector organisations can now use information and communication technology (allowing real-time interaction with customers) to relocate parts of their operation anywhere that can provide an equivalent but cheaper service. In addition to voice services, paper-based operations (e.g. customer complaints, application forms, financial trans-actions) can take place in remote locations without it affecting the quality of service. This global shift in the location of customer service work means that skill increase in one location may be matched with a decline in other locations, as organisations find new means of sustaining and accumulating profit – and, of course, this is not at all surprising to supporters of the deskilling thesis.

3.4 | Extract

Cyber coolies in India?

A research institute funded by the Indian government has produced a damning report on the working conditions inside call centres. It has labelled the educated, intelligent graduates who work there as 'cyber coolies', and claims that they are wasting their talents on undertaking mindless, repetitive work for Western organisations.

According to *The Observer* newspaper, the study claims that the call centre workers are employed under constant surveillance, in an atmosphere similar to that in 'nineteenth century prisons or Roman slave ships'. Despite the relatively high salaries, and modern working environments, the study concludes that 'most of these youngsters are in fact burning out their formative years as cyber coolies' doing low-end jobs.

The true monotony of the work is disguised by 'camouflaging work as fun' – introducing cafes, popcorn booths and ping-pong tables into the offices. Meanwhile, quotas for calls or emails successfully attended to are often fixed at such a high level 'that the agent has to burn out to fulfil it', the report claims.

With employees working through the night to cater for clients in different time zones, the work requires staff 'to live as Indian by day and Westerner after sundown' and takes a 'heavy toll' on agents' physical and mental health, the study states. But more importantly, call centre work 'leads to a wastage of human resources and de-skilling of workers' which will have a high impact on Indian industry in the long-term.

Source: *The Observer* (2005) 'Painful truth of the call centre cyber coolies', 30 October.

3.4 | Exercise

What do you think?

Consider criticism number 5 of the upskilling thesis and read Extract 3.5.

1 What limitations might there be to offshoring that could mean some skilled jobs in the service sector could not be transferred to places such as India?
2 To what extent is technology playing a role in the offshoring process?
3 Have the so-called cyber coolies been upskilled or deskilled by the offshoring? Explain your reasoning.
4 Who are the winners and losers in the case of offshoring to India?

TO SUM UP

The upskilling thesis is as ambitious as the deskilling thesis in attempting to arrive at a theoretical framework that reflects a general tendency of skill change. However, in both cases the unidirectional argument needs to be qualified, as the various criticisms have shown. It is highly problematic to answer whether the dynamics of skill change can be simplified in such a way. A more robust theoretical approach might be to hypothesise multidirectional change within different sectors, industries, occupations and tasks. Three approaches which address such a synthesis are examined in the next section.

SYNTHESES – POLARISATION, COMPENSATION AND THE DUAL IMPACT OF AUTOMATING AND INFORMATING

There have been various attempts to synthesise the perspectives of deskilling and upskilling by arguing that both are occurring, with some people being upskilled while others are deskilled. This section reviews three different approaches to explain how and why this might occur: polarisation, compensation and the dual impact of technology. There is some common ground between the three approaches, and they should not be seen as competing theories but rather as complementary explanations of the effects of upskilling and deskilling.

The polarisation of skills

The polarisation of skills perspective argues that different segments of the workforce will be affected in different ways. For instance, higher occupational groups such as professionals and managers might see their skill levels increase, while those lower in the occupational hierarchy, such as operatives, might experience a diminution in skill. Similarly, those workers on permanent, full-time contracts might be upskilled while their co-workers on part-time or fixed-term contracts (and other non-standard arrangements) might find they are given fewer opportunities to increase their skill levels. Polarisation approaches might also argue that the differences could be linked to structural features, such as the sector or industry, or argue that other contingencies, such as whether or not employees can exert influence through trade unions, will affect the likelihood of being upskilled or deskilled.

Research in the Netherlands (see Extract 3.5) and the United States reveals the differential impact of technological and organisational change on the work of different employees. Milkman's (1997) case study of the General Motors' plant in Linden, New Jersey, depicts a complex picture of work transformation, but it reveals how skilled workers were given opportunities to acquire new skills and retrain, while their semi-skilled counterparts on the production line were denied such opportunities. Similarly, in an entirely different industry (case studies of software and data processing) in a different country (the UK), the same pattern was found whereby changes in skill requirements had the effect of advantaging those already highly skilled 'depriving others of not only the few skills they have but also any hope of a route out of a low skills, low income trap' (Grugulis and Vincent, 2009). The common feature across these case studies is the consequence of upskilling for one group and deskilling for the other: a polarisation effect.

3.5 | Extract

Skill polarisation in the Netherlands

As part of a research programme examining the effects of automation on job content, de Witte and Steijn (2000) analysed the responses of 1022 Dutch employees to a questionnaire. The respondents were asked about:

○ the amount of autonomy (freedom or control) they had in their work;
○ the complexity of their jobs;
○ the extent of automation in their work.

From analysis of the responses to these and other background questions, de Witte and Steijn, conclude:

o There is a general trend in upskilling associated with increasing automation.
o Professionals and white-collar workers experience the most upskilling.
o Blue-collar workers are least likely to experience upskilling.
o Some blue-collar workers experience substantial deskilling.

To explain deskilling amongst blue-collar workers, de Witte and Steijn suggest that 'internal differentiation' is occurring. This term means that automation leads to an *increase* in the complexity of the job *but not* the autonomy of the job. However, this internal differentiation is less likely to occur amongst the professional and white-collar workers; for them automation brings an increase in both complexity *and* autonomy.

The compensatory theory of skill

The argument put forward by proponents of the compensatory theory (Penn, 1990; Penn, Gasteen, Scattergood and Sewel, 1994; Penn and Scattergood, 1985) is that the general theories of both upskilling and deskilling are inadequate to explain the complexity of skill change. Instead, 'middle-range' explanations based on actual data offer a better way forward. This is because technological change generates both deskilling and upskilling, and in different forms. First, the effects are international: 'the shift of routine manufacturing from advanced, core economies to less developed, peripheral economies, and the increasing internationalisation of the capital goods (machinery) industry' (Penn, 1990: 25). Second, the effects differ between and within occupations: some groups are advantaged by having a more skilled and central role, while others find themselves deskilled and marginalised. More specifically:

> technological changes tend to deskill *direct productive roles* but put an increased premium on a range of *ancillary skilled tasks* that are associated with the installation, maintenance and programming of automated machinery. This is because modern machinery incorporating micro-electronics tends to simplify many production skills but renders maintenance work far more complex.... [However] within maintenance work itself...there is a far greater need for new electronic based maintenance skills than for traditional mechanical maintenance skills.
>
> (Ibid, emphasis in original)

This position highlights the importance of a broader picture of skill change across occupational groups, industries and national contexts.

Automating and informating – the dual impact on skill change

The important role of advanced technology in reconfiguring skills is explored in detail by Zuboff (1988). She argues that a distinction must be drawn between the processes of automating and informating, since they have impacted upon skills in different ways. Automating work operations involves replacing people with technology and so it is characterised by a deskilling of work and a reassertion of management control over the work process. However, technological developments also provide opportunities to generate detailed information about work operations. These could, if systematically gathered and analysed, increase the visibility of the productive and administrative work undertaken in an organisation. In other words, technology is informating the work process, and that data requires interpretation using cognitive ability. This constitutes an upskilling of work and provides 'a deeper level of transparency to activities that had been either partially or completely opaque' (Zuboff, 1988: 9).

Taken together, the processes of automating and informating lead to a reduction in action-centred skills (doing), but an increase in intellective skills (analysing). At the same time:

> these dual capacities of information technology are not opposites; they are hierarchically integrated. Informating derives from and builds upon automation. Automation is a necessary but not sufficient condition for informating.
>
> (Ibid: 11)

Zuboff also argues that although automating displaces people, it is not yet clear what the full effects of informating are. While managers can choose either to exploit or to ignore the informating process, her own case study evidence suggests that the tendency has been for managers to stress the automating process and ignore the informating potential. This is not surprising because the informating capacities of advanced technology force managers to rethink traditional structures, work organisation and forms of control:

> The shifting grounds of knowledge invite managers to recognize the emergent demands for intellective skills and develop a learning environment in which such skills can develop. That very recognition contains a threat to managerial authority, which depends in part upon control over the organization's knowledge base…. Managers who must prove and defend their own legitimacy do not easily share knowledge or engage in inquiry. Workers who feel the requirements of subordination are not enthusiastic learners…. Techniques of control that are meant to safeguard authority create suspicion and animosity, which is particularly dysfunctional when an organization needs to apply its human energies to inventing an alternative form of work organization better suited to the new technological context.
>
> (Ibid: 391–2)

The analysis presented by Zuboff is detailed, so this summary cannot really do justice to the subtlety of her argument. Still, it illustrates how both the deskilling and upskilling theses are inadequate as single explanations of skill change. While the former concentrates on the process of automating, the latter is focused on the process of informating. As a result, both approaches overlook the dual impact of advanced technology.

TO SUM UP

The syntheses above are more firmly based on empirical research than either the deskilling or the upskilling thesis. All three syntheses identify the possibility of deskilling and upskilling occurring simultaneously, and therefore they reject the notion of an overall general tendency in one direction only. In moving away from general theorising to context-specific understanding of skill change, they can more easily take account of the diversity of empirical evidence. These syntheses also converge in concluding that the overall picture is one of differing experiences of skill change.

DISCUSSION

Possible trends in work transformation, as represented by the various approaches above, can be depicted using a simple framework. As with any model that seeks to simplify the complexities embedded in work organisation, this is limited, but it does allow us to make some important analytical distinctions. The framework draws on Fox (1974), Friedmann (1961) and Littler (1982) by proposing that work can be described as varying along two dimensions:

○ *The range of work*. Work can vary according to the range of tasks that the employee performs. At one extreme, an employee will perform a very narrow range of tasks, while at the other extreme the employee will be expected to perform a wide range of different tasks.

○ *The discretion in work*. This refers to the extent to which employees have the ability to exercise choice over how the work is performed, deciding such aspects as the pace, quality, quantity and scheduling of work. At one extreme there will be very little opportunity for employees to use their discretion in this way, while at the other extreme work will require employees to use discretion constantly.

By combining these two dimensions as in Figure 3.1, it is possible to visualise the way jobs may vary and to plot four ideal-type (abstract) cases:

1 *Specialist work*: high discretion over a narrow range of work.
2 *Specialised work*: a narrow range of prescribed tasks.
3 *Generalised work*: a wide range of prescribed tasks.
4 *Generalist work*: high discretion over a wide range of work.

A good way to illustrate this typology is to look at a single work setting and assess how different jobs within that setting can be placed in one of these four categories. In a hospital, the paramedics and nurses are undertaking generalised work, the doctors perform generalist work, the porters do specialised work and the surgeons are responsible for specialist work. To take another example, in a nightclub the manager is doing generalist work, the DJ is doing specialist work, the bar staff are doing generalised work and the bouncers are doing specialised work. This type of categorisation can be undertaken for any workplace. Of course not all jobs will fit neatly into one category (some nurses are specialists and have a great deal of discretion, for instance), but that is always a limitation of such frameworks. However, if a job does not fit neatly into

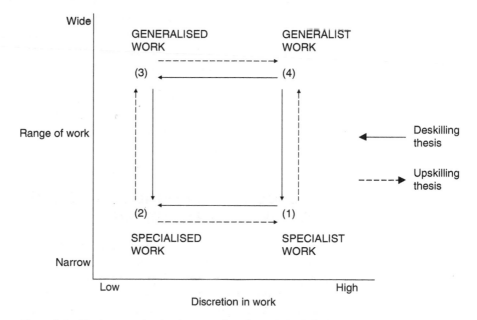

Figure 3.1 – Work categorisation framework and trends in skill change

a category it may indicate that the work is undergoing a transition – the sort of skill change that we discussed above and elaborate below.

3.5 | Exercise

What do you think?

Think of a workplace with which you are familiar, list the main jobs and attempt to categorise them using the work categorisation framework. Remember, this framework cannot tell us about the importance of the work. It does not indicate the value of the work, but it helps us to classify the nature of the work.

Now take several of these jobs and speculate how they could change along the two dimensions (range and discretion) in line with the two theses. You will need to think about the specific tasks required by the jobs.

Mapping the skill changes

In addition to classifying the nature of jobs, the work categorisation framework can be used to show the trends proposed by the skill change theses:

- The deskilling thesis is based on the idea that there is a general trend towards low-discretion jobs comprising a narrow range of tasks. This reveals itself in the form of a degradation of work along the 'discretion' dimension. In other words, discretion is removed from generalist work (making it more generalised) or from specialist work (making it more specialised). Similarly the deskilling thesis suggests a simplification of work along the 'range' dimension, so the work would entail a narrower range of tasks. This would turn generalised work into specialised work, and generalist work initially into specialist work, and then into specialised work through the degradation process. These trends are represented by the solid arrows in Figure 3.1.
- The upskilling thesis identifies an opposite trend towards high-discretion jobs comprising a wide range of tasks. There is an enrichment of work along the 'discretion' dimension: by increasing the extent of discretion, specialised work becomes increasingly specialist and generalised work becomes increasingly generalist. In addition, the upskilling thesis suggests that multi-tasking is becoming a feature of all work, so there are changes along the 'range' dimension. Specialised work is becoming more generalised and specialist work is becoming more generalist. The broken arrows in Figure 3.1 show these trends.
- Those researchers who reject a general tendency of either deskilling or upskilling would argue that a mixed pattern emerges. This means that change could occur along any of the paths represented by the arrows, and such changes are likely to vary greatly both between and within countries, sectors, industries, occupations, workplaces and workgroups.

CONCLUSION – MAPPING SKILL CHANGE ONTO WORK ORGANISATION PARADIGMS

Finally, we can return to the issue of work organisation with which we began the chapter. We argued that Taylorist and Fordist methods have had a dominant influence on work organisation, so how do these relate to the different theories of skill change? In Figure 3.2, the work categorisation framework is drawn again, but this time we have mapped onto it the dominant forms of work organisation that can be associated with each work category. The term 'paradigm' – which here means a

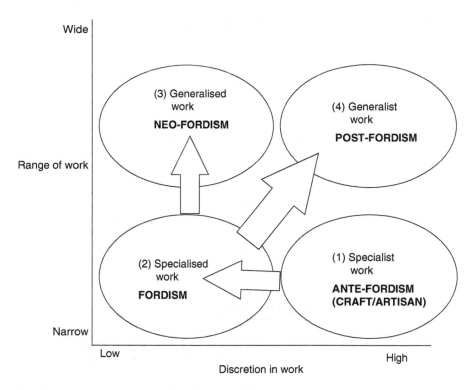

Figure 3.2 – Work categorisation framework and paradigms of work organisation

distinctive pattern or approach – can describe these forms of work organisation. So we can refer to the Fordist paradigm (a pattern of work similar to that developed by Ford). What do these paradigm terms mean, and how do they relate to the theories of skill change?

The word 'Fordism' appears in all the paradigms. This is no accident because the Fordist paradigm had a massive impact on how work was organised during the twentieth century. That is why we discussed it so much at the beginning of this chapter. Because of its impact, other paradigms of work organisation can be defined in relation to Fordism. So:

- Post-Fordism: means 'after Fordism' and refers to types of work organisation that do not rely on the principles of Taylor or the methods of Ford.
- Neo-Fordism: means 'new Fordism' and refers to types of work organisation that have adopted many of the basic methods of Ford but have adapted them – particularly through more flexible working practices – to fit contemporary circumstances.
- Ante-Fordism: means 'before Fordism' and refers to types of work organisation that rely on craft-based skills, often associated with the independent, self-employed artisan (craft worker).

The deskilling and upskilling theses both accept that (in general terms) craft/artisan production in the nineteenth century gave way to Fordism, which dominated the majority of the twentieth century. However, they offer contrasting interpretations of how work organisation is now changing. The upskilling thesis suggests a dramatic change has taken place in advanced capitalist economies in recent decades. This 'paradigm shift' to post-Fordism is based on new concepts of work organisation (incorporating multiskilled workers, self-managed teams, networked organisations and teleworking), an increasingly dominant service-based economy, and frequently characterised as the post-industrial society in which knowledge workers dominate.

In contrast, the deskilling thesis suggests that Fordism is continually being renewed as the dominant mode of work organisation, so there has been no paradigm shift. The consequence is specialised work comprising a narrow range of low-discretion tasks. A variant of this deskilling approach comes from commentators who suggest that Fordism has evolved into neo-Fordism (e.g. Harvey, 1989). This perspective suggests that multi-tasking, new management techniques (such as just-in-time, lean production and business process re-engineering) and increasingly automated and internationalised production processes have revitalised Fordism. Proponents of this view (e.g. Aglietta, 1979) stress the importance of continuity with the past, rather than characterising change as a quantum leap into a new dimension of capitalism. From this perspective, new forms of work organisation continue to reproduce traditional divisions of labour and essentially dispiriting and alienating experiences for employees. Employees cope with these in the best way they can, and sometimes join for collective support to make their voices heard.

REFERENCES

Aglietta, M. (1979) *A Theory of Capitalist Regulation*, London: New Left Books.

Armstrong, P. (1988) 'Labour and monopoly capital', in R. Hyman and W. Streeck (eds), *New Technology and Industrial Relations*, Oxford: Blackwell: 143–59.

Armstrong, P. (1989) 'Management, labour process and agency', *Work, Employment and Society*, 3 (3): 307–22.

Armstrong, P. (1995) 'Accountancy and HRM', in J. Storey (ed.), HRM: *A Critical Text*, London: Routledge: 142–63.

Bain, P., Watson, A., Mulvey, G., Taylor, P. and Gall, G. (2002) 'Taylorism, targets and the pursuit of quality by call centre management', *New Technology, Work and Employment*, 17 (3): 170–85.

Batstone, E., Gourlay, S., Levie, H. and Moore, R. (1987) *New Technology and the Process of Labour Regulation*, Oxford: Clarendon.

Becker, G. (1964) *Human Capital*, New York: National Bureau of Economic Research.

Beechey, V. (1982) 'The sexual division of labour and the labour process: a critical assessment of Braverman', in S. Wood (ed.), *The Degradation of Work?*, London: Hutchinson: 54–73.

Bell, D. (1973) *The Coming of Post-Industrial Society*, New York: Basic Books.

Benders, J., Huijen, F. and Pekruhl, U. (2001) 'Measuring group work: findings and lesions from a European survey', *New Technology, Work and Employment*, 16 (3):204–17.

Beynon, H. (1973) *Working for Ford*, Harmondsworth: Penguin.

Blauner, R. (1964) *Alienation and Freedom*, Chicago: University of Chicago Press.

Braverman, H. (1974) *Labor and Monopoly Capital*, New York: Monthly Review Press.

Buchanan, D. A. (1986) 'Management objectives in technical change', in D. Knights and H. Willnott (eds), *Managing the Labour Process*, Aldershot: Gower: 67–84.

Buchanan, D. and Boddy, D. (1983) *Organisations in the Computer Age: Technological Imperatives and Strategic Choice*, Aldershot: Gower.

Burawoy, M. (1979) *Manufacturing Consent*, Chicago: University of Chicago Press.

Cavendish, R. (1982) *Women on the Line*, London: Routledge.

Child, J. (1985) 'Managerial strategies, new technology and the labour process', in D. Knights, H. Willmott and D. Collinson (eds), *Job Redesign*, Aldershot: Gower: 107–41.

Crompton, R. and Jones, G. (1984) *White Collar Proletariat*, London: Macmillan.

De Witte, M. and Steijn, B. (2000) 'Automation, job content and underemployment', *Work, Employment and Society*, 14 (2): 245–64.

Delbridge, R., Turnbull, P. and Wilkinson, B. (1992) 'Pushing back the frontiers: management control and work intensification under JIT/TQM factory regimes', *New Technology*, Work and Employment, 7 (2): 97–106.

Edwards, R. (1979) *Contested Terrain: The Transformation of the Workplace in the Twentieth Century*, London: Heinemann.

Felstead, A., Gallie, D. and Green, F. (2002) *Work Skills in Britain, 1986–2001*, London: Department for Education and Skills.

Felstead, A., Gallie, D. and Green, F. (2004) 'Job complexity and task discretion', in C. Warhurst, I. Grugulis and E. Keep (eds), *The Skills That Matter*, Basingstoke: Palgrave: 148–69.

Fox, A. (1974) *Beyond Contract*, London: Faber and Faber.

Frenkel, S. J., Korczynski, M., Shire, K. A. and Tam, M. (1999) *On the Front Line: Organization of Work in the Information Economy*, New York: Cornell UniversityPress.

Friedman, A. (1977a) *Industry and Labour: Class Struggle at Work and Monopoly Capitalism*, London: Macmillan.

Friedman, A. (1977b) 'Responsible autonomy versus direct control over the labour process', *Capital and Class*, 1 (Spring): 43–57.

Friedman, A. (1990) 'Managerial activities, techniques and technology: towards a complex theory of the labour process', in D. Knights and H. Willmott (eds), *Labour Process Theory*, London: Macmillan: 177–208.

Friedmann, G. (1961) *The Anatomy of Work*, London: Heinemann.

Fuchs, V. (1968) *The Service Economy*, New York: Basic Books.

Gallie, D. (2005) 'Work pressures in Europe 1996–2001: trends and determinants', *British Journal of Industrial Relations*, 43 (3): 351–75.

Gallie, D., Felstead, A. and Green, F. (2004) 'Changing patterns of task discretion in Britain', Work, *Employment and Society*, 18 (2): 243–66.

Grimshaw, D., Beynon, H., Rubery, J. and Ward, K. (2002) 'The restructuring ofcareer paths in large service sector organizations: delayering, upskilling and polarisation', *Sociological Review*, 50 (1): 89–116.

Hammer, M. and Champy, J. (1993) *Reengineering the Corporation: A Manifesto for Business Revolution*. New York: Harper Business.

Harvey, D. (1989) *The Condition of Postmodernity*, Oxford: Blackwell.

Hyman, R. (1991) 'Plus ça change? The theory of production and the production of theory', in A. Pollert (ed.), *Farewell to Flexibility?* Oxford: Blackwell: 259–83.

Kelly, J. (1982) *Scientific Management, Job Redesign and Work Performance*, London: Academic Press.

Kerr, C., Dunlop, J. T., Harbison, F. H. and Myers, C. A. (1960) *Industrialism and Industrial Man*, London: Heinemann.

Knights, D. and Willmott, H. (eds) (1990) *Labour Process Theory*, London: Macmillan.

Korczynski, M. (2002) *Human Resource Management in Service Work*, Basingstoke: Palgrave.

Korczynski, M. (2004) 'Back-office service work: bureaucracy challenged?', *Work, Employment and Society*, 18 (1): 97–114.

Korczynski, M., Shire, K., Frenkel, S. and Tam, M. (1996) 'Front line work in the "new model service firm": Australian and Japanese comparisons', *Human Resource Management Journal*, 6 (2): 72–87.

Lewis, A. (1995) 'The deskilling thesis revisited: on Peter Armstrong's defence of Braverman', *Sociological Review*, 43 (3): 478–500.

Littler, C. R. (1982) *The Development of the Labour Process in Capitalist Societies*, Aldershot: Gower.

Littler, C. R. (1985) 'Taylorism, Fordism and job design' in D. Knights, H. Willmott and D. Collinson (eds), *Job Redesign*, Aldershot: Gower: 10–29.

Littler, C. R. and Salaman, G. (1982) 'Bravermania and beyond: recent theories ofthe labour process', *Sociology*, 16 (2): 251–69.

McLoughlin, I. and Clark, J. (1994) *Technological Change at Work*, 2nd edn, Milton Keynes: Open University Press.

Meyer, S. (1981) *The Five-Dollar Day: Labor Management and Social Control in the Ford Motor Co., 1908–21*, Albany, NY: SUNY Press.

Milkman, R. (1997) *Farewell to the Factory: Auto Workers in the Late Twentieth Century*, Berkeley: University of California Press.

Morgan, G. (1986) *Images of Organization*, London: Sage.

O'Doherty, D. and H. Willmott (2001) 'Debating labour process theory: the issue ofsubjectiv-ity and the relevance of poststructuralism', *Sociology* 35: 457–76.

Palmer, B. (1975) 'Class, conception and conflict', *Review of Radical Political Economics*, 7 (2): 31–49.

Penn, R. (1983) 'Theories of skill and class structure', *Sociological Review*, 31 (1): 22–38.

Penn, R. (1990) *Class, Power and Technology*, Cambridge: Polity Press.

Penn, R. and Scattergood, H. (1985) 'Deskilling or enskilling? An empirical investigation of recent theories of the labour process', *British Journal of Sociology*, 36 (4): 611–30.

Penn, R., Gasteen, A., Scattergood, H. and Sewel, J. (1994) 'Technical change and the division of labour in Rochdale and Aberdeen', in R. Penn, M. Rose and J.Rubery (eds), *Skill and Occupational Change*, Oxford: Oxford University Press: 130–56.

Piore, M. J. and Sabel, C. F. (1984) *The Second Industrial Divide*, New York: Basic Books.

Pollert, A. (1981) *Girls, Wives, Factory Lives*, London: Macmillan.

Pollert, A. (ed.) (1991) *Farewell to Flexibility?*, Oxford: Blackwell.

Procter, S. and Mueller, F (eds) (2000) *Teamworking*, Basingstoke: Macmillan.

Purcell, J. (1989) 'The impact of corporate strategy on human resource management', in J. Storey (ed.), *New Perspectives on Human Resource Management*, London: Routledge: 67–91.

Purcell, J. (1995) 'Corporate strategy and its link with human resource management strategy', in J. Storey (ed.), *Human Resource Management: A Critical Text London*: Routledge: 63–86.

Ritzer, G. (1993) *The McDonaldization of Society*, Thousand Oaks, Calif.: Pine ForgePress.

Ritzer, G. (1998) *The McDonaldization Thesis*, London: Sage.

Rose, M. (1988) *Industrial Behaviour*, 2nd edn, Harmondsworth: Penguin.

Sabel, C. F. (1982) *Work and Politics: The Division of Labour in Industry*, Cambridge: Cambridge University Press.

Schein, E. H. (1965) *Organizational Psychology*, Englewood Cliff, NJ: Prentice-Hall.

Sewell, G and Wilkinson, B. (1992a) 'Empowerment or emasculation? Shop floor surveillance in a total quality organisation', in P. Blyton and P. Turnbull (eds), *Reassessing Human Resource Management*, London: Sage: 97–115.

Smith, C. (1989) 'Flexible specialisation, automation and mass production', *Work, Employment and Society*, 3 (2): 203–22.

Sorge, A., Hartman, G., Warner, M. and Nicholas, I. (1983) *Microelectronics and Manpower in Manufacturing Applications of Computer Numerical Control in Great Britain and West Germany*, Aldershot: Gower.

Spencer, D. (2000) 'Braverman and the contribution of labour process analysis tothe critique of capitalist production: twenty-five years on', *Work, Employment and Society*, 14 (2): 223–43.

Sturdy, A. (1992) 'Clerical consent', in A. Sturdy, D. Knights and H. Willmott (eds), *Skill and Consent*, London: Routledge.

Taylor, F. W. (1911) *The Principles of Scientific Management*, New York: Harper.

Taylor, P. and Bain, P. (1999) '"An assembly line in the head": work and employee relations in the call centre', *Industrial Relations Journal*, 30 (2): 101–17.

Taylor, P., Hyman, J., Mulvey, G. and Bain, P. (2002) 'Work organisation, control and the experience of work in call centres', *Work, Employment and Society*, 16 (1): 133–50.

Thompson, P. (1989) *The Nature of Work*, 2nd edn, London: Macmillan.

Tinker, T. (2002) 'Spectres of Marx and Braverman in the twilight of postmodernistlabour process research', *Work, Employment and Society*, 16 (2): 251–81.

Westwood, S. (1984) *All Day Every Day*, London: Pluto.

Williams, C. L. (1992). 'The glass escalator: hidden advantages for men in the"female" professions', *Social Problems*, 39: 253–66.

Williams, K., Cutler, T., Williams, J. and Haslam, C. (1987) 'The end of mass production?', *Economy and Society*, 16 (3): 405–39.

Williams, K., Haslam, C. and Williams, J. (1992) 'Ford versus "Fordism": the beginning of mass production?' *Work, Employment and Society*, 6 (4): 517–55.

Womack, J. P., Jones, D. T. and Roos, D. (1990) *The Machine that Changed the World*, New York: Rawson Macmillan.

Wood, S. (ed.) (1989) *The Transformation of Work?* London: Unwin Hyman.

Zuboff, S. (1988) *In the Age of the Smart Machine*, Oxford: Heinemann.

ORGANIZATIONAL DESIGN

CHAPTER OUTLINE

- Introduction
- Organizational structure and design
- Dimensions of structure
- Typologies of organizational structure
- Determinants of organizational structure: making strategic choices
- Organizational restructuring: a conceptual framework
- Traditional designs of organizational structure: bureaucracy
- Emerging organizational designs: post-bureaucracy?
- Gender, sexuality and organizational design
- Summary and end-of-chapter features
- Chapter case study 1: Strategy and design in Australia's tourist industry
- Chapter case study 2: ABC's just-in-time supply chain

CHAPTER OBJECTIVES

After studying this chapter, you should be able to:

- identify and define the foundation concepts of organizational structure and design
- understand the meaning and significance of complexity, formalization and centralization
- explain the relationships between strategy, size, technology and capitalist development, and the different forms of organizational design
- describe the difference between classical and modern thinking about organizational design
- describe some of the emerging contemporary forms of organizational design and identify the potential impact on workplace behaviour
- explain and illustrate the basis of criticism of managerial thinking about organizational design with reference to power, gender and sexuality

INTRODUCTION

In his influential book *Beyond Reengineering*,[1] Michael Hammer cited the Ford Motor Company as an exemplar of how a few American corporations had restructured and transformed 'beyond recognition' their old ways of doing things in order to meet the challenges of global competition. In February 2009, Ford chairman and CEO Bill Ford and other CEOs from General Motors and Chrysler were publicly explaining to the US Senate banking committee why they needed US$17 billion of emergency financial infusion to prevent bankruptcy. And in March 2009, US President Barack Obama rejected General Motors' and Chrysler's restructuring plans that had been submitted in February, while demanding the resignation of General Motors' CEO, Rick Wagoner, as part of the government's offer to help General Motors to accelerate and deepen their restructuring plans (see OB in focus, below).

In the same period, corporate bail-outs and the restructuring of European companies such as Fiat SpA, Renault SA, Volvo and Opel were reported. These restructuring initiatives were not unique to the manufacturing sector. Accelerated by dysfunctional financial markets and deteriorating global trade, venerable financial firms such as American International Group, Fannie Mae, Freddie Mac, Citigroup, Bank of America, Northern Rock, Bradford and Bingley, Royal Bank of Scotland and HBOS have been bailed out, restructured or nationalized.

Organizational restructuring entails a significant decrease in the resources that it allocates to process activities or product markets in which it has previously engaged, or a reallocation of resources to new geographical locations.[2] A plethora of studies have analysed such a 'downsizing' as part of a process of 'outsourcing' many functions originally assigned to permanent employees. Restructuring has been wrapped in the mantra of flexibility, lean and mean and competitiveness.[3-12] These studies emphasize that 'corporate anorexia' can fundamentally change how work is performed as well as reshape employment relations. Thus, the study of organizational structure and design is essential for a deeper understanding of workplace behaviour. What exactly are senior managers 'restructuring'? What determines organizational design? What is the right relationship between the centre of a company and its periphery? How does the psychological contract between the worker and the employer change after restructuring? And how does organizational design and redesign modify behaviour?

The answer to these questions is the focus of this chapter. We begin by explaining the meaning and nature of organizational structure and design. To help with our analysis of different organizational forms, we offer a conceptual framework of the various types of organizational reconfiguring. We then move on to examine some traditional **formal organizational** designs: functional, product/service, divisional and matrix. New organizational designs that have allegedly supplanted the traditional

formal organization: a highly structured group formed for the purpose of completing certain tasks or achieving specific goals

OB in focus

OB in focus: Corporate restructuring and the car industry

Since the start of the recession, downsizing has become the management trend around the world, and corporate restructuring has become key to survival. In just one week in November 2008, Britain's BT, Canada's Nortel and German-owned DHL were just three of many firms announcing massive job cuts. In addition to having to trim down the number of employees, businesses are having to rethink the organization of their headquarters. Many are struggling with the problem of maintaining the right relationship between the centre and the periphery. In the 1970s, large multinationals created large headquarters. In the 1990s, the fashion changed to modest, simple centres. In the twenty-first century, headquarters were beginning to expand again – but the recession will probably force organizations to revert to minimalism.

The car industry has been hit especially hard by the recent economic downturn. Three of the largest US car manufacturers – General Motors (GM), Chrysler and Ford – have been forced to make significant changes to how they operate, while the government has had to step in to help out. All three organizations were in the midst of implementing vast restructuring and cost-cutting strategies when they were knocked back again by tightening credit and rising oil prices. The revelation that GM was in danger of running out of cash concentrated executive minds. Although not quite as desperate, Ford was in a similar position, while Cerberus Capital Management (which owned 80 per cent of Chrysler) sought to offload the car maker to another firm. So the struggling car manufacturers were left with just two options: either the US government would have to come to the rescue, or the biggest car companies in America would have to seek bankruptcy protection.

Chrysler did in the end file for bankruptcy (despite evidence that customers would be likely to abandon the products of a car manufacturer that took this step). The US government bailed out GM, and President Obama expressed his hope that the company would emerge 'leaner and meaner' as a result of its financial woes. In some ways, it seems that the Obama administration's automotive task force holds the fate of the US car industry and its future structure in its hands.

Sources: Anonymous (2008) 'Centres of attention', *The Economist*, November 13; Anonymous (2008) 'Follow the money', *The Economist*, October 18, p. 72; Anonymous (2008) 'On the edge', *The Economist*, November 15, 2008, p. 75; Keenan, G. (2009) 'Losses force GM to question its future', *Globe and Mail*, February 27, p. B1; http://news.bbc.co.uk/1/hi/business/8065760.stm.

stop reflect
Think about an organization where you have worked or studied. Can you identify a set of characteristics that help to describe its structure?

organizational structure: the formal reporting relationships, groups, departments and systems of the organization

organizational design: the process of creating and modifying organizational structures

forms are also examined. We conclude this chapter with a discussion on the links between gender, sexuality and organizational design.

ORGANIZATIONAL STRUCTURE AND DESIGN

Organizations are created to produce goods or services and to pursue dominant goals that individuals acting alone cannot achieve. According to Peter Drucker, the purpose of the work organization 'is to get the work done'.[13] However, organizational structure is not easy to define because it is not a physical reality, but rather a conceptual one. Let us begin to explain the concept in this way. To accomplish its strategic goals, an organization typically has to do two things: divide the work to be done among its members, and then coordinate the work. **Organizational structure** refers to the formal division of work and the formal configuration of relationships that coordinate and control organizational activities. The **organizational design** is the planning and implementation of a structural configuration of roles and modes of operation. Arguably, theories of organizational structure are a product of modernity,

Plate 1 – In a small restaurant, the horizontal divisions might be divided into three main work activities: preparing the food, service and running the bar. A vertical division of labour would describe the coordinating and directing work of the head chef, the restaurant supervisor and the head bar tender, all of whom report to the restaurant manager.
Source: istock photo.

because they are largely based on Weber's notions of rationality and bureaucratic specialization.

Thus, work is divided horizontally into distinct tasks that need to be done, either into jobs, subunits or departments. This horizontal division of labour is associated with specialization on the part of the workforce. The vertical division of labour is concerned with apportioning authority for planning, decision making, monitoring and controlling: who will tell whom what to do? For example, in a small restaurant, the horizontal divisions might be divided into three main work activities: preparing the food, service and running the bar. A vertical division of labour would describe the coordinating and directing work of the head chef, the restaurant supervisor and the head bar tender, all of whom report to the restaurant manager.

This small business has a simple structure. However, the structure could become more complex as more people were hired and as coordination and control became more difficult. As business expanded and management became more complicated, the manager might not have enough time to deal with the accounts and hiring and training of new staff. To solve these problems, the restaurant manager might hire an accountant and a human resource manager, which would increase the vertical division of labour. The growth of an organization might therefore lead to a greater degree of specialization of its workforce.

Alternatively, the restaurant manager might create work teams and allow the team members to coordinate their work activities and hire and train their members. This limited 'empowerment' of the workers would then free up time for the head chef, the restaurant supervisor and the head bar tender to handle the accounts for their departments.

specialization: the allocation of work tasks to categories of employee or groups. Also known as division of labour

Specialization occurs when people focus their effort on a particular skill, task, customer or territorial area. Our simple example of the restaurant illustrates two important points: managers have choices over how to divide labour, and different organizational configurations impact on people's work experience. (For instance, if teams were introduced, additional tasks would have to be learnt and the pace of work might intensify.)

organization chart: a diagram showing the grouping of activities and people within a formal organization to achieve the goals of the organization efficiently

An **organization chart** graphically shows the various parts as boxes, and the coordination and control by lines that connect the boxes. This system is used in Figure 4.1 to demonstrate the simple structure of the restaurant just described, and is used in the sample organization charts that follow. Organizational design refers to the process of creating a structure that best fits a strategy, technology and environment. For example, Ford Motor Company has created a structure on a product basis, with separate divisions for specific models. So why do managers redesign structures? Management designs new structures in order to reduce costs, to respond to changing customer buying patterns or business boundaries, to reset priorities, to shift people and align capabilities, to shift perceptions of service among users, or to 'shake things up'.[14]

Why is organizational structure important? From a managerial perspective, structure may make the task of managing employees more complex, bringing into play the questions of efficiency and consistency that are likely to arise more often when different groups report directly to departmental managers, rather than to a single owner or manager in an organization employing relatively few people. Structure therefore defines lines of responsibility and authority. In terms of organizational performance, a 'good' structure is not a panacea, but it is very important, argues management guru Peter Drucker: 'Good organizational structure does not by itself produce good performance ... But a poor organization structure makes good performance impossible, no matter how good the individual managers may be' (ref. 15, p. 4). The structure of an

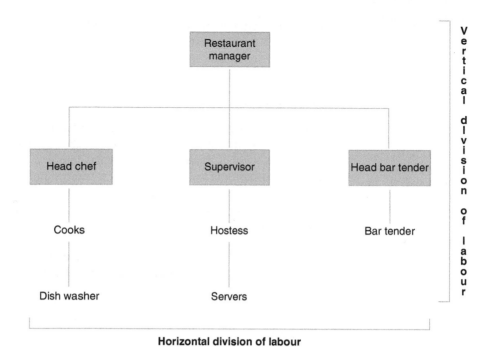

Figure 4.1 – An example of a simple organizational structure

organization also affects the ability of workers to learn, to be creative, to innovate and to participate in decision making.[16,17]

From a worker's perspective, different structural configurations affect not only productivity and economic results, defined by the marketplace, but also job satisfaction, commitment, motivation and perceptions about expectations and obligations. Redesigning organizational structure will therefore affect the intangible 'psychological contract' of each individual worker.

The concept of the psychological contract has an important implication for those redesigning organizational structures. Each individual employee will have different perceptions of his or her psychological contract, even when the structure within which he or she works is identical. Therefore, there will be no universal notion of mutual expectations and obligations.[18] Changes in the organization's structure also affect employee relations and organizational governance. All this serves to remind us that organizational success and failure depend on the behaviour of people, who work within the formal structure and who mould and imprint their personality into their work activities.

So far, we have given what could be described as the orthodox or mainstream position, in which organizational structure is rationally designed by managers to meet dominant organizational goals in as efficient a way as possible within the constraints they perceive. However, a critical approach to studying organizational behaviour examines the **informal aspects of structure**, which consist in part of unofficial working arrangements, social **networking** cabals and the internal **politicking** of people. Conceptually, it is argued that these two aspects of organizational structure – the formal and the informal – are dialectically related, in that they are influenced by each other, and activities in one encourage activities in the other.[19,20] For example, a team-based organizational structure designed by senior management to increase

informal structure: a term used to describe the aspect of organizational life in which participants' day-to-day activities and interactions ignore, bypass or do not correspond with the official rules and procedures of the bureaucracy

networking: cultivating social relationships with others to accomplish one's goals

organizational politics: behaviours that others perceive as self-serving tactics for personal gain at the expense of other people and possibly the organization

flexibility may invite unofficial strategies among line managers who choose to resist being relocated. An organizational structure reflects internal power relationships.[21,22]

DIMENSIONS OF STRUCTURE

stop reflect
Think about an organization where you or someone you know well has worked. Can you identify a management practice that was designed to encourage one behaviour but also resulted in another behaviour that impacted on the activity?

A variety of dimensions can be used to conceptualize organizational structure. There is a disagreement among theorists over what makes up the term 'structure', but a relatively recent way of thinking about organizations and structure is as 'discursive metaphors'. Advocates of this approach suggest that organizations are 'texts', created through discourses, which have symbolic meaning for managers and workers. These meanings are open to multiple readings even when particular meanings become sufficiently privileged and concrete. Here, we take a more orthodox approach to examine how researchers have analysed structure, before discussing how it affects organizational behaviour.[23] While we acknowledge the elastic definitions and various labels attached to organizational phenomena, here we examine three aspects: complexity, formalization and centralization.

Complexity

complexity: the intricate departmental and interpersonal relationships that exist within a work organization

Complexity is the degree of differentiation in the organization. Complexity measures the degree of division of tasks, levels of hierarchy and geographical locations of work units in the organization. The more tasks are divided among individuals, the more the organization is *horizontally complex*. The most visible evidence in the organization of horizontal complexity is specialization and departmentalization.

weblink
Go to www.shell.com for an example of team-based organizational design

Specialization refers to the particular grouping of activities performed by an employee. Division of labour – for example, accounting activities – creates groups of specialists (in this case, accountants). The way these specialists are grouped is referred to as departmentalization. As the vertical chain of command lengthens, more formal authority layers are inserted between top management and front-line workers. In such circumstances, the organization becomes more *vertically complex*. Therefore, vertical complexity refers to the depth of the organization's hierarchy: the number of levels between senior management and the workers. Organizations with the same number of workers need not have the same degree of vertical complexity. Organizations can be 'flat', with few layers of hierarchy, or 'tall', with many levels of management between the top CEO and front-line employees (Figure 4.2).

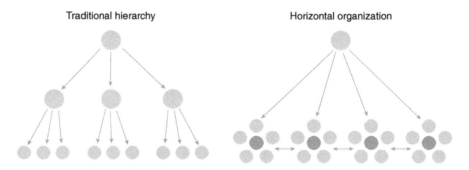

Figure 4.2 – A tall organization structure versus a flat (team-based) structure

During the last decade, organizations have moved towards flatter configurations by eliminating whole levels of middle managers and generally 'doing more with less'. This form of restructuring, commonly called 'downsizing', increases the span of control for the managers who remain. The **span of control** defines the number of subordinates that a single manager or administrator can supervise effectively. If this span is narrow, managers have few subordinates reporting to them. If it is wide, managers are responsible for many subordinates. The larger the span, the less potential there is for control by direct supervision. When work tasks are routine, the control of subordinates through technology and output performance substitutes for direct supervision. At lower operational levels, it is not unusual to have spans of control of up to 20 individuals. In the managerial ranks, work is less routine, and spans of control tend to be smaller. Thus, the complexity of the task often dictates the span of control.

Vertical complexity can also affect managerial behaviour by impacting on other factors such as communication networks and manager–worker dynamics. For example, a wide span of control makes it more difficult for a manager to hold face-to-face meetings.

An organization can perform the same work activities in geographically separate locations, a fact emphasized by globalization. The existence of multiple workplaces increases complexity. *Spatial complexity* refers to the degree to which the organization's operations and core workforce are geographically dispersed. As spatial complexity increases, managers face coordination, control and communication challenges relating to their subordinates.[24]

span of control: the number of people directly reporting to the next level in the organizational hierarchy

Formalization

formalization: the degree to which organizations standardize behaviour through rules, procedures, formal training and related mechanisms

Formalization is the second core dimension of organizational structure, and describes the degree of standardization of work and jobs in the organization. It refers to the extent to which work is defined and controlled by rules. The more rules there are about what is to be done, when it is to be done and how it should be done, the more an organization is formalized. Where formalization is low, employees are given freedom to exercise discretion in their work. The degree of formalization can vary widely within and among organizations.

The extent of formalization typically varies with the nature of the work performed and the size of the organization.[25] The most complex and creative paid work is amenable to low degrees of formalization. Formalization also tends to be inversely related to the hierarchical level in the organization. Individuals lower in the organization are engaged in activities that are relatively simple and repetitive, and therefore these people are most likely to work in a highly formalized environment. Although formalization regulates workers' behaviour, it can also impose constraints on managers and subordinates. In a unionized workplace, for instance, contract rules negotiated by union and management can constrain managers' ability to mobilize the skills, creativity, commitment and values of their subordinates.[26]

Centralization

centralization: the degree to which formal decision authority is held by a small group of people, typically those at the top of the organizational hierarchy

Centralization, the third core dimension of organizational structure, refers to the degree to which decision making is concentrated at a single point in the organization. In essence, it addresses the question, who makes the decisions in the organization? A decentralized organization is one in which senior managers solicit input from members when making key decisions. The more input members provide or the more autonomy they are given to make decisions, the more decentralized the organization.

The degree of centralization affects workers' ability to make decisions, levels of motivation and the manager–subordinate interface. An ongoing challenge for managers is to balance the degree of centralization necessary to achieve control on the one hand, and to gain commitment through participation and work-related learning on the other.

TYPOLOGIES OF ORGANIZATIONAL STRUCTURE

mechanistic organization: an organizational structure with a narrow span of control and high degrees of formalization and centralization

organic organization: an organizational structure with a wide span of control, little formalization and decentralized decision making

stop reflect
Can you identify organizations that have organic features and organizations that display mechanistic features?

The three core dimensions of formal organizational structure – complexity, formalization and centralization – can be combined into a number of different types or models. Two popular descriptive models have received much attention: the mechanistic model and the organic model.[27]

The **mechanistic organization** has been characterized as a machine. It has high complexity, high formalization and high centralization. A mechanistic organization resembles a bureaucracy. It is characterized by highly specialized tasks that tend to be rigidly defined, a hierarchical authority and control structure, and communications that primarily take the form of edicts and decisions issued by managers to subordinates. Communication typically flows vertically from the top down.

Organic organizations are the antithesis of mechanistic organizations. They are characterized by being low in complexity, formality and centralization. An organic organization is said to be flexible and informally coordinated, and managers use participative decision-making behaviours. Communication is both horizontal (across different departments) and vertical (down and up the hierarchy), depending on where the information resides.

DETERMINANTS OF ORGANIZATIONAL STRUCTURE: MAKING STRATEGIC CHOICES

competitive advantage: the ability of a work organization to add more value for its customers and shareholders than its rivals, and thus gain a position of advantage in the marketplace

weblink
Visit http://www.12manage. com/methods_ contingency_theory.html and http://changingminds. org/disciplines/ leadership/theories/ contingency_theory.htm for more information on contingency theory

The underlying rationale for mechanistic and organic organizations is, according to conventional organizational theory, explained by the choice of competitive strategy. The mechanistic organization strives for **competitive advantage** by maximizing efficiency and productivity, whereas an organic organization's competitive strategy is based on maximum adaptability and flexibility. Thus, structural characteristics concern contextual factors within the organization and affect the management process. So far, although we have examined a number of core organizational design concepts, we have not provided much insight into why organizational structures vary so much, or into the forces behind corporate restructuring. The purpose of this section is to discuss theories of organizational design in terms of their relevance for understanding current restructuring endeavours.

Early management theorists put forward universalistic organizational structure theories: that is, the 'one size fits all' principle applied to organizations. Over the last 30 years, organizational analysts have modified the classical approach by suggesting that organizational structure is contingent (or depends) on a variety of variables or contextual factors. The contingency approach to organizational design takes the view that there is no 'one best' universal structure, and emphasizes the need for flexibility. The significant contingency variables are strategy, size, technology and environment.

Strategy and structure

Strategy can be viewed as a pattern of activity over time to achieve performance goals. The classical position that 'structure follows strategy' assumes that managers choose the structure they have: 'A new strategy required a new or at least refashioned structure' (ref. 28, p. 15). This hypothesis is represented in Figure 4.3.

For example, if top management chooses to compete through product and service innovation and high quality – a differentiation strategy – then managers need to adopt an organic or horizontal organizational structure. A cost leadership strategy, on the other hand, requires products or services to be standardized with minimum costs. A mechanistic, functional structure with more formalization and centralization is most appropriate with this strategy, so that managers can closely control quality and costs.

A counter-thesis sees strategy as related less directly to organizational design. In this view, 'strategy follows structure'.[29] The design of the organization is the context in which top managers form the business strategy. Thus, the existing organizational configuration affects top managers' perceptions of internal strengths, weaknesses, threats and opportunities (SWOT) outside the organization, and helps shape a strategy.

Empirical research offers support for both views of strategy affecting the design of an organization; this is illustrated in Figure 4.3 by a two-headed arrow between structure and strategy. This recognizes that the link between strategy and structure is affected by other contingency factors, such as size, technology and environment.

In her book *No Logo*, globalization critic Naomi Klein provides a more controversial account of the link between corporate strategy – a focus on 'branding' and the relocation of manufacturing capacity from the core capitalist economy to the periphery, where wage levels are low – and multifaceted structures spanning national frontiers:

> The astronomical growth in the wealth and cultural influence of multinational corporations over the last fifteen years can arguably be traced back to a single, seemingly innocuous idea developed by management theorists in the mid-1980s, that successful corporations must primarily produce brands, as opposed to products ... The very process of producing – running one's own factories, being responsible for the tens of thousands of full-time, permanent employees – began to look less like the route to success and more like a clunky liability.
>
> At around this time a new kind of corporation began to rival the traditional all-American manufacturers for market share; these were the Nikes and Microsoft, and later, the Tommy Hilfigers and Intels ... What these companies

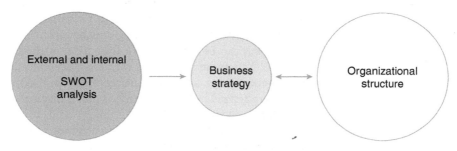

Figure 4.3 – The strategy- structure thesis

produced primarily were not things, they said, but images of their brands. Their real work lay not in manufacturing but in marketing. This formula, needless to say, has proved enormously profitable, and its success has companies competing in a race towards weightlessness: whoever owns the least, has the fewest employees on the payroll and produces the most powerful images, as opposed to products, wins the race.

(ref. 30, p. 4)

weblink
Visit www.corpwatch.org, a US-based organization that monitors and critiques global capitalism through education and social action

Of course, as globalization theorists have observed, the notion of 'weightlessness' is only feasible because of the developments in transportation, namely containerization and the Internet.

Size and structure

Most studies define organizational size as the total number of employees, and researchers suggest that larger organizations have different structures from smaller organizations. As organizations increase in size, they tend to develop more written rules and procedures, and division of labour becomes more specialized. A number of theorists have argued that size is an important factor affecting organizational design.[31-33] It seems credible that there is a positive relationship between size and the degree of formalization, specialization and centralization.

Critics of the size imperative have countered that neither formalization nor complexity can be inferred from organizational size. An equally valid alternative interpretation of early empirical data is that size is the result, not the cause, of structure.[34] The key point here is that there are obvious structural differences between large and small organizations, but a statistically significant relationship between size and structural dimensions does not imply causation. For example, technology influences structure, which in turn determines size.

Technology and structure

Technological change is quintessentially a defining feature of the 'knowledge economy', and is also another important contingency variable explaining organizational structure. Researchers have adopted either a restrictive or an expansive definition of technology, and the early research on technology suggests a positive relationship between type of technology and organizational structure.[35,36]

The 'technology–structure' thesis has sought to analyse technology as an independent explanatory variable. The British academic Joan Woodward, for example, classified production technology into three main categories for analysis: unit production (as in a tailor's shop), mass production (as in an automotive plant), and continuous process production (like that of a pulp mill). Perrow classified four types of technology: routine, engineering, craft and non-routine. Routine technologies have few exceptions and easy-to-analyse problems (for example, pulp and paper mills or chemical plants belong to this category). Engineering technologies have a large number of exceptions, but can be managed in a systematic manner (as with the construction of bridges). Craft technologies deal with relatively difficult problems with a limited set of exceptions (such as in hand-crafted furniture making). Non-routine technologies are characterized by many exceptions and difficult-to-analyse problems (as with research and development).

The research found evidence of different types of technology being associated with different organizational designs. Non-routine technology, for instance, is positively associated with high complexity. So as the work becomes more customized, the span of control narrows. Studies also suggest that routine technology is positively related to formalization. Routine technologies allow leaders to implement rules and regulations because the work is well understood by their followers. It has been proposed that routine technology might lead to centralized decision making and control systems if formalization is low. Within this theoretical framework, it is suggested that technology mediates mechanical and integrated forms of management control, which are incorporated into the technology itself. Thus, employee performance is subject to control by technology rather than by direct human supervision.

Joan Woodward died in 1971, but her thesis that technology is a crucial contingency influenced the American sociologist Howard Aldrich. For Aldrich in 2002, as for Woodward, the technology in use in the organization had high priority in accounting for the degree of organizational structure.[37] Both structure and technology are multidimensional concepts, and it is not realistic to relate technology to structure in any simple manner. In addition, all the technological paradigms have their strengths and weaknesses. Conceptualizing technology by degrees of 'routineness' leads to a generalizable conclusion that technology will shape structure in terms of size, complexity and formalization. The strategic choice discourse also suggests that it is managerial behaviour at critical points in the process of organizational change – possibly in negotiation with trade unions – that is critical in reshaping managerial processes and outcomes, including organizational structure.

Environment and structure

environment: refers to the broad economic, political, legal and social forces that are present in the minds of the organization's members and may influence their decision making and constrain their strategic choices, such as the national business system

stop reflect
Can you think of any developments in the UK or Europe that have changed organizational design?

The **environment** is everything outside the organization's boundary. The case for the environmental imperative argues that organizations are embedded in society, and therefore a multitude of economic, political, social and legal factors will affect organizational design decisions. The attack on the World Trade Center on September 11, 2001 and the global economic recession that began in 2008–09 are two catastrophes outside organizations that resulted in major restructuring within many airlines and banks.

An early study by Burns and Stalker in 1966 proposed an environment–structure thesis.[27] In essence, their study of UK firms distinguished five different kinds of environment, ranging from 'stable' to 'least predictable', and two divergent patterns of managerial behaviour and organizational structure – the organic and the mechanistic configurations. They suggested that both types of structural regime represented a 'rational' form of organization that could be created and sustained according to the external conditions facing the organization. For instance, uncertainty in the environment might cause top managers to restructure in order to be more responsive to the changing marketplace.

An organization's environment can also range from *munificent* to *hostile*. Organizations located in a hostile environment face more competition, an adversarial union–management relationship and resource scarcity.

These four distinct dimensions of environments shape structure. The more dynamic the environment, the more 'organic' the structure, and the more complex the environment, the more 'decentralized' the structure.[38] The explosive growth of e-commerce, for example, has created a dynamic complex environment for much of the retail book and clothing industry, and is therefore spawning highly flexible network structures. Despite the criticisms of contingency theory, it has provided insights into understanding complex situational variables that help to shape organizational structure.

Globalization and organizational restructuring

Our aim in this chapter is to offer a multidimensional understanding of organizational structure and restructuring. Existing organizational behaviour texts tend to be more narrowly focused, and give limited, if any, coverage to the causation and consequences of global capitalism.

globalization: when an organization extends its activities to other parts of the world, actively participates in other markets, and competes against organizations located in other countries

As a field of study, the term **globalization** is controversial, as are its alleged effects. Clearly, a detailed study of globalization is beyond the scope of this chapter, but to ground the arguments on organizational structure we need to at least acknowledge the interplay of continuity, restructuring and the diversity of experiences of globalization.

For some, globalization involves the spread of transplanetary connections between people.[39] For others, globalization primarily revolves around two main phenomena.

Work and Society: Fordism for doctors?

For those who study occupational change, the professions represent an interesting case. 'Professional' occupations span a broad range of areas – from established occupations such as doctor or lawyer, to so-called 'semi-professional' occupations such as teacher or social worker. What makes the professions unique is that they appear to have resisted many of the trends that have changed the face of work in the twentieth century. Although specialized, the professional worker is not alienated. He or she enjoys considerable discretion over how work is done, the settings in which it is done, and the ways in which it is evaluated. Traditionally, professional workers have maintained control over their work processes, despite efforts by managers and consumers to challenge that control.

The world of professional work has undergone significant change in the last two decades. Professional authority has been contested, and there have been efforts to subordinate professional authority to managerial authority. Some of the more dramatic instances of this kind of challenge have occurred in Britain's National Health Service (NHS). Referring to specific moments in this process of reform, David Hunter (1994), a Professor at the Nuffield Institute for Health, offers the following analysis:

> Much of the impetus beyond the 1989 reform proposals ... can be seen as an attempt to secure a shift in the balance of power between doctors and managers in favour of the latter. They seek to achieve such a shift in the context of advocating improved efficiency in the use of resources and in the provision of services. Much of the management problem in the NHS has centered on the notion of undermanagement in respect of the medical side of the service. Getting a grip on the freedom enjoyed by clinicians and holding them to account for expenditure they incur is seen as the last unmanaged frontier in the NHS. (p. 6)

As Hunter suggests, the rationale behind this attempt to limit the professional power of doctors was efficiency. But what is the larger historical context of this managerial initiative? Richard Sennett argues that the rationale for reform of this kind can be traced back to Henry Ford's views on how work should be organized. In Sennett's view, 'Fordism' entails a particular perspective on the division of labour: 'each worker does one task, measured as precisely as possible by time-and-motion studies; output is measured in terms of targets that are ... entirely quantitative' (Sennett, 2008, p. 47). Sennett goes on to suggest how Fordism has shaped reforms in the NHS: 'Fordism monitors the time doctors and nurses spend with each patient; a medical treatment system based on dealing with auto parts, it tends to treat cancerous livers or broken backs rather than patients in the round' (p. 47).

How effective has this approach been to managing the clinical world of healthcare? Hunter maintains that while the power of doctors was constrained in some ways, doctors continued to exert considerable influence over how health and disease should be understood, and consequently on how the work of producing health and preventing illness should be organized. Moreover, as Sennett notes, 'doctors create paper fictions' to circumvent the practice guidelines imposed by managers in the NHS: 'Doctors in the NHS often assign a patient a disease in order to justify the time spent exploring a puzzling body' (p. 49).

The challenge of how to organize and manage professional work remains a central issue in the field of organizational design. We have yet to answer the question of what might constitute the optimal balance between professional and managerial power. Perhaps the best way to approach this question is to attempt to envision a situation where shared power enhances productivity and quality in the provision of healthcare.

stop!   Taking the doctor as an example, where would you position the threshold beyond which too much managerial power might erode productivity and decrease the quality of patient care? Provide some concrete examples to illustrate how a sharing of power between professionals (including allied professionals, such as nurses) and managers will enhance the overall effectiveness of the NHS and national health systems more generally.

Can you identify the major source of managerial authority in a system like that of the USA where private corporations play a key role in the delivery of healthcare?

Consider how these issues may apply to other professions, such as law and teaching.

Sources and further information

Freidson, E. (1998) *Professionalism Reborn*, Chicago: University of Chicago Press.

Hunter, D. (1994) 'From tribalism to corporatism: the managerial challenge to medical dominance', pp. 1–22 in J. Gabe, D. Kelleher and G. Williams (eds), *Challenging Medicine*, London: Routledge.

Sennett, R. (2008) *The Craftsman*, New Haven, CT: Yale University Press.

Note: This feature was written by David MacLennan, Assistant Professor at Thompson Rivers University, BC, Canada.

First is the emergence of a capitalist global economy based on a sophisticated system of production, finance, transportation and communication driven by transnational corporations (TNCs). Second is the notion of global culture, which focuses on the spread of particular patterns of consumption and the ideology of consumerism at the global level.[40]

The more radical globalization literature helps us to locate the main driver of organizational design and restructuring in the dialectical development of global capitalism. This argument is based on the theory that organizational restructuring occurs because of systematic contradictions.[41] This approach, which has occupied an immense space in Marxist literature, searches for inherent tendencies in the global capitalist system that create tension and bring about their own conflicts, until such a system can no longer maintain itself without far-reaching structural adjustments. Thus, every phase of capitalist expansion is characterized by the particular model through which business organizations 'make their profits'. In Marxist literature, this is referred to as 'accumulation'.

To apply accumulation theory to the various restructuring initiatives shown in Figure 4.5, below, profit maximization was achieved in the first half of the twentieth century through the use of bureaucracies modelled on Fordist-style production and employment relations. The whole point about bureaucratic Fordism as a profitable undertaking is that it achieves economies of scale: the system produces standardized products at relatively low unit costs.

However, the downside to Taylorism and Fordism is that the success of the operation depends on an expanding market for the same standard product, and mass production cannot readily adjust to changing consumer tastes. The offer to consumers of 'Any colour of car provided it's black' is less compelling when the market is saturated with black cars and competitors are offering a choice of colours. It is perhaps not surprising that, in order to maintain profitability, an early response of employers to the catalogue of problems associated with bureaucratic Fordism was to decentralize and transplant assembly-line systems from core capitalist countries (such as Germany) to the periphery (for example, to Mexico), where wage levels were very low. The systematic contradiction of Fordism and corporate imperatives created divisionalized structures, including strategic business units, as manufacturing was relocated to the newly industrialized economies (NIEs) of South-East Asia, Brazil and Mexico.

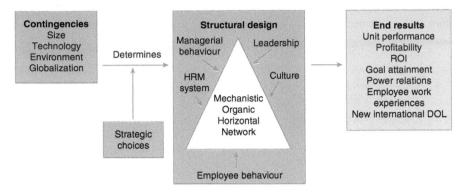

Figure 4.4 – Determinants of organizational structure and end-results. DOL, division of labour: ROI, return on investment

weblink
Visit https://www.cia.gov/ library/publications/ the-world-factbook for more information on the relative size, by revenue, of TNCs

In recent years, market changes compelled further restructuring and 'downsizing' towards 'horizontal' or 'lean' organizations. As two US management theorists write, 'American companies were weighted down with cumbersome organizational charts and many layers of management' (ref. 42, p. xiii). Critical accounts of organizational restructuring also describe the associated changes in social relations: non-standard or precarious employment, and a new 'international division of labour' in which a small number of NIEs participate in the global dispersal of manufacturing by TNCs.

Feminist scholars have highlighted the exploitative and patriarchal nature of the new international division of labour. The critics of global capitalism argue that, as the dominance of the capitalist global system spreads and deepens, it simultaneously sows the seeds of organizational restructuring by providing resources, forms of organizational capacity and the ideological rationale.[40]

Figure 4.4 offers a synthesis of current thinking. It suggests that organizational structure is influenced by business strategy, size, technology, environment and the economics of global capitalism. It is also influenced by internal situational variables, such as culture, managerial and worker behaviour, and the strategic choices available to dominant organizational decision makers. The end results include increased profits for corporations and a new international division of labour.

ORGANIZATIONAL RESTRUCTURING: A CONCEPTUAL FRAMEWORK

Much discussion on organizational structure in standard organizational behaviour textbooks tends to be historically blind, economically shallow, culturally illiterate and politically naive. Although organizational structure and redesign are widely assumed to influence behaviour in the workplace, most treatment of the subject gives scant attention to the complex interplay of organizational structure, management strategies and changes in global capitalist development. To help the analysis of the interplay of different dimensions that appear to have been critical in recent organizational restructuring, we have drawn upon the work of Mabey and his colleagues[43] and constructed a conceptual framework using four interconnected dimensions. Each of these is shown in Figure 4.5.

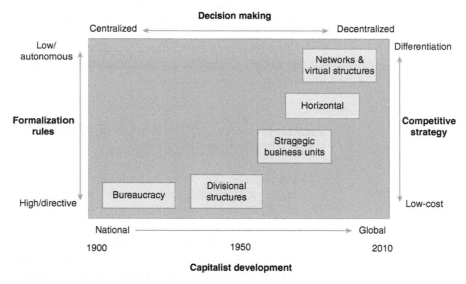

Figure 4.5 – Types of organizational restructuring
Source: Adapted from Mabey, Salaman and Storey (1998),[43] p. 235

On the bottom horizontal axis is the dimension of capitalist global development over the last century, from national economies to a global scale. On the right vertical axis is the dimension of competitive strategy, covering the spectrum from low cost to differentiation. On the left vertical axis is the dimension of formalization, showing the contrast between high/directive and low/autonomous, and on the horizontal axis at the top of the figure is the dimension relating to decision making, which contrasts centralized and decentralized modes.

At the risk of oversimplification, some alternative structural designs are shown for illustrative purposes. In the first half of the twentieth century, at the lower left of Figure 4.5, the bureaucratic form is located to suggest a low-cost, mass-production competitive strategy, a high degree of formalization and direction, and a centralized decision-making mode. Ascending and moving to the right in the figure, from about the 1960s, we see the development of divisionalized configurations, to the development of strategic business units and then networks and virtual organizations.

In addition to the changes in conventional structural boundaries, organizations have recently undertaken other types of restructuring involving new commercial relationships. Manufacturing companies have outsourced the production of some parts – note the influence of just-in-time systems – and services (such as payroll, training and benefits handling), and in the public sector so-called non-core activities (such as laundry, catering and cleaning) have been privatized.

This framework is useful in illustrating the different organizational forms and design options facing top managers, when considered in relation to the core dimensions of formal organizational structure and in relation to each other. The argument of this book is that if we are to understand contemporary workplaces and explain what is happening in them, we need to locate restructuring initiatives in a multidimensional framework that includes capitalist global development. While we believe that the actions of TNCs and the international division of labour are intimately interconnected with organizational design and restructuring, the inclusion in the framework of capitalist global development does not suggest any inevitable linear progression.[39,43] We must remember that millions of people still work in 'sweatshops' and bureaucratic organizations in core economies and NIEs, and these traditional modes of organizing work exist alongside 'new' horizontal and process-based forms and 'frame-breaking' network-based organizations.

The next two sections review the traditional and contemporary types of organizational structure shown in Figure 4.5.

TRADITIONAL DESIGNS OF ORGANIZATIONAL STRUCTURE: BUREAUCRACY

In Henry Mintzberg's *Structure in Fives: Designing Effective Organizations*,[44] he suggests that any work organization has five core parts, which vary in size and importance (Figure 4.6). Three line roles include senior management (the strategic apex), middle management (the middle line), and the production (operating, technical) core. The production core consists of those who do the work of the organization, making its products or servicing its customers. Two staff roles include technical support (technological structure) and clerical support (support staff). The model suggests that, given these five different parts, organizations can adopt a wide variety of structural configurations, depending on which part is in control.

At its simplest, work organizations must perform four essential functions to survive and grow in a capitalist economy:

1 A product or a service must be developed that has value.
2 The product must be manufactured or the service rendered by employees who rely on paid work as their only or major source of income.
3 The product or service must be marketed and made available to those who are to use it.
4 Financial resources are needed in order to develop, create and distribute the product or service provided.

These 'task' functions are the basic activities of the organization, and are undertaken within each of Mintzberg's five basic elements: developing (support), manufacturing the product or providing the service (technostructure and operating core), marketing the product and service (support), and financing the organization (strategic apex and support).

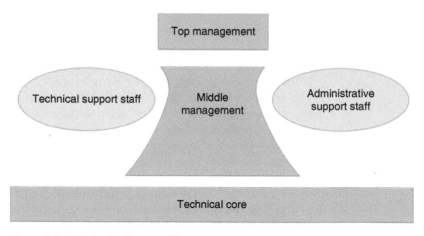

Figure 4.6 – Five basic elements of an organizational structure

Plate 2 – Government organizations are typically bureaucratic. They have numerous rules and procedures that white-collar workers must follow, and concentrate decision making with high-ranking bureaucrats. This photo shows part of the parliament building in Wellington, New Zealand.
Source: iStockphoto

The process of developing, manufacturing the product or providing the service, and marketing it in a capitalist economy also results in a number of organizational imperatives (an imperative being something that dictates something) that centre on issues of control. For those who sit at the strategic apex and for middle-line managers, producing for a market creates pressures to control costs and control uncertainties. Organizations that compete in the marketplace typically face two types of competitive pressure: pressure for cost reductions and pressure to be responsive to changing customer tastes.

Responding to pressures for cost reductions means that managers must try to minimize unit costs by, for example, producing a standardized product and achieving economies of scale. On the other hand, responding to pressures to be responsive to customers requires that managers differentiate the firm's product offering in an effort to accommodate differences in consumers' tastes and preferences. These two types of competitive pressure are even more intense in the global marketplace.[45]

Additionally, the indeterminacy of employees' job performance creates pressures to render individual behaviour predictable and manageable. The control imperatives inherent in capitalist production and employee relations create a need for other managerial behaviour that is supportive of the operating functions of the organization, including human resource management (HRM), industrial relations and public relations. Together, the pressures arising from 'task' functions and 'control' functions shape formal organizational structure as a hierarchy, where decision making is top-down, with subunits or departments, and with managers hired to control employee behaviour.

In the industrial technology era, the organizational dynamics just described caused managers to adopt one of four common structural configurations. They could structure the organization by:

- function
- product/service
- division
- function and product, a matrix.

No formulas exist to guide the choices for organizational structure. Each structure has advantages and disadvantages. The guiding principle is that although there is no one right organizational structure, the right structure for top managers is the one that offers the most advantages and the fewest limitations, or, to put it another way, the one that 'makes their profits'.

Several newer contemporary forms of organizational design have evolved over the last two decades, and are well established in the organizational discourse. These new designs focus on processes or work teams, or the electronic connection of widely dispersed locations and people to form an extended 'virtual' organization. Understanding the strengths and limitations of each structural design helps us to understand what informs design choices, as well as the interplay between different structural configurations and organizational behaviour.

functional configuration: an organizational structure that organizes employees around specific knowledge or other resources

A **functional configuration** is one in which managers and subordinates are grouped around certain important and continuing functions. For example, in an engineering company, all design engineers and planners might be grouped together in one department, and all marketing specialists grouped together in another department (Figure 4.7). In a functionally designed organization, the functional department managers hold most of the authority and power. Key advantages of functional organizations include the development of technical expertise and economies of scale: it is the

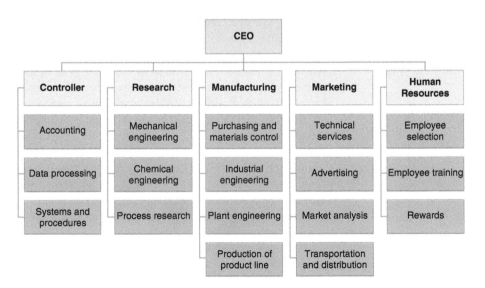

Figure 4.7 – Engineering company with a functional design

classic bureaucratic structure. Disadvantages can include the encouragement of narrow perspectives in functional groups, alienation and demotivation, and poor coordination of interdepartmental activities.

A *product or service design* arrangement is one in which managers and subordinates are grouped together by the product or service they deliver to the customer. For example, at Volvo Motors there is a car division, a truck division and so on (as schematized in Figure 4.8). Another example is a hospital where a medical team and support workers are grouped together in different departments or units dealing with particular treatments, such as maternity, orthopaedic surgery and emergencies.

The advantages of product or service structures include increased coordination of functional departments, improvements in decision making, and the location of accountability for production and profit. Disadvantages of product or service structures can include a loss of economies of scale, the duplication of scarce resources and the discouragement of cooperation between divisions.

A **divisional structural** arrangement uses decentralization as its basic approach. The decentralized divisions can group employees together in one of three ways: by the products or services on which they work, by the sets of customers they serve, or by the geographical locations in which they operate. In the 1980s, these divisional structures developed into **strategic business units,** often with 20 levels of management between the corporate CEO and front-line employees in the business units.

The Body Shop uses a divisional structure based on its major operating regions around the world. The company's products are sold in different markets in different parts of the globe. This is based on the premise that marketing The Body Shop's products in Canada is different from marketing skin and hair products in the UK or the Asian region.

Figure 4.9 shows one possible conception of a multidivisional corporation with strategic business units, built around core products and core competencies. Organizations often evolve from a functional design to a divisional arrangement. As the external environment changes and becomes more complex and uncertain, management might find that it must diversify its operations to remain competitive.[24,45,46] Divisional organizational design emphasizes autonomy in divisional managers' decision making.

There are several advantages associated with a divisional configuration. It improves decision making by allowing many decisions to be delegated to divisional managers, who are generally more knowledgeable about the local markets. Divisional managers

divisional structure: an organizational structure that groups employees around geographical areas, clients or outputs

strategic business unit: a term to describe corporate development that divides the corporation's operations into strategic business units, which allows comparisons between each strategic business unit. According to advocates, corporate managers are better able to determine whether they need to change the mix of businesses in their portfolio

Figure 4.8 – An auto company with a product design

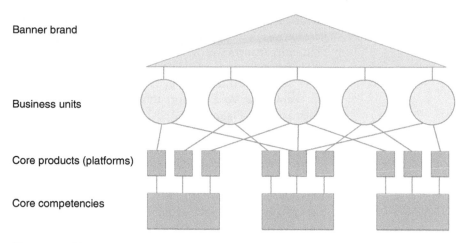

Banner brand

Business units

Core products (platforms)

Core competencies

Figure 4.9 – Divisional organizational structure based on strategic business units
Source: Hamel and Prahalad (1994),[24] p. 279

are more accountable for their decisions. In many divisional organizations, units are 'profit centres', and divisional managers are evaluated on the overall performance of their unit.

The disadvantages of a divisional structure come partly from its decentralized activities. Economies of scale are lost because many task functions of the organization, such as marketing, and control functions, such as accounting and HRM, are duplicated in each division. Specialists in one division may not be able or willing to share information with similar specialists in other divisions. Thus, the autonomy given to each division to pursue its own performance goals becomes an obstacle to achieving overall corporate goals. As a consequence, warn Hamel and Prahalad in *Competing for the Future*, 'corporate' strategy is little more than 'an amalgamation of individual business unit plans' and managerial strategic behaviour tends to be parochial, focusing only on existing business units (ref. 24, p. 309). From a worker's perspective, the outcome can be catastrophic: relocating to another geographical location means job loss as the firm's products or services are relocated to typically low-wage economies or outsourced and, in the case of public corporations, privatized.

In the **matrix structure**, both functional specialities and product or service orientation are maintained, and there are functional managers and product managers. Functional managers are responsible for the selection, training and development of technically competent workers in their functional area. Product managers, on the other hand, are responsible for coordinating the activities of workers from different functional areas who are working on the same product or service to customers. In a matrix design, employees report to two managers rather than to one (Figure 4.10).

EMERGING ORGANIZATIONAL DESIGNS: POST-BUREAUCRACY?

Since the 1980s, faced with accelerated changes in global capitalism, the limitations of bureaucracy and new technologies, such as the Internet, new post-bureaucratic forms of organization have emerged in the management literature: the flexible firm,[47] the cellular configuration,[48,49] the adhocracy configuration,[38] the postmodern

weblink
Go to www.starbucks.com/aboutus/international.asp to examine Starbucks' matrix structure, which combines functional and product divisions, with employees reporting to two heads

matrix structure: a type of departmentalization that overlays a divisionalized structure (typically a project team) with a functional structure

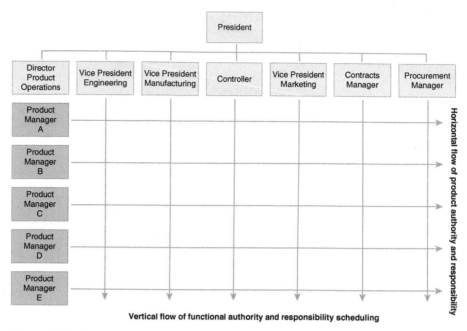

Figure 4.10 – An engineering company with a matrix design

organization,[50] the individualized corporation,[51] the re-engineered corporation,[52] and the virtual[53] and the networked[54] organization. All the post-bureaucratic forms of organization are conceived as substituting a hierarchical model of structure and implementing a more flexible work regime that gives workers limited empowerment.[55] A centre-piece of employment relations in the post-bureaucratic organization is a 'new pay' paradigm linking individual or group performance to rewards.[56,57] Three leading-edge post-bureaucratic configurations, which we examine here, are shown in Figure 4.5, above: horizontal, virtual and network.

The **horizontal or 'lean' structure** is the division of work into teams or 'cells' that are responsible for completing a whole process. A team-based organization uses decentralization to move decisions to the work teams, and gives limited autonomy to those teams to decide about product and service design, process design, quality and customer service. Typically, work-based regimes are accompanied by other management techniques such as just-in-time and total quality management.

Business process re-engineering

One design methodology with a process emphasis in a horizontal structure is **business process re-engineering** (BPR). According to the re-engineering guru James Champy, BPR is 'about changing our managerial work, the way we think about, organize, inspire, deploy, enable, measure, and reward the value-adding operational work. It is about changing management itself' (ref. 26, p. 3).

Structurally, the typical pyramid-shaped industrial model is stood on its head, management structures are leaner or 'delayered', and decision making is pushed down to the 'front line' to meet the contemporary demands for quality, flexibility, low cost and entrepreneurial autonomy. Some writers have described these anti-hierarchical characteristics in organizational design as a shift from 'modernist' to 'postmodernist' organizational forms and employee relations practices.[52]

horizontal or 'lean' structure: an integrated system of manufacturing, originally developed by Toyota in Japan. The emphasis is on flexibility and team work

business process re-engineering: a radical change of business processes by applying information technology to integrate operations, and maximizing their value-added content

Table 4.1 – The re-engineered and virtual organization

Characteristic	Bureaucratic model	Re-engineered model
Market	Domestic	Global
Competitive advantage	Cost	Speed and quality
Resources	Capital	Information
Quality	What is affordable	No compromise
Focal point	Profit	Customer
Structural design	Hierarchical	Flattened
Control	Centralized	Decentralized
Leadership	Autocratic	Shared
Labour	Homogeneous	Culturally diverse
Organization of work	Specialized and individual	Flexible and in teams
Communications	Vertical	Horizontal

emotional labour:
the effort, planning and control needed to express organizationally desired emotions during interpersonal transactions

weblink
Visit www.wbs.ac.uk/ faculty/research, the website at the University of Warwick, for information on publications on BPR. Alternatively, visit www. accenture.com and search for 'business process engineering'

'virtual' organization: an organization composed of people who are connected by video-teleconferences, the Internet and computer-aided design systems, and who may rarely, if ever, meet face to face

core competency: the underlying core characteristics of an organization's workforce that result in effective performance and give a competitive advantage to the firm

The re-engineered organization allegedly has a number of common characteristics (Table 4.1). Central to these organizational forms is the 'reconceptualization' of core employees, from being considered to be a variable cost to being represented as a valuable asset; capable of serving the customer without the need for a directive style of organizational leadership.[58] With the ascendancy of 'customer democracy', employees are encouraged not only to exercise initiative, but also to display **emotional labour** in creating value for customers. According to BPR proponent Hammer, 'Loyalty and hard work are by themselves quaint relics ... organizations must now urge employees to put loyalty to the customer ... because that is the only way the company will survive' (ref. 1, pp. 158–9). Unlike earlier movements in organizational design, re-engineering is market driven – the 'dictatorship of the customariat' – and, by focusing on the social interaction between the buyer and seller of services, rather than the relationship between employer and employee, BPR emphasizes emotional labour as a key aspect of competitiveness.

Re-engineering has been criticized largely by academics.[58–63] It is argued, for example, that the 'leaner' organization actually gives more power to a few: 'Removing some of the middle layers of organizations is not the same as altering the basic power structure ... By cutting out intermediary levels [of management] ... the power resources of those at the top can be increased' (ref. 60, p. 192).

Virtual organizations

In the age of the Internet, it is not unsurprising that the **'virtual' organization** has captured the attention of organizational analysts. The virtual organization is a temporary or permanent arrangement of otherwise independent companies or individuals, with a lead firm, to produce a product or service by sharing costs and core competencies. This ever-changing constellation of organizations is connected not through formal rules, but rather through virtual networks. A **core competency** is a knowledge and expertise base that resides in the organization.[24] The Internet, the

World Wide Web and information technology connect members of the network wherever they are in the world. Typically, data are electronically transferred around the virtual network and separate competency sets work on the data either sequentially or in parallel.[64] Several factors have driven organizations to adopt network-based modes of organizing: an increased requirement for flexibility and global learning, reducing market uncertainty, managing joint production, a high-tech base and the perceived need to manage cultural diversity.[65]

Corporate global network connections have forerunners in the eighteenth and nineteenth centuries, but they have figured as a pervasive, major aspect of organizational life in the twenty-first century.[39] A **networked organization** is a constellation of several independent organizations or communities of people, usually linked on a large project basis, such as aerospace alliances between specialist engineering firms. The firms or groups in the network have a more formal and long-term commercial relationship than in the virtual organization.[66] Hierarchy is sacrificed in order to speed decision making, and vertical integration is supplanted by horizontal integration across group boundaries. Each group in the network focuses on a set of competencies. This structure enables each community of people to be flexible and responsive to changes.[64]

Networks, argues Castells, have had a transformational effect on structures.[67] Examples of network structures exist at Amazon.com, Cisco Systems, Dell Computers and Mozilla Corporation. Perhaps the best-known company using a network structure is Amazon.com, a virtual bookstore with no inventory, online ordering and electronic links to its customers. Cisco Systems, another exemplar, produces 80 per cent of the world's Internet hardware using a global network of employees and suppliers using web-based technology. In a recent book, Clay Shirky argues that Internet technologies make it increasingly easy to create constellations of networked project groups (see the Critical Insight 'Business without Organizations', below).[68]

A virtual or network structure has neither a corporate head office nor an organizational chart. Mitchell Baker, the CEO of Mozilla Corporation, developer of the Firefox web browser, for example, describes her role not as head of the organization but as 'the coordinator and motivator of a group effort'.[69] Bartlett and Ghoshal describe an integrated global network structure with, for example, a firm in France receiving flows of components from across the globe.[70] The concept of an integrated networked structure emphasizes the shift from inflexible to permeable structures and processes, accompanied by significant flows of components, resources, information and people. Unilever is an example of a networked company that has pursued a transnational strategy, with 17 different and largely decentralized detergent plants in Europe alone.

The network structure offers employers access to wider markets, lower production costs, and the potential to respond quickly to new product and service developments and markets. The weakness of the network arrangement is that associates have little direct control over the functions done by other members of the network. The number of independent members in the network creates a high-dependency relationship between each company within the network. This requires new behaviours and a high trust in network members. Managers and knowledge workers need to radically modify their behaviours as strategic planning, for example, is no longer an independent activity, but a process needing coordination, information sharing and global learning.[70]

Although the networked organization may have been the favoured paradigm of the 1990s, the global economic recession of 2008/09 has caused firms to reassess the efficacy of the networked model. As *The Economist* reported, management wisdom had for two decades been to make companies as lean as possible,

network structure: a set of strategic alliances that an organization creates with suppliers, distributors and manufacturers to produce and market a product. Members of the network work together on a long-term basis to find new ways to improve efficiency and increase the quality of their products expanding just-in-time supplier networks around the globe and outsourcing all but core competencies, lubricated by cheap credit. In September 2008, the abrupt closure of the overnight commercial paper market to lubricate the system meant that most companies need to accumulate cash to meet such basic obligations as paying their employees. Thus, 'ultra-lean supply chains no longer look like a brilliant idea when you have to find cash to keep a supplier afloat that cannot get even basic trade credit' (ref. 71, p. 17). A case perhaps of 'just-in-time' being substituted for a 'just-in-case' network.

More sceptical analysts have found the 'dark side' of networks. A characteristic signature of networks is the exploitation of the less powerful by the more powerful members. Buttressing this assertion is evidence that employees experience 'uncertainty, ambiguity and frustration' in their attempts to enact their professional roles within this organizational form.[72] Countering the academic hype around 'post-bureaucratic' organizations is a recent study by Pulignano and Stewart. Analysing primarily qualitative data from global automotive companies, they persuasively argue that new employment arrangements have, paradoxically, revitalized Weber's typology of bureaucracy. According to the researchers, new employee performance-related incentives have generated behavioural rules that reinforce bureaucratic control at Fiat, VW and Renault: 'Thus, intriguingly, the use of bureaucratic control emerges as the main element of labour control in this type of workplace' (ref. 56, p. 104). Arguably, the binary bureaucratic/post-bureaucratic view of organizational design is a somewhat misleading analytical paradigm. In reality, new organizational structures are likely to be hybrids, new forms coexisting alongside some old enduring elements of bureaucracy.[73]

Critical insight

Business without organizations

The Internet and social networking sites are bringing people together like never before. Websites such as Facebook and Bebo make it extraordinarily easy to meet like-minded people, join groups and exchange ideas. What impact might this be having on business? Clay Shirky, author of the recent book *Here Comes Everybody: The Power of Organizing Without Organizations*,[68] argues that these new technologies could revolutionize the way in which businesses operate. But how? The story of rival web browsers Microsoft Internet Explorer and Mozilla Firefox provides an excellent example.

In the early 1990s, Internet Explorer appeared to have an unassailable lead in the web browser market, with an estimated market share of around 95 per cent in 2002. Microsoft's supremacy seemed assured when rival company AOL abandoned its own Netscape browser, leaving Internet Explorer with a near-monopoly. What happened next is a lesson in the growing power of informal networks and their increasing ability to take on big business. Former Netscape employees grouped together under the title The Mozilla Foundation and, using a small investment from AOL, began work on a new web browser. But The Mozilla Foundation was (and still is) no ordinary company: it is a non-profit-making organization, made up of not only staff, but also a network of volunteers and contributors – essentially, a community of Mozilla enthusiasts whose efforts are organized and coordinated electronically using the open-source model. In the words of Mozilla's CEO, Mitchell Baker, 'we build software, but we also build communities of people who build software and share a particular vision for what the future of the Internet should look like'.

This open-source model has enabled Mozilla to draw on a vast array of talent and creativity without having to become a huge, unwieldy corporation – and in this way, it gains competitive advantage over more traditional business set-ups. Any given individual might only contribute one idea to the development of the browser – their output could be very limited, but their input to the project could be crucial. Mozilla can harness the skills of such individuals without having to employ them full time – meaning that it can avoid becoming a vast, bureaucratic and hierarchical organization.

The success of Mozilla's model speaks for itself: Firefox's market share has increased to around 20 per cent since its foundation, and it now has over 100 million users worldwide – an incredible achievement and a very speedy growth rate, particularly given that it was pitting itself against the fearsome might of an established Microsoft product.

Consider the following question: Do you think that traditional corporations are the *solution* to our problems or *are* the problem? How can Facebook and Twitter transform organizational structure and design?

Source: Based on an article by Ken Hunt (2009), 'The chaos theory of organization', *Report on Business*, March, pp. 16–18.

Further research: Shirky, C. (2008) *Here Comes Everybody: The Power of Organizing Without Organizations*, New York: Penguin.[88]

Implications for organizational behaviour

The downsizing and restructuring to create 'lean and mean' high-performance workplaces hit employees across the globe with cataclysmic force in the global economic recession that emerged in 2008–09. By definition, downsizing and restructuring include both high and poor performers. Employees are therefore usually correct in predicting job losses, extensive changes in the way they perform their work, work intensification, skill changes and changes in employee relations.

It is well documented that relocating operations to an NIE or outsourcing and privatizing a service in a public sector organization can have major employment implications. Downsizing has a chilling effect on the psychological climate, much as high levels of unemployment depress wage rates. Well-documented empirical research shows that, for the survivors of corporate restructuring, there can be detrimental effects on work motivation and commitment building, as well as fundamentally redefining the contours of employment relations.[43] The trauma of downsizing has predictable negative effects on the psychological well-being of individuals. 'Survivors typically are less loyal and less willing to provide service to customers and support for fellow employees,' opines Denise Rousseau (ref. 74, p. 212). The effects of the global recession and downsizing on the psychological climate also include negative perceptions about corporate leaders and decreased trust in management on the part of the survivors and the public generally.[75]

GENDER, SEXUALITY AND ORGANIZATIONAL DESIGN

Alongside management debates on organizational structures, there is a body of critical literature that focuses on relationships between gender, sexuality and organizational design. The term 'sexuality' refers to sexual characters and sexual behaviour in the workplace. Sexuality pervades organizations through pornographic pin-ups, innuendo, gossip and sexist joking. While it serves to affirm men's sense of shared masculinity, sexuality can, in a male-dominated workplace, serve to make women feel uncomfortable. Leaving the organization is often seen as the only alternative.[76,77]

Studies of the gendering of organizations emphasize that gender and sexuality make an overwhelming difference to organizational reality.[78–82] The studies draw attention to the double problem of women entering work organizations: discrimination and gender harassment. The first part of the problem is entering occupations and professions that have traditionally been occupied by men (for example, manual trades and white-collar professions).[83] The notion that 'gendered occupations', that is, ones that associate job requirements with the perceived qualities of a particular sex, has generated debate in organizational studies over the extent to which organizations and their hierarchical structures can be considered as gendered. The second part of the problem is that, once in the organization, many women face gender harassment, making it difficult for women to move into positions of authority. This is often referred to as a 'glass ceiling' – invisible, informal barriers to promotion to higher positions of authority in the organizational hierarchy.

Legislation making direct gender discrimination and harassment unlawful means that it is more common for male and even some female subordinates to hinder in indirect ways the promotion of women. Indirect gender harassment may be an identifiable element of an organization's culture. Gender analysis questions research findings and analysis that segregate studies of organizational behaviour from those of gender divisions in the labour market, patriarchal power, issues of workplace inequality and 'dual-role' work–family issues.[84] More importantly, however, including the 'gender and sexuality paradigm' in the study of the organizational structure and restructuring has pushed the boundaries of organizational behaviour by examining the people who are deemed to be the 'recipients' of organizational design.

As sociologist Judy Wajcman observes in her insightful study, the individual and the modern bureaucracy are not gender-neutral. Indeed, more controversially perhaps, she presents a powerful argument for gender-inclusive organizational theories if we accept her main premise that 'gender is woven into the very fabric of bureaucratic hierarchy and authority relations' (ref. 84, p. 47).

OB and globalization

Gender equality in times of economic transition: women workers in Russia

The late twentieth century brought significant changes to world of work in Eastern Europe and the former Soviet Union. The fall of Communist state governments was accompanied by a massive restructuring of national and local economies, and of the social lives of the workers who populated these institutions. While old-order policies and practices were pushed aside in favour of open markets, social and cultural attitudes about gender endured, often extending into the offices and boardrooms of organizations navigating this massive capitalist shift.

By the late 1990s, the new Russian economy was starting to look up, buoyed by successes in high-tech and natural resource sectors. Russian women, in particular, made strides in the new economy, creating successful businesses catering to the burgeoning Russian consumer culture. Two decades after this transition, scholars and journalists are turning a critical eye to how gendered experiences of work in post-Soviet Russia continue to be affected by enduring cultural attitudes about women in Russian society.

According to Russian *Vogue* magazine editor Alyona Doletskaya, although career opportunities for women in Russia have changed significantly over the past few decades, women workers continue to overpopulate sectors such as fashion, service and public relations (Weir, 2005). Furthermore, women's salaries are substantially lower than those of their male counterparts. Weir writes, 'A recent survey of living standards … suggested that of the poorest 15 percent of Russians, 68 percent are women. Many of the poor are well-educated women who find their skills unrewarded in the new economic order.'

The contemporary experiences of Russian women in the workforce can be linked to the Soviet era, when women were often relegated to undesirable, low-wage work, a pattern that reflected state support for, and reproduction of, wider cultural attitudes about gender roles. Today, although the transition to a free market economy has resulted in access to new types of work for Russian women workers, enduring cultural attitudes about gender roles continue to affect women's abilities to participate fully in the new Russian economy. This period of economic, political and social transition in Russia provides us with an opportunity to consider how cultural attitudes about gender can span major systemic changes, influencing local people's experience of such transitions. It also raises questions about how, over time, the new economic and political orders in Russia will affect local constructions of gender.

stop!   Using gender as an example, consider the often-entwined relationships between cultural beliefs and economic and governance systems. How do local attitudes about gender influence government and economic policy and practice? How do governments and economies influence local constructions of gender?

What kinds of societal attitude and practice related to gender extend into workplaces where you live? Who should be responsible for regulating gender roles and gender equity in the workplace?

How should 'gender equality' be defined? Are there different organizational approaches to achieving equity?

In times of political and economic upheaval, support for social conservatism can surge. How might this claim be used to explain – or dispute – the experiences of Russian women workers described above?

Sources and further information

Ashwin, S. (2005) *Adapting to Russia's New Labour Market: Gender and Employment Strategy*, New York: Routledge.
Brainerd, E. (1998) 'Winners and losers in Russia's economic transition', *American Economic Review*, 88(5), pp. 94–115.
McGregor, C. (2003) 'Getting beyond the glass ceiling', *Moscow Times*, February 10. Available at: www.clumba.com/news.asp?ob_no=2927 (accessed October 2, 2009).
Weir, F. (2005) 'For Moscow's businesswomen, a powerful new role', *Christian Science Monitor*. Available at: www.csmonitor.com/2005/0308/p07s01-woeu.html; www.usatoday.com/news/world/2005-03-07-russsia-women_x.htm (accessed October 2, 2009).
Note: This feature was written by Gretchen Fox, PhD, Anthropologist, Timberline Natural Resource Group, Canada.

CHAPTER SUMMARY

○ We have attempted to cover a wide range of complex issues in this chapter. Organizational structure refers to the formal division of work or labour, and the formal pattern of relationships that coordinate and control organizational activities, whereas organizational design refers to the process of creating a structure that best fits a strategy, technology and environment.

○ The three core dimensions of formal organizational structure – complexity, formalization and centralization – can be combined into different types or models. Three descriptive models were examined: mechanistic, bureaucratic and organic. The mechanistic organization has been likened to a machine. It is characterized by highly specialized tasks that tend to be rigidly defined, a hierarchical authority and control structure, and communications that primarily take the form of edicts and decisions issued by managers to subordinates. Communication typically flows vertically from the top down. Thus, it has high complexity, high formalization and high centralization. A mechanistic organization resembles a bureaucracy. A bureaucratic organization is a rational and systematic division of work. Within it, rules and techniques of control are precisely defined. A bureaucratic design allows for large-scale accomplishments. The disadvantages associated with bureaucracy include suppression of initiative through overcontrol.

○ Organic organizations are the antithesis of mechanistic organizations. They are characterized by being low in complexity, formality and centralization. A post-bureaucratic organizational structure, such as team-based structures and those produced by BPR, is organic and highly adaptable. However, the binary bureaucratic/post-bureaucratic view of organizational design may be a somewhat misleading analytical device.

○ The contingency view of formal organizational design focuses on strategy, size, technology and environment. A change in business strategy may require changing the manufacturing process and the organizational design, for example moving from a functional to a team-based organizational structure. Large organizations will tend to be more centralized and have more rules and techniques of control. Organizations with complex non-routine technologies will tend to have more complex organizational arrangements. Organizations with routine technologies will tend to use written rules and procedures to control people's behaviour, and decision making will be more centralized than in establishments using non-routine technologies.

○ An organization's external environment can range from 'stable' to' dynamic' and from 'hostile' to 'munificent'. Distinct external environments help to explain divergent patterns of managerial behaviour and organizational structure. For example, organic configurations are better suited to dynamic and hostile environments so that organizational members can adapt more quickly to changes.

○ The external context has a significant impact on managerial and employee behaviour. The external domain influences the formal structure and functioning of a work organization, and in turn the organization's leaders influence the wider society. The linkage between external contexts and the search for competitive advantage through employee performance and managerial activities is complex. We have therefore emphasized that organizational behaviour studies must be able to deal with the new complexities and nuances. Caught up in the drama of severe economic recession, there is a need for a multidimensional approach to the study of organizational behaviour.

○ The analysis offered here provides a guide to how formal organizational structure helps to shape the behaviour of managers and employees. The contingency elements identified – strategy, size, technology, environment, culture and HRM systems – are not separate, but are integrated and linked in complex ways. It is within this integrated framework that interpretations of competing resources, conversations and interests take place, and influence people's behaviour in many ways.

KEY CONCEPTS

bureaucracy
horizontal
mechanistic
network structure
organic
technological change
virtual organization

VOCAB CHECKLIST FOR ESL STUDENTS

○ Artefacts
○ Business process re-engineering
○ Capitalist, capitalism, capitalize
○ Centralization, centralize, central
○ Competitive advantage
○ Complexity, complex
○ Core competency
○ Divisional structure
○ Emotional labour
○ Environment, environmental
○ Formal organization
○ Formalization
○ Functional configuration
○ Globalization, globalist, globalize, global
○ Horizontal structure

- Information structure
- Lean structure
- Matrix structure
- Mechanism organization
- Networking, network
- Network structure
- Organic organization
- Organization chart
- Organizational design
- Organizational politics
- Organizational structure
- Span of control
- Specialization, special, specialize
- Strategic business unit
- Virtual organization

CHAPTER REVIEW QUESTIONS

1 Compare and contrast a 'mechanistic' and a 're-engineered' organization. What is it like to be a manager making decisions in these two types of organization? What employees' behaviours are likely to be rewarded? What type of competitive strategy is each best suited to?
2 Why is there no 'one best way' to design an organization's structure?
3 What is the link between organizational structure and technology?
4 Why do organizations in fast-change and unstable environments have different structures from those in stable environments?
5 Review the 'new' forms of organizational design described in this chapter. Discuss the designs that you and other students finding appealing and challenging. Explain your reasons.
6 Does Internet web-based technology have the potential to demolish bureaucracy?

CHAPTER RESEARCH QUESTIONS

1 Read the Critical Insight 'Business without Organizations', above. Form a study group. Thinking about how you use Facebook and Twitter, sketch out how new social networking sites (a) provide an opportunity to change the form of organizational structure and design, (b) can create new services or products, and (c) can enhance the delivery of your orgnizational behaviour course and other courses in your university programme.
2 Obtain a copy of *The Oxford Handbook of Work and Organization* (see Further Reading). 'Post-bureaucracy?', discuss why the authors believe that emerging post-bureaucratic forms operate more as a means of *legitimating* change and innovation than as a concrete indicator of changing forms of work organization.
3 Read the article by Jonathan Morris et al. (2008), listed in Further Reading. What empirical evidence do the researchers provide of a shift towards new governance post-bureaucratic forms of work organization?

FURTHER READING

Acker, J. (2008) 'Helpful men and feminist support: more than double strangeness', *Gender, Work and Organizations*, **15**(3), pp. 288–93.

Alvesson, M. and Thompson, P. (2006) 'Post-bureaucracy?', pp. 485–507 in S. Ackroyd, R. Batt, P. Thompson and P. Tolbert, (eds), *The Oxford Handbook of Work and Organization*, York New: Oxford University Press.

Armstrong-Stassen, M. and Schlosser, F. (2008) 'Taking a positive approach to organizational downsizing', *Canadian Journal of Administrative Science*, **25**, pp. 93–106.

Bakan, J. (2004) *The Corporation*, London: Penguin.

Currie, G., Finn, R. and Martin, G. (2008) 'Accounting for the "dark side" of new organizational forms: the case of healthcare professionals', *Human Relations*, **61**(4), pp. 539–64.

Du Gay, P. (2000) *In Praise of Bureaucracy*. London: Sage.

Fulop, L., Hayward, H., and Lilley, S. (2009) 'Managing structure', pp. 195–237 in S. Linstead, L. Fulop and S. Lilley (eds), *Management and Organization: A Critical Text* (2nd edn), Basingstoke: Palgrave.

Grey, C. (2005) *A Very Short, Fairly Interesting and Reasonably Cheap Book about Studying Organizations*, London: Sage.

Hammer, M. (1997) *Beyond Reengineering*, New York: Harper Business.

Lazonick, W. (2006) 'Corporate restructuring', pp. 577–601 in S. Ackroyd, R. Batt, P. Thompson and P. S. Tolbert (eds), *The Oxford Handbook of Work and Organization*, Oxford: Oxford University Press.

Morris, J., Hassard, J. and McCann, L. (2008) 'The resilience of institutionalized capitalism: managing managers under "shareholder capitalism" and "managerial capitalism"', *Human Relations*, **61**(5), pp. 687–710.

Pulignano, V. and Stewart, P. (2006) 'Bureaucracy transcended? New patterns of employment regulation and labour control in the international automotive industry', *New Technology, Work and Employment*, **21**(2), pp. 90–106.

Tyler, M. and Wilkinson, A. (2007) 'The tyranny of corporate slenderness: "corporate anorexia" as a metaphor for our age', *Work, Employment and Society*, **21**(3), pp. 537–49.

Chapter case study 1

Strategy and design in Australia's tourism industry

Setting

Tourism is a strong contributor to Australia's economy, with over a half million people employed in the sector, and tourism spending reaching over $85 billion a year. The country promotes its beautiful landscapes, Aboriginal art and culture, coastal lifestyles and the outback as main attractions for visitors.

Australia's top five international tourism markets are New Zealand, the UK, Japan, the USA and China. Visitor numbers from the emerging markets of China and India have grown strongly, while the numbers of Japanese and Korean tourists have declined in the last few years. China is now Australia's fifth largest international tourism market, bringing it into second place with New Zealand, and this is set to grow over the next decade.

However, Australia's share of global tourism continues to drop, with a decrease of 14 per cent between 1995 and 2008. Since its peak in 2001, it has also declined as a proportion of Australia's gross domestic product. The Australian tourism industry continues to struggle from the effects of a series of crises, starting with a pilot strike in 1989 and the worldwide economic outfalls of the Iraq War and the SARS outbreak in more recent years. Skilled staff shortages are also contributing to the industry's troubles, with an estimated 42,000 employees needed by 2015.

The problem

Established in the early 1990s, Outback Inc. is an adventure-based tour company located in Sydney, Australia. The company offers a variety of services, including guided tours, accommodation and meals, to those wishing to visit remote and regional areas of Australia. Outback's comprehensive packages of services appeal to travellers from all over the world, particularly visitors from Japan, who typically make up over 80 per cent of their client base. However, despite increased marketing efforts aimed at the general Asian market, the company has seen a decrease in bookings from its traditionally reliable Japanese sector. Outback has yet to attract new clients from China or other Asian countries experiencing more favourable economic conditions.

Although Outback grew from a small, family-owned business in the early 1990s to a moderately sized company with sales of several million dollars a year, it still retains its original functional organizational structure. Outback's managers, typically members of the company's founding family, head up the various departments, which are structured around traditional functions such as marketing, finance and human resources. Although the company does have its own website, management has been hesitant to move away from using standard travel agencies for their client booking purposes.

As with most organizations in the hospitality field, the Outback management uses a traditional leadership style, with decisions made at the top levels of management and communicated downwards. The majority of Outback's employees are young, highly motivated and eager for learning opportunities, but the company struggles to retain them, facing a turnover rate higher than even what is expected in an industry with a notorious turnover culture.

Management recently made the decision to hire a consultant whom they hoped could make some recommendations to help attract new clients and stop the flow of employees walking out of the door.

Tasks

As a consultant hired by the Outback management, prepare a short presentation addressing the following questions:

1 Would you recommend a change in the company's functional structural arrangement? If yes, which of the other three common structural configurations (product/service, division, matrix) would you recommend? Why?
2 How does your recommended structure fit with a strategy that could help with Outback's goal to attract new clients?
3 Would you characterize Outback as a mechanistic organization? How might this contribute to a high turnover of its staff?

Essential reading

Navickas, V. (2007) 'The reasons and consequences of changes in organizational structures of tourism companies', *Economics and Management*, pp. 809–13.

Ogaard, T., Marnburg, E. and Larsen, S. (2008) 'Perceptions of organizational structure in the hospitality industry: consequences for commitment, job satisfaction and perceived performance', *Tourism Management*, **29**(4), pp. 661–71.

Tribe, J. (1997) *Corporate Strategy for Tourism*, London: International Thomson Business Press.

For more information on Australia's tourism industry and the challenges it faces, go to www.tourism.australia.com/home.asp

Note

This is a fictional case study. It was written by Lori Rilkoff, MSc, CHRP, Senior Human Resources Manager at the City of Kamloops, and lecturer in HRM at Thompson Rivers University, BC, Canada.

Chapter case study 2

ABC's just-in-time supply chain

Visit www.palgrave.com/business/brattonob2e to view this case study.

WEB-BASED ASSIGNMENT

This chapter discusses the different types of organizational design, and the interconnectedness between structure and restructuring, and organizational behaviour. Organizations can adopt a large number of structures to match their strategy, size, technology and profit-making imperative. Restructuring affects job design and individual workers' perception of the employer and work motivation.

This web-based assignment requires you to explore the web to find a site that displays an organizational chart, or that discusses a method of managing its structure. For example, enter the website of Dell Computers (www.dell.com), Canadian TV and media company Globalmedia (www.globalmedia.ca) or car manufacturer Saturn (www.saturn.com) for an example of a 'flatter' organizational structure.

Consider these questions:

⊚ What kind of organizational structure does the company have (for example, in terms of decision making, is it centralized or decentralized)?
⊚ In what ways is the organizational structure appropriate for the company?

OB IN FILMS

The documentary film *The Corporation* (2003) offers an excellent collection of case studies, anecdotes and true confessions from corporate elites, which reveal structural contradictions and behind-the-scenes tensions. The documentary also features many critical perspectives, including interviews with Noam Chomsky, Michael Moore, Maude Barlow and Naomi Klein.

What examples are given to substantiate the claim that corporations, if left unregulated, behave much like individuals with 'a psychopathic personality', creating destruction? What examples of corporate crime does the film illustrate?

REFERENCES

1. Hammer, M. (1997) *Beyond Reengineering*, New York: Harper Business.
2. Lazonick, W. (2006) 'Corporate restructuring', pp. 577–601 in S. Ackroyd, R. Batt, P. Thompson and P. S. Tolbert (eds), *The Oxford Handbook of Work & Organization*, Oxford: Oxford University Press.
3. Baumol, J. W., Blinder, S. A. and Wolff, N. E. (2003) *Downsizing in America*, New York: Russell Sage Foundation Press.
4. Delbridge, R. (1998) *Life on the Line in Contemporary Manufacturing*, Oxford: Oxford University Press.
5. Gowing, M. K., Kraft, J. D. and Campbell Quick, J. (eds) (1997) *New Organizational Reality: Downsizing, Restructuring, and Revitalization*, Washington, DC: American Psychological Association.
6. Hales, C. (2002) 'Bureacracy-lite and continuities in management work', *British Journal of Management*, **13**(1), pp. 51–66.
7. Innes, P. and Littler, C. (2004) 'A decade of downsizing: understanding the contours of change in Australia, 1990–99', *Asia Pacific Journal of Human Resources*, **42**(2), pp. 229–42.
8. Legge, K. (2000) 'Personal management in the lean organization', pp. 43–69 in S. Bach and K. Sisson (eds), *Personal Management*, Oxford: Blackwell.
9. Littler, C. and Innes, P. (2004) 'The paradox of managerial downsizing', *Organizational Studies*, **25**(7), pp. 1159–84.
10. Moody, K. (1997) *Workers in a Lean World*, London: Verso.
11. Womack, J., Jones, D. and Roos, D. (1990) *The Machine that Changed the World*, London: HarperCollins.
12. Tyler, M. and Wilkinson, A. (2007) 'The tyranny of corporate slenderness: "corporate anorexia" as a metaphor for our age', *Work, Employment and Society*, **21**(3), pp. 537–49.
13. Drucker, P. F. (1997) 'Toward the new organization', pp. 1–5 in F. Hesselbein, M. Goldsmith and R. Beckhard (eds), *The Organization of the Future*, San Francisco: Jossey-Bass.
14. Gadiesh, O. and Olivet, S. (1997) 'Designing for implementability', pp. 53–78 in F. Hesselbein, M. Goldsmith and R. Beckhard (eds), *The Organization of the Future*, San Francisco: Jossey-Bass.

15. Drucker, P. (1954/1993) *The Practice of Management*, New York: HarperCollins.
16. Galbraith, J. R. (1996) 'Designing the innovative organization', pp. 156–81 in K. Starkey (ed.), *How Organizations Learn*, London: International Thomson Business Press.
17. Bratton, J. (1999) 'Gaps in the workplace learning paradigm: labour flexibility and job design', in Conference Proceeding of Researching Work and Learning, First International Conference, University of Leeds, UK.
18. Herriot, P. (1998) 'The role of human resource management in building a new proposition', pp. 106–16 in P. Sparrow and M. Marchington (eds), *Human Resource Management: A New Agenda*, London: Financial Times Management.
19. Watson, T. (1995) *Sociology of Work and Industry* (3rd edn), London: Routledge.
20. Thompson, P. and McHugh, D. (2006) *Work Organizations: A Critical Introduction* (4th edn), Basingstoke: Palgrave.
21. Clegg, S. and Dunkerley, D. (1980) *Organization, Class and Control*, London: Routledge & Kegan Paul.
22. Hardy, C. and Clegg, S. R. (1999) 'Some dare call it power', pp. 368–87 in S. R. Clegg and C. Hardy (eds), *Studying Organization*, London: Sage.
23. Clegg, S., Hardy, C. and Nord, W. (eds) (1999) *Managing Organizations: Current Issues,* Thousand Oaks, CA: Sage.
24. Hamel, G. and Prahalad, C. K. (1994) *Competing for the Future*, Boston, MA: Harvard Business School Press.
25. Daft, R. (2001) *Organization Theory and Design* (7th edn), Cincinnati, OH: South-Western.
26. Champy, J. (1996) *Reengineering Management*, New York: HarperCollins.
27. Burns, T. and Stalker, G. M. (1966) *The Management of Innovation* (2nd edn), London: Tavistock.
28. Chandler, A. (1962) *Strategy and Structure*, Cambridge, MA: MIT Press.
29. Keats, B. W. and Hitt, M. (1988) 'A causal model of linkages among environmental dimensions, macro organizational characteristics, and performance', *Academy of Management Journal*, September, pp. 570–98.
30. Klein, N. (2000) *No Logo*, London: Flamingo.
31. Blau, P. M. and Schoenherr, R. A. (1971) *The Structure of Organizations*, New York: Basic Books.
32. Pugh, D., Hickson, C, Hining, R. and Turner, C. (1969) 'The context of organization structures', *Administrative Science Quarterly*, **14**, pp. 91–114.
33. Child, J. (1972) 'Organizational structure, environment and performance: the role of strategic choice', *Sociology*, **6**(1), pp. 331–50.
34. Aldrich, H. (1972) 'Technology and organizational structure: a re-examination of the findings of the Aston Group', *Administrative Science Quarterly*, **17**(1), pp. 26–43.
35. Woodward, J. (1965) *Industrial Organizations: Theory and Practice*, London: Oxford University Press.
36. Thompson, J. D. (1967) *Organizations in Action*, New York: McGraw-Hill.
37. Aldrich, H. E. (2002) 'Technology and organizational structure: a reexamination of the findings of the findings of the Aston Group', pp. 344–66 in S. R. Clegg (ed.), *Central Currents in Organization Studies,* London: Sage
38. Mintzberg, H. (1993) *Structure in Fives: Designing Effective Organizations* (7th edn), Englewood Cliffs, NJ: Prentice Hall.
39. Scholte, J. A. (2005) *Globalization: A Critical Introduction*, Basingstoke: Palgrave Macmillan.
40. Sklair, L. (2002) *Globalization: Capitalism and its Alternatives*, Oxford: Oxford University Press.
41. Hoogvelt, A. (2001) *Globalization and the Postcolonial World* (2nd edn), Basingstoke: Palgrave.
42. Orsburn, J. and Moran, L. (2000) *The New Self-Directed Work Teams*, New York: McGraw-Hill.
43. Mabey, C., Salaman, G. and Storey, J. (1998) *Human Resource Management: A Strategic Introduction* (2nd edn), Oxford: Blackwell.
44. Mintzberg, H. (1983) *Structure in Fives: Designing Effective Organizations*, Englewood Cliffs, NJ: Prentice Hall.

45. Hill, C. and Jones, G. (2004) *Strategic Management Theory*, New York: Houghton Mifflin.
46. Jacoby, S. M. (2005) *The Embedded Corporation: Corporate Governance and Employment Relations in Japan and the United States*, Princeton, NJ: Princeton University Press.
47. Atkinson, J. (1984) 'Manpower strategies for flexible organizations', *Personnel Management*, August, pp. 14–25.
48. Bratton, J. A. (1992) *The Japanization of Work*, London: Macmillan.
49. Miles R. E., Snow, C. C., Matthews, J. A. and Coleman, H. J. (1997) 'Organizing in the knowledge area: anticipating the cellular form', *Academy of Management Executive*, **11**(4), pp. 7–20.
50. Hassard, J. and Parker, M. (1993) *Postmodernism and Organizations*, London: Sage.
51. Ghoshal, S. and Bartlett, C. A. (1997) *The Individualized Corporation: A Fundamentally New Approach to Management: Great Companies Are Defined by Purpose, Process, and People.* New York: Harper Business.
52. Hammer, M. and Champy, J. (1993) *Reengineering the Corporation: A Manifesto for Business Revolution*, New York: Harper Business.
53. Goldman, S. L., Nagel, R. N. and Preiss, K. (1995) *Agile Competition and Virtual Organizations: Strategies for Enriching the Customer*, New York: Van Nostrand Reinhold.
54. Powell, W. W. (2003) 'Neither market nor hierarchy: network forms of organization', pp. 315–30 in M. J. Handel (ed.), *The Sociology of Organizations*, Thousand Oaks, CA: Sage.
55. Clarke, T. and Clegg, S. R. (1998) *Changing Paradigms: The Transformation of Management for the 21st Century*, London: Collins.
56. Pulignano, V. and Stewart, P. (2006) 'Bureaucracy transcended? New patterns of employment regulation and labour control in the international automotive industry', *New Technology, Work and Employment*, **21**(2), pp. 90–106.
57. Corby, S., Palmer, S. and Lindop, E. (2009) *Rethinking Reward*, Basingstoke: Palgrave.
58. Willmott, H., (1995) 'The odd couple?: re-engineering business processes: managing human relations', *New/Technology, Work and Employment*, **10**(2), pp. 89–98.
59. Reed, M. I. (1993) 'Organizations and modernity: continuity and discontinuity in organization theory', pp. 163–82 in J. Hassard and M. Parker (eds), *Postmodernism and Organizations*, London: Sage.
60. Thompson, P. (1993) 'Fatal distraction: postmodernism and organizational theory', in. J. Hassard and M. Parker (eds), *Postmodernism and Organizations*, London: Sage.
61. Craig, J. and Yetton, P. (1993) 'Business process redesigns critique of *Process Innovation* by Thomas Davenport as a case study in the literature', *Australian Journal of Management*, **17**(2), pp. 285–306.
62. Oliver, J. (1993) 'Shocking to the core', *Management Today*, August, pp. 18–21.
63. Grint, K. and Willcocks, L. (1995) 'Business process re-engineering in theory and practice: business paradise regained?', *New Technology, Work and Employment*, **10**(2), pp. 99–108.
64. Davidow, W. H. and Malone, M. A. (1992) *The Virtual Corporation: Structuring and Revitalizing the Corporation for the 21st Century*, New York: HarperCollins.
65. Ferlie, E. and Pettigrew, A. (1998) 'Managing through networks', pp. 200–22 in C. Mabey, G. Salaman and J. Storey (eds), *Strategic Human Resource Management: A Reader*, London: Sage.
66. Rocket, J. F. and Short, J. E. (1991) 'The networked organization and the management of interdependence', in M. S. Scott Morton (ed.), *The Corporation of the 1990s: Information Technology and Organizational Transformation*, Oxford: Oxford University Press.
67. Castells, M. (2000) *The Information Age: Economy, Society and Culture*, Volume 1: *The Rise of Network Society* (2nd edn), London: Blackwell.
68. Shirky, C. (2008) *Here Comes Everybody: The Power of Organizing Without Organizations*, New York: Penguin.
69. Baker, M. Quoted in Hunt, K. (2009) 'The chaos theory of organization', *Report on Business*, March, p. 18.
70. Bartlett C. A. and Ghoshal, S. (1989) *Managing Across Borders: The Transnational Solution*, London: Random House.

71. Anonymous (2008) 'All you need is cash', *Economist,* November 22, p. 17.

72. Currie, G., Finn, R. and Martin, G. (2008) 'Accounting for the "dark side" of new organizational forms: the case of healthcare professionals', *Human Relations*, **61**(4), pp. 539–64.

73. Dunford, R., Palmer, I., Benveniste, J. and Crawford, J. (2007) 'Coexistence of "old" and "new" organizational practices: transitory phenomenon or enduring feature?', *Asia Pacific Journal of Human Resources*, **45**(1), pp. 24–43.

74. Rousseau, D. M. (1995) *Psychological Contracts in Organizations*, Thousand Oaks, CA: Sage.

75. Clarke, J. and Koonce, R. (1995) 'Engaging organizational survivors', *Training and Development*, **49**(8), pp. 22–30.

76. Mills, A. and Tancred, P. (eds) (1992) *Gendering Organizational Analysis*, Newbury Park, CA: Sage.

77. Hearn, J., Sheppard, D., Tancred-Sheriff, R. and Burrell, G. (eds) (1989) *The Sexuality of Organization*, London: Sage.

78. Dex, S. (1988) 'Gender and the labour market', pp. 281–309 in D. Gallie (ed.), *Employment in Britain*, Oxford: Blackwell.

79. Witz, A. (1986) 'Patriarchy and the labour market: occupational control strategies and the medical division of labour', in D. Knights and H. Willmott (eds), *Gender and the Labour Process*, Aldershot: Gower.

80. Knights, D. and Willmott, H. (eds) (1986) *Gender and the Labour Process*, Aldershot: Gower.

81. Phillips, R. and Phillips, E. (1993) *Women and Work: Inequality in the Canadian Labour Market*, Toronto: Lorimer.

82. Wilson, F. M. (2003) *Organizational Behaviour and Gender*, Farnham: Ashgate.

83. Ledwith, S. and Colgan, F. (eds.) (1996) *Women in Organizations: Challenging Gender Politics*, London: Palgrave Macmillan.

84. Wajcman, J. (1998) *Managing Like a Man: Women and Men in Corporate Management*, Cambridge, MA: Polity Press/Penn State University Press.

Chapter
5

MANAGING THE HUMAN FACTOR

Before 1912–13, engineering, accounting, and economics were the only bodies of knowledge relevant to systematic management. If consolidations of the 'human factor' were at all involved, they were based on philosophy, ethics and religion.

(Shenhav, 1999: 181)

Managers had, by the early part of the twentieth century, already drawn on the expertise of people such as Taylor and other consultants in order to develop systems of controlling the labour process. It was not enough. As Baritz observes in his brilliant account of the historical uses of social science in American industry, 'Increasingly the men who manage and direct industry, find themselves incapable of effectively controlling their organisations' (1960: 3). After the First World War, some major corporations began financing industrial psychology and endowing business schools as part of a process of research and experimentation. That interaction was eventually to result in the emergence of the *human relations* approach to management. The two approaches have traditionally been seen as opposites. Perrow's somewhat tongue-in-cheek description sums it up: 'From the beginning, the forces of light and darkness have polarised the field of organisational analysis, and the struggle has been protracted and inconclusive' (1973: 2). However, the forces of darkness and light may not be as far apart as they seem. As we shall show, corporate co-operation with social scientists arose from the same source as links with Taylorism: the vulnerability of management to the appeal of planning and science.

The aims of this chapter are to:

- Explore the historical development of human relations ideas and practices, their links to Scientific Management and early corporate life.
- Set out the distinctive characteristics of human relations and the extent to which they derive from the Hawthorne Studies and Mayo's perspectives.
- Examine the (often limited) legacies left for modern management, from work design to corporate culture.
- Demonstrate how human resource management (HRM) emerged from the personnel function and corporate welfare to claim the territory of management of the human factor.

SOCIAL SCIENCE AND INDUSTRY: A COURTSHIP

The courtship between social science and industry began with the promise of a dowry in the form of a battery of tests and measurements offered to fit people to jobs. While this does represent a shift from measurement of work to measurement of people, it was not wholly new. This kind of intervention represented a version of Taylor's 'scientific selection of the worker' by other means. In fact the *Bulletin of the Taylor Society* carried articles discussing issues of human personality and arguing that newly recruited workers should be tested for personality, character and temperament. In 1915, an article about one factory noted that:

> A system of cards was used, one side of each card contained information about the worker's identity, parents, ethnic origins and previous employment; the other contained a certain amount of medico-psychological information ('anaemic', 'nonchalant') and notes on the individual's degree of motivation and way of life ('father out of work', 'mother agreed to take care of child', etc.). This was followed by his medical record (doctor, optician, dentist) and by basic health advice on the need for rest and fresh air.
>
> (Doray, 1988: 188)

This was part of a growing interest shown by engineers in the human factor and employment issues. Professional journals began to run articles such as 'Personality in the Shop Psychology of the Female Employee' (see Shenhav, 1999: 182).

This primitive psychology was openly geared towards manipulation of the 'uncertainties of human nature' (Shenhav, 1999: 174). In this sense, far from being a different academic species, it is arguable that the human relations current was partly prefigured in engineering discourses and derived from a form of Taylorist revisionism. Nor did it challenge Taylorism on its traditional territory of organisation of work. Nevertheless the battle cry of 'neglect of the human factor' did represent a partial critique that was directed against the costs of scientific management in terms of resistance and disenchantment. The simple appeal and apparent applicability of the variety of tests convinced a growing minority of employers. Problems arose when naïve enthusiasm and unrealistic expectations quickly ran up against the crude nature and limited results arising from the techniques. By the mid-1920s, and in changed economic circumstances, the tests had been abandoned by most companies (Baritz, 1960: 71).

Though a similar overlap in topics with scientific management can be observed (see Table 4.1), accounts of the development of British industrial psychology (M. Rose, 1975: 65–87; G. Brown, 1977: 213–28) show it to be more sober, centralised, less consultancy-based and affecting even fewer firms. It took a particular interest – derived from experiences of the Industrial Fatigue Research Board during the war – in monotony. Fatigue was, as we have seen, an issue that also concerned the scientific management movement, linked as it was to the need for the successful measurement of work. Common interests and client relations again meant, as in the US, 'a large proportion of their problems had to be taken over from the scientific managers' (M. Rose, 1975: 86). But despite sharing some common assumptions about efficiency, productivity and work organisation, British researchers established a distance, criticising, for instance, the anti-social and abnormal assumptions underlying notions of work rate under Taylorism (Myers, 1926: 81). Myers perceptively noted the hostility generated among workers by scientific management through its attack on skills, and the effects of speed-up and time and motion study. He made attacks on the notion of 'one best way', rightly pointing to the greater complexity of behaviour and industrial conditions. This critique was linked to a more sympathetic consideration of the need to convince the trade unions of the validity of social science interventions, and to win more generally the consent of the workforce. The relatively progressive stance of British industrial psychologists is further illustrated by their alliance with a small group of employers centred on the Quaker families such as Rowntree, who shared their enthusiasm for 'scientific planning' and dislike for the harsher aspects of Taylorism. When those companies began to utilise psychologists, however, there

Table 5.1 – Contents page of Industrial Psychology, ed. Charles Myers

Chapter
1 Introduction – Charles S. Myers, MD, ScD, FRS
2 The Human Factor in Industrial Relations – J. Drever, MA, BSc, DPhil
3 Work and Environment – A. M. Hudson Davies, MA
4 Work and Rest – Rex Knight, MA
5 Ease and Speed of Work – G. H. Miles, DSc, and A. B. B. Eyre
6 Unproductive Working Time – A. Angles, BCom
7 Industrial Accidents – A. Stephenson, BSc
8 The Measurement of Intelligence and Aptitudes – F. M. Earle, MEd, BSc
9 Choosing a Career – Angus Macrae, MA, MB, ChB
10 Square Pegs and Square Holes – Winifred Spielman, BSc
11 Industrial Psychology and Welfare Work – Sheila Bevington, BSc
12 The Economic Aspects of Industrial Psychology – F. W. Lawe, MA, FSS
13 Industrial Psychology and Agriculture – W. R. Dunlop

Source: Myers (1929).

was still considerable suspicion and resistance from employees, particularly when it was introduced at the same time as scientific management methods (G. Brown, 1977: 216). The Quaker tapestry firm, Lee's, divided the managerial responsibility for 'psychology' and Taylorist 'mechanics' between the owner's two sons (Johnson and Moore, 1986). Most British employers, however, still preferred to cut costs simply by squeezing wages and exploiting favourable market circumstances.

But industrial psychology was not as isolated a phenomenon as it appeared. In the US particularly it was part of a wider period of experimentation involving human relations and Taylorist management, as employers chose within and between the new techniques. Richard Edwards (1979: 102) gives an interesting example of the Bancroft textile company employing a consultant to introduce welfare work in 1902, and Taylor's follower Gantt to reorganise production in 1905! Welfarism was a significant part of that context. A paternalistic concern for the well-being of employees in return for loyalty and hard work, had a long pedigree in some companies. Company towns were one manifestation, as employers provided houses, schools, stores, sanitation and lighting in order to attract an adequate labour force. But the rhetoric had shifted from older themes of community and improving the workingman to ones of entitlements and better working conditions (Barley and Kunda, 1992: 372).

Welfare work was also present in conventional circumstances. An increasing number of firms began to employ welfare secretaries whose role ranged from encouraging a 'proper moral atmosphere' to the provision of social and medical facilities. This interest was not philanthropic – 'Capital will not invest in sentiment', as one leading employer put it (quoted in Nelson, 1975: 104). It arose from attempts to grapple with the recruitment and motivation problems deriving from the increasing size of the labour force and a new industrial relations situation shaped by declining loyalty and rising unrest. There was a parallel development in the growth of employment or personnel departments as a means of dealing 'scientifically' with such issues – again showing an overlap with Taylorism. In the US and Britain, professional personnel bodies grew from the seeds of welfare work. But in the latter country, welfarism was strongly connected to the study of fatigue in the laboratory of wartime factories. As in the US, British welfarism was described by one of its leading members as combining 'pity and profit' (quoted in G. Brown, 1977: 185). Lee's issued 'partnership certificates' to employees who had shown a genuine interest in the company. Many workers, particularly the women who were its prime object, saw its motivation as directed primarily towards profit, given the emphasis on improving conditions for the sole purpose of maximising output. After the war, changing economic circumstances saw the decline of welfare initiatives. But in the US, to a greater extent than Britain, there was a broader framework of 'welfare capitalism'. Companies such as General Electric, International Harvester and US Steel continued policies of off-the-job benefits in the form of insurance, healthcare, pensions, social clubs, profit-sharing schemes and other measures (R. Edwards, 1979: 91–7).

The process took many different forms. Take Ford, for example. The company had only limited social provision, but it had social control potential. The 'Sociological Department' had investigators who were empowered to visit homes to check on absentees and monitor an employee's family, values and habits. But this social control mechanism did not exist in the abstract. To act as a counterweight to the assembly line and associated problems of labour turnover and unionisation, Ford had profit-sharing schemes and the famed five-dollar day. The Department could therefore ascertain the 'fitness' of workers for these generous rewards!

In a period in which space was opened up for employers by defeated industrial militancy and repression of socialist organising, welfarism in the US also had close ties to the development of company unions. This was different from the kind of enterprise unions initiated more recently by Japanese employers. The former arose primarily from wartime attempts to institute limited forms of worker representation such as works councils. After the war many large companies, often utilising their new personnel departments, were quick to consolidate this trend by initiating company unions as a focus for formal grievance procedures, thus alleviating the need for independent union representation (Edwards, 1979: 106). There was some success in delaying or undermining unionism, and employers learnt some important lessons on the importance of controlled employee involvement and formal procedures. But, as in Britain, little survived the economic changes associated with the growing depression and sharpening social polarisation. Company unionism and welfarism did not provide an adequate means of pursuing collective interests of workers, while at the same time they became a financial burden for employers without solving any of their fundamental control problems inside the factory.

HAWTHORNE AND BEYOND

The Hawthorne studies occupy a pivotal place in organisational theory. Begun in the mid-1920s, the research was carried out in the large Hawthorne plant employing 29,000 workers making electrical appliances for Bell as a subsidiary of American Telegraph and Telephone (AT&T). Management regarded themselves as progressive, but this was with regard to a willingness to experiment rather than their general attitudes, for they were strongly anti-union. The significance of Hawthorne does not lie in the results of the research as such, for both its findings and methods are widely regarded as highly questionable (Carey, 1967; Silver, 1987). Rather it reflects two factors. First is the sustained nature of the intervention itself, combining psychologists, sociologists and anthropologists. In this way the courtship between social science and industry became something of a formal engagement. Second, the interpretation of the results became the core of human relations theory and subsequent managerial practices. This was partly due to the propagandising work of Elton Mayo (1946), despite the fact that he did not join the team properly until 1928 and was much more peripheral than those who actually wrote up the detailed research such as Roethlisberger and Dickson (1939/1964) and, to a lesser extent, Whitehead (1938).

Let us retrace these steps briefly. Early experiments centred on varying the lighting for two small test groups of women workers. The purpose was to identify conditions affecting worker performance. Unfortunately no firm conclusions could be drawn, as productivity increased under every level of illumination and even for the control group that was not being subjected to any changes at all! At the time this caused great puzzlement, but it was later theorised that the real change had been the segregation of a small group, which blossomed under special attention and treatment. Thus the 'Hawthorne effect' was born, through which it was recognised that the research intervention itself is an independent variable in its effects on human behaviour. Initially the puzzlement led to a further stage of experiments on groups of women selected for their degree of friendship with one another. Again the emphasis was on manipulation of environmental variables, this time of a greater variety: rest pauses, length of working day, group bonus schemes and so on. Observers, initially placed in a test room, were gradually encouraged to act like supervisors and become more friendly with the group. Until 1929, in almost all cases output rose, with the only consistent factor again the effects of creating a special group with its identity strengthened by the replacement of two 'unco-operative' members. However, worker interest in experiments declined and output fell with the onset of the depression. Furthermore, additional experiments with two other groups to further test the effects of incentives and rest pauses had inconclusive results, both experiments being discontinued amidst some discord.

All this confusion might appear to be grounds for giving up. But a more positive line was taken that a constant factor was the significance of employee attitudes and the influence of supervisory techniques upon them. The successful experiments were those that allowed the individuals to coalesce into a group, though it is difficult to imagine how the special conditions could be transferred.

> Right now I couldn't ask for anything better than I have. I just can't explain what it is but I sure like it in the test room.... I think we work for the most wonderful man in the Western Electric Company. We have no boss. Mr. ____ simply waits on us.... We have privileges that a lot of the other girls don't have. We are allowed to go down and lie on the couch when we are tired or don't feel good, and the matron was told not to say anything to us. Of course, none of us have done that yet because we always feel pretty good and we have rest periods and can do anything we want to in those ten minutes.
>
> (Roethlisberger and Dickson, 1964: 144)

Attitudes are not simply created by interaction with management. Employee preoccupations arise from a variety of sources, so further means were found of identifying them. Even while the above experiments were going on, the company and researchers had initiated an interviewing programme to explore the relations between employee morale and supervision. 'Counsellors' were trained by researchers to play the role of the observers in the illumination phase. Over a long period of time, a variety of formal and more open-ended techniques of interviewing were utilised as a means of gaining information and of detecting, diverting and redirecting dissatisfactions.

The counsellor was told by the company, 'to watch constantly for signs of unrest and to try to assuage the tension of the worker by discussion before the unrest became active' (quoted in Fischer and Sirriani, 1984: 182). Employee complaints were treated as unreliable due to their vagueness (hot, cold, damp, smoky or dusty were apparently inferior to 'the temperature in the room was 67°F'); or because they really revealed some personal, external disturbance. Even when told of grievances, management did not act on them. Aside from letting off steam, the process could also be used to adjust employees to the work situation and screen out effective counsellors as management material.

A final phase of research linked together the concern with employee attitudes and the earlier focus on the group. The famed 'bank wiring room' experiments were based on an existing workgroup carrying out wiring, soldering and inspecting tasks with a supposedly unobtrusive observer present. What was 'discovered' on the face of it was no different from Taylor's observations in the steel industry: the workgroup systematically controlled and restricted output on the basis of their own conception of a fair day's work and enforced group norms on any fellow workers who deviated by overproducing (rate busters) or under-working (chisellers).

> One day an interviewer entered a department unobserved. There was a buzz of conversation and the men seemed to be working at great speed. Suddenly there was a sharp hissing sound. The conversation died away, and there was a noticeable slowing up in the work pace. The interviewer later discovered from an acquaintance in the department that he had been mistaken for a rate setter. One of the workmen, who acted as a lookout, had stepped on a valve releasing compressed air, a prearranged signal for slowing down.
>
> (Roethlisberger and Dickson, 1964: 386)

The interpretation and reaction were, however, sharply different. Despite the restrictions, cliques and hostilities, a more accommodating picture was endorsed of group identities. Instead of suppressing the group and attempting to individualise its members, human relations is concerned to cultivate its sentiments and switch its loyalties to management. Roethlisberger and Dickson note: 'It is as well to recognise that informal organisation is not "bad", as they are sometimes assumed to be' (1964: 559). As it is fruitless to try and destroy it, management's task is to achieve a greater harmony between the informal and formal organisation. This can be done through controlled participation, effective communication and socially skilled, humane supervision. Referring to the experience of one of the Hawthorne experimental groups, Mayo commented that, 'Before every change of program, the group is consulted. Their comments are listened to and discussed; sometimes their objections are allowed to negative a suggestion. The group undoubtedly develops a sense of participation in the critical determination and becomes something of a social unit' (quoted in Baritz, 1960: 88–9). Here we can see the seeds of every superficial consultation exercise in the managerial toolkit!

As an alternative managerial *tactic* this new way of managing the small group made a lot of sense; indeed a minority of British employers were reaching similar conclusions (G. Brown, 1977: 243). Today, as we shall see later, it is applied in new and more sophisticated ways in current teamwork practices. The problem, however, arises from how Mayo and the human relations tradition theorised their understanding of Hawthorne. They were determined to fashion a general theory of behaviour in organisations. Later management theorists have dubbed a key element of this approach 'social man' (Schein, 1965). For Mayo, this started from a critique of the so-called 'rabble hypothesis' he attributed to economists and management theorists such as Taylor, in which individuals act solely according to rational self-interest. In contrast, 'social man' proceeds from the assumption that the major human need is for social solidarity that can be satisfied through group association. Naturally, this downplays the role of economic incentives. Such associations are seen to create social routines that substitute for logical and individual self-interest. Mayo preferred the term 'non-logical' to 'irrational', but the essential message is clear: workers act according to sentiments and emotions.

Contrary to some accounts, he did not believe that management was by definition and contrast rational, for all individuals were held to be governed by the same abstract instincts and needs. Rather managers and administrators could *become* rational, precisely because they can free themselves from social routines and the accompanying emotional involvement. This is an extremely curious notion, as any analysis of management shows that it has *its own* routines and 'illogicalities'. But it indicates the uncritical attitude of human relations writers towards the economic élites. Interestingly the new theorists of corporate culture manage to maintain the emphasis on emotions, symbolism and 'irrationality' without separating management and workforce in the same way.

It must also be said that the empirical basis for Mayo's assertions in the Hawthorne experience is very shaky. Group solidarity was carefully engineered through the selection and treatment of those workers involved, even to the point of replacing 'unco-operative' workers. Even this did not sustain co-operative activity. Mayo interpreted restriction of output as a combination of group sentiments and lack of trust in management. But there are alternative and simpler explanations: 'Restriction of output by voluntary norms was a rational response by primarily economically-oriented agents to the increasingly likely prospect of unemployment' (Clegg and Dunkerley, 1980: 131). Environmental influences on employee attitudes were recognised, but it was held that the consequences could be dealt with and 'adjusted' inside the enterprise.

The denial of economic factors led to some absurd psychologisms. Mayo used the curious term 'pessimistic reveries' to account for industrial unrest of any kind. Put another way, strikes and other actions that restrict output are obsessive preoccupations and signs of maladjustment, even to the point of identifying industrial unrest with mental breakdown and casting trade union leaders as psychological deviants! Not surprisingly, unions very rarely get mentioned in Mayo's writings. That did not stop later followers. The psychologist McMurry argued that not only were unions unnecessary when management acted fairly, but workers joined unions not to protect their jobs and improve pay but because of unconscious cravings to improve the emotional situation at work (Baritz, 1960: 175). Seemingly, social science had not improved much on the primitive psychology of engineering discourses, which two decades earlier had been describing striking employees as 'explosive workers' with strike-prone personalities and backgrounds of juvenile delinquency (see Shenhav, 1999: 189)!

It would, however, be misleading to view human relations through its excesses. To add to 'social man', a second highly influential level of theorisation emphasised the essentially co-operative nature of the enterprise. In fact the two were linked, as Mayo continually referred to the supposed eager desire of workers for co-operative activity. It is easy to dismiss this kind of analysis, particularly given the capacity of human relations researchers to systematically ignore or reinterpret conflictual processes. But they *had* identified significant changes in the socio-economic sphere that brought the issue of co-operation to the fore. They pointed to the disparity between the attention paid to technical efficiency and economic functions, and the absence of 'the development of skills and techniques for securing co-operation' (Roethlisberger and Dickson, 1964: 552). The need to improve the latter was especially important because, as Mayo recognised, the balance between technical and social skills had been disrupted as workers' traditional forms of craft socialisation and identity had been undermined by mechanisation and the assembly line.

Emphasis is therefore put on the role of management to use the formal organisation to intervene in the *informal*, so as to create and sustain consent. Only in this context can we understand what appear to be the superficial solutions of human relations practices, with their prescriptions of 'democratic' supervision, good communications, teamwork and socially skilled leadership. Mayo's 'lifelong obsession with social harmony' (M. Rose, 1975: 115) was not based merely on his distorted empirical observations; it was underwritten by an organic model of society in which equilibrium and stability are the natural order of things, while structural divisions and conflicts are pathological. Mayo was worried about the 'extensive maladjustment of our times' as a period of rapid change undermined values and atomised individuals. The task was to recreate a sense of community inside the workplace.

During the same period Chester Barnard, the President of New Jersey Bell Telephone Company, was developing an even heavier emphasis on the basis for human co-operation, which was to have a major impact on later mainstream theorists (Perrow, 1979). Co-operation necessary to the survival of society could be most clearly observed in organisations. Unequal power and resources were irrelevant against the 'fact' that individuals voluntarily entered and submitted themselves to a common goal unachievable without collective effort. Organisations were rational and individuals were not. But this virtual deification of the formal organisation, like Mayo, still reserved the key role for management. The rationality of the 'non-personal' organisation was in practice again located with the executive élite who, as decision-makers, had responsibility for what Peters and Waterman, in praising Barnard, describe as 'managing the values of the organisation' (1982: 26). For co-ordination was still required to make a system, particularly as a sense of common purpose was not always present among the 'lower participants'. Barnard therefore reinforced the emphasis, not just on co-operation, but on the balance of formal and informal. As Perrow points out, this is the most extreme identification with the formal organisation, devoid of any concern about the negative effects of power and domination, or even the stress in human relations on sympathetic supervision and controlled participation.

CONSOLIDATING HUMAN RELATIONS

> Many managers would agree that the effectiveness of their organisations would be at least doubled if they discover how to tap the unrealised potential present in their organisations.
>
> (Douglas McGregor, 1960: 4)

Recognising the significance of co-operative activity was an advance, but it was wrong to transfer the analysis from the workgroup to the organisation as a whole. The fundamental contradiction at the heart of human relations and of Barnard is that co-operation, even of the 'spontaneous' kind, has to be created. Reed refers to an intellectual schizophrenia whereby, 'a theoretical framework is forced to reconcile the contradictions generated by a metaphysic that assumes collective moral consensus as a social given and at the same time advocates the adoption of techniques whereby this may be engineered' (1985: 6). There is a therefore a wide consensus among the critics we have discussed that the significance of the tradition is to be located in its *ideological appeal*. Michael Rose (1975: 124) puts this most succinctly in his memorable comment that Mayoism was the twentieth century's most seductive managerial ideology, in which social scientists and managers fashioned each other in their own image.

There is a great deal of accuracy in the view that one of its major functions was to legitimate the power and authority of both emergent professional 'classes' of managers and industrial consultants. The problem is that such an analysis can slip into giving the impression that human relations was a gigantic, if dangerous, contrick with no purchase on reality. In part the reverse is true, for it makes sense only as a reaction to and means of shaping new realities. The depth of economic and political crisis meant that 'by the 1930s corporate America felt under siege' (Neimark and Tinker, 1986: 25). Congress had passed corporatist legislation allowing companies greater control over markets and pricing in return for acceptance of codes governing minimum wages and maximum hours, plus guarantees of union membership and collective bargaining rights. In addition, the country was experiencing a huge strike wave of sit-down strikes and factory occupations. Large corporations bitterly resisted the 'New Deal' institutions and the union organising drive. But the more perceptive of them also realised that 'the crisis generated critical problems of social control and legitimation for management' (Boreham, 1980: 25). A second front was opened, drawing extensively on the human relations package of better communication, democratic leadership, co-operation and social integration. This went hand-in-hand with early versions of the managerial revolution thesis, General Motors claiming that the organisation was a community of stakeholders for which management was a trustee.

The success of strikes and union organising drives only consolidated a recognition of the importance of consent and attention to employee attitudes in the more general writings of human relations theorists such as T. N. Whitehead in his *Leadership in a Free Society* (1936). Despite the weakness of the tradition in Britain, Whitehead's book was well received in progressive management circles worried about the changing position of business in a more democratic community. Human relations was able to provide greater legitimation of management authority than Taylor, because it went beyond the narrow confines of 'science' and formal organisation to address issues more in tune with the times. But it would not have made the same impact merely as a body of ideas. It had to help generate new practices.

Though it was still confined to a minority of even the largest employers throughout the 1930s, Bendix, Baritz and other researchers show that an increasing number of firms such as General Electric, General Motors and Proctor and Gamble developed programmes influenced by human relations. The Hawthorne researchers had put considerable emphasis on 'personnel work' in its broadest sense of 'adequate diagnosis and understanding of the actual human situations – both individual and group – within the factory' (Roethlisberger and Dickson, 1964: 591). With this background, greater consideration in many large companies was given to the training of managers and supervisors in the arts of intensive communication, social skills and non-authoritarian leadership that would motivate as well as command. Personnel departments grew further, alongside more use of attitude surveys. General Motors managed to neatly combine them with spying on union activists by employing Pinkerton detectives to carry out the tests! As previously, the war acted as a spur, large companies and the state finding the use of tests an invaluable means of dealing with the problems associated with the sudden employment of thousands of new workers. Despite a sustained attack by more critical academics, the diverse applications and effects of human relations theories had established a bridgehead for the social sciences in industry and, by the 1940s, the movement had gained substantial institutional support (Barley and Kunda, 1992: 374).

The 1950s saw the relationship between social science and industry blossom still further. This was facilitated both by the development of OB and related disciplines in business schools that specialised in the human side of the enterprise, and by the training of middle and senior executives in leadership and management development (Barley and Kunda, 1992: 375). The practices or solutions were not necessarily any less superficial than Hawthorne's. Bendix (1956: 326–7) remarks that the National Association of Manufacturer's newfound attachment to 'two-way communica-tion' was based on the assumption that employers relayed *facts* to the workforce to promote co-operation, whereas what workers say is *information* which management can use to 'eliminate misunderstandings'.

Despite the over-emphasis on solving problems through issues of poor interpersonal relations, and the re-rise of harder managerial 'sciences' such as opera-tions research and systems analysis with their associated quantitative and financial techniques, human relations did not disappear. The body of research and to a lesser extent practical intervention moved on to new topics. Some researchers continued to examine leadership styles or search for the qualities of good leadership. Others focused on group processes and dynamics, including the well-known socio-technical studies of the Tavistock Institute in Britain. Rhetorical claims, however, foundered on a failure to demonstrate an exact and direct relationship between theory and practice. Perrow, for example, has written sceptically of the 'thirty year history of the effort to link morale and leadership to productivity' (1979: 97). In the piece quoted at the begin-ning of the chapter, Perrow was dismissive of the contributions from 'the forces of light'. From the vantage point of that decade it looked as if studies of the influence of technology and organisational environments, associated with systems theory, had triumphed: 'management should be advised that the attempt to produce change in an organisation through managerial grids, sensitivity training, and even job enrichment and job enlargement is likely to be fairly ineffective for all but a few organisations' (1973: 14).

COMPETITORS AND CONTINUITIES: THE RISE OF HUMAN RESOURCE MANAGEMENT

There were competitors to the new influences. The human relations school gradually became less visible, giving way, even within the territory of managing the human factor, to behavioural psychology. Mayo and others had always provided, in Bendix's words, a vocabulary of motivation. What developed in its wake was a fully-fledged theory of motivation, promoted by figures such as Maslow, McGregor and Herzberg, which had the additional advantage of challenging Taylorism on questions of job design. But Perrow was wrong to believe that a hard structure and systems approach had achieved a durable dominance. The earlier human relations tradition that had lain dormant and often abused for its naïveté suddenly became influential again in the 1980s. Nor was it a question of a particular soft style simply becoming fashion-able again. Human relations thinking contained genuine insights within a flawed general framework. The idea that the internal dynamics of the small group could be turned around so that a degree of self-governance could favour management resur-faced in the substantial wave of interest in teamworking from the 1980s onwards. At broadly the same time, management theorists and practitioners were also rediscovering the benefits of creating social cohesion and value consensus through organisational 'communities'. The advocates of corporate cultures such as Peters and Waterman (1982) explicitly acknowledged the influence of earlier human relations writers.

Despite such influences, human relations theory as such is still largely regarded as a ghost from a past banquet. When people talk now of managing the human factor, human resource management (HRM) is what comes to mind. We can tell this, in part, as a story about changes in functional structures and practices, though this requires us to retrace a few steps. This chapter has already demonstrated that the origins of personnel work lie in the human relations tradition. As a more specific function was consolidated, the humanistic rhetoric was complemented by practices that reflected the forms of adaptation to 'local' environments. Notable in this were the dominant rule-based and hierarchical systems of bureaucratic control developed in large organisations, and the expanded legal regulation of the employment relationship established as part of the post-war settlement between capital, labour and the state. The outcome expanded the domain and expertise of the personnel function, but created practices that were largely procedural, reactive and low trust.

As part of the general shift in workplace practices and organisational restructuring in the 1980s, these orientations were put into question. The personnel function was recast as HRM, though in this incarnation it was not to be the exclusive property of a narrow functional department (Tichy et al., 1982; Beer et al., 1985). This was a matter not just of territory but of content. HRM always had a dual usage, signifying a new way of describing the field of people management, and a distinctive approach to managing the employment relationship (Mabey, Salaman and Storey, 1998: 1). The emphasis is on the integration of 'personnel' issues within the overall business strategy; with employees becoming a 'resource' equivalent to something like finance, with ownership of HR issues diffused down to other actors, notably line managers. 'Strategic management' is a term continually invoked to refer to the management of employees at all levels, directed towards the creating and sustaining of competitive advantage (P. M. Miller, 1989; Kamoche, 1994).

From the beginning, the various usages have been open to dispute. Some have questioned whether the approach genuinely reflects substantial shifts of policy from the old personnel departments, or is simply 'old wine in new bottles' (M. Armstrong, 1987). Many more have queried whether something radically different was actually being delivered in the practice of managing of the employment relationship. The latter is important, but need not detain us here – our emphasis is on the continuities and changes from human relations to human resource management.

To project itself as something that was not 'simply a new sign tacked on the personnel manager's door' (Thomas, 1988: 3), HRM had to sell itself as a theoretical and normative narrative as well. As one of us has explained in more detail elsewhere (Thompson, 2007), this has centred on the concept of human capital. Though borrowed from the debates about educational performance, the idea of human capital has helped HRM make a business case for the role of the quality and skills of the workforce in competitive advantage. Individual employees had a responsibility invest in the attitudes and expertise that could enhance their usefulness to the firm. Meanwhile, a strategic approach to HRM is said to be marked by investment in the workforce and this would be associated with enhanced skills, training, career structures and skill and knowledge – based reward systems. In turn, this forms the basis for mutual gains and shared interests through the employment relationship. The management of people is thus given a potential seat at the top table. Typical of this approach was Pfeffer's (1994) 'profits through people' message. He examined seven practices that successful organisations needed to have in order to make a difference, including employment security, selective hiring, self-managed teams and decentralized decision – making, high compensation linked to organizational performance, training, minimal status differences and extensive openness in sharing information. Though HRM retains a link with the 'treat people nicely and they will behave better' traditions of human relations, its newfound legitimacy lies in its capacity to escape the association of managing people purely with soft, developmental approaches. The argument is not free-floating. From the middle of the 1980s HRM theorists began to make a more contingent argument that changes in the external environment were making the internal assets of the firm more significant and strategic. More special-ised, dynamic markets and technologies required more flexible, better trained labour. The HRM model was cast explicitly in terms of human capital and high involvement (Kaufman, 2003).

The unifying and often derided slogan, was 'people are our most important asset', but beneath the surface lurked two widely observed variants. First, there is a 'hard' version in which HRM is a much more systematic, rational instrument that can support organisational change through effective mobilisation and measurement of human capabilities and performance (Devanna, Fombrun and Tichy, 1984; Huselid, 1995). There is obvious continuity here with more traditional functional practices, but it is the extent to which reward and other forms of performance management are tied in to overall strategy and bottom-line outcomes that is considered to be decisive.

A softer, normative variant can be identified (Kochan, Katz and McKersie, 1986; Guest, 1987), which links HRM primarily to a transformation of employment rela-tionships based on higher levels of employee commitment and involvement. This orientation received a considerable boost with the development of the excellence literature genre, which promoted culture change as a primary managerial resource. In many firms this enabled the HR department to take a leading role in change programmes, as the definer and measurer of value change (Marks et al., 1997). The variants could and should come together through the pathway of high-performance work systems (HPWS). While this can be interpreted as covering all HRM territo-ries (Huselid, 1995), it is more common for it to be associated with a workplace level and issues such as teamwork, quality and continuous improvement (Kochan and Osterman, 1994). This impacts upon the practices of employee relations. As Guest notes, the underlying goal is to get employees to go 'beyond contract' and away from old-style adversarial collectivism, 'thereby reducing the potential for the effort bargain to operate as a potential focus for conflict and grievance' (1998: 239).

While the intent to restructure the employment relationship away from low-trust industrial relations systems is widely approved, the association with an attack on collectivism and trade unions is more controversial. The rise of HRM, with its unita-rist philosophy, more individualistic relations between employer and employee, and direct communication between company and workforce, has undoubtedly coincided with some diminution of the significance of collective bargaining and union power (Blyton and Turnbull, 1998: 9). That is not the only controversy. It is certainly possi-ble to produce *models* that integrate different types of practices, of which the 'mutual gains enterprise', which combines strategic, functional and workplace dimensions, is attractive and coherent (Kochan and Osterman, 1994). However, practices on differ-ent territories and through hard and soft mechanisms are easier to reconcile rhetori-cally than in practice (Legge, 1995). While debates focus on conceptual tensions, they are dwarfed by the problem of holding the different facets of the HRM model together in the context of contemporary organisational restructuring. In particular, performance goals such as greater productivity and flexibility in work organisa-tion are proving difficult to reconcile with changes in employment that undermine loyalty, career and stability. In this context, critical commentators argue that hard, cost-driven approaches are predominating over softer, commitment and trust based policies (Blyton and Turnbull, 1992; Storey, 1992, 1995).

SUMMARY AND KEY POINTS

It is conventional wisdom that Taylorism and human relations are at best opposite ends of a spectrum and worst, deadly enemies. This chapter has shown that they shared many of the same origins and concerns in attempting to apply 'science' to the understanding and control human behaviour, or the 'labour problem' as it was known at the beginning of the twentieth century. There, was, admittedly a difference of territory. Taylorism focused largely on the design of work, human relations on employee adjustment to it. While this is frequently described in mainstream writing as technical and human organisation and the need to integrate the two, it may be more accurately thought of in terms of overlapping or sometimes competing control systems. Whatever its record of patchy practices and inflated theoretical claims about social harmony and the power of leadership and communication, human relations would not exist if it did not bring something distinctive to the table. That distinctiveness is a focus on the informal dimension of organisational life – represented in practices such as teamworking and culture change – which Scientific Management wrongly thought could be excluded or marginalised. This recognition is, in part, retrospective and by the time it came, the human factor franchise had been largely taken up by HRM. We began that discussion with a quote from McGregor, of Theory X and Theory Y fame. Despite being written at the end of the 1950s, its language is identical to that of contemporary HRM. Though he goes on to argue that the major thing holding back the efficient and scientific management of the human factor is the adolescence of the social sciences (1960: 5), we would draw a different conclusion. Influenced by conceptions of human capital, HRM is a more coherent set of ideas and better embedded in managerial practices, but its sustainability is as much about social *life* as the social sciences. While the franchise may have changed hands, it is still proving difficult to produce a durable formula that can transform the conflicting, albeit complex, interests that lie at the heart of the labour process and employment relationship.

FURTHER READING

Once again, Shenhav is good on the links between Taylorism and human relations. Baritz's classic Servants of Power is an indispensable account of the way that social science began to be used by management. If you can get hold of it, Browns' Sabotage is a British variant that also shows how workers resisted the new trends. When examining human relations and the Hawthorne studies it's good to access the original writings, notably Roesthlisberger and Dickson, but the various editions of Rose are a decent substitute. Perrow sets out the conventional scepticism of the more scientific end of organisation theory. On the move from personnel/industrial relations to HRM, Legge and the articles of Guest are a useful start.

Baritz, L. (1960) *The Servants of Power*, Middletown: Wesleyan University Press.

Brown, G. (1977) *Sabotage*, Nottingham: Spokesman.

Guest, D. E. (1987) 'Human Resource Management and Industrial Relations', *Journal of Management Studies*, 24. 5: 503–21.

Guest, D. E. (1989) 'Personnel and HRM: Can You Tell the Difference?' *Personnel Management*, January: 48–51.

Legge, K. (1995, 2nd edn 2005) *Human Resource Management: The Rhetorics, the Realities*, London: Macmillan.

Perrow, C. (1973) 'The Short and Glorious History of Organisational Theory', *Organisational Dynamics*, Summer, 2–15.

Roethlisberger, F. G. and Dickson, W. J. (1964) *Management and the Worker*, New York: Wiley.

Rose, M. (1975, 1986) *Industrial Behaviour*, Harmondsworth: Penguin.

Shenhav, Y. (1999) *Manufacturing Rationality: The Engineering Foundations of the Managerial Revolution*, Oxford: Oxford University Press.

REFERENCES

Armstrong, M. (1987) 'Human Resource Management: A Case of the Emperor's New Clothes?' *Personnel Management*, 19. 8: 30–5.

Baritz, L. (1960) *The Servants of Power*, Middletown, CT: Wesleyan University Press.

Barley, S. R. and Kunda, G. (1992) 'Design and Devotion: Surges of Rational and Normative Ideologies of Control in Managerial Discourse', *Administrative Science Quarterly*, 37: 363–99.

Barnard, C. (1938) *The Functions of the Executive*, Cambridge, MA: Harvard University Press.

Beer, M., Spector, B., Lawrence, P., Quin Mills, D. and Walton, R. (1985) *Human Resource Management: A General Manager's Perspective*, Glencoe, IL: Free Press.

Bendix, R. (1956) *Work and Authority in Industry*, New York: Harper & Row.

Blyton, P. and Turnbull, P. (1992) *Reassessing Human Resource Management*, London: Sage.

Blyton, P. and Turnbull, P. (1998) *The Dynamics of Employee Relations* (2nd edn), London: Macmillan.

Boreham, P. (1980) 'The Dialectic of Theory and Control: Capitalist Crisis and the Organisation of Labour', in D. Dunkerley and G. Salaman (eds), *Control and Ideology in Organizations*, Milton Keynes: Open University Press.

Brown, G. (1977) *Sabotage*, Nottingham: Spokesman.

Buchanan, D. (2000) 'An Eager and Enduring Embrace: The Ongoing Rediscovery of Teamworking as a Management Idea', in S. Proctor and F. Mueller (eds), *Teamworking*, London: Macmillan.

Carey, A. (1967) 'The Hawthorne Studies: A Radical Criticism', *American Sociological Review*, 32: 403–16.

Clegg, S. and Dunkerley, D. (1980) *Organisation, Class and Control*, London: Routledge & Kegan Paul.

Devanna, M. A., Fornbrun, C. J. and Tichy, N. M. (1984) 'A Framework for Strategic Human Resource Management', in C. J. Fornbrun, N. M. Tichy and M. A. Devanna (eds), *Strategic Human Resource Management*, New York: Wiley.

Doray, B. (1988) *A Rational Madness: From Taylorism to Fordism*, London: Free Association.

Edwards, R. (1979) *Contested Terrain: The Transformation of the Workplace in the Twentieth Century*, London: Heinemann.

Fischer, F. and Sirriani, C. (eds) (1984) *Critical Studies in Organisation and Bureaucracy*, Philadelphia: Temple University Press.

Guest, D. E. (1987) 'Human Resource Management and Industrial Relations', *Journal of Management Studies*, 24. 5: 503–21.

Huselid, M. (1995) 'The Impact of Human Resource Management Practices on Turnover, Production and Corporate Financial Performance', *Academy of Management Journal*, 38: 635–72.

Johnson, I. and Moore, K. (1986) *The Tapestry Makers: Life and Work at Lee's Tapestry Works*, Birkenhead: Merseyside Docklands Community Project.

Kamoche, K. (1994) 'A Critique and a Proposed Reformulation of Strategic Human Resource Management', *Human Resource Management Journal*, 4. 4: 29–47.

Kaufman, P. (2003) Learning to *Not* Labor: How Working-Class Individuals Construct Middle-Class Identities, *Sociological Quarterly*, 44. 3, June: 481–504.

Kochan, T. and Osterman, P. (1994) *The Mutual Gains Enterprise*, Boston, MA: Harvard Business School Press.

Kochan, T., Katz, H. C. and McKersie, R. B. (1986) *The Transformation of American Industrial Relations*, New York: Basic Books.

Legge, K. (1995) *Human Resource Management: The Rhetorics, the Realities*, London: Macmillan.

Mabey, C., Salaman, G. and Storey, J. (1998) 'Strategic Human Resource Management: The Theory of Practice and the Practice of Theory', in C. Mabey, G. Salaman and J. Storey (eds), *Strategic Human Resource Management*, London: Sage.

Marks, A., Findlay, P., Hine, J., McKinlay, A. and Thompson, P. (1997) 'Handmaid's Tale or Midwives of Change? HR Managers and Organisational Innovation', *Journal of Strategic Change*, 6: 469–80.

Mayo, E. (1946) *Human Problems of an Industrial Civilisation*, New York: Macmillan.

McGregor, D. (1960) *The Human Side of the Enterprise*, New York: Harper & Row.

Miller, P. M. (1989) 'Strategic HRM: What it Is and What it Isn't', *Personnel Management*, February.

Myers, C. S. (1926) *Industrial Psychology in Great Britain*, London: Jonathan Cape.

Myers, C. S. (ed.) (1929) *Industrial Psychology*, London: Thornton Butterworth.

Neimark, M. and Tinker, T. (1986) 'On Rediscovering Marx: Dissolving Agency–Structure in Dialectical Unity', paper presented to the Conference on the Labour Process, Aston-UMIST.

Nelson, D. (1975) *Managers and Workers: Origins of the New Factory System in the United States 1880–1920*, Madison: University of Wisconsin Press.

Perrow, C. (1973) 'The Short and Glorious History of Organisational Theory', *Organisational Dynamics*, Summer: 2–15.

Perrow, C. (1979) *Complex Organizations: A Critical Essay (2nd edn)*, Glenview, IL: Scott Foreman.

Peters, T. J. and Waterman, R. H. (1982) *In Search of Excellence: Lessons from America's Best-Run Companies*, New York: Harper & Row.

Pfeffer, J. (1994) *Competitive Advantage through People: Unleashing the Power of the Work Force*, Cambridge, MA: Harvard University Press.

Roethlisberger, F. G. and Dickson, W. J. (1939/1964) *Management and the Worker*, Science Editions, New York: Wiley.

Rose, M. (1975, 1986) *Industrial Behaviour*, Harmondsworth: Penguin.

Schein, E. H. (1965) *Organisational Psychology*, Englewood Cliffs, N.J.: Prentice Hall (also 1980, 3rd edn.).

Shenhav, Y. (1999) *Manufacturing Rationality: The Engineering Foundations of the Managerial Revolution*, Oxford: Oxford University Press.

Silver, J. (1987) 'The Ideology of Excellence: Management and Neo-Conservatism', *Studies in Political Economy*, 24, Autumn: 105–29.

Storey, J. (1992) *Developments in the Management of Human Resources*, Oxford: Blackwell.

Thomas, R. J. (1988) 'What is Human Resource Management?' *Work, Employment and Society*, 2. 3: 392–402.

Tichy, N., Fombrun, C. and Devanna, M. A. (1982) 'Strategic Human Resource Management', *Sloan Management Review*: 47–61.

Whitehead, T. N. (1938) *The Industrial Worker*, London: Oxford University Press.

SOCIAL NATURE OF WORK

CHAPTER OUTLINE

- Introduction
- Work and non-work
- The development of work
- Work in organizations: an integration of ideas
- Gender and the sexual division of work
- Work less, live better? Managing the work–life balance
- Summary and end-of-chapter features
- Chapter case study 1: Service with a smile: McJobs in China
- Chapter case study 2: Home-working at Matherdom City Council

CHAPTER OBJECTIVES

After completing this chapter, you should be able to:
- explain the function and meaning of work
- explain the relationship between work and an individual's personal and social identity
- summarise the historical dimensions of work, pre-industry, the factory system, occupational changes, and the emergence of knowledge work in the virtual worksite
- identify some key strategic issues involved in designing work
- discuss the debates around issues of emotional work and work–life balance

INTRODUCTION

It is a paradox of life that its recognizable features are often the most difficult to understand. This observation is highly relevant to the topic of this chapter: work. Benjamin Franklin said that 'in this world nothing can be said to be certain, except death and taxes'. He was wrong. There is another certainty for most of us, and that is work. Whether defined in conventional economic terms as 'paid work' or defined more inclusively as a broad range of activities beyond the boundaries of paid employment, work is an almost inescapable feature of industrialized societies. Decisions about how paid work is organized and performed have created many different and contrasting types of work and employment relationships.

Since the Industrial Revolution, as factories have become more capital intensive, manual labour has undergone a transformation. Most traditional 'trade' or 'craft' jobs based on tacit knowledge have disappeared or have been 'deskilled', lessening control by craft workers. Factory work has increasingly been influenced by the 'scientific management' principle of 'one best way' of organizing particular work tasks. As employment shifted from manufacturing to the service sector, the process of **deindustrialization**, the principles of scientific management became incorporated into clerical labour and professional work. A trend throughout the twentieth century has been the growing presence of women in virtually all **occupations**. Another noticeable trend, especially since the 1990s, has been the global growth of flexible labour, a plethora of employment contracts that are part time, fixed term, short term or seasonal and create what has become known as 'precarious' employment.

The essence of being human is to engage in waged labour, but most people have little influence over how their labour is designed and performed. Organizations can be regarded as the architects of waged work, as it is within organizations that work is structured, jobs are designed and the employment relationship is formed.[1] Paid work for most individuals and families is the primary source of income that determines their standard of living. But it is important for more than economic reasons. Bolton and Houlihan's latest book, *Work Matters*,[2] juxtaposes both the bad and the good aspects of work. Waged work can be arduous, tedious, dirty, unhealthy and at times dangerous, but it can also bring connections and friendship, be a principal source of individuals' self-fulfilment and form part of their social identity. At the society level, how and where work is performed has consequences not only for the individuals who do it, but also for families and for the communities they live in.

Writing about the 'transformation of work' might be described as a cottage industry. Since the late 1970s, many books and research articles have been published, offering optimistic and pessimistic accounts of the effects of globalization and technological change on the nature of work. The optimistic scenario focuses on the liberating effect of information technology. Andre Gorz in 1982 predicted 'the liberation of time and the abolition of work' (ref. 3, p. 1). For more than a decade, Gorz set the trend for polemical 'future of work' books.[5-12] More recently, Jeremy Rifkin has argued that sophisticated 'Information Age' technologies are 'freeing up' the talent of men and women to create social capital in local communities.[4] Similarly, Microsoft's Bill Gates has argued that computers allow us to increase leisure time.[6] Both Rifkin and Gates write very persuasively, and their material has reached a wide audience.

Critical scholarship offers strikingly different accounts of work found in the Information Age rhetoric and captures the realities of lower-skilled work. Such accounts argue that the latest idiom of **flexibility** creates regimes that lead to the intensification of work, deskilling, tighter managerial control over work activities, and work-based inequalities.[5,7-12] With a particular eye to the gendering of work, it is argued that 'Where the goal of most employers throughout the world is to get the work of one full-time male done for one part-time female at a fraction of the cost, talk of the new liberation from toil can sound offensive' (ref. 5, p. 752). There is a growing consensus that there is currently a shortage of 'decent' work, with 'good' work being the preserve of a privileged minority in the new 'labour aristocracy' found in the professional, high-tech and creative industries loosely defined as 'knowledge workers'.[2]

This chapter has a very bold objective: to explain the nature of work in advanced capitalist societies, and why the design of work is important to understanding behaviour in organizations. This requires us to trace the evolution of work from early capitalism to late modernity. We look at the historical dimension of work in the belief that present problems associated with work are an outcome of the past, and that the problems of the future are embedded in the social relations of work designed in the present. The broader context of work provides an essential background for understanding the connection between work, identity, work and private life, and behavioural decisions in the workplace, and the implications for managing the employment relationship.

WORK AND NON-WORK

'What kind of work do you do?' is such a classic question that it is repeatedly asked in social conversation. This question is significant because it underscores the fact that paid work – employment – is generally considered to be a central defining feature of our identity. It is also one important means by which we judge others. Adults with paid jobs usually name their occupation by way of an answer, but we can see this question in a wider sense too. It invites us to explore the nature of work in relation to time, space and **social structure**.

social structure: the stable pattern of social relationships that exist within a particular group or society

Consider this everyday scene in any Western town or city. It is 2 o'clock in the afternoon, and a neighbourhood park is busy with adults and children enjoying themselves. Some are walking quickly through the park, perhaps going back to their office or store after their lunch break. A city employee is pruning roses in one of the flower beds. Near the bandstand, three musicians are playing a saxophone, a clarinet and a violin. Two people are playing tennis. Others are watching young children play. A man sitting on a bench is reading a book, a woman is using a mobile phone, and a teenager is completing a printed form. This scene draws attention to the blurred boundary between work and non-work activity. It gives us an entry point for answering the question, 'What is work?'

If we try to define some of these individual activities as work, the confusion and ambiguity about the meaning of work will become apparent. For example, the people walking back to their offices or to the shops might prune the roses in their gardens at the weekend, but they are unlikely to see the task in the same way as the gardener who is employed to do tasks such as pruning. The three musicians might be playing for amusement, or they might be rehearsing for an evening performance for which they will be paid. An amateur who plays tennis for fun and fitness does not experience or think of the game in the same way as a professional tennis player. Similarly, a parent keeping an eye on a child playing does not experience child-minding in the same way as a professional nanny. The person using the mobile phone might be talking to a friend, but she could be, say, a financial adviser phoning a client. The person filling in the form might be applying for a student grant, or a clerical worker catching up with an overdue job during his lunch hour. We can see from these examples that work cannot be defined simply by the activities that are carried out.

stop reflect
Write down your own definition of 'work'. To help you, consider a chef preparing a meal at a five-star hotel, and the same chef going home and preparing the family meal. Are both activities 'work'?

So what is work, exactly? 'Work' can be contrasted with 'labour'. According to Williams, labour has a 'strong medieval sense of pain and toil' (ref. 13, p. 335), and 'work' can be distinguished from 'occupation', which is derived from a Latin word meaning 'to occupy or to seize' (ref. 14, p. 2). The terms 'work', 'occupation' and 'job' have become interchangeable: work is not just an activity, something one *does*, but something a person *has*.[3] Conventionally, to 'have worked' or to 'have a job' is to use a place (or space) and sell time.

A substantial number of people have an *instrumental* orientation to work. They work for economic rewards in order to do non-work or leisure activity that they 'really enjoy'. For these people, life begins when work ends. Different occupations provide different levels of pay, so those doing them have different life chances and opportunities in terms of health, education, leisure pursuits and quality of life. Among people who 'have work', it is not simply the case that people need to work in order to have enough money to live on. People do paid work to earn money to acquire 'consumer power'. Thus, paid work for many is a means to an end – commodity consumption (buying designer clothes, fast cars, mobile phones and so on) or social consumption (such as drinking, dining out and holidaying). The central differentiating feature between people 'out of work' and those 'in work' is that the latter have much higher levels of consumer power and more choice about their lifestyle.

However, pay is only part of the equation. Research suggests that many people do paid work not primarily for extrinsic rewards (such as pay), but for the intrinsic rewards that work can bring, such as self-esteem, friendship, enjoyment and the social purpose of work. Traditionally, people occupying higher positions in an organization's hierarchy obtain more prestige and self-esteem than those in lower positions, and most people get satisfaction from participating in activities that demonstrably contribute to human well-being.[15,16]

We can begin to understand the complexity of work and its social ramifications by exploring the following definition:

> Work refers to physical and mental activity that is carried out to produce or achieve something of value at a particular place and time; it involves a degree of obligation and explicit or implicit instructions, in return for pay or reward.

This definition draws attention to some central features of work.[17] First, the most obvious purpose of work is an economic one. The notion of 'physical and mental' and 'value' suggests that the activities of both a construction worker and a computer systems analyst can be considered as work. The 'mental activity' also includes the commercialization of human feeling, or what is called 'emotional labour'.

Second, work is structured spatiality – how social life is organized geographically – and by time, and people's spatial embedding shapes work and management practices.[18] Throughout most of the twentieth century, work was typically carried

Plate 1 – Work in the service sector often requires workers to provide more than physical labour. Jobs such as flight attendants, shop assistants and waiting at tables require workers to manage their feelings in order to create a publicly observable facial display: what Hochschild calls 'emotional labour'.
Source: Getty Images

out away from home and at set periods of the day or night. Thus 'place and time' locates work within a social context. However, in advanced capitalist economies, there are new expectations of spatial mobility and temporal flexibility.[19,20] The mass timetable of the '8 to 5' factory world, of the '9 to 5' office world and of recreational Sundays has given way to a flexi-place, flexi-time world. The Internet means that the timing of the working day may be shaped by working times in a number of time zones.

Third, work always involves social relations between people: between employer and employee, between co-workers, between management and trade unions, and between suppliers and customers. Social relations in the workplace can be cooperative or conflictual, hierarchical or egalitarian. When a parent cooks dinner for the family, he or she does tasks similar to those performed by a cook employed by a hospital to prepare meals for patients. However, the social relations involved are quite different. Hospital cooks have more in common (in this sense) with factory or office workers than with parents, because their activities are governed by rules and regulations. They accept 'instructions' from the employer or the employer's agent, a manager. Obviously, then, it is not the nature of the activity that determines whether it is considered 'work', but rather the nature of the social relations in which the activity is embedded. Thus, to be 'in work' is to have a definite relationship with some other who has control of the time, place and activity.

Finally, work is remunerated (that is, there is a reward for it). There are two types of reward, **extrinsic** and **intrinsic**. The worker provides physical effort and/or mental application, and accepts fatigue and the loss of control over his or her time. In return, the extrinsic work rewards that he or she usually receives consist (primarily) of wages and bonuses. The intrinsic rewards he or she might get from the job include status and recognition from his or her peers.

Although our definition helps us to identify key features of work, it is too narrow and restrictive. First, not all work, either physical or mental, is remunerated. We cannot assume that there is a simple relationship in which 'work' means a paid employment or occupation, 'real' work that is remunerated. Our definition obscures as much as it reveals. Most people would agree that some activities that are unpaid count as work. This work can be exhilarating or exhausting. Some of it is household-based work – cooking, child rearing, cleaning and so on – and some of it is done voluntarily, for the good of society – for instance, working for the Citizen's Advice Bureau. The activities that are done in the course of this unpaid or 'hidden' work are identical to those in some paid jobs, such as working in a nursery or advising people on their legal rights. Is it fair to exclude it simply because it is not paid?

Furthermore, whether an activity is experienced as work or non-work or leisure is dependent on social relations, cultural conditions, social attitudes and how various activities are perceived by others. So, for example, 'an active woman, running a house and bringing up children, is distinguished from a woman who works: that is to say, takes paid employment' (ref. 13, p. 335). Historically, unpaid work is undertaken disproportionately by one-half of the population: women. This book concentrates on paid work, and as a consequence we largely omit the critically important area of women's unpaid work in the household, but that is not to suggest that we see it as unimportant.

Second, our definition of paid work says little about how employment opportunities are shaped by gender, ethnicity, age and abilities or disabilities. For example, when women do have access to paid work, they tend to receive less pay than men doing similar work. Women are disproportionately represented in paid work that involves tasks similar to those they carry out in their domestic life – catering,

extrinsic reward: a wide range of external outcomes or rewards to motivate employees

intrinsic reward: inner satisfaction following some action (such as recognition by an employer or co-workers) or intrinsic pleasures derived from an activity (such as playing a musical instrument for pleasure)

weblink
Go to the following websites for more information on employment trends: in Britain (www.statistics.gov.uk), Canada (www.statcan.ca/start.html and the Canadian Labour Force Development Board www.hrmguide.net/canada/), the European Union (www.eurofound.europa.eu/eiro), the USA (www.bls.gov and www.hreonline.com, South Africa (www.statssa.gov.za) and Brazil (www.ibge.gov.br/english/)

nursing, teaching, clerical and retail employment. Ethnic and racially defined minorities experience chronic disadvantage in paid work because of racism in organizations and in recruitment. The likelihood of participating in paid work varies with age and certain types of work. For example, young people are disproportionately represented in more physically demanding paid work. Disabled adults, especially disabled young adults, experience higher levels of unemployment and under-employment than do those who are able bodied.[21]

Third, paid work can be dangerous and unhealthy, but the hazards are not distributed evenly. Manual workers face more work-related hazards, and have more accidents at work, than do (for example) office workers. It has been argued that this unequal distribution of work-related accidents is not only related to the risks the individuals face, but is also influenced by **values** and economic pressures.

Our approach to understanding the issue of inequality surrounding work involves an analysis of the differential treatment of people based on class, gender and race. We need to look at who does what job, analysing the social and sexual division of labour. We need to consider what sort of occupations there are, and who exercises power or control over the social institutions.

Fourth, our definition obscures an important element of the employment relationship: the *psychological contract*.[22-25] The 'psychological contract' is a metaphor that captures a wide variety of largely unwritten expectations and understandings of the two parties (employer and employee) about their mutual obligations. Denise Rousseau defines it as 'individual beliefs, shaped by the organization, regarding terms of an exchange agreement between individuals and their organization' (ref. 25, p. 9). Most commentators view the concept as a two-way exchange of perceived promises and obligations. The concept has been around since the early 1960s, but in recent years it has become a 'fashionable' framework to support the development of more nuanced understandings of large and small organization employment relationships.[26] Work shapes the employment relationship, the behaviour of all employees, and the relations between men and women inside and outside the workplace, and it has a significant bearing upon personal identity, fulfilment and social life.[27,28]

THE DEVELOPMENT OF WORK

The structure of the labour market and paid work is not static: it reflects patterns of substantial change in the ways in which work is organized in specific industrial sectors. This is the essence of industrialization and a new emerging form of life – modernity. In this section, we trace the emergence of new work forms, starting with the **Industrial Revolution** (around 1780–1830) in Britain and finishing with a look at employment in what has been called 'post-industrial' work.

We provide this brief historical overview of work because, in our view, it provides a perspective on contemporary work issues and problems, which often result from decisions made in the past. Additionally, when we look at how work forms have developed, it becomes apparent that most 'new' work forms have deep historical roots. Contemporary management gurus might claim to have 'discovered' the importance of informal work-related learning, but such a mode of learning was important in the apprenticeship system of pre-industrial Europe. Similarly, that 'virtual' home-based work reduces the need for office space and costs was well understood by employers in the eighteenth century who operated the 'putting-out' system of home-working discussed below. In effect, these claims of 'new' or 'innovative', when viewed through

value: a collective idea about what is right or wrong, good or bad, and desirable or undesirable in a particular culture
values: stable, long-lasting beliefs about what is important in a variety of situations

stop reflect
Do you think that managers need to manage the employment relationship differently for knowledge workers and for manual industrial workers? Why and how?

Industrial Revolution: the relatively rapid economic transformation that began in Britain in the 1780s. It involved a factory- and technology-driven shift from agriculture and small cottage-based manufacturing to manufacturing industries, and the consequences of that shift for virtually all human activities

the economy: the social institution that ensures the maintenance of society through the production, distribution and consumption of goods and services

stop reflect
To what extent does a 'good' or 'bad' work design depend on which approach we use and which theorist we believe?

a historical lens, might be a rediscovery of past practices that had been forgotten or abandoned.

Before we retrace the organization of work in **the economy**, we need to take a moment to make some general observations and highlight some challenges that this task presents. The history of work emphasizes that work is a social activity, not an individual one. Even those who work alone do so within a socially constructed network of relations among people associated with the pursuit of economic activity. History tends to contradict the suggestion that divisions on the basis of class, gender and race are systematic features created by, and found solely in, industrial capitalism. The social inequality of work, however, long predates the rise of capitalism. The history of industrial capitalism fosters the image of work as a predominantly male activity, separate from, and unrelated to, the home. Again, this is historically atypical: 'home and the place of work have always been, and still are, intimately connected by a seamless web of social interdependence' (ref. 29, p. 46).

Studying work and organizational forms from a historical perspective is a challenge for a number of reasons. By its very nature, such an exercise involves a compression of time periods and of different ways of organizing work. As Eric Hobsbawm wrote, 'The past is a permanent dimension of the human consciousness, an inevitable component of institutions, values and other patterns of human society (ref. 30, p. 10). The problem for social theorists is to avoid presenting the emergence of new work forms as a coherent, orderly and inevitable process of change.

Looking back from the vantage point of the early twenty-first century, it might seem reasonable to talk of the emergence of the factory, or of new forms of management control. But, as others have pointed out, the development of new work forms and social relations took place piecemeal, sporadically and slowly – and frequently they were resisted. Many features of work in the pre-industrial economy (the period before 1780) survived until late into the nineteenth and twentieth centuries, and similarly many twentieth work forms survive in the early twenty-first century. When we outline general trends, this not only compresses wide variations and collapses time periods, but also attaches a coherent pattern to these changes, which they did not show in reality.[31,32]

With this caveat, the rest of this section examines pre-industrial work, the transition to factory forms of work, the significance of concentrated production, the rise of trade unions and the interventions of the state.[30]

Pre-industrial work

In the middle of the eighteenth century, the most striking feature of the economy in Europe was the importance of agriculture as a basic human activity. Manufacturing operated on a small scale, employed labour-intensive methods and used little fixed capital. Agricultural and industrial work was characterized by low productivity. Population growth created an ever-growing class of landless labourers who were compelled to relocate to towns and sell their **labour power** to survive. The human movement to the new cities was critical for industrial capitalism to develop. As Max Weber explained, 'only where ... workers under the compulsion of the whip of hunger, offer themselves' to employers does capitalism develop.[33]

labour power: the potential gap between a worker's capacity or potential to work and its exercise

Before 1780, the English economy was characterized by regulation. The central government intervened in the economy. The Statute of Artificers of 1563, for example, set the level of wages and conditions of employment, regulated the mobility of labour (as the government did during the Second World War, 1939–45), and protected and promoted, by force if necessary, domestic manufacturing and trade. In the towns, craft guilds regulated all activities related to their trade, including apprenticeship training, wages and prices, and standards of work.

Away from the town-based guilds, the rural-based **putting-out system** was a feature of the pre-Industrial Revolution manufacturing of woollen garments and many branches of metal working. The putting-out system was a decentralized method of manufacturing that, in the case of producing woollen cloth for example, involved the various processes of combing, spinning and weaving the wool usually being performed by different workers in their cottages. Such a form of work organization had profound consequences for the social organization of work and the nature of workers' reactions to the Industrial Revolution:

> It could not be used in industries requiring bulky plant and power-driven machinery. Neither was it suitable for crafts demanding a high degree of skill or which needed close supervision ... Even when technical conditions were favourable to the use of out-workers, high costs of distribution and losses arising from pilfering and fraud by the workers were serious weaknesses.
>
> (ref. 34, p. 102)

Thus, the putting-out system, a pre-modern variant of home-working, contained considerable rigidities and inefficiencies, which were apparent when markets expanded and there was a need for large-scale manufacturing.

Gender-based patterns of work predate industrial capitalism. In the pre-industrial European family, both men and women produced goods for the household and were also engaged in paid work as part of the putting-out system, but depending on local norms and customs, there were 'rather strict ideas about women's work and men's work within the specific community' (ref. 35, p. 55). Moreover, work was 'a social activity circumscribed by custom and traditions that went deeper than the cash nexus' (ref. 29, p. 52), and work and family life were not regarded as separate spheres.

Factory-based work

The traditional work rhythms and practices of pre-industrial society gave way to the specialization and discipline of the **factory system**. We can describe the Industrial Revolution as a fundamental change in the structure of the economy, in which the capitalists' pursuit and accumulation of profit guided the mode of organizing work, harnessing technology and determining the social relations of work. The change was characterized by the rise of the factory, a combination of power technology and specialized machines with specialized occupations. The significance of the concentration of workers lay in the potential for extending the division of labour, installing machines, regulating the flow of raw materials, and controlling and moulding workers' behaviour to meet the specific needs of large-scale production.

Here, the focus is on the **division of labour** within the factory organized by the owner. The factory offered the opportunity to improve each specialized task through the use of innovative technology, more than was possible with the decentralized putting-out system: 'The very division of labour ... prepared the ground from which mechanical invention could eventually spring,' wrote one historian (ref. 36, p. 145). The factory also enabled a tighter control of the work in process than was possible with the domestic system. With the putting-out system, it was difficult to control the behaviour of cottage-based workers because the employer had 'no way of compelling his [sic] workers to do a given number of hours of labour; the domestic weaver or craftsman was master of his time, starting and stopping when he [sic] desired' (ref. 37, p. 59). The factory system offered new opportunities for controlling the pace and quality of work by the 'discipline of mechanization' – the actual speed of the machine – and by a hierarchy of control over the work in process.

putting-out system: a pre-industrial, home-based form of production in which the dispersed productive functions were coordinated by an entrepreneur

factory system: a relatively large work unit that concentrated people and machines in one building, enabling the specialization of productive functions and, at the same time, a closer supervision of employees than did the pre-industrial putting-out system. Importantly, the factory system gave rise to the need for a new conception of time and organizational behaviour

division of labour: the allocation of work tasks to various groups or categories of employee

Work and Society: Were socialist firms inefficient?

In a study published over two decades ago, Michael Burawoy asked a provocative question: 'Can state socialist firms be as efficient as capitalist firms?' To answer this question, he and a colleague, Janos Lukacs, studied two machine shops – one in the USA (which they called Allied) and one in Hungary (which they called Banki). Their answer may surprise some readers. In the conclusion to their analysis of the two firms, Burawoy and his co-investigator offered the following summary of their key ideas:

> We have argued that the technical efficiency at Banki's machine shop was greater than at Allied's. In comparison to Allied, Banki operators work as hard if not harder and produce higher quality work, norms are better adjusted to jobs, pressure for innovation is more continuous, planning on the shop floor is more effective, the external labor market is better able to tie rewards to skills and experience, and bureaucratic rules that interfere with production are more limited. (p. 734)

Among the rationales for this study was a belief that existing views of work in socialist societies were dominated by stereotypes. Burawoy and Lukacs hoped that their research would help readers move beyond these stereotypes towards a more accurate picture of work in the two kinds of society. Their article succeeds in unmasking some of the myths that have led to false or superficial accounts of the differences between capitalist and socialist ways of organizing work.

This is no small achievement. In the period after the Second World War, the war of ideology (the Cold War) between the West and the USSR made it difficult to engage in objective comparative analysis of different aspects of life in capitalist and socialist societies. Burawoy and Lukacs broke new ground in their efforts to demonstrate how such research ought to be conducted.

Two features of their research stand out as particularly noteworthy. Both Burawoy and Lukacs spent time working at the machine shops they studied. As a result, they offer detailed accounts of what was actually happening on the shop floor. An accurate description of what is happening in two different contexts is a necessary element of high-quality comparative research.

But an accurate and detailed description of social reality is not the only strength of this particular research study. Burawoy and Lukacs also devote considerable attention to the question of causal mechanisms. Put differently: not only do they describe *how* the two patterns of work organization vary, but they also develop an explanation of *why* the two patterns of work organization vary. For example, a key difference between the two firms was the willingness of workers and local management to innovate. In the socialist firm levels of innovation were relatively high, while in the capitalist firm levels of innovation were relatively low. How do Burawoy and Lukacs explain this counter-intuitive finding?

They argue that, as a division of a large multinational company, the capitalist firm was forced to adhere to strict rules for organizing production imposed by its corporate headquarters. The capitalist firm had to produce a predetermined number of engines of a specified type, and there was no incentive to innovate. For the socialist firm, however, there was an incentive to innovate. There was some pressure to reduce over time the amount workers would be paid for a specified output (to 'tighten' production norms). However, production norms would be relaxed if management introduced 'New machines or new products' (p. 729). The prospect of looser production norms appealed to both management and workers. As a result, there were higher levels of innovation in the socialist firm. This incentive for innovation is evident in other socialist firms as well: 'in the Hungarian steel industry,' Burawoy and Lukacs note, 'managers [could] more than double their income through sponsoring innovations' (p. 729).

One may question the causal analysis offered by Burawoy and Lukacs, and suggest other possible causes of the innovations they observed in the socialist firm. Perhaps, for example, this willingness to innovate reflected local craft traditions that existed before the industrial revolution and before the socialist takeover of Hungary. It would also be instructive to look at one of Toyota's machine shops to understand how the Japanese system supports or fails to support innovation.

stop!   This article encourages you to examine your assumptions about the superiority of particular ways of organizing work. Many successful businesses assumed that their success would last for ever. They assumed further that their approach to organizing work was superior to all others. Can you think of once-successful companies whose current difficulties stem in part from complacency with regard to the organization of work? How might successful companies avoid the trap of complacency?

Sources and further information

Burawoy, M. and Lukacs, J. (1985) 'Mythologies of work: a comparison of firms in state socialism and advanced capitalism', *American Sociological Review*, 50(6), pp. 723–37.

Harvard Business Review on Manufacturing Excellence at Toyota, Boston, MA: Harvard Business School Press, 2008.

Ragin, C. (1994) *Constructing Social Research*, Thousand Oaks, CA: Pine Forge Press.

Note: This feature was written by David MacLennan, Assistant Professor at Thompson Rivers University, BC, Canada.

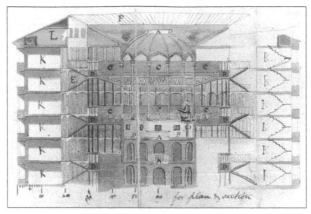

Figure 6.1 – The panopticon building

Historians have debated the role of technology in factory work organization. For example, it is argued that the origins of management within capitalist production lie not in the extended division of labour created by technical developments, but in the desire for social control on the part of capitalists, so that levels of exploitation could be increased.[38] Factories were not the inevitable results of technical change, nor were they the inexorable results of the search for simple efficiency. The architecture of the new factories had much in common with prisons. Jeremy Bentham coined the term 'panopticon' in 1816 to describe a circular building that could provide 'hierarchical observation' and 'normalizing judgement' (Figure 6.1). Observing Victorian architecture and Bentham's idea of a panopticon, the twentieth-century philosopher Michel Foucault asked, 'Is it surprising that prison resembles factories, schools, barracks, hospitals, which all resemble prisons?' (ref. 33, p. 30). The suggestion is that the factory, with its specialization and logical flows of processes, provided capitalists with a formal role as managers or coordinators. An alternative interpretation for the new forms of organizing work emphasizes the inadequacy of the family-based putting-out system in the face of expanding markets.[39]

The new factory system transformed the social organization of work. Factories needed a disciplined workforce. In this lay another key development associated with factory-based work – the shaping of workers' behaviour based on new concepts of commitment and time. In the early period of industrialization, changing workers' behaviour had a number of aspects: both entering the factory itself, and the **work ethic**. Workers, particularly men, were reluctant to enter the factories, with their unaccustomed rules and discipline, because they 'lost their birthright, independence' (ref. 40, p. 51). The majority of workers were women and children, who were more pliant and easier to manage.

work ethic: a set of values that stresses the importance of work to the identity and sense of worth of the individual and encourages an attitude of diligence in the mind of the people

OB in focus

The working week – a matter for the law?

These days, people increasingly expect businesses to be open all hours – yet many companies are having to lay off workers as a result of a downturn in the global economy. As a result, staff are under increasing pressure to deliver more and work harder. Does the law need to intervene?

The European Union Working Time Directive states that working hours should not exceed 48 hours per week, which is causing problems in the UK, as the National Health Service struggles to comply with this rule and reduce doctors' working hours without compromising on care (1). Across the Channel in France, the much-vaunted 35 hour working week, introduced in 2000, has effectively been abolished under a new law passed in 2008 allowing companies to 'strike individual deals with unions on working hours and overtime'(2). Canada is grappling with similar issues as it considers whether middle managers (who are currently 'not covered by labour standards legislation'(3)) should be offered protection.

What do *you* think? What role should the law, and trade unions, play in determining working conditions? Should these laws apply equally to all job types? Are there any cases where 'long hours come with the territory?'(3).

Sources: (1) 'Doctors warn over working rules', BBC news online, May 27, 2009. (2) 'MPs scrap France's 35-hour week', BBC news online, July 24, 2008. (3) Gate, V. (2005) 'Worn-out middle managers may get protection: Labour Code review could expand reach', *Globe and Mail*, January 3, p. B1.

Once in the factory, the employers had to develop 'appropriate' and 'responsible' behaviour that met the needs of the new work regime. This involved the management instilling in workers attitudes of obedience to factory regulations and punctuality. What the employers required was a 'new breed of worker' whose behaviour reacted favourably to the inexorable demands of the pace-setting machine, factory rationality and the 'tyranny of the clock'. The process took several generations: 'by the division of labour; the supervision of labour; fines; bells and clocks; money incentives; preaching and schooling; the suppression of fairs and sports – new labour habits were formed, and a new time-discipline was imposed' (ref. 41, p. 90). From the preoccupation with workers' work motivation and behaviour, there eventually emerged a specialized branch of management: personnel, or human resource management.

Taylorism and Fordism

In this section, we turn to what others call 'classical' work organization – Taylorism and Fordism. They are considered classical partly because they represent the earliest contributions to modern management theory, but they are also classical because they identify ideas and issues that keep occurring in contemporary organizational behaviour and management literature, although writers now tend to use a different vocabulary.[42] We will now consider each of these influential classical approaches to work organization.

Plate 2 – The First World War (1914-18) saw large numbers of women finding employment in the munitions and engineering factories.
Source: Nick Hedges

Taylorism

Taylorism: a process of determining the division of work into its smallest possible skill elements, and how the process of completing each task can be standardized to achieve maximum efficiency. Also referred to as scientific management

The American Frederick W. Taylor (1856–1915) pioneered the scientific management approach to work organization, hence the term **Taylorism**. Taylor developed his ideas on work organization while working as superintendent at the Midvale Steel Company in Pennsylvania, USA. Taylorism represents both a set of management practices and a system of ideological assumptions.[27] The autonomy (freedom from control) of craft workers was potentially a threat to managerial control. For the craft worker, the exercise of control over work practices was closely linked to his personality, as this description of 'craft pride', taken from the trade journal *Machinery* in 1915, suggests:

> [The craftsman] is engaged in tasks where the capacity for original thought is exercised: he has refined and critical perceptions of the things pertaining to his craft. His work creates a feeling of self-reliance ... he lives a full and satisfying life.

(ref. 43, p. 97)

As a first-line manager, Taylor not surprisingly viewed the position of skilled shop-floor workers differently. He was appalled by what he regarded as inefficient working practices and the tendency of his subordinates not to put in a full day's work, what Taylor called 'natural soldiering'. He believed that workers who did manual work were motivated solely by money – the image of the 'greedy robot' – and were too stupid to develop the most efficient way of performing a task – the 'one best way'. The role of management was to analyse 'scientifically' all the tasks to be undertaken, and then to design jobs to eliminate time and motion waste.

Taylor's approach to work organization and employment relations was based on the following five principles:

- maximum job fragmentation
- separate planning and doing
- separate 'direct' and 'indirect' labour
- a minimization of skill requirements
- a minimization of handling component parts and material.

The centrepiece of scientific management is the separation of tasks into their simplest constituent elements – 'routinization of work' (the first principle). Most manual workers were viewed as sinful and stupid, and therefore all decision-making functions had to be removed from their hands (the second principle). All preparation and servicing tasks should be taken away from the skilled worker (direct labour), and, drawing on Charles Babbage's principle, performed by unskilled and cheaper labour (indirect labour, in the third principle). Minimizing the skill requirements to perform a task would reduce the worker's control over work activities or the labour process (the fourth principle). Finally, management should ensure that the layout of the machines on the factory floor minimized the movement of people and materials to shorten the time taken (the fifth principle).

stop reflect
Can you think of jobs in the retail and service sector that would support the charge that work systems in the modern workplace continue to be affected by neo-Taylorism?

While the logic of work fragmentation and routinization is simple and compelling, the principles of Taylorism reflect the class antagonism that is found in employment relations. When Taylor's principles were applied to work organization, they led to the intensification of work: to 'speeding up', 'deskilling' and new techniques to control workers, as shown in Figure 6.2. And since gender, as we have discussed, is both a system of classification and a structure of power relations, it should not surprise us that Taylorism contributed to the shift in the gender composition of engineering firms. As millions of men were recruited into the armed forces for the First World War (1914–18), job fragmentation and the production of standardized items such as rifles, guns and munitions enabled women 'dilutees' to be employed in what had previously been skilled jobs reserved exclusively for men.[43]

Some writers argue that Taylorism was a relatively short-lived phenomenon, which died in the economic depression of the 1930s.[44] However, others have argued that this view underestimates the spread and influence of Taylor's principles: 'the popular notion that Taylorism has been "superseded" by later schools of "human relations", that it "failed" … represents a woeful misreading of the actual dynamics of the development of management' (ref. 45, p. 56). Similarly, others have made a persuasive case that, 'In general the direct and indirect influence of Taylorism on factory jobs has been extensive, so that in Britain job design and technology design have become imbued with neo-Taylorism' (ref. 10, p. 73).

Fordism

Henry Ford (1863–1947) applied the major principles of scientific management in his car plant, as well as installing specialized machines and adding a crucial innovation to

Figure 6.2 – A craft union response to Taylorism

Fordism: a term used to describe mass production using assembly-line technology that allowed for greater division of labour and time and motion management, techniques pioneered by the American car manufacturer Henry Ford in the early twentieth century

Taylorism: the flow-line principle of assembly work. This kind of work organization has come to be called **Fordism**. The moving assembly line had a major impact on employment relations. It exerted greater control over how workers performed their tasks, and it involved the intensification of work and labour productivity through ever-greater job fragmentation and short task-cycle times. In 1922, Henry Ford stated his approach to managing shop-floor workers: 'The idea is that man ... must have every second necessary but not a single unnecessary second' (ref. 46, p. 33).

The speed of work on the assembly line is determined by the technology itself rather than by a series of written instructions. Management's control of the work process was also enhanced by a detailed time and motion study inaugurated by Taylor. Work study engineers attempted to discover the shortest possible task-cycle time. Recording job times meant that managers could monitor more closely their subordinates' effort levels and performance. Task measurement therefore acted as the basis of a new structure of control.

Fordism is also characterized by two other essential features. The first was the introduction of an interlinking system of conveyor lines that fed components to different work stations to be worked on, and the second was the standardization of commodities to gain economies of scale. Thus, Fordism established the long-term principle of the mass production of standardized commodities at a reduced cost.

Ford's production system was, however, not without its problems. Workers found the repetitive work boring and unchallenging, and their job dissatisfaction was expressed in high rates of absenteeism and turnover. In 1913, for example, the turnover of Ford workers was more than 50,000. The management techniques developed by Ford in response to these employment problems serve further to differentiate Fordism from Taylorism. Henry Ford introduced the 'five dollar day' – double the pay and shorter hours for those who qualified. Benefits depended on a factory worker's lifestyle being deemed satisfactory, which included abstaining from alcohol. Ford's style of paternalism attempted to inculcate new social habits, as well as new labour habits, that would facilitate job performance.

Taylorism and Fordism became the predominant approaches to job design in vehicle and electrical engineering – the large-batch production industries – in the USA and Britain.[10,46]

Post-Fordism

As a strategy of organizing work and people, Taylorism and Fordism had their limitations. First, work simplification led to boredom and dissatisfaction, and tended to encourage adversarial relations and conflict, including frequent work stoppages. Second, Taylor-style work involves control and coordination costs. As specialization increases, so do indirect labour costs as more production planners, supervisors and quality control inspectors are employed. The economies associated with the division of labour tend to be offset by the diseconomies of management control costs.

Third, Taylorism and Fordism affect what might be called 'cooperation costs'. As management's control over the quantity and quality of workers' performance increases, workers experience increased frustration and dissatisfaction, which leads to a withdrawal of their commitment to the organization. The relationship between controller and controlled can deteriorate so much that it results in a further increase in management control. The principles of Taylorism and Fordism thus reveal a basic paradox, 'that the tighter the control of labour power, the more control is needed' (ref. 10, pp. 36–7). The adverse reactions to the extreme division of labour led to the development of new approaches to work organization that attempted to address these problems.

The 'human relations' movement attempted to address the limitations of Taylorism and Fordism by shifting attention to the perceived psychological and social needs of workers. The movement grew out of the Hawthorne experiments conducted by Elton Mayo in the 1920s. Mayo set up an experiment in the relay assembly room at the Hawthorne Works in Chicago, USA, which was designed to test the effects on productivity of variations in working conditions (lighting, temperature and ventilation). The Hawthorne research team found no clear relationship between any of these factors and productivity. However, the study led the researchers to develop concepts that might explain the factors affecting worker motivation. They concluded that more than just economic incentives and the work environment motivated workers: recognition and social cohesion were important too.

The message for management was also quite clear: rather than depending on management controls and financial incentives, it needed to influence the work group by cultivating a culture that met the social needs of workers. The human relations movement advocated various techniques such as worker participation and non-authoritarian supervisors, which would, it was thought, promote a climate of good (neo)-human relations in which the quantity and quality needs of management could be met. This largely forgotten history, which examined concepts such as atmosphere, informal structures and organizational climate, reminds us that twenty-first-century culturalist scholarship is not a completely new development in the thinking about organizations.[47]

Criticisms of the human relations approach charged managerial bias and the fact that its advocates tended to play down the basic economic conflict of interest between the employer and employee. Critics pointed out that when the techniques were tested, it became apparent that workers did not inevitably respond as predicted. The human relations approach also neglects wider socioeconomic factors (see ref. 12 for an excellent critical analysis of this approach to work). Despite these criticisms, however, the human relations approach to job design began to have some impact on management practices in the post-Second World War environment of full employment.

In the 1970s, new approaches to work design stressed the principles of closure, whereby the scope of the job is such that it includes all the tasks to complete a product or process, and task variety, whereby the worker acquires a range of different skills so that job flexibility is possible and the worker can personally monitor the quantity and quality of the work. This thinking spawned new techniques such as 'job enrichment', which gave the worker a wider range of tasks to perform and some discretion over how those tasks were done. For example, in the context of a fast-food outlet, an employee's job would, instead of being limited to grilling burgers, be enlarged to grilling the burgers, preparing the salad, ordering the produce from the wholesaler and inspecting the quality of the food on delivery.

Some theorists have been critical of these new work designs. An influential study argues that although job enrichment techniques may increase job satisfaction and commitment, the key focus remains managerial control. Although post-Fordism work design strategies gave individuals or work groups a wider measure of discretion over their work, or 'responsible autonomy', the strategy is a 'tool of self-discipline' and a means of maintaining or even intensifying managerial control.

With the growth of call centres over the past decade, critical research has drawn attention to 'new' forms of Taylorism. It is alleged that sophisticated electronic eavesdropping on salesperson–client conversations, and peer group scrutiny, have created 'electronic sweatshops' or a form of 'electronic Taylorism'.[12,48–50]

Work teams and high-performance workplaces

weblink
Go to the 2004 Workplace Employee Relations Survey website www.berr.gov.uk for more information on trends in work organization

The favoured work configuration over the last two decades has been team working. The focus on work teams has grown out of, drawn upon and sometimes reacted against Taylorism and Fordism.[42] The centrepiece of team working is functional flexibility, with members undertaking a wide range of tasks with a high degree of autonomy.

In the 1980s, Japanese work and employment practices were held up as a model for the struggling UK and North American manufacturing sectors.[51–55] The Japanese model has been a 'contested concept' in its description, interpretation and explanation.[56] Pioneering interpretations of the model identify three notable elements: flexibility, quality control and minimum waste.

Flexibility is achieved by arranging machinery in a group – what is known as 'cellular technology' – and by employing a multiskilled workforce. Thus, the work organization is the opposite of that of 'Taylorism': a generalized, skilled machinist with flexible job boundaries is a substitute for the specialized machinist operating one machine in one particular workstation. Higher-quality standards are achieved by making quality every worker's responsibility. Minimum waste, the third element of the Japanese model, is achieved by just-in-time techniques. As the name suggests, this is a hand-to-mouth mode of manufacture that aims to produce no more than the necessary components, in the necessary quantities, of the necessary quality and at the necessary time. Team working has a cultural and social dimension. The practices aim to generate social cohesion and a 'moral commitment' to common organizational goals.

The managerial mantra of the 1990s was flexibility, although various terms were used to describe these fashions in work organization: flexible specialization or 'flexspec', 'lean production', 're-engineering' and 'high-performance work systems' are well established in the literature. In the late 1990s, Japan experienced slow economic growth, and thereafter the US model of work organization was again held up as the exemplar. The new debate focused on whether the high-performance workplace, comprising a combination of work and employment variables or 'bundles' of 'best' practices, can deliver comparative advantage.

Post-industrial work

The 'Information Revolution', which we date from 1980 with the development of the silicon chip, marks, as does the Industrial Revolution 200 years earlier, a fundamental transformation of human activity. One theme running through this chapter has been the continuities as well as the discontinuities across time. There is no doubt that, for many people, paid work has changed profoundly during the Information Age, but these changes must be set in a historical context if we are to appreciate their significance and relevance.

Critical insight

As you study organizational behaviour, you should look at less orthodox material – expanding voices – as well as the established experts in the field. Leslie Salzinger's book *Genders in Production* is an example of the kinds of other voice it is useful to consider.[57] Through case studies of employment and management in four different transnational factories, the author provides a sophisticated analysis of gender relations in the workplace. She explains the variability and flexibility of concepts of femininity and masculinity, and the fact that they are context-dependent behaviours.

As Salzinger asserts, in a globalized world the creation of 'cheap labour' is central to the economic process. However, although the young women at the factories she studied are generally perceived to be intrinsically 'cheap, docile, and dextrous', she comments that 'Panoptimex, like all effective arenas of production, makes not only TVs but workers.'

Obtain a copy of Salzinger's book, 'Producing women – femininity on the line'. What does Salzinger mean when she states that Panoptimex makes not only TVs but also workers?

Knowledge work

knowledge work: paid work that is of an intellectual nature, non-repetitive and result-oriented, engages scientific and/or artistic knowledge, and demands continuous learning and creativity

The emergence of **knowledge work** – intellectual capital – and the 'knowledge worker' – employees who carry knowledge as a powerful resource which they, rather than the organization, own – is closely associated with the contemporary, sophisticated, Internet-based information technologies. Defining the notion of knowledge work and knowledge worker has proven problematic. Following Horwitz et al., however, we can say that knowledge work is characterized as 'ambiguity intensive', and a knowledge worker is an individual with the ability to communicate and apply professional knowledge, as well as manage other employees (see ref. 58, p. 31).

The nature of knowledge work is said to be fundamentally different from what we have traditionally associated with the 'machine age' and mass production, and hence it requires a different order of employment relations. It should not be confused with routine clerical work. It requires knowledge workers to learn a broad range of skills and knowledge, often with a focus around problems or customers, and to work in small groups or project teams to co-create new insights. It is also said to require a different employment relationship, with a psychological contract that has implications for employee commitment and career trajectory.

These differences in the nature of traditional work and knowledge work are spelled out in Table 6.1. In the Information Age, when an organization's wealth and ability to compete may exist 'principally in the heads of its employees' and human competitiveness can effectively 'walk out the gates' every day, it is not surprising that organizations are concerned with 'better' human resource practices and 'knowledge management' (ref. 59, p. 48). Information technology, new employment contracts and knowledge work have changed the 'spatiality' of work: some people do paid work at home, and others undertake more short-term work assignments as organizations

Table 6.1 – The nature of traditional work and knowledge work

	Traditional work	**Knowledge work**
Skill/knowledge sets	Narrow and often functional	Specialized and deep, but often with diffuse peripheral focuses
Locus of work	Around individuals	In groups and projects
Focus of work	Tasks, objectives, performance	Customers, problems, issues
Skill obsolescence	Gradual	Rapid
Activity/feedback cycles	Primary and of an immediate nature	Lengthy from a business perspective
Performance measures	Task deliverables Little (as planned), but regular and dependable	Process effectiveness Potentially great, but often erratic
Career formation	Internal to the organization through training, development, rules and prescriptive career schemes	External to the organization, through years of education and socialization
Employee's loyalty	To organization and his or her career systems	To professions, networks and peers
Impact on company success	Many small contributions that support the master plan	A few major contributions of strategic and long-term importance

Source: adapted from Despres and Hiltrop (1995)[102] and Boud and Garrick (1999)[59]

reduce their 'core' employees and contract work out.[19] Critical accounts of contemporary work in advanced capitalist economies offer a counterweight to the bullish management perspectives on the knowledge economy and provide data showing that the International Labour Organization's definition of 'decent work' remains elusive only for the privileged minority.[60,61] As European studies attest, there are too many businesses taking the 'low road' and striving for competitive advantage on the basis of a low-skill and low-pay workplace.[2]

Emotional work

With the growth of routinized service work, with its demands of customer sovereignty – such as fast food, tourism, hotels and call centres – new kinds of social relationship and aspects of the self have developed and come under scrutiny. As the service sector has grown in importance, there has, not surprisingly, been a growing interest in the embodied attributes and dispositions that are stereotypically feminine, such as patience, deference to the customer and a pleasant demeanour, associated with what sociologists call 'emotional labour'. Much has been written in recent years on how emotion is an important part of the effort–wage exchange, that workplaces in general have 'emotions',[62,63] and that 'strong' cultures strive to engender emotional energy, affection and even love for the organization.

Although the sociological analysis of workplace emotions is an expanding field of research, the classical sociological canons of Marx, Durkheim and Weber do contain important ideas about emotions. For instance, alienation engendered feelings of anger, and sentimentality was eliminated in bureaucracies gripped in the 'iron cage' of rationality. Modern critical scholarship emphasizes the servility of routine interactive workers within the service interface.[64]

It was the pioneering work of Arlie Hochschild that drew attention to the significance of social interaction as a crucial element of service provision. She considered emotional labour as part of the employment contract when 'the emotional style of offering the service is part of the service itself'.[65] Although servers in restaurants have always been trained to 'serve with a smile', there has been growing recognition that emotional labour is far more significant for a larger proportion than this of service employees, as management theorists emphasize 'customer service' as a vital aspect of business competitiveness. Emotional labour exists when workers are required, as part of the wage–effort bargain, to show emotions with the specific aim of causing customers or clients to feel and respond in a particular way. They might do this by verbal means – 'Good morning, sir/madam' – or non-verbal means, for example by smiling. Thus, the recent interest in emotional labour is focused on mobilizing emotions into the 'service' of the organization as an added dimension of the 'self' that the organization can appropriate, as has traditionally occurred with physical and mental labour.[66]

It is important to understand that emotional labour, like physical and intellectual labour, is bought by the employer for a wage. It requires a specific set of attributes and behaviours, and it can be a potential source of stress and alienation. Emotional labour 'carries the potential for individuals to become self-estranged – detached from their own "real" feelings – which in turn might threaten their sense of their own identity' (ref. 15, p. 193). The embodied attributes and skills associated with emotional labour compromise a particular type of working-class masculine identity. Manual labour has traditionally been a key source of identity, self-esteem and power for many working-class men. Emotional labour, however, is antithetical to muscular masculine identity. A study by Nixon in 2009 suggests that unskilled unemployed male workers were psychologically mismatched to the demands of customer sovereignty.[67] He found that those men who had been employed in service jobs did not last long: 'I've got no patience with people basically. I can't put a smiley face on, that's not my sort of thing,' said one 24-year-old unskilled manual worker. Others said they disliked the pressure to 'chase customers', and found work at call centres involved 'Too much talking' (ref. 67, pp. 314–15). The seismic shifts associated with the 'new economy' appear to have eliminated not only particular types of jobs, but also a type of masculine identity.

Our brief history of work organization suggests that when an economy enjoys economic success, its work and management practices will often be regarded as a model by slower-growing economies.[68] Consistent with this prediction, European organizations adopted US management ideas for most of the twentieth century, and adopted the 'Japanese model' in the 1980s, including team working. The 2004 Workplace and Employee Relations Survey (WERS) provides data on how these work practices are applied in UK workplaces.

Much of the literature on 'new' forms of work simplifies the analysis to a polar comparison between 'traditional' Fordism and new 'post-Fordism' work team characteristics. But although it looks elegant to draw up lists of opposite characteristics, this is not a good reflection of reality.[69,70] We can today still witness old 'boring' work forms existing alongside new 'decent' work configurations. Work in post-industrial capitalism is still routinized in both the manufacturing and the service sectors. In this brave new world of work, task variety is low, skill requirements are low, security and

stop reflect

A major theme of this section has been the continuities as well as the discontinuities across time in paid work. Can you see any similarities between knowledge work in home-based distributed environments and the putting-out system? Look at Plate 7 (page 43), showing a scene of customers and a server. What does the picture reveal about emotional labour? Have you ever been in a situation at work where you had to manage your feelings before customers? If so, what did it do to your sense of self?

weblink

Go to the following websites for more information and statistics on economic trends and gender relations in the workplace: www. statistics.gov.uk; www. eiro.eurofound.ie; www. un.org/womenwatch; www. isreview.org (search for Eleanor Burke Leacock)

dignity are low, and managerial control, reminiscent of Frederick Taylor's philosophy of a century ago, remains rule bound. All this suggests that the nature of work remains largely unchanged for millions of workers, that the design of work is not a smooth transition from one model to another, and that contemporary work regimes are most likely to resemble a hybrid configuration, with elements from the old work design and parts of the new.

WORK IN ORGANIZATIONS: AN INTEGRATION OF IDEAS

In discussing post-Fordism, we emphasized competing claims over whether new forms of work lead to an enrichment of work or the degradation of work. Managerial optimists argue that new work structures empower employees, and celebrate the claim that managerial behaviour has shifted its focus from 'control' to 'commitment'.[71] Critical analysts contend that some new work regimes are 'electronic sweatshops', and are basically a euphemism for work intensification. To capture the new realities of the modern workplace, critics often use the term 'McWorld' or '**McDonaldization**', meaning that a vast amount of work experience, especially for young people, women and workers of colour, involves menial tasks, part-time contracts, close monitoring of performance and entrenched job insecurity (for a good critical review of this trend, see refs 50 and 72–75).

In Figure 6.3, we draw together the developments in work and employment practices over the last 200 years, by highlighting four paradigms or distinctive approaches: craft/artisan, Taylorism/Fordism, neo-Fordism and post-Fordism. Work is shown to vary along two dimensions: the *variety of work* – the extent to which employees have an opportunity to do a range of tasks using their various skills and knowledge – and the *autonomy in work* – the degree of initiative that employees can exercise over how their immediate work is performed.

McDonaldization (also known as 'McWork' or 'McJobs'): a term used to symbolize the new realities of corporate-driven globalization that engulf young people in the twenty-first century, including simple work patterns, electronic controls, low pay and part-time and temporary employment

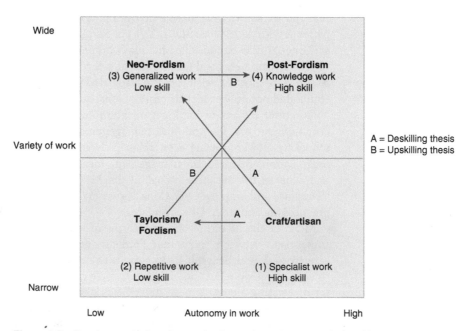

Figure 6.3 – Development of work organization and employment relationships

Here, *craft/artisan* means the types of work organization that are based on craft-based skills and often associated with a narrow range of specialized tasks, a high level of skill and a high degree of autonomy. Taylorism/Fordism means the adoption of basic scientific management principles and the assembly-line methods pioneered by Henry Ford, and **neo-Fordism** refers to a work configuration that has modified the core principles of Fordism through flexible working practices to fit contemporary operations. In contrast to the craft/artisan paradigm, the Taylorism/Fordism and neo-Fordism paradigms are often associated with a narrow variety of tasks, a low level of skill and a low degree of autonomy in work. **Post-Fordism** refers to organizations that do not rely on the principles of Taylorism or Fordism, and is often associated with 'high-performance work systems', with self-management and with a high degree of autonomy in work.

As others have mentioned, the strength of this conceptual model is as a heuristic device – a teaching aid – to help us summarise the complex development of work organization and employment relations. The research on the trends in work design suggests that Taylorism and Fordism have dominated the managerial approaches to work organization.

In addition to the four broad classifications of work organization, the model shows two trends proposed by the proponents of the 'deskilling' and 'upskilling' theses. The deskilling thesis maintains that, in Western capitalist economies, there is a general trend in paid work towards a narrow variety of tasks and low autonomy; the arrows marked 'A' represent this trend in the diagram. The upskilling thesis suggests an opposite trend towards a wide variety of tasks and high autonomy in work; the arrows marked 'B' represents this trend. It is important to understand that different regimes of work organization affect the nature of the employment relationship, whether or not this is explicitly acknowledged in the writings of organizational theorists. For example, if work is reorganized to deskill or upskill employees, this will change the degree of interdependency, and typically the power dynamics, between the employer and employee.

To sum up, some of the more recent empirically based literature offers a context-sensitive understanding of the development of work, and rejects a general tendency towards either deskilling or upskilling. The 'context-sensitive' view makes the point that new work structures do not have uniform outcomes, but are likely to be 'mixed' and contingent on a number of variables, such as business strategy, the nature of new technology, the degree of employee involvement in decision making, union involvement in the change process, and the extent to which 'bundles' of employment practices support the new work regime. In sum, the identification of potential benefits and costs for workers from new work configurations provides a more complex picture, one that strongly supports the **hypothesis** that changes in the nature of work can strengthen or threaten the 'psychological contract'.

neo-Fordism/ post-Fordism: the development from mass production assembly lines to more flexible manufacturing processes

hypotheses: statements making empirically testable declarations that certain variables and their corresponding measure are related in a specific way proposed by theory
hypothesis: in search studies, a tentative statement of the relationship between two or more concepts or variables

GENDER AND THE SEXUAL DIVISION OF WORK

Figure 6.3 does not, however, show how gender ideologies shape work or the sexual division of work. To understand contemporary issues of gender – by which we mean the processes of gender roles, inequalities in society and women's subordination and exploitation – we need to look at the historical developments of gender–work patterns.

Gender-based patterns of work and gender inequality were universal in early industrial capitalism. In 1838, over 70 per cent of factory textile workers were adult women and children. Family labour, with women and their children working together, was a feature of employment relations in the new factory system. The factory owner did not accept direct responsibility for the conditions of employment or supervision of the workforce, but subcontracted these people-management functions to an intermediary. Factory owners negotiated with the heads of families for the whole family unit. There is evidence that the worst conditions of employment under industrial capitalism existed in these circumstances. Child labour began at the age of 4 in some cases in order to oblige parents, but most child workers started between the ages of 7 and 10. An adult man entered the new textile factories with his family, and the 'fact that discipline was imposed on the children largely by their own parents made the harshness of the new disciplines socially tolerable' (ref. 76, p. 202).

After 1850, with the exception of waged work in domestic service and textiles, industrial capitalism tended to create a clear distinction between the paid work opportunities of women (particularly married women) and of men. With the spread of the factory system, the need for cheap labour power provided opportunities for working-class women to do wage work in areas unrelated to their former work in the home. Large-scale food-processing factories – for example, bakeries – were female dominated in the late nineteenth century. In working-class families, women often remained in the labour market to support the family income. When middle-class women married, they were primarily expected to withdraw from paid employment to take care of the house and children. Reinforcing the belief that work and family life were two separate spheres – the stereotypes of men as strong and competitive and women as frail and nurturing – began to emerge: 'images that depicted men as naturally suited to the highly competitive nineteenth-century workplace and women as too delicate for the world of commerce' (ref. 77, p. 21).

Gender-based patterns of work changed when war broke out in Europe in 1914. The First World War was the first 'mass' war in the sense that it required the mobilization of massive quantities of products and people. Whereas Napoleon waged war against Prussia in 1806 using no more than 1500 rounds of artillery shells, in 1917 the French munitions industry had to produce 200,000 shells a day: 'Mass war required mass production' (ref. 78, p. 45). It also made it necessary to rethink the social organization of work. As Britain mobilized 12.5 per cent of its able-bodied men for the armed forces, the government encouraged women to enter the munitions and engineering factories, and this led to a revolution in waged work for women outside the household. It resulted in several occupations turning permanently into female preserves, including offices, hotels, shops, cinemas and to a lesser extent transport. In other occupations, such as engineering, men were reabsorbed in 1919 and women went back to pre-war patterns of paid or unpaid work.

Did industrial capitalism segregate the home from work, and allocate women to the former and men to the latter? Gender-based patterns of work and family-located sites of work are forms that predate capitalism: they are not the results of social changes induced by capitalism. Women's work tended to be concentrated around six human activities that predate capitalism: to bear children, to feed them and other members of the family, to clothe the family, to care for the young and old when sick, to educate children, and to take care of the home.[35,79] Explanations for why some work was men's and some was women's are almost as various as the patterns of wages that have existed. In the pre-Industrial Revolution period, there is some evidence that women did a much greater variety of jobs, but even then gender influenced the allocation and reward of work. A disproportionate number of women undertook the most menial, poorly paid and domestically related jobs.

Evidence about work-related gender relations before the nineteenth century is sparse. Contemporary accounts emphasize that the gender division of work is socially constructed, and that work tended to be labelled female or male on the basis of socially changeable expectations about how to view, judge and treat the two sexes. Part of the long historical process of gender inequality at work can be explained by the activities of the pre-industrial craft guilds and the **trade unions**. The town-based craft guilds, the forerunners of trade unions, tended to be exclusively male oriented, with severe restrictions on women's membership. In the context of competitive pressure to reduce labour costs and the economic effect of female workers in terms of depressing wages, male-dominated trade unions worked hard to maintain or restore wage levels and traditional employment privileges.[80]

Trade union bargaining strategies developed gender-based occupational segregation. One function of trade unionism, according to one union leader, was 'to bring about a condition ... where wives and daughters would be in their proper sphere at home, instead of being dragged into competition for livelihood against the great and strong men of the world' (ref. 81, p. 185). Prior to 1858, women participated in medicine quite widely, but thereafter, as in other traditional professions, the work became a male preserve. With the exception of midwifery and nursing, a combination of government legislation and male tactics excluded middle-class women from all medical practices.[82] Feminist critiques of the sociology of work have demonstrated in important ways the manner in which both the theory and practice of work and work behaviour have excluded women as subjects, as well as their experiences and voices.[83]

Married women were systematically removed from waged work after the initial phase of the Industrial Revolution. The new factory system proved beneficial to working-class women, particularly unmarried women, providing waged work outside the grossly exploitative decentralized putting-out system. Throughout the nineteenth century and well into the twentieth century, men managed to effectively exclude working-class and middle-class women from participating in many trade and professional occupations, by retaining old 'skills' or monopolizing new ones, using their professional privilege and power, using strategies of closure and demarcation, and encouraging the concepts of 'skill' and 'profession' to be seen as male property.[84]

In the twenty-first century, although the realities of workplaces have changed, ideas about them have lagged far behind.[85] Many Europeans and North Americans still believe in the 'traditional' male breadwinner/female home-keeper model, even though household lives and financial imperatives no longer reflect it. In Germany, for example, the traditional sense of family roles remains strong, and women who do paid work can be called *Rabenmutter*, meaning a raven mother. Commenting on German social values in 2006, Reiner Klingholz, head of the Berlin Institute for Population and Development, said, 'These old-fashioned ideas about the sexes aren't really part of mainstream German thought any more, but it's still embedded in the neurons of our brains that women have to stay home and take care of the children' (quoted in ref. 86).

WORK LESS, LIVE BETTER? MANAGING THE WORK–LIFE BALANCE

The interplay between working life, the family and the community, often expressed as '**work–life balance**', is a 'hot' topic of debate and research that is receiving increasing attention from policy makers and managers.[87–89] The main message of

trade union: an organization whose purpose is to represent the collective interest of workers

weblink
Go to the following websites for more information on the history of trade unions and current statistics on trade union organization: www.tuc.org.uk; www.icftu.org; www.cosatu.org.za

weblink
Go to the following websites for more information and statistics on women employed in advanced capitalist societies: http://europa.eu/index_en.htm; www.statistics.gov.uk; www.iegd.org

work–life balance: the interplay between working life, the family and the community, in terms of both time and space

discourse: a way of talking about and conceptual-izing an issue, presented through concepts, ideas and vocabulary that recur in texts

the debate is that a balance between work and life is desirable, and that too much work has negative effects on private life – in effect, a more sophisticated version of the popular proverb 'All work and no play makes Jack a dull boy.' In spite of the spate of literature, for Warhurst and his colleagues, the current debate on work–life balance remains problematic both empirically and conceptually.[90] Empirical research does indeed reveal a significant degree of interest in many organizations, but data show a mismatch between the work–life balance **discourse** and the reality in most workplaces.

This gap is illustrated by the findings from WERS 2006. The European Union Social Charter of 1961 obliged Member States to ensure 'reasonable and weekly working hours', yet research indicates that British workers work the longest hours in the EU-15 Member States.[91] Not surprising, therefore, the UK labour market has been characterized as the 'long hours culture'.[92] Setting a limit on the number of hours an employee must work in a working day and week most directly affects the work–life balance.

The boundary between work and private life is influenced by flexible working arrangements, such as 'home-working'. UK survey data show that the incidence of 'home-working' increased 12 per cent between 1998 and 2004. Women were more likely than men to have access to home-working arrangements, yet home-working was slightly more prevalent in workplaces where women were not in the majority.[93] There are a number of possible causes for this, including inadequate child care provision, non-standard or precarious employment and perhaps, in more recent years, a 'flight to work' in a period of economic uncertainty.

The concept at the centre of the work–life balance debate is problematic. The notion of work–life balance has been defined as 'the relationship between the institutional and cultural times and spaces of work and non-work in societies where income is predominantly generated and distributed through labour markets' (ref. 94, p. 56). Warhurst et al. argue that the concept of work–life *balance* is based on a traditional, large-scale workplace model which presumes that paid work and life constitute two distinct spheres, separated by time and space (Figure 6.4).[90] This orthodox binary interpretation adopts a particular interpretation of labour under capitalism, viewing paid work as an encroachment on people's 'real' private life, particularly family life, and seeing it as something that therefore has to be contained. As the examples and case studies included throughout this book suggest, work can be boring and alienating – a 'blank patch' between morning and evening – unhealthy and at times dangerous. Yet work brings fulfilment and friendship, and people can potentially derive joy from it.[2] Work brings structure to people's lives, dignity and satisfaction, and is an important source of identity.

Paid work	Life
Tasks	Child care
Projects	Housework
Deadlines	Elder care
Travel	Community activities
Meetings	Hobbies
Client demands	Holidays

Figure 6.4 – The notion of the work–life balance

Plate 3 – The interpenetration between work and life is most obvious in contemporary home-working, which allows professionals to engage in paid work and domestic activities in the same physical space, and perhaps even on occasion at the same time.
Source: Getty Images

Warhurst's et al. premise is that the work–life interface is not best articulated as one of 'balance' because 'interpenetration' occurs between the two spheres.[90] This interpenetration between work and life is most obvious in contemporary home-working, which, through information and communication technology, allows professionals to engage in paid work and domestic activities in the same physical space and maybe at the same time. Thus, the concept of work–life balance, with its suggestions of a binary opposition between 'work' and 'life', does not indicate how the complex interplay of personal choice and constraints, competing interests and power relations, shapes the relationship between work and life.

People are what Anthony Giddens[95] has called 'knowledgeable agents' – that is, they construct perceptions of work and life – and through their agency they produce social practices, which can be translated into what Warhurst et al.[90] call 'work–life patterns'. These social patterns and practices that human beings construct relate to work, family activities, maintaining friendships and the pursuit of leisure activities.

Naturally, depending on the individual's context, the way in which work–life patterns are experienced can vary markedly between individuals. The advocates of the work–life pattern approach identify four implications for researchers and discerning managers:

1 The focus of praxis proposes an analysis of actual work practices and the impact these have on work–life patterns. For example, if work is takes place in a fixed and unmovable location (for example, assembly-line work), work–life patterns are likely to exhibit a clear delineation between work and life.

2 Employment analysts and practitioners need to understand the structural constraints (economic, social and cultural resources) that fashion work–life patterns. For example, economic capital can buy additional time for work (for example, hiring a nanny) or life (for example, only part-time paid work); cultural (for example, education) and social (for example, extended family) resources also affect job opportunities and work–life choices and opportunities.

3 Lifestyles – values, beliefs and work-related perceptions – influence individual practices and work–life patterns. Max Weber first proposed a connection between lifestyle (religion and asceticism) and work–life patterns.[96] The lifestyle of artists, musicians or theatre actors, for example, might promote a fusing or 'amalgamation' of a work–life pattern. Thus, creative artists are more likely to regard 'work as life, and life as work' (ref. 90, p. 14). Neither is the notion of a fusing of a work–life pattern restricted to artistic labour. As Michelle Gillies, a recently unemployed professional who had been a promotion manager and producer in the Canadian broadcasting sector, said, 'My job was me. I spent 10 years so closely linked to what I did there that there were no lines separating the two' (quoted in ref. 97). Examples of work–life amalgamation illustrate that experience of work and life cannot be understood using a simple model that separates the two spheres and sets them into opposition.

4 Work–life patterns are constructed following a range of logics, depending on the context. Whereas work centres on exchanges between effort and pay, life embraces a multitude of logics, such as unconditional love for family, the reciprocity of friendships and self-gratification through conspicuous consumption. These logics of work and life coexist, allowing individuals 'a fairly frictionless *alternation* between the two distinct spheres' (ref. 90, p. 15).

Work–life patterns are continually (re)constructed as employees' work and life cycles change. Examples of such changes might include:

⊙ the shift from independent single person to mid-life with family dependants and so on
⊙ a change in perceived economic insecurity
⊙ government incentives and regulations to help individuals achieve work–life goals.[98]

Complex and problematic though the idea of work–life 'balance' may be, employers' strategies in this area can have important benefits for the organization. For example, work–life policies and practices might be important for attracting and motivating professionals and innovative behaviours[99,100] – and conversely, failure to introduce such policies and practices can have a detrimental effect. Many law firms in North America, for example, retain 'a dominant male hierarchy and a suspicion of women who crave a balance between work and family', and the industry is losing talented professionals as a result. As one anonymous lawyer attests, 'A lot of male lawyers … were extremely unhappy about losing these really high-calibre people'.[101]

weblink
Go to the following website for more information on the European Union Working Time Developments:www.eurofound.europa.eu/eiro/studies/tn0804029s/tn0804029s.htm. Information is also available for preceding years, and can be accessed at www.eurofound.europa.eu/eiro/comparative_index.htm

However, the idea of achieving a work–life 'balance' still seems remote for millions of low-income families. As we have seen, the work–life pattern approach is more complex than the notion of 'balance' between two separable spheres, and it is a perspective that has important implications for how work and people are managed in the workplace. We move on to examine how developments in work have been conceptualized and theorized.

OB and globalization

A family affair – cross-cultural adjustment to overseas work

The rapid growth of multinational organizations has been accompanied by an increase in the number of expatriate workers – people who work for a foreign branch of a parent company based in their home country. Sometimes, expatriate workers leave their families in the home country while they travel abroad for work. At other times, the parent company encourages workers' families to accompany them overseas.

Studies have shown that the rate of failure for overseas placements is high, with many workers returning home before the end of their overseas assignment. One of the top reasons given for this failure is the inability of workers' families to adjust to life in the host country. The failure of overseas work assignments can be personally stressful and defeating for the workers, can cost the parent company money, and can result in damage to business relationships with the host country. A 2008 *New York Times* article (Mohn, 2008) describes the interconnected challenges to work and family life that can accompany overseas work assignments:

> *The initial excitement of an exotic new posting can turn to culture shock, loneliness, identity loss and depression, and it is often the employee's spouse and children – without the familiar routine of work – who are most affected.*

When an employee's family does not adapt well to an overseas work assignment, familial happiness is not the only thing at stake. According to workforce mobility expert Brenda Fender, overseas postings can fail when employees' families are unhappy, resulting in substantial financial losses to companies (Mohn, 2008). This outcome is far from inevitable. Increasingly, organizations relying on expatriate workers to manage overseas operations are recognizing the relationship between organizational success and the ability of workers' families to adjust to life abroad, and they are developing strategies to support both business success and family happiness.

Caligiuri et al. (1998) emphasize the importance of organizations providing cross-cultural support, such as language training, to help expatriate workers and their families achieve social and cultural adjustment in the host country. When expatriate families felt that their cultural and social adjustment was supported by the organization, they were more likely to support the family member working for the organization, which in turn resulted in success for the worker and for the organization.

stop!   Imagine that you or a family member is posted to a job overseas. What types of cross-cultural support or information might be important for your adjustment to your new environment?

As an employee posted overseas, how might your sense of 'work–life balance' be affected by the experiences of other members of your family? What is the role of workers' families in organizational culture?

Sources and further information

Caligiuri, P. M., Hyland M. M., Bross A. S. and Joshi, A. (1998) 'Testing a theoretical model for examining the relationship between family adjustment and expatriates' work adjustment', *Journal of Applied Psychology*, **83**(4), pp. 598–614.

Expat Finder Blog. Available at: www.expatfinder.com/blog.

Mohn, T. (2008) 'The dislocated Americans', *New York Times*, December 1, 2008. Available at: www.nytimes.com/2008/12/02/business/worldbusiness/02expat.html.

Sharples, J. (2005) 'Regrets and resentment over relocation', *Daily Telegraph*, January 19, 2005. Available at: http://www.telegraph.co.uk/expat/4194833/Regrets-and-resentment-over-relocation.html.

Note: This feature was written by Gretchen Fox, PhD, Anthropologist, Timberline Natural Resource Group, Canada.

CHAPTER SUMMARY

○ One of the major themes running through the study of paid work has been the continuities as well as the discontinuities across time. There is no doubt that changes occur all the time, but these must be adequately contextualized if we are to appreciate their relevance. Thus, we can only really talk about a rise in instrumental orientations to work if we know what previously existed.

○ Trying to summarise the experience of work over several millennia is a difficult task. There is so much material to cover that no text of conventional size would be able to deal adequately with the complexities. However, this chapter has been written on the assumption that some knowledge is preferable to complete ignorance, especially if, to understand the present, we have to situate it against the past. The chapter has tended to highlight gender issues in the workplace to balance out the conventional preference for male history.

○ The complexity of the experience of work defies any simple assumptions about the significance of work. However, we can perhaps salvage from the past a conclusion that illuminates the significance of the social. Work, like other institutions, is inherently and irreducibly constructed, interpreted and organized through social actions and social discourse.

○ We explained how, with the growth of routinized service work, new kinds of social relations and aspects of the self have developed and come under scrutiny. As the service workforce has grown in importance, we noted the growing interest in 'emotional work', pioneered by Arlie Hochschild.

○ The persistence of gender ideologies on work, discrimination and the sexual division of paid work have been discussed, as has the persistent belief in the 'traditional' male breadwinner/female home-keeper model, particularly in periods of economic recession.

○ We have explored the concept of work–life balance and why this orthodox binary view is based on traditional large-scale work and life patterns separated by time and space. As such, paid work is regarded as an activity that is an encroachment on people's private life. A more complex approach is represented by the notion of work–life patterns, which sees the activity of labour itself as an important source of identity and satisfaction.

KEY CONCEPTS

cellular technology
control
division of labour
emotional labour
factory system
gender-based patterns of work
Industrial Revolution
knowledge work
labour power
McJobs
putting-out system
trade unions
work

work–life balance
work–life patterns

VOCAB CHECKLIST FOR ESL STUDENTS

- Artisan
- Control
- Corporation, corporate
- Deindustrialization
- Deskilling
- Discourse
- Division of labour
- Emotional work
- Extrinsic reward
- Factory system
- Flexibility, flexible
- Fordism
- Hypotheses
- Hypothesis
- Industrial Revolution
- Intrinsic reward
- Knowledge work
- Labour power
- Neo-Fordism
- Occupation, occupy
- Post-Fordism
- Post-industrial
- Pre-industrial
- Putting-out system
- Quality of working life
- Social structure
- Taylorism
- Trade union
- Upskilling
- Values, valuable
- Work ethic

CHAPTER REVIEW QUESTIONS

1 What is work?
2 What were the advantages and disadvantages of the putting-out system?
3 Why were men reluctant to enter the new factories during the Industrial Revolution?
4 Why were male trade unionists so hostile to women entering traditional occupations?
5 Explain the importance of 'control' in a factory system.
6 How does knowledge work different from traditional work?
7 How does emotional labour differ from traditional paid work?

8   What is the difference between work–life balance and work–life patterns? Why is it considered important for managers to understand these concepts?

CHAPTER RESEARCH QUESTIONS

1   Form a study group of three to five people. Look at Figure 6.3, which draws together the development of paid work and employment relations. As a group, discuss how each major job/organization design influences the job of a manager. What intrinsic rewards do employees obtain when working under (a) craft, and (b) post-Fordism? What are the advantages/disadvantages of home-working for (a) the employer, and (b) the employee? Why, if at all, is it important to manage work–life patterns?

2   Obtain a copy of Chris Warhurst's et al.'s (2008) *Work Less, Live More?*[90] Read, 'On the edge of the time bind: time and market culture'. How does the 'market culture' affect the modern family? How can the 'logic of work' crowd out 'life logics', and why is this important in understanding the debate on work–life patterns?

3   Retrieve and read Carol Emslie and Kate Hunt's (2009) article, '"Live to work" or "work to Live"? A qualitative study of gender and work–life balance among men and women in mid-life' (see Further Reading, below). Why should managers understand the work–life interface through a gender lens? How does the author explain how individual choices about work–life patterns are constrained by their socioeconomic resources and cultural norms?

FURTHER READING

Bolton, S. and Boyd, C. (2003) 'Trolley dolly or skilled emotion manager? Moving on from Hochschild's managed heart', *Work, Employment and Society*, **17**(2), pp. 289–308.

Bolton, S. C. and Houlihan M. (2009) *Work Matters*, Basingstoke: Palgrave Macmillan.

Edgell, S. (2006) *The Sociology of Work*, London: Sage.

Emslie, C. and Hunt, K. (2009) '"Live to work" or "work to live"? A qualitative study of gender and work–life balance among men and women in mid-life', *Gender, Work and Organization*, **16**(1), pp. 151–72.

Frenkel, S. J. (2006) 'Service workers in search of decent work', pp. 356–75 in S. Ackroyd, R. Batt, P. Thompson and P. Tolbert (eds), *The Oxford Handbook of Work and Organization*, New York: Oxford University Press.

Hardill, L. and Green, A. (2003) 'Remote working – altering the spatial contours of work and home in the new economy', *New Technology Work and Employment*, **18**(3), pp. 212–22.

Kelan, E. (2008) 'Gender, risk and employment insecurity: the masculine breadwinner subtext', *Human Relations*, **61**(9), pp. 1171–202.

Kvande, E. (2009) 'Work–life balance for fathers in globalized knowledge work. Some insights from the Norwegian context', *Gender, Work and Organization*, **16**(1), pp. 58–72.

Lewchuk, W., Clarke, M. and de Wolff, A. (2008) 'Working without commitments: precarious employment and health', *Work, Employment and Society*, **22**(3), pp. 387–406.

McCormick, K. (2007) 'Sociologists and "the Japanese model": a passing enthusiasm?', *Work, Employment and Society*, **21**(4), pp. 751–71.

McIvor, A. (2001) *A History of Work in Britain, 1880–1950*, Basingstoke: Palgrave Macmillan.

McKinlay, A. and Smith, C. (2009) *Creative Labour*, Basingstoke: Palgrave Macmillan.

Noon, M. and Blyton, P. (2009) *The Realities of Work*, Basingstoke: Palgrave Macmillan.

Salzinger, L. (2003) *Genders in Production*, Berkley, CA: University of California Press.

Warhurst, C., Eikhof, D. R. and Haunschild, A. (2008) *Work Less, Live More?*, Basingstoke: Palgrave.

Chapter case study 1

Service with a smile: McJobs in China

Setting

Although McDonald's is well known for its Fordist method of food production, China has had experience using an assembly-line approach to feed many people for over two centuries. As early as the nineteenth century, Chinese public dining halls had perfected breaking down the cooking process into basic procedures performed by a separate team of workers.

McDonald's brought its own brand of food production and management to China in 1990 when it opened its first restaurant in a city called Shenzhen. In 1992, the world's largest McDonald's was opened in Beijing, serving 40,000 customers on that first day. McDonald's now operates 1000 restaurants in more than 190 Chinese cities, with further expansion plans well underway.

More than 70 per cent of McDonald's restaurants worldwide are owned and operated independently by local men and women. In recent years, McDonald's future growth strategy has focused on China's smaller urban areas, known as second- and third-tier cities. McDonald's is not alone as many multinational and domestic companies are now looking to expand outside the traditional economic bases in the larger Chinese centres. McDonald's faces particularly stiff competition from KFC, a fellow American fast-food restaurant chain, which dominates the Chinese market.

While Chinese fast food operators do not deal with the high turnover rates seen in American cities (sometimes as high as 300 per cent for non-managerial employees), the rapid expansion by multiple companies has resulted in competition for quality workers and rising wage costs in the new tighter labour markets.

Problem

Hai Yan is one of the new owners of a McDonald's franchise in an area several hours outside Beijing. As with other franchisees, Hai relied on the McDonald's corporation to assist him with recruiting and training his new employees to bring them in line with the company's expectations.

Peter Bepple, a new Human Resources Manager assigned to the region, flew in from New York to help. Peter had never worked in China before and was looking forward to getting the new franchises up and running. He had been briefed on the recruiting issues and was told that although the Chinese were hard workers who respected management authority and leadership, they also expected their managers to build supportive relationships with them.

Upon his arrival in Hai's area, Peter immediately set up recruitment advertising on the company website, interviewed applicants on the phone, and made arrangements for selected candidates to come into Hai's restaurant for 3 days of work. Accompanied by a McDonald's employee, each candidate tried various roles from waiter to assistant manager in the restaurant. To Hai's dismay, 80 per cent of the candidates were not offered permanent employment. He became concerned that he would not find enough suitable workers to serve customers on his restaurant's opening day. Hai decided to approach Peter to find out why so many of the candidates had not been successful during the recruitment process.

Peter was sympathetic but explained to Hai that he had observed each failed candidate's reactions to the customers and was not impressed. 'The main challenge is to maintain a positive attitude and provide good service,' Peter told Hai. 'The most important characteristic is the willingness to communicate with others and that is best reflected with a smile. Those candidates simply did not smile enough.'

Hai was taken aback by the comment. 'Here in China customers are suspicious of workers who smile on the job,' he said to Peter.

Peter was surprised by this, but decided to check with his counterparts in other McDonald's locations in China to see if this was actually the case. They confirmed what Hai had said. 'Customers in China expect employees to be serious about their work,' he was told. 'The customers are more concerned about the efficiency, reliability and cleanliness of the restaurant than if the worker smiles at them.'

Before returning to New York, Peter's head office called and asked him to prepare a report on what he had learned on his first overseas assignment.

Tasks

Prepare a short report, incorporating answers to the following questions:

1　How important is it for the McDonald's customer service strategy to insist on having its employees provide 'service with a smile'?
2　What possible effects will forcing smiles have on the Chinese workers?
3　How could Peter have better prepared himself for working in China?
4　To what extent do you think the success of the US-based McDonald's corporation influences local Chinese companies to adopt its management practices, despite the cultural differences?

Essential reading

Deery, S. (2005) 'Customer service work, emotional labour and performance', Chapter 13 in S. Bach (ed.), *Managing Human Resources: Personnel Management in Transition*, Oxford: Blackwell.

Earnhardt, M. (2009) 'The successful expatriate leader in China', *Graziado Business Report*, 12(1). Available at: http://gbr.pepperdine.edu/091/expatriatesinchina.html.

Mujtaba, B. and Patel, B. (2007) 'McDonald's success strategy and global expansion through customer and brand loyalty', *Journal of Business Case Studies*, 3(3), pp. 55–66.

Watson, J. (2006) *Golden Arches East: McDonald's in East Asia*, Stanford: Stanford University Press.

Note

This case study was written by Lori Rilkoff, MSc, CHRP, Senior Human Resources Manager at the City of Kamloops, and lecturer in HRM at Thompson Rivers University, BC, Canada.

Chapter case study 2

Home-working in Matherdom City Council

Visit www.palgrave.com/business/brattonob2e to view this case study.

WEB-BASED ASSIGNMENT

Central to the advance of organizational behaviour as a field of critical inquiry is an openness to expanding our understanding of both work and the 'workplace'. We believe it is important to understand that work expands beyond the boundaries of 'paid work', and importantly, the place where work is performed extends beyond the formal organization. The notion of work–life pattern has increasing relevance to workers, particularly to women, in the early twenty-first century.

On an individual basis, or working in a small group, visit the following websites and write a brief report of the research and practical issues associated with (a) home-working, and (b) work–life balance: www.berr.gov.uk; www.tca.org.uk; www.thework-foundation.com/difference/e4wlb.aspx.

OB IN FILM

The film *Modern Times* (1936) features Charlie Chaplin in a scathing portrayal of North American assembly-line work. The first 15 minutes of the film humorously illustrate the meaning of Taylorism and the stress associated with working on an assembly line. The film led Charlie Chaplin to be banned from the USA and some of the actors to be investigated by the Federal Bureau of Investigation.

Watch the first 15 minutes of the film. What does the film tell us about Taylorism? How would you rate Chaplin's job in terms of 'job enrichment' techniques?

REFERENCES

1. Rubery, J. (2006) 'Labour markets and flexibility', pp. 31–51 in S. Ackroyd, R. Batt, P. Thompson and P. Tolbert (eds), *The Oxford Handbook of Work and Organization*, New York: Oxford University Press.
2. Bolton, S. C. and Houlihan, M. (eds) *Work Matters*, Basingstoke: Palgrave.
3. Gorz, A. (1982) *Farewell to the Working Class*, London: Pluto.
4. Rifkin, J. (1996) *The End of Work*, New York: Tarcher/Putnam.
5. Pahl, R. E. (ed.) (1988) *On Work*, Oxford: Blackwell.
6. Gates, W., with Myhrvold, N. and Rinearson, P. (1996) *The Road Ahead*, New York: Penguin.
7. Wood, S. (ed.) (1982) *The Transformation of Work?*, London: Unwin Hyman.
8. Zuboff, S. (1988) *In the Age of the Smart Machine*, New York: Basic Books.
9. Hearn, J., Sheppard, D., Tancred-Sheriff, P. and Rand Burrell, G. (eds) (1989) *The Sexuality of Organization*, London: Sage.
10. Littler, C. R. and Salaman, G. (1984) *Class at Work: The Design, Allocation and Control of Jobs*, London: Batsford.
11. Mills, A. and Tancred, P. (eds) (1992) *Gendering Organizational Analysis*, Newbury Park, CA: Sage.
12. Thompson, P. (1989) *The Nature of Work* (2nd edn), London: Macmillan.
13. Williams, R. (1983) *Keywords*, New York: Oxford University Press.
14. Christiansen, C. H. and Townsend, E. A. (2004) *Introduction to Occupation: The Art and Science of Living*, Upper Saddle River, NJ: Prentice Hall.
15. Noon, M. and Blyton, P. (2002) *The Realities of Work*, Basingstoke: Palgrave Macmillan.
16. Rinehart, J. W. (2006) *The Tyranny of Work: Alienation and the Labour Process* (4th edn), Scarborough, ON: Nelson Thomson.
17. Thomas, K. (1999) 'Introduction', pp. xiii–xxiii in K. Thomas (ed.), *The Oxford Book of Work*, Oxford: Oxford University Press.
18. Herod, A., Rainnie, A. and McGrath-Champ, S. (2007) 'Working space: why incorporating the geographical is central to theorizing work and employment practices', *Work, Employment and Society*, **21**(2), pp. 247–64.
19. Hardill, L. and Green, A. (2003) 'Remote working – altering the spatial contours of work and home in the new economy', *New Technology, Work and Employment*, **18**(3), pp. 212–22.
20. Coyle-Shapiro, J. A.-M., Shore, L., Taylor, M. S. and Tetrick, L. (2005) *The Employment Relationship*, Oxford: Oxford University Press.
21. Barnes, C. (1996) 'What next? Disability, the 1995 Disability Discrimination Act and the Campaign for Disabled Peoples' Rights', National Bureau for Disabled Students Annual Conference, March 2, Leeds, UK.
22. Guest, D. E. and Conway, N. (2002) 'Communicating the psychological contract: an employer perspective', *Human Resource Management Journal*, **12**(2), pp. 22–38.
23. Herriot, P. (1998) 'The role of human resource management in building a new proposition', pp. 106–16 in P. Sparrow and M. Marchington (eds), *Human Resource Management: A New Agenda*, London: Financial Times Management.
24. Kramer, R. M. and Tyler, T. R. (1996) *Trust in Organizations: Frontiers of Theory and Research*, Newbury Park, CA: Sage.
25. Rousseau, D. M. (1995) *Psychological Contracts in Organisations: Understanding Written and Unwritten Agreements*, Thousand Oaks, CA: Sage.
26. Atkinson, C. (2008) 'An exploration of small firm psychological contracts', *Work, Employment and Society*, **22**(3), pp. 447–65.

27. Sveiby, K. E. (1997) *The New Organizational Wealth: Managing and Measuring Organizational Wealth*, San Francisco, CA: Berrett-Koehler.
28. Hodson, R. and Sullivan, T. A. (2002) *The Social Organization of Work* (3rd edn), Belmont, CA: Wadsworth/Thomson Learning.
29. Grint, K. (1998) *The Sociology of Work* (2nd edn), Cambridge: Polity Press.
30. Hobsbawm, E. (1997) *On History*, London: Weidenfeld & Nicolson.
31. Littler, C. R. (1982) *The Development of the Labour Process in Capitalist Societies*, London: Heinemann.
32. Salaman, G. (1981) *Class and the Corporation*, London: Fontana.
33. Weber, M. (1927/2003) *General Economic History*, New York: Dover Publications.
34. Clarkson, L. A. (1971) *The Pre-Industrial Economy of England, 1500–1750*, London: Batsford.
35. Alvesson, M. and Due Billing, Y (1997) *Understanding Gender in Organizations*, London: Sage.
36. Dobb, M. (1963) *Studies in the Development of Capitalism*, London: Routledge.
37. Landes, D. S. (1969) *The Unbound Prometheus*, Cambridge: Cambridge University Press.
38. Marglin, S. (1982) 'What do bosses do?: the origins and functions of hierarchy in capitalist production', in A. Giddens and D. Held (eds), *Classes, Power and Conflict*, Basingstoke: Macmillan.
39. Kelly, J. (1985) 'Management's redesign of work: labour process, labour markets and product markets', in D. Knights, H. Willmott and D. Collinson (eds), *Job Redesign: Critical Perspectives on the Labour Process*, Aldershot: Gower.
40. Hobsbawm, E. (1968) *Industry and Empire*, London: Weidenfeld & Nicolson.
41. Thompson, E. P. (1967) 'Time, work and discipline, and industrial capitalism,' *Past and Present*, **38**, pp. 56–97.
42. Grey, C. (2005) *A Very Short, Fairly Interesting and Reasonably Cheap Book about Studying Organizations*, London: Sage.
43. Hinton, J. (1973) *The First Shop Stewards Movement*, London: Allen & Unwin.
44. Rose, M. (1988) *Industrial Behaviour*, London: Penguin.
45. Braverman, H. (1974) *Labor and Monopoly Capitalism: The Degradation of Work in the Twentieth Century*, New York: Monthly Review Press.
46. Beynon, H. (1984) *Working for Ford*, Harmondsworth: Penguin.
47. Parker, M. (2000) *Organizational Culture and Identity*, London: Sage.
48. Friedman, A. (1977) *Industry and Labour: Class Struggle at Work and Monopoly Capitalism*, London: Macmillan.
49. Callaghan, G. and Thompson, P. (2001) 'Edwards revisited: technical control and worker agency in callcentres', *Economic and Industrial Democracy*, **22**, pp. 13–37.
50. Sewell, G. (1998) 'The discipline of teams: the control of team-based industrial work through electronic and peer surveillance', *Administrative Science Quarterly*, **43**, pp. 406–69.
51. Bratton, J. (1992) *Japanization at Work*, Basingstoke: Macmillan.
52. Elger, T. and Smith, C. (eds) (1994) *Global Japanization?*, London: Routledge.
53. Thompson, P. and McHugh, D. (2006) *Work Organizations: A Critical Introduction* (4th edn), Basingstoke: Palgrave.
54. Womack, J., Jones, D. and Roos, D. (1990) *The Machine that Changed the World*, New York: Rawson Associates.
55. Oliver, N. and Wilkinson, B. (1992) *The Japanization of British Industry*, Oxford: Blackwell.
56. McCormick, K. (2007) 'Sociologists and "the Japanese model": a passing enthusiasm?', *Work, Employment and Society*, **21**(4), pp. 751–71.
57. Salzinger, L. (2003) *Genders in Production*, Berkeley: University of California Press.
58. Horwitz, F. M., Chan Feng Heng and Quazi, H. A. (2003) 'Finders, keepers? Attracting, motivating and retaining knowledge workers', *Human Resource Management Journal*, **13**(4), pp. 23–44.
59. Boud, D. and Garrick, J. (eds) (1999) *Understanding Learning at Work*, London: Routledge.
60. Ackroyd, S., Batt, R., Thompson, P. and Tolbert, P. (2005) *The Oxford Handbook of Work and Organization*, Oxford: Oxford University Press.

61. Baldry, C., Bain, P., Taylor, P. et al. (2007) *The Meaning of Work in the New Economy*, Basingstoke: Palgrave.
62. Bolton, S. C. (2005) *Emotion Management in the Workplace*, Basingstoke: Palgrave.
63. Fineman, S. (2003) *Understanding Emotion at Work*, London: Sage.
64. Warhurst, C. and Nickson, D. (2007), 'A new labour aristocracy? Aesthetic labour and routine interactive service', *Work, Employment and Society*, **21**(4), pp. 785–98.
65. Hochschild, A. (2003) *The Second Shift*, New York: Penguin.
66. Linstead, S., Fulop, L. and Lilley, S. (2009) *Management and Organization: A Critical Text* (2nd edn), Basingstoke: Palgrave.
67. Nixon, D. (2009) '"I can't put a smiley face on": working-class masculinity, emotional labour and service work in the "new economy"', *Gender, Work and Organization*, **16**(3), pp. 300–22.
68. Jacoby, S. M. (2005) *The Embedded Corporation: Corporate Governance and Employment Relations in Japan and the United States*, Princeton, NJ: Princeton University Press.
69. Jaffee, D. (2001) *Organization Theory: Tension and Change*, Boston, MA: McGraw-Hill.
70. Vallas, S. (1999) 'Re-thinking post-Fordism: the meaning of workplace flexibility', *Sociological Theory*, **17**(1), pp. 68–85.
71. Walton, R. (1985) 'From control to commitment in the workplace', *Harvard Business Review*, March/April, pp. 77–84.
72. Hyman, R. and Mason, B. (1995) *Managing Employee Involvement and Participation*, London: Sage.
73. Reiter, E. (1992) *Making Fast Food: From the Frying Pan into the Fryer*, Montreal: McGill-Queen's University Press.
74. Ritzer, G. (2000) *The McDonaldization of Society*, Thousand Oaks, CA: Pine Forge Press.
75. Leidner, R. (1993) *Fast Food, Fast Talk: Service Work and the Routinization of Everyday Life*, Berkeley, CA: University of California Press.
76. Mathias, P. (1969) *The First Industrial Nation*, London: Methuen.
77. Reskin, B. and Padavic, I. (1994) *Women and Men at Work*, Thousand Oaks, CA: Sage.
78. Hobsbawm, E. (1994) *Age of Extremes*, London: Abacus.
79. Berg, M. (1988) 'Women's work, mechanization and early industrialization', in R. E. Pahl (ed.), *On Work*, Oxford: Blackwell.
80. Bradley, H. (1986) 'Technological change, management strategies, and the development of gender-based job segregation in the labour process', pp. 54–73 in D. Knights and H. Willmott (eds), *Gender and the Labour Process*, Aldershot: Gower.
81. Turner, H. A. (1962) *Trade Union Growth, Structure and Policy: A Comparative Study of the Cotton Unions*, London: Allen & Unwin.
82. Witz, A. (1986) 'Patriarchy and the labour market: occupational control strategies and the medical division of labour', in D. Knights and H. Willmott (eds), *Gender and the Labour Process*, Aldershot: Gower.
83. Sydie, R. A. (1994) *Natural Women, Cultured Men*, Vancouver: UBC Press.
84. Knights, D. and Willmott, H. (eds) (1986) *Gender and the Labour Process*, Aldershot: Gower.
85. Kimmel, M. (2004) *The Gendered Society* (2nd edn), New York: Oxford University Press.
86. Saunders, D. (2006) 'Politician-mom seeks to change dated German social values', *Globe and Mail*, June 22, p. A3.
87. Greenhaus, J. H. (2008), 'Innovations in the study of the work–family interface: introduction to the Special Section', *Journal of Occupational and Organizational Psychology*, **81**, pp. 343–8.
88. Purcell, J., Purcell, K., and Tailby, S. (2004) 'Temporary work agencies: here today, gone tomorrow?', *British Journal of Industrial Relations*, **42**(4), pp. 705–25.
89. Sturges, J. and Guest, D. (2004) 'Working to live or living to work: work/life balance and organizational commitment amongst graduates', *Human Resources Management Journal*, **14**(4), pp. 5–20.
90. Warhurst, C., Eikhof, D. R. and Haunschild, A. (2008) *Work Less, Live More?*, Basingstoke: Palgrave.

91. European Trade Union Confederation. 'Factsheet: Working Time Directive'. Available at: http://www.etuc.org/a/504 (accessed November 2, 2009).

92. Bonney, N. (2005) 'Overworked Britains?: part-time work and work–life balance', *Work, Employment and Society*, **19**(2), pp. 391–401.

93. Kersley, B., Alpin, C., Forth, J. et al. (2006) *Inside the Workplace: Findings from the 2004 Workplace Employment Relations Survey*, London: Routledge.

94. Felstead, A., Gallie, D. and Green, F. (2002) *Work Skills in Britain: 1986–2001*, London: HMSO.

95. Giddens, A. (1984) *The Constitution of Society*, Cambridge: Polity Press.

96. Weber, M. (1905/2002) *The Protestant Ethic and the 'Spirit' of Capitalism*, London: Penguin.

97. *Globe and Mail*, April 22, 2009, p. C1.

98. Kvande, E. (2009) 'Work–life balance for fathers in globalized knowledge work. Some insights from the Norwegian context', *Gender, Work and Organization*, **16**(1), pp. 58–72.

99. Scholarios, D. and Marks, A. (2004) 'Work–life balance and the software worker', *Human Resource Management Journal*, **14**(2), pp. 54–74.

100. De Cieri, H., Holmes, B., Abbot, J. and Pettit, T. (2002) *Work/Life Balance Strategies: Progress and Problems in Australian Organizations*. Working Paper 58/02. Melbourne: Department of Management, Monash University.

101. Makin, K.(2009) 'Lawyer-moms aim to change law firms' punishing work culture', *Globe and Mail*, April 11, p. 4.

102. Despres, C. and Hiltrop, J-M. (1995) 'Human resource management in the knowledge age: current practice and perspectives on the future', *Employee Relations*, **17**(1), pp. 9–23.

WORK GROUPS & TEAMS

CHAPTER OUTLINE

- Introduction
- Work groups and work teams
- Group dynamics
- Work teams and management theory
- Work teams: ending bureaucracy and extending employee empowerment?
- Paradox in team-based work systems
- Summary and end-of-chapter features
- Chapter case study 1: Building cars in Brazil
- Chapter case study 2: Teams at Land Rock Alliance Insurance

CHAPTER OBJECTIVES

After completing this chapter, you should be able to:

- distinguish between informal and formal work groups
- explain the current popularity of teams in work organizations
- articulate how group norms and cohesiveness exert influence on individual and group behaviour
- describe and critically evaluate the theories of team development
- explain the pros and cons of using groups to make decisions
- identify the different theoretical perspectives and paradoxes related to work teams

INTRODUCTION

Without doubt, everyone will find him- or herself at some point in life to be a member of a group. You have probably already experienced group membership through participating in a sports team, climbing or caving club, jury service, church, political party or study group. In many organizations, people are called upon to work in groups. Work groups influence the behaviour of their members, often enhancing job satisfaction, promoting learning and increasing individual and unit productivity and more effective decision making.

Work groups are not something invented by management consultants. History shows that they have been part of human social development since ancient times. For thousands of years, men and women lived in small hunting and gathering groups, and later they lived in small farming or fishing groups. It is only in the last 200 years, with the advent of industrial capitalism, that small groups have become the exception rather than the rule.[1] The factory system ushered in a minute division of labour and close direct supervision, which substantially improved labour productivity and profits. By the late twentieth century, however, extensive specialization and hierarchical forms of work organization were identified as a 'problem'.

A host of mainstream management literature proselytized the notion that traditional work organization was an obstacle to innovation and competitiveness.[2-4] Team work as a system of paid work is intended to transcend the alleged problems of inflexibility, poor quality, low employee commitment and motivation associated with traditional work structures. Its increased prevalence in Europe and North America is a recognition by employers that competitive advantage comes from so-called lean organizations, the full utilization of their human capital, and a set or 'bundle' of 'soft' human resource management practices that form part of an integrated high-performance workplace (HPW).[5] In the critical literature, team work and HPW initiatives are a means of increasing work intensification, obtaining higher productivity, increasing workplace stress and controlling workers indirectly through a culture of self-control.[5-9]

If you paused and thought about the questions we asked in the 'Stop and reflect' box above, you should appreciate that understanding groups and teams in work organizations is important for several reasons. Team work has become a significant feature of organizational life. Individuals behave differently when in a work group from how they do when they work independently. Team synergy can potentially transform moribund productivity and improve organizational performance. Finally, understanding group dynamics is seen to be an important aspect of managing (controlling) people more effectively.

This chapter introduces the complex phenomenon of work groups and work teams in organizations. It begins by examining the background, nature and behavioural implications of work groups. We also explore the nature of work groups through the concepts of group norms, cohesiveness and learning. Finally, we go beyond management rhetoric, and present arguments and evidence to suggest that self-managed teams shift the focus away from the hierarchy, and direct and bureaucratic **control** processes, to a culture of self-control.

WORK GROUPS AND WORK TEAMS

What are work groups?

The term 'group' can be used to describe a cluster of individuals watching a hockey game or queuing for a bank teller. When studying the behaviour of groups, it is important to distinguish between a mere cluster of individuals and what organizational theorists call a 'psychological group'. This term is used to describe individuals who perceive themselves to be in a group, who have a shared sense of collective identity, and who relate to each other in a meaningful way. We can define a **work group** as two or more people who are in face-to-face interaction, each aware of their membership in the group, and striving to accomplish assigned work tasks.

The first part of this definition suggests that there must be an opportunity for people to interact socially with each other, that is, to communicate with each other, to behave in each other's presence, and to be affected by the other's behaviour. Over time, group members who regularly interact socially become aware of each other's values, feelings and goals, which then influence their behaviour. Although a work group can theoretically range from two members to an unspecified upper limit, the need to interact limits the size of the group.

The second part of the definition refers to group members' perceptions of the group itself. Members of the group are able to distinguish who is and who is not in the group, and are aware that an action affecting one member is likely to affect all. This part of the definition helps us to exclude mere clusters of people who are simply individuals who happen to be assembled at the same location at a particular time (such as soccer fans, bank customers or airline travellers). These individuals do not consider themselves a part of any identifiable unit, nor do they relate to one another in any meaningful fashion, despite their close proximity.

On the other hand, a soccer team, an airline crew or a project team at the Bank of Scotland would fulfil the criteria for a work group. In a situation of extreme danger – such as the hijacking of an airline – an aggregate of passengers could be transformed into a group. For example, several passengers on US United Airlines Flight 93, which crashed on September 11, 2001, apparently formed a group that stormed the cockpit to prevent the hijackers from carrying out any further terrorist acts.

The third part of the definition implies that group members have common goals, which they work collectively to accomplish. Six individuals drinking coffee in the company rest area at the same time would not necessarily be considered a group. They do not have common goals, nor are they dependent on the outcome of each other's actions. However, six union shop stewards drinking coffee together regularly to discuss health and safety issues or grievances would be considered a work group.

Groups in organizations can be formal or informal. Organizational decision makers create formal work groups to permit collective action on assigned task(s). In this sense, the rationale for creating work groups can be linked to an organization's competitive strategy. A manufacturing strategy that emphasizes flexibility can result in tasks and responsibilities being reassigned from individual employees and supervisors to a group of employees. This process of dividing up the tasks, assigning responsibility and so on, is called **job design**, and it is through the restructuring of work that formal work groups are created and consciously designed. Managers are interested in ensuring that the behaviour of the formal group is directed toward organizational goals. Not surprisingly, therefore, much of mainstream organizational behaviour research focuses on the dynamics of formal work groups.

In addition to formal work groups, organizations also contain **informal work groups**. Managers do not specifically establish these work-based groups; they emerge from the social interaction of workers. Although an organization employs people for their intellectual capital, unlike with other forms of capital, the organization gets the whole person. People bring their personal needs to the workplace. Organizational behaviour theorists suggest that informal work groups are formed as an outcome of psychological processes: the perception of a shared social identity and to fulfil social needs for affiliation and supportive relationships. A cluster of employees can become an informal work group when members influence others' behaviour and contribute to needs satisfaction. Informal work groups are important in that they can help shape communication flows in the organization.

What are work teams?

The words 'group' and 'team' are often used as substitutes. In the management literature, the word '**team**' is more likely to be used in a normative sense as a special type of group with positive traits.[10] Like a soccer team, it has connotations of collaboration, mutual support and shared skill and decision making.[11] The observation and

job design: the process of assigning tasks to a job, including the interdependency of those tasks with other jobs

informal group: two or more people who form a unifying relationship around personal rather than organizational goals

teams: groups of two or more people who interact and influence each other, are mutually accountable for achieving common objectives, and perceive themselves as a social entity within an organization

implied criticism that 'He is not a team player' or 'This group is not a team' expresses the difference in meaning between 'group' and 'team' in the management lexicon. A mainstream text defines a team as 'a set of interpersonal interactions structured to achieve established goals' (ref. 1, p. 539), and two popular writers define a team as 'a small number of people with complementary skills who are committed to a common purpose, performance goals, and approach for which they hold themselves mutually accountable' (ref. 2, p. 45).

self-managed work teams: cross-functional work groups organized around work processes that complete an entire piece of work requiring several interdependent tasks, and that have substantial autonomy over the execution of those tasks

Another variant of 'teams' has become part of current managerial rhetoric – the words '**self-managed work team**' (SMWT). The SMWT, which suggests a new way of organizing work, is not the same as a 'work group': an SMWT is 'a group of employees who are responsible for managing and performing technical tasks that result in a product or service being delivered to an internal or external customer' (ref. 12, p. xiii). The difference between work groups and SMWTs is explained in terms of the degree of interdependency and accountability. The interdependence among SMWT members is typically high, and the accountability for the work focuses primarily on the team as a whole rather than the individual group member. Another distinguishing feature of SMWTs is their longevity: SMWTs are typically an integral part of a redesigned organizational structure, brought together for long-term performance goals.

Work teams can be classified according to their position in the organization's hierarchy and their assigned tasks. Figure 7.1 shows three types of work team most

Plate 1 – A self-managed work team allows employees in the core work unit to have sufficient autonomy to manage the work process.
Source: Getty Images

commonly found in organizations. Teams that plan and run things are positioned in the top echelon (senior level) of the organization, teams that monitor things occupy the middle levels, and teams that make things occupy the lower levels of the organization. It is important to emphasize, however, that the nature of teams varies considerably among organizations, depending on whether they are engaged in value-added activities in small batches or large batches, or whether they provide financial or other services.

The formal definitions of work teams are not so different from the definition of a formal work group, which might explain why both words are used interchangeably in the organizational behaviour literature. However, the conscious use of the word 'team' is not simply a question of semantics. Mainstream management rhetoric is awash with what Bendix called 'a vocabulary of motivation'.[13] In this instance, communication emphasizes the 'team' (with phrases like 'We must all pull together') and the 'family' (suggesting that employees are brothers and sisters and customers are family guests), using these metaphors to obfuscate the power differentials and conflicting interests between management and workers. Whether employees are organized into a 'work group' or a 'work team', the effectiveness of the work configuration will be the outcome of complex group behaviours and processes, which is the focus of the next section.

weblink
www.managementhelp.org/grp_skll/slf_drct/slf_drct.htm is an online library devoted to self-managed teams. At http://groups.yahoo.com, people form their own social groups to exchange ideas. Visit the site and see how 'virtual groups' work

GROUP DYNAMICS

group dynamics: the systematic study of human behaviour in groups, including the nature of groups, group development, and the interrelations between individuals and groups, other groups and other elements of formal organizations

Group dynamics is the study of human behaviour in groups.[1] The field studies the nature of groups, group development and the interrelations between individuals and groups. Group dynamics or processes emphasize changes in the pattern of activities, the subjective perceptions of individual group members and their active involvement in group life. Studies on group dynamics by mainstream researchers draw attention to two sets of process that underlie group processes: task-oriented activities and maintenance-oriented activities. Task-oriented activities undertaken by the group are aimed at accomplishing goals or 'getting the job done'. Maintenance-oriented activities, on the other hand, point to the subjective perceptions of group members and their active involvement in keeping acceptable standards of behaviour and a general state of well-being within the group. Conventional wisdom argues that the two processes constantly seek to coexist, and an overemphasis of one realm at the

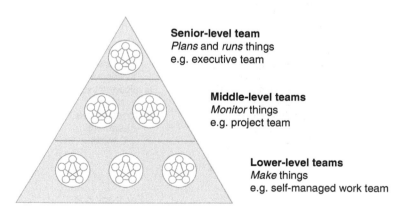

Senior-level team
Plans and *runs* things
e.g. executive team

Middle-level teams
Monitor things
e.g. project team

Lower-level teams
Make things
e.g. self-managed work team

Figure 7.1 – Classification of work teams

expense of the other leads to discontent and withdrawal. An effective group or team is one that creates a reasonable compromise between both realms.[10,14,15]

Some of the major factors influencing group dynamics are shown in Figure 7.2. The framework does not attempt to offer a theory of group dynamics, nor does it necessarily follow that all elements of the model must, or can, be applied to every work group. We offer it here as a useful heuristic for understanding the complexities of group dynamics. Four major elements are graphically depicted in the model: a context, team structure and processes, group effectiveness, and a feedback loop that links the outcomes back to the other main components. We look at each of the first three elements over the next few pages.

Group context

Although the work group or team is a structure in itself, it is also a subset of a larger structure, the organization. Thus, the work group is constrained to operate within the structure of the organization, and **group context** refers to organizational and job design, organizational control systems, resources and the external political economy and economic forces.

The implementation of team-based working requires organizational restructuring, by which we mean changing the core dimensions of the organization: its centralization, complexity and formality. Tasks and responsibilities must be designated within and between teams. Task interdependence, which refers to the level of relationship among members in the work activities, can affect group structure, processes and outcomes. Alternative work configurations are typically followed by alternative control systems. For example, when work groups are introduced, the direct supervisory control of employees is typically replaced by a computer-based control of group performance. The adoption of team work is normally contingent on management installing a system to control the redesigned work process.[6]

Resources are another contextual factor affecting group structure and processes. The amount of resources management is willing to commit to teams is directly related to the organizational context. Specifically, the policies and procedures of the organization must provide for sufficient physical (such as computer software), financial and human resources to enable the team to function and complete the task. Inadequate

group context: refers to anything from the specific task a work group is engaged in to the broad environmental forces that are present in the minds of group members and may influence them

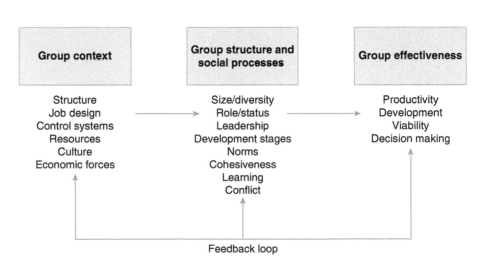

Figure 7.2 – A model of group dynamics

resources, it is argued, will delay group development and have a negative impact on group outcomes.[3]

Group structure

group structure: a stable pattern of social interaction among work group members created by a role structure and group norms

Work groups and teams have a structure that influences the way in which members relate to and interact with one another, and makes it possible to explain individual behaviour within the group. Have you ever noticed that, when people come together in a new group, some listen while others talk? Such differences between group members serve as a basis for the formation of group structure. As differentiation takes place, social relations are formed between members. The stable pattern of relationships among the differentiated elements in the group is called **group structure**.

weblink
The notion of diversity and balance in teams is central to Belbin's team role theory. Visit www. belbin.com for more information and www. palgrave.com/business/brattonob2e for an activity on team roles

The group can be differentiated by a number of variables including size, roles, status and leadership. The *size* of the group plays a critical role in how group members interact with one another. The German sociologist Georg Simmel pointed out that increasing the size alters the group's dynamics, since the increased number of relationships results in different interactions.[16] Figure 7.3 shows the incremental impact of group size on relationships. Two individuals form a single relationship; adding a third person results in three relations; a group of seven, however, has 21 relationships. According to Simmel, as groups grow beyond three people, the personal attachments between individuals become looser, and coalitions emerge in which some group members align themselves against other group members. Thus, the more impersonal relationships need additional formal rules and regulations. At the same time, the group's growth allows it to become more stable, because the intensity of the interactions is reduced, and because it becomes better able to withstand the loss of some of its members.

The *composition* or diversity of work groups is another key variable that influences individual behaviour in a group setting. Work group composition can be diverse in terms of gender, ethnicity, age, hierarchical status, performance levels and

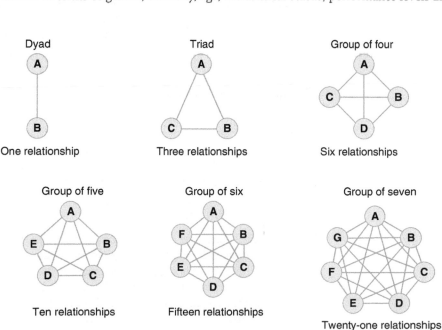

Figure 7.3 – The incremental effects of group size on relationships

educational background. Research suggests that group composition is a predictor of members' creative behaviour and the quality of decision making. Gender and hierarchical status diversity tended to decrease a member's creative behaviour, and this negative effect appeared to be particularly strong for women members in a minority and 'low-power' group situation. The group's composition may also impede the shared exchange, discussion and integration of information, with negative effects on decision quality.[17,18]

role: a set of behaviours that people are expected to perform because they hold certain positions in a team and organization

All group members are expected to carry out certain functions. The set of expected behaviours associated with a position within the group constitutes the **role** of the occupant of that position. The role concept helps us understand how a member's behaviour is structured by the prescriptive dictates of the group and/or organization. A team-based culture will influence the roles individuals play within the organization. With HPW forms of organization, a premium is placed on values such as cooperative behaviour with team members, sharing information and expertise with others, and more generally on promoting a social network necessary for effective team performance. Role definition is often used as a diagnostic tool by management consultants to determine causes of poor team performance. Problems of **role ambiguity** – uncertainty on the group member's part about what exactly he or she is supposed to do – and **role conflict** – conflicting requests from more than one source – allegedly have far-reaching negative outcomes on group performance.[3] Role ambiguity and role conflict affect the socialization of new employees into existing work groups.[19]

role ambiguity: uncertainty about job duties, performance expectations, level of authority and other job conditions

role conflict: conflict that occurs when people face competing demands

status: the social ranking of people; the position an individual occupies in society or in a social group or work organization

Status is the relative ranking that a member holds, and indicates the value of that member as perceived by the group. Status is important because it motivates individuals and has consequences for their behaviour. Almost every work group has either a formal or an informal leader, who can influence communications, decision making, learning and similar processes, thereby playing an important part in group's outcomes.

It is necessary, but not sufficient for team efficacy, to have an organizational design strategy that incorporates adequate resources, effective control systems, role clarity and leadership. To be effective, managers and group members must learn to work in the new work structure. The group processes responsible for group development, norms, cohesiveness and learning are extremely important.

Group social processes

group processes: refers to group member actions, communications and decision making

The term **group social processes** refers to the manner in which various aspects of group behaviour are constructed on a continuing basis, and the behaviour that serves to encourage or discourage group learning and to ameliorate or exacerbate group conflict. Understanding group social processes is important in so far as they are often considered to be key predictors of group effectiveness.

Group development

Organizational behaviour theorists typically highlight the importance of understanding the developmental stages that a group must pass through: groups are born, they mature and they die. It is suggested that a group must reach the mature stage before it achieves maximum performance. Of course, it is also acknowledged that not all groups pass through all these stages, and some groups can become fixed in the early stage and remain ineffective and inefficient. A good example of the life-cycle metaphor is Tuckman and Jensen's five-stage cycle of group development model: forming, storming, norming, performing and adjourning (Figure 7.4).[20]

In the *forming* stage, individuals are brought together and there tends to be ambiguity about roles and tasks. Group members are polite as they learn about each other and attempt to establish 'ground rules' for accomplishing the assigned task(s). Dependency on the group leader is said to be high at this stage.

In the *storming* stage, individual members become more proactive by taking on specific roles and responsibilities. Members frequently compete for positions in the group, and conflict occurs between individuals, and/or alliances are formed between members. The group leader must be able to facilitate dialogue and handle conflict at this stage.

When group members begin to accept differences of opinion, conform to their roles and cooperate (for instance, sharing information), the group has reached what is called the *norming* stage. As a consensus forms around the group's goals and means of attainment, group cohesion grows.

High productivity is typically achieved at the *performing* stage of group development. A high level of trust in each group member is prevalent at this phase, and there is 'consensual validation' in the sense that members are positively valued for their specific attributes and qualities.

A work group does not exist infinitely. The *adjourning* stage refers to individuals leaving the group and being replaced by others, or to the group's disbandment. Social rituals, such as having a party, often accompany group disbandment.

Tuckman and Jensen's model is based on the premise that a group must go through each stage before being able to move on to the next, and every transition holds the potential risk of regression to an earlier stage. Organizational behaviour theorists taking a managerialist perspective have tended to interpret the five-stage model in terms of levels of performance, with group productivity being higher after the second stage. While this assumption may be correct, what makes a work group effective is more complex than this model acknowledges. Although the model has become entrenched in mainstream organizational behaviour texts and in management training, it has more recently been shown 'to be of little or no assistance in getting teams to perform better' (ref. 3, p. 34).

An earlier critique of Tuckman and Jensen's five-stage model found the phenomenon of 'punctuated equilibrium' to be a more useful concept to explain group development.[21] Specifically, a team does not accomplish a great deal up to about the halfway point to completion (this midpoint occurring regardless of the time-frame

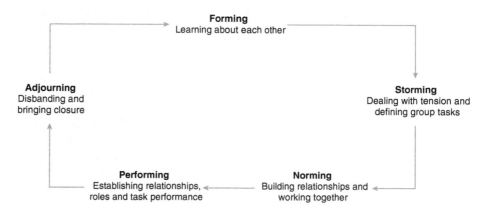

Figure 7.4 – Five phases of group development
Source: Tuckman and Jensen (1977)[20]

involved). At the midpoint, there is an acceleration of activity by members to accomplish their assigned work. In essence, the 'punctuated equilibrium' model characterizes work groups as exhibiting long periods of inertia interspersed with shorter bursts of activity, initiated primarily by their members' awareness of the impending completion deadline. This would suggest, therefore, that not all groups develop in a universal linear fashion.

The research on group development has drawn criticism because much of it has tended to be laboratory-based rather than workplace-based research. For example, old favourites like Tuckman and Jensen's model were developed from work with therapy, laboratory or training groups, not 'real teams in real contexts'. Group development models that predict linear sequential phases have particularly been criticized. As Kline graphically points out:

> Imagine the following situation. The cockpit crew of a 747 boards the plane twenty minutes before take-off. You are seated in seat 117B, and as the airplane rushes down runway nine you hope like hell that this team is past the storming stage of group development.

(ref. 3, p. 5)

Kline argues that there is something, personalities aside, about the aircrew that enables them to fly the aircraft safely, even when they have just met one another. These 'contextual variables', she asserts, are powerful tools for understanding group dynamics and group performance.

Although alternative research suggests that every group does not go through all the development stages, Tuckman and Jensen's model can be a useful heuristic for understanding group dynamics and why some groups fail to perform. A group might be ineffective and inefficient because individuals are pulling in different directions, since the goals of the group have not been agreed. Alternatively, individuals might have a tendency to dismiss or ridicule others' thoughts, ideas and feelings, which leads to low trust among the group. For all these reasons, effective group functioning and learning might be hindered. The main conclusion drawn from the group development models presented here is that a team-based organizational structure does not imply an effective and efficient organization. Top managers introducing team-based work structures need to attend to the development of group interactions.

Group norms

Have you ever noticed that professors do not normally criticize other professors? Why? The answer is 'norms'. Groups significantly influence their members' behaviour through the operation of norms. Social norms are a set of expected patterns of behaviour that are established and shared by the group's members. Norms inform members on what they ought and ought not to do under certain situations. A group's norms do not occur in a vacuum: they represent the interaction of historical, social and psychological processes. In the workplace, for example, a new employee joining a group will assess the norms for work effort from how most individuals in the group behave. In turn, members of the group observe the extent to which the new member's behaviour matches the group's norms. Norms develop in work groups around work activities (the means and speed), around attitudes and opinions that should be held by group members regarding the workplace, and around communications, concerning appropriate language.

group norms: the unwritten rules and expectations that specify or shape appropriate human behaviour in a work group or team

The Hawthorne studies[22] highlighted the importance of **group norms** to management theorists. The researchers identified three important norms: no 'rate-busting'

Plate 2 – Organizations send their employees to outdoor corporate training centres where they learn to work as teams.
Source: Getty Images

(working too hard), no 'chiselling' (working too little) and no 'squealing' (telling the supervisor anything that could undermine the group). Group members who significantly deviated from these norms were subjected to either ridicule or physical punishment. Groups typically enforce norms that:

- facilitate the group's survival
- allow members to express the central values of the group
- reduce embarrassing interpersonal problems for group members – for instance, a ban on discussing religion or politics at work.[23]

Norms are communicated to new employees through a process called 'group socialization', whereby the new member learns the group's principal values and how these values are articulated through norms. Emergent group leaders differ from their peers in that they make more attempts to influence the group and play a role in forming team norms.[24]

Group cohesiveness

cohesiveness: refers to all the positive and negative forces or social pressures that cause individuals to maintain their membership in specific groups

The term **cohesiveness** refers to the complex forces that give rise to the perceptions by members of group identity and attractiveness of group membership. The cohesiveness of a group has a major effect on the behaviour of its members, because higher cohesion amplifies the potency of group norms. A series of experiments conducted by Solomon Asch in 1952 and Stanley Milgram in 1963 suggested that group membership can engender conformity, and also that members are likely to follow the directions of group authority figures, even when it means inflicting pain on another individual. These psychological experiments can be used to help explain the brutalizing acts inflicted on prisoners by both male and female US guards at Abu Ghraib prison.[25]

weblink
For more information on Milgram's classic psychological prison experiment, go to Stanford University's site: www.prisonexp.org

A cohesive group can develop norms that can be a great asset to the organization, for example a norm that prescribes voluntary overtime working when required. Equally, a cohesive group can undermine organizational goals, for example by enforcing conformity to a work effort below what is considered acceptable by managers. Not surprisingly, therefore, sources of group cohesiveness are of considerable interest to mainstream organizational behaviour theorists and managers. For example, a recent study contends that humour can have a positive effect on a variety of group or team processes including group cohesiveness and the management of emotion.[26]

The attractiveness of a group is partly determined by its composition. Members of the group need to get along with each other, which might be difficult if members have very different values, attitudes towards work or interests. Research suggests that behaviour in work groups is shaped by a sex difference in aggressiveness, with male members engaging in more dominating behaviour than female members. Studies have found that, in groups, men talk more frequently, interrupt others and express anger more than women (see ref. 27, especially pp. 181–3). As a result, more men than women are chosen as group leaders. In institutions of learning, the experiences of work groups by women and faculty members from racial and ethnic minorities tend to differ significantly from the experiences of white male group members.[28]

groupthink: the tendency of highly cohesive groups to value consensus at the price of decision quality

Ensuring diversity in a work group or team is not only an equity matter – a lack of diversity might inhibit some of the benefits of group working. An early study suggests that moderate heterogeneity in a work group balances the requirements of cohesion and productivity.[29] As we will examine in the next section, one notable disadvantage of groups that are *too* cohesive is that their decision-making ability can be impaired by what Janis termed '**groupthink**'.[30] He defined this group phenomenon as a psychological drive for consensus at any cost, which suppresses dissent and the evaluation of alternatives in cohesive decision-making groups.

weblink
For more information on how 'groupthink' can influence decision making, visit www.afirstlook.com; www.abacon.com. Search for 'groupthink'

Group learning

We turn now to another aspect of social interaction within groups and teams: work-based learning. It will be apparent from this review of team theory and practice that expanding workers' skill sets and **empowering** workers to make prescribed decisions has significant implications for learning in the workplace. Rather than learning a narrow set of skills, the need for flexibility and interchangeability necessitates that workers acquire new knowledge and technical skills to perform the new repertoire of tasks. In addition, the experience of 'lived reality' – decision making, trial and error experimentation – and the social relations associated with teams create their own dynamic environment for enhancing informal work-based learning.

empowerment: a psychological concept in which people experience more self-determination, meaning, competence and impact regarding their role in the organization

If the group or team is going to make its own decisions, control quality and control its own behaviour, members must engage in learning. Adult educators and human resource development theorists have suggested that, in order for a group or team to learn, individual members of the unit must be able to learn: that is, to experiment, reflect on previous action, engage in dialogue, and share and build on their individual knowledge.[31,32] Adopting a culture of learning in the workplace impacts on innovation, employment relations and leadership style.

Group conflict

Work groups do not exist in isolation: they are located within capitalist workplace dynamics and linked by a network of relationships with other groups. Unsurprisingly, with the proliferation of teams in organizations, there is more research on behaviours that serve to ameliorate or exacerbate the effect that group conflict has on their effectiveness. In the critical studies, analysts have highlighted the inevitable tensions between team-based HPW rhetoric and the reality of work intensification and job insecurity.[33] Mainstream research on group conflict is, however, generally limited to investigating how dysfunctional behaviour at individual or group level affects the variance in groups' performance generally. There are many definitions for the term *conflict*. A broad definition describes conflict as 'that behaviour by organization members which is expended in opposition to other members' (ref. 34, p. 411).

Researchers widely recognize that group conflict is comprised of two dimensions: task and emotional conflict.[35] *Task conflict* refers to disputes over group members' tasks or the extent to which members disagree on the utilization of resources or ideas related to group tasks. *Emotional conflict*, which is also known as relational conflict, is more personal and involves personality clashes within groups and incompatibilities among team members, or the extent to which tension or verbal or non-verbal friction characterizes members' interaction within the group. Exemplars of specific types of behaviour associated with task and emotional conflict are shown in Table 7.1.

Psychological studies confirm the notion that individuals' personalities are part of the contributions that group members make to work groups, and, moreover, a mix of these individuals' personalities plays a key role in how intragroup conflict unfolds. It is well documented how many occupations regard team work and support from team members as 'lifelines' in coping with the various demands of work. For example, nurses and air cabin crew are known to rely upon support from fellow co-workers to help them deal with work-related emotion and difficult situations.[36] Studies on the consequences of members' emotions on team performance show that the team members' shared negative emotion, or what is called 'negative affective tone', is inversely related to team performance.[37] A conceptual framework for linking dysfunctional group behaviour and group effectiveness is shown in Figure 7.5.

The proposed sequence of incidents depicted in the model begins with dysfunctional group behaviour causing an increase in what is labelled groups' 'negative affective tone' – groups' collective shared experience of negative emotions. In turn, it is hypothesized that that greater levels of negative group affective tone tend to reduce

Table 7.1 – Task-related and emotion-related behaviours in groups

Task-related behaviours	Emotion-related behaviours
Goal setting	Criticizing
Integrating	Judging
Utilizing resources	Violence
Calculating	Bullying
Compromising	Favouritism
Decision making	Teasing
Evaluating	Sexual harassment

Source: Adapted from Proctor et al. (2009)[90]

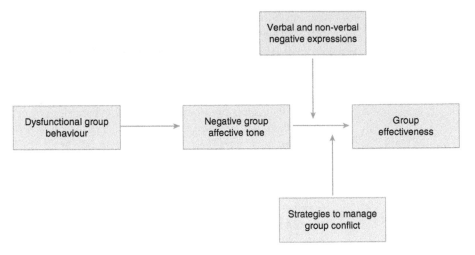

Figure 7.5 – A conceptual framework for examining intragroup conflict
Source: Adapted from Cole, Walter and Bruch (2008),[37] p. 946, itself based on Brown et al (2005),[91] p. 793

group effectiveness. It also proposes that 'display rules' capable of adjusting or varying the expression of negative emotions through verbal and non-verbal (for example, facial or body) cues is critical to groups' goal-directed behaviour and effectiveness. A study by Dunlop and Lee found that dysfunctional behaviour predicted 24 per cent of the variance in groups' performance.[38] With this assertion in mind, the model further proposes that emotion management strategies will mediate the effect of negative group affective tone.[37]

Research findings suggest that how well conflict resolution strategies address a group-level balance between task and emotion management is what yields superior group productivity and viability.[39] On the basis of reported results, when work groups withhold displays of negative emotionality, it seems they are better able to control the detrimental performance implications of dysfunctional behaviour.[37]

Intergroup conflict might also occur. One explanation for intergroup conflict is that when a group is successful, members' self-esteem increases, and conversely when group members' self-esteem is threatened, they are more prone to disparage members of other groups.[40-43] Another alternative explanation contends that intergroup conflict is the result of one group's perceiving another group as a threat to its goal attainment.[1,3,44]

The traditional managerial perspective tends to hold that conflicts between individuals and groups, and between workers and management, are a bad thing. An alternative perspective, the *interactionist theory*, holds that conflicts in work groups are productive and can increase rather than decrease job performance.[45] The view holds that group leaders should encourage an ongoing 'optimum' level of conflict, which allows the group to be self-critical, creative and viable. But notions of 'win–lose' scenarios complicate estimates of what constitutes an 'optimal level' of conflict. It has been suggested, for instance, that the more the intergroup conflict is defined as a 'win–lose' situation, the more predictable are the effects of the conflict on the social relationships within the group and on relations between work groups.[1]

Work and Society: Making it work

With the emergence of the idea of 'positive psychology', there has been a pronounced effort to shift research attention away from its traditional focus on abnormal or problematic patterns of human functioning, and towards the study of optimal functioning and human flourishing. This shift in attention away from the problematic and towards the optimal is evident in many fields of study – from organizational behaviour research to studies of marriage. For example, in a pioneering analysis of marriage dynamics, Frank Fincham and his colleagues argue (2007) that the traditional preoccupation with conflict in marriage must be corrected. Their article focuses on 'naturally occurring marital self-repair processes' (p. 282) and seeks to understand the mechanisms that enable some couples to bounce back from conflict while others separate or continue to live together unhappily.

Does this research on marriages have anything to tell us about group dynamics? Obviously, the differences between small work groups and marriages are fundamental, and there is no need to review those differences here. The question is, are there enough similarities between work groups and marriages to derive some insights into group dynamics from recent research on marriages? You be the judge. Consider the following synopsis of the work of Fincham and his colleagues.

Inspired by the move toward positive psychology, Fincham and his co-investigators set out to identify what distinguishes marriages that endure (or 'bounce back' after trouble) from marriages that fall apart. They found that couples who stay together do not necessarily experience conflict-free relationships. What distinguishes these resilient couples from couples who separate are mechanisms that work to defuse conflict, often without the help of external interventions. One might say that spouses in these resilient couples exhibit capacities for 'self-regulation' and the couples themselves are capable of 'self-repair'.

To understand how this works, Fincham and his colleagues suggest we consider how conflicts unfold in time. An initial disagreement or problematic event will often escalate over time as couples become locked into cyclical patterns of 'tit-for-tat' responding. Resilient couples seem to be able to avoid this pattern. They do so by engaging in two kinds of regulation: they regulate both 'the degree to which a negative partner behaviour elicits a correspondingly negative response' and 'the extent to which negative partner behavior produces a change in the overall view of the relationship' (2007, p. 283). With regard to this second kind of regulation, one can imagine a wife (or husband) coming to the realization: this marriage is not worth saving. Spouses in resilient couples seem to be able to avoid these profound and irreversible changes of heart.

The two kinds of regulation associated with resilient couples are clearly relevant to work groups. Work groups experience internal conflict, and people in work groups become locked into cyclical patterns of 'tit-for-tat' responding. As with couples, the likelihood that members of work groups can resolve their conflicts without resorting to external mediation will depend on their capacity to engage in the kinds of regulation identified by Fincham and his colleagues.

Readers may feel comfortable with the analogy between marriages and work group thus far. But consider the proposed explanation of why some couples more than others are able to engage in effective self-regulation. Fincham and his colleagues offer the following list of factors that they believe enhance a couple's capacity for self-regulation and repair:

Without methods for changing negative processes over time, or for changing direction once negative interactions begin, even the best marital skills for dealing with conflict may provide couples with insufficient basis for long-term marital satisfaction. The framework [described in this article has] ... the potential to help us understand the impact [on self-regulatory processes] of forgiveness ... commitment ... valuing sacrifice ... and sanctification. (p. 287)

stop! Fincham and his colleagues associate this list of qualities – forgiveness, commitment, valuing sacrifice and sanctification – with couples who engage in effective self-regulation. Would these same qualities be associated with the optimal functioning of work groups? How would each of the four qualities contribute to higher levels of self-regulation among work group members?

Given its links to organized religion, the idea of sanctification may seem irrelevant to many work groups. Is there a secular version of sanctification that might be relevant to a broader range of work groups?

Sources and further information

Bakkle, A. and Schaufeli, W. (2008) 'Positive organizational behavior: engaged employees in flourishing organizations', *Journal of Organizational Behavior*, **29**, pp. 147–54.

Fincham, F., Stanley, S. and Beach, S. (2007) 'Transformative processes in marriage: an analysis of emerging trends', *Journal of Marriage and the Family*, **69**, pp. 275–92.

Note: This feature was written by David MacLennan, Assistant Professor at Thompson Rivers University, BC, Canada.

stop reflect
Sociologists maintain that relationships formed in groups shape members' behaviour. Think about your own experience of working in a group. What norms and values did the group exhibit? Did any particular members challenge a particular group norm? If so, how did the other group members respond to the challenge? If they did not, why not?

job satisfaction:
a person's attitude regarding his or her job and work content

Group effectiveness

Most group theory examines group effectiveness or outcomes in terms of group performance and group decision making. Since the widespread proliferation of team work, much research has been occupied with investigating the link between work teams and performance. Two aspects of group effectiveness are examined in this section: performance and decision making.

Group performance

Research on group performance has often drawn upon Hackman's normative theory of group effectiveness, where effectiveness consists of (1) productivity, (2) employee development, or the opportunity of the individual team member to learn from her or his experiences within the team as well as from other team members, and (3) team viability, or the degree to which members of the team are able to continue working together in the future.[46] The group literature contends that a combination of high-level cohesion and norms, consistent with organizational objectives, will have a positive effect on team productivity.[47–49] Figure 7.6 illustrates the relationship between group cohesiveness and group performance norms. Improved productivity of employees in SMWTs is said to stem from the fact that the interrelationship between the configuration of job design and employment practices inevitably leads to more intrinsic **job satisfaction**, higher team member commitment and the mobilization of greater discretionary effort from employees.[50,51]

Group decision making

In theory, one advantage of cohesive groups is that, by combining member resources, they make better decisions than those made by a single individual. In mathematical logic, this phenomenon of groups, called synergy, suggests that 2 + 2 is greater than 4.

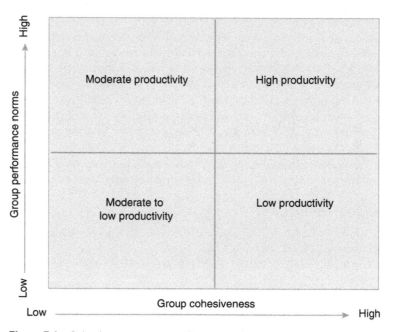

Figure 7.6 – Cohesiveness, norms and group performance

The concept is used extensively in mainstream texts to understand group processes and to justify the implementation of work teams. The general assumption is that moderately cohesive work teams (sufficiently diverse to avoid groupthink), together with better communications and 'enlightened' leadership, are best able to encourage the sharing of information and group learning – which results in superior decision-making outcomes. In terms of group decision making, here we examine some important concepts and empirical research on the decision-making performance of groups.

An important concept that might cause groups not to live up to their decision-making potential is *conformity* for people to change their behaviour to fit the norms of a group or team. It may make sense to follow others' behaviour or judgement when you are inexperienced or when the situation is ambiguous, but just how strongly do group norms influence individual behaviour and decision making when the situation is unmistakable?

Research by Solomon Asch and Stanley Milgram provided the answer to this question.[52,53] Asch recruited several groups of students, allegedly to study visual perception. Before the experiment began, he explained to all the students, apart from one student in each group, that the real purpose was to put pressure on the one selected student. Each group of students was asked to estimate the lengths of lines presented on a card. A sample line was shown at the left, and the group was to choose which of the three lines on the right matched it (Figure 7.7). Group members were seated so that the subject answered last. Group pressure did not affect the subjects' perception, but it did affect their behaviour. Initially, as planned, group members made the correct matches (B on Card 2). When, however, Asch's accomplices made incorrect responses, the uninformed subject became uncomfortable, and 76 per cent of the subjects chose to conform by answering incorrectly on at least one trial. The study shows how strong the tendency to conform can be, even when the pressure comes from people we do not know.

In Milgram's controversial study, a researcher explained to male recruits that they would be participating in an experiment on how physical punishment affects adult learning. The learner, actually an accomplice of Milgram's, was seated in a fake electric chair, with electrodes fastened to the wrist and secured by leather straps. In an adjoining room, the subject, playing the role of educator, was seated in front of a replica 'shock generator' with the capacity to administer an electric 'shock' of between 15 and 315 'volts' to the learner. The educator was directed to read aloud pairs of words, and

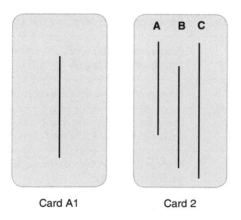

Card A1   Card 2

Figure 7.7 – An example of the cards used in Asch's experiment in group conformity

the learner was asked to recall the second word. Whenever the adult learner failed to answer correctly, the educator was instructed to apply an electric shock. Although the educator heard moans and then screams as the level of voltage increased, none of the subjects questioned the experiment. Milgram's research suggests that people are likely to follow the directions of 'legitimate authority figures', even when it means inflicting pain on another individual. To learn about how this classic experiment by Milgram has been related to contemporary events, see ref. 54.

As previously mentioned, Irving Janis's study illustrates how 'experts' can succumb to group pressure.[30] Interestingly, to illustrate the concept of groupthink, Janis analysed the ill-fated attempt by President Kennedy's administrative team to invade Cuba in 1961. He argues that the executive group advising the US President displayed all the symptoms of groupthink: they were convinced of their invulnerability, and 'self-censorship' prevented members from expressing alternative views even when intelligence information did not align with the group's beliefs. There was, according to Janis, an illusion of unanimity, with silence being interpreted as consent. In other words, the pressures for conformity that can arise in a highly cohesive group can cloud members' judgement and the decision-making process. Table 7.2 outlines some symptoms of groupthink.

Obviously, groupthink results in low-quality decisions. More seriously, it has been implicated in the decision processes that led to NASA's fatal launch of the space shuttle Challenger in 2003, and the US and UK invasion of Iraq in 2003. Prior to the invasion, the US official position was that Iraq illegally possessed weapons of mass destruction in violation of UN Security Council Resolution 1441 and had to be disarmed by force. The decision to embark on the Iraq invasion, termed 'Operation Iraqi Freedom' was made by President George W. Bush and a small group of military and intelligence advisers. After investigating the events, which continue to shape the course of twenty-first century history as we write, a US Senate Committee found that the Central Intelligence Agency had dismissed alternative reports, and that the intelligence community as a whole suffered from 'collective group think'.[55] The research by Asch, Milgram and Janis tells us that groups influence the behaviour of their members, altering perceptions of reality and often promoting conformity, which can lead to imperfect and even catastrophic decisions.

Table 7.2 – Symptoms of groupthink

Symptom	Description
Illusion of invulnerability	Group members are arrogant and ignore obvious danger signals
Illusion of morality	Groups decision(s) are not only perceived as sensible, they are also perceived as morally correct
Rationalization	Counter-arguments are rationalized away
Stereotypes of outsiders	Members construct unfavourable stereotypes of those outside the group who are the targets of their decisions
Self-censorship	Members perceive that unanimous support exists for their decisions and action
Mindguard	Individual(s) within the group shield the group from information that goes against its decisions

The phenomenon of groupthink, therefore, has the potential to undermine the group's ability to appraise alternative choices and make quality decisions. Another phenomenon that has the potential to adversely affect decision making is group polarization. This refers to the tendency of groups to make more extreme decisions than managers and employees working alone. For example, suppose that a board of governors of a college meets to make a decision on the future of a new sports complex for the college. Individual board members might come to the meeting with various degrees of support or opposition to the project. However, by the end of the board meeting, it is highly possible that the board of governors will agree on a more ambitious (that is, a higher financial cost) plan than the average individual had when the board meeting began.

One reason for the more ambitious preference is that individual board members feel less personally responsible for the decision consequences because the entire board of governors makes the decision. Another reason is that board members become comfortable with more extreme positions when they realize that co-members also support the same position. Persuasive arguments favouring the dominant position convince doubtful members and help form a consensus around the most ambitious or extreme option. So persuasion, group support and shifting responsibility explain why groups make more extreme decisions.

OB and globalization

Power and culture in work team relations

The globalization of work has opened new opportunities for workers from different cultural backgrounds to work closely with each other – both in person and remotely. Diverse work teams can have positive effects on productivity and problem solving by generating a greater number of innovative ideas and approaches (Earley and Gibson, 2002). Many organizations with overseas operations, however, have also encountered challenges in managing multicultural work teams. These challenges are primarily related to team members' different cultural understandings about their role in the team (and within the larger organization) and how the work should be accomplished.

In an insightful study, Mutabazi and Derr (2003) explore the cultural and historical roots of a breakdown in work team relationships at a Franco-Senegalese organization the authors call Socometal, whose work teams were made up of French expatriates and local Senegalese workers. Mutabazi and Derr concluded that inefficiencies and misunderstandings in these multicultural work teams were, to a great extent, connected with the enduring legacy of colonialism. They explain:

> the problem associated with multiculturalism [on work teams] comes from preexisting attitudes about relations between Africa and the West. This is a deeply-rooted relationship with perceptions distorted by historical consternation. On one side, the West as the dominant partner overemphasizes its own culture, ideals and conceptions of the world ... the resulting tendency is to impose this cultural determination upon the party that is considered inferior ... [and] this characteristic of multiculturalism becomes embedded in the relationship creating a vicious cycle of misunderstanding. (p. 3)

At Socometal, French managers and work team members did not understand the Senegalese community-based approach to team work, which relies on the circulation of people, goods, services and information through local social and economic networks. Likewise, the Senegalese workers did not understand the approaches of the French expatriate managers and workers, mistaking their focus on top-down decision making and individual competition as an assertion of superiority. The result was the reproduction of colonial power relationships between French and Senegalese workers, and work teams that were 'characterized by indifference toward the values and perspectives of fellow team members ... The professional and personal difficulties that [ensued led] to a breakdown of operations' (Mutabazi and Derr, 2003, p. 4).

This case highlights the centrality of power and culture in organizational behaviour. Gibson and Zellmer-Bruhn (2001) remind us that workplaces are culturally situated, and that relationships within organizations are shaped by culturally and historically embedded power relationships. Misunderstandings about work team relationships and responsibilities can be exacerbated in situations where team members make assumptions about their colleagues' capabilities and motivations based on preconceived notions. The potential of multicultural work teams to excel will remain untapped as long as they are managed according to a single cultural paradigm. Effective management approaches in these situations must address cultural misunderstandings and power imbalances head on, and provide enough flexibility to incorporate multiple approaches to team work and decision making into the organization.

stop!   Have you ever worked on a project or a work team with members from different cultural backgrounds? Discuss any culturally based misunderstandings or 'disconnects' that you or your colleagues might have encountered while working on the project. How did you address your differences?

Can you think of any other examples of how historical relationships between nations or cultures could affect organizational behaviour if members of those groups were assigned to the same work team?

Sources and further information

Earley, P. C. and Gibson, C. B. (2002) *Multinational Work Teams: A New Perspective*, Mahwah, NJ: Lawrence Erlbaum Associates.

Gibson, C. B. and Zellmer-Bruhn, M. E. (2001) 'Metaphors and meaning: an intercultural analysis of the concept of teamwork', *Administrative Science Quarterly*, **46**(2), pp. 274–303.

Mutabazi, E. and Derr, C. B. (2003) 'The management of multicultural teams: the experience of Afro-Occidental teams', Research Paper 13, *European Entrepreneurial Learning*. Available at: www.em-lyon.com/%5Cressources%5Cge%5Cdocuments%5Cpublications%5Cwp%5C2003-13.pdf; http://cat.inist.fr/?aModele=afficheN&cpsidt=18098760 (accessed September 22, 2009).

Note: This feature was written by Gretchen Fox, Anthropologist, Timberline Natural Resource Group, Canada.

Research has repeatedly demonstrated that group decision making is not always superior. In reality, groups sometimes do perform better than the average group member but rarely do better than the best member.[56] One explanation is that even relatively homogeneous groups often fail to exchange their members' unique resources. One key assumption underpinning the enthusiasm for group-based decision making is the expectation to benefit from group members' distributed experiences and informational resources. This point is particularly important with regard to group diversity enhancing the quality of group decisions. Increasingly, diversity is an organizational fact of life, and many work groups are diverse in terms of the characteristics of their membership, bringing together members who may differ in gender, ethnicity, age, disability, hierarchical status, educational background and so forth.

Research on diversity in work teams has shown mixed results regarding the effects of group diversity on team decision making. On the one hand, the processing of decision-relevant information may benefit from a wider pool, variety of perspectives and life experiences in more diverse groups. On the other hand, diversity may actually impede the exchange, discussion and integration of decision-relevant information, with consequential negative effects on decision quality.[18] Others suggest that increasing diversity can have both positive and negative effects on group information processing and decision making contingent on 'individuals' beliefs about diversity'.[57] Thus, educating employees in diverse organizations to value diversity can improve the quality of decisions. Furthermore, the positive effects of diversity might be propagated through several structured group processes that are designed to improve the exchange of group members' unique information and the decision quality. These structured group decision-making processes include brainstorming, the nominal group technique and the stepladder technique.

weblink
For examples of team working in European and North American companies, visit: www. honda.com; www.sony. com; http://ptcpartners. com/Team/home. htm; www.dti.gov.uk/ employment/useful-links/ index.html. Search for '2004 employee relations survey'. This site gives a summary of the UK 2004 survey, including a section on work teams

Clearly, group social processes are complex and contentious, and are strongly influenced by the individual characteristics of team members and by dominant gender, race and power patterns. The wealth of research and interest in work teams over the last decade is related to the changing fashion in US and European management theory on how to compete in conditions of globalized capitalism.

WORK TEAMS AND MANAGEMENT THEORY

The theoretical interest in work groups or teams draws upon human relations, sociotechnical and Japanese perspectives on organizational design.[5,6,12,58] Pioneering work on human relations by Roethlisberger and Dickson, Mayo, Maslow and McGregor focused top managers' attention on the importance of social relations within work groups.[22,59–61]

The collaborative research by Roethlisberger, an industrial psychologist from Harvard University, and Dickson, a manager at the Western Electric plant, involved studying the job performance of two groups of front-line workers doing identical work but in separate rooms. Each work group's productivity was carefully monitored. One work group – the study group – experienced ergonomic changes including increasing the intensity of the lighting in the workshop. The study group's productivity increased. The other work group – the control group – experienced no changes in lighting. However, to the astonishment of the researchers, its productivity increased also. Even more mystifying to the researchers, when the level of light intensity was lowered for the study group, the results showed that output continued to go up. After repeated experiments over many years, the researchers began to make connections between social interaction and job performance. In 1939, Roethlisberger and Dickson wrote:

stop reflect
Think about your experience of working in a group. Do Roethlisberger and Dickson's findings resonate with any aspect of your own view on group working? Why?

> The study of the bank wiremen showed that their behaviour at work could not be understood without considering the informal organization of the group and the relation of this informal organization to the total social organization of the company. The work activities of the group, together with their satisfactions and dissatisfactions, had to be viewed as manifestations of a complex pattern of interrelations.

(ref. 59, pp. 551–2)

After the Second World War, the work of Maslow and McGregor helped US human relations advocates to clarify their perspective, with its focus on the interrelations between workers and the quality of the employment relationship.

systems theory: a set of theories based on the assumption that social entities, such as work organizations, can be viewed as if they were self-regulating bodies exploiting resources from their environment (inputs) and transforming the resources (exchanging and processing) to provide goods and services (outputs) in order to survive

In Europe, much of the early research on work teams was conducted within the framework of sociotechnical **systems theory**. This theory developed from work in 1951 on autonomous work teams in the British coal-mining industry under the supervision of Trist and Bamforth. These researchers proposed that 'responsible autonomy' should be granted to primary work groups, and that group members should learn more than one role, so that an interchangeability of tasks would be possible within the group. The flexibility would permit the completion of sub-whole units. The studies showed that the labour process in mining could be better understood in terms of two systems: the technical system – including machinery and equipment – and the social system, including the social relations and interactions among the miners.

Later advocates of the sociotechnical systems approach to organizational design argued that work teams provide a work regime for achieving the 'best match' between technical and social considerations or 'systems'. The term 'best match' is used to

describe the relationship between the social and technological systems of the organization, where each is sensitive to the demands of the other.[12]

Attempts to implement the sociotechnical systems approach have included work
redesign to 'enrich' jobs. The concept of '**job enrichment**' refers to a number of
different processes of **rotating**, **enlarging** and aggregating tasks. It increases the
range of tasks, skills and control that workers have over the way they work, either
individually or in teams. Job enrichment theory, also known as **job characteristics**
theory, was given theoretical prominence by the work of Turner and Lawrence,
and Hackman and Oldham.[29,62] As a counter to the thinking underlying Taylorism
and Fordism, the job enrichment model has been influential in the design of work
teams. It suggests a casual relationship between five core job characteristics and the
worker's psychological state. If this relationship is positive, it leads in turn to positive
outcomes. The five core job characteristics contained in the model are defined as:

1 *skill variety*: the degree to which the job requires a variety of different activities
  in carrying out the work, requiring the use of a number of the worker's skills and
  talents
2 *task identity*: the degree to which the job requires completion of a whole and
  identifiable piece of work
3 *task significance*: the degree to which the job has a substantial impact on the lives
  or work of other people
4 *autonomy*: the degree to which the job provides substantial freedom, independence and discretion to the worker in scheduling the work and in determining the
  procedures to be used in carrying it out
5 *feedback*: the degree to which the worker possesses information on the actual
  results of her or his performance.

The more that a job possesses the five core job characteristics, the greater the motivating potential of the job (Figure 7.8).

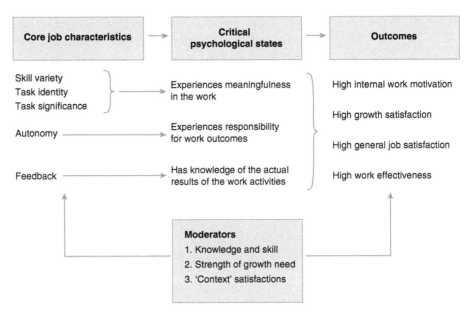

Figure 7.8 – Oldham and Hackman's job characteristics model
Source: Oldham and Hackman (1980)[29]

The model also recognizes the importance of learning to achieve motivation and outcome goals. Workers' work-related learning is implicitly linked to the existence of the 'moderators' – knowledge and skills, growth need strength and context satisfaction – contained in the model. The presence of moderators is used to explain why jobs that are theoretically high in motivating potential will not automatically generate high levels of motivation and satisfaction for all workers.

The argument goes that an employee with a low 'growth need' is less likely to experience a positive outcome when her or his work is 'enriched'. Thus, the neo-human relations approach to job design in general, and the job characteristic model in particular, emphasized the fulfilment of social or relatedness needs by recomposing fragmented jobs. In certain circumstances, self-managed teams could provide an alternative to individual job enrichment.

The quality of work and work-related learning in small SMWTs rests on five principles of 'good' job design:

- The first principle is *wholeness*: the scope of the job is such that it includes all the tasks to complete a product or process.
- The second principle involves individual and group *learning and development*. Opportunities exist to engage in a variety of fulfilling and meaningful tasks, allowing team members to learn a range of skills within a community of practice, and facilitating job flexibility.[63]
- The third principle relates to *governance and self-regulation*. With the focus on product differentiation and the rise of knowledge-based economies, the imperatives of work do not permit managers to master all the challenges. As a result, they must allow team and project members to assume responsibility for the pace of work, problem solving and quality control.
- The fourth principle involves occupational *wellness and safety*. Work is designed to maintain the safety and wellness of team members and to support a good work–life balance.[64]
- Finally, the fifth principle is *social interaction*. The job design permits interaction, cooperation and reflexivity among team members.

Drawing upon the work of Klein and McKinlay et al.,[65] the principles of 'good' job design are achieved by management interventions in the technical, governance and sociocultural dimensions of work (Figure 7.9).

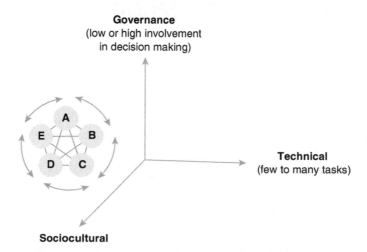

Figure 7.9 – The three dimensions of group work: technical, governance and social

The horizontal axis in Figure 7.9 represents the functional or technical tasks that are required to produce the product or service. Group working involves combining a number of tasks on the horizontal axis to increase the cycle times and create more complete and hence more meaningful jobs. The technical dimension is then regarded as the central purpose of work teams, and is concerned with the range of tasks undertaken by members, multiskilling and functional flexibility. The vertical axis represents the governance aspects of the labour process, and shows the extent of workers' autonomy on the job. The third axis, the diagonal, represents the sociocultural aspects of work, one of which is the social interaction that takes place in work groups. The sociocultural dimension is perhaps the most interesting as far as organizational behaviour is concerned, since it represents the behaviour or 'normative' considerations – what ought to happen – to secure effective team performance. This dimension of group work recognizes that employees' compliance and cooperation depend upon the complex interplay of social interactions in the group. It should be noted that, in a five-member team, there are 10 relationships (see Figure 7.3, above).

The SMWT represents an *ideal-type* work regime because it restores the craft paradigm by enlarging tasks on the horizontal axis and by giving members greater autonomy over how the work is accomplished on the vertical axis: a reversal of Taylorism. The movement along the diagonal axis represents the implications of group working in terms of group norms, group cohesion and organizational culture. The three dimensions of work organization in Figure 7.9 help to illustrate the point that top managers make strategic choices regarding how work is designed, and alternative work structures have an impact on social behaviour and organizational culture.

Critical insight

Workplace observers agree there is evidence that, in organizations that have been successful in devolving decision making to work groups, there have been benefits for management and workers: a 'win–win' situation. Visit www.jobquality.ca and 'High-performance working' at www.cipd.co.uk. Read also Andy Danford et al. (2008), 'Partnership, high-performance work systems and the quality of working life', *New Technology, Work and Employment*, 23(3), pp. 151–66. Who are the prime beneficiaries of team-based working? Do SMWTs reduce workplace stress?

WORK TEAMS: ENDING BUREAUCRACY AND EXTENDING EMPLOYEE EMPOWERMENT?

Whereas groups as social entities go back thousands of years, management interest in work teams is much more recent. From early experiments in sociotechnical job design techniques in the 1970s, teams became the hallmark of postmodern work organizations in the 1990s. Team work has been popularized by mainstream organizational behaviour theorists and management consultants as a panacea for curing inflexible work systems and allegedly inefficient bureaucratic structures, and for enhancing employee higher-order 'growth' and 'relatedness' needs by job enrichment and empowerment.

Motivated by the prospect of connecting the synergy of work teams with corporate goals, managers have focused on teams to help improve organizational performance. In Sweden, the most celebrated example of work teams was introduced at the new Volvo car plant in Uddevalla in 1987. It was reported that the new assembly line avoided the classic problems associated with Fordism.[66] However, in 1992 Volvo closed its Uddevalla factory. For many organizational behaviour researchers, the Swedish plant had become an icon for a European, human-centred and productive organization, and its closure suggested that Taylorist and neo-Taylorist solutions still dominate management thinking in the automobile industry.[67]

In critical accounts of team work, in which group practices are connected to the class power relations in which they are embedded, there is considerable debate over whether or not these regimes constitute a significant departure from Western-style 'high-autonomy' work teams.[5,68] Some argue that the difference lies in the fact that team work utilizes a control orientation that depends upon 'self-control'. Others persuasively argue that self-managed teams create a culture that enhances management control via self-regulation. This insight into group dynamics focuses on the socialization and organization culture, and on the behaviour deemed necessary to make teams work effectively.[69]

The discussion on different group and team concepts highlights the array of definitions, and the need for commentators to define work groups carefully if comparisons are to be made. As mentioned earlier, the reason that so many organizations have 're-engineered' work processes around teams is that managers are looking for improvements in productivity resulting from the positive synergy associated with teams. Thus, the perceived connections between the way work is designed and organizational performance need to be appreciated to understand the current wave of corporate interest in teams.

In standard accounts of team work, such regimes do not necessarily lead to improved organizational performance. People must learn to work in team-based structures: clearly a lesson from sociotechnical theory, which acknowledges the importance of the dialectic relationship between the technical and social aspects of work. In critical accounts of teams, there is deep scepticism. Work teams do not eradicate the three chronic capitalist antagonisms that centre on issues of managerial control: producing goods and services for a global market, which creates uncertainty and pressure to control costs; designing work structures and employee relations systems that maximize shareholder interests; and managerial top-down control over employee behaviour, in contrast to employee autonomy.

Contrary to the management rhetoric, work teams involve elaborate computer information systems developed to support a control-oriented management philosophy.[12] This observation illustrates the work of critical scholars who tend to be interested in understanding the power relations in team design. For example, one study found that while team members had increased their autonomy in performing their work and additional responsibilities, managers had actually increased their control over value-added activities through a computerized production system. This control-oriented approach can be given the name 'computer-controlled autonomy'.[6] Another study offered a scathing account of team working in white-collar work, arguing 'that workers experience forms of team organization as being no less coercive than classically understood Taylorism' (ref. 70, pp. 168–9).

PARADOX IN TEAM-BASED WORK SYSTEMS

How are we to interpret the effects of group membership on employee behaviour? As with the other aspects of organizational behaviour we cover in this text, it depends on the author's approach to the subject. For some, team synergy can be a panacea to bureaucratic ills: 'Teams foster a sense of dignity, self-worth, and a greater commitment to achieving the performance that makes an organization competitive' (ref. 71, p. 10). More critical sociological analysis serves as an antidote to the mainstream assumptions that team work is inherently favourable. The employee commitment implications of team work are not entirely positive. As an empirical reality, working in self-directed teams had no significant effect on employee commitment to the organization, whereas it was associated with higher work-related stress.[72] For others, team work, far from being 'empowering', actually intensifies management control over workers by cultivating a form of self-management through constant peer and self-monitoring.[73] This critical perspective focuses on, among other things, the effect of team ideology and behaviour on the working lives of workers. Whereas the managerialist approach found in most mainstream organizational behaviour texts focuses on the technical and the empowering dimensions of teams and team efficacy, a feature of a critical approach is a focus on the normative dimension of groups and teams, the 'tyranny' arising from team work and paradoxes in team-based work structures.

A paradox involves ambiguity and inconsistency, and both are evident in work group design. A central pillar of team work involves combining a number of tasks on the horizontal axis. This has led many traditional scholars to argue that SMWTs reverse Tayloristic deskilling tendencies by enhancing workers' skills. It is suggested that SMWTs exemplify the re-emergence of the craft model.[74] Critical organizational theorists, however, have challenged the popular logic that SMWTs lead to a more highly skilled workforce. Detractors argue that although they apparently give limited empowerment to workers, they do not necessarily reverse the general 'deskilling' trend, but generate new forms of control that assist management in extracting higher productivity from workers via work intensification as the range of horizontal and vertical tasks expands.[75–80]

Those subscribing to this critique almost invariably draw parallels with Taylorism and Fordism. A number of accounts stress that, with the assistance of microtechnology, re-engineering work into teams is an 'up-dating of Taylor's crusade against custom

Plate 3 – Team members can perceive a moral obligation to increase their level of effort on a job, and 'put in a full day' (or more) because of peer group pressure, or 'clan control', thereby unwittingly creating a control culture system.
Source: iStockphoto

and practice in which the silicon chip plays an equivalent role in [re-engineering] to that performed by the stop watch in Scientific Management' (ref. 81, p. 96). In other words, it provides a disguised form of intensified managerial control. Others offer more optimistic analyses, in which the outcomes of team working are less deterministic. Whether work teams result in the 'upskilling' or 'deskilling' of workers depends, among other things, on factors such as batch size, managerial choice and negotiation.[6]

Critical organizational theorists have illustrated the paradox in another way. The behavioural dimension of the team work model emphasizes worker empowerment while simultaneously increasing management's control over the labour process. This is achieved using both 'hard' technology (such as computers) and 'social' technology (such as group norms). When decision making is devolved to the team, members begin to think and act like managers, and they internalize company values. In this way, team work influences the attitude and behaviour of the team's members by creating a work culture that reproduces the conditions of employees' own subordination. In other words, team members perceive a moral obligation to increase their level of effort on the job, and 'put in a full day' because of peer group pressure or 'clan control', thereby unwittingly creating a control culture system.[8,9,82–85] Critical studies have found team members' discipline to be more punitive than that of the managers: 'Team members are tougher on fellow workers than management is' (ref. 9, p. 75). A 50-year-old male explained how peer group surveillance influenced the behaviour of the team's members like this:

> I think it's a matter of conscience. A person who under the old system might go away for an hour, now he will think twice: Are they [co-workers] going to think they are carrying me because I've been away? … Because you are a close-knit community in the [team] system. You get niggly remarks: 'Where have you been all morning?' That sort of thing and it gradually works its way in psychologically.
>
> (ref. 6, p. 186)

In their account of team learning processes, Kasl and colleagues unwittingly provide further evidence of the control culture generated by work teams.[86] When one particular work team 'failed', some team members left the company, while others worked on 'disheartened'. Moreover:

> The team became the laughing stock of the whole company and the people who weren't involved in it at all, the people who worked on a different floor, would walk right in and say, 'How's logistics, ha ha ha?' They heard about it, it was like this big disaster.
>
> (ref. 86, p. 238)

OB in focus

Few employees have a 'good' job

Despite the hype about improved quality of work arising from the growth of team working, it is reported that 'only 39 per cent of workers think that their job is "good", according to new research from the Chartered Institute of Personnel and Development (CIPD)'. 'Good' roles are defined as 'exciting but not too stressful', according to a new report from the UK institute, *Reflections on Employee Well-Being and the Psychological Contract*.

The research explored how employees felt about their job and their relationships with managers and colleagues. It concluded that employers should make jobs more appealing and interesting to improve commitment from employees. 'Most jobs can be made interesting or even exciting if they are well managed,' Mike Emmott, CIPD employee relations adviser, said. An interesting and exciting job was one with variety and security, and where the role of the employee was clear. Many workers did not believe that their job had these qualities. A fifth of respondents thought that the demands of their job were unrealistic, and the same proportion found their jobs either very or extremely stressful.

Nic Marks, head of well-being research at the New Economics Foundation and co-author of the report, said that interest and excitement were key elements in the psychological contract between employers and employees. 'If employees don't feel their role is exciting, this will be reflected in underperformance and their lack of commitment and satisfaction,' he said.

Source: adapted from Julie Griffiths, 'Only 39 per cent of employees have a "good" job', *People Management Online*, August 9, 2005.

There is another paradox. The managerial literature views team work as organizational synergy unifying people and thus developing members' capacities through dialogue and learning. Critical reflection in workplace learning literature presumes that if team members can just detect their dysfunctional or inefficient practices, they are free to find more creative and efficient ways of doing and thus improve their performance in the workplace. One mainstream assumption is that all members of the work team are equal. Recent empirical research on multiprofessional team work in the health sector, however, contends that, rather than unifying health professions, team work produces unintended divisive effects.[87] It is argued that power relations and the language used by the health professionals both reflect and reproduce structural inequality between surgeons, anaesthetists and nurses within the team. In reality, where team work is characterized by social structures of inequality and clinical power – for example, surgeons and anaesthetists over nurses – critical reflection and dialogue, and thus the mobilization of alternative practices, are suppressed.

The discourse on work teams illustrates competing interpretations. On the one hand, the thinking and prescriptions in mainstream accounts tend to focus on the technical and the 'growth need' dimension of team-based work configurations, as well as the links between group processes and group performance. On the other hand, critical evaluations of team work focus on paradoxes and the effect of team ideology and behaviour on workers. Thus, team work arguably resembles Morgan's 'psychic prison' in the sense that peer pressure and self-surveillance are the norm, and this more accurately resembles reality than the optimistic notion of the learning-empowering, self-managed work team. In his book *Images of Organizations*,[88] Morgan explains that the notion of organizations as psychic prisons is a metaphor that connects the idea that organizations are a psychic phenomenon, in the sense that they are ultimately constructed and sustained by conscious and unconscious processes, with the belief that people can actually become imprisoned or confined by the ideas, thoughts and actions to which these processes give rise.

CHAPTER SUMMARY

○ In this chapter, we have examined the background, nature and behavioural implications of work groups. We have suggested that the current wave of interest in work teams, often located within a cluster of other employment practices constituting what is called a 'high-performance workplace', is linked to lean forms of work organizations and the perceived shortcomings of large bureaucratic organizational structures.

○ The chapter has emphasized that understanding group processes, such as groupthink, group leadership, informal group learning and intragroup conflict, is imperative for the successful management of the HPW system.

○ Management tries to persuade workers of the need to work beyond their contract for the 'common' good and to engage in self-regulatory norms. The SMWT is said to be upskilling and empowering workers.

- However, we have also gone beyond management rhetoric, and presented arguments and evidence to suggest that self-managed teams shift the focus away from the hierarchy, directive and bureaucratic control processes, to a culture of self-control mechanisms.
- The discussion has emphasized that orthodox and critical accounts of team working provide very different views of this form of work organization and employment relations. Both perspectives, however, conceptualize team working as influencing individual behaviour and contributing to improved organizational performance. While both approaches make employee autonomy central to their analyses, each conceptualizes team membership as having a different influence. Additionally, autonomy is theorized as leading to different outcomes (such as growth need versus self-regulation) in each perspective.

KEY CONCEPTS

group dynamics
group processes
group structure
job characteristic model
peer pressure
psychic prison
work group
work team

VOCAB CHECKLIST FOR ESL STUDENTS

- Cohesiveness
- Empowerment, empower
- Formal work group
- Group context
- Group dynamics
- Group norms
- Group processes
- Group structure
- Groupthink
- Increment, incremental
- Informal group
- Job characteristics model
- Job design
- Job enlargement
- Job enrichment
- Job rotation
- Job satisfaction
- Paradox, paradoxical
- Role
- Role ambiguity
- Role conflict
- Role perceptions
- Self-managed work teams

- ○ Systems theory
- ○ Status
- ○ Teams
- ○ Work group

CHAPTER REVIEW QUESTIONS

1 How useful are group development models for understanding group or team behaviour?

2 What effect, if any, do you expect workforce diversity to have on group processes and outcomes?

3 Explain how the size of the work group might affect group dynamics and performance?

4 'Self-managed work teams are simply attempts by managers to control individuals at work by mobilizing group processes.' Do you agree or disagree? Discuss.

5 Students often complain about doing group projects. Why? Relate your answer to group processes and the critique of self-managed work teams.

6 What is meant by 'group think', and how important is it in deciding group performance?

CHAPTER RESEARCH QUESTIONS

1 Diversity is an organizational fact of life. In a group, we would like you to examine your own beliefs about diversity and how people stereotype others. Form a study group. (a) Post each term from the following list on separate sheets of paper: Male, Roman Catholic, Asian, Generation Y, Disabled, American, Muslim, Female, Irish, Single mother, Over age 60, West Indian. (b) Circulate the sheets around the group, and write down one stereotype you have heard under each heading. Avoid repeating anything that is already written down. (c) After everyone has finished writing, each group member takes turns to read all the stereotypes under each category. (d) Group members should then discuss (i) their personal reaction, (ii) what they have learned about stereotyping others, and (iii) what managers can do to experience positive effects of diversity.

2 Obtain a copy of Bolton and Houlihan's book *Work Matters: Critical Reflections on Contemporary Work* (see Further Reading). After reading pages 162–79, explain how team working was introduced into a major supermarket chain. How much autonomy did the teams have? How did the leadership style differ between the teams? How was team productivity measured? How did team work help members cope with work-related stress? How might team diversity impact on the team dynamics?

3 Read Rolf van Dick et al.'s article, 'Group diversity and group identification: the moderating role of diversity beliefs' (see Further Reading). Does group diversity positively or negatively affect group decision making? What can managers do to improve the quality of group decision making?

FURTHER READING

Behfar, K., Peterson, R., Mannix, E. and Trochim, W. (2008) 'The critical role of conflict resolution in teams: a closer look at the links between conflict type, conflict management strategies, and team outcomes', *Journal of Applied Psychology*, **93**(1), pp. 170–88.

Belbin, R. M. (1993) *Team Roles at Work*, London: Butterworth/Heinemann.

Bolton, S. and Houlihan, M. (eds) (2009) *Work Matters: Critical Reflections on Contemporary Work*, Basingstoke: Palgrave.

Cole, M. S., Walter, F. and Bruch, H. (2008) 'Affective mechanisms linking dysfunctional behavior to performance in work teams: a moderated mediation study', *Journal of Applied Psychology*, **93**(5), pp. 945–58.

Cordery, J. (2002) 'Team working', pp. 326–50 in P. Warr (ed.), *Psychology of Work*, London: Penguin.

Danford, A., Richardson, M., Stewart, P., Tailby, S. and Upchurch, M. (2008) 'Partnership, high performance work systems and quality of working life', *New Technology, Work and Employment*, **23**(3), pp. 151–66.

Kasl, E., Marsick, V. and Dechant, K. (1997) 'Teams as learners', *Journal of Applied Behavioral Sciences*, **33**(2), pp. 227–46.

Kooij-de Bode, H. J. M., Hanneke J. M., van Knippenberg, D. and van Ginkel, W. P. (2008) 'Ethnic diversity and distributed information in group decision making: the importance of information elaboration', *Group Dynamics: Theory, Research and Practice*, **12**(4), pp. 307–20.

Proctor, S., Fulop, L., Linstead, S., Mueller, F. and Sewell, G. (2009) 'Managing teams', pp. 539–73 in S. Linstead, L. Fulop and S. Lilley (eds), *Management and Organization: A Critical Text* (2nd edn), Basingstoke: Palgrave.

Russell, N. and Gregory, R. (2005) 'Making the undoable doable: Milgram, the Holocaust, and modern government', *American Review of Public Administration*, **35**(4), pp. 327–49.

Sewell, G. (1998) 'The discipline of teams: the control of team-based industrial work through electronic and peer surveillance', *Administrative Science Quarterly*, **43**, pp. 406–69.

Taggar, S. and Robert Ellis, R. (2007) 'The role of leaders in shaping formal team norms', *Leadership Quarterly*, **18**, pp. 105–20.

van Dick, R., van Knippenburg, D., Hagele, S., Guillaume, Y. R. F. and Brodbeck, F. (2008) 'Group diversity and group identification: the moderating role of diversity beliefs', *Human Relations*, **61**(10), pp. 1463–92.

Chapter case study 1

Building cars in Brazil

Setting

Founded in the earlier part of the century, the Cable Motor Company was a traditional, North American automobile manufacturer. They used Fordist management techniques and traditional assembly line production, and worked with a highly unionized workforce. By the mid-1980s, with their sales slumping, the company made the decision to purchase an obsolete automotive assembly plant in Brazil. The company quickly proceeded to upgrade the plant, resulting in a very large, modern, single-storey building of approximately 1.4 million square feet with four major manufacturing centres: stamping, body, paint and final assembly. The plan was to adopt the use of cooperative work teams, which had been used by Swedish car manufacturers such as Saab and Volvo, and to implement the Japanese lean production system originally created by Toyota and later adapted by Mazda.

The company spared no expense in planning for the workforce that would fit the plant's new approach to job design. There were extensive pre-employment screening and selection techniques used to recruit the 1200 people needed for the production run. Unlike the minimalist training normally provided under the Ford system, the company provided intensive classroom time and continuous on-the-job training for employees on the subject of self-managed work teams. Group decision making, integral to team success, was a strong focus.

The company found that the union representing the workers, the National Union of Cable Motor Company Workers, had little influence in the new Brazilian plant. This resulted in a much quicker implementation of the flexible production system. Production shifts of about 100 persons were scheduled with workers performing operations individually and in self-directed two-, three- or four-person teams. Any team member could pull a car off the line to check a quality issue. In such a case, a group walk-around decided if a car needed 'finessing'.

CEO John Miner was impressed with the initial look of the new production system. 'Minimal supervision and a self-directed workforce are what we strive to maintain and encourage,' he remarked. 'We will not get bogged down in traditional thinking, processes or paperwork. All workers are encouraged to be free-thinking and to get creative.'

The problem

The selection of the team leaders was conducted by the senior management group. Maria Lopez, a 30-year-old clerical worker, was moved from the administration office to head up one of the teams. Shortly after, production manager Clive Richards began to notice that Maria's team's production cycle times were increasing. He also noticed conflicts within her group. Clive decided to approach one of Maria's team members, Juan Fernandez, who had formerly worked in a team at another car company's assembly plant in Brazil. 'We can't work with Maria as our team leader,' Juan said. 'The team finds it hard because she is a woman. You have to remove her.'

While Clive struggled to decide what to do with Maria, other problems emerged. Employees were arriving to work late on a consistent basis. City buses, the main source of transportation for the plant workers, ran late if they ran at all. This was beginning to impact the continual on-the-job training as it required workers to arrive at work on time. Other employees were hesitant to do quality checks on their own work, saying that it would create the impression that the supervisors did not trust them.

Clive decided to meet with the CEO to let him know about the increasing issues so that action could be taken before the problems got worse. John was concerned when he heard what was happening at the new plant as he had just returned from a meeting where there were preliminary discussions on opening another in a different Brazilian location. 'I need you to do a presentation for the Board of Directors,' John said to Clive. 'We have to show what we've learned from this experience and how we can move forward.'

Tasks

Prepare a short presentation, incorporating the answers to the following questions:

1 How did Brazilian culture or work ideology contribute to the problems the company experienced with its use of teams?
2 In what alternative way could the team leader have been chosen which may have been more acceptable to the team members?
3 Should the conflicts in Maria's group only be viewed as a negative development?

Ask yourself:

4 Why do you think the use of teams could weaken a union's influence or power in the workplace?

Essential reading

Katz, H. C., Lee, W. and Lee, J. (2004) *The New Structure of Labour Relations*, New York: Cornell University Press.

Proctor, S., Fulop, L., Linstead, S., Mueller, F. and Sewell, G. (2009) 'Managing teams', pp. 539–73 in S. Linstead, L. Fulop and S. Lilley (eds), *Management and Organization: A Critical Text* (2nd edn), Basingstoke: Palgrave.

Note

Cable Motor Company is a fictitious company, but the background material for the case is derived from Muller, Rehder and Bannister (1998).[89] Some circumstances of the case organization have been altered. This case study was written by Lori Rilkoff, MSc, CHRP, Senior Human Resources Manager at the City of Kamloops, and lecturer in HRM at Thompson Rivers University, BC, Canada.

Chapter case study 2

Teams at Land Rock Alliance Insurance

Visit www.palgrave.com/business/brattonob2e to view this case study

WEB-BASED ASSIGNMENT

Work groups and teams is one of the most important topics of organizational behaviour, and given that many students have experienced group working and will be called upon to work in groups in organizations, it is important to reflect on how groups influence human behaviour.

For this assignment, we would like you to gain more information on work teams by visiting www.workteams.org and www.berr.gov.uk. In addition, you are asked to explore examples of team working in European and North American companies by visiting the following websites: www.honda.com; www.sony.com; http://ptcpartners.com/Team/home.htm; www.berr.gov.uk.

What main principles can be identified as 'good' job design when applied to work teams? Looking at the companies that have introduced teams, what behaviours or 'norms' are expected of employees? How does the team-based model impact on other aspects of management such as human resource management? Discuss your findings with other students on your course.

OB IN FILM

The film *Twelve Angry Men* (1957) examines the behaviour of 12 members of a jury who have to decide on the innocence or guilt of a young man from a working-class background. At the beginning, 11 jurors are convinced of the youth's guilt and wish to declare him guilty without further discussion. One member of the jury (played by Henry Fonda) has reservations and persuades the other members to review the evidence. After reviewing the evidence, the jury acquits the defendant.

A modern version of this film can be seen in a 2005 episode of the television series *Judge John Deed*, in which Judge Deed (played by Martin Shaw) serves as a member of a jury and persuades the other members to review the evidence in a sexual assault case.

What group concepts do the film or the *Judge John Deed* episode illustrate? What types of power are possessed by the characters played by Henry Fonda and Martin Shaw? What pattern of influencing behaviour is followed by Henry Fonda and Martin Shaw?

REFERENCES

1. Johnson, D. W. and Johnson, F. P. (2000) *Joining Together: Group Theory and Group Skills* (7th edn), Boston: Allyn & Bacon.
2. Katzenbach, J. R. and Smith, D. (1994) *The Wisdom of Teams*, New York: Harper Business.
3. Kline, T. (1999) *Remaking Teams*, San Francisco: Jossey-Bass.
4. Orsburn, J. and Moran, L. (2000) *The New Self-directed Work Teams*, New York: McGraw-Hill.
5. Procter, S. and Mueller, F. (2000) *Teamworking*, Basingstoke: Palgrave Macmillan.
6. Bratton, J. (1992) *Japanization at Work*, Basingstoke: Macmillan.
7. Thompson, R and Ackroyd, S. (1995) 'All quiet on the workplace front: a critique of recent trends in British industrial sociology', *Sociology*, **29**(4), pp. 615–33.
8. Sewell, G. (1998) 'The discipline of teams: the control of team-based industrial work through electronic and peer surveillance', *Administrative Science Quarterly*, **43**, pp. 406–69.
9. Wells, D. (1993) 'Are strong unions compatible with the new model of human resource management?', *Relations Industrielles/Industrial Relations*, **48**(1), pp. 56–84.

10. Hertog, J. F. and Tolner, T. (1998) 'Groups and teams', pp. 62–71 in M. Poole and M. Watner (eds), *The Handbook of Human Resource Management*, London: International Thomson Business Press.

11. Buchanan, D. (2000) 'An eager and enduring embrace: the ongoing rediscovery of teamworking as a management idea', in S. Procter and F. Mueller (eds), *Teamworking*, London: Macmillan.

12. Yeatts, D. E. and Hyten, C. (1998) *High-performing Self-managed Work Teams*, Thousand Oaks, CA: Sage.

13. Bendix, R. (1956) *Work and Authority in Industry*, New York: Wiley.

14. Crawley, J. (1978) 'The lifestyles of the group', *Small Groups Newsletter*, **2**(1), pp. 26–39.

15. Gil, R., Rico, R., Alcover, C. M. and Barrasa, A. (2005) 'Change-oriented leadership, satisfaction and performance in work groups: effects of team climate and group potency', *Journal of Managerial Psychology*, **20**(3/4), pp. 312–29.

16. Simmel, G. (1908/1950) 'Subordination under a principle', pp. 250–67 in *The Sociology of Georg Simmel* (ed. and trans. K. Wolff), New York: Free Press.

17. Choi, J. N. (2007) 'Group composition and employee creative behaviour in a Korean electronics company: distinct effects of relational demography and group diversity', *Journal of Occupational and Organizational Psychology*, **80**, pp. 213–34.

18. Kooij-de Bode, H. J. M., van Knippenberg, D. and van Ginkel, W. P. (2008) 'Ethnic diversity and distributed information in group decision making: the importance of information elaboration', *Group Dynamics: Theory, Research and Practice*, **12**(4), pp. 307–20.

19. Slaughter, J. E. and Zicker, M. J. (2006) 'A new look at the role of insiders in the newcomer socialization process', *Group & Organization Management*, **31**(2), pp. 264–90.

20. Tuckman, B. and Jensen, M. (1977) 'Stages of small group development revisited', *Group and Organization Management*, **2**, pp. 419–27.

21. Gersick, C. J. (1988) 'Time and transition in workteams: towards a new model of group development', *Academy of Management Journal*, **31**, pp. 47–53.

22. Mayo, E. (1946) *The Human Problems of an Industrial Civilization*, New York: Macmillan.

23. Feldman, D. C. (1984) 'The development and enforcement of group norms', *Academy of Management Review*, **1**, pp. 47–53.

24. Taggar, S. and Ellis, R. (2007) 'The role of leaders in shaping formal team norms', *Leadership Quarterly*, **18**, pp. 105–20.

25. Zimbardo, P. (2008) BBC *Hardtalk* interview, April 22, 2008.

26. Romero, E. and Pescosolido, A. (2008) 'Humor and group effectiveness', *Human Relations*, **61**(3), pp. 395–418.

27. Wilson, F. M. (2003) *Organizational Behaviour and Gender*, Farnham: Ashgate.

28. Smith, J. W. and Calasanti, T. (2005) 'The influences of gender, race and ethnicity on workplace experiences of institutions and social isolation: an exploratory study of university faculty', *Sociological Spectrum*, **25**(3), pp. 307–34.

29. Hackman, J. and Oldham, G. (1980) *Work Redesign*, Reading, MA: Addison-Wesley.

30. Janis, I. L. (1972) *Victims of Groupthink*, Boston, MA: Houghton Mifflin.

31. Senge, P. (1990) *The Fifth Discipline*, New York: Doubleday.

32. O'Brien, D. and Buono, C. (1996) 'Building effective learning teams: lessons from the field', *SAM Advanced Management Journal*, **61**(3), pp. 4–11.

33. Jenkins, J. (2008) 'Pressurised partnership: a case of perishable compromise in contested terrain', *New Technology, Work and Employment*, **23**(3), pp. 167–80.

34. Thompson (1960). Cited in Robbins, S. P. (1990) *Organization Theory: Structure, Design, and Applications* (3rd edn), Englewood Cliffs, NJ: Prentice-Hall, p. 411.

35. Varela, O. E., Burke, M. J. and Landis, R. S. (2008) 'A model of emergence and dysfunctional effects of emotional conflicts in groups', *Group Dynamics: Theory, Research and Practice*, **12**(2), pp. 112–26.

36. Bolton, S. (2005) *Emotion Management in the Workplace*, Basingstoke: Palgrave.

37. Cole, M. S., Walter, F. and Bruch, H. (2008) 'Affective mechanisms linking dysfunctional behavior to performance in work teams: a moderated mediation study', *Journal of Applied Psychology*, **93**(5), pp. 945–58.

38. Dunlop, P.D. and Lee, K. (2004) 'Workplace deviance, organizational citizenship behavior, and business unit performance: the bad apples do spoil the whole barrel', *Journal of Organizational Behavior*, **25**, 67–80.

39. Behfar, K., Peterson, R., Mannix, E. and Trochim, W. (2008) 'The critical role of conflict resolution in teams: a closer look at the links between conflict type, conflict management strategies, and team outcomes', *Journal of Applied Psychology*, **93**(1), pp. 170–88.

40. Tajfel, H. (1978) 'Social categorization, social identity, and social comparison', pp. 61–76 in H. Tajfel (ed.), *Differentiation between Social Groups*, London: Academic Press.

41. Tajfel, H. (1981) 'Social stereotypes and social groups', in J. C. Turner and H. Giles (eds), *Intergroup Behaviour*, Oxford: Blackwell.

42. Turner, J. (1987) *Rediscovering the Social Group: A Self-categorization Theory*, New York: Basic Books.

43. Miller, N. and Brewer, M. B. (eds) (1984) *Groups in Contact: The Psychology of Desegregation*, New York: Academic Press.

44. Sherif, M., Harvey, O. J., White, B. J., Hood, W. R. and Sherif, C. W. (1961) *Intergroup Conflict and Cooperation*, Norman, OK: Oklahoma Book Exchange.

45. De Dreu, C. and Van de Vliert, E. (eds) (1997) *Using Conflict in Organizations*, London: Sage.

46. Hackman, H. R. (1986) 'The psychology of self-management in organizations', pp. 89–136 in M. S. Pallack and Perloff, R. O. (eds), *Psychology and Work: Productivity, Change and Employment*, Washington, DC: American Psychological Association.

47. Banker, R. D., Field, J. M., Schroeder, R. G. and Sinha, K. (1996) 'Impact of work teams on manufacturing performance: a longitudinal study', *Academy of Management Journal*, **39**(2), pp. 867–90.

48. Cohen, S. G. and Bailey, D. E. (1997) 'What makes team work: group effectiveness research from the shop floor to the executive suite', *Journal of Management*, **23**(3), pp. 239–90.

49. Steiner, I. D. (1972) *Group Processes and Productivity*, New York: Academic Press.

50. Horwitz, F. M., Chan feng Heng and Quazi, H. A. (2003) 'Finders, keepers? Attracting, motivating and retaining knowledge workers', *Human Resource Management Journal*, **13**(4), pp. 23–44.

51. Stewart, P. and Danford, A. (2008) 'Editorial: Union strategies and worker engagement with new forms of work and employment', *New Technology, Work and Employment*, **23**(3), pp. 146–50.

52. Asch, S. E. (1951) 'Effects of group pressure upon modification and distortion of judgements', in H. Guetzkow (ed.), *Groups, Leadership and Men*, New York: Carnegie Press.

53. Milgram, S. (1973) *Obedience and Authority*, London: Tavistock.

54. Russell, N. and Gregory, R. (2005) 'Making the undoable doable: Milgram, the Holocaust, and modern government', *American Review of Public Administration*, **35**(4), pp. 327–49.

55. Koring, P. (2004) 'Iraq war based on "flawed" reports', *Globe and Mail*, p. A11.

56. Winquist, J. and Franz, T. (2008) 'Does the stepladder technique improve group decision making? A series of failed replications', *Group Dynamics: Theory, Research and Practice*, **12**(4), pp. 255–67.

57. van Dick, R., van Knippenburg, D., Hagele, S., Guillaume, Y. R. F. and Brodbeck, F. (2008) 'Group diversity and group identification: the moderating role of diversity beliefs', *Human Relations*, **61**(10), pp. 1463–92.

58. Benders, J. and Van Hootegem, G. (1999) 'Teams and their context: moving team discussion beyond existing dichotomies', *Journal of Management Studies*, **36**(5), pp. 609–28.

59. Roethlisberger, F. J. and Dickson, W. J. (1939) *Management and the Worker*, Cambridge, MA: Harvard University Press.

60. Maslow, A. H. (1954) *Motivation and Personality*, New York: Harper.

61. McGregor, D. (1960) *The Human Side of Enterprise*, New York: McGraw-Hill.

62. Turner, A. N. and Lawrence, P. R. (1965) *Industrial Jobs and the Worker*, Boston: Harvard University, Graduate School of Business Administration.

63. Hoeve, A. and Nieuwenhuis, L. (2006) 'Learning routines in innovation processes', *Journal of Workplace Learning*, **18**(3), pp. 171–85.

64. Lowe, G. (2000) *The Quality of Work: A People-centred Agenda*, New York: Oxford University Press.

65. Klein, J. (1994) 'Maintaining expertise in multi-skilled teams', *Advances in Interdisciplinary Studies of Work Teams*, **1**, pp. 145–65.

66. 'Volvo's radical new assembly plant: "the death of the assembly line"?', *Business Week*, August 28, 1989.

67. Cressey, P. (1993) 'Kalmar and Uddevalla: the demise of Volvo as a European icon', *New Technology, Work and Employment*, **8**(2), pp. 88–96.

68. Elger, T. and Smith, C. (eds) (1994) *Global Japanization?*, London: Routledge.

69. Thompson, P. and Wallace, T. (1996) 'Redesigning production through teamworking', *International Journal of Operations and Production Management*, **16**(2), pp. 103–18.

70. Baldry, C, Bain, P. and Taylor, P. (1998) '"Bright satanic offices": intensification, control and team Taylorism', pp. 163–83 in P. Thompson and C. Warhurst (eds), *Workplaces of the Future*, Basingstoke: Macmillan.

71. Manz, C. C. and Sims, H. P. Jr. (1993). *Business Without Bosses*, New York: Wiley.

72. Danford, A., Richardson, M., Stewart, P., Tailby, S. and Upchurch, M. (2008) 'Partnership, high performance work systems and quality of working life', *New Technology, Work and Employment*, **23**(3), pp. 151–66.

73. Thompson, P. and McHugh, D. (2006) *Work Organizations: A Critical Introduction* (4th edn), Basingstoke: Palgrave.

74. Piore, M. and Sabel, C. (1984) *The Second Industrial Divide*, New York: Basic Books.

75. Turnbull, P. (1986) 'The Japanisation of British industrial relations at Lucas', *Industrial Relations Journal*, **17**(3), pp. 193–206.

76. Sayer, A. (1986) 'New developments in manufacturing: the just-in-time system', *Capital and Class*, **30**, pp. 43–72.

77. Tomaney, J. (1990) 'The reality of workplace flexibility', *Capital and Class*, **40**, pp. 29–60.

78. Clarke, L. (1997) 'Changing work systems, changing social relations? A Canadian General Motors Plant', *Relations Industrielle/Industrial Relations*, **52**(4), pp. 839–65.

79. Malloch, H. (1997) 'Strategic and HRM aspects of kaizen: a case study', *New Technology, Work and Employment*, **12**(2), pp. 108–22.

80. Willmott, H., (1995) 'The odd couple?: re-engineering business processes: managing human relations', *New/Technology, Work and Employment*, **10**(2), pp. 89–98.

81. Thompson, P. (1989) *The Nature of Work* (2nd edn), London: Macmillan.

82. Burawoy, M. (1979) *Manufacturing Consent*, Chicago: University of Chicago Press.

83. Burawoy, M. (2002) 'What happened to the working class?', pp. 69–76 in K. Leicht (ed.), *The Future of the Market Transition*, New York: JAI Press.

84. Shalla, V. (1997) 'Technology and the deskilling of work: the case of passenger agents at Air Canada', in A. Duffy, D. Glenday and N. Pupo (eds), *Good Jobs, Bad Jobs, No Jobs: The Transformation of Work in the 21st Century*, Toronto: Harcourt.

85. Wood, S. (1986) 'The cooperative labour strategy in the U.S. auto industry', *Economic and Industrial Democracy*, **7**(4), pp. 415–48.

86. Kasl, E., Marsick, V. and Dechant, K. (1997) 'Teams as learners', *Journal of Applied Behavioral Science*, **33**(2), pp. 227–46.

87. Finn, R. (2008) 'The language of teamwork: reproducing professional divisions in the operating theatre', *Human Relations* **61**(1), pp. 103–30.

88. Morgan, G. (1997) *Images of Organization* (2nd edn), Thousand Oaks, CA: Sage.

89. Muller, H. J., Rehder, R. R. and Bannister, G. (1998) 'The Mexican–Japanese–U.S. model for auto assembly in Northern Mexico', *Latin American Business Review*, **2**(1), pp. 47–67.

90. Proctor, S., Fulop, L., Linstead, S., Mueller, F. and Sewell, G. (2009) 'Managing teams', pp. 539–73 in S. Linstead, L. Fulop and S. Lilley (eds), *Management and Organization: A Critical Text* (2nd edn), Basingstoke: Palgrave.

91. Brown, S. P., Westbrook, R. A. and Challagalla, G. (2005) 'Good cope, bad cope: adaptive and maladaptive coping strategies following a critical negative work event', *Journal of Applied Psychology*, **90**, 792–8.

IDENTITY WORK, MANAGING AND RESEARCHING

INTRODUCTION

In this chapter I shall illustrate the value of paying attention to the interplay between the 'self' and the 'social category' aspects in studying human *identity work* by reflecting on the way my own identity work over the years has influenced and been influenced by the research work I have done on the identity work of managers. I shall use conceptual tools which I have devised in my most recent work to do this. One can only look back to earlier work from where one is currently conceptually located.

Increasing attention is being paid by organization and management scholars to 'identities'. As well as looking at 'organizational identities' (Hatch and Schultz 2004, for example), researchers are investigating so-called 'professional identities' (Dent and Whitehead 2001, for example), 'entrepreneurial identities' (Cohen and Musson 2000, for example) and 'managerial identities' (Sveningsson and Alvesson 2003, for example). My own research has taken me into each of these latter three areas. But note that I have distanced myself from these expressions with inverted commas and the tag 'so-called'. Why is this? It is because I feel that these terms encourage us to beg the question of whether, say, a 'managerial identity' is part of some people's notions of self or is a social category which exists 'in society'. To what extent is a 'managerial identity' part of what we become as a person if we occupy a managerial role in a work organization and to what extent is it a characterization of a type of individual to be found in novels, newspapers or workplace conversations?

All the issues that arise with regard to human identities, I suggest, have a 'self' dimension and a 'social category' dimension to them. To understand what happens in work organizations and the lives of managerial and other workers, we need to look at both the social categories that relate to those people and the varying ways in which individuals embrace or refuse to embrace those categories. What needs to be investigated is the nature of the relationship between social categories and 'selves'. It is therefore important for research and theorizing to start with concepts that do not prejudge or close off the variety of empirical possibilities that arise. To keep open the relationship between issues of self and issues of social categorization, it would be much more helpful to talk of 'entrepreneurial', 'professional', 'managerial' *aspects of human identities*, rather than of 'managerial identities' and the rest, as such.

Thus, I shall now set out the key concepts to be used and then go back to what I believe are the biographical roots of my research career, moving from childhood through to undergraduate learning and on to participant observation research in managerial settings and to later reflections on what I now choose to conceptualize as 'identity work' as it relates to the working aspects of people's lives.

IDENTITY WORK, SELF AND SOCIAL IDENTITIES

What I mean by *identity work* is the mutually constitutive set of processes whereby people strive to shape a relatively coherent and distinctive notion of personal self-identity. To do this they struggle to come to terms with and – within limits – influence the various social identities which pertain to them in the various milieux in which they conduct their lives. This characterization distinguishes between self-identity and social identities, it will be noticed. These are seen as two aspects of the broad concept of *human identity*. And 'human identity' is simply the notion of who or what a particular person is, in relation to others. It defines the ways in which any given person is like other people and the ways in which they differ from others. *Self-identity* refers to the internal aspects of human identity. It is the individual's own notion of who and what they are and it is something that has to be 'worked at'. To be sane and effective social actors, we all have to achieve a degree of coherence and consistency in our conception of who we are. But we can only achieve this through relating to the social world. And to understand this it is necessary to consider how we are influenced by or choose to relate to *social identities*: cultural, discursive or institutional notions of who or what any individual might be. And these social identities take three different forms. First, there are *category identities* of class, gender, nationality and ethnicity; second there are *formal role identities* of occupation, rank, citizenship and so on; third, there are *local-personal identities* whereby individuals are characterized in terms of what various others make of an individual, in the context of specific situations or events ('the departmental clown', 'a bullying manager'...).

These analytical categories represent a personal attempt to develop a conceptual apparatus to be applied to the people and organizational settings that I am studying. But they can also be understood as revealing my own understanding of the personal and social world in which I exist, all the time privately coming to terms with my own life circumstances and publicly producing analyses of the social world that I hope will be of value to the people who read my work or participate in my classes and my discussions with organizational practitioners – these two aspects of my life, like anyone else's, being tightly interrelated. Making the latter statement is in itself clearly a piece of 'identity work', as that activity was defined earlier. I am presenting a notion of the type of person I am, or aspire to being, both to myself and to you, the reader. I am using social categories like those of 'teacher' and 'writer' and relating these to personal aspects of self: presenting my-self as someone who cares about the people he tries to serve, wants to say things that are relevant to organizational actors and so on. At this point we can move into autobiographical mode to make some sense of this.

WHO AM I, WHERE DO I COME FROM?

The personal identity work that we all do has to answer questions of who we are and where we come from, even if we leave such questions in the background of our personal taken-for-grantedness most of the time. And such questions necessarily take us back into our childhoods. I shall do this shortly but, to help connect this autobiographical reflection to social scientific issues, I shall frame my account in terms of some thinking that I did in my late teen/early adult years as sociology student.

Before settling for a sociology course, I had been tempted some of the time to study English literature, sometimes to study psychology and sometimes to study history, or perhaps politics. But sociology turned out to be precisely the subject to deal with the concerns around which my interests were crystallizing. At the core of this was the issue of the relationship between individual human beings and the bigger patterns of history, society and politics. When I read English literature I was fascinated not only by the texts in their own terms, but also by the writers of those texts and their lives and times. When I thought about history I was fascinated not only by patterns of change, but also by the role that key individuals played in those patterns. This, I was to discover on reading Wright Mills, could be understood in terms of *the sociological imagination* – that style of thinking in which one shifts up from a concern with the 'personal troubles' of individuals to the level of 'public issues' (Mills 1970).

It was reading Bendix's (1966) 'intellectual portrait' of Max Weber and its emphasis on Weber's concern to link individual thinkers, group material interests and massive social change which confirmed for me that sociological ideas were vital for relating who we all are, as unique individuals, to the social world. But how did I link this to my own biography and my desire to make sense of my own life? As I remember, it happened not so much as a result of reading the analytical content of the work of people like Weber, Durkheim, Veblen or Mills, as a result of my reflecting on what it was about the lives of these figures that pushed them towards a sociological style of thinking about the world. To put this question in more contemporary terms: I was wondering about a possible personal *identity work* dimension to their writing. Without now remembering the details of my rough analysis of the lives of these 'founding fathers of sociology' (as the texts of the time tended to characterize them), I remember so clearly coming to the conclusion that they were all in some way socially or psychologically *marginal* in the circumstances of their origins and/or their subsequent lives. They had a capacity or a need to 'stand back' and look with a critical eye at a social world of which they did not feel they were unproblematically a part.

This idea that a sociological (or perhaps an 'anthropological') imagination could relate to some degree of marginality in a writer/researcher's life experience might not stand up to serious intellectual examination. But it was invaluable to me as an 'identity work' resource. It resonated loudly with how I remembered my own childhood. There were practically no other children around in the English East Midlands near-slum back-street in which I spent the first two and a half years of my life. And then, to my delight, I found myself with a whole lot of friends to play with when we eventually moved into a new (and very fine) house on a public housing estate. But I soon became aware of the fact that the other people on the street spoke differently from me. Although my mother is English, she and my father had moved to England from the north of Scotland and lots of the expressions that the people on the street used, and the ways in which they pronounced words, were quite different from what I was used to (both my mother's Wiltshire and my father's Highland speech – and hence, presumably my own, contained rhoticity – the pronouncing of the letter 'r' in words like mother and father – something missing in the English Midlands). I clearly remember seeing puzzled faces when I referred to one friend's baby sister as 'a girning bairn'. And I was equally puzzled myself when I heard another friend being accused of being a 'mardy bum'. I was experiencing here what I later learned to call cultural variation and relativity!

Nothing in these circumstances was powerful enough to be described as 'culture shock'. Nevertheless, continuous recognition of social differences between people, in addition to the more obvious individual differences, led to a life-long tendency to ask 'why is this like this?', 'what is going on here?' A striking memory is that of visiting a friend's home for tea and seeing on the table a plate of bread that had already been cut and buttered. As soon as I got home I asked my parents about what seemed to me to be peculiar behavior. It wasn't just that we cut slices from the loaf as we needed it in our house, and then buttered it. It also seemed to me to be wasteful to butter bread that might not be consumed. When later, as a student, I read Weber's reference to 'the ghosts of dead religious beliefs' haunting our lives, I reflected back on this incident, going beyond my parents' explanations of the bread-buttering phenomenon in terms of English/ Scottish and social class differences to new thoughts about the possible influence in our (non-churchgoing) family of deep-down currents of Scottish Calvinism.

Much later in life I have reflected on this 'bread and butter' experience, and others like it, when people have asked me why doing ethnographic research has been so important to me in my academic career. The truth, I tend to think, is that I find it hard to conceive of 'real research' which does not involve one in thinking/theorizing/ explaining events in the process of closely observing and, if possible, experiencing them. I lived in what was effectively a Scottish home in an English town. And, yes, like for so many fellow diaspora semi-Scots there were the Jimmy Shand records and a wee kilt to wear at family weddings. Also, I lived in a council house with a father, who, in spite of his *social category identity* as a factory worker, was well educated and well read. All of this, it could be said, made me marginal in ethnic and class terms. And, generally speaking, I was not uncomfortable with this. I rather liked it, in fact. It was a good training for a participant observation researcher, one could say with hindsight.

INTO THE FIELD

Within weeks of graduating from the sociology course (in which there was an excellent industrial sociology option), I was working as an industrial relations officer in the foundry of the aero-engine division of Rolls-Royce.

I also registered to do a research degree at a nearby university. Both of these moves were deliberately planned as a preparation for an intended move into an academic post in three years' time (which happened exactly as planned). The research study focused on a major organizational change in the foundry and, as my managerial job was involved with the 'human facilitating' of that change, I quickly found myself doing participant observation research. And what does such research inevitably both push and pull one into? Yes, marginality. Participant observation involves switching back and forth between being a 'native' and being a 'stranger', as we are all told on our research methods courses. It is when one tiptoes along the margin between, in this case, being a fully active junior manager and being a reflective sociological researcher that one produces one's best insights. Well, that is what I persuaded myself as I switched about between the two very divergent *formal role identities* of suited and 'street-wise' (very) young manager and thoughtful, theory-hungry research student. When managers wanted to oppose what I was doing (and the job meant this would inevitably happen) they could attack me by drawing on and pejoratively shaping discursive resources from *category identities* ('typical over-educated graduate'), *formal* role identities ('another Personnel parasite') or a *local-personal identity* ('another straight-out-of-college careerist who will be gone from here as soon as he can get a promotion'). My outward-facing identity work meant countering this with a presentation of self, in *category identity* terms, as 'a boy from a factory-working background who is loyal to his roots'. (This, incidentally, would have been an 'identity of choice' for many sociology students at the time.) And there was a presentation of self in *formal role identity* terms, as 'someone in Personnel who actually wants to support line managers' and, in *local-personal identity* terms as, well, 'a friendly and interested colleague' – or something like that.

I don't remember the identity-management issues in the business context worrying me too much. But I do remember being more challenged, in self-identity terms, when one or two university colleagues tried to make me feel uncomfortable for working for 'a capitalist company' or being 'a servant of power'. To handle this, my external-facing identity work involved my pointing out the necessity of gaining sociological understandings of managerial processes from inside management and by arguing that this could be done without compromising, in any way, one's personal and political values (I argue this further in Watson 2000). And my father helped me significantly in this self-identity maintenance in two respects. First, he said that he had slogged through the heavy factory work and the hours of overtime in part to give his sons the chance to do work above and beyond the working class. And, second, he argued that those people who worked on the shop floor would often be much better placed if the managers in charge of the factory had a better understanding of 'good management'. 'With your education', he said, 'you might be able to do something about that – and have a much more comfortable life than I have had.'

What about the research itself then? This examined the process of the move of more than a thousand employees from Rolls-Royce's 'dirty old foundry' to what they referred to as the 'ultra modern precision casting facility' – the 'PCF'. At the center of the analysis was a consideration of the changing work orientations and implicit contracts of the various groups in the foundry (Watson 1982). The differing social class and work experience aspects of what we might now call these people's 'identities' were central to the analysis. As an illustration of the thinking here, I would pick on one detail of how the senior managers' orientations related to their commitment or otherwise to the new venture. All but two of the senior managers in the foundry were enthusiastic about the new PCF. This made sense, given that they saw involvement in this major business investment as highly career-enhancing. I talked at length, over a period of time, with these two men. After a period of mutual trust-building, they admitted to me that they were unhappy with what was happening. And it became clear that a higher level managerial career was not pertinent to their self-identities. Each of them, we could say, preferred to relate to different *formal role* identities from those embraced by their peers. One of them told me that he valued much more his international reputation as an expert on certain aspects of quality control. And the other man told me how he felt uncomfortable with the managerial level that he was currently at. He saw himself much more as craft plant-management person than as a career line manager. He told me that he was tired of having to present himself to people inside and outside the company as 'a manager'. He would welcome a chance to work at a senior technical level. He had told no one else about this, in part, he explained, because he had 'taken his eye off the ball a couple of times' with costly results. As I understood it, these failures were managerial rather than technical ones.

This piece of detail from my first research study can be interpreted in terms of personal identity issues having implications for managerial behavior and, indeed, managerial effectiveness. And coming back to my own identity work and the importance of this of my claims for the virtues of ethnographic research, I would claim that what I learned here about these two men's identity work would not have been discovered by a researcher simply calling at the plant to interview managers in a more traditional way. This latter type of data collection, however, was what most of the other research students I knew were doing. They might 'name-call' me 'management boy'. But I could counter this with a claim to be 'the researcher who gets the better data'. Yah boo. Most identity work has an element of this kind of label-sticking and label-resisting to it!

MARGINALITY, MANAGEMENT AND PERSONNEL WORK

Self-labelling is something in which personnel managers have shown a particular interest over recent decades. They have re-presented themselves to the world as human resource (HR) professionals. And their occupational spokespersons have shown considerable *discursive ingenuity* in building on this – going as far as to redefine the very idea of a 'profession' (Watson 2002). Why have such efforts been so important? It is because members of this occupation have always had to handle the problem of, guess what? Yes, marginality. The analysis which I first set out in my 1970s study of the personnel management occupation (Watson 1977) stands to the present day, I believe. Whether or not particular 'employment management' specialists present themselves to the world as personnel or HR managers, they have continually to struggle to win credibility – above all in the eyes of other managers. These are men and women whom HR managers are required, at the same time, both to advise/assist and to constrain/control. I learned about the implications of this from the very first day of being located in a personnel department at Rolls-Royce. Within days of starting work I realized that being a member of the 'Personnel and Administration' department made one suspect with other managers and required the type of outward-facing identity work to which I referred earlier. Whether one liked it or not, one had to deal with what I called 'conflict, marginality and ambivalence' (Watson 1977: 58) every working day.

The personnel worker is employed as an 'agent' of the employer. Yet it does not always seem as straightforward as that, in practice. It is normal for HR managers to have to come to terms with a situation which, when I joined the Rolls-Royce 'Personnel and Administration' department, immediately reminded me of the classic industrial sociology studies of foremen whom Wray (1949) called the 'marginal men of industry' and Roethlisberger (1945) referred to as 'master[s] and victim[s] of double talk'. Part of the rationale for my undertaking a study of the personnel management occupation was one of making sense *in sociological terms* of what I had experienced as a young manager doing personnel and industrial relations work. (The other part of the rationale, it has to be recognized, was the career-making one of writing a significant book about an occupation that had previously been practically untouched sociologically.) In personnel work one would, in day-to-day terms at least, 'side' with a managerial group at one moment and with trade union representatives at another. One would 'side' on certain occasions with a corporate management initiative and, at another time, with local management resistance (or vice versa). All of these moves, of course, occurred within a logic of strategically servicing long-term corporate interests. This was firmly argued in *The Personnel Managers*. The daily identity work (both inward- and outward-facing) of the personnel managers whom I studied was related to what was conceptualized in that study as the logic of handling aspects of the conflicts and contradictions of an industrial, capitalist, political economy. In the spirit of the sociological imagination (Mills 1970), we can thus see that the 'personal troubles' and individual identity work that I and the hundred personnel managers studied for the book engaged in were only understandable in terms of 'public issues' and societal structures. Although the expression 'identity work' was not used in the study, much of the analysis of the values, orientations and stratagems of the personnel managers can be understood in such terms.

The study of the personnel management occupation was carried out primarily by visiting a range of organizations, from large to small enterprises and from public sector to private sector undertakings, to interview employment management specialists. One of the research aims was to find out the extent to which there were occupational characteristics in common across different organizational settings. In terms of personal identity, I felt a need to gain knowledge of organizations other than a large engineering one. This was important to my authority as an industrial sociologist or organization theorist, I believed, as well as to my credibility as a business school teacher. How could one speak about organizations and management generally to students and others when one only had experience of a large aerospace business?

A question I asked myself about the personnel manager study was whether I might be seen as turning away from the ethnographer/participant observer element of both my self-identity and my social identity within the academic community. The way my internal identity work handled this question was to persuade myself that the interview-based study was deeply rooted in the ethnographic experience of working as a participant in a personnel function. And I remain persuaded of this. In so far as there were hypotheses being examined in the study, they were ones formed during my full-time industrial experience. And what about outward-facing identity work? Here my claimed background as a 'former personnel specialist' or as someone 'who worked for some time in industrial relations' (the precise formula depending on who I was addressing) was invaluable. It was helpful in gaining access to organizations and senior management offices and it was utterly invaluable in establishing a level of rapport with individuals which would not have been possible for a complete 'civilian'. And this rapport enabled me, I believe, rapidly to establish the level of trust which is so vital to the obtaining of high quality information from research respondents. Such a level was going to be even more important in another large research undertaking.

BACK TO THE FIELD: SEARCHING FOR MANAGEMENT

After 20 or so years of teaching and researching in a full-time business school post following the publication of the personnel manager study, I remember a sense of unease once again developing around 1990 about the gap between the occupational dimension of my identity as a business school 'expert' on the managing of organizations and the fact that my organizational and managerial experience was now almost completely confined to the organizing and managing of academic activity. At the same time I felt the need to undertake a significant empirical study. What do I mean by 'felt the need'? Perhaps I should recast this in terms of identity work. Yes, I should. I had written two textbooks in a row (three, if one includes a second edition of one of these) and I did not want to take on a work-related identity as 'mainly a textbook writer'. Earlier in this chapter, I conceptualized human identity as the notion of who or what a particular person is, in relation to others. And I emphasized how it defines not only how any particular person is similar to others but also how they differ from them. Establishing who *one is not* is as important in identity work as establishing who *one is*. I did not want to be seen as someone who, after producing one successful research monograph in the 1970s, was in the 1990s producing books which did not present new research material and theorizing.

In the middle of this self-reflection, two opportunities presented themselves to me. The first of these was the opportunity to be released from normal academic duties for a year to concentrate on personal research. 'What about taking a fellowship abroad or getting an attachment to a leading business school somewhere where you can have plenty free time to write another book?', I was asked by the head of the business school. To put it in very simple terms, I felt that neither of these things was 'me'. 'Essentialist' as this statement might seem, it most effectively describes the feeling that I remember (feelings surely being significant parts of all identity-maintenance work). And foolishly puritanical as it may sound, I felt that either of these possibilities would be somewhat parasitic. Could one really take a salary for this? Perhaps I should take a 'real' job for a year. And that really would give me something to write about.

The moral aspect of human identity is perhaps coming into play here: the need to believe that one is a 'good' person. And a good person would not live parasitically off others. But is 'need' the right word? Perhaps not. It might simply have been the old ghost of dead Protestant beliefs coming back to haunt me. It would be unworthy to take time away from one's normal duties without producing something that engaged with the 'this-worldly'. This would not happen if one confined oneself to the 'other-worldly' pseudo-monastic world of the university library or set off on the equivalent of the old leisure-class gentleman's 'grand tour'. There would be little monastic, gentlemanly or 'other-worldly', however, about working in a factory for a year. But perhaps these reflections amount to little more than my putting a moral gloss on a simple desire to satisfy my curiosity about what was going on 'out there' in the big corporate world by going out into the field 'in search of management' – as I came to characterize my research adventure when I later wrote about it (Watson 2001a, originally 1994). But I suspect that all of these factors were important, together with others I do not remember. And this is where the second opportunity came in. I found myself in conversation with the manager in charge of an ambitious 'change programme' in the Nottingham-based businesses of GPT (GEC Plessey Telecommunications or 'ZTC' in earlier publications). To help them with their change programme, the management was proposing to employ consultants to undertake a number of specific tasks. One of these, for example, was to 'identify the management competences that the business needs'. Given the sabbatical opportunity that I had been offered and, I must admit, given that the company was in easy walking range of my own house, I offered to help. I argued that it was a bad idea to think of employing consultants to do such sensitive work. If they were willing to give me a senior post for a year, I would undertake these tasks *from within management*. And after some interesting negotiations, in which I clearly had to establish that I had some really 'practical' ideas about management as well the necessary managerial experience, the deal was done. I once again found myself with an office in the HR function of a large company. And I had a list of research questions on one side of my desk and a list of management tasks to fulfil on the other.

I could write at length about the extremely challenging outward-facing identity work which had to be done for me to establish the necessary credibility and rapport with the managers with whom I was working in GPT. However, I can cut this short by referring to my earlier account of the identity work that had to be done when I was a new sociology graduate and junior manager in Rolls-Royce. The 'distancing' from personnel was again very important. So was the need to establish that someone can be academically accomplished and still capable of 'making a difference' in the rough and tumble of managerial politics and problem solving. At least this time I was a 'senior' man working among people of my own age group. But the main difference from the earlier fieldwork experience lay in the vital need to establish with everyone, at every level, that I was not a consultant. Earlier I referred to how 'internal' identity work has to deal with *who one is not* as much as *who one is*. Here we see the importance of establishing in 'external' identity work what one is not. Someone even offered to make me a badge saying in large bright letters 'I am not a consultant'. This was a label, if not a literal one, that I needed. The managers had to be absolutely sure that I was not a consultant if I was going to be accepted as a working colleague. And without that I would neither be able to carry out effective managerial work nor produce worthwhile research.

As at Rolls-Royce, I worked hard to make it clear that I was being paid to act managerially, as a manager, in management's interest. I was not acting in any way whatsoever as an independent professional 'expert'. I was anxious to remove any ambiguity about this for both ethical reasons and in order to make my research observations fully 'participant'. The difference this time was that I had to overcome the suspicion that I was, as it was put to me, 'yet another consultant who takes up our managerial time and then writes a report saying what crap we managers are'. I heard some grim war stories about consultants they had endured. I thus had to repeat time and again that I was part of the management team and that I would bring to bear on events whatever expertise and outside experience I had during my everyday work with them. In this external identity work I was careful not to throw away the academic part of my social identity. This formed a necessary part of my claim to expertise. But it also enabled me to make sense for them of what I wanted from the project materially. I made a promise, which was well received, that I was never going to write any kind of report to top management. I was, however, going to write a research-based book. This, I said, would be published for academic and public consumption (with the confidences of my informants respected throughout and, as I jokingly put it a couple of times, 'the identities of guilty colleagues protected').

The research carried out at GPT, which combined 12 months of participant observation ethnography with the formal interviewing of managers, focused on the activities and accommodations of managers managing their lives and identities within the structural circumstances which prevailed over the year of the study. A key question was that of how managers were handling the 'double control problem' of having, at the same time, to handle all the personal and existential challenges of their personal lives and all the interpersonal, political and economic challenges of managing the activities and meanings of others in the workplace. The study used the notion of 'identity work' albeit in a rather informal way (Watson 2001a: 58). The term was not used as a formal part of the study's conceptual framework. And the managers themselves did not use an explicit notion of 'identity'. A number of them, however, made significant use of a notion of 'the sort of person I am'. This can be seen as an interesting 'lay' concept which is close to what, in the social sciences, we call 'identity'. It is a resource which individuals could utilize in doing what I now formally conceptualize as 'identity work'.

The thinking process of human individuals is theorized in the study as a 'rhetorical' one (Billig 1987) with use being made by these managers in their inward- and outward-facing identity work of a variety of *discursive resources* (ranging from sources in childhood experience to the talk of management change agents) to help them cope with both the existential and the mundane challenges of managing their lives at the same time as they have to manage the work of others. I got personally close to a lot of these managers, by working closely with them and discussing day-in and day-out the pleasures and pains of the work we were doing (as well as many interpersonal, career and family problems that a lot of colleagues sought me out to speak about). But a significant element of my 'closeness' to the managers can be understood in terms of that fact that I, in coming out of the academic world into the rough and tumble of commercial life in a threatened factory, had as much challenging identity work to do to 'stay sane' and to meet the often over-numerous and indeed contradictory demands of a variety of work tasks as did the managers themselves.

The pressures on me as a researcher in this situation were considerable, as indeed they would be on any organizational ethnographer, especially if he or she were participating in the sort of performance-focused activities that managers carry out. And the pressures on the managers were no less considerable. A threat of losing their jobs hung over many of these men and women. I did not face the same threat of redundancy as these people, of course. But I did experience such agonies as that of being involved in decision-making processes which led to the selection for redundancy of one's own managerial colleagues. In that year, the managers of GPT were challenged in their notions of who they were and what they were doing with their lives. So was I. Identity work for everyone involved in that company during that year was hard work, it could be said. And I have only been able to tell the stories of those managers and provide glimpses into their experiences by relating them to my own story. As is often, if not always, the case when one writes about the lives of others, I can only write about stories of these managers in the context of telling my own.

A CONTINUING STORY

After completing the GPT ethnography and writing the *In Search of Management* book (a research monograph which, I believe, has sold well over 10,000 copies), I have examined human identity work, in the spirit of the sociological imagination, in a number of other contexts. These vary from 'whole' managerial careers (Watson 2001b) and ethical aspects of managerial work (Watson 2003a) to strategy-making work (Watson 2003b) and entrepreneurship (Fletcher and Watson 2007). I am currently researching in a small business context where attention is being paid to the ways in which the principals in the business have simultaneously shaped their personal lives and their business over several decades. I am also following up the GPT study and looking in depth at the lifetime's identity work engaged in by one of the managers who worked there (Watson forthcoming).

In this continuing work I am very conscious of my own presence within the research and the significance of what Johnson and Duberley call *epistemic reflexivity*. The present chapter meets the call that these authors make for researchers to account for themselves in a spirit of epistemic reflexivity where 'systematic attempts are made to relate research outcomes to the knowledge-constraining and -constituting impact of the researcher's own beliefs which derive from their own socio-historical location or "habitus" ' (Johnson and Duberley 2000: 178). I have written about some of my research in this chapter and put it in the context of 'where I have come from' intellectually, historically, philosophically and so on. This has not been done as an end in itself but as a means towards contributing to more general thinking about identity work. In this spirit, perhaps, a tentative theoretical generalization can be put forward, to the following effect. Most of the time, we human beings do not reflect consciously about 'who we are' and how we 'fit into society'. If we did, we would probably go mad.

Instead, our culture does this worrying for us, in a way parallel to how institutions can be said to do a lot of our *thinking* for us (Douglas 1986). Although it is normal for people to worry away 'at the edge' of such matters, most of us take our identities for granted most of the time, given the templates, roles, labels, social categories and all the rest that our culture provides for us. However, once we find ourselves operating between or across cultures we can no longer take for granted who we are and how we should behave. This means that the more culturally marginal a person is, the more significant both their both inward-and outward-facing identity work becomes in their lives.

The matter is nowhere near as simple as this tentative theorizing suggests, I am sure. Just considering my own experience, I suspect there will always be an element of personal temperament at play. That is something that will have to be considered in future theoretical work, as will the issues about the moral and emotional dimension of identity work which have surfaced in the process of writing this chapter. But what will personally have to be considered in future work will be the danger of allowing my personal predilection towards strong control over self, career and social location to push me towards overemphasizing theoretically the role of conscious agency and choice in the identity work that people do generally. Doing research on relatively self-assertive people like managers, professionals and entrepreneurs, as opposed to studying the lives of the poor and dispossessed of the earth, might also lead one into such a danger.

We all need to be epistemologically reflexive and conscious of how our own life experiences and our own identity work can both inspire and constrain our research creativity. And we need also to keep in mind the sociological imagination and remain aware at all times that personal circumstances and experiences can only ever be understood within the public, historical and structural contexts of which they are a part. This applies equally to ourselves as researchers and to the people we involve in our research.

REFERENCES

Bendix, R. (1966) *Max Weber: A Sociological Portrait*. London: Methuen.

Billig, M. (1987) *Arguing and Thinking: A Rhetorical Approach to Social Psychology*. Cambridge: Cambridge University Press.

Cohen, L. and Musson, G. (2000) 'Entrepreneurial identities: Reflections from two case studies'. *Organization* 79(1): 31–415.

Dent, M. and Whitehead, S. (eds) (2001) *Managing Professional Identities*. London: Routledge.

Douglas, M. (1986) *How Institutions Think*. Syracuse, NY: Syracuse University Press.

Fletcher, D. E. and Watson, T. J. (2007) 'Entrepreneurship, management learning and negotiated narratives: 'making it otherwise for us – otherwise for them', *Management Learning*. 18(1): pp. 9–26.

Hatch, M. J. and Schultz, M. (eds) (2004) *Organizational Identity: A Reader*. Oxford: Oxford University Press.

Johnson, P. and Duberley, J. (2000) *Understanding Management Research*. London: Sage.

Mills, C. W. (1970) *The Sociological Imagination*. Harmondsworth: Penguin.

Roethlisberger, F. J. (1945) 'The foreman: master and victim of double talk'. *Harvard Business Review* 23.

Sveningsson, S. and Alvesson, M. (2003) 'Managing managerial identities: organizational fragmentation, discourse and identity struggle'. *Human Relations* 56(10): 1163–1193.

Watson, T. J. (1977) *The Personnel Managers: A Study in the Sociology of Work and Employment*. London: Routledge and Kegan Paul.

Watson, T. J. (1982) 'Group ideologies and organisational change'. *Journal of Management Studies* 19(3): 259–275.

Watson, T. J. (2000) 'Managerial practice and interactive social science'. *Science and Public Policy* 27(3): 31–38.

Watson, T. J. (2001a) *In Search of Management (revised edition)*. London: Thomson Learning (Originally Routledge 1994).

Watson, T. J. (2001b) 'The emergent manager and processes of management pre-learning'. *Management Learning* 32(2): 221–235.

Watson, T. J. (2002) 'Speaking professionally – occupational anxiety and discursive ingenuity among human resourcing specialists'. In Whitehead, S. and Dent, M. (eds) *Managing Professional Identities*. London: Routledge.

Watson, T. J. (2003a) 'Ethical choice in managerial work: the scope for managerial choices in an ethically irrational world'. *Human Relations* 56(2): 167–185.

Watson, T. J. (2003b) 'Strategists and strategy-making: strategic exchange and the shaping of individual lives and organisational futures'. *Journal of Management Studies* 40(5): 1305–1323.

Watson, T. J. (forthcoming) 'Identity work, managers and managing'. *Organization*.

Wray, D. (1949) 'Marginal men of industry: the foremen'. *American Journal of Sociology* 54.

Chapter

MANAGING CULTURE

QUESTIONS ABOUT CULTURE

1   What is organizational culture? What is it good for?
2   Are companies with strong cultures always successful?
3   What are the dysfunctions of culture?
4   What are subcultures, and are they healthy?
5   How is organizational culture related to national culture?

Case Study Culture at Company T

Company T is a Canadian automobile assembly plant employing some 1300 people. In response to increased foreign competition, the corporation decided to implement a participative management programme focused on quality. In 1980, the plant hired consultants to help implement a quality of working life (QWL) programme. The union refused to participate, but approved a participative management programme and the plant management decided to go ahead.

The plant was functionally organized, with a plant manager, assistant plant manager and six department managers, including industrial relations, controller, quality, operations, manufacturing engineering and materials. The plant ran two shifts a day and in addition to the operations manager, there were 2 production managers (one responsible for each shift), 8 superintendents, 22 general supervisors, 7 utility supervisors and 66 foremen, each of whom supervised up to 50 hourly workers.

As a result of problems encountered in the implementation of the QWL programme after two years, it became clear that while both consultants and managers had originally engaged in a process with social and technical redesign goals, the real challenge was one of cultural change and personal transformation. They were up against a distinctive and extremely strong company culture, whose assumptions were working a kind of sea change with their interventions, distorting their purpose and twisting their outcomes.

Aggression: 2 × 4 management

The culture of Company T was distinctive even by the estimation of company members. It positively sanctioned an aggressive macho management style, termed '2 × 4 management', which consisted of reprimands in the form of intensive verbal abuse ('yelling and screaming'), dramatic confrontations, and generally, figuratively, 'beating up' on offenders. Extreme examples of this behaviour had become myth in the organization and perpetrators were spoken of as something of folk heroes:

> In the old days here, there used to be a lot of grandstanding, but a lot of it was for show. I can remember one day, 'X' came out onto the floor and he saw a piece that he did not like, and he started jumping up and down on it and he bashed it all in and yelling and screaming and then he said, 'Now throw it out, because it is not good for anything' and when he turned around, he winked at me. It was a show, it was fun, it was a game. It was just like a John Wayne movie, as soon as the movie was over with, they became human again.

The perception was that those who were good at 2 × 4 management got promoted at Company T:

> If your boss catches you out, catches something wrong with the product in your area, you can respond in one of two ways. You can say, 'OK, I'll find out what's wrong', or you can say, 'God damn it, it's John Smith. I'm going to call him in here and chew him out.' The second way looks much better, more glory in it.

This macho style was seen by many as being quite anachronistic, as representing a culture very distinct from the 'larger' culture in which managers spent their family, civic and recreational lives. Some experienced embarrassment when describing their work environment to their friends and families:

> My brother, who is an accountant, says he cannot believe this place, that it is like a game instead of a workplace, but he thinks everything about this place is ridiculous.

And even the worst 2 × 4 managers were recognized as being quite different away from work:

> Mind you, he was a fine fellow outside. He used to tell me that he kept his leopard skin suit in the guard house and would put it on when he came in. In the past, if you wanted to get ahead, you had to do a little more of the 2 × 4. The idea was, if you did not beat, you got beaten.

Managers referred to the company culture as a jungle, the workers as 'animals', the extreme 2 × 4 type managers as 'monsters', and yet, while many expressed aversion to the harsh style, others found it tough, 'honest' and hence, appealing:

> I prefer the straightforward approach. I don't like the foul language. But I do not think people listen to you if you are a nice guy. I don't think people listen to [the assistant plant manager] as much as they used to. People are scared of someone who chews them out.

Competitiveness: 'shiftitus' and empire building

If the tough macho management style was one of the salient values underlying the Company T culture, the other was an intense competitiveness which manifested itself in two forms of behaviour: competition between shifts ('shiftitus') and lack of cooperation between functions ('empire building'). Both these forms of competition were highly valued. 'Shiftitus', with its disease-like connotations, was defined by one manager as 'we do not like to see the other shift run as well as we do'. It was intense in Company T. As mentioned earlier, there were two shifts, A and B. The two shifts were constantly compared and invited to compete in order to encourage people to work hard. At times, however, it got out of hand:

> It is a big game, to get the other guy. There is a lot of resentment and competition. We base everything on results and so people will resort to things like counting back on the line [including items made on the production line but not packed or despatched as shift output] to get a better count for their shift. Sometimes the foreman will lock up his tools so that the other people on the next shift will not get them. We have to do process books, to make sure things like tools and materials are exchanged, otherwise people start breaking into each other's lockers. Rivalry is good but you have to keep the lid on.

Despite the recognized damage and waste incurred by the competition, it had some defenders. These fell into two categories. There were those who felt that, in general, it was healthy because it fostered 'good, clean competition'. Others felt that it was part of the fun of working at Company T. It was a macho, competitive, street-fighting world:

> I knew everything about the machines in my area and I used to turn up the speed on the line for brief periods of time so that my boys could produce more units than the other shift. Sometimes the foreman from the other shift would sneak in early to make sure I was not going on overtime. But I just knew to regulate the line and get things done faster and I had everyone behind me, my boys loved to do it that way. They loved to shove it in their [the other shift's] face.

Similarly, functional loyalty was very strong in Company T. This was sometimes referred to as 'empire building' and permeated all levels of the organization from the operating committee down:

> It is really incredible how one unit pits itself against another in this place. It is as if there is a wall at the end of each unit, and anything that passes through that wall is no longer a problem for that unit. People pass things along because there is always pressure, there is always pressure to deliver the numbers. Despite all the lip service about quality being most important, if you do not get the numbers, you get nothing.

Lying, cheating and stealing culture

While the two values of 2 × 4 management and competitiveness formed the basis of the company culture, pursuit of these values on the individual level was commonly recognized as resulting in a set of interconnected assumptions about behaviour which was widely recognized as dysfunctional. On an individual level, the 2 × 4 management led to considerable fear of being exposed and humiliated and forced people into a secretive, self-defensive, mode termed 'covering ass':

> I've had it solid, with that 2 × 4 style – it nullifies you. You just start covering ass and playing your cards close to the vest. You collect a lot of excuses and you are ready to hand them out if anything comes up. So the problems never get solved.

The competitiveness, on the other hand, meant that functions and shifts worked actively to pass the buck, passing poor quality products from one department to another, failing to take responsibility for product defects, and rushing faulty products out the door in an effort to 'beat' the other production shift in a race for numbers. This activity was known in the culture as 'shipping shit':

> The biggest problem around here is that there is no trust, no one wants to get blamed for anything. So say the sealer goes bad and you know how to fix it, but you do not fix it; what you do is to call maintenance or to call industrial engineering. That way they get stuck with the problem and you do not get chewed up for it. It could be that it was your fault, that your guys screwed up the gun, but you try to cover that up and get it pinned on maintenance and engineering. For example, if you had a big hole, it might be something you could fix, but if you fixed it too many times, then it would become your responsibility, you would pick up the job and you can't hold that job.

The need to hide personal and functional problems and failures, fuelled by the desire to be competitive and to win, combined with the fear of retaliation resulted in tacit acceptance of all kinds of rule breaking which managers in Company T called 'lying, cheating and stealing'. Essentially, these terms referred to the concealing of information, parts and personnel which was viewed as a 'survival tactic':

> This culture [lying, cheating and stealing] is still important, this is how they survive. If someone gets on their back, they say 'we know how to fix that: lie, cheat and steal'. There is not real progress there. There is a recognition that it is a problem, but to tell you the truth I think [the assistant plant manager] does it as well. He lies, cheats and steals to get the plant manager off his ass.

'Lying, cheating and stealing' also involved concealing (stockpiling) parts, hiding personnel (giving them fictitious jobs to do so that they won't be transferred) and falsifying reports concerning injuries, defects and manpower:

> The book records say that we have a million dollars of obsolete material. But before the last launch, we shipped it out and it turned out to be 2 million dollars worth. There are kitties all over the place. Foremen squirrel things away that they think they need. Foremen get hit over the head all the time for scrap, so it is better to hide it away and call it lost stock. I think I would do the same thing. But it makes for a lot of waste in the system.
>
> Another example is, if you are running rough on certain parts of the line and defects come up, someone will stamp it off so that it does not show up as a loss for our department. That is dangerous; it is just bad for the company. We are more concerned about covering ass than quality or quantity. We would rather run with one man less than we need to do the job properly. We expect the repairmen to pick up the slack. If the repair does not get it, it goes out and the warranty gets it.

Again, as with competition and the macho style, lying, cheating and stealing, while felt by some to be dysfunctional, were seen by others as simple flexibility, with the goal of getting the job done. This perspective is not unusual and often forms an important aspect of the informal value system of organizations:

> We all fight to keep down costs, but … costs are still way out of control. But you know, it is mostly the new supervisors whose budgets are way over. If they understood the old system better, they maybe would lie, cheat and steal a little and would be better off. Old supervisors who know the ropes, his budget will always be under … lying, cheating and stealing is a system which has worked. Everyone watched what they spent and they stayed on their toes … Most seasoned supervisors can keep it within limits.

Finally, of course, there were those who perceived the lying, cheating and stealing as part of the fun of Company T culture. It represented a kind of freedom to wheel and deal, to live by your wits. It was perceived as a game with its own challenges and satisfactions, a healthy environment for those that survived. Part of the difficulty in introducing change was that many managers liked the excitement and the subterfuge. They had survived in Company T because they were good at playing a game and holding a job which required considerable skill, knowledge and personal toughness.

SOURCE: Adapted from Frances Westley (1990) 'The eye of the needle: Cultural and personal transformation in a traditional organization', *Human Relations* **43**(3): 273–93. Reprinted by permission of Sage Publications Ltd. Copyright © The Tavistock Institute 1990.

QUESTIONS ABOUT THE CASE

1 Does Company T have a shared culture?
2 Is Company T a 'strong' culture?
3 What are the problems of the culture?
4 Do you think the company can be changed?

INTRODUCTION

Organizational culture has become an essential element in our understanding of organizations. There is an interrelatedness between this and other concepts such as leadership, organizational structure, motivation, power and strategy. The rise of the popularity of the organizational culture concept in the 1970s and 1980s, promising as it did to secure employee commitment, coincided with the relative decline in both the popularity of and broader research interest in the field of motivation. Although culture was often presented as the 'answer' to the problems of failing companies, Peter Anthony (1994: 6), in discussing one of the few longitudinal studies of organizational change, notes that 'the attempt to change corporate culture was accompanied by complex political processes and structural adjustment' and later comments 'the case for culture cannot win: if change is confined to culture it will not work, if accompanied by structural change it cannot be isolated as crucial to success' (Anthony 1994: 15). More recently, there has been a growing recognition that it is impossible to extricate culture as a 'variable' from other elements of the organizational context. Nevertheless, one of the main reasons for the rise in interest in organizational culture was to understand how it impacts on organizational change: for a time it was seen as the hidden obstacle to success.

The growing concern with the economic ascendancy of Japanese companies and the need to dismantle the crumbling industrial bureaucracies of the West at the end of the 1970s fuelled the dramatic rise of the organizational culture or 'excellence' literature (see Pascale and Athos 1980; Deal and Kennedy 1982; Peters and Waterman 1982). Old structures and the old-fashioned values associated with them needed to be replaced, but with what? Thomas Peters and Robert Waterman and Terrence Deal and Allen Kennedy were in no doubt that 'strong' cultures were the key to prosperity. The suggestion was simple, timely, flattering and inspiring in its concern with success, and comforting in its implication that for a company to become successful it simply had to change its core values (Guest 1992; Anthony 1994: 16).

Unfortunately, most of the major culture changes of the 1980s were accompanied by major downsizing or divestment and depended significantly on size and growth strategies. This is not to deny that culture is an important dimension of organization, although it does seem to be easier to argue for culture as a barrier to change (Johnson 1992) than as a guarantor of success. Steven Feldman (1996) argues that culture is neither one thing nor the other, and is simultaneously both an obstacle to change and a ground for creative development – it forms the *context* for action. Frances Westley (1990), as we have seen above, provides an example of a culture with which no one was happy but to which almost everyone subscribed, in an organization that was committed to conflict, violent and abusive management and internal competition. Company T, as Westley calls it, was proud of its '2 × 4' management, which dealt with people verbally as though they were hitting them with a 2 × 4 inch plank of wood; 'shiftitus' where shifts doing the same job would strive to better each other to the extent of damaging overall performance; and 'lying, cheating and stealing', which was basically do or say anything to make yourself and your group look good and everyone else look bad. The people who worked in this system did not like it: nevertheless it was powerful and they felt unable to change it. As a culture it was just as 'strong' and pervasive as McDonald's or IBM but worked against organizational effectiveness.

THE ORIGINS OF ORGANIZATIONAL CULTURE

The idea of culture in relation to organizations has a long but tortuous history (Chan and Clegg 2002). The initiatives of nineteenth-century work reformers such as Robert Owen, mentioned in the Introduction to this book, were foundational in setting an agenda for industrial organization in cultural as much as organizational terms, and ethical Quaker capitalists such as Joseph Rowntree and Edward Cadbury saw their mission in sociocultural as well as business terms. Even F.W. Taylor's scientific management had important cultural objectives, which threatened the subcultural influences of both organized labour and management. After the 1920s, at least, it was overtly recognized from the Hawthorne Studies that the social dimensions of work are important elements of effectiveness and the Studies also identified the critical function of the supervisor or shop-floor leadership. But it was Elliott Jaques (1952) who perhaps first coined the term 'culture' specifically in relation to work organiza-tion in *The Changing Culture of a Factory*, which was part of a series of accounts of participatory management in the Glacier Metal Company, although structure (that is, size and design of the organization), reward systems and the use of hierarchy (that is, different layers of authority from top management to shop-floor supervisors) were also important to the success of the project.

During subsequent years, organizational psychologists such as Chris Argyris (1964) were beginning to note the importance of the subconscious dimensions of organization and its psychological health. In the 1950s Alvin Gouldner, an American sociologist, also identified the importance of the implicit dimensions of working life that were taken for granted, in two books, *Wildcat Strike* (1955) and *Patterns of Industrial Bureaucracy* (1954). In the former he tells the story of a gypsum mine in which the local managers had been accustomed to letting the men have little favours – borrowing equipment, leaving early, taking breaks and so on – in return for working committedly when necessary. The mine was taken over by new management from outside the area – 'cosmopolitans' – who did not understand the implicit system of concessions and obligations (which Gouldner called the 'indulgency pattern') and immediately tightened up discipline and rules. The workforce did not like this and performance dropped, culminating in a 'wildcat strike' when one of the workforce was dismissed for an infringement which had been customarily overlooked as normal practice under the old regime.

Another related development in the 1960s was the discovery of *negotiated order theory*, which was based on work done in psychiatric hospitals by Anselm Strauss and his colleagues (1963). What Strauss et al. argued was that hospitals are composed of different groups or 'congeries' of professionals and non-professionals. Each of these groups has an interest in how, for example, a patient is managed, treated by drugs, given occupational therapy or cared for on the ward, and each has an influence over how the actual treatment happens in practice (think of a time you may have spent in hospital: did you prefer it when one doctor saw you rather than another? When one shift of nursing staff was working rather than another? How about the cleaners or voluntary workers? How did the presence and behaviour of the other patients affect your treatment? Did you ever notice any tensions between groups of staff?). Strauss et al. argued that each of these groups had a view about what made their job easier, what should be their responsibility and into what decisions they should have an input; each also had a view about what was morally and ethically desirable behaviour. In addition, individuals within groups developed relationships with particular patients and shared these perceptions over time, individuals have careers and even patients can have 'sick careers', and there were always issues of power and resource allocation in the background. Strauss et al. argued that the way things were done was constantly shifting and realigned from time to time; there were implicit rules as well as explicit ones, and groups customarily negotiated the order of how things happened, consciously and unconsciously. A good film to watch that relates to negotiated order, power and culture is *One Flew Over the Cuckoo's Nest* (1975) starring Jack Nicholson and directed by Milos Forman.

Around the same time, Harold Garfinkel (1984 [1967]) was developing *ethnomethodology*, a form of sociology which concentrated on the ways in which people make sense of their social situations, that stressed the importance of unspoken rules, talk, common sense and the taken-for-granted aspects of social life. The idea of membership was also important to Garfinkel, and particularly the things people had to learn to become a 'member' of a social group. Much of Garfinkel's work overlapped with the work of anthropologists, who customarily studied exotic societies, and in 1971 Barry Turner (who was influenced by the work of Garfinkel and the banker-philosopher Alfred Schütz, on whose work Garfinkel based many of his ideas) published *Exploring the Industrial Sub-Culture*, the first book to bring the two disciplines together in looking at the way stories, rites, rituals and humour shaped behaviour in organizations. Turner's book did not have immediate impact but is now recognized as having been pioneering.

Related to the emphasis of this work on the non-obvious, and the importance of the implicit and taken-for-granted in forming our experience of organizations, some social psychologists involved in organizational change, who called themselves organizational development (OD) specialists, began to recognize the significance of the unsaid as a barrier to transformation. They often argued that their work was to bring out the unconscious obstacles to organizational change, as a form of cultural intervention. So ideas of culture, in relation to organization and organizational change, had been around for quite a while before the 'excellence' literature picked them up, but in contrast to that literature they emphasized the implicit and unconscious elements of experience and the processes of sense-making and meaning-making rather than the content of communication and the explicitly expressed values.

Jim Olila (1995) argued that in the tradition of the study of the non-obvious, anthropologists who study organizations are interested in the tensions that people experience as a series of 'gaps' in their organizational experience. Not exactly creating a definition of culture, he suggested that in practical terms cultural *tension* as the object of investigation could be seen as 'gaps'. These gaps he described as:

- *the ideal/real culture gap* (the tension between what ought to be done and what actually takes place)
- *the formal/informal culture gap* (the tension between the official, often written description of who, what, why and when in an organization versus the unofficial, unwritten, yet frequently the most comfortable, traditional or successful ways of

getting things done by those who are deemed best, most fun or most compatible for the job or task regardless of their official position, title or duties)

○ *the overt/covert culture gap* (the tension between known and publicly acknowledged ways of thinking, feeling and doing and those known ways which are never spoken about, the shadowed or occluded areas of the culture)

○ *the conscious/unconscious gap* (the tension between ways of thinking, feeling and doing in which we are aware we participate and those in which we engage but are not aware are taking place).

He also argued that this approach recognizes the complexity of everyday life: rather than having single identities, loyalties and experiencing the same reality, we all have multiple identities, loyalties and experiences of reality, and the exciting thing about investigating organizational cultures is teasing out this tissue of differences and seeing how it works, doesn't work, or can work better. In a management sense, we are talking about the management of diversity.

Charles Hampden-Turner (1990) also draws on anthropological sources and argues similarly that culture is a response to human *dilemmas*, a means of problem solving. Human beings are faced with alternatives in living their lives in a very fundamental way: how to develop communities; how or whether to cultivate the land; whether to be dominating or cooperative as a society; how to arrange for procreation and the succession of the race; how to manage time and adapt to the climate; whether to be individualistic or group-oriented. Some of these things, through mutual interaction over time, become shared and common; others become more elaborated and differentiated, a result of the difference that Olila identifies. In organizational terms, these dilemmas become formulated in such terms as 'the need to adapt the organization to a changing environment' versus 'the need to integrate members of the organization internally'; or 'the need for periodic change' versus 'the need to preserve key continuities'. Culture is what evolves to bridge these gaps.

DEFINING CULTURE

Myriad attempts have been made to define culture, but this does not necessarily mean that the concept is elusive – on the contrary, the manifestations of culture are often very concrete in buildings and behaviours. Andrew Brown (1998) gives a list of what he calls definitions of culture, but in actuality, taken out of the context of the pieces of which they were originally part, most of them are just partial *descriptions* of culture, and all of them make some sense (see Exhibit 9.1). Brown also attempts to classify these into a rather crude structured hierarchy, but this is a confused and confusing exercise, as is his account of the development of theories of culture.

A useful collection of definitions can also be found in Martin (2002: 57–8) and Alvesson (2002) is also helpful in identifying the scope of the culture concept. Paul Bate (1994: 20) seeks to examine what other writers have tried to define culture as, and he also comes up with a wide variety of types of definition. But his approach is both more subtle and theoretically alert than is Brown's. What Bate argues is that culture and strategy are not just related, or similar, but that strategy is itself a cultural phenomenon (an outcome of cultural processes) and culture is strategic (a way of dealing with problems so that living becomes easier). Applied to organizations, this does not mean that the culture of a company and its strategy will be seamless and supportive, but that work needs to take place in both areas simultaneously if either is to change. However, given Peter Anthony's argument that every organizational culture change process tends to take place at the same time as a structural change, so its effects are hard to measure, it is little wonder that the many attempts to isolate and measure 'culture' as a variable (from the early 'climate' studies onward) have tended to founder. This empirical confusion has given rise to some theoretical confusion as well, as can be seen in Exhibit 9.2. Here Drennan (1992) identifies causal factors that determine culture, but of these several are structural factors, and some are environmental. Items 1 and 6 might be components of *corporate* culture, but only item 12 would be considered to be part of *organizational* culture. Culture is not, as in Drennan's functionalist approach, about the content of causal chains; on the contrary it is about how factors that may or may not occur within causal chains are interpreted and become meaningful in the context of social action by members of the organization.

9.1 | Exhibit

Some definitions of organizational culture

○ The culture of the factory is its customary and traditional way of thinking and doing things, which is shared to a greater or lesser degree by all its members, and which new members must learn, and at least partially accept, in order to be accepted into service in the firm. Culture in this sense covers a wide range of behaviour: the methods of production; job skills and technical knowledge; attitudes towards discipline and punishment; the customs and habits of managerial behaviour; the objectives of the concern; its way of doing business; the methods of payment; the values placed on different types of work; beliefs in democratic living and joint consultation; and the less conscious conventions and taboos (Jaques 1952: 251).

○ The culture of an organization refers to the unique configuration of norms, values, beliefs, ways of behaving and so on that characterize the manner in which groups and individuals combine to get things done. The distinctiveness of a particular organization is intimately bound up with its history and the character-building effects of past decisions and past leaders. It is manifested in the folklore, mores and the ideology to which members defer, as well as in the strategic choices made by the organization as a whole (Eldridge and Crombie 1974: 89).

○ A set of understandings or meanings shared by a group of people. The meanings are largely tacit among members, clearly relevant to the particular group and distinctive to the group. Meanings are passed on to new group members (Louis 1980).

○ Culture is a pattern of beliefs and expectations shared by the organization's members. These beliefs and expectations produce norms that powerfully shape the behaviour of individuals and groups in the organization (Schwartz and Davis 1981: 33).

○ Organizational culture is not just another piece of the puzzle, it is the puzzle. From our point of view, a culture is not something an organization has; a culture is something an organization is (Pacanowsky and O'Donnell-Trujillo 1982: 126).

○ A pattern of basic assumptions – invented, discovered or developed by a given group as it learns to cope with its problems of external adaptation and internal integration – that has worked well enough to be considered valid and, therefore, to be taught to new members as the correct way to perceive, think and feel in relation to those problems (Schein 1985: 9).

○ The shared beliefs that top managers in a company have about how they should manage themselves and other employees, and how they should conduct their business(es). These beliefs are often invisible to top managers but have a major impact on their thoughts and actions (Lorsch 1986: 95).

○ Culture is 'how things are done around here'. It is what is typical of the organization, the habits, prevailing attitudes and grown-up pattern of accepted and expected behaviour (Drennan 1992: 3).

Source: Adapted from Andrew Brown (1998) *Organizational Culture*, London: Financial Times/Prentice Hall, p. 6.

9.2 | Exhibit

The sources of an organization's culture

According to David Drennan the twelve key causal factors which shape a company's culture are:

1. Influence of a dominant leader
2. Company history and tradition
3. Technology, products and services
4. The industry and its competition
5. Customers
6. Company expectations
7. Information and control systems
8. Legislation and company environment
9. Procedures and policies
10. Rewards systems and measurement
11. Organization and resources
12. Goals, values and beliefs

Source: Andrew Brown (1998) *Organizational Culture*, London: Financial Times/Prentice Hall, p. 42. Adapted from D. Drennan (1992) *Transforming Company Culture*, London: McGraw-Hill.

The question then remains: Is the nature of an organization's culture a factor for success? Despite the views of managers and consultants, research has been unable to demonstrate it, although there does seem to be some evidence that it has impact in particular combinations of factors, including economic climate, and that it can be a *barrier* to success (Barney 1986).

Culture is a means of finding a way to resolve differences and of helping people work together, often through symbols that work effectively without our having to think about them (see also Johnson 1992). We 'know' what things mean, without having to be too specific – in other words, symbols work best as an umbrella which is sufficiently general to contain a diversity of orientations (like the national flag of a country: the Union Jack of the UK actually combines elements of the national flags of England, Scotland and Northern Ireland within it) rather than having a great deal of specificity. Ed Young (1989) and Stephen Linstead and Robert Grafton Small (1992) also argue that rather than culture being an exclusive expression of shared values, where it is most strongly expressed it is an attempt to contain potentially divisive difference and conflict. In short, if we all think the same we do not need to express it, we tend to accept it. In fact, we are not even aware that we do all think the same, because we accept our views as reality and don't positively choose to accept or reject alternatives as we don't recognize alternatives as such. Jorge Luis Borges (1962:181) cites the (apparently mistaken) observation by the historian Edward Gibbon in his *History of the Decline and Fall of the Roman Empire*, where he observed that there is a complete absence of camels in the text of the Qur'an. For Borges this is the most convincing indication of the text's authenticity, the one feature that indicates that the Qur'an was written by an Arab. A Westerner trying to write a Middle Eastern document would think that camels were an important symbol of authenticity and would remark on them repeatedly; an Arab who saw them constantly, however, would take them for granted and think them not worthy of remark. This raises a major question about 'strong' visible cultures – to what unspoken problems are they a response, and what conflicts are being avoided or suppressed? Paradoxically, perhaps where cultures are most visible is where we should expect the deepest conflict and divergence of opinions.

Of course, organizational culture still relates in many ways to a system of shared meaning held by members that distinguishes the organization from other organizations, but this may not always be easy to articulate for the members. In fact, the concept of 'culture' relates to something that most of us can recognize from our experience of organizations, but is rather elusive when we attempt to define it. For Deal and Kennedy (1982) and Peters and Waterman (1982), culture is 'the way we do things around here' or 'the rules of the game for getting along in the organization'. For Linda Smircich (1983), culture is 'not something an organization has, but something an organization is'. In other words, an organization is a place where cultural processes happen, but it is also an outcome of those processes working in society. The organization itself is both a product and a producer of culture. This dual dimension is often missed by the more managerialist of commentators who seem to see culture as an object. But we can go further to suggest that cultural processes do not operate in a unified way – they are fragmentary, incomplete, contradictory, disrupted and neither stop nor start when we want them to. Although culture cannot be completely controlled, it can still be open to some manipulation.

Edgar Schein (1985) defines culture as 'the deeper level of basic assumptions and beliefs that are shared by members of an organization, that operate unconsciously, and that define in a basic, "taken-for-granted" fashion, an organization's view of itself and its environment'. Schein has a model that identifies three levels of culture (as described in Figure 9.1). The three levels are composed of: *artefacts and creations* (objects, buildings, uniforms, technology and so on); underpinned by *values* that are not visible, but of which we are or can be made aware; and *basic assumptions*, which are taken for granted, invisible, preconscious and hard to access. Furthermore, he argues that the culture reveals itself when it is most stressed, when presented with problems and challenges, rather than in its routine, which is similar to Hampden-Turner's dilemma-centred view of culture. This has an important consequence: to observe what a culture does when faced by problems, you have to be there, you cannot rely on questionnaires. Further, if culture is unconscious, it cannot be easily articulated. Questionnaires can therefore only access the known, visible and pretty unremarkable aspects of culture. Nevertheless, many 'culture investigations', both academic and commercial, rely on such instruments. Whatever it is that these instruments elicit, Schein and others (especially social anthropologists) would argue, it is not culture.

Linstead and Grafton Small (1992: 333) argue that a distinction can be made between 'corporate culture' and 'organizational culture'. The former is:

> devised by management and transmitted, marketed, sold or imposed on the rest of the organization, with both internal and external images yet also including action and belief – the rites, rituals, stories and values which are offered to organizational members as part of the seductive process of achieving membership and gaining commitment.

The latter, however, is that which 'grows or emerges within the organization and which emphasizes the creativity of organizational members as culture-makers, perhaps resisting the dominant culture'. In other words, the organizational culture may consist of subcultures, and it may be fragmented, but it will be the outcome of cultural processes which take place wherever human beings attempt to achieve a collective understanding of their everyday world by making it meaningful.

Joanne Martin (2002: 111–14) notes that there are distinctions that need to be made between the related concepts of organizational culture – organizational climate, organizational identity and organizational image (Ashkanasy et al. 2000). *Organizational climate* (Denison 1990) tends to take a psychological approach to the

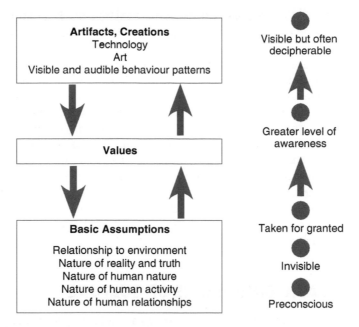

Figure 9.1 – Schein's three levels of culture

Source: Edgar Schein (1985) *Organizational Culture and Leadership*, p. 14. Copyright © Edgar Schein 1985. Reprinted by permission of John Wiley & Sons, Inc.

Plate 1 – Personalization can extend to some unusual workplaces
Source: Photo © Garance Maréchal

measurement of content themes (beliefs, values, basic assumptions) or informal practices (behavioural norms) while neglecting the cultural and symbolic forms – stories, physical arrangements, rituals, jargon – that are the core of organizational culture research. Climate studies therefore tend to take a narrow approach to cultural issues, and, insofar as they assume consistency of culture and climate, assume that the manifestations of culture in symbolic forms would be consistent with and predicted by the key measures upon which they concentrate their attention. Many culture researchers would disagree, and would argue that the distinction between the two lies in how they define meaning and what phenomena they consider to be significantly meaningful. *Organizational identity* (Hatch and Schultz 1997) refers broadly to what members perceive, feel and think about their organization and is thus less broad than culture. *Organizational image* is what the organization's audiences – customers, shareholders, regulators, key publics – believe to be its values and beliefs and their own values and beliefs about the company. These images are projected outward and may then be absorbed back into the company's meaning system to affect its identity, that is, who we are and who we think we are is always in interaction with who others think we are. In this chapter, we will concentrate on the idea of culture only, but there will inevitably be points at which questions of image overlap.

BASIC DIMENSIONS OF CULTURE

Organizational cultures, viewed as a whole, may vary along different dimensions. Brown (1998: 58) argues that the key dimensions are *transparency/opaqueness* and *simplicity/complexity* (see Figure 9.2). The first dimension relates to whether the culture is easily understood in terms of clarity, whether things are what they appear to be, whether the 'ropes' and rules of the culture are immediately accessible or whether they need to be discerned through experience and insight. This varies according to how tightly or loosely coupled the various elements of the culture are, and whether the *actual* culture corresponds to the *espoused* culture. The simplicity/complexity dimension refers to the quantity of cultural artefacts, beliefs and assumptions; the diversity of such items; and the number of embedded subcultures and their relationships to the dominant culture. Where a culture is both complex and opaque, it will take a newcomer considerably more time to learn how to 'fit in'.

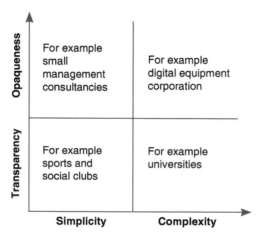

Figure 9.2 – Culture and socialization
Source: Andrew Brown (1998) *Organizational Culture*, London: Financial Times/Prentice Hall, p. 59.

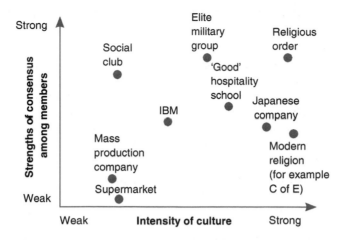

Figure 9.3 – Examples of strong and weak cultures
Source: Andrew Brown (1998) *Organizational Culture*, London: Financial Times/Prentice Hall, p. 76. Adapted from Roy Payne (1990) 'The Concepts of Culture and Climate', *Working Paper 202*, Manchester Business School.

Another commonly mentioned measure of organizational culture is strength or weakness. Brown adapts a formulation by Payne (1990) which regards strength as a production of the interaction of the widespread distribution of beliefs, or strength of consensus, and the intensity with which beliefs are held, or strength of feeling. These dimensions are illustrated in a range of organizations from supermarkets to religious organizations as shown in Figure 9.3. Taken in combination with the dimensions of transparency/opacity and simplicity/complexity, the textural variety of cultures is readily apparent, although such schematic treatments of culture inevitably sacrifice subtlety and detail for the ability to contain a broad picture of cultural possibilities.

STRONG CULTURES

Despite the variations to be observed in cultural strength, the literature has not been obsessed with cultural processes but with 'strong cultures' and how they can be created. Traditional control processes in organizations tend to operate through direct orders or programmes and procedures. Cultural control strategies tend, however, to operate by generating the consent of the workforce through the diffusion and popularization of either the culture of the senior management, or a culture which senior management popularize without actually sharing (Bate 1994: 39). The values and norms are first disseminated; then there may be some denial and censorship of alternative or oppositional views; finally there will be some attempt to define and limit the parameters of what is able to be discussed, and eventually people will internalize this and just avoid certain topics and lines of critique (Kirkbride 1983: 238). Interestingly, people tend to leave organizations when this happens. However, control is increasingly being exercised over sensory, aesthetic and emotional responses – people are being told what to feel as well as what to think, and these feelings are played on by culture manipulators. Omar Aktouf (1996), in Exhibit 9.3, outlines some of the characteristics which managers seek to disseminate among the brewery workers he studied.

9.3 | Exhibit

Supervisory culture in Algiers and Montreal: Managers' views

The good employee (who has the potential to become a foreman) is:

○ submissive: ever consenting, obedient and disciplined;
○ punctual: doesn't lose a half-minute of production time;
○ serious: 'doesn't talk', totally absorbed in his task;
○ malleable: lets himself be 'formed', acquires the 'right' bent;
○ ambitious: 'wants it', 'works his guts out' to succeed, gives 'his maximum'.

Foremen should (in order of importance):

○ achieve their assigned objectives: quotas are first and foremost, everything else comes 'after';
○ set an example: particularly concerning the points listed above;
○ be 'firm': never yield on any issue, do not be 'soft', output before all else;
○ be a policeman with 'velvet gloves': supervise and obtain productivity without problems;
○ 'have a grip': able to boss the men, be inflexible and uncompromising;
○ not 'try to please': 'to please' the employees is 'playing their game';
○ know how to be tough: 'deal severely with', 'sanction' and 'make an example of offenders to avoid shirking' on the part of the employees;
○ be 'able to solve his own problems': 'to show initiative';
○ but all the same, know how to 'communicate' while 'maintaining discipline' and 'not going further than he's asked'.

Formal criteria for the evaluation of foremen in Montreal:

○ Production per line
○ Production per machine
○ Production per job
○ Number of breakdowns
○ Number of conflicts.

Source: Omar Aktouf (1996) 'Competence, symbolic activity and promotability', in Stephen Linstead, Robert Grafton Small and Paul Jeffcutt (eds) *Understanding Management*, London: Sage, pp. 66–77.

Strong cultures are intended to engender commitment, dedication and devotion, enthusiasm, passion and even love in employees. And they can work: at least they can have great impact. If employees 'feel' for the company, if it touches them in some way, they will follow its leaders anywhere because they value, even idolize, everything it stands for. Or so the argument runs. Arlie Russell Hochschild's book *The Managed Heart* (1983) looks at the issue of emotional labour, where employees are required to manage their selves sufficiently to generate a display of emotion for the benefit of the company. Flight attendants are required to 'smile from the inside' and debt collectors have to project the sort of self-image that would make debtors pay their bills. Hochschild argues that human feeling has been commercialized, manipulated for competitive advantage. Companies expect their employees artificially to generate sincere feelings. The job of the leader then is not just the management of meaning (Smircich and Morgan 1982), but also the management of feeling (Bate 1994; Hancock and Tyler 2001: 125–49).

Employees, as Deal and Kennedy (1982) argue, are uncertain about not only what to think in the modern world, but also what to feel, and whether they are worthy to be in that world. Companies with strong cultures offer to fill these mental and emotional gaps; 'think this', 'feel this' and act accordingly and you will be worthy, they say (Schwartz 1990). Dedicate yourself to the company, constantly go the extra mile, love its products and services – Ray Kroc of McDonald's constantly urged his employees to love the beauty of a burger, an aesthetic that still escapes many of us in the age of *Super Size Me* – and success is virtually ensured.

Bate (1994) goes on to look at how order is maintained in strong cultures. He identifies six processes:

1. *Taking care of people* – making them feel safe, valued, comfortable and secure, fully employed and protected. But it also means, as Deal and Kennedy (1982: 56) put it, 'not permitting them to fail'. This is sometimes known as 'tough love'.
2. *Giving people their head* – people are given freedom, responsibility and considerable autonomy in how the task is achieved. But this freedom depends entirely on whether they 'deliver'. It requires the employee to take the corporate mission personally, to literally take it to heart. This is referred to as 'loose–tight' control (Peters and Waterman 1982: 318).
3. *Having fun* – criticism and resistance to control can be disarmed by encouraging an atmosphere of playfulness and a sense of fun. In many companies with strong cultures, joking is common, parties frequent, fancy dress, pranks and humorous gifts and spoof awards habitual. Everyone joins in; affection, loyalty and community are developed; having a good time and laughing at oneself are encouraged, while questioning the point of the event is discouraged. Not that employees do not see through the hokum – they acknowledge it *and* value it for its playfulness, its non-seriousness. In this way, criticism is neutralized (Willmott 1991: 10).
4. *Giving personal gifts* – companies can reward employees with personal gifts direct from the CEO after good performance. Scandinavian Airline Systems (SAS) in Sweden did this in 1982 with Jan Carlzon, the managing director, himself sending each employee a gold watch after a year in which the company returned to profitability (Carlzon 1987: 113). The range of gifts, being direct and personal, is supposed to have more impact than a mere monetary bonus. Bate argues that this affects the individual cognitively, that is, accepting the gift from the leader is tantamount to accepting the leader's definition of the corporate mission, and emotionally, as such a gift can physically trigger positive emotions about the company which can be recalled for a long period.
5. *Spelling it out* – the vagueness of feelings is always grounded in specific rules which define standards. Even if these rules are informal and implicit, violation of them can be serious to the point of termination.
6. *Getting heavy* – strong cultures, in short, need their 'bastards' to make them stick (Deal and Kennedy 1982: 56). Making visible public examples of people – one executive at National Cash Register (NCR) in the USA returned from lunch to find his desk and chair on the pavement and in flames – reminds everyone what the rules are and who has the power.

Finally, not only do strong cultures have to manage the positive, softer emotions like love and affection, but fear, anger and jealousy can be powerfully manipulated too. They might not produce the apparent degree of unity behind the corporate mission or the sense of dedication and loyalty that the celebratory cultures do, but they are deeply ingrained and hard to dislodge. Both types of culture 'trap' people. Company T is an example of such a culture, as were many of the big engineering-based industrial bureaucracies that dominated Western smokestack industry for most of the twentieth century. Some of these companies have become dramatically smaller since the 1980s, but little seems to have changed in their cultures. Organizations with strong cultures not only seek complete loyalty and compliance from members but also try to become the dominant basis for a member's identity. Some regard these organizations as 'greedy institutions' that make extraordinary demands on individuals (Flam 1993: 62). Nevertheless, as Thompson and McHugh (2002: 207) note, because the vast majority of organizations have varieties of weak culture, and strong cultures remain comparatively rare, we should be cautious in employing approaches which may lead to 'underestimating both the fragility of corporate culture and the creative appropriation, modification and resistance to such programmes'.

CULTURAL HETEROGENEITY

Organizational cultures, even when they do represent a common perception held by the organization's members, or a system of shared meaning, are not uniform cultures. Large organizations, like British Airways, might have one dominant culture expressing the core values of the corporation, which in a very general way are shared by most of the organization's members. They also have sets of subcultures typically, but not exclusively, defined by department designations and geographical separation (see Parker 2000 for a thorough discussion of the importance of subcultures supported by empirical evidence). However, as Hampden-Turner (1990) argues, the corporate response to tension between subcultures, as in that between the service elements and the operational elements in British Airways (BA), is what shapes the culture itself. His approach to culture seeks to identify key dilemmas. In BA, despite the undoubted success of the airline in turning itself round from public loss maker to private profit maker, there were divergences between the rhetoric of the corporate culture and its professed values, and what people reported as the reality. These tensions persisted throughout the next decade and a half, and as Brewis (2007) summarizes, a succession of CEOs struggled to understand and ultimately failed to resolve this tension – with consequences for the airline's performance. Aktouf (1996), in his ethnographic study of breweries in Algiers and Montreal, noted the same thing at an empirical level. There was a strongly articulated idealized view by the managers as to what their criteria for promoting supervisors were, as we saw in Exhibit 9.3, yet the workers' more realistic view of what was actually necessary to get promoted diverged strongly from this, as we see in Exhibit 9.4.

9.4 | Exhibit

Supervisory culture in Algiers and Montreal: The workers' view

The workers' profile of an ideal foreman:

- 'competent', firstly;
- has confidence in us, doesn't feel obliged to be incessantly on the workers' backs;
- we can trust him, isn't 'two-faced';
- a man of his word, dignified, a 'true example';
- talks to the employees, listens, 'has a heart';
- 'respects' the employees, treats them like 'people';
- is fair;
- is not 'tense' (obsessed with output, and who transfers obsession to everybody).

The profile of the typical real foreman:

- 'Most of the guys are chosen [to become foremen] not because they're competent hard workers, but because they're "two-faced" or "hard-headed"; these are guys who climb over the backs of their colleagues, I don't like that.'

○ 'They don't know anything, don't do anything except try to catch you out just to shame you! Those are the types that are encouraged.'
○ 'Good or bad, they're all the same. A dog doesn't eat dog, so they close ranks against us.'
○ 'There are some here who only want to crush you – crush you with work and filth.'
○ 'They never stop pushing. One might think they're only here to make trouble.'
○ 'One time I injured my hand, blood was pissing out of me, and all the boss was interested in was that I fill out a report before going to the hospital! And they come around every year to shake your hand!'

Source: Omar Aktouf (1996) 'Competence, symbolic activity and promotability', in Stephen Linstead, Robert Grafton Small and Paul Jeffcutt (eds) *Understanding Management*, London: Sage, pp. 66–77.

Some commentators have attempted to identify basic types of culture found in organizations. These typologies are necessarily crude and general, but may nevertheless have value in broadly characterizing organizations. Perhaps the earliest such attempt was by Roger Harrison (1972) and later developed by Charles Handy (1993). Harrison uses dimensions of centralization and formalization to identify four cultures – *role culture*, *task culture*, *power culture* and *atomistic culture* (which Handy calls a *person* culture) as shown in Figure 9.4. *Formalization* refers to the extent to which rules, policies and procedures dominate organizational activities, while *centralization* refers to how much power and authority is concentrated at the top levels of an organization. Centralization is most evident in terms of what types of decision are allowed at various levels of an organization, particularly in authorizing and giving rewards to employees.

Ironically, Harrison's dimensions are in fact structural dimensions rather than cognitive or behavioural ones and are certainly not symbolic ones! However, what he is saying is that there are typical sets of behaviours, and associated mindsets,

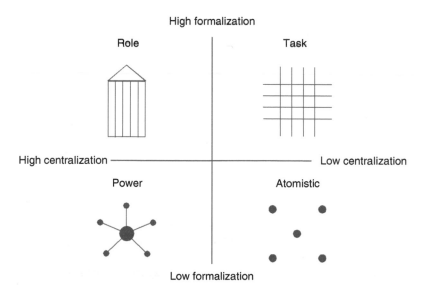

Figure 9.4 – Culture quadrant by Roger Harrison
Source: Reprinted by permission of *Harvard Business Review*. From 'Understanding your organization's character' by Roger Harrison, May/June 1972, pp. 119–28. Copyright © 1972 by Harvard Business School of Publishing Coroporation. All rights reserved.

that tend to go along with particular structures, examples being project teams, big bureaucracies, small entrepreneurial companies or chambers of lawyers. Andrew Kakabadse, Ron Ludlow and Susan Vinnicombe (1988: 225–37) took the same framework but looked at what they called *power levers*, that is, the characteristic and different types of influence which work best in each culture. Again, in this example, culture is difficult to separate from power and structure. Their framework is described in Table 9.1.

Another typology was also attempted by Deal and Kennedy (1982) as shown in Figure 9.5. They related the amount of risk involved in the core activities of the company to the speed of feedback from the environment on the consequences of those activities to categorize four main cultural types.

Deal and Kennedy's cultures are characterized as follows:

- *The tough-guy macho culture*: A world of individualists who regularly take high risks and get quick feedback on whether their actions were right or wrong.
- The *work hard, play hard culture*: Fun and action are the rule here, and employees take few risks, all with quick feedback; to succeed, the culture encourages them to maintain a high level of low-risk activity.
- *The bet-your-company culture*: Cultures with big-stakes decisions, where years pass before employees know whether decisions have paid off. A high-risk, slow-feedback environment.
- *The process culture*: A world of little or no feedback where employees find it hard to measure what they do; instead they concentrate on how it's done. We have another name for this culture when the processes get out of control – bureaucracy!

In Deal and Kennedy's scheme, the major influencing factor on the culture seems to be the task of the organization, coupled with the financial consequences of its operations. But feedback about task performance also affects the identity of employees, their sense of who they are in these companies. Collectively, groups develop patterns of behaviour which may become ritualistic; symbols and symbolic behaviours (or meanings associated with particular behaviours) which are peculiar to them; their own language and jargon; and stories, legends and traditions. These features help to establish meanings and beliefs and they are transmitted – as

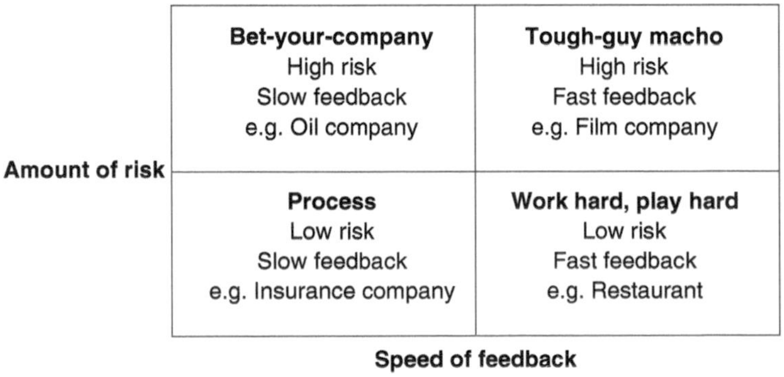

Amount of risk	Bet-your-company High risk Slow feedback e.g. Oil company	Tough-guy macho High risk Fast feedback e.g. Film company
	Process Low risk Slow feedback e.g. Insurance company	Work hard, play hard Low risk Fast feedback e.g. Restaurant

Speed of feedback

Figure 9.5 – Simple quadrant by Deal and Kennedy
Source: Adapted from the model of a simple quadrant from T.E. Deal and A.A. Kennedy *Corporate Cultures: The Rites and Rituals of Corporate Life* (Penguin books 1988). Copyright © Terence E. Deal, Allan A. Kennedy 1988.

Table 9.1 – Relationships between power-related behaviours and cultures

Types of power lever	Power culture	Role culture	Task culture	Person culture
Reward levers	Rewards offered for supporting key power figures	Rewards offered for following existing rules, regulations and procedures	Rewards for high task performance, project leadership and so on	Acceptance by peers
Coercive levers	Mistakes, misdemeanours and actions punished if they threaten key power figures	Punishment for working outside role requirements or breaking rules, procedures or communication patterns	Focuses on low task performances or differences of expert opinion. Rejection from elite group or cancellation of project possible	Threatened by/with group expulsion
Legitimate levers	Rules and regulations can be broken by key power figures	Behaviour in keeping with defined authority, relationships, rules, procedures, job outlines and descriptions	Problem-solving ability through technical expertise. Senior management can be challenged on technical grounds	Behaviour according to needs of individuals in situation. Loyalty to those with whom one interacts, with allegiance to organization as a whole
Personal levers	Strong, decisive, uncompromising, charismatic behaviour. Manipulation by leaders. Low support for those who are not key power figures	Personal power from perceived rightful issuing, observance and interpretation of rules, procedures and allocation of work. Personal support offered only to fulfil role requirements	Status and charisma derived from problem-solving skills	Personal power through sharing and partnership. Personal growth, developing supportive environment
Expert levers	Knowledge and performance standards based not on professional criteria but on influence over others – political	Working solely within one's specialist role – not crossing boundaries or disturbing existing role structure	Constant skills development to solve new and more complex problems. Driving standards higher	Behaviour and work standards developed by group members at any one time. Individuals expected to adhere to current informal standards
Information levers	Information valued only if it helps achieve personal ends	Information flows according to role prescriptives and established patterns and procedures	Driving to acquire and share new information for better problem solving	Any relevant information to be shared among the group
Connection levers	Making numerous contacts and connections is vital, within and without the organization. Generates a closed shop culture	Contacts and connections only required to fulfil role demands according to regulations – e.g. health and safety advisers	Extensive network of experts inside and outside the organization. Loyalty to experts (profession, discipline) rather than organization	A personal sympathetic/ emotional link with others. Satisfy a need to be with people one likes

Source: Adapted from Andrew Kakabadse, Ron Ludlow and Susan Vinnicombe (1988) *Working in Organizations*, Aldershot: Penguin, pp. 228, 229, 232, 234.

culture is a communicative phenomenon – through formal and informal socialization processes. The formal processes emphasized in much of the culture literature include:

○ education and training
○ selection and appraisal
○ role modelling by superiors and peers
○ leadership.

CULTURE AND LEADERSHIP

In particular, leaders can exert a powerful influence on the culture of their organization, especially if they are the founder. Organizations are replete with stories and myths about founders, and significant leaders who came after the founder. Leaders can shape the culture of their organizations by:

○ what they pay attention to and notice
○ their reactions to problems and crises
○ role modelling, coaching, mentoring and teaching
○ their criteria for selection, reward, promotion and punishment/sanction
○ their influence on organizational structure and policy.

This is in general reinforced, or may be undermined, by its consistency of fit with:

○ mechanisms of control in the organization (for example meetings, budgets, peer surveillance)
○ organizational structure (for example size of sub-units, levels of hierarchy, number of sites, distance of divisions from headquarters)
○ organizational systems (for example types of production technology, operating procedures)
○ formal statements (for example policies, reports, manuals, press releases).

We might think of the leader's actions (the first list) as the reality and the more formal arrangements (the second list) as the rhetoric or the difference between doing and saying. Sometimes bringing policy and practice into alignment is referred to as the need to 'walk the talk', which is not always easy to achieve. The study by Aktouf cited earlier revealed a glaring dichotomy, as he says:

> the organization (that is, its members) does the utmost to maintain an official discourse, and then acts in direct opposition to that discourse. When asked about the reasons for the systematic promotions of foremen whose behaviour and attitude are a blatant contradiction of the organization's official position, managers inevitably answer that it was 'because the workers did not want to be promoted'!

When companies are small and the leaders can be visible and lead by example, the influence they can have over the development of their companies can be much more directly felt than when they are CEOs of large multidivisional companies. Communication then becomes critical, but it is often seen as being one-way, the problem being defined as spreading the CEO's word to get people to follow, rather than increasing upward and lateral flows of communication to improve sharing, if shared meaning is really what culture is about. Two examples of this are illustrated below.

In 1988, at a management development seminar held at the Basingstoke Hilton in the UK, the arrival of the company's human resources director was preceded by a flurry of activity to present a well-ordered reception. He had masterminded the company's much vaunted and very successful culture change over the previous three years. The great man arrived, his acolytes running before him to announce his coming. The conference room was hushed. 'Now,' he began, 'the first thing I'd like to see is you all holding up your mission cards!' A forest of small cards rustled across the room as hands were raised in the apparent expression of a common faith. Within a year, the company and the great man parted abruptly at the chief executive's instigation.

On another occasion, at the end of a management development course, managers gathered at the company's country house management development centre. The chief executive was to arrive en route to the airport to take a flight to the Far East. He would interrupt his progress to present awards to the assembled managers. The morning was spent in preparation, scripting, the preparation of the ceremonials, the formal dressing, the arrangement of the setting, the rehearsal of the presentations, the preparation of the appropriate frame of mind. The great man arrived. His limousine pulled up outside the centre and course participants, tutors and staff of the centre alike mentally came to attention. His hand was raised, the signal given and the ceremony began. The course participants went forward one at a time to shake hands with the incarnate author of their corporate performance. It was a dignified and solemn moment. He exchanged a few words with each of the managers in turn and many commented afterwards that he seemed 'quite human'. The performance completed, he gestured his valediction. A chauffeur ushered him to his waiting car, to the airport and to other incarnations, other performances.

Source: Adapted from Heather Höpfl (1996) 'Authority and the pursuit of order in organizational performance', in Paul Jeffcutt, Robert Grafton Small and Stephen Linstead (eds) *Organization and Theatre*, special issue of *Studies in Cultures, Organizations, and Societies* 2(1): 73–4.

The above quite empty incidents demonstrate how difficult it is for the CEO to change anything so 'deep' as culture with the customary methods in use. Much of the culture literature recognizes that meaning and common-sense understanding are the bedrock of culture, and that they are transmitted in some circumstances by stories, myths, rites and rituals. But primarily they are imparted by experience, especially shared experience, and the everyday occurrence of events which may be weakly and metaphorically described as rites, or storytelling. These rites have the advantage of being living and organic, changing and developing, rather than having the dead quality of the contrived stories which most companies now construct or stage-manage about their senior managers. For example, Michael Levin, the consultant who helped BA to change its culture in the 1980s, tells this story of the first day of the relaunched Super Shuttle service from London to Manchester, which provided hot breakfasts and newspapers for the first time:

> We then had 96 people lined up in front of the BA desks. I was frantic. We were not clearing them fast enough. I tried to get some four-stripers [supervisors] to help but they said 'We are four-stripers, we can't do that'. But then I happened to see out of the corner of my eye that one of the managers was helping. Guess who it was – Marshall [the CEO]. They were in horror, they were aghast. (Young, D. 1989: 3)

While one might wonder what the CEO was doing at the check-in desks, and who on earth had trained him to use the computer system, it makes a good story. BA modelled its changes on those at SAS, which had been described in the bestselling book *Moments of Truth* by Jan Carlzon (1987), its managing director. In the book, Carlzon tells an almost identical story of himself helping with the baggage on a flight, saying that he did it to emphasize to the workers that everyone at every level is responsible to the customer and if necessary should help out. BA and Marshall must have not only copied this example, with the slight change to check-in desks, but also contrived it, as Marshall had no skills and no experience in the airline industry, so, if he was not to make things worse, he must have been trained beforehand. If the incident ever happened, of course (other than Levin, neither the author nor his colleagues in several years of working and researching in BA were ever able to find anyone who actually witnessed the incident). Ironically, in June 1997, while BA was negotiating with the unions on a pay cuts and redundancy package, it was revealed that it was training its managers to operate flights and check-in procedures in preparation for a strike. It was widely felt that BA engineered the strike to break the union, and it completely backfired on management and the high-profile CEO Bob Ayling, who no doubt was planning a similar publicity stunt himself. However, by the time of the strike he was so unpopular with the customers he would have found it difficult to show his face in the check-in area. BA subsequently tried strenuously to rebuild both its public image and its culture, by reaffirming the importance of people with mixed success – and Ayling was forced to step down in 2000. In 2001 the British foot and mouth crisis was followed by 9/11, resulting in 7000 redundancies, with a further 5800 the following year. Although wining service awards in 2002, industrial action in 2003 and staff shortages in 2004 led to further disastrous impacts on service, and in 2008 the airline, already rated Europe's worst for lost luggage and second-worst for delayed bags, cancelled 200 flights and lost 15,000 bags due to problems at the new Terminal 5 at London's Heathrow (Walsh 1997; Brewis 2007; Bloomberg News 2008).

Additionally, no matter how hard the CEO might try to motivate with corporate symbolism and ritual and the issuing of mission statement cards to everyone, even if the message is successfully bought by the shop floor, the level where culture hits a problem is the level where organizational politics is most keenly felt. Sometimes this is in senior management, sometimes at supervisory level, as in this short example.

Sometimes, workers find that managerial politics gets in the way of their motivation to perform well in accordance with the 'mission' of the organization. Meeting production targets and delivering a quality product or service often conflict, and 'culture' is supposed to resolve these kinds of dilemmas. In a bakery in the north of England, where the workers in question were making mince pies for the early Christmas market, the workforce frequently showed considerable concern for their product's quality. They would often fail to pack pies which they considered to be substandard. Once a pie was made, the policy according to supervision was 'pack as much as we can get away with', although quality control had other ideas. When confused about what to pack and what not to pack, and finding the criterion of whether they would like to purchase the goods themselves in such a condition of no help, and caught between supervision and quality control, they resorted to the management for arbitration. 'Who pays your wages?' said Jack (the production manager), 'me or quality?' The workers, in some puzzlement, replied that they thought it was the company.

It was very difficult for workers in this organization, with an understanding of the organization's mission and what the customer (who could easily be themselves) would want, to find that these considerations were overridden by internecine warfare between the plant manager and quality control. This is also difficult for CEOs to understand and hear about: people generally will not tell them; it will not appear as a response in a survey; and generally employees will be reluctant to reveal it to inquirers. Middle managers also experience difficulties with corporate culture initiatives, according to Anthony (1994: 64–77), because top management often engineers its culture change with staged performances, such as we have discussed, with the only real objective being to improve financial performance, not to change values. But it sells it to middle managers as the great new initiative, and expects them to sell it to supervision and the shop floor. Supervision and the shop-floor workers have, of course, seen it all before and are typically cynical. They go along with change for a while but expect that top management will eventually show its 'true colours' with dismissals, redundancies, savage cuts, disciplinary measures or just plain heartlessness. Eventually this might happen, especially if top management never believed in the 'new order', but got its efficiency gains. The shop floor expected to be sold out and they were, and the middle managers who believed in and worked for the new cultural changes often feel deeply betrayed and cheated. It is now quite common to find managers still working long hours effectively, but who claim to have lower morale than ever. They work because of their professionalism, they say, not because of their 'commitment'.

SYMBOLIC ACTION

Jeffrey Pfeffer (1981) introduced the distinction between symbolic management and substantive management in the early 1980s, to distinguish between those acts of a manager that were done deliberately to carry extra meaning, and those that were part of the normal run of things. This distinction has been widely propagated, mostly by writers who have little understanding of the symbolic process. The corollary of this is that managers often believe that anything can become symbolic, but just because they think it ought to be does not make it symbolic. Neither does it make it inevitable that if it does become symbolic, the manager's preferred meaning will be the one that is taken (Feldman 1996). Of course, if you are the CEO and have the power, you are more likely to be able to make your meaning stick, at least in public. The stories about Marshall and Carlzon above were of 'symbolic' management, yet there is little evidence as to how these stories were received, although they were widely retold. But they were powerful images, and as such would be likely to circulate and have impact. Jack's rebuttal of the workers on the quality issue (see Box above) was no less symbolic, and delivered a powerful message to those involved, but it was not a memorable image.

Sometimes humour will be used to undermine the intended symbolic message. Acting symbolically is more a matter of acting publicly, in ways that give off powerful images which can easily be associated with the other more content-laden messages that are being given out. Ralph Halpern, for example, former chairman of the UK Burton Group, a menswear manufacturer and retailer, always wore the group's clothes and insisted from the start that the companies' employees would 'wear the strategy' – actually wear the clothes which they were selling to the public. This gave a powerful message to the employees. Some years later, when the 50-something Halpern, now Sir Ralph, was exposed for having an affair with an 18-year-old topless model, she revealed that he still insisted that she wear the group's products during their erotic assignations (luckily the group had by that time diversified into sexy lingerie!). The shareholders found this consistency symbolically reassuring, perhaps additionally consoled by his reported demands for sex 'up to five times a night'. Four days after his exposure they voted him Britain's best CEO remuneration package of £2 million p.a. and called him 'the greatest Englishman since Churchill'. Halpern was clearly no novice in the art of symbolic management as Gerry Johnson (1989: 547) points out. Back in 1977 when the Burton Group was in crisis, he obtained a reduction in capacity, which could have just as easily been obtained by closing several small plants, by closing the main headquarters plant in Leeds. He did this because the headquarters 'castle' symbolized the stability and complacency he wanted to challenge, and closing it down signalled that manufacturing was not the heart of the company, giving a much-needed boost to the retail section. The Burton turnaround was spectacular, with it becoming Britain's most profitable retailing group less than 10 years after posting a £13 million loss.

So although the idea of symbolic management is theoretically flawed and practically difficult to control, acts with strong symbolic associations and high image quality do seem to have an impact upon and help to change people's minds about a company, often without their knowing it, because symbols are effective, to the extent that they mean something without the 'reader' having to think about it. Some companies then fall into the trap of contriving images and events and symbolic performances, while others do not. The example below illustrates one extended metaphor that in the end had the opposite effect to what was intended.

Case Example What were you doing the day the war ended?

The British Airways UK Sales Conference: September 1989

The following account of a piece of organizational theatre was provided by a participant. It demonstrates how meanings are invested in performance and what happens when the performance becomes insupportable.

That autumn the airline business was buoyant. The company was achieving most of its revenue targets and people in the sales department were charged with anticipation. Every September, all members of the sales department, some three hundred people, are invited to participate in the annual sales conference and this particular year everyone felt they really had something to celebrate.

The location and theme of the conference is always a fairly well kept secret. This adds to the general air of expectancy. Stories and anecdotes concerning previous conferences were rife. Rumours, predictions and theories about who, where and what were put forward by just about everybody in the weeks before the event.

The suspense was eased yet stimulated by the arrival of 'The Invitation'. The location was Gatwick or rather a four star hotel very close to it. The theme was announced as, 'What were you doing the day the War ended?' The Invitation itself came from the Allied HQ and was printed in a 1940s style. All those attending the conference were requested to dress in the attire which they felt best fitted in with the theme of the conference.

The conference itself started on a warm Saturday afternoon in September. It was to run through to Monday morning. A large majority of the participants had requested a day off for the Monday aware that alcohol and sheer exhaustion would necessitate at least 18 hours sleep after a 'good sales conference'.

The next thing to do was to hire a costume. This turned out to be quite costly despite sales teams using the same fancy dress hire shop and getting a bulk order discount. The cost of hiring the costumes, £35 for the weekend (washing, if necessary, was extra) promised to be well worth it. The first opportunity to 'dress up' came on Sunday morning. The scene at breakfast was extraordinary. Italian generals ate cornflakes with women from the French Resistance. An American five-star general with foot long epaulettes on each shoulder politely ordered bacon, sausage and tomato. The Field Sales Manager, Adolf Hitler, swapped jokes with two young London evacuees who were fully kitted out with gas masks and name labels. The feeling of excitement continued as everyone boarded coaches taking them to the venue for the main conference seminar. Here an introduction to the proceedings was given by the Field Marshal, General Manager UK Sales. His role was to explain the campaign strategy, to identify the location of enemy action. He prowled up and down, pointing with his swagger stick to the battle lines drawn up on a wall chart.

And so the day went on. All the presentations contained innumerable references to war. The evacuees, French Resistance, Gestapo, American Generals, the Home Guard and the Medical Corps all listened dutifully. Lunchtime continued with the war-time theme. Wooden trestle tables, benches, masking tape crosses on the windows and a catering company's idea of what 1940s army rations might have been kept 'the troops' in the mood. Indeed, all the day's events were planned to keep people 'in the mood' but by 4.30 in the afternoon the proceedings began to drag. The novelty of being dressed as a Japanese Admiral or a Desert Rat began to wear off. The team from Northern England Sales who were all dressed as clowns began to have trouble with their face make-up. The Japanese Admiral finally discarded his heavy overcoat with a sigh of relief.

The presentations ran on. The event should have finished by 6.00 p.m. but it was 6.30 p.m. when the Field Marshal rose to give his final address. It was too late. He was confronted by a weary and lacklustre assembly of ridiculously overdressed, tired and irritated individuals who had had enough of the 'performance'. As their leader tried to rouse them with exhortations to future performance targets, their own performance and participation had become unbearable. They had thrown off their roles and the props which supported them.

Source: Heather Höpfl (1996) 'Authority and the pursuit of order in organizational performance', in Paul Jeffcutt, Robert Grafton Small and Stephen Linstead (eds) *Organization and Theatre*, special issue of *Studies in Cultures, Organizations, and Societies* **2**(1): 74–5.

CULTURE AND CONTROL

One of the earliest writers to publish a sociological critique of organizational culture, utilizing the work of Durkheim, Carol Axtell Ray (1986) argues that in the early years of the twentieth century, scientific management and associated techniques established what Weber (1964) termed 'bureaucratic control'. In essence, the manipulation of rewards established, or rather bought, the workers' loyalty, which led to the organization's ultimate objective, increased productivity. After the impact of the Hawthorne Studies, recognition of the social needs of the workforce was increasingly taken into account. In this model of humanistic control, it was the provision of a satisfying task or work group life that produced worker loyalty, which in turn led to increased productivity. In more recent times, culture control has been achieved. By a manipulation of culture, including myth and ritual, the workforce comes to love the firm and its goals and, as a result, we find increased productivity. Of course, reality is rather more complex than this, but the critique does have substance. For some commentators, cultural management is just the latest control strategy, a direct descendant of Taylorism, except that human control replaces technical control.

In a similar vein, Smith and Wilkinson (1996) offer an unusual account of what they call a totalitarian culture. Sherwoods, the company they studied, is a progressive, non-hierarchical company, a very successful part of a hugely successful multinational. Pursuing 'furious interaction' and 'knocking the corners off politics' with a religious fervour that places everyone, even top management, in an open-plan office, they produce a self-policing conformity. Managers can be demoted by their subordinates if they are not performing, and they are paid well in excess of the industry norms in order to keep them – the 'golden handcuffs'. Smith and Wilkinson raise some disturbing questions about how conflict is apparently obliterated in this company, arguing that Sherwoods takes on a nightmarish quality 'because tight control coexists with a high degree of autonomy and an almost citizen status for members. If there is an analogy with penal institutions, it is the open prison'(1996: 131).

Case Example Sherwoods

The central feature of this organization is that it is both an open system and yet achieves unusually complete control. There is little scope for privacy. Managers have been active in bringing this about. 'We are our own policemen.' They are not passive 'cogs in a machine'. The family who own the company would not want them to behave mechanically. Anti-bureaucratic, relatively undifferentiated, this organization is not an organization. Yet its reach is very complete. This degree of control is exceptional: the institutionalization of cooperation; the exorcism of politics through the 'cleansing' effect of 'free speech'; job rotation between functions for managers – 'safer promotions'; and through keeping the characteristics of new recruits within known and agreed parameters – the 'sheep dip'. Sherwoods is a somewhat totalitarian system not in a fascist, violent sense, but because, except for research scientists who work in a separate building, it is total. It is full of methods for creating consent. Several of its officers reported that when they first came, they thought Sherwoods 'a bit funny', but they can 'see it as natural now'.

This lack of privacy precludes serious dissent. Criticism is encouraged, but only within bounds. Excepting the unchallenged, strategic rules of ROTA (the accounting system – return on total assets), open management and FAN (social responsibility, lobbying and supplier control policy – friends and neighbours), day-to-day restrictions are set by the evolving collective conscience of the organization itself. Control is not imposed by officers. Control does not have a specific location. 'Everybody is at the heart of things', but everybody also has several others within their gaze, and everybody is clearly observed by others. Everybody is central both as a necessary agent and in terms of the encircling attention of co-agents.

Attentiveness is probably the best approximation of the way Sherwoods works. In any organization there are dividing lines and points of censure. But few would devote the attention that Sherwoods gives to happy 'separations', nor the obsessive degree of quality control, for which Sherwoods is well known. In this attentive organization, members are also held to attention. They are their own policemen.

Source: Adapted from Steve Smith and Barry Wilkinson (1996) 'No doors on offices, no secrets: We are our own policemen. Capitalism without conflict?', in Stephen Linstead, Robert Grafton Small and Paul Jeffcutt (eds) *Understanding Management*, London: Sage, pp. 130–44. Reprinted by permission of Sage Publications Ltd. Copyright © Sage Publications 1996.

Drawing on these critiques and examples, we can pick up two lines of critique which are essentially postmodern – that culture can be seen either in terms of *surveillance*, where control is exercised through a combination of vertical and horizontal peer observation and self-discipline, which was the case in Enron (Swartz and Watkins 2003). In fact, while not being as extreme as Enron, many companies nowadays maintain cultural control through a combination of both these strategies, as can be illustrated in Disneyland or McDonald's, where fantasy images of the company are used to sell the product. Surface pleasantry is vital, but behind the smile are two very Tayloristic and disciplinarian corporations (see Ritzer 1990/2003, 1999; Van Maanen 1991; Boje 1995; Bryman 2004).

The move from bureaucratic to symbolic control is in fact difficult for most organizations, but particularly those in which there are concentrations of

9.5 | Exhibit

The comedy of winners

Enron liked to close its meetings with humor, and this year was no exception. A videotaped skit began to roll, purporting to show how Enron innovated. It opened with a tired cleaning woman emptying a trash can in the office of an overworked young associate. 'Gee,' she tells him. 'you guys should find something to do with all this paper you throw away!' The junior associate slumped over his desk from the rigors of his eighty hour work week, suddenly sits bolt upright. Cut to the next morning. He dashes to the head of Enron's trading group and breathlessly shares his idea: Enron should create the market for trading recycled paper and pulp. 'It's huge!' he promises, spreading his arms wide.

As soon as the associate leaves, the head trader, who was cool to the idea, leaps from his chair and speeds to the office of the head of the Wholesale trading group, played by Greg Whatley, the real head of Wholesale trading. The head trader starts to sell Whatley on *his* idea of creating a paper trading business. 'It's a very inefficient market,' he stresses. 'We can make a killing!'

Whatley, a man well known for his aggressive style, grabs the trader by the lapels, puts a finger to his lips and pulls him into a restroom, the only place, everyone in the audience knows, that Enron's hidden cameras and listening devices can't go. Whatley peeks under every stall. Then he listens intently to the pitch again. 'We should develop the business plan and go to Skilling [then COO],' he says. 'Get cracking.'

But Whatley and the trader have not been careful enough. A low-level employee has overheard their conversation through an air-conditioning vent. While the executives dither, he races back to his desk and makes a phone call. Jeff Skilling's secretary answers and gives him an appointment to discuss *his* idea – for creating a market in paper and pulp. The low-level employee is played by David Cox, who in real life went from a minor job running Enron's graphics department to creating the company's paper and pulp trading division. He was now, true to form, another Enron multimillionaire.

The audience applauded wildly when the skit ended – sure, the culture at Enron was treacherous, but that was the point. Enron hired the best and the brightest: so fighting your way to the top was tougher. But once you got there, you knew – it was incontestable, incontrovertible – that you were a winner.

Source: Extracted from Mimi Swartz with Sherron Watkins (2003) *Power Failure: The Inside Story of the Collapse of Enron*, New York: Doubleday, pp. 13–14.

professionals, such as hospitals, universities and other areas of public service. A number of studies have drawn attention to how public sector employees tend to have stronger union affiliations, strong client-based relations, weak identification with the employing organization, stronger identification with professional bodies and peers, considerable expert power, and are more likely to be oriented to ethical as opposed to commercial values (Sinclair 1991: 326–7). In recent cases, such as Enron (beautifully illustrated in the film *The Smartest Guys in the Room*) a group of professionals within an organization may develop unethical values (see Exhibits 9.5 and 9.6 for aspects of how culture can reinforce such values regardless of the manager's personal attitude towards them (Swartz and Watkins 2003)). Research from which these observations are made supports the view that professional public sector employees, such as clinicians, nurses, academics, welfare workers and engineers, are less likely to tolerate management-imposed constraints, will treat the organization as a means to an end and as a place to do the work they have chosen as a vocation or career. These professionals tend to strive for high levels of autonomy or freedom and generally have high expectations of achieving intrinsic self-fulfilment without strong identification with the organizations in which they work. Strong beliefs about public service, dedication or almost a 'calling' to the job, especially where there are heavily client-based relations, such as with clinicians, strengthens the view that strong subcultures or multicultures flourish in these types of organizations (Eastman and Fulop 1997, citing Sinclair 1991 and Bovens 1992). As Amanda Sinclair comments, control through a dominant culture, especially one based on private sector models, such as McDonald's, might not be an appropriate management approach to integrate, accommodate or exploit the differences in organizations with strong multicultures (1991: 328–9). Moreover, many public sector organizations are recognized as having a range of governance or control structures, including collegial, bureaucratic and professional ones – the typical *knowledge organization* with a high concentration of experts – that defy one all-embracing culture (Sinclair 1991: 328, citing Benveniste 1987).

9.6 | Exhibit

Winners and losers in the 'World's Best Company'

Sherron Watkins went to the Enron Corporation's November management conference in the year 2000 determined she wouldn't be taken for a loser. The year before, at her first such meeting after being promoted to vice president she had blown it. Booked into the Hill Country Hyatt and Resort for three days of corporate team building she had opted, in the recreational hours for the company-sponsored salsa-making class. At affairs such as these where Enron took over the entire hotel and offered an array of afternoon networking and socializing activities, it was to important to pick one that advanced your career. A smart, ambitious employee would never sign up for the afternoon of fly fishing, for instance, because you couldn't lose the smell of fish in time for the evening cocktail party, and because you could wind up wasting your afternoon with guys who worked in the once crucial but now irrelevant pipeline division. That left, as career-building activities, skeet shooting, the road rally, tennis, golf, facials, pedicures, outlet shopping and antiquing in a nearby Hill Country town.

To understand the loaded nature of the choices you had to understand the loaded nature of life at Enron. Salsa making, for instance, had turned out to be a disaster. One of the small hotel conference rooms had been converted into a kitchen for the occasion; Sherron had entered straight from her facial without makeup, without combing her hair and she was chopping jalapeños with three pipeline guys – middle-aged men shaped like bumpy Bosc pears – when the then COO, soon to be CEO, Jeff Skilling, had walked in. Or rather, he'd poked his head into the room, narrowed his eyes, and raised his peaked nose, as if to test the air. It had not pleased him. At just that moment he'd caught sight of her. 'Uh, hi, Sherron,' Skilling had said, and then whoosh, he was gone. In his wake Sherron found herself enveloped in that uniquely Enronian sense of dread: she knew she'd been caught with a bunch of losers, far, far away from Skilling's winning team.

Once, the pipeline guys had mattered but that was long ago. In the 1980s Enron was one of the largest pipeline companies in North America, moving natural gas from the Gulf Coast to the East Coast, the West Coast, the Midwest and beyond. But as Jeff Skilling's influence over CEO Ken Lay grew, Enron changed identities several times. It always positioned itself as the company of vision but it supplemented its base. In the late 1980s and early 1990s Enron revolutionized the way natural gas was bought and sold by operating more like a finance company than a gas company. In the mid-1990s, Enron started selling and trading power, battling across the country to deregulate entrenched electric utilities.

Lately, with the boom in dot.com and high-tech companies, Enron was vigorously morphing into an Internet–telecommunications conglomerate. Enron Online, the company's online trading platform was already the largest e-commerce site in the world and now 'broadband' was the new buzzword inside the company. Enron was gearing up to trade space available on high-speed telephone lanes in order to deliver movies and more into private homes over its Enron Intelligent Network, a new and improved Internet. It was poised to dominate AT&T and all the other behemoths.

This corporate shape shifting made Enron seem to Wall Street less like an IBM or an Exxon and more like the poster child for the new economy, a business so fast paced, so protean, and so forward looking that it could change its stripes, virtually overnight, to suit the Zeitgeist. So if you wanted to get ahead at Enron, you had to be able to change too.

○ Does Enron have a 'strong' culture?
○ Is it possible to have a culture of change?
○ How does Enron's culture affect individual identity?

Source: Adapted from Mimi Swartz with Sherron Watkins (2003) *Power Failure: The Inside Story of the Collapse of Enron*, New York: Doubleday, pp. 1–3.

In many organizations there might also be different operational demands that encourage a 'culture' that is not easily brought under any group or individual's control. Members of the University of California, Berkeley, have for some years been studying organizations that they describe as 'high-reliability organizations'. They have studied aircraft carriers, nuclear power plants, air traffic control systems and the operation of large electric power grids – organizations all likely to be involved in major crises, needing rapid response capacities and even having to deal with major catastrophes (Pool 1997: 44). In high-reliability organizations there is no one permanent structure or pattern of activity, in the sense that some groups operate bureaucratically and in

Plate 2 – National culture – or kitsch?
Source: Photo © Chris Poulson.

a hierarchical manner, others in a professional and collegial way (as described above), while others operate in an emergency mode. The high-reliability organizations, or the ones that seem to outperform others in their industry, have the capacity to have everyone switch between these modes of operating, depending on the situation. At any one time, all members might be operating in an emergency or crisis mode for a period of time. Communication in these organizations is intense, frequent and encouraged, as is the practice of challenging rules and procedures or looking for what can go wrong before it happens. Mistakes are not punished when someone is trying to do the 'right' thing. An inbuilt tolerance or expectation of ambiguity and uncertainty in management practices is the norm, which the researchers noted was one of the most unsettling aspects of these organizations. Often managers and employees alike struggle with this ambiguity because they believe that a well-functioning organization always knows what it is doing next and how (Pool 1997: 44–5). To sustain 'high reliability' literally means working with and encouraging multicultures as the basis of encouraging a 'culture' of learning (see also Pauchant and Mitroff 1988).

THE CULTURAL RELATIVITY OF MANAGEMENT

Another reason why values might be difficult to change could be the extent to which they are connected to wider cultural values which support them. Workforce diversity is increasingly a worldwide phenomenon, and besides the multicultural composition of a workforce based in a single country, many companies coordinate operations based in several countries, manufacturing and assembling products across different locations. Parochial attitudes and ethnocentric views persist in developed, less-developed and underdeveloped economies, even when a society is multicultural in its composition. Whether these biases translate into a predominantly monolingual society or an intolerance towards other cultural norms, it can prevent a country or organization from taking full advantage of the new global opportunities in faster growing regions like China, India and the Asia-Pacific. That companies need to 'Think Global: Act Local', or practise globalization in the new world markets, has become something of a cliché (see Torrington 1994). However, some writers have examined the consequences of the developing global–local dilemma (Humes 1993) and found that despite the visionary rhetoric, the practice itself is anything but simple. Hari Bedi (1991) provides an insightful analysis of globalization from the practising Asian manager's point of view, critiquing the extension of Western practices (ersatz capitalism) into other cultures, which themselves have long histories of civilization and their own complex social arrangements and values.

However, as Edward Hall (1959) argues, cultures are communicated by more languages than simply the verbal. Consider the following questions:

1 You arrive for a meeting with a business client at the scheduled time of 10:00. By 10:45 the client is still not ready to see you. What do you think?
2 You arrive for a meeting with an agent whose performance is likely to be very important to your operations. The agent's office is small, crowded and cluttered and in a seedy part of town. How is your confidence affected?
3 You arrive at the offices of a major supplier who has told you how well the business is doing. However, the managing director's office is almost bare, with simple furniture and little decoration. Do you still believe the company is doing well?
4 Your company asks you to review the restaurant of a friend as a venue for entertaining clients. The food is awful. Your friend tells you that he really needs the business and is relying on you for a good review. What do you do?

5 You have clinched the deal and shaken hands on it, but when you try to set a date to meet and sign formal contracts, the other party is reluctant to commit. What do you do?

Each of these situations would normally be interpreted as a warning signal in Australia, Canada, the UK or the USA. But they would be interpreted quite differently in other cultures, such as South America, East Africa or Japan (where the Western haste to do business is often a disadvantage); the Middle East (where a crowded office is a good sign that the agent is busy and in touch with the action); Japan (where minimalist furnishing is a sign of great discernment and can even be more expensive than opulence); various parts of Southeast Asia, the Middle East and South America where personal relationships incur obligations (that is, you would give the good public review but tell the friend in private that the food required improvement – and they would take the responsibility of not making you a liar on their behalf); and parts of Asia and Africa where a 'gentleman's agreement' is considered more binding than a written contract (where personal obligation, being based on moral principles, is more powerful than the technicalities of legal compulsion). Hall identifies five non-verbal languages which communicate information to us without anyone speaking, and they correspond to each of the five questions above: time, space, things, relationships and agreements. Hall's point is that we all have a characteristic way of 'reading' these things according to our cultural background, and we do this without thinking. When we go into other cultures, however, we may be making the wrong reading, and we need to be on our guard against this.

Two other early macro-frameworks were also developed to help identify the differences in cross-cultural understanding. Robert Westwood (1992) gives a useful outline of the theory behind the concept of culture, including the framework developed by Kluckhohn and Strodtbeck (1961; see also Adler 1991). These two frameworks identify five basic orientations or core dimensions of culture as responses to questions which all societies must answer:

1 What is the essence of human nature?
2 How do/should people relate to their environment?
3 What is the basic time orientation of people?
4 What state of being and action are people basically predisposed to?
5 What is the basis for a relationship between people?

The frameworks then identify three states of possible cultural responses – positive, negative and neutral – which are tabulated horizontally against the five vertical dimensions, as shown in Table 9.2. Although the columns in Table 9.2 may be vertically related, the orientations may also vary horizontally between questions. In other words, because you believe that people are basically evil does not necessarily mean that you think they are subservient to nature – a negative response to one item does not automatically entail a negative response to all. So, any culture may not necessarily have all its scores in one column, and may have items of value in all three as part of its basic cultural matrix. Understanding this cultural underpinning can often help to make inexplicable actions – like the Arab car mechanic who refuses to commit to a time for having your car repaired – explicable (Arab cultures would score in column 1 in Table 9.2 across the dimensions of 'time', 'being' and 'relationships', a common phrase being 'inshallah' or 'if Allah wills'). Having respect for the past, they value traditional obligations highly, and lineal obligations can at any time take precedence over work-related ones. This also poses problems for the introduction of quality initiatives which require the statement in advance of performance standards, service standards and benchmarks We also gave the example where many management fads were difficult to copy in Asia and one reason for this was the strong basis of family ties in businesses (that is, scoring in column 1 on 'relationships').

A series of much cited studies and commentaries by Geert Hofstede (1980, 1991, 1998, 1999, 2001; Hofstede et al. 1990; Hofstede and Peterson 2000) saw the development of an influential but controversial framework of cultural differentiation along four continuums, to which Hofstede and Michael Bond (1988) added a fifth:

- *Individualism–collectivism* (is it more important to stand out as an individual, or to be established as a member of a group?)
- *Power distance* (tall societies with the very poor and very rich, and authority structures in which those in authority do not respond to the wishes of those below, are distinct from those egalitarian societies in which many voices are heard and taken into account)
- *Uncertainty avoidance* (the need for certainty, risk avoidance, caution)
- *Masculinity–femininity* (quantity, measurement, regulation and order as against quality of life, caring, concern with feelings and expression)
- *Long-term–short-term orientation* (Confucian dynamism – the ability to pursue long-term and general goals as against short-term gain and advantage).

These dimensions, when related to each other, produced cultural maps of the world which enabled countries to be located relative to each other. This classification has not been without its critics and controversies. Cultural assumptions are very deep, and are expressed in a variety of ways, of which verbal language is just one. Learning to read the other non-verbal languages of culture is an important skill, which international managers of the future must acquire.

Table 9.2 – Dimensions of basic cultural assumptions

Core dimensions	Cultural assumptions		
	1	2	3
What is the essence of human nature?	People are basically evil	People are a mixture of good and evil	People are basically good
How do/should people relate to the environment?	People are subservient to nature	People are in harmony with nature	People should be masters of nature
What is the basic time orientation of people?	To the past	To the present	To the future
What state of being and action are people basically predisposed to?	The desirable state is simply to 'be'; to act spontaneously and without long-term expectations	People should act and strive towards their own self-development and actualization	People should act so as to achieve measurable accomplishments
What is the basis for a relationship between people?	Lineal – orientation is towards the group – is based on family ties; continuance of family line is a prime goal	Collateral – orientation towards a group – less emphasis on blood-ties. Continuance through time	Individual – the individual person is the focus. Individual interests take precedence over group interests

Source: Robert Westwood (1992) *Organizational Behaviour*, Hong Kong: Longmans, p. 43, adapted from Kluckhohn and Strodtbeck (1961).

For Hofstede, these five continuums are the assumptions, shared meanings and relativities which underpin social and organizational life in different national cultures and inevitably shape behaviour. In terms of the power distance dimension, we would appreciate power differently, for example, according to whether we lived in a society in which a few people had wealth and influence and many people had little wealth and no influence, such as India, or whether we lived in a society in which most people had a good standard of living and a chance to participate in decision making, such as Sweden. Similarly, our view of knowledge, in terms of what we may know and how we may know it, could vary: high power distance societies often restrict the flow of information from the few to the many, regarding most people as not worthy of knowledge; while low power distance societies are more open and communicative about a variety of matters, regarding most people as having great ability to learn and improve themselves. So the concepts of organizational learning and the learning organization are likely to be highly culturally relative: in Hong Kong, for example, it has often been difficult for researchers to gain access to a sufficient range of companies to gather significant evidence. Cultural differences, especially as argued by Hofstede (1980, 1991), are associated with these forms of power and knowledge and traditional justifications such as membership of certain clans or castes, religious rituals, veneration of ancestors and so on, and are often used to maintain the exclusion of the many from access to knowledge and power. Patriarchs in societies who encourage headship not leadership do not want their employees to learn too much. Similarly, in certain collective cultures with high power distance, where members of certain family groups or tribes have job security, such as parts of the Middle East, there is often little incentive for managers to develop themselves, and initiatives such as total quality management (TQM) have had great difficulty in getting a foothold. Many of the concepts that Western businesses use to talk about 'competitiveness', 'efficiency' and 'profitability' are technique-driven and ignore the harder aspects of culture, both national and organizational (Negandhi 1986).

These cultural substructures have expressive forms in social and organizational institutions like the education system, the property system or the tax system, and are represented in language and symbol. Thinking again of institutions in terms of the power distance idea, high power distance societies would tend to have an elitist education system for the children of the wealthy, whereas more egalitarian societies would tend to provide education for all those who were able to benefit. Political systems would usually offer at best a restricted participation in high power distance societies and would more often be dictatorships, even if paternal ones. Low power distance societies would tend to have more participatory, democratic systems. In terms of specific practices and behaviours, high power distance societies would have more rules of exclusion restricting individual freedom, more initiation rituals and more taboos, while low power distance societies would have rules conferring individual rights and guaranteeing access to information. Privately, individuals in high power distance societies would tend to have more topics that they would discuss in open conversation, such as religion or politics, whereas in low power distance societies these would often be the subject of popular debate and satirical humour.

Non-verbal artefacts (things, objects, social and organizational arrangements) can carry cultural meaning as well as verbal ones. Hierarchy, as a structure, is a highly significant symbol of life in high power distance societies, and in some societies such as Japan it is necessary for a person to know the exact social level of another before he or she can determine the correct way to address that person. Position in the hierarchy here carries privilege and respect and requires others to act in a deferential way. In low power distance societies, such as the USA and the UK, hierarchy is regarded more loosely, and in terms of function in the organization not in terms of personal worth, and is less meaningful. To be the managing director of a company in Hong Kong is far more socially significant than being the managing director of a similar company in Huddersfield, Houston, Helsinki or Hyderabad. Societies where place, time, body language, buildings, dress, property and other non-verbal symbols are regarded as important are known as 'high-context societies', where the primary focus is on who is speaking rather than the content, and many Asian and Middle Eastern societies fit this description. Western societies, where what people say tends to be taken at face value, are known as 'low-context societies', and here the focus is on *what* is being said rather than on who said it. In a high-context culture, criticism of a speech is seen as criticism of the speaker and as disrespectful; in a low-context culture it is seen as criticism of the words only, and no disrespect is implied. It is very difficult for low-status managers from a low-context culture, where they may have been used to speaking freely in front of the managing director and having their opinions listened to, to move into a high-context culture where they will find themselves ignored and will run the risk of giving great offence to the senior managers there.

Nonetheless, the notion that a unified, homogeneous national culture can adequately explain all or even most patterns of behaviour at the organizational level is highly problematic, and many of the findings of Hofstede's own research and similar research following his approach have been contradictory. Many studies do not differentiate between national and organizational culture and often treat organizational culture as homogeneous because it exists in a particular country (Tayeb 1988: 41). Even though perceptions of power are heavily influenced by wider cultural influences, Monir Tayeb suggests that such things as education, age and the seniority of a manager are also likely to affect perceptions of power and these demographics might explain differences found in organizations in similar cultures. National culture does impact strongly at the organizational level in areas such as autonomy and freedom, economic rewards, job expectations and management approaches (Tayeb 1988). Attitudes, values and norms relating to autonomy and freedom influence expectations about delegation and hence authority within organizations as well as devolution or the decentralization of such things as decision making. Thus, as previously stated, the extent to which participatory and democratic practices are possible in organizations is largely culture-specific. As a result, many management approaches are, according to Tayeb, also strongly related to the national culture. Thus, whether or not egalitarian and democratic management approaches, as opposed to inegalitarian, paternalistic and autocratic ones, are considered appropriate in an organization is largely a by-product of national culture and extremely difficult to change. Formalization, or the degree to which people accept rules, policies and procedures, is also determined to a large extent by national culture and thus impacts more directly on organizational culture. Values relating to privacy and independence of the individual over the group are the key determinants of how much formalization is tolerated in workplaces.

A range of other societal factors, such as the labour market composition (for example level of skills, levels of employment, degree of unionization, extent of casual versus full-time employees), the industrial relations system (laws covering employment and work conditions, conciliation and arbitration of disputes and union and employer rights) and the class system of a country (for example how wealth and opportunities for social mobility are distributed) also affect how organizations operate and the cultures within them. These are often referred to as institutional factors. Commitment and trust of employees by management, for example, are two particularly important aspects of organizations that can also be heavily influenced by such things as the labour market and industrial relations systems within countries (Tayeb 1988: Chapters 8 and 9). Other national factors, such as the economic system (for example capitalist, socialist, mixed economy, closed economy), systems of government (for example elected, dictatorship) and the legal system (for example nature of civil and commercial law) also affect certain work practices and the cultures of organizations. Both the social and national factors are embedded in national cultures, but they are often more easily changed or manipulated than widely held attitudes and values (see Fulop 1992: 361–9; Schwartz and Sagie 2000). For many years Japanese companies offered such things as lifetime employment, which many observers attributed to something paternal or clan-like in the culture of Japan, and hence its organizations. Yet when hard economic times arose these practices were quickly questioned and ceased in many large companies (Fulop 1992: 367).

At the organizational level, a number of other factors sometimes called 'contingency variables' also influence both the type of organizational structure and culture that might emerge. Thus the size of an organization might mean that larger organizations tend to be more bureaucratic and therefore centralized, no matter where they might be located. The markets that organizations enter are likely to influence how they practise management; for example, many Japanese 'transplant' companies in the car industry have had to modify their management practices to operate in countries such as Australia, the USA and the UK. Technologies can also influence how organizations develop their management practices, for example certain computer technologies, mass production and assembly methods produce similar problems across a range of countries irrespective of national culture. It is no surprise to realize that core aspects of scientific management were adopted in many parts of the world – Guillén (2006) even argues that its principles were influential in the development of modernist architecture and maps that development across several countries. The form of ownership of the company or business (for example limited liability shareholders versus owner-managers) can affect the degree of centralization and hierarchy in organizations, probably more than national culture (Tayeb 1988).

The neglect of these considerations has been part of growing criticism of Hofstede's work. The cross-cultural psychologist Harry Triandis (1993) makes the point that Hofstede does not attempt to integrate his work with any of the growing number of studies in the broader social science literature, developing only his own agenda, and unnecessarily polarizes his value pairs, when in reality 'two can coexist and are simply emphasized more or less' varying situationally – we can all behave individualistically or collectively, rigidly or flexibly, opportunistically or far-sightedly, trustingly or suspiciously and so on (Triandis 199: 42). Shalom Schwartz (1992: 2–3), for example, found that the organizational levels and national level of culture tended to be dynamic and closely integrated rather than stable and independent as in Hofstede's research. Schwartz (1992) also points out, as have others, that the 'normative ideals' of a culture cannot be inferred from a statistical average of individual responses, and furthermore that unless the value set investigated is comprehensive, significant values that interrelate with the values studied could be ignored, distorting the whole picture (see also Schwartz 1999, 2004, 2006). Schwartz's research on human values generated seven dimensions rather than the five of Hofstede, and he considered them to be quite different (Schwartz 1994: 116). Further, Hofstede did not check for equivalence of meaning of terms and concepts across contexts, which renders his comparisons 'virtually meaningless' (Schwartz 1994: 94). Trompenaars and Hampden-Turner, although working in the shadow of Hofstede and seeking to build an even larger database with similar assumptions, nevertheless argue that similarly positive or negative responses can frequently be found in compared countries but for very different reasons, and these differences are important (Hampden-Turner and Trompenaars 1993; Trompenaars and Hampden-Turner 1998; for critical appraisals see French et al. 2001; Jacob 2005).

Hofstede's most recent and most virulent critic, Brendan McSweeney (2002a, 2002b) takes him ferociously to task for his methodology; for the deterministic way in which he defines national culture as distinct from organizational and occupational cultures while nevertheless being implicit, core, systematically causal, territorially unique and relatively uniformly shared; and for neglecting other possible explanations for the phenomena he identified, such as other (non-national) cultural causes like ethnicity or gender; non-cultural causes, such as political changes, economic circumstances or even civil wars; and national heterogeneity. Hofstede's (2002) replies are somewhat evasive, but do indicate that Hofstede has both expressed some caution about the nature and use of the constructs while accumulating validation evidence from a considerable number of studies by, and in some cases with, others. McSweeney (2002b) maintains that the problems are with *both the analysis and the validation procedures* because 'fallacious assumptions necessarily lead to inaccurate empirical descriptions regardless of the quantity of data and statistical manipulation used' (McSweeney 2002a: 112). Peter Smith (2002) acknowledges the substantial scholarship behind Hofstede's contribution, including his willingness to engage his critics, but identifies several significant continuing general and specific criticisms of Hofstede's extrapolating move from identifying certain work-related values and goals to the cultural characteristics of societies, noting in particular Hofstede's unwillingness to entertain that 'increasing social change may require us to study not just how societies hold together, but also how they fragment' (Smith 2002: 129).

The criticisms are summarized in a thorough and balanced way by Magala (2005 Chapter 2, section 3 ff.). Magala (2005: 73) notes that Hofstede has two major concerns underpinning his work – the first is *the problems of multicultural workforces* in globally operating corporations, the second, *political instability* in the face of persistent inequalities and conflicts. Nation states are controversially given a privileged status in Hofstede's thinking because they provide the prefabricated building blocks of identity through the management of cultural heritage. The processes of socialization into particular identities are carried out through large and small institutions and organizations. This owes much to the conservative thinking of influential mid-twentieth-century American sociologist Talcott Parsons. Much of Hofstede's subsequent research preserves this demographic imperialism – regardless of how arbitrary the historical origins of particular geo-political boundaries might be – and its structural-functionalist ideology (McSweeney 2002a). Yet Hofstede's Cold War theory has both implicit and explicit exceptions: it was never intended to apply to the Warsaw Pact countries, for example, where the national cultures of such countries as Poland, Hungary, Czechoslovakia, Bulgaria and Romania were repressed by a totalitarian political system with an integrated military arm and institutional, occupational and organizational arrangements were standardized and imposed (Magala 2005: 76). Yugoslavia, conveniently treated as a homogeneous culture by Hofstede and well known for its participatory organizational forms, was not recognized in terms of its historical background as a fragile compromise solution after the First World War to the Balkan problem that resulted from the disintegration of the Austro-Hungarian Empire. Its violent fragmentation in the 1990s indicated how profound the cultural differences contained under a military dictatorship could be (Schwartz and Bardi 1997, 2000; Schwartz et al. 2000; McSweeney 2002a: 110–11). Hofstede (2001: 464–5) does caution researchers that his methodology is effective for some levels of culture but not all, that subcultural influences based on age, gender, class and specific organizational features elude it, and that detecting differences within cultures requires different methods. His view is that these elements are minor variations – but this is a typical assumption of neocolonial thought and severely contested by postcolonial commentators (Banerjee and Linstead 2001; Smircich and Calás 2006). Magala (2005: 77–85) identifies the characteristics of the criticisms of Hofstede:

○ *In-built Western bias*
Despite Hofstede's own critique of Western theories of motivation and leadership, his original four-dimensional model showed a discernible Western European bias that he later tried to correct by adding a fifth dimension from Chinese research. However, subsequent studies were predominantly carried out by Western or Western-trained researchers who were insensitive to dimensions of other cultures that remained 'tacit' – knowledge was either ignored or reconstructed within the existing model. Magala (2005: 77) gives the example of 'shame' versus 'guilt' typologies of societies (common for example in contrasting Japan with the West) that were disregarded as being a variant manifestation of 'high-context' versus 'low-context' cultures. Somewhat weakly given his broader claims, Hofstede (2001: 465) argues against the charge of 'sophisticated stereotyping', that his instrument only measures differences between the cultures of a large multi-national (IBM), and that other instruments and qualitative methods should be used to detect 'the essence of cultural differences in other populations'. But as Magala notes, the problem of Eurocentrism is not just Hofstede's, and most cross-cultural studies tend to reproduce the view that the rest of the world is a source of raw material (data) for the West's (and North's) 'ideas factory'. The ideas themselves are developed from generalizations from Western social research and disregard any indigenous social inquiry. There is also an inherent universalist ideological bias, that the continuation of the enlightened modernization of the less- or under-developed world requires both parliamentary democracy and free-market capitalism. As postcolonial theorists have pointed out, this tends to extend the injuries of 'empire' beyond colonial rule and by other means and occludes alternative models – justifying them with a circular reliance on its own 'science' (Banerjee and Linstead 2001; 2004; 2006).

○ *In-built static and conservative nature of the dimensional model*
The culture of one organization may be a weave of subcultures or multicultures, overcrossed by a variety of external cultural, social, national and contingency factors. Culture, structure and strategy are not separate 'variables', as some theorists might wish to argue, but rather need to be seen as inseparable and treated holistically as suggested by Bate (1994) and Anthony (1994). Because culture is not an 'independent' variable, you cannot change structure or strategy without affecting culture. This is particularly so at the organizational level, but at any level culture does change over time (Roberts and Boyacigiller 1984; Lytle et al. 1995). Even Hofstede's own research shows changes occurring among certain dimensions but does not understand them as signs of major change (Smith 2002: 111–12). Hofstede's model is leaden-footed in this because he bases his assumptions

of how cultural identity is formed on a Parsonian functionalist model that sees the factories of socialization as being family, school, workplace and the political sphere. Not only is the whole area covered by media and cultural studies, and the sociology of consumption, ignored, but the smooth functioning of institutions and bureaucracies under the umbrella of the nation state is assumed – an assumption that flies in the face of contemporary research on identity across several disciplines (Giddens 1991; Castells 1997; Bauman 2004; Hatch and Schultz 2004; Pullen and Linstead 2005; Pullen 2006). The nuclear family as an institution is not simply different across cultures, it has changed dramatically in the past 50 years, in the West in particular. Communications technologies with the Internet and mobile phones in particular have given young people access to a far wider range of social networks than previously possible, workplaces are far more multicultural and multiethnic, organizations are constantly re-engineering themselves, and the concept of shifting and multiple identities has emerged as a characteristic of post-modern society. Identities are not necessarily consistent any more – if they ever were – and their relation to culture is complex (Beech and McInnes 2005). Exhibit 9.7 offers a humorous real example of postmodern identity-play in a pub football team. This is not to say that *everything* changes or is unstable, but Hofstede's whole approach – concepts, theory, method, analysis, practice – is firmly rooted in a modernist style of thinking and finds contemporary post-industrial social dynamics problematic.

9.7 | Exhibit

Identity and culture: What's in a name?

Lynam Athletic, named after the dapper sports presenter Des, had a terrible first season. They finished bottom of the lowest division in the South Birmingham Sunday League. So they decided to act.

First, they transferred to the Coronation League – the thinking being that with more teams in the Coronation's lowest division they had less chance of finishing bottom again. Next, they sought assistance from the professionals. The self-proclaimed 'worst team in the Midlands' entered the Carling Pub Football awards in the 'Team Most In Need of Help' category and for the first time they tasted triumph.

The prize was a training session with the Plymouth Argyle manager, Ian Holloway – a man known for getting the best out of underperformers. Holloway asked why Athletic needed help. Well, they said, they weren't awful footballers exactly, but they just couldn't do it as a team and were tired of losing by scores of up to 13–0. Holloway told them this was already promising. 'Most teams think they're really great and are arrogant,' he said, 'so you lot knowing you're crap is great. It means we can start from somewhere.'

But as Holloway said, this was only the start. Lynam Athletic decided to take serious collective action. If Lynam Athletic were going to be winners, they needed a new identity. So, one by one, they changed their names by deed poll. Darren Yeomans became Thierry Henry [Barcelona and France], Kevin Alban became Cristiano Ronaldo [Manchester United and Portugal], Majid Ali became Ronaldinho [Barcelona and Brazil]. Out went Jon Barber, Paul Blears, Dan Branch, Darryl Brown, Marc Clifton, Connor Edgcumbe, Ian Flatt, Chris Gray, Pete Hall, Nick Hall, Neil Kimpton, Andrew Mullan, Jon Robins and Ben White. In came Jamie Carragher [Liverpool and England], Dani Alves [Sevilla and Brazil], Cafu [AC Milan and Brazil], Michael Essien [Chelsea and France], Ruud van Nistelrooy [Real Madrid and Holland], Steven Gerrard [Liverpool and England], John Terry [Chelsea and England captain], Lionel Messi [Barcelona and Argentina], Kaka [AC Milan and Brazil], Iker Casillas [Real Madrid and Spain], Fabio Cannavaro [Real Madrid and Italy], Hernán Crespo [Inter Milan and Argentina], Petr Cech [Chelsea and Czech Republic] and Wayne Rooney [Manchester United and England]. A team of world-beaters.

I phone Alves to see how he's coping with life as a sporting superstar.

'Hello, is that Dani?'

'No, it's Paul.' He stops. 'Oops, yes, it's Dani. It's hard to remember.' He giggles. 'My girlfriend keeps asking me why everyone's calling me Dani.'.

Why did they decide to change their names? 'It was all a bit of a laugh really. Thierry Henry came up with the idea after a match.'

Henry says: 'We wanted to strike fear into the opposition and we certainly weren't going to do that with our football skills.' He realizes there is work to be done – Van Nistelrooy smokes 20 a day and Gerrard rarely plays sober.

In the week, Henry, Terry, Kaka and Messi work for a games development company but on Sunday they will play their first game as the all-stars. How does Alves feel their opponents, Coldland, will react? 'They'll probably think we reckon we're good, calling ourselves these names. We expect they'll kick us a lot. Lucky I play at the back.'

The deed poll commits Athletic's players to using their new name at all times and on all formal documents. They believe it will be worth it.

My phone rings. 'Hi, it's Michael Essien, I heard you wanted to talk to me.' Essien, in a gentle Brummie brogue, says his mates didn't give all this a great deal of thought. For example, he's just discovered that he'll need a new passport. 'But it's no problem. I've no immediate plans and we won't be playing in Europe this season.'

Essien is convinced the name change will improve his game. And that's not all. 'I think it's going to make a big impact with the ladies.'

In terms of motivation and self-belief, it makes a kind of sense. But one thing puzzles me. I call Alves, a driving instructor by day, and tell him I have a personal question. 'Go on,' he says.

Why on earth did you choose the relatively un-celebrated Dani Alves? 'Well,' he says, 'we chose our names according to the position we play, and we decided they had to have played in the Champions League to qualify. The only right-backs I could think of were Dani Alves and Gary Neville [Manchester United and England] … and who wants to be Gary Neville?'

Source: Adapted from Simon Hattenstone 'Big names make Lynam Athletic a des res' *Guardian* Wednesday 26 September 2007 (http://sport.guardian.co.uk/columnists/story/0,,2177280,00.html).

○ *In-built methodological bias*

Apart from the fact that Hofstede has criticized the Western bias of concepts such as motivation and leadership in organization studies, his own work almost inevitably displays some aspects of such a bias. This is inevitable when a cluster of concepts are condensed into a small number of 'master' concepts. An attitude survey can be contested as an appropriate (simplistic) tool for the investigation of culture, in that it cannot access the taken-for-granted or subconscious aspects of culture that it prioritizes; the reliability of its respondents can be challenged; its ability to recognize and discriminate between organizational, professional, occupational and national cultures can be disputed; and because of its tendency to 'zip-up' subdimensions. On this last point, Magala (2005: 82) notes that a construct like Uncertainty Avoidance actually contains three *themes* – the *closure of the individual mind* (open to new ideas or conservative of old ones?), *the question of freedom* (does one embrace ambiguity as an occasion to be creative, or try to avoid having to take the initiative?) and *the question of organizational culture* (is my action structured and constrained by rules, or do I have flexibility in how I operate?). Furthermore, there is the problem of *perspective* – are respondents avoiding uncertainty in means (how things are done) but being flexible about goals (what is done), or flexible about the means of achieving stable goals? Difference on this issue leads Hofstede to rate the Greeks (flexible of means, certain of goals) as the least uncertainty-avoiding nation while House makes it the Swiss (certain of means, adaptable on goals). Furthermore, are respondents themselves able to distinguish sufficiently between *reality* (what they do) and *desirability* (what they think should be done). An old question but an important one given the evidence that Hofstede (Hofstede et al. 1990) himself generated in a study of Dutch and German organizations, where differences between organizational sub-units were attributable to *practices*, while at individual and cultural levels they were attributable to *values*.

Differences in approach therefore make a difference. The most recent significant study has been the GLOBE (Global Leadership and Organizational Behaviour Effectiveness) project by House et al. (2004) who found they had to 'unpack' or 'unzip' some of Hofstede's dimensions into:

- Future orientation
- Gender equality
- Assertiveness
- Humane orientation
- In-group collectivism
- Institutional collectivism
- Performance orientation
- Power distance
- Uncertainty avoidance.

But House's team found that on seven out of nine dimensions there was a negative correlation between values and practices. The assumption behind much of the culture literature, certainly in Hofstede and most obviously in Schein's (1985) culture model, is that values and beliefs shape action, which is their expression. However, values may emerge from the observation of pragmatic action, whether positive (this should be the case in future) or negative (that should not happen again). More practically oriented cultures will display little difference between practice and values; more abstract, aspirational or principled cultures will display potentially considerable difference from time to time. The relationship, House argues, can be complex – although he seems to argue for a managerial form of value practice engineering, which we have critiqued earlier in this chapter. Nevertheless, the modest critique of this approach signals a characteristic of all critical approaches to cultural issues related to organizations, whether heterodox economics, cultural sociology, political history, or critical psychology – the need to unpack assumptions, to trace influences carefully, and to deconstruct the object of investigation.

GENDER AND CULTURE

Talk is an important part of culture. Therefore, if men and women communicate differently we might anticipate differences in the kinds of cultures which develop where one or the other is dominant. We might also expect that the way people are customarily required to communicate will make it easier for one or the other gender to become successful in that culture. Men and women have never been viewed as, or treated as, equals in the workplace. Jobs have been differentiated and even whole occupations, especially those in service industries, have been designated 'women's work'. Fewer than 20 per cent of all managerial posts are held by women, and at more senior levels this falls to 10 per cent. Men are often seen to be rational, calculating and resilient whereas women are seen as being emotional, changeable and lacking resolution. This forms the background to what men and women do in any real organization, but Deborah Tannen (1990) indicates that men and women actually talk differently and thus communicate different things when they speak. As Tannen (1990) argues, women tend to learn styles of speaking which make them appear less confident and self-assured than they really are, and as a result they lose out on those organizational issues, like promotion, that depend on appearing confident. Women tend to say 'we' rather than 'I' when discussing work, and as a result get less credit for what they do. They tend to boast less and ask more questions, which can often make them seem

Table 9.3 – Gherardi's classification of women's cultural positioning

| Male positioning | Women's reciprocal positioning | | |
	Accepted	Contested	Imposed
Friendly	*The guest* A cooperative position	*The holidaymaker* A mismatched position	*The newcomer* An open-ended position
Hostile	*The marginal* A stigmatized position	*The snake in the grass* A contested position	*The intruder* A unilaterally imposed position

Source: Silvia Gherardi (1995) *Gender, Symbolism and Organizational Cultures*, London: Sage, p. 109. Reprinted by permission of Sage Publications Ltd. Copyright © Sage Publications 1995.

less sure of themselves. Women downplay their certainty while men minimize their doubts. Men are more likely to save their own face in a problem situation. Above all, powerful people, which usually means men, are more likely to reward people with similar language styles to their own.

To give another example: a New York psychiatrist in the mid-1980s joined one of the earliest Internet chat groups in order to try to develop a new way of counselling and helping people. He chose as his name 'Doctor', which he had not fully realized was gender-neutral. One day he was chatting in a side room with a woman and he realized that she had thought that he too was female. He was astonished by the richness and openness of the communication that he was receiving and assumed that this was the way women talked to each other. As a result, he created a false identity for himself as a woman, an easy thing to do on the Internet. He was able to build some very loyal friendships in this way and helped many people, but he wearied of the strain of constantly having to be someone else, and so he joined the group under his own identity, his female alter ego introducing him as a great guy and a lovely person, a fine doctor and so on. He hoped that he would build relationships with all his friends and the female alter ego could disappear from the picture. Unfortunately, none of his friends from his other identity could get along with him when he was being himself, and they found him stiff and a bit cold! As a man, he could not communicate in the same way – they did not expect it and were unreceptive to it – and they did not communicate with him in the same manner either (Stone 1995: 63–87).

So what you say and how you say it are different depending on your gender, and this may both open and close doors to you depending on your gender's position within the organization's culture. Of course an organization that only rewards one communicative style is losing its ability to hear a wide range of information and increase the flexibility of its actions, but it does not stop there. As Silvia Gherardi (1995) notes, organizations tend to write stories for their participants, with gendered roles for women to play. She identifies six discursive positions that were offered to or imposed on women in her studies, in which men were basically either friendly or hostile and women's positions were either accepted, contested or imposed (see Table 3.3). Women could be accepted in a friendly manner, as a guest, treated pleasantly, but politely circumscribed and not allowed to be a 'real' member of the culture like the men were. Gherardi's respondent Giovanna tells us:

> I felt as if I was a guest. Just as a guest is placed at the head of a table, treated politely, and never allowed to wash the dishes, so I was surrounded by a web

of polite but invisible restraints. I began to suspect something when I saw the other women when they arrived and were, so to speak, 'integrated'. For example, I almost never go into the production department to talk with the workers. My older male colleagues go because they like it. They go and see their friends, and then they pretend that they are protecting me from the 'uncouthness of the working class'. So I find myself constantly on the phone dealing with the editorial office, the commercial office, the administration. I'm almost always in the office. *It's as if I'm at home and they're always out.* It's true that they are better at what they do, and I'm better at what I do, or we women are, but constantly being their guest is getting me down. (Gherardi 1995: 110–11, emphasis added)

We might recall the argument of Marta Calás and Linda Smircich on how women are being used to domesticate the workforce and free up males for international assignments, apparently because of women's greater interpersonal and caring skills. It is part of the permanent guest role that women are being asked to play. However, things could be more unpleasant if the males were hostile. Gherardi's respondent Fiorella tells of her experience of being marginalized:

I felt I'd become invisible, I thought I was transparent. There's no point in recounting individual episodes or blaming things on hostility. Formally, every-thing was as it should be, and they treated me politely, like gentlemen, but I counted for nothing. I discovered this little by little and it was tough admitting it to myself. What had I got to complain about? The situations were quite clear, the solutions were reasonable, indeed they were the only ones feasible. Everything was already decided and all I had to do was agree and implement. There was no need to open my mouth at meetings. I realized I had been pushed to one side even though my expertise was publicly praised. (Gherardi 1995: 112)

These kinds of examples show how limited by organizational culture the equal opportunities and positive discrimination approaches can be. Nothing was done wrong in either of these situations and the men were reasonable, polite and even gentlemanly. However, the women were 'second-class citizens' and powerless.

In Gherardi's other examples, the positions are more uncomfortable. If the woman is in the *holidaymaker* position, then everyone else is just waiting for her to move on, nothing really changes, and they all make contingency plans behind her back; if seen as a *snake in the grass*, then they plot to get rid of her and make her fail; if seen as a *newcomer*, then they reserve judgement, for long periods of time, are anxious and make it hard to get commitments to projects and participation in processes; and if seen as an *intruder*, she will be constantly openly challenged. Many of these categories could apply to men in some situations, but the question is clearly one of degree; women start off by being *other*, whereas men at the very least receive the benefit of the doubt and the 'testing' of a new male appointee is not likely to last for years but to be resolved fairly quickly. The feeling of being trapped by invisible nets is a typi-cal indicator that the problem is cultural, and making these invisible nets visible is difficult, particularly when the 'nets' are often constructed and enacted by those with the power to change the situation.

CONCLUSION

Despite the fact that it is difficult to define, the idea of culture captures some dimensions of human social organizing that other strictly psychological, sociological or economic approaches cannot adequately address. It is about interaction, shared-ness, distinctiveness, similarity and difference, meaning and significance, signs and symbols, rituals and tokens, leadership, common sense and the taken-for-granted. It is also about problem solving, thinking strategically, devising and operating within structures and, perhaps surprisingly, change. It is not entirely separable from these activities, and is affected by power relations, gender, ethnicity, time and place. In the late 1970s and the 1980s the main concern of studies of culture was with creating new cultures of excellence in performance; in the late 1980s and the 1990s the concern developed into changing cultures which were a drag on performance and perception of the environment. In first decade of the new century, the focus has shifted as a result of such cases as Enron to address how and whether cultures that are excellent in terms of performance can also excel morally. Culture has so many facets that as research on culture and the application of ideas of managing culture are put into practice, new emphases continually emerge. Although it became something of a fad in the 1980s, as this chapter has shown, culture has a firm basis in a range of underlying theories across disciplines and remains one of the most important concepts we have in management and organization theory.

Let us now revisit our questions on culture at the beginning of the chapter.

ANSWERS TO QUESTIONS ABOUT CULTURE

1 **What is organizational culture? What is it good for?** Organizational culture is a complex phenomenon, usually related to shared values and shared meanings in an organization, but also related to common ways of dealing with, or ignoring, commonly experienced problems. It is a form of common sense, an outcome of cultural processes at work in a particular setting. The benefits of paying attention to culture are that it focuses on people but in particular on the symbolic significance of almost every aspect of organizational life. It emphasizes shared meanings, even if implicit, and alerts us to the influencing potential of values, beliefs, ideology, language, norms, ceremonies, rituals, myths and stories. It constructs leaders as shapers of meaning. It also emphasizes the importance of communication and learning, and the importance of how others perceive us; and it alerts us to the fact that organizational environments are also socially constructed.

2 **Are companies with strong cultures always successful?** No! Strong cultures can be a barrier to change if they are negative cultures, but, even so, with the happiest, most creative culture there are still other factors that can frustrate performance, such as the economic climate and competitive situation, that are out of the organization's control.

3 **What are the dysfunctions of culture?** Culture tends to select and socialize people who are alike, and so often there is a lack of diversity and critical thinking in strong cultures, and the tendency to stick to old recipes even when things change. There can be a focus on the emotional and non-rational, to the extent that simple but important technicalities, like structural arrangements, inventory control or quantitative analysis of the market, can be neglected.

4 **What are subcultures and are they healthy?** Subcultures are groups of people who are part of a wider group, subscribing to the overall culture but with some distinctly different values of their own. Large companies will certainly have many of these; sometimes they will be associated with functions – marketing, maintenance and so on – or with professions – engineering, legal, accounting. But they can occur even in small companies and may not be related to any company features. They can

be a source of creativity or division and destructive conflict, depending on the nature of their values and how they differ from those of the rest of the company.

5 **How is organizational culture related to national culture?** Organizational culture is often influenced by the background culture in which it is located, sometimes explicitly. Indeed, in the 1990s BA removed the British flag from the tailplanes of its jets and replaced it with a variety of different ethnic tailplane designs to reflect the diversity of its business and its increasingly global culture, or at least give that impression. There are several underlying assumptions about the world, which are characteristic of different national cultures and affect the ways in which people habitually think and orient them towards particular organizational preferences. However, these assumptions are not intractable, although it should not be assumed that they can be easily changed or set aside. Culture is a complex concept and other variables such as national and contingency ones need to be considered when trying to make sense of organizational cultures and subcultures.

Revisiting the Case Study

Let us take a look at the questions we raised on the case study in the light of our discussion.

1 Does company T have a shared culture?

The answer here is broadly 'yes'. Although many people declare themselves unhappy with it, because of the 'sink or swim' nature of the culture, they go along with it and play the game. One feature of culture is that if a culture is shared this does not mean it is shared equally; not everyone will believe in it to the same extent, some may be enthusiastic, some may hate it, some just comply. The culture, however, is not one which unites them behind a collective objective – the shared culture is a divisive one of every shift/department for itself.

2 Is company T a 'strong' culture?

The answer here is again 'yes'. It is not a positive one in the sense that the literature talks about companies like McDonald's, Hewlett-Packard, Marks & Spencer and Ben and Jerry's, of which commitment, dedication and love of the company are hallmarks, and few people seem to be having fun, but it is one which quickly sanctions those who are not part of it. You suffer if you do not play the game. It is also very explicit and dramatic, but the performances are not formally staged on occasions; people do the 'staging' on an everyday basis, which suggests that the behaviour is habitual and ingrained and will consequently be hard to shift.

3 What are the problems of the culture?

Well first of all, it is divisive and defensive. It sets sections up against each other and produces senseless internal competition. Managers try to look good and cover up problems, and no one is working towards a mutual goal or goals. The lying, cheating and stealing means that the organization has systems and procedures that do not work and those new managers who try to follow them end up failing. The organization is not getting the information it needs passed up the hierarchy, and as a result it cannot be a learning organization. Development will be difficult, if not impossible. At an individual level, the 2 × 4 culture makes people anxious, perhaps bitter, but certainly risk averse. Fear is the worst climate for creativity and problem solving. In addition, although there is no evidence on the gender balance of the company, it would appear to have a masculinist culture, which would affect the potential benefits to be gained from a greater diversity of approaches.

4 Can the company be changed?

Well, any culture can be changed given time. The consultants in this case worked with key managers at an interpersonal level, exploring with them the problems they were facing and the effects of the culture, and tried to get them to change their behaviour. This was not always easy for them – people who have been 'beaten up' every day have a tendency to miss the beatings when they stop and crave the structure that the old ways gave them. Additionally, any change produces a period of mourning for the old way before the new behaviour is internalized, and so plenty of support and reinforcement is necessary. However, managers involved in this type of individual change can provide mutual support for each other. It is also essential in opening up channels of communication. At the right time, top-down support will also be an important reinforcement, especially if changes in structure and procedure are complementary to and require changes in behaviour. So change will be difficult, but it is possible, given effort across a range of mutually supporting areas.

REFERENCES

Adler, N. (1991) *International Dimensions of Organizational Behaviour*, Boston, MA: PWS-Kent.

Aktouf, O. (1996) 'Competence, symbolic activity and promotability', in Linstead, S., Grafton Small, R. and Jeffcutt, P. (eds) *Understanding Management*, London: Sage.

Alvesson, M. (2002) *Understanding Organizational Culture*, London: Sage.

Anthony, P. (1994) *Managing Culture*, Buckingham: Open University Press.

Argyris, C. (1964) *Integrating the Individual and the Organization*, New York: John Wiley.

Ashkanasy, N.M., Wilderom, C.P.M. and Peterson, M.F. (2000) *Handbook of Organizational Culture and Climate*, Thousand Oaks, CA: Sage.

Banerjee, S.B. and Linstead, S.A. (2001) 'Globalization, multiculturalism and other fictions: Colonialism for the new millennium?', *Organization* **8**(4): 683–722.

Banerjee, S.B. and Linstead, S.A. (2004) 'Masking subversion: Neocolonial embeddedness in anthropological accounts of indigenous management', *Human Relations* **57**(2): 221–47.

Banerjee, S.B. and Linstead, S.A. (2006) 'Make that sixty-seven: A rejoinder to Whiteman and Cooper's "Sixty-six ways to get it wrong"', *Human Relations* **59**(3): 429–42.

Barney, J. (1986) 'Organizational culture: Can it be a source of sustained competitive advantage?', *Academy of Management Review* **2**(3): 656–65.

Bate, S.P. (1994) *Strategies for Cultural Change*, London: Butterworth Heinemann.

Bauman, Z. (2004) *Identity*, Cambridge: Polity.

Bedi, H. (1991) *Understanding the Asian Manager*, Sydney, NSW: Allen & Unwin.

Beech, N. and McInnes, P. (2005) 'Now where was I? Questioning assumptions of consistent identity', in Pullen, A. and Linstead, S. (eds) *Organization and Identity*, London: Routledge.

Benveniste, G. (1987) *Professionalizing the Organization*, San Francisco, CA: Jossey-Bass.

Bloomberg News (2008) 'British Airways' Terminal 5 problems at Heathrow spill over to 4th day', *International Herald Tribune*, 30 March http://iht.com/articles/2008/03/30/business/30heathrow.php (accessed 1 April 2008).

Boje, D.M. (1995) 'Stories of the storytelling organization: A postmodern analysis of Disney as "Tamara-Land"', *Academy of Management Journal* **38**(4): 997–1035.

Boje, D.M. and Winsor, R.D. (1993) 'The resurrection of Taylorism: Total quality management's hidden agenda', *Journal of Organizational Change Management* **6**(4): 57–70.

Borges, J-L (1962) 'Pierre Menard, author of the Quixote' in Irby, J.E and Yates, D.A (ed. and trans.) *Labyrinths: Selected Stories and Other Writings*, New York: New Directions Publishing Corporation.

Bovens, M. (1992) 'Conflicting loyalties: Ethical pluralism in administrative life', paper presented at the *First International Productivity Network Conference*, 21–24 July, Canberra, Australia.

Brewis, J. (2007) 'Culture', in Knights, D. and Willmott, H. (eds) *Introducing Organizational Behaviour and Management*, London: Thomson.

Brown, A. (1998) *Organizational Culture* (2nd edn), London: Financial Times/Pitman.

Bryman, A. (2004) *The Disneyization of Society, London: Sage*.

Carlzon, J. (1987) *Moments of Truth*, New York: Harper & Row.

Castells, M. (1997) *The Power of Identity*, Oxford: Blackwell.

Chan, A. and Clegg, S. (2002) 'History, culture and organization studies', *Culture and Organization* **8**(4): 259–73.

Deal, T.E. and Kennedy, A.A. (1982) *Corporate Cultures: The Rites and Rituals of Corporate Life*, New York: Addison-Wesley.

Deal, T.E. and Kennedy, A.A. (1988) *Corporate Cultures: The Rites and Rituals of Corporate Life*, London: Penguin.

Denison, D. (1990) *Corporate Culture and Organizational Effectiveness*, New York: John Wiley.

Drennan, D. (1992) *Transforming Company Culture*, London: McGraw-Hill.

Eastman, C. and Fulop, L. (1997) 'Management for clinicians or the case of "bringing the mountain to Mohammed"', *International Journal of Production Economics* **52**: 15–30.

Eldridge, J.E.T. and Crombie, A.D. (1974) *A Sociology of Organizations*, London: Allen & Unwin.

Feldman, S. (1996) 'Management in context: Culture and organizational change', in Linstead, S., Grafton Small, R. and Jeffcutt, P. (eds) *Understanding Management*, London: Sage.

Flam, H. (1993) 'Fear, loyalty and greedy organizations', in Fineman, S. (ed.) *Emotion in Organizations*, London: Sage.

French, W., Zeiss, H. and Georg Scherer, A.G. (2001) 'Intercultural discourse ethics: Testing Trompenaars' and Hampden-Turner's conclusions about Americans and the French', *Journal of Business Ethics* **34**: 145–59.

Fulop, L. (1992) 'Management in the international context', in Fulop, L., Frith, F. and Hayward, H. (eds) *Management for Australian Business: A Critical Text*, Melbourne: Macmillan.

Garfinkel, H. (1984 [1967]) *Studies in Ethnomethodology*, Cambridge: Polity Press.

Gherardi, S. (1995) *Gender, Symbolism and Organizational Cultures*, London: Sage.

Giddens, A. (1991) *Modernity and Self-Identity*, Cambridge: Polity.

Gouldner, A. (1954) *Patterns of Industrial Bureaucracy*, New York: The Free Press.

Gouldner, A. (1955) *Wildcat Strike*, London: Routledge & Kegan Paul.

Guest, D. (1992) 'Right enough to be dangerously wrong: An analysis of the "In Search of Excellence" phenomenon', in Salaman, G. (ed.) *Human Resource Strategies*, London: Sage.

Guillén, M. (2006) *The Taylorized Beauty of the Mechanical: Scientific Management and the Rise of Modernist Architecture*, Princeton, NJ: Princeton University Press.

Hall, E. (1959) *The Silent Language*, New York: Doubleday.

Hampden-Turner, C. (1990) *Corporate Culture: From Vicious to Virtuous Circles*, London: Economist Books/Hutchinson.

Hampden-Turner, C. and Trompenaars, A. (1993) *The Seven Cultures of Capitalism*, New York: Currency Doubleday.

Hancock, P. and Tyler, M. (2001) *Work, Postmodernism and Organization*, London: Sage.

Handy, C. (1993) *Understanding Organizations*, London: Penguin.

Harrison, R. (1972) 'How to describe your organization', *Harvard Business Review* **50**(3): 119–28.

Hatch, M.J. and Schultz, M. (1997) 'Relations between organizational culture, identity and image', *European Journal of Marketing* **31**: 356–65.

Hatch, M.J. and Schultz, M. (2004) *Organizational Identity: A Reader*, Oxford: Oxford University Press.

Hochschild, A.R. (1983) *The Managed Heart*, Berkeley, CA: University of California Press.

Hofstede, G. (1980/2001) *Culture's Consequences: International Differences in Work-Related Values*, London: Sage.

Hofstede, G. (1991) *Cultures and Organizations: Software of the Mind*, London: Harper Collins.

Hofstede, G. (1998) 'Attitudes, values and organizational culture: Disentangling the concepts', *Organization Studies* **19**(3): 477–92.

Hofstede, G. (1999) 'The universal and the specific in 21st-century global management', *Organizational Dynamics*, (summer): 34–43.

Hofstede, G. (2002) 'Dimensions do not exist: A reply to Brendan McSweeney', *Human Relations* **55**(11): 1355–61.

Hofstede, G. and Bond, M.H. (1988) 'The Confucian connection: From cultural roots to economic growth', *Organizational Dynamics* **16**(4): 4–21.

Hofstede, G. and Peterson, M.F. (2000) 'National values and organizational practices', in Ashkanasy, N.M., Wilderom, C.P.M. and Peterson, M.F. (eds) *Handbook of Organizational Culture and Climate*, London: Sage.

Hofstede, G., Neuijen, B., Ohayv, D. and Sanders, G. (1990) 'Measuring organizational cultures: A qualitative and quantitative study across twenty cases', *Administrative Science Quarterly* **35**: 286–316.

Höpfl, H. (1996) 'Authority and the pursuit of order in organizational performance', in Jeffcutt, P., Grafton Small, R. and Linstead, S. (eds) *Organization and Theatre*, special issue of *Studies in Cultures, Organizations, and Societies* **2**(1): 67–80.

House, R.J., Hanges, P., Mansour, J., Dorfman, P. and Gupta, V. (2004) *Culture, Leadership and Organizations: The GLOBE Study of 62 Societies*, Thousand Oaks, CA: Sage.

Humes, S. (1993) *Managing the Multinational: Confronting the Global–Local Dilemma*, New York: Prentice Hall.

Jacob, N. (2005) 'Cross-cultural investigations: Emerging concepts', *Journal of Organizational Change Management* **18**(5): 514–28.

Jaques, E. (1952) *The Changing Culture of a Factory*, New York: Dryden Press.

Johnson, G. (1989) 'The Burton Group (B)', in Johnson, G. and Scholes, K. (eds) *Exploring Corporate Strategy*, London: Prentice Hall.

Johnson, G. (1992) 'Managing strategic change: Strategy, culture and action', *Long Range Planning* **25**(1): 28–36.

Kakabadse, A., Ludlow, R. and Vinnicombe, S. (1988) *Working in Organizations*, London: Penguin.

Kirkbride, P.S. (1983) 'Power in the workplace', unpublished PhD thesis, University of Bath, UK.

Kluckhohn, F.R. and Strodtbeck, F.L. (1961) *Variations in Value Orientations*, Evanston, IL: Row, Peterson.

Linstead, S.A. and Grafton Small, R. (1992) 'On reading organizational culture', *Organization Studies* **13**(3): 331–55.

Lorsch, J. (1986) 'Managing culture: The invisible barrier to strategic change', *California Management Review* **28**(2): 95–109.

Louis, M.R. (1980) 'Organizations as culture-bearing milieux', in Pondy, L.R., Frost, P.J., Morgan, G. and Dandridge, T.C. (eds) *Organizational Symbolism*, Greenwich, CT: JAI Press.

Lytle, A.L., Brett, J.M., Barsness, Z., Tinsley, C.H., and Janssens, M., (1995) 'A paradigm for quantitative cross-cultural research in organizational behavior', in B.M. Staw and L.L. Cummings (eds) *Research in Organizational Behavior*, vol. 17, pp. 167–214.

Magala, S. (2005) *Cross-cultural Competence*, London: Routledge.

Martin, J. (2002) *Organizational Culture: Mapping the Terrain*, Thousand Oaks, CA: Sage.

McSweeney, B. (2002a) 'Hofstede's model of national cultural differences and their consequences: A triumph of faith, a failure of analysis', *Human Relations* **55**(1): 89–118.

McSweeney, B. (2002b) 'The essentials of scholarship: A reply to Geert Hofstede', *Human Relations* **55**(11): 1163–72.

Negandhi, A.R. (1986) 'Three decades of cross-cultural management research', in Clegg, S.R., Dunphy, D.C. and Redding, S.G. (eds) *The Enterprise and Management in South-East Asia*, Hong Kong: Centre for Asian Studies, University of Hong Kong.

Olila, J. (1995) 'Corporate anthropology and organizational change', unpublished working paper, Erasmus University, Rotterdam.

Pacanowsky, M.E. and O'Donnell-Trujillo, N. (1982) 'Communication and organizational culture', *The Western Journal of Speech and Communication* **46**(spring): 115–30.

Parker, M. (2000) *Organizational Culture and Identity*, London: Sage.

Pascale, R.T. and Athos, A.G. (1980) *The Art of Japanese Management*, London: Penguin.

Pauchant, T. and Mitroff, I. (1988) 'Crisis prone versus crisis avoiding organizations: Is your company's culture its own worst enemy in creating crisis?', *Industrial Crisis Quarterly* **2**: 53–63.

Payne, R. (1990) *The Concepts of Culture and Climate*, Working Paper 202, Manchester Business School.

Peters, T. and Waterman, R.H. (1982) *In Search of Excellence*, New York: Harper & Row.

Pfeffer, J. (1981) 'Management as symbolic action: The creation and maintenance of organizational paradigms', in Cummings, L.L. and Staw, B. (eds) *Research in Organizational Behaviour* **3**(1): 1–52.

Pool, R. (1997) 'When failure is not an option', *Technology Review* July: 38–45.

Pullen, A. (2006) *Managing Identity*, London: Palgrave Macmillan.

Pullen, A. and Linstead S. (2005) *Organization and Identity* London: Routledge.

Ray, C.A. (1986) 'Corporate culture: The last frontier of control?', *Journal of Management Studies* **23**(3): 287–98.

Ritzer, G. (1990/2003) *The McDonaldization of Society*, Thousand Oaks, CA: Pine Forge Press.

Ritzer, G. (1999) *Enchanting a Disenchanted World: Revolutionizing the Means of Consumption*, Thousand Oaks, CA: Pine Forge Press.

Roberts, K.H. and Boyacigiller, N. (1984) 'Cross national organizational research: The grasp of the blind men', in L.L. Cummings and B.M. Staw (eds) *Research in Organizational Behavior*, vol. 6, Greenwich, CT: JAI Press, pp. 455–88.

Schein, E. (1985) *Organizational Culture and Leadership*, San Francisco, CA: Jossey-Bass.

Schwartz, H. (1990) *Narcissistic Process and Corporate Decay*, New York: NYU Press.

Schwartz, H. and Davis, S.M. (1981) 'Matching corporate culture and business strategy', *Organizational Dynamics* **10**: 30–48.

Schwartz, S.H. (1992) 'Universals in the content and structure of values: Theoretical advances and empirical tests in 20 countries', in Zanna, M. (ed.) *Advances in Experimental Social Psychology*, vol. 25, New York: Academic Press, pp. 1–65.

Schwartz, S.H. (1994) 'Beyond individualism/collectivism: New cultural dimensions of values', in Kim, U., Triandis, H.C., Kagitcibasi, C., Choi, S-C. and Yoon, G. (eds) *Individualism and Collectivism: Theory, Methods and Applications*, London: Sage, pp. 85–119.

Schwartz, S.H. (1999) 'Cultural value differences: Some implications for work', *Applied Psychology: An International Review*, **48**: 23–47.

Schwartz, S.H. (2004) 'Mapping and interpreting cultural differences around the world', in Vinken, H., Soeters, J. and Ester, P. (eds) *Comparing Cultures, Dimensions of Culture in a Comparative Perspective*, Leiden, The Netherlands: Brill.

Schwartz, S.H. (2006) 'Value orientations: Measurement, antecedents and consequences across nations', in Jowell, R., Roberts, C., Fitzgerald, R. and Eva, G. (eds) *Measuring Attitudes Cross-nationally: Lessons from the European Social Survey*, London: Sage.

Schwartz, S.H. and Bardi, A. (1997) 'Influences of adaptation to communist rule on value priorities in Eastern Europe', *Political Psychology* **18**: 385–410.

Schwartz, S.H. and Bardi, A. (2000) 'Moral dialogue across cultures: An empirical perspective', in E.W. Lehman (ed.) *Autonomy and order: A communitarian anthology*. Lanham, MD: Rowman & Littlefield.

Schwartz, S.H., Bardi, A. and Bianchi, G. (2000) 'Value adaptation to the imposition and collapse of Communist regimes in Eastern Europe', in Renshon, S.A. and Duckitt, J. (eds) *Political Psychology: Cultural and Cross Cultural Perspectives*, London: Macmillan – now Palgrave Macmillan, pp. 217–37.

Schwartz, S.H. and Sagie, G. (2000) 'Value consensus and importance : A cross-national study', *Journal of Cross-Cultural Psychology* **31**(4): 465–97.

Sinclair, A. (1991) 'After excellence: Models of organisational culture for the public sector', *Australian Journal of Public Administration* **50**(3): 321–32.

Smircich, L. (1983) 'Concepts of culture and organizational analysis', *Administrative Science Quarterly*, **28**(3): 339–58.

Smircich, L. and Calás, M. (2006) 'From the woman's point of view ten years later: Towards a feminist organization studies', in Clegg, S., Hardy C., Lawrence, T. and Nord, W. *Handbook of Organization Studies,* London: Sage, pp. 284–346.

Smircich, L. and Morgan, G. (1982) 'Leadership: The management of meaning', *Journal of Applied Behavioural Science* **18**(2): 257–73.

Smith, P.B. (2002) 'Culture's consequences: Something old and something new', *Human Relations* **55**(1): 119–35.

Smith, S. and Wilkinson, B. (1996) 'No doors on offices, no secrets: We are our own policemen: Capitalism without conflict?', in Linstead, S., Grafton Small, R. and Jeffcutt, P. (eds) *Understanding Management*, London: Sage.

Stone, A.R. (1995) *The War of Desire and Technology at the Close of the Mechanical Age*, Boston, MA: MIT Press.

Strauss, A., Schatzman, L., Ehrlich, D., Bucher, R. and Sabshin, M. (1963) 'The hospital and its negotiated order', in Friedson, E. (ed.) *The Hospital in Modern Society*, New York: Macmillan.

Swartz, M. and Watkins, S. (2003) *Power Failure: The Inside Story of the Collapse of Enron*, New York: Doubleday.

Tannen, D. (1990) *You Just Don't Understand: Men and Women in Conversation*, New York: William Morrow.

Tayeb, M.H. (1988) *Organisations and National Culture*, London: Sage.

Thompson, P. and McHugh, D. (2002) *Work Organisations: A Critical Introduction*, London: Palgrave Macmillan.

Torrington, D. (1994) *International Human Resource Management*, New York: Prentice Hall.

Triandis, H.C. (1993) 'Review of cultures and organizations: Software of the mind', *Administrative Science Quarterly*, **38**(2): 132–4.

Triandis H.C. (1994) *Culture and social behavior*, New York, NY: McGraw-Hill.

Trompenaars, F. and Hampden-Turner, C. (1998) *Riding the Waves of Culture: Understanding Cultural Diversity in Global Business* (2nd edn), New York: McGraw-Hill.

Turner, B.A. (1971) *Exploring the Industrial Sub-Culture*, London: Macmillan – now Palgrave Macmillan.

Van Maanen, J. (1991) 'The smile factory: Work at Disneyland', in Frost, P., Moore, L.F., Louis, M.R., Lundberg, C.C. and Martin, J. (eds) *Reframing Organizational Culture*, Newbury Park, CA: Sage.

Walsh, J. (1997) 'BA hopes to clear air with top-flight moves', *People Management* **23**(October): 11.

Weber, M. (1964) *The Theory of Social Economic Organizations*, London: Heinemann.

Westley, F.R. (1990) 'The eye of the needle: Cultural and personal transformation in a traditional organization', *Human Relations* **43**(3): 273–93.

Westwood, R. (1992) *Organizational Behaviour*, Hong Kong: Longmans.

Willmott, H. (1991) 'Strength is ignorance; slavery is freedom: Managing culture in modern organizations', *Journal of Management Studies* **30**(4): 515–52.

Young, D. (1989) 'British Airways: Putting the customer first', unpublished paper, Ashridge Strategic Management Centre, Ashridge Management College, UK.

Young, E. (1989) 'On the Naming of the Rose: Interests and multiple meanings as elements of organizational culture', *Organization Studies* **10**(2): 187–206.

Chapter 10

ENTREPRENEURSHIP IN THE 21ST CENTURY

- The stuff of dreams
- The entrepreneurial revolution
- The economics of entrepreneurship
- Entrepreneurs and owner-managers
- Small firms
- The differences between small and large firms
- Lifestyle and growth firms
- The UK small firms sector
- Global Entrepreneurship Monitor (GEM)
- Summary

CASE INSIGHTS

- Bill Gates and Microsoft
- Michael Dell and the Dell Corporation
- Richard Branson and Virgin
- Shaa Wasmund and Brightstation Ventures
- Marc Demarquette
- Joseph Bamford and JCB

CASES WITH QUESTIONS

- Julie Spurgeon
- Sara Murray – serial entrepreneur

LEARNING OUTCOMES

By the end of this chapter you should be able to:
- Explain why small firms and entrepreneurs are so important to the economies of modern countries;
- Describe the influences that have contributed to their increasing importance;
- Explain the economic underpinning for entrepreneurship;
- Explain the meaning of the terms entrepreneur and owner-manager and how they are different;
- Explain the differing statistical definitions of small firms;

- Describe the relationship between small firms and entrepreneurship;
- Describe the characteristics of the UK small firms sector compared to other countries and the significant contribution it makes to the economy;
- Explain the consequences of differing policy options for stimulating SMEs;
- Explain what data is gathered by the annual GEM surveys.

THE STUFF OF DREAMS

Over the last thirty years the business world has fallen in love with the idea of entrepreneurship. Entrepreneurs have evolved to become super-heroes who valiantly and single-handedly battle to make the most of business opportunities, pulling together resources they do not own, finding willing suppliers and eager customers and, just sometimes, against all the odds, winning out to become millionaires. The entrepreneur has emerged as a new 'cultural hero' (Cannon, 1991; Carr and Beaver, 2002). This is the stuff of dreams. Entrepreneurs are held up as role models. They are said to embody ephemeral qualities that we ought to emulate – freedom of spirit, creativity, vision, zeal. Above all, they have the courage and self-belief to turn their dreams into reality. Is it any wonder that we envy them?

Entrepreneurs, like super-heroes, valiantly make the most of opportunities

Yet take time to get a perspective on this. As we entered the twentieth century, the focus was on big. Big was beautiful and size really mattered. Big was respectable, it was political-establishment. Big was the future. It offered economies of scale; mass production that brought well being, if not wealth, to the masses. It was how the Western democracies would keep the common man, not only in food, shelter and life's necessities, but also in his place. It even spawned its own professional elite – managers. Whilst running a business has been a fundamental activity throughout history, the recognition and study of it as a discipline and profession is a thoroughly modern, twentieth century phenomenon. Harvard Business School awarded its first Masters degree in the discipline in 1910. And all of this was based upon the best practices in large corporations. Business schools have reflected the wider establishment view;

they have traditionally eschewed the arts of running a small business and largely ignored the skills of entrepreneurialism (Crainer and Dearlove, 1998).

But have small firms, like David, suddenly triumphed over the Goliath of large firms? In fact small firms, new firms and entrepreneurs never went away. And in the later part of the twentieth century reality began to dawn. In 1974 E.F. Schumacher, in his somewhat romantic book *Small is Beautiful*, asserted that giant organisations and increased specialisation resulted in economic inefficiency, environmental pollution and inhumane working conditions, and he proposed a system of intermediate technology based on smaller working units. Others began to doubt even the hard-nosed economic orthodoxy. In 1983 Jim Dewhurst wrote:

> In all the short history of modern business there is nothing so strange as this. On the one hand we have the traditional belief in the rightness and power of size. Rationalisation, standardisation and concentration are the watchwords. Economies of scale rule the industrial world. And in the UK we have gone further along this road of concentration than any other country in the world. Yet this predilection for economic orthodoxy has not brought us economic success.
>
> Dewhurst and Burns, 1983

The reality is that large firms were not so much the future of business but the natural consequence of businesses being set up by entrepreneurs and then growing. Unfortunately, like many things in life, they have a natural life expectancy and prolonging this is not always beneficial – to the firm or to society. According to Arie de Geus (1997) large organisations have proved amazingly inept at survival. He quoted a Dutch survey showing that the average corporate life expectancy in Japan and Europe was 12.5 years. 'The average life expectancy of a multinational corporation – the Fortune 500 or equivalent – is between 40 and 50 years.' The reality is that large companies die young, or at least their ownership changes fairly quickly.

Since the late twentieth century we have come to realise that new firms have done more to create wealth than firms at any time before them – ever! Ninety-five per cent of the wealth of the USA has been created since 1980. When Bill Gates founded Microsoft, IBM dominated the computer market with over 70 per cent of the market and more cash on its balance sheet than the sales of the rest of the industry. During the early 1990s IBM's share price plummeted and its workforce was slashed as it struggled to stay alive, while the new entrepreneurial companies, like Microsoft and Dell, prospered. By the start of the twenty-first century, one in every three households in the USA – 37 per cent or 35 million households – had at least one person who was involved in a primary role in a new or emerging business (*Economic News*, 1997).

Furthermore, people have begun to appreciate the sheer proportion of firms that can be described as small – by any definition, in any country. Small firms, virtually no matter how they are defined, make up at least 95 per cent of enterprises in the European Community. Their contribution to the economies of their countries also began to be appreciated around 1980. It was David Birch (1979) who, arguably, started this process with his seminal research which showed that 81.5 per cent of net new jobs in the USA, between 1969 and 1976, were created by small firms (under 500 employees). The general pattern has been repeated since. Small, growing firms have outstripped large ones in terms of job generation, year after year. At times when larger companies retrenched, smaller firms continued to offer job opportunities. There are now about 10 million self-employed people in the USA and it has been estimated that small firms generate some 50 per cent of GDP, with over 50 per cent of exports coming from firms employing less than 20 people.

Case insight

Bill Gates and Microsoft

We start with what is probably the outstanding business success story of a generation. Born in 1955 in Seattle, Bill Gates and his friend Paul Allen, 'begged, borrowed and bootlegged' time on his school's computer to undertake software commissions. The two went to Harvard University together, using the University's computer to start their own business. Bill's big break came when he approached Altair, a computer company in Albuquerque, New Mexico, trying to sell it a customised version of the programming language, BASIC, for its PC. The only problem was that, at the time, he and Paul Allen had not finished writing it. He had a vision of what it would look like and how it would operate, but no software. That was not finished until some weeks later and with it Microsoft came about. The package was later licensed to Apple, Commodore and IBM. IBM then commissioned Microsoft to develop its own operating system and that was how Microsoft Disk Operating System (MS DOS) was born. Founded in the late 1970s, by 1980 Microsoft was seen as a successful start-up with turnover of $8 million from just 38 employees. The company floated its shares on the US stock market in 1986; the ensuing rise of the company's stock price has made four billionaires and an estimated 12 000 millionaires from Microsoft employees.

Microsoft's growth has been amazing. With a turnover of over $58 billion and 93 000 employees, Microsoft is now the world's largest software company, producing a range of products and services that includes the Windows operating system and Microsoft Office software suite. And its ambitions are still anything but small. The company has expanded into markets such as video game consoles (Xbox), interactive television, internet access (MSN) and search engines (Bing). With its core markets maturing, it is targeting services for growth, looking to transform its software applications into web-based services.

In 2008 Bill Gates retired from day-to day-activities in the company a multimillionaire. He remains Chairman of the Board of Directors, and will continue to act as an advisor on key projects.

Up-to-date information on Microsoft can be found on their website: www.microsoft.com

---

Small firms are just as important in Europe. In 2005 enterprises employing up to 249 employees made up 98.8 per cent of all firms in the EU – a total of 19.6 million enterprises (Eurostat, 2008). That compares to 84 per cent in the USA – although this data is not exactly comparable as it relates to 'establishments' rather than enterprises (OECD, 2008). These small firms in the EU generated 67.1 per cent of employment and 57.6 per cent of value added (Eurostat, op. cit.). By just about any measure the contribution small firms make to the economy of any country is considerable and their importance is now fully recognised.

But the focus is not just on small firms. It is also on high-growth firms. Despite being few in number, high-growth businesses are disproportionately important to national economies. Harrison and Taylor (1996) claim that in the USA it has been estimated that, whilst 15 000 medium sized businesses represent just 1 per cent of all businesses, they generate a quarter of all sales and they employ a fifth of all private sector labour. In the UK, Storey et al. (1987) asserted that 'out of every 100 small firms, the fastest growing four firms will create half the jobs in the group over a decade' – an assertion that has stood the test of time.

This book looks at a range of things that make up this whole romanticised, but blurred, vision of entrepreneurs and small business. It looks at entrepreneurs – how they start up businesses, grow them, and nurture them to maturity, many failing on the way. It links theory – how things ought to be done – with practice – how they are done in the real world – to find best practice through the minefield of starting and growing a business. It looks in depth at:

○ *Entrepreneurs*. Who are they? Are all owner-managers entrepreneurial? What is their link with the process of innovation and economic growth, so loved by governments in most countries? Are they born rather than made and how are they shaped? Can they manage large firms or do they have to change as the business grows? Are they any different from managers or leaders in larger firms? Can they adapt to work in social enterprises with not-for-profit objectives? And, the important question for this millennium, can entrepreneurship be engendered in larger companies or other sorts of organisations?

- The *start-up*. How do you develop a business idea, one that is viable? How do you develop a plan that allows you to successfully launch the business – linking the marketing strategy that has the best chance of success with the resources you need to implement it? And where might those resources come from? Indeed once set up, what controls do you need to put in place to run the business?

- The *growth* of small firms. What growth strategies give the best chance of success? How do you find new customers or introduce new products or services? How do you develop a business plan that will get the backing of financiers? And what are the things that might go wrong and lead the business to failure, or how might you cash in on your success and sell the business?

- The *maturity* of these businesses. How do family firms pass from generation to generation – or not? How does the entrepreneur have to change with the business as it grows if he wants to lead it effectively? Can we put in place the structures, systems and processes that ensure that the firm continues to be entrepreneurial as it grows? Can we understand the DNA of the entrepreneur sufficiently to transplant it into the very architecture of a large firm?

This book attempts to answer these questions. With over thirty years of research into entrepreneurship and small business there are now many answers. We do know what to do and what not to do, what works and what does not. This book will take a conceptual perspective to develop a theoretical framework for understanding the area and, based on this, move forward to show how many of these concepts may be operationalised and developed into practical help in successfully launching and growing a business – indeed any organisation. In other words it will link theory with practice to show that organisations can successfully start up, grow and stay entrepreneurial in their maturity.

Case insight

Michael Dell and the Dell Computer Corporation

Michael Dell purchased his first computer – an Apple II – in 1980 and immediately took it apart to see how it was built. Only three years later he started a lucrative business selling upgraded PCs and add-on components out of his dormitory room at the University of Texas with capital of only $1000. Securing capital of $300 000 through his family, Michael registered the name Dell Computer Corporation in 1984 when he decided to leave college and start selling custom-built computers directly to end-users, ignoring the more normal channel of selling mass-produced computers through computer resellers. This not only eliminated the substantial middleman mark-up, but also the costly inventories required. In 1985, the company produced the first computer of its own design, the 'Turbo PC', which sold for $795.

'We built the company around a systematic process: give customers the high-quality computers they want at a competitive price as quickly as possible, backed by great service.'

Dell, 1999

In the 1980s Dell pioneered the 'configure to order' approach to manufacturing, producing individual PCs configured to customers' specifications and, in so doing, minimising its inventories and its costs. In contrast, most manufacturers at that time delivered large orders to intermediaries on a quarterly basis. Dell currently sells PCs, servers, data storage devices, network switches, software, and computer peripherals. It also sells HDTVs, cameras, printers, MP3 players and other electronics built by other manufacturers. Dell grew during the 1980s and 1990s to become, for a time, the biggest marketer of PCs and servers. It is currently the second largest company in the industry after Hewlett-Packard and employs over 76 500 people worldwide.

In 2004 Michael Dell stepped aside as CEO of Dell while retaining his position as Chairman of the Board. Kevin Rollins became the new CEO but Michael Dell returned in 2007 to become CEO once more. Like Bill Gates, he also is a multimillionaire and has become a truly exceptional entrepreneurial leader.

Up-to-date information on Dell can be found on their website: www.dell.com

THE ENTREPRENEURIAL REVOLUTION

What we are seeing now is nothing short of an entrepreneurial revolution. The major factors causing this are change and the pace at which it is accelerating. Change itself has changed to become discontinuous, abrupt but all pervasive. And small, entrepreneurial firms are better able to cope. Their flexibility and speed of response to changing market circumstances is well documented. In a turbulent world, full of uncertainties, they seem better able to survive and prosper. This is the essence of their success – their ability to spot an opportunity arising out of change or even to create it and then focus resources on delivering what the market wants quickly. In essence they are expert in innovation. And that often means taking risks that larger businesses are unwilling or unable to take. This all boils down to one word – entrepreneurship. It is the entrepreneurial small firms that have been able to capitalise most on the turbulent world we face today – entrepreneurial firms led by founders like Bill Gates, Michael Dell and Richard Branson.

> *The Entrepreneurial Revolution is here to stay, having set the genetic code of the US and global economy for the 21st century, and having sounded the death knell for Brontosaurus Capitalism of yesteryear. Entrepreneurs are the creators, the innovators, and the leaders who give back to society, as philanthropists, directors and trustees, and who, more than any others, change the way people live, work, learn, play, and lead. Entrepreneurs create new technologies, products, processes, and services that become the next wave of new industries. Entrepreneurs create value with high potential, high growth companies which are the job creation engines of the US economy.*

Jeffrey Timmons, author, 1999

A number of other influences have accelerated this trend towards smaller firms. Firstly there has been the shift in most economies away from manufacturing towards the service sectors where small firms often flourish because of their ability to deliver a personalised, flexible, tailor-made service at a local level. The 'deconstruction' of larger firms into smaller, more responsive units concentrating on their core activities, often sub-contracting many of their other activities to smaller firms, has also contributed to the trend. Large firms and even the public sector became leaner and fitter in the 1980s in a bid to reduce fixed costs and reduce risks. Small firms have benefited, although they may be seen as dependent on large ones.

Technology has played its part. It has influenced the trend in three ways. Firstly, the new technologies that swept the late twentieth century – computers and the internet – were pioneered by new, rapidly growing firms. Secondly, these technologies actually facilitated the growth of self-employment and small business by easing communication, encouraging working from home and allowing smaller and smaller market segments to be serviced. Indeed information has become a product in its own right and one that can be generated anywhere around the world and transported at the touch of a button. Thirdly, many new technologies, for example in printing, have reduced fixed costs so that production can be profitable in smaller, more flexible units.

> *We now stand on the threshold of a new age -- the age of revolution. In our minds, we know the new age has already arrived: in our bellies, we're not sure we like it. For we know it is going to be an age of upheaval, of tumult, of fortunes made and unmade at head-snapping speed. For change has changed. No longer is it additive. No longer does it move in a straight line. In the twenty first century, change is discontinuous, abrupt, seditious.*

Gary Hamel, author, 2000

Social and market trends have also accelerated the growth of small firms. Firstly, customers increasingly expect firms to address their particular needs. Market niches are becoming slimmer and markets more competitive – better served by smaller firms. Secondly, people want to control their own destiny more. After periods of high unemployment, they may see self-employment as more attractive and more secure than employment. In the late twentieth century, redundancy pushed many people into self-employment at the same time as the new 'enterprise culture' gave it political and social respectability. The growth of 'new age' culture and 'alternative' lifestyles also encouraged the growth of a whole new range of self-employment opportunities.

THE ECONOMICS OF ENTREPRENEURSHIP

The question arises as to whether there are any underlying theories to explain the growth in number and importance of small firms. Marxist theory predicts that capitalism will degenerate into economies dominated by a small number of large firms and society will polarise between those that own them and those that work in them. To a Marxist, the rise of small firms is just another, subtler way for this trend to manifest itself. Small firms are dependent upon larger firms for their custom and well being; they absorb risk and push down pay and conditions for workers as they are rarely unionised. However, the successful growth of so many small firms since the 1980s, the increasing fragmentation of industries and markets and the increasing popularity of self-employment by choice would seem to belie this theory.

People like Fritz Schumacher (1974) would have us believe that the growth of small firms is part of a social trend towards a more democratic and responsive society – 'small is beautiful'. To him the quality of life is more important than materialism. He is very much in favour of 'intermediate technology' – simpler, cheaper and easier to use – with production on a smaller scale and more locally based. However, the technologies that fuelled the growth of small firms at the end of the twentieth century were far from simple and, for many, quality of life improved alongside materialism. This leads us on to free-market economics. At one extreme the growth of small firms can be seen as the triumph of the free market and the success of the 'enterprise culture' promulgated by politicians like Ronald Reagan and Margaret Thatcher. Increasing numbers of small firms are the natural result of increased competition and a drive to prevent private and public monopoly. But what exactly does economic theory have to say about the creation of small firms?

Traditional industrial economists would explain the growth of new firms in terms of industry profitability, growth, barriers to entry and concentration. However, they are more concerned with 'entry' to an industry, rather than whether this is by a new or an existing firm. They assume an endless supply of potential new entrants. They would say that entry to an industry is high when expected profits and growth are high. It is deterred by high barriers to entry and high concentration, when collusion between existing firms can take place. However, much of this work does not specifically consider the role of new or smaller firms. Indeed, Acs and Audretsch (1989) show that entry by small, primarily new, firms is not the same as entry by large firms and that the birth of small firms is lower in highly concentrated industries and ones where innovation plays an important part.

By way of contrast, labour market economists have been more interested in what influences individuals to become potential entrants to an industry by becoming self-employed. Psychologists have also contributed greatly to this work, which has focused on the character or personality of the individual, the antecedent influences on them, such as age, sex, education, employment status, experience and ethnicity, as well as other societal influences. This work has proved far more successful and informative.

The link between entrepreneurship – the creation of new firms – and economic growth has until recently been far from clear, as far as economists are concerned. Traditional theories tended to suggest that entrepreneurship impeded rather than encouraged growth. Classical economics focused on optimising existing resources within a stable environment and treated any disruptions, such as entrepreneurial new firms creating whole new industries, as 'god sent' external forces. It was Joseph Schumpeter (1934), an Austrian economist, who created the link between entrepreneurship, innovation and growth. Schumpeter sought to explain economic development as a process caused by enterprise – or innovation – and carried out by entrepreneurs. This process of 'creative destruction', whereby new entrants displaced inefficient firms was formally restated by Aghion and Howitt (1992).

More recent theories of 'industrial evolution' have linked entrepreneurship and economic growth directly (Jovanovic, 1982; Lambson, 1991; Hopenhayn, 1992; Audretsch, 1995; Ericson and Pakes, 1995; Klepper, 1996). These theories focus on change as the central phenomenon and emphasise the role knowledge plays in charting a way through this. Innovation is seen as the key to entry, growth and survival for an enterprise and the way entire industries change over time. But the information they need in order to innovate is crucial – being inherently uncertain, asymmetric (one party may have more than another) and associated with high transaction costs. As a result there are differences in the expected value of new ideas, and people therefore have an incentive to leave secure employment to start up a new enterprise in order to capitalise on a commercial idea they believe in more than others. Once established, if economies of scale are important, the enterprise must grow, simply to survive. In this way the economic performance of nations is linked to how well the potential from innovation is tapped – start-ups encouraged and growth facilitated. And inherent in the process is churning – firms being displaced by newer, more innovative rivals.

These new evolutionary theories, supported by empirical evidence, therefore state that entrepreneurship encourages economic growth for three reasons:

1 It encourages competition by increasing the number of enterprises. Whilst this increases growth in itself, it is a cumulative phenomenon because competition is more conducive to knowledge externalities – new ideas – than is local monopoly. And so entrepreneurship encourages entrepreneurship.

2 It is a mechanism for 'knowledge spillovers' – transmission of knowledge from its point of origin to other individuals or organisations. Knowledge spillover is an important mechanism underlying endogenous growth, and start-ups – entrepreneurs – are seen as being particularly adept at appropriating knowledge from other sources. In other words entrepreneurs spot opportunities and innovate.

3 It generates diversity and variety among enterprises in any location. Each enterprise is in some way different or unique and this influences economic growth.

ENTREPRENEURS AND OWNER-MANAGERS

Before we go much further we need to define some terms. There is no universally accepted definition of the term 'entrepreneur'. The *Oxford English Dictionary* defines an entrepreneur as 'a person who attempts to profit by risk and initiative'. This definition emphasises that entrepreneurs exercise a high degree of initiative and are willing to take a high degree of risk. But it covers a wide range of occupations, including that of paid assassin. No wonder there is an old adage that if you scratch an entrepreneur you will find a 'spiv' (somebody who makes a living from unlawful work). The difference is more than just one of legality. Therefore a question you might ask is, how do they do it?

> *We learned the importance of ignoring conventional wisdom and doing things our way ... It's fun to do things that people don't think are possible or likely. It's also exciting to achieve the unexpected.*

Michael Dell, 1999

Back in the 1800s, Jean-Baptist Say, the French economist, said: 'entrepreneurs shift economic resources from an area of lower productivity into an area of higher productivity and greater yield' (1803). In other words entrepreneurs create value by exploiting some form of change, for example in technology, materials, prices or demographics. We call this process innovation and this is an essential tool for entrepreneurs. Entrepreneurs, therefore, create new demand or find new ways of exploiting existing markets. They identify a commercial opportunity and then exploit it.

Central to all of this is change. Change causes disequilibrium in markets out of which come the commercial opportunities that entrepreneurs thrive upon. To them change creates opportunities that they can exploit. Sometimes they initiate the change themselves – they innovate in some way. At other times they exploit changes created by the external environment. Often, in doing so, they destroy the established order and complacency of existing social and economic systems. How entrepreneurs manage and deal with change is central to their character and essential if they are to be successful. Most 'ordinary people' find change threatening. Entrepreneurs welcome it because it creates opportunities that can be exploited and they often create it through innovation.

How entrepreneurs deal with change is a key part of their success

Another key feature of entrepreneurs is their willingness to accept risk and uncertainty. In part this is simply the consequence of their eagerness to exploit change. However, the scale of uncertainty they are willing to accept is altogether different from that of other managers. It reflects itself in the risks they take for the business and for themselves. And for some this can be so addictive that they become 'serial entrepreneurs', best suited to continuing to start up businesses and unwilling to face the tedium of day-to-day management.

It is no wonder that entrepreneurship has been described as 'a slippery concept ... not easy to work into a formal analysis because it is so closely associated with the temperament or personal qualities of individuals' (Penrose, 1959). Where we attempt to differentiate entrepreneurs from others by their character traits. We shall also address the question of whether entrepreneurs are born or made.

Notice that in these definitions that there is no mention of small firms. Indeed, Richard Branson, a successful entrepreneur in his own right, is quoted as saying:

> I am often asked what it is to be an 'entrepreneur' and there is no simple answer. It is clear that successful entrepreneurs are vital for a healthy, vibrant and competitive economy. If you look around you, most of the largest companies have their foundations in one or two individuals who have the determination to turn a vision into reality.
>
> Anderson, 1995

The point is that entrepreneurs are defined by their actions, not by the size of organisation they happen to work within. Any manager can be entrepreneurial. The manager of a small firm may not be an entrepreneur – an important distinction that is often missed in the literature. Equally, entrepreneurs can exist within large firms, even ones that they did not set up themselves.

Case insight

Richard Branson and Virgin

Richard Branson is probably the best known entrepreneur in Britain today and his name is closely associated with the many businesses that carry the Virgin brand name. He is outward-going and an excellent self-publicist. He has been called an 'adventurer', taking risks that few others would contemplate. This shows itself in his personal life, with his transatlantic power boating and round-the-world ballooning exploits, as well as in his business life where he has challenged established firms like British Airways and Coca-Cola. He is a multimillionaire with what has been described as a charismatic leadership style. The Virgin Group is characterised as being informal and information driven – one that is bottom-heavy rather than strangled by top-heavy management.

Now in his sixties, Richard Branson's business life started as an 18-year-old schoolboy when he launched Student magazine, selling advertising space from a phone booth. He started selling mail-order records but soon decided he needed a retail site. In 1972 he got his first store, above a shoe shop on London's Oxford Street, rent-free on the grounds that it could not be let and would generate more customers for the shoe shop. It was a great success and Richard earned enough money from it to buy a country estate, in which he installed a recording studio and started Virgin Records.

Since those early days the Virgin brand has found its way onto aircraft, trains, cola, vodka, mobile phones, cinemas, a radio station, financial services and most recently the internet. Virgin Atlantic Airways was launched in 1984. In 1986 Virgin was floated but later reprivatised because Richard did not like to be accountable for his actions to institutional shareholders. In 1992, to keep his airline company afloat, he sold the Virgin record label to EMI for $1 billion. In 1999 a 49 per cent stake in the airline was sold to Singapore Airlines. In the same year Virgin Mobile was launched. Today Virgin describes itself as a 'branded venture capital company', comprising over 360 separate businesses.

'Virgin is not a big company – it's a big brand made up of lots of small companies. Our priorities are the opposite of our large competitors ... For us our employees matter most. It just seems common sense that if you have a happy, well motivated workforce, you're much more likely to have happy customers. And in due course the resulting profits will make your shareholders happy. Convention dictates that big is beautiful, but every time one of our ventures gets too big we divide it up into smaller units … Each time we do this, the people involved haven't had much more work to do, but necessarily they have a greater incentive to perform and a greater zest for their work.'

Branson, 1998

Up-to-date information on the Virgin Group can be found on their website: www.virgin.com

The way our notion of entrepreneur has been crafted has a long history, dating back to Cantillon (1755). Table 10.1 summarises some of the major developments in the concept. It charts the academic history and maps the antecedence of modern entrepreneurship. Trying to combine these shifting concepts and definitions with elements of character, I would propose the following definition for this elusive term:

> Entrepreneurs use innovation to exploit or create change and opportunity for the purpose of making profit. They do this by shifting economic resources from an area of lower productivity into an area of higher productivity and greater yield, accepting a high degree of risk and uncertainty in doing so.

You do not have to own a firm to manage it. However, some managers do own the firms they manage and these make up the majority of managers of small firms. These are owner-managers. Sole traders are owner-managers. Limited companies, however, have share capital. The term owner-manager, therefore, needs further refinement. An obvious one would be that to qualify as an owner-manager requires ownership (or beneficial ownership) of over 50 per cent of the share capital, thereby giving control of the business.

These definitions are, however, restrictive. For example, if a company is owned equally by two managers they would not be called owner-managers. Would this be any different if it were a partnership? Many people would call the managers in both situations 'owner-managers'. But where does this dilution begin and end? How many managers owning part of the business do you need before they cease being called owner-managers? Are all the employees of the John Lewis Partnership owner-managers? The real issue is not ownership, but control. Owner-managers significantly control the operations of their firm on a day-to-day basis. Notice, however, that this is a question of judgement and therefore this term, as with 'entrepreneur', is likely to be used very loosely.

Notice also that, using these definitions, owner-managers need not be entrepreneurs. Indeed, most owner-managers are not entrepreneurial. This book argues that entrepreneurs can be described in terms of their character and judged by their actions and one of the major factors differentiating them from owner-managers is the degree of innovation they practise.

Many managers of small firms do not own or control the firm they are employed by. The firm may be controlled by its larger, parent company. The manager is therefore not an owner-manager. Paradoxically, however, they might be entrepreneurs, depending on the way they act. Figure 10.1 shows these relationships. Whilst managers are different from owner-managers, both can be entrepreneurial. Similarly both managers and owner-managers may not be entrepreneurial. The entrepreneur is a unique individual with characteristics that are found in both owner-managers and managers.

Table 10.1 – The antecedence of modern entrepreneurship

Date	Author	Concept
1755	Cantillon	Introduced the concept of entrepreneur from 'entreprendre' (ability to take charge).
1803, 1817	Say	Emphasised the ability of the entrepreneur to 'marshal' resources in order to respond to unfulfilled opportunities.
1871	Menger	Noted the ability of entrepreneurs to distinguish between 'economic goods' – those with a market or exchange value – and all others.
1893	Ely and Hess	Attributed to entrepreneurs the ability to take integrated action in the enterprise as a whole, combining roles in capital, labour, enterprise and entrepreneur.
1911, 1928	Schumpeter	Envisioned that entrepreneurs proactively 'created' opportunity using 'innovative combinations' which often included 'creative destruction' of passive or lethargic economic markets.
1921	Knight	Suggested that entrepreneurs were concerned with the 'efficiency' in economic factors by continually reducing waste, increasing savings and thereby creating value, implicitly understanding the opportunity-risk-reward relationship.
1948, 1952, 1967	Hayek	Continued the Austrian tradition of analytical entrepreneurs giving them capabilities of discovery and action, recognising the existence of information asymmetry which they could exploit.
1973, 1979, 1997, 1999	Kirzner	Attributed to entrepreneurs a sense of 'alertness' to identify opportunities and exploit them accordingly.
1974	Drucker	Attributed to entrepreneurs the capacity to 'foresee' market trends and make a timely response.
1975, 1984, 1985	Shapero	Attributed a 'judgement' ability to entrepreneurs to identify 'credible opportunities' depending on two critical antecedents – perceptions of 'desirability' and 'feasibility' from both personal and social viewpoints.

Source: Adapted from Etemad (2004).

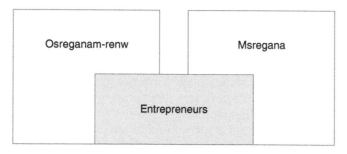

Figure 10.1 – Entrepreneurs, managers and owner-managers

SMALL FIRMS

As with the other terms, there is no uniformly acceptable definition of a small firm. Back in 1971, the Bolton Report (Bolton, 1971), which is usually held to be a definitive

Case insight

Shaa Wasmund and Brightstation Ventures

Shaa Wasmund is a graduate of the London School of Economics. In her last year at the London School of Economics she won a writing competition which led to a chance to interview the boxer Chris Eubank for *Cosmopolitan*. Eubank was impressed with Shaa and the interview led to a job with him, promoting his fights. After Eubank retired in 1994 she set up her first business, a PR and marketing company, with James Dyson as her first client. In 1999, a chance meeting with pop star and businessman Sir Bob Geldof led her to join him in launching the travel company Deckchair.com.

A year later, Shaa raised £6 million to launch her own company Mykindaplace.com a combination of online teenage girls' magazine and an early social networking site. By working with large companies like BSkyB and Freeserve – who also provided funding – to drive traffic to the site, the business prospered. So much so that by 2006 it was worth £10–£15 million and she decided to sell half her share in the business to BSkyB.

In 2007, together with entrepreneur Dan Wagner, she launched Brightstation Ventures, an investment vehicle with $100 million of capital dedicated to investing in internally generated ideas and seeding young companies that use information technology in innovative ways.

In a podcast interview for *Leadership Week* in 2008, she reflected on her experience:

Business is like a relay race and I am very, very good at the first leg and I am very, very good at the last leg, and I'm really not the best person to do the second and third legs. So you have to learn to pass that baton over to somebody else and more often than not that person will be somebody from a more corporate background than you, who has probably more experience at systems and procedures and who ... and enjoys developing and growing the business but also managing the business, whereas an entrepreneur will typically really enjoy the first part – getting the business off the ground, getting the funds in and making the ideas happen, probably to the point of bringing a business to profitability ... At that point I start to lose focus and so that's when you need to recognise what your strengths and your weaknesses are and then you come back in to sell the business. It's not that you disengage completely during the second and third legs, but you certainly pass the responsibility over to somebody who is more capable than you.

I believe in as flat a management structure as possible ... in leading without title ... I never put any emphasis on my title. I most certainly try to lead by example and I'm very much a big believer in making all of my mistakes public so that other people feel confident and comfortable to be able to air their own mistakes.

Management Today 18 July 2008, www.managementtoday.co.uk

Up-to-date information on Brightstation Ventures can be found on their website: www.brightstation.com

report on the state of small business in Britain at the time, made heavy weather of providing a statistical definition. Recognising that one definition would not cover industries as divergent as manufacturing and service, it used eight definitions for various industry groups. These ranged from under 200 employees for manufacturing firms to over £50000 turnover (in 1971) for retailing, and up to five vehicles or less for road transport. So many definitions clearly cause practical problems. What is more, definitions based on financial criteria suffer from inherent problems related to inflation and currency translation.

The European Commission coined the now widely used term 'small and medium enterprise' (SME) and in 1996 defined it as an organisation employing fewer than

250 people – a criterion that continues to be used for most statistical purposes. It defines these further categories:

	Number of employees
Micro	0–9
Small	10–49
Medium	50–249
Large	250 or more

The EU goes further to define the SME as having a turnover of less than €50 million and an annual balance sheet total of €43 million when it comes to establishing which SMEs might benefit from EU programmes, policies and competitiveness rules.

Being a small firm is not just about size, defined in simple statistical terms. Small firms also have important defining characteristics. The Bolton Committee described a small firm as satisfying three criteria, all of which defy practical statistical application:

1 *Market influence.* In economic terms, the small firm has a small share of the market. Therefore it is not large enough to influence the prices or national quantities of the good or service that it provides. Unfortunately, two fundamental problems arise with this, firstly with the definition of market and secondly with the ability of the small firm to influence price and the quantity sold in that market. Many of the most successful small firms operate in market niches so slim that they dominate that market segment, with no clear competition, and they can and do influence both price and quantity sold. In that respect Bolton's definition looks naïve and dated and was probably influenced by the economists' definition of perfect competition. It is certainly not one that most entrepreneurs would agree with.

2 *Independence.* The small firm is independent in the sense that it does not form part of a larger enterprise and that the owner-managers are free from outside control in taking their principal decisions. This means that only owner-managed firms are considered small firms. This is clearly unsatisfactory if you believe that there are certain specific characteristics about managing a small firm that mark it out as different from a large one.

3 *Personal influence.* The small firm is managed in a personalised way and not through the medium of a formalised management structure. This person is involved in all aspects of the management of the business and is involved in all major decision-making. Frequently there is little devolution or delegation of authority.

Case insight

Richard Branson and Virgin

Half French and half Chinese, Marc Demarquette was born and lives in London. He was a management consultant until an accident caused him to reconsider his priorities. His interest in catering led him to the prestigious Maison Lenôtre in Paris to learn the art of making chocolate and then to the Alps to work with a master chocolatier. In 2006 he opened an up-market chocolate shop, Demarquette, in Fulham, in south west London, and a small production facility nearby with the help of a £40 000 bank loan. He employed a chocolatier to help him create his range of high quality chocolates.

Three years later the business was well established. The £40 000 was spent within the first six months but since then the business has been entirely funded out of cash flow. Marc now produces a range of chocolates for Fortnum & Mason, but about one-third of sales come through the website. He has talked to other stores around the world about producing bespoke ranges of chocolate for them but has not moved forward on any of these. He also thought about opening a second shop in 2008, but decided not to because of the economic down turn. Since then his margins have been squeezed as chocolate prices rose by some 40 per cent in 2008 at a time when Marc felt unable to increase his prices. Marc still employs the chocolatier.

> 'After week one you can rip up your business plan because, although theories are wonderful, you have to respond to the real market. You need to have nerves of steel but it has been a fantastic experience. I'm loving it. I just wish I had a couple of extra hours in the day to enjoy my own life.'

Sunday Times, 24 May 2009

Up-to-date information on Marc Demarquette can be found on his website: www.demarquette.com

Small firms start to make managerial appointments when they have some 10–20 employees and at this point they begin to take on the appearance of more formal structures (Atkinson and Meager, 1994). Nevertheless, this third point is the key to a definition of the real small firm – the one with potential, the one that economists cannot understand, the one that makes it so different from the large firm. Essentially the real small firm can be described as having 'two arms, two legs and a giant ego'. In other words it is an extension of a person – the owner-manager or entrepreneur and their character traits – into the firm. Their personality is imprinted on the way it operates. The risks they and their family face if the firm fails influences how business decisions are made.

THE DIFFERENCES BETWEEN SMALL AND LARGE FIRMS

Small firms are not just scaled down versions of large ones. They go about their business in a number of fundamentally different ways. The key to understanding how a particular small firm goes about management and why and how decisions are made is to understand the personality of the owner-manager. Their personality and their behavioural characteristics will strongly influence this. More than large firms, small firms are social entities that revolve around personal relationships. They approach risk and uncertainty in a particular way that sometimes seems far from rational, which may explain why they are so little understood by economists.

There are a number of other characteristics that are typical of small firms and underline their different approach to management and business. The first is that they are typically short of cash. They cannot raise capital in the same way that a large company can. This has major strategic implications. Firstly, it constrains the strategies that they can adopt. For example, they cannot afford to adopt expensive advertising and promotion campaigns, so instead managers develop close relationships with customers and prospective customers, investing their time rather than money. Secondly, it dictates that business decisions must have a quick pay-off and therefore decision-making is short-term. For a growing business it means that raising finance becomes a major strategic issue and relationships with financing institutions such as banks and venture capitalists can become a major resource issue.

The second characteristic is that small firms are likely to operate in a single market, or a small number of markets, probably offering a limited range of products or services. This means that their scope of operations is, or at least should be, limited. In that sense they face fewer strategic issues than larger firms and often business strategy is synonymous with marketing strategy. However, unlike large firms, they find it difficult to diversify their business risk, which is another reason why they find it hard to raise finance.

Related to this is the characteristic that most small firms are over-reliant on a small number of customers. This means that they are particularly vulnerable to losing any one customer and the effect on the firm of such a loss will be disproportionately large. This is yet another reason why they are riskier prospects than large firms and find difficulty raising finance.

The fourth characteristic is the effect of scale on the economics of the business and how that translates into financial evaluation and decision-making. Most business finance textbooks are written with large companies in mind; consequently, whilst the principles they espouse are sound, the examples they use and generalisations that result are not. For example, taking on an additional member of staff for a small firm is a major strategic decision involving relatively large sums of money that represent a step increase in their fixed costs. Consequently they are reluctant to do so unless absolutely necessary. Yet in most business finance textbooks wage costs are treated as a variable cost, a view that can only be justified when there is a large number of employees. This error can lead to quite incorrect business decisions being made. It is little wonder that managers of small firms have little faith in professional advisors and accountants. Banks have for some time realised that traditional financial analysis says little about the health of the small firm and have started to broaden their approach.

These characteristics start to combine to distinguish small firms from large ones on a basis other than scale. Wynarczyk et al. (1993), strongly influenced by Casson (1982), argue that the much greater role played by uncertainty, innovation and firm evolution is the real defining characteristic of small firms. Small firms face more uncertain markets than large firms. They have a limited customer base and often cannot influence price. The owner-manager's own aspirations and motivations may also be uncertain. The effect of this high degree of uncertainty is to force decision-making to become short-term. Small firms also innovate in a particular way that makes them different from large firms. The final distinguishing characteristic is evolution – the recognition that the nature, style and functions of management change considerably as the small firm grows and evolves. Once more, we shall explore this in detail, in particular looking at the 'stage theories' of how firms grow.

LIFESTYLE AND GROWTH FIRMS

Small firms and entrepreneurship have often been linked together in a very loose fashion. They are broadly overlapping sets. As Storey and Sykes (1996) explain:

> the small firm is less concerned with formal systems and its decision-making process will be more judgemental, involving fewer individuals, and can therefore be quicker. It can be much more responsive to changes in the market-place but, conversely, is much less able to influence such developments. Hence the small firm is likely to adjust more quickly than the large firm to situations of market disequilibrium and, in these senses, embodies the characteristics of the classic entrepreneur.

However, this is a question of scale and, just as it was necessary to distinguish between owner-managers and entrepreneurs, it might be useful to distinguish between two categories of small firms:

1 *Lifestyle firms.* These are businesses that are set up primarily to undertake an activity that the owner-manager enjoys or gets some comfort from whilst also providing an adequate income, for example craft-based businesses. They are not set up to grow and, therefore, once a level of activity that provides the adequate income is reached, management becomes routine and tactical. There is probably little thought about strategic management unless things start to go wrong, and the most likely thing to go wrong is that the market changes without the owner-manager realising it. These firms are rarely managed by entrepreneurs and, if they are, the entrepreneur will be extremely frustrated. Most owner-managed firms fall into this category. Many are sole traders (unincorporated businesses). However, a lifestyle business can change if the owner-manager's motivations change and they have the entrepreneurial qualities to see it through.

2 *Growth firms.* These are set up with the intention of growth, usually by entrepreneurs. Occasionally a lifestyle business can turn into a growth business unintentionally. However, if the manager does not have entrepreneurial characteristics they are unlikely to succeed in the long run. Rapid growth is risky and creates major problems that must be addressed within very short time frames. Effective strategic management is vital if the firm is to succeed, indeed possibly survive. Notwithstanding this, these firms will face numerous problems and crises as they grow, some of which are predictable, others that are not. This is the classic entrepreneurial firm so beloved by the financial press.

It is important to realise that the small firm sector is far from homogeneous. Consider issues of size and age of business, sector, location, growth and decline, economic and market conditions. What is more, the people that manage them are many and varied. You do not have to own a small firm to manage it and you certainly do not have to be an entrepreneur. Consider also issues of age, sex, ethnicity, social origins, family relationships and then you start to realise the scale of the complexity.

Generalisations about small firms and the people that manage them are therefore just that – vast generalisations that are supposed to cover what makes up some 95 per cent of firms in most countries. Small firms are not homogeneous but, notwithstanding this, let us try to paint a broad picture of their nature and role in the UK.

Case with questions

Julie Spurgeon

In her mid-forties, Julie Spurgeon graduated with a first in ceramic design from London's Central Saint Martin's College of Art and Design in the summer of 2008. As part of her final project to design a range of tableware she had to seek critical appraisal from retailers and industry experts. One of the firms she contacted was up-market retailer Fortnum & Mason and they were sufficiently impressed to commission a range of bone china tableware, called Material Pleasures, that was launched in August 2009.

The trade mark Material Pleasures, which goes on the reverse of each piece, is registered (cost £200) and Julie joined Anti Copying in Design (ACID), which allowed her to log her design trail as proof against copying. Julie has had to pay for tooling and manufacturing costs herself. The moulds cost £5000 and the factory in Stoke on Trent required a minimum order of 250 pieces. The contract with Fortnum's involved exclusivity for six months. All this was funded with a £5000 loan from the Creative Seed Fund and a part-time job.

> 'In the future I'd like to continue creating specialist tableware, as well as handmade pieces. Material Pleasures stands for individual design, not big-batch production.'
>
> *Sunday Telegraph*, 12 July 2009

Questions

1 In your opinion, is Julie's a lifestyle or a growth business?
2 How do you differentiate between the two?

THE UK SMALL FIRMS SECTOR

During much of the twentieth century, the UK saw a decrease in the importance of small firms, measured in terms of their share of manufacturing employment and output. The proportion of the UK labour force classified as self-employed was at its lowest point in the 1960s. It was no wonder that the Bolton Committee (op. cit.), set up in the late 1960s to investigate the role of small firms in the economy, concluded that 'the small firm sector was in a state of long-term decline, both in size and its share of economic activity'. From the 1970s the situation has been reversed. Small firms have increased in importance, measured in terms of their number and their share of employment and turnover, and the number of small firms continues to rise, as does the number of people classified as self-employed. In 1979 there were only 2.4 million SMEs in the UK (see preceding definition). By 2007 this had grown to 4.7 million – an increase of almost 96 per cent in 28 years.

In the UK a range of SME statistics are produced and are available free on www. statistics.gov.uk. These are updated annually. The statistics for 2007 (Table 10.2) show that 99.9 per cent of firms were SMEs (all but 6000 out of 4.7 million) and they generated 59.2 per cent of employment (out of 22.7 million) and 51.5 per cent of turnover (out of £2.8 billion).

However, the detailed statistics also show that 73.9 per cent of all firms in the UK had no employees (3.5 million). These comprise sole proprietors, partnerships with only self-employed partners and companies with only an employee/director. These firms generated 16.6 per cent of UK employment for their proprietors (3.8 million) and 7.6 per cent of UK turnover (£222 billion).

These statistics reinforce the view that most UK small firms really are small, offering no more than self-employment. Most of these are probably lifestyle businesses. Few firms grow to any significant size. What is more, employment in small firms varies widely from sector to sector. Over 70 per cent of employment in both construction and agriculture is in SMEs. At the other extreme, less than 10 per cent of employment in financial intermediaries and mining is in SMEs. Small firms are not a homogeneous group.

In fact, small firms are increasing in number in most advanced countries, as is their share of employment. In 2005, 99.8 per cent of enterprises in the EU were SMEs which generated 67.1 per cent of employment and 57.6 per cent of value added (Eurostat, op. cit.). They employed on average 4.3 people, varying between 12 people in Slovakia and upwards of 7 in Estonia, Ireland Latvia and Germany, to less than 3 in the Czech Republic and Greece. SMEs are a vital part of all EU economies. They dominate many service sectors, particularly hotels, catering, retailing and wholesaling, and are important in construction. What is more, SMEs in the EU display many of the same characteristics as those in the UK. Most display modest growth rates and only about 50 per cent survive beyond their fifth year.

An EU report (European Commission, 2008) comparing EU to US SMEs found that US SMEs were on average larger than EU firms with proportionately fewer micro firms generating less employment. It observed that entry, exit and survival rates were roughly comparable and that the main differences were:

o in the US new firms expand more rapidly than in the EU;
o in the US new firms display a higher dispersion of productivity;
o in the US the more productive firms have a stronger tendency to increase their market shares than in the EU.

The report concluded that the US market was probably therefore more competitive than the EU and had fewer barriers to growth.

Table 10.2 – Comparison of UK enterprises by size, 2007

	Number (%)	Employment (%)	Turnover (%)
Micro	95.7	33.2	22.8
Small	3.6	14.3	14.6
Medium	0.6	11.7	14.1
Large	0.1	40.8	48.5

The issue about encouraging survival and growth for SMEs pervades much of government policy. Some academics, like Storey and Greene (2010), remain unconvinced by the arguments for government intervention, except in cases of 'market failure'. For them governments cannot justify policy interventions related to provision of finance, advice and assistance for particular groups and the general creation of an 'enterprise culture'. They only remain convinced of intervention in support of technology business in terms of R&D support and the case for a publicly-funded loan guarantee scheme. Others support the view that there is little evidence of success in government interventions in supporting SMEs (Bill et al., 2009; Bridge et al., 2009; Davidsson, 2008). Not withstanding these reservations. Hölzl et al. (2006) provided a stylised typology for looking at the issue of government intervention, reproduced as Figure 10.2. The horizontal axis depicts the degree of successful exploitation of opportunities in terms of survival and growth, and the vertical axis represents the smoothed frequency distribution of firms. The strongly skewed shape of the curve reflects the large number of start-ups that may be thought about (latent or nascent entrepreneurship), with decreasing numbers of businesses that are actually set up only to fail, those that survive and those that go on to grow. Policy might simply encourage more start-ups, but this is likely to lead to more start-ups failing early. On the other hand, a policy of encouraging surviving firms to grow – even if it does not involve 'picking winners', which most policy advisors would be sceptic of the ability of government to do – may result in fewer start-ups because of reduced opportunities. As with so many things, there is a balance to be achieved – that is of course, if you believe in government intervention at all. But whilst many academics feel these micro-economic policies might be ineffectual, even Storey and Greene (op. cit.) would agree that the broader macro-economic policies of taxation, regulation, competition and even immigration can have a powerful effect on SMEs, simply because they affect the economic environment in which they operate.

In the UK, there are also a range of VAT statistics that inform us about SMEs. These are available free from the Office of National Statistics in a series called

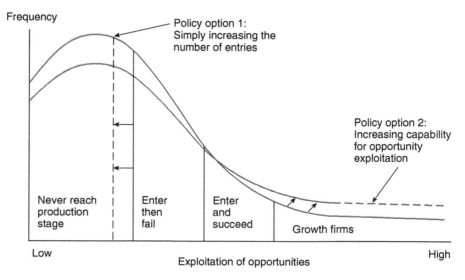

Figure 10.2 – Policy options for encouraging survival and growth
Source: Hölzl et al. (2006), quoted in European Commission (2008)

'Business Demography' (www.statistics.gov.uk). Information about VAT registrations and deregistrations is widely used as the best guide to patterns of change in the small-firm sector – levels of entrepreneurship and the health of the business population. They are also used in regional and local economic planning. The net change in business stocks is a particularly important figure that is often reported in national newspapers. The net change in stock tends to be highly related to the state of the economy. Small firms are particularly vulnerable to economic changes because of their frequently precarious financing situation. In times when the economy is in recession there tends to be a net decrease in the stock of businesses and vice versa. So, the 1980s saw a large increase in the stock of registered companies, whereas the stock decreased between 1991 and 1994. From 1995 net stocks have increased. 2008 saw a net increase of 2 per cent or 51 000 firms (270 000 registrations less 219 000 deregistrations) – down from 57 900 in 2007. These statistics are also broken down by sector and region. The highest birth rate in 2008 was in business administration and support services (16.2 per cent), followed by professional, scientific and technical (14.6 per cent). London had both the highest birth and death rates at 15.0 and 10.3 per cent, respectively. Northern Ireland had the lowest birth and death rates at 9.5 and 7.3 per cent, respectively. One interesting point is that areas with high registrations, like London, also tend to have high deregistrations – an effect called 'churning' – indicating that high economic growth may cause or be caused by more firms

Case insight

Joseph Bamford and JCB

Stories of successful entrepreneurs always make good reading. And successful entrepreneurs have been with us for many, many years in Britain. Joseph Cyril Bamford gave his initials to the ubiquitous yellow hydraulic excavator and digger seen on just about every building site or road works – the JCB. In fact JCB became one of the few post-war British industrial success stories. By the time of Joseph Bamford's death in 2001 the company employed over 4500 people across three continents and had a turnover of £833 million. Over 70 per cent of JCB production is for overseas markets.

Joseph Bamford came from a prosperous Staffordshire engineering family which had been making agricultural equipment since mid-Victorian times. When he returned to civilian life after the Second World War he decided to start up on his own doing what he knew best. Starting his business with only an electric welder he bought for £2.50, he started producing tipping farm trailers from a garage in Uttoxeter, using materials from old air-raid shelters. These sold well, but in 1948 he decided to branch out into hydraulic equipment and, in 1953, went into partnership to produce a range of earth-moving machines before eventually coming up with the famous backhoe loader that combined the two functions of excavator and shovel and became the visual embodiment of the initials JCB.

Joseph Bamford was a paternalistic employer, who provided a social club and a fishing lake next to his factory in Rochester. He ran a tight ship but rewarded effort. He also knew how to get PR. In 1964, when he famously paid his workers £250 000 in bonuses because the company's turnover had topped £8 million, he personally handed out the bonus to each employee, standing on the first farm tractor he had designed in 1947.

Joseph Bamford made JCB into one of the most successful privately owned companies in Britain. Eventually the company diversified from his central control into a group of several operating companies. He gave up his chairmanship of the group in 1975, handing it over to his eldest son, now Sir Anthony Bamford, and retired to Montreux, Switzerland where he enjoyed yacht designing and landscape gardening. Today the company is the third-biggest maker of construction equipment in the world, with about 12 per cent of the global market. It employs around 7000 people on 4 continents and sells its products in 150 countries through 1500 dealer depot locations. It remains a family business.

Up-to-date information on JCB can be found on their website: www.jcb.com

coming into existence (registering) but the increased competition means that more will cease (deregister).

These VAT statistics have also been used to show that the most dangerous time for a new business is its first three years of existence. Almost 50 per cent of businesses will cease trading within that period. This does not, of course, mean that the closures represent failure in terms of leaving creditors and unpaid debts. Most are simply wound down. Businesses that cease trading do so for a number of reasons. Some will close because the business ceases to be lucrative. Others because of the death or retirement of the proprietor, or changes in their personal motivations and aspirations. Some will simply close to move on to other, more lucrative opportunities. This 'churning effect' of small firms closing and opening is part of the dynamism of the sector as they respond to changing opportunities in the market place and is why the net change in the stock of businesses is more important than the individual number of failures.

Other studies have given an insight into the UK small firms sector. Small firms tend to have lower productivity than large firms, even in the same industry – a conclusion supported across Europe (Eurostat, 2009). Firms with fewer than 200 employees had 55 per cent of the productivity (measured in value added per employee) of firms with 1000 or more employees. In the computer and office machinery sectors SME productivity is only one-third that of larger firms'. These differences are largely because of lower capital backing. Research also indicates that SMEs have a disproportionately high number of 'bad jobs' (McGovern et al., 2004) and higher accident rates (Walters, 2001). The availability of flexible working practices to encourage family-friendly working appears arbitrary in SMEs (Dex and Smith, 2002) and there is low take-up of training initiatives such as NVQs (national vocational qualifications) and IIP (Investors in People) (Matlay, 2002). However it would be wrong to characterise SMEs as poor employers as there is enormous diversity of practice (Barrett and Rainnie, 2002; Ram and Edwards, 2003).

GLOBAL ENTREPRENEURSHIP MONITOR (GEM)

GEM is a research programme which was started in 1999 in 10 countries. By 2008 it had been extended to 43 countries. It is a harmonised assessment of the level of national entrepreneurial activity in each of the countries. In the UK it is based upon an annual survey of 32 000 adults of working age. It asks a number of questions but a central one is whether or not they are starting up a business (nascent entrepreneurs – the stage at which individuals begin to commit resources, such as time or money, to starting a business), or already own or manage a business (new business owner-managers – those whose business are paying income, such as salaries or drawings). From this information a figure for total entrepreneurial activity (TEA) is calculated for each country as the proportion of nascent entrepreneurs and new business owner-managers. In 2008 the TEA index for the UK was 5.5 per cent, the same as in 2007' – in other words 5.5 per cent of the UK population were engaged in some form of entrepreneurial activity (GEM, 2009). As you might expect, the USA with a score of 10.8 per cent ranked higher. This continued a long-term pattern in the UK of lower TEA rates than the USA, Canada, Brazil, India and China, and higher TEA rates than other G7 nations and Russia. The UK TEA rate has closely tracked the G7 average since 2002. The report also showed that the UK had intermediate rates of established business ownership and business 'churn'

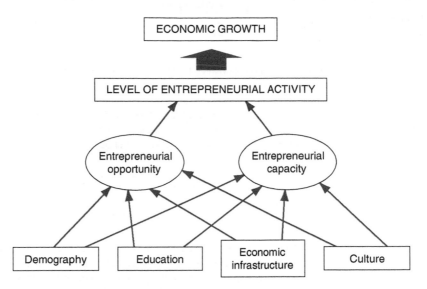

Figure 10.3 – The GEM approach to measuring entrepreneurial activity
Source: Adapted from GEM (2001) Executive Report

in comparison to other G7 nations. The proportion of entrepreneurs reporting high growth expectations, new product/market combinations, and new technology applications was also intermediate. 'Necessity-driven' entrepreneurship in the UK was relatively low.

GEM 2008 came up with some interesting conclusions about gender and race. It found that in most high-income countries, men are around twice as likely to be entrepreneurially active as women. The UK rate of TEA in males was 7.4 per cent compared to 3.6 per cent for women. It found that immigrants who identify with the white British ethnic group have higher rates of TEA than UK-born white British. UK-born and immigrant mixed ethnic individuals have similar TEA rates. Black and Asian immigrants have lower TEA rates than their UK-born peers.

Central to the GEM approach is the hypothesis of a causal relationship between entrepreneurial activity in the economy and the level of economic growth. The GEM model is shown in Figure 10.3. The demand side is represented by entrepreneurial opportunity and the supply side by entrepreneurial capacity. These are affected in different ways by demography, education, economic infrastructure and culture.

GEM is an enormous research endeavour generating quantitative data that can be used for both cross-sectional analysis and, probably most importantly, longitudinal analysis, allowing us to track individuals from entrepreneurial aspiration ('nascent entrepreneurship') to action. Obvious methodological problems exist. For example, GEM does not attempt to measure differences in culture. Also the use of a single questionnaire across all the countries is clearly problematic. Nevertheless data from GEM is increasingly being pored over by econometricians eager to find statistical relationships of any kind, no matter how unsupported by theory or other research. GEM reports can be downloaded free of charge from www.gem consortium.org.

Case with questions

Sara Murray – Serial entrepreneur

Sara Murray is a serial entrepreneur, having set up three businesses so far. Born in 1968 to professional parents (her father was a manager at Chloride and her mother was a teacher), Sara graduated from Oxford University in 1990 with an MA in physiology, psychology and philosophy. She started work as a management consultant with ZS Associates in the USA and in 1991 moved to Hambros Bank in London to work in asset finance. In 1993 she started her first business, called Ninah Consulting. It used technology to improve companies' marketing effectiveness, working for blue-chip clients like Coca-Cola and SmithKline Beecham. In 1999 she started her second business, inspop.com, an insurance comparison website. She expanded the site to more than 250 000 customers within 18 months and then sold it to Admiral Group who renamed it 'Confused.com'. In 2002 Sara sold Ninah to Publicis, the French media group.

Sara is married with one daughter and three step-children. She is a keen sportswoman – a runner, skier and yachts-woman who helmed an America's Cup boat across the Atlantic. She claims that her mother encouraged her to set up her own business, telling her she would be in 'control' and that it was 'better for having a family'.

The idea for Sara's latest business came when her daughter disappeared in a supermarket and she wondered whether there was a technological solution to this problem. She decided to find a satellite navigation tracking device that could be used in such situations and eventually found a company in California that had already spent $180 million on developing one. However it was not yet on sale and, anyway, would only work in US metropolitan areas. Having set up businesses before and with a range of contacts in finance through her brief City career, Sara decided to investigate the opportunity herself. A friend introduced her to two engineers.

'I decided to make one myself … I knew the difficult thing would be building the hardware, because I had never done it before … I was completely consumer-orientated. I said – this is what I would like it to do for my child. They were completely technology-orientated. There was a gap … Most technology companies build technology and look at where they can sell it.'

The Times, 3 January 2009

Sara spent £200 000 of her own money on building a working prototype. Relying heavily on her network of finance contacts she then went on to obtain the first round of funding from business angels in 2005. The first Buddi device went on sale in 2007.

A Buddi is about the size of a wrist watch and is hung around the neck. It sells for a small fixed amount above the cost of manufacture plus a monthly charge for unlimited use. By logging on to the Buddi website it is possible to find some-one's whereabouts on the relevant page of Google Maps. Their movements can even be tracked in real time. The device also contains a panic button, which alerts one of two constantly monitored call centres and has an audio feed to assess whether there is a real emergency. If there is an emergency, the centres contact a nominated guardian. It can be used for any vulnerable people, not just children, and operates anywhere in the world.

So far the venture has cost just over £1.3 million, funded by two rounds of calls on business angels and further injections of cash will be necessary. Turnover in 2008 was £3 million

Up-to-date information on Buddi can be found on their website: www.buddi.co.uk

Questions

1 In what ways is Sara different from most women? How might these characteristics contribute to her drive and determination in setting up her own firms?
2 What challenges has Sara faced in setting up her businesses? How has she overcome them?
3 How much of what she has achieved has been down to luck?

SUMMARY

○ In the late twentieth century the focus of business interest shifted from large to small firms. Their contribution to the economy became recognised, as did the shortcomings of large companies. Start-up entrepreneurs like **Bill Gates**, founder of **Microsoft**, **Michael Dell**, founder of **Dell Computer Corporation**, **Richard Branson,** founder of **Virgin** and **Joseph Bamford**, founder of **JCB**, demonstrated they could become world-class, outstanding successes very quickly, and at the same time they became 'the stuff of dreams' – at least in the financial press. Some entrepreneurs, like **Shaa Wasmund** and **Sara Murray**, become 'serial entrepreneurs, starting up and selling multiple businesses.

○ Many politicians would claim that the growth of small firms is a manifestation of the success of free-market capitalism, although Marxist theory does seem to be able to accommodate it. But whilst industrial economists would have little to say to explain the phenomenon, labour economists and psychologists have been more successful. It was Schumpeter who first linked entrepreneurs with economic growth through innovation and 'creative destruction'. Theories of 'industrial evolution' link entrepreneurship and economic growth through the tendency of entrepreneurial companies to increase competition, make the most of knowledge spillovers and create increased diversity.

○ Entrepreneurs use innovation to exploit or create change and opportunity for the purpose of making profit. They do this by shifting economic resources from an area of lower productivity into an area of higher productivity and greater yield, accepting a high degree of risk and uncertainty in doing so.

○ Owner-managers own the business they manage. Sole traders are owner-managers. Managers of companies owning over 50 per cent of the share capital, and thereby controlling the business, are owner-managers. However, the term is also used loosely when a small group of managers own and control the business. Not all owner-managers are entrepreneurs.

○ Small firms and entrepreneurship are broadly overlapping sets. However, the two concepts are not necessarily synonymous. We broadly characterise small firms as either lifestyle – set up to allow the owner-manager to pursue an activity they enjoy – or growth – set up to make money and grow. Some owners, like **Julie Spurgeon**, have lifestyle businesses by choice. Others, like **Marc Demarquette**, have businesses that might grow if opportunities present themselves.

○ Entrepreneurs are defined primarily by their actions although, they can have certain identifiable personal characteristics. They are the particular type of owner-manager that the financial press love so much. They make 'the stuff of dreams' come true.

○ A small or medium-sized enterprise (SME) is one with fewer than 250 employees. A micro business has up to 9 employees, a small business up to 49 employees and a medium-sized business up to 249 employees. A defining characteristic of the small firm is the influence of the owner-manager. It is managed in an informal, personalised way and the character and preoccupations of the manager are significant influences on decision-making.

○ SMEs have a number of other significant characteristics, which include shortage of cash and difficulty in raising finance, limitations in product or service range and the markets they operate in, reliance on a small number of customers and the effects of their small scale on financial evaluation and decision-making. But the other defining characteristics of entrepreneurial SMEs are uncertainty, innovation and firm evolution.

○ Until the 1960s the UK saw a decrease in the importance of small firms. Since the 1970s this has been reversed and SMEs are now an important part of the UK and EU economies, generating significant employment and wealth. However, most small firms in the UK do not grow to any size. The increasing number of small firms is a result of many trends – the move from manufacturing to the service sectors, the 'deconstruction' of many large firms and the trend towards sub-contracting, the influence of new technologies, and social and market changes.

FURTHER RESOURCES ARE AVAILABLE AT WWW. PALGRAVE.COM/BUSINESS/BURNS

ESSAYS AND DISCUSSION TOPICS

1. Are small firms worthy of special treatment? If so, by whom and what form should it take?
2. List the pros and cons of running your own business.
3. Do you think you might have what it takes to be an entrepreneur?
4. Do you dream of starting your own business? If so, why? If not, why not? What do you think will be the main challenges you would face?
5. Do you think the definition of an entrepreneur is adequate?
6. How does the management of a small firm differ from the management of a large one?
7. What are the characteristics of small firms that distinguish them from large firms and what are their implications? Do these mean that small firms really are sufficiently different to warrant special study?
8. Are small firms sufficiently homogeneous to justify special study? What further segmentation might you suggest and what are the special and different characteristics of these segments?
9. Is it good that so many businesses close in their first three years?
10. Why has the number of small firms been increasing in the UK since the late 1960s?
11. Does Marxism say anything to explain the increasing number of small firms?
12. How does entrepreneurship encourage economic growth?
13. How might entrepreneurship be encouraged?
14. Should governments encourage an increase in the number of start-ups or encourage opportunity exploitation? Are the two mutually exclusive?
15. How can you encourage opportunity exploitation?
16. Are lifestyle firms worth encouraging?
17. Should art students who want to be self-employed be taught entrepreneurship?
18. Should all students at university be taught entrepreneurship?
19. Is small really beautiful?
20. What are the real defining characteristics of a small firm?
21. What are nascent entrepreneurs? What does their number tell us that start-up statistics do not?
22. Do you see any similarities between the entrepreneurs profiled in this chapter?

EXERCISES AND ASSIGNMENTS

1. Research the history and profile of an entrepreneur who set up their own business and grew it successfully.
2. Update the statistics on small firms in Britain and in the EU. Alternatively, obtain similar statistics on the performance of small firms in your country. What does this tell you about recent developments? Summarise your findings in a report.
3. Access the latest GEM report for your country and summarise its findings in a report.

REFERENCES

Acs, Z.J. and Audretsch, D.B. (1989) 'Births and Firm Size', *Southern Economic Journal*, 55.

Aghion, P. and Howitt, P. (1992) 'A Model for Growth through Creative Destruction', *Econometrica*, 60.

Anderson, J. (1995) *Local Heroes*, Glasgow: Scottish Enterprise.

Atkinson, J. and Meager, N. (1994) 'Running to Stand Still: The Small Business in the Labour Market', in J. Atkinson and D.J. Storey (eds), *Employment, The Small Firm and the Labour Market*, London: Routledge.

Audretsch, D.B. (1995) *Innovation and Industry Evolution*, Cambridge: MIT Press.

Barrett, R. and Rainnie, A. (2002) 'What's So Special About Small Firms? Developing an Integrated Approach to Analysing Small Firm Industrial Relations', *Work, Employment and Society*, 16(3).

Bill, F., Johannisson, B. and Olaison, L. (2009) 'The Incubus Paradox: Attempts at Foundational Rethinking of the "SME Support Genre"', *European Planning Studies*, 17(8).

Birch, D.L. (1979) 'The Job Creation Process', unpublished report, MIT Program on Neighbourhood and Regional Change, prepared for the Economic Development Administration, US Department of Commerce, Washington, DC.

Bolton, J.E. (1971) *Report of the Committee of Inquiry on Small Firms*, Cmnd. 4811, London: HMSO.

Branson, R. (1998) *Losing my Virginity*, London: Virgin.

Bridge, S., O'Neill, K. and Martin, F. (2009) *Understanding Enterprise, Entrepreneurship and Small Business*, Basingstoke: Palgrave Macmillan.

Cannon, T. (1991) *Enterprise: Creation, Development and Growth*, Oxford: Butterworth-Heinemann.

Cantillon, R. (1755) *Essai sur la Nature du Commerce en General*, London and Paris: R. Gyles (trans. H. Higgs (1931), London: Macmillan). See also www.newschool.edu/nssr/het/profiles/cantillon.htm.

Carr, P. and Beaver, G. (2002) 'The Enterprise Vulture: Understanding a Misunderstood Concept', *Strategic Change*, 11.

Casson, M. (1982) *The Entrepreneur: An Economic Theory*, Oxford: Martin Robertson.

Crainer, S. and Dearlove, D. (1998) *Gravy Training: Inside the Shadowy World of Business Schools*, Oxford: Capstone.

Davidsson, P. (2008), 'Some Conclusions about Entrepreneurship and its Support', Paper presented at the World Entrepreneurship forum, November, Evian, France.

de Geus, A. (1997) *The Living Company*, Boston, MA: Harvard Business Press.

Dell, M. (1999) *Direct from Dell: Strategies that Revolutionised an Industry*, New York: Harper Business.

Dewhurst, J. and Burns, P. (1983) *Small Business Finance and Control*, London: Macmillan – now Basingstoke: Palgrave Macmillan.

Dex, S. and Smith, C. (2002) *The Nature and Pattern of Family-Friendly Employment Policies in the UK*, Abingdon: Policy Press.

Drucker, P.F. (1974) *Management Tasks, Responsibilities, Practices*, New York: Harper & Row.

Economic News (1997) 'The Small Business Advocate', February 1997, Washington, DC, Office of Advocacy, SEA.

Ely, R.T. and Hess, R.H. (1893) *Outline of Economics*, New York: Macmillan.

Ericson, R. and Pakes, A. (1995) 'Markov-Perfect Industry Dynamics: A Framework for Empirical Work', *Review of Economic Studies*, 62.

Etemad, H. (2004) 'International Entrepreneurship as a Dynamic Adaptive System: Towards a Grounded Theory', *Journal of International Entrepreneurship*, 2.

European Commission (2008) *European Competitiveness Report 2008*, available free online at www.ec.europa.eu/enterprise.

Eurostat (2008) *Enterprises by Size Class – Overview of SMEs in the EU, Statistics in Focus, 31/2008*. Available on epp.eurostat.ec.europa.eu.

Eurostat (2009) *European Business Facts and Figures, 2009 Edition*, Luxembourg: Eurostat. Available on epp.eurostat.ec.europa.eu.

GEM (2001) *Executive Report*, Babson College, Boston, USA/London Business School.

GEM (2009) *Global Entrepreneurship Monitor 2008*, reports by individual GEM national teams available free online at www.gemconsortium.org.

Harrison, J. and Taylor, B. (1996) *Supergrowth Companies: Entrepreneurs in Action*, Oxford: Butterworth-Heinemann.

Hayek, F.A. (1948) 'The Use of Knowledge in Society', in *Studies in Philosophy, Politics and Economics*, Chicago: University of Chicago Press.

Hayek, F.A. (1952) *The Sensory Order*, Chicago: University of Chicago Press.

Hayek, F.A. (1967a) 'Competition as a Discovery Procedure', in Hayek, *New Studies in Philosophy, Politics, Economics and History of Ideas*, Chicago: Chicago University Press.

Hayek, F.A. (1967b) 'The Results of Human Action, but not Human Design', in Hayek, *New Studies in Philosophy, Politics, Economics and History of Ideas*, Chicago: Chicago University Press.

Hölzl, W., Huber, P., Kaniovski, S. and Peneder, M. (2006) 'Neugründung und Entwicklung von Unternehmen, Teilstudie 20', in K. Aiginger, G. Tichy and E. Walterskirchen (eds), *WIFO-Weißbuch: Mehr Beschäftigung durch Wachstum auf Basis von Innovation und Qualifikation*, Vienna: WIFO.

Hopenhayn, H.A. (1992) 'Entry, Exit and Firm Dynamics in Long Run Equilibrium', *Econometrica*, 60.

Jovanovic, B. (1982) 'Favorable Selection with Asymmetrical Information', *Quarterly Journal of Economics*, 97(3).

Kirzner, I.M. (1973) *Competition and Entrepreneurship*, Chicago: University of Chicago Press.

Kirzner, I.M. (1979) *Perception, Opportunity and Profit: Studies in the Theory of Entrepreneurship*, Chicago: University of Chicago Press.

Kirzner, I.M. (1997) 'Entrepreneurial Discovery and Competitive Market Processes: An Austrian Approach', *Journal of Economic Literature*, 35.

Kirzner, I.M. (1999) 'Creativity and/or Alertness: A Reconsideration of the Schumpeterian Entrepreneur', *Review of Austrian Economics*, 11.

Klepper, S. (1996) 'Entry, Exit, Growth and Innovation over the Product Life Cycle', *American Economic Review*, 86(3).

Knight, F. (1921) *Risk, Uncertainty and Profit*, Chicago: University of Chicago Press.

Lambson, V.E. (1991) 'Industry Evolution with Sunk Costs and Uncertain Market Conditions', *International Journal of Industrial Organisations*, 9.

Matlay, H. (2002) 'Training and HRD Strategies in Family and Non-Family Owned Small Business: A Comparative Approach', *Education and Training*, 44.

McGovern, P., Smeaton, D. and Hill, S. (2004), 'Bad Jobs in Britain: Non-standard Employment and Job Quality', *Work and Occupations*, 31.

Menger, C. (1871/1981) *Principles of Economics*, New York: New York University Press.

OECD (2008) *Measuring Entrepreneurship: A Digest of Indicators*, Paris: OECD. Available on www.oecd.org.

Penrose, E.T. (1959) *The Theory of the Growth of Firms*, Oxford: Basil Blackwell.

Ram, M. and Edwards, P. (2003) 'Praising Caesar Not Burying Him – What We Know About Employment in Small Firms', *Work, Employment and Society*, 17(4).

Say, J.B. (1803) *Trait d'Economie Politique ou Simple Exposition de la Manière dont se Forment, se Distribuent, et se Consomment les Riches*; revised (1819); translated (1830) by R. Prinsep, *A Treatise on Political Economy: On Familiar Conversations on the Manner in Which Wealth is Produced, Distributed and Consumed by Society*, Philadelphia: John Grigg and Elliot. See also Resources for Say at cepa.newschool.edu/het/profiles/say.htm.

Say, J.B. (1817) *Catechisme d'Economie Politique*, translated (1821) by John Richter, *Catechism of Political Economy*, London: Sherwood, Neely & Jones.

Schumacher, E.F. (1974) *Small is Beautiful*, London: Abacus.

Schumpeter J.A. (1928) 'The Instability of Capitalism', *Economic Journal*, 38.

Schumpeter J.A. (1934) *The Theory of Economic Development: An Inquiry into Profits, Capital, Credit and Interest and the Business Cycle* (trans. R. Opie), Cambridge, MA: Harvard University Press. (First published in 1911 as *Theorie der Wirtschaftlichen Entwicklung*, Munich and Leipzig: Dunker und Humblat).

Shapero, A. (1975) 'The Displaced, Uncomfortable Entrepreneur', *Psychology Today*, 8.

Shapero, A. (1984) 'The Entrepreneurial Event', in C. Kent (ed.) *Environment for Entrepreneurship*, Lexington, MA: DC Heath.

Shapero, A. (1985) 'Why Entrepreneurship?', *Journal of Small Business Management*, 23(4).

Storey, D. and Greene, F.J. (2010) *Small Business and Entrepreneurship*, Harlow: Pearson Education.

Storey, D. and Sykes, N. (1996) 'Uncertainty, Innovation and Management', in P. Burns and J. Dewhurst (eds), *Small Business and Entrepreneurship*, London: Macmillan – now Basingstoke: Palgrave Macmillan.

Storey, D., Keasey, K., Watson, R. and Wynarczyk, P. (1987) *The Performance of Small Firms, Profits, Jobs and Failure*, London: BCA.

Timmons, J.A. (1999) *New Venture Creation: Entrepreneurship for the 21st Century*, Boston: Irwin/McGraw-Hill.

Walters, D. (2001) *Health and Safety in Small Enterprise*, Oxford: PIE Peter Lang.

Wynarczyk, P., Watson, R., Storey, D.J., Short, H. and Keasey, K. (1993) *The Managerial Labour Market in Small and Medium Sized Enterprises*, London: Routledge.

CONTROL & RESISTANCE

Asked what the secret of successful automotive management was, a senior General Motors executive replied, 'Control. Deal control. Product control. Labour control.'

(Quoted in Huczynski, 1993: 185)

The aims of this chapter are to:

- ⊚ Assert the significance of control against a tendency of mainstream analyses to present it as marginal or of diminishing relevance.
- ⊚ To elaborate critical perspectives on control, particularly those that derive from labour process theory and its emphasis on a variety of managerial strategies within the contested terrain of the workplace.
- ⊚ To examine various objections to labour process concepts and to make a qualified defence of them.
- ⊚ To discuss and evaluate more recent research on control, particularly those that argue for a decisive shift towards surveillance and self-discipline, ultimately pointing to patterns of continuity as well as change.

Yet why and how is strongly contested between mainstream and critical approaches. This chapter examines contrasting perspectives on understanding control. It is primarily about conceptualisation rather than current evidence of the *outcomes* of control strategies and techniques.

MAINSTREAM MIS/UNDERSTANDINGS

The treatment of control in mainstream writing is ambiguous at best, marginal at worst. Frameworks that assume goal consensus can often simply ignore or trivialise the issue. When it is discussed explicitly in standard textbooks, the chapters devoted to it are sometimes of a rather bizarre nature in almost omitting any reference to conflicts between groups. The talk is of technical inputs and outputs in a self-adjusting system, performance standards and feedback mechanisms. It is also seen in a unitary way: 'controlled performance' with an assumption of goal-consensus. Control is reduced to a *monitoring* device, with management's role to check progress, ensure that actions occur as planned, correct any deviation, or reassure us that what we are doing is appropriate (O'Reilly and Chatman, 1996). Some writers (Lawlor, 1976) put an emphasis on people desiring control, for example getting enjoyment from dependence on higher authority. This is the other side of the coin from attributing control to the pathological desires of particular individuals – those that are described as 'control freaks'. Resistance is smuggled in occasionally when discussing the *behavioural* implications as people 'react' to control processes, requiring management to adjust strategies accordingly.

This apparent absence of control from the mainstream is, however, somewhat misleading. The issues are there but they are articulated in different language and concepts. As the influential mainstream writer Pfeffer notes, 'control is at once the essential problem of management and organisation and the implicit focus of much of organisation studies' (1997: 100). The key term here is *implicit*. When control is discussed it is often alongside co-ordination. Any complex division of labour requires mechanisms to set goals, allocate responsibilities and evaluate the effectiveness of performance. Co-ordination is a more neutral term than control and more compatible with an assumption that management is a largely neutral set of techniques and competencies.

Even when texts do have chapters with control in the title, they often pass over quickly into other issues such as job design, organisational structure or leadership. In the first instance, debate is focused on designing structures which facilitate levels of control and co-ordination appropriate to types of work that require different levels of discretion and standardisation. In the second, discussion of leadership styles such as the classic polarity of authoritarian versus democratic is a way of discussing control, but through the language of influence and motivation. So what is described in mainstream writing as technical and human organisation and the need to integrate the two could be alternatively thought of in terms of competing control systems. For example, in their historical survey of American managerial discourse, Barley and Kunda (1992) distinguish between rational (for example, scientific management, systems theories) and normative (for example, human relations, organisational culture) ideologies of control. Rather than one simply displacing another, there are successive and alternate waves paralleling broad cycles of economic expansion and contraction.

We do accept that not all control processes arise from, or are structured by, antagonistic interests. Stock inventories and financial budgeting are necessary and not always conflictual features of any system of work organisation. A written job description may under certain conditions actually allow employees to assert power or control. But most control processes remain difficult to separate from the social relations of work, even when they appear to be neutral. This was the important conclusion of Blau and Schoenherr (1971), who used the concept of *insidious* controls to highlight the way in which management can utilise impersonal and unobtrusive means. Examples include selective recruitment of staff whose sense of professionalism or expertise enables them to work without direct controls; use of resource allocation as a financial discipline; and controls embodied in technology. Thus even those staff who exercise considerable work autonomy, such as those in higher education, have a series of indirect constraints over their actions.

In practice mainstream theory is more uncomfortable with its own marginalisation of control than the above discussion might suggest. The simple indication of that can be seen in the frequency with which the death of Taylorism or bureaucracy is announced. Implicit in these pronouncements is the recognition that control does exist, but the preference that it *shouldn't*. From the human relations writers of the 1950s, with their distinctions between (bad) theory X and (good) theory Y, to the advocates of 1970s-style job enrichment, control has been presented as unnecessary and outdated. Democratic leadership styles and autonomous workgroups have been seen as the basic precondition for job satisfaction and high productivity. Recent formulations have moved the debate further on. It is said that we now live in a world where change is so frequent and expertise so fundamental to the work process that 'command and control' is not merely undesirable, it is actually bad for business.

Picking up on themes from the academic literature (Walton, 1985), the editor of a Scottish business journal asserts that:

> The pyramidal, hierarchical school of management is, at long last, being dragged to its knees and kicked to death. Command and control is not an option in what is rapidly becoming an economy founded on knowledge and the skills of those who have it. In such an economy it seems employees will have to be involved in strategic decision-making if organisational goals are to be achieved.

(B. Millar, *Scottish Business Insider*, October 1998)

The language of contemporary management theory and practice has therefore been based around two axes: empowerment and commitment. The former suggests that organisations are delegating control to project groups and work teams, so that they become *self*-managing; the latter implies that values rather than rules have become the prime means of co-ordination. As indicated earlier, it is not our intention to examine these claims at this point. We will merely observe that they represent a continued evasion of the relevant issues. Control is either rhetorically abolished or presented in softer, more neutral terms. One of the problems with such approaches is their aspirational nature and the subsequent tendency to conflate prescription and description. Take, for example, the empowerment literature. In an incisive review, Hales (2000: 503) comments that, 'the burgeoning prescriptive or celebratory literature is replete with conceptions of empowerment which display equivocation, tautology and contradiction in equal measure'. He suggests that it is not clear whether power is to be achieved or received, what kind of powers are being enhanced (voice in decisions or choice over actions?), or the extent to which individuals or teams are expected to exercise delegated responsibilities. Such ambiguities tend to be terms – such as 'directed autonomy' – that paper over in words what is likely to be contradictory in practice (Waterman, 1988). Mainstream theory lacks conceptual frameworks that are robust enough to deal with the nature, types and levels of control. For this we have to turn elsewhere.

CRITICAL PERSPECTIVES: LABOUR PROCESS THEORIES OF CONTROL AND RESISTANCE

Pfeffer rightly observes that 'the ambivalence about the effects (if not the effectiveness) of social control is in part responsible for the development of a critical perspective on organisations and their control practices' (1997: 135). In contrast to mainstream theorists, radical writers on organisation and management frequently *begin* from an analysis of control relations. Whereas mainstream perspectives treat control and co-ordination together, radical theorists argue that management performs a *dual* function in the enterprise (Carchedi, 1977; R. Edwards, 1979). Managerial practices are a necessary means of *co-ordinating* diverse activities, but they also bear the imprint of conflicting interests in the labour process, a conflict that reflects the unique nature of labour as a commodity. This orientation was reflected in the first radical text to make a major impact as organisation theory, which began by defining the theoretical rationale of organisational analysis: 'For this volume we have proposed as such an object the concept of organisation as control of the labour process' (Clegg and Dunkerley, 1980: 1). This framework derived from Marx's analysis of the capitalist labour process, which was updated and revitalised by Braverman (1974) and a range of other 'labour process' theorists discussed below.

All societies have labour processes, but under capitalism they have specific characteristics. The most significant is what Marx referred to as the transformation of labour power into labour. In other words, when capital purchases labour it has only a potential or capacity to work. To ensure profitable production, capital must organise the conditions under which labour operates to its own advantage. But workers pursue their own interests for job security, higher rewards and satisfying work, developing their own counter-organisation through informal job controls, restriction of output, and the like.

To resolve this problem, and because they are under competitive pressure from other firms to cut costs and raise productivity, employers seek to control the conditions under which work takes place. This argument is often misunderstood. Pfeffer says that Marxist analysis 'asserts that control, not efficiency, is the object of organising arrangements' (1997: 180). While radical approaches would challenge particular conceptions of efficiency, control is not an end in itself, but a means to transform the capacity to work, established by the wage relation, into profitable production. It is a term summarising a set of mechanisms and practices that regulates the labour process (P. K. Edwards, 1990). Richard Edwards (1979: 18) distinguishes three elements in any system of control:

1 direction and specification of work tasks
2 evaluation, monitoring and assessment of performance
3 the apparatus of discipline and reward to elicit co-operation and compliance.

Such elements may, however, be best described as detailed control, in that they are normally connected to immediate work processes, whereas general control refers to management's capacity to subordinate labour to their direction of the production process as a whole. This distinction made by P. K. Edwards (1990) and other writers is of significance in that it allows for recognition of tremendous variations in how detailed control is exercised. Such a model can even allow for employers giving workers significant discretion over tasks, as in semi-autonomous work groups, if it maintains their overall control. Control is also not absolute, but, at least at the immediate level, a contested relationship. Conflict is built into the wage–effort bargain, with even mainstream writers recognising that an employment contract outlining required performance runs up against employees with their own goals and wants. As each 'party' seeks to exert its influence over the formal and informal aspects of the employment relationship, the outcome is a constantly changing 'frontier of control' (Goodrich, 1975) or 'contested terrain' (R. Edwards, 1979).

This latter point illustrates the centrality of resistance to labour process analysis. Richard Edward's research shows how control and resistance exist in dialectical relation. In other words, forms of worker self-organisation and action stimulate management to develop control practices, out of which a systematic pattern might emerge (such 'strategies' are discussed in the next section). Over a period of time, workers learn new ways of resisting those practices, and so on. Labour process accounts became known as a 'control and resistance' model. One of the best illustrations came from the British researchers Edwards and Scullion (1982). Detailed case studies show how workers adapt their behaviour, through actions such as diverse as absence, labour turnover and sabotage to particular modes of control over work organisation or rewards. Equally, they are able to demonstrate how management develop policies and practices on issues such as the provision of overtime as a means of trying to counter powerful shop-floor controls. In another important contribution, Hodson (1995; 2001) examines a range of ethnographic studies to illustrate how forms of resistance, ranging from sabotage to pilferage, develop through openings created by managerial control systems.

What about the role of management? Claims of independent actors carrying out a neutral role are disputed by evidence concerning the top strata of management (Zeitlin, 1974). By their motivation, social background and connections, rewards and shareholdings in corporations, most managers are part of the capitalist class. While a useful corrective, this 'sociological' analysis is not the crucial point. For example, a number of entrepreneurs are from a traditional working-class background. But what matter are the structural location and functions in the organisation. If anything, entrepreneurs from this background tend to identify even more closely with their new role. These roles require management to carry out functions of control and surveillance, exercising hierarchical authority over workers separated from the means of production. While it is not always clear that it is possible to distinguish between a 'neutral' co-ordination and an 'antagonistic' control, managers do act as agents carrying out the 'global functions' of capital, functions which, were delegated as part of the bureaucratisation of production. The idea of agency conjures up rather crude images of conspiracies and empty vessels: 'In the capitalist system, the principal function of management is to exploit labour power to the maximum in order to secure profits for the owners of capital' (Berkeley Thomas, 1993: 61). But the generality 'to the maximum' is meaningless. There are only specific and diverse means through which the requirements of capital are brought about, in which management takes an active rather than predetermined role.

Critical analyses sometimes get tangled up in attempts to designate managers to precise class positions. This theme does not concern us here (though see Johnston, 1986 for a critical account). What is important is that we have available a framework for understanding management practices which provides an alternative to the dominant combination of behavioural and managerial revolution theories. The fact, for example, that executives of a large corporation have the formal status of employees is, as Braverman observes, merely the form given to the domination of capital in modern society:

> Their formal attribute of being part of the same payroll as the production workers, clerks and porters of the corporation no more robs them of the powers of decision and command over the others in the enterprise than does the fact that the general, like the private, wears the military uniform, or the pope and the cardinal pronounce the same liturgy as the parish priest.
>
> (Braverman, 1974: 405)

Instead of the separation of ownership and control, radical writers distinguish between real or economic ownership and agents holding actual possession (De Vroey, 1975; Carchedi, 1977). Managerial agents are governed by the external constraints imposed by the dynamics of competition and capital accumulation, with profitability remaining the crucial criteria through which the successful management work is judged. If anything, this is enhanced by property ownership and related forms of control becoming increasingly depersonalised with the rise of finance, pension funds and other institutional shareholders. Individual enterprises become 'simply units in a structure of intercorporate relations' (J. Scott, 1985: 142), the division of ownership and possession resulting in greater vulnerability for managers who know they may be removed from office (Holland, 1975). A structural analysis does not imply that the growth of new forms of managerial labour is irrelevant. The heterogeneity of management has increased with the sheer extent and diversity of delegated functions and the competing groups, such as accountants and engineers, who lay claim to them.

MANAGEMENT STRATEGIES

Critical perspectives have been conditioned by Braverman's (1974) argument that the twentieth century saw the tightening of managerial control, primarily through the application of Taylorist and scientific management strategies. Detailed evidence is provided of the extension of such methods from simple to complex production and its use in the transformation of clerical labour. When allied to managerial shaping of science and technology through mechanisation and automation, work design and organisation continue to embody key Taylorist principles such as task fragmentation and the separation of conception and execution. Braverman provided an important corrective to the widespread view that Taylorism was a failed system, superseded by more sophisticated behavioural theories to be used for motivational and job design tools (see M. Rose, 1975).

But it is widely recognised that Braverman overestimated the dominance of Taylorist strategies and practices, and underestimated the varied and uneven implementation, influenced by worker hostility, management suspicion and appropriateness to given environments. If Taylorism is taken to be part of a broader movement towards 'scientific' management focused on fragmentation of tasks and their subjection to increasing job measurement and evaluation, as well as the structuring of work processes so that skills and planning activities are located off the factory and office floors, then particular elements remain a highly significant component of control strategies, though seldom on their own.

Precisely because Braverman confused a particular system of control with management control in general, the question of *strategy* was put firmly on the agenda because of the resulting debate on alternatives. This is not to say that issues of strategy had no place in the existing organisational literature. How Chandler (1962) regarded strategy, defined as long-term planning and resource allocation to carry out goals, as the characteristic feature of the modern multidivisional firm. But control over employees was not systematically dealt with. Strategy has also been increasingly part of the agenda of the business policy and corporate management literature (Steiner and Miner, 1978). Radical perspectives differ from both in avoiding the prescriptive search for the 'best way'; remaining free to analyse what management does, rather than what it should do.

What of the alternative strategies raised in the labour process debate? As we noted earlier, Richard Edward's (1979) model is based on historically successive dominant modes of control, which reflect worker resistance and changing socio-economic conditions. A nineteenth-century system of *simple* or *personal* control by employers exercising direct authority gave way to more complex *structural* forms with the transition from small business, competitive capitalism to corporate monopolies. The first of these forms was *technical* control typified by the use of the assembly line that can pace and direct the labour process. The contradiction for management is that it created a common work experience and basis for unified shop-floor opposition. In contrast, a system of *bureaucratic* control, embedded in the social and organisational structure of the firm rather than in personal authority, offers management a means of re-dividing the workforce and tying it to impersonal rules and regulations. With his co-thinkers among radical economists (R. Edwards, Reich and Gordon, 1975; Gordon, Edwards and Reich, 1982), Edwards has also argued that employers consciously create *segmented* labour markets as a response to economic crises and as a divide-and-rule strategy, particularly using gender and race.

In contrast, Friedman (1977) rightly eschews the notion of stages, preferring to set out ideal types or strategic poles of responsible autonomy and direct control which run parallel throughout the history of capitalism. Each strategy generates its own inflexibilities in areas such as hiring and firing and task specification. The choice of strategy is governed by variations in the stability of labour and product markets, mediated by the interplay of worker resistance and managerial pressure. There is, however, an element of common ground in the belief that there has been a gradual historical tendency towards more consensual, integrative strategies; utilising internal markets, institutionalised rules and in some cases, work humanisation schemes. This is also the view of the other major control theorist, Burawoy (1979). He periodises the development of capitalist work organisation in terms of the transition from *despotic* to *hegemonic* regimes. The former involved relations of dependence and coercion that did not prove viable for capital or labour. Workers sought collective representation and social protection from the state. Capital also had an interest in state regulation of conflict and a minimal social wage that would boost purchasing power. The shift to hegemonic regimes was also based on an internal state in the workplace that provided an 'industrial citizenship', utilising grievance machinery and regulated bargaining which minimised likely resistance and class solidarity.

Subsequent events have not been kind to such models. The 1980s and 1990s have seen organisational restructuring based on downsizing and de-layering, the search for flexibility in work and employment, a move away from collective and joint regulation of the workplace and a growth in job insecurity. It is always possible, of course, to adjust the model, which Burawoy does by defining the new dominant factory regime as one of *hegemonic despotism*. This is not a return to arbitrary tyranny, but the apparently 'rational' power of a capital that is mobile across the globe, over the workforce (1985: 150). However, the problem is not just with specific projections, but linear thinking more generally. New conceptual categories of this nature merely illustrate the fundamental problem of the control theories we have been examining. Alternative strategies have been put on the map, but too often within what has been described as the 'panacea fallacy' (Littler and Salaman, 1982) or 'monism' (Storey, 1985), that is, the idea that capital always seeks and finds definitive and comprehensive modes of control as the solution to its problems. Admittedly, this is somewhat less true of Friedman, who in his own defence argues that responsible autonomy and direct control have in-built contradictions and are 'two directions towards which managers can move, rather than two predefined states between which managers choose' (1987: 3). But there is still a sense of a search for all-embracing categories, which have their parallels in behavioural theory, such as Etzioni's (1961) structures of compliance, or Schein's (1965) linear models of economic, social and complex man.

Nevertheless, the control debate sparked an extensive and useful amount of empirical work influenced by labour process theory. Early case studies tended to focus on reaffirmation of theses of deskilling and tighter controls (Zimbalist, 1979), or critiques of them highlighting mediating factors such as markets and worker resistance (Wood, 1982). Subsequent efforts were concerned to establish trends in their own right. Studies dealing with the introduction of new technology have stressed that deskilling and direct control represents only one of a range of management strategies (Wilkinson, 1986). Child's (1985) research shows even more clearly how ideas of strategy can be used, while recognising variations in goals and environments. He identified a variety of strategies including elimination of direct labour, sub-contracting, polyvalence or multi-tasking and job degradation. These were connected to an even wider set of influences, including those of national economic cycles, government policy and the culture of organisations.

Other research applied models to specific industries, but without any claims for universality. A good example is the use by researchers of Richard Edwards' control concepts. Murray and Wickham (1985) studied two Irish electronics factories employing mainly female semi-skilled workers, showing that direction, discipline and evaluation are all carried out according to explicit rules rather than direct controls. Supervisors do not monitor production performance and enforce discipline. This is left to inspectors on the basis of statistical records that can identify the operators responsible. Supervisors, however, are central to processes of evaluating the social character of the 'good worker' in order to facilitate promotion through the internal labour market. The elaborate and artificial hierarchy created at the plants meant that one third of workers had been promoted from the basic assembly grade, thus confirming Edwards's view that employees are given positive material reasons for complying with bureaucratic rules. More recently Callaghan and Thompson (2001) used the growth of call centres to revisit Edwards, observing the similarities between automated call distribution systems and previous descriptions of technical control in which managerial authority is embedded within supposed objective mechanisms of work distribution and measurement. We return to this issue and study in the final section of the chapter.

A further direction was to focus on specific strategies and processes of control such as recruitment policies (Fevre, 1986; Maguire, 1986; Winstanley, 1986; Callaghan and Thompson, 2002) that were neglected in an exclusive focus on the labour process. The most extensive research was initially carried out on *gender*. Socially-defined notions of femininity as a form of control have been observed in multinationals operating in the third world (Pearson, 1986). Plant management consciously exploits cultures of passivity and subordination by combining an image of the company as a patriarchal family system with the manager as father figure, Western-style beauty competitions and classes (Grossman, 1979). In the West, Grieco and Whipp's overview argues that 'managerial strategies of control make use of and enhance the sexual divisions in society' (1985: 136). Studies of office and factory workers (Glenn and Feldberg, 1979; Pollert, 1981; Westwood, 1984; Bradley, 1986) show that management uses women's marginality to work, arising from the family, to frame its labour control policies.

In reflecting on the above debates, a degree of common ground emerged. Product and labour markets, worker resistance and a range of other external and internal factors are recognised as mediating control strategies and shaping power relations in the frontier of control between capital and labour. The variations in strategy that result are not random, but reflect the fundamental tension we have talked of between management's need to control and discipline, while engaging workers' commitment and co-operation. Strategies therefore contain inherent contradictions (Storey, 1985; Hyman, 1987). These are enhanced by the difficulty of harmonising the different managerial functions, sites of intervention and decision-making, which includes technology, social organisation of labour and relations with the representative bodies of employees. Hyman notes that 'there is no "one best way" of managing these contradictions, only different routes to partial failure' (1987: 30). Management of large organisations is therefore likely to try combinations of control strategies and practices, appropriate to particular environments or sections of the workforce. As one of us has remarked elsewhere:

> The most consistent weakness of existing theory has been to counterpoise one form of control to another. ... No one has convincingly demonstrated that a particular form of control is necessary or inevitable for capitalism to function successfully.

(Thompson, 1989: 151)

Whatever the limitations of the ideas, as Pfeffer notes, 'labour process theorists have been enormously influential in stimulating a discussion of work place control, not from the point of view of organisational efficiency or management but from the point of view of its determinants and its effects on workers' (1997: 184). The above 'consensus' fails to satisfy those within and outside the radical perspective, who are critical of the explanatory power of concepts concerned with management control strategy. For some, the problem with a Marxist-influenced agenda is that, like more orthodox accounts, it wrongly assumes high levels of rationality, this time applied to top management (Bryman, 1984: 401; Grint, 1995: 51). Others go beyond the previously noted criticism of 'panacea fallacies' to object to the treatment of management as omniscient, omnipotent and monolithic. Based on her study of chemical plants, Harris mocks the image of managers who have the attributes of deity and 'papal inerrancy' when dealing with workers, commenting that radical writers assume that senior management 'always know what is in capital's interests and unfailingly order things so that they work together for its greater good' (1987: 70). There are conflicts within management reflecting contending interest groups and the difficulty of carrying out integrative functions. Nor is it always possible to draw a neat dividing line from workers given that managers are also wage labourers subject to controls. The distortions in such analyses are held to derive from a wider determinism and functionalism in which 'managers are regarded as unproblematic agents of capital who dispatch their "global functions" in a rationalistic manner' (Storey, 1985: 195).

Capital's interests are not given and management practices cannot be 'read-off' from them. Assumptions of a 'tight-coupling' underestimate the diversity and complexity of such practices, and the significance for decision-making processes within the enterprise. It is also the case that in addition to the responsibilities that managers have to the control apparatus of the enterprise, they need to control their own personal identities and make sense of their own work in the employing organisation. Managerial work therefore has a 'double control' aspect in which there is a strategic exchange between individuals and organisations (Watson, 1994). The consequence of the above critiques is the belief that too few insights are generated into what 'flesh and blood' managers actually do.

At a general level many of these criticisms would be accepted across a wide spectrum. But some carry it much further: 'current uses of the terms "strategy" and "control" are somewhat misleading guides both to actual management conduct and to the causes of particular outcomes in work organisation and industrial relations' (Rose and Jones, 1985: 82). We can break this down into two issues: do identifiable management strategies exist and are practices centred on controlling workers?

QUESTIONING STRATEGY

Those who argue against the idea of coherent strategies with a fixity of purpose believe that management activities are more likely to be piecemeal, unco-ordinated and fragmented, with at best a striving for logical incrementalism. Management is concerned primarily with 'keeping the show on the road' (Tomlinson, 1982: 128), corresponding with the 'realist' views discussed earlier.

Supportive research was outlined in areas such as work reorganisation schemes (Rose and Jones, 1985) and new technology and skills in engineering (Campbell and Currie, 1987). Any strategic capacity is held to be inevitably undermined by a plethora of sites of decision-making, varied objectives among different management specialists and interest groups, the need to smooth over diverse and contradictory practices, and the requirement of sustaining a consensual accommodation with employee organisations. The result is an unpredictable variety of managerial intentions characterised by a 'plant particularism' (Rose and Jones, 1985: 96), and control structures as merely 'temporary outcomes' (Storey, 1985). Campbell and Currie plump for the idea of 'negotiated preferences' and there is a general orientation towards explanations based on *practices* rather than strategy.

Some of these differences may reflect the sector being researched. For example, engineering is well known for its 'seat-of-the-pants' approach to management, whereas other sectors such as food or chemicals are noted for more strategic methods. Nevertheless, this kind of approach is confirmed by some writers on industrial relations (Purcell and Sissons, 1983), who note the problems created by the absence of management strategies towards their own employees, particularly ones that are integrated into overall business objectives. Instead there is a continued dominance of reactive and opportunistic practices directed towards immediate problem solving (Thurley and Wood, 1983: 209). What *kind* of strategy is said to be absent is not always made explicit. But the basic model used is similar to that popularised by Chandler, which, like many other adaptations to the business sphere, is strongly influenced by military experience and terminology (Shaw, 1990). That is, it posits detailed and co-ordinated plans of campaign in which conscious, long-term planning based on corporate goals is supported by appropriate courses of action and allocation of resources. This can be seen in the business policy debate (Steiner and Miner, 1978; Porter, 1980) in which generations of students are warned of the negative consequences of the absence of corporate strategy, and scholars debate different models of structure, strategy and competitiveness. Similarly, standard models of strategic HRM emphasise the need for coherence and integration both within its component parts and with wider business strategy (Tichy *et al.*, 1982). Indeed, HRM is sometimes seen only to offer something new if it has strategic value (Kamoche, 1994).

The problem with mainstream notions of strategy is that it is all too easy to counter textbook ideal types of coherence and integration with the messy reality of real companies and sectors. The insights of social science have been applied to demonstrate how organisations muddle through rather than plan rationally. The promise of complete knowledge and controllable environments is seen as neither desirable nor feasible in fragmented, turbulent, postmodern times. As a result, in the last decade strategy has gone from buzzword to boo-word. It has been 'problematised' to the point that the concept is no longer fashionable even in strategic management circles (for a useful overview, see Whipp, 1996). Complaining that discourses of strategy are primarily about shoring up the power of senior managers and consultants, Knights and Morgan reject the concept altogether: 'Nothing new is really added by talking the discourse of strategy; on the contrary, a limit is put on our understanding of the special phenomenon because we are forcing action into a particular rationalistic and individualistic framework' (1990: 480).

But conceptions of management strategy in the above frameworks are in themselves problematic. A stereotyped polarity is set up between a conception of objective rationality that implies perfect foresight, choice and follow-through; and a bounded rationality of constrained choice in complex realities. Too often the critics collude in forcing action into a conceptual straitjacket. By adopting a straw man of 'strong' strategy, they have set criteria for strategy so stringently that it becomes impossible to meet them (Child, 1985). While it is wrong to attribute coherent, rational intent to management, it is equally mistaken to assume that strategy has to be seen as always consistent, systematic and without contradiction. Strategies may not always be effectively followed through at the implementation stage, as with the introduction of new technology. They may not constitute a coherent package for the whole operations of a company, perhaps manifesting a disjuncture between job design plans and employee relations. Coherence is an important variable, but it has to be set against the knowledge of inevitable contradictions and the likelihood of 'loose-coupling' between planning and practices. Strategies are likely to be accompanied by bargaining within management and with the workforce, so making the end result uncertain. As Friedman rightly notes, 'Irrationality, inconsistency, lack of system certainly exist and must be allowed for; however, a more useful concept to introduce is failure' (1987: 294). Even where changes are introduced without clear intent, they can establish the preconditions for subsequent strategy (Hyman, 1987: 47).

While managers frequently act on the world with poor information, they can and do act strategically. It is only necessary for researchers to show a degree of intent or planning, and to infer a logic over a period of time from the frequency and pattern of action, or from 'emergent outcomes' (Hales, 1988: 12). Boxall and Purcell make a similar point in a different way: 'It is possible to find strategy in every business because it is embedded in the important choices the managers and staff of the firm make about what to do and how to do it' (2003: 28). The same criteria apply to the activities of workers. Groups such as printers or doctors do not always behave in a fully conscious or coherent manner. But observation reveals a clear pattern of occupational and job controls, and strategies of closure aimed at excluding competitors, often women (Cockburn, 1983; Witz, 1986). The latter point reinforces research on households that shows that strategies emerge from 'bottom-up', day-to-day activities – a weaker, but still legitimate sense of strategy that relies on social scientists observing and analysing predictable patterns (Wallace, 1993).

Of course, the capacity for strategy is not random. Certain external conditions are likely to push management in that direction. Streek (1987) puts forward a persuasive case that economic crisis and rapidly changing market environments have created a 'general strategic problem' whose core element is the need for *flexibility*. However, the very nature of uncertainty and varied conditions in sectors and countries produces different strategic responses. For example, countries such as Germany and Austria with traditions of tripartite state, union and employer bargaining have seen moves towards economic liberalisation and labour flexibility that retain a strong union role and corporatist regulation of wages, labour and product markets. The hostility of all economic actors in Germany to the prospective takeover of telecommunications giant Mannesman by a UK competitor in 1999 was a case in point. Streek's analysis not only builds in an explanation of such variations, but it also provides a framework for understanding the general conditions under which strategies develop. At times of crisis and readjustment, 'the variety of strategies and structures within the collectivity of firms is bound to increase at least until a new standard of "best practice" has been established' (1987: 284). In other words, there is always ebb and flow in intensity and direction of organisational practices, but strategic patterns do emerge and can be observed, particularly in the cauldron of highly internationalised sectors where a small number of giants compete for dominance.

QUESTIONING CONTROL OVER LABOUR

The second strand of critique questions whether the centrality given to control of labour is actually reflective of managerial behaviour. It is argued that we cannot view management strategies and tactics from the vantage point of the labour process, but must consider the role of product and labour markets, and technologies. Control proceeds in a complex cycle from planning to implementation, involving groups such as accountants and industrial engineers. It is also true that labour costs may be only a relatively small proportion of the total, particularly in capital-intensive industries, so the emphasis of managerial controls may be elsewhere. With such factors in mind, some argue that analysis should focus on the 'multiple constituents' of management expertise beyond the confrontation of capital and labour in the control of the work-place (Miller and O'Leary, 1987: 10). Such a critique can be presented in a Marxist form. Accumulation and costs of production are what matter to capital and its agents, not control. If anything, managers are dominated by problems of the *outcomes* of the labour process, including sales, marketing, supply and cash flow. Kelly uses the concept of the full circuit of capital to argue that we must be concerned not only with the *extraction* of surplus value through controlling the labour process, but its *realisation* through the sale of commodities, as well as the prior *purchase* of labour. On these grounds, 'there is no sound reason for privileging any moment in the circuit' (1985: 32).

Morgan and Hooper used a similar framework in their research into the Imperial Tobacco Group in the 1970s to distinguish between three circuits of capital. *Industrial* capital refers to that used in the management and design of the production process itself; *commercial* to the sphere of buying and selling and therefore functions such as marketing and advertising; and *banking* to the process of capital used in lending and borrowing, governed by accountancy and financial controls.

These distinctions are used to argue that critical theories of the labour process have often lost sight of the role of capital and ownership because of the emphasis on management control. The case study shows a series of strategies pursued in tandem, representing the particular circuits. To break out of a static tobacco market, top management prioritised commercial and banking strategies, rather than developing existing labour processes. In particular, companies such as Imperial were drawn into investments in the share and gilts markets. These proved successful, but when the resultant money was invested in production this had disastrous results. Firms are thus conceptualised as 'sites of a complex integration of circuits of capital' (Morgan and Hooper, 1987: 623), which management must integrate and control. This takes us back to the opening quote of the chapter in which the General Motors executive was seeking control in a number of spheres.

During this period of debate, other writers questioned whether control can be regarded as the factor that distinguishes between a dominant management and a subordinate labour. Management has non-control functions and characteristics of employees, while workers exercise job controls and may be involved in the regulation of others (Melling, 1982: 249). At a more theoretical level, Cressey and MacInnes (1980) observe that workers have an interest in the viability of their own units of capital as well as resisting subordination, matching capital's dual relationship with labour as a commodity and as a source of co-operation necessary for profitable production. Some mainstream writers use their own research into the chemical industry (Harris, 1987) and those of chemicals, engineering and biscuits (Buchanan, 1986) to argue that workers basically accept managerial authority, give commitment and effort willingly, and have convergent interests with management, thus negating any preoccupation with control. This is likely to be linked to a rejection of 'zero-sum' conceptions of power in which one side necessarily gains at the expense of the other (Harris, 1987: 77). Even some radical writers believe that capital and management are not necessarily dominant, with unions having considerably more power, even in a recession, than usually acknowledged (Kelly, 1985: 49; Rose and Jones, 1985: 101).

It is certainly true that, as Hyman observes; 'If most orthodox literature on business strategy ignores or marginalises the conflict between capital and labour, most Marxist literature perceives nothing else' (1987: 34). This has a curious parallel with the virtual total emphasis in organisation behaviour on 'man-management'. So the full circuit of capital is a very useful and necessary concept for understanding the capitalist enterprise. Furthermore, change and crisis often arise from disarticulation of the moments of the circuit (Kelly, 1985), as we saw in the Imperial example. Such concepts can be combined with more orthodox accounts of the changing pattern of *corporate control* which plot how large firms seek to solve their competitive problems by reshaping structures and forms of intervention in the market (Fligstein, 1990). Such 'modes of control' have included vertical and horizontal integration, the multidivisional form and, more recently, financial means of integrating diverse portfolios built up through acquisition.

However, these perspectives do not invalidate a specific emphasis on relations of control between capital and labour. This is not just another process equivalent to marketing or financial accounting. The management of workers and work remains at the heart of the enterprise and indeed of economic reproduction as a whole. But such an orientation need have no marginalising effect on the analysis of other social relations. As P. K. Edwards (1990) observes, the problem of 'privileging' one part of the circuit arises only if the analysis assumes that this one part determines what happens in the others.

As we made clear at the start of the chapter, we are not saying that control is normally the *goal* of management, but rather a *means* embodied in strategies and techniques. It is true that management strategies are not always developed with labour's role in mind. But it is ultimately difficult to separate a concern with 'outcomes' such as product quality of financial targets from acting on labour in some way. Strategies towards markets or technologies will often be constrained or mediated by labour policies and the practices of workers (Friedman, 1987). In addition, as Child notes, 'strategies which are unspecific towards the labour process may still have relevance for it' (1985: 110). An example is the introduction of new technology which, much research shows, is frequently used as a means of more general work reorganisation. Finally, irrespective of the detail of arguments about the outcomes of high-performance work systems, it is widely accepted that labour productivity is the most appropriate measure of human resource management of the firm (Boxall and Purcell, 2003: 8). Given the inherently incomplete nature of employment contracts, a strong focus on labour controls – of various types – is an inevitable corollary, particularly in a mainly labour-intensive service economy.

On the issue of the existence of co-operation and common interests, we would wholly concur. In fact we would go further. As one of us has observed: 'Workers do not always need to be overtly controlled. They may effectively "control" themselves' (Thompson, 1989: 153). Participation in routine practices to create interest or increase rewards can generate *consent* to existing structures of control and power, as Burawoy's (1979) famous studies of production 'games' indicate. What is puzzling is why some writers insist on co-operative and consensual processes being counterposed to those of control and conflict. It is increasingly recognised that all have to be theorised as different products of the contradictory relations within the enterprise. Not only do consent and control coexist; 'the mobilisation of consent' through culture strategies forms an increasingly central part of management–employee relations strategies in many sectors.

We also accept that workers exercise controls, but it would be a serious mistake to regard them as *equivalent* to those of management. This would fail to distinguish between *types* of control, particularly between the general and detailed dimensions.

At the general level of direction of production, managerial dominance is guaranteed by their stewardship of the crucial organisational resources. This is not 'zero-sum' because it cannot be 'added up'. Clearly, however, control of immediate work processes is largely zero-sum, in that if workers control a given item, then management cannot also do so (P. K. Edwards, 1990).

NEW DIRECTIONS – SURVEILLANCE AND SHIFTING THE LOCUS OF CONTROL

Having gone through successive forms of criticism concerning ideas of control strategy, the more recent period has seen the emphasis move back to new accounts of control. Some of these arise from empirical shifts in work and employment. For example, the growth of front-line service work means that the *customer* may mediate the standard management–worker dyad, providing information on employees, and directing their behaviour or values (Frenkel *et al.*, 1999; Sturdy *et al.*, 2001). The most significant challenge to established labour process frameworks, however, comes from the argument that the locus of control has shifted from external to internal. We have already identified one version of this earlier in the chapter. A move to seeking employee commitment can be seen as a form of *internalised control* that does not rely on external rewards and sanctions, or rule-following. Cultural controls rely primarily on acceptance of values and peer enforcement. In one of the earliest contributions, Ray (1986) argued that control by corporate culture was the last frontier, in that it had enabled organisations to generate sentiment and emotion, simultaneously internalising control and linking personal with corporate identity. It is argued that the expansion of work that has a higher discretionary content and more ambiguity leads management to give less direction and elicit more reciprocated trust through 'info-normative control' (Frenkel *et al.*, 1995).

At this stage we want to concentrate on a parallel argument about a shifting locus, this time with the emphasis on surveillance replacing, or becoming the dominant mechanism of, control. On the surface this does not appear to be consistent with an internalised direction. After all, surveillance is normally associated with collecting and storing information, using it to monitor behaviour and establish discipline (Dandeker, 1990). However, the argument is less about mechanisms than their *effects*. Case studies (Zuboff, 1988; Sewell and Wilkinson, 1992; Sewell, 1998) of high-tech manufacturing make much of the enhanced capacity of management to collect, display and attribute performance data through electronic surveillance. Because stockpiles of labour and parts are eliminated through quality (TQM) and just-in-time (JIT) systems, production arrangements are highly visible. The information is generated from and fed back through teams of employees that appear to have autonomy, but in practice internalise production norms and discipline themselves through systems such as Nissan's 'Neighbour Watch' (Garrahan and Stewart, 1992). Such information is unobtrusive and perceived to be objective, therefore accentuating its legitimacy. Teams may produce self-surveillance independently of an information-driven process. Delegated responsibilities, whether for routine production decisions or, more exceptionally, induction and evaluation of team members, mean that employees have to develop their own disciplinary 'rules', thus collaborating with management to identify and reward the 'good worker' (Barker, 1993; McKinlay and P. Taylor, 1996). Such studies argue that as a consequence of such discipline and the removal of any 'slack' from the production system, 'worker counter-control (in the sense described by Roy and many others) is effectively eliminated... the ultimate goal of management under a TQM/JIT regime must be recognised to be Total Management Control' (Delbridge, Turnbull and Wilkinson, 1992: 105).

The growth of call centres has also boosted new theories of control. Surveillance undoubtedly plays a pivotal role in the way that integrated telephone and computer technologies facilitate the access and retrieval of data in the service interaction between desk-bound employee and external customer. Of particular importance is a sophisticated capacity remotely to record and assess the speed and 'quality' of the work. Not only are performance data made public, but also a proportion of the calls will be monitored remotely and used to reward and discipline employees. As a result, the previously identified 'objectivity' of the statistics is combined with constant, but unseen surveillance. Not only do employees internalise controls, but also the controllers are redundant: 'In call centres the agents are constantly visible and supervisor's power has indeed been "rendered perfect" – via the computer monitoring screen – and therefore its actual use unnecessary' (Fernie and Metcalf, 1997: 29).

In the most developed theorisation of such trends, Sewell (1998) argues that the interaction of 'vertical' electronic surveillance and 'horizontal' peer-group scrutiny has produced a new model of control, countering the optimistic gloss of the empowerment and team literatures, while moving beyond the limits of traditional labour process theory. The implication of Sewell's argument is that such a combination solves the direct control/responsible autonomy dilemma that has historically troubled generations of managers, to say nothing of management theorists.

Surveillance is not a new phenomenon, many writers have described the early factory in terms of the attempted subordination and surveillance of recalcitrant workers, using the work of historians to illustrate how employers used new systems of rules and control techniques to induce 'appropriate' morals and work habits. In the most detailed examination of the issues, Dandeker (1990) links surveillance primarily to processes of bureaucratic rationalisation that have developed throughout this century. By 1990, 10 million workers in the US, including many professional and managerial employees, had become subject to electronic performance monitoring (Pfeffer, 1997: 114). Given these trends and recent socio-technical systems, it is difficult to deny that *some* shift towards electronic and self-surveillance has taken place in *some* industries.

Whether this constitutes an overarching development requiring an entirely new conceptualisation is a different matter. Many practices highlighted in the manufacturing case studies were identified by earlier writers making a critique of lean production (Parker and Slaughter, 1988b). Yet they were described as a form of work intensification – 'management by stress' – in other words, more a shift in the effort bargain than the frontier of control. The idea that electronic surveillance is unobtrusive is a strange one. Performance display is characterised by its visibility to management and employees. It can therefore only be unobtrusive if the information it relays is accepted as objective. Yet there is considerable evidence that employees challenge the accuracy of the data, or use them for their own purposes against management (Zuboff, 1988; Bain and P. Taylor, 2000).

Call centres are clearly a new development, but do we need new concepts to explain them? Callaghan and Thompson (2001) argue that Richard Edwards' control framework provides better insights than recent 'electronic sweatshop' perspectives. His three dimensions of a system of control and distinction between stages of direct, technical and bureaucratic control strategies have been fully outlined earlier in the chapter. Call centres predominantly use a system of technical control. In terms of Edwards' first dimension, automated call distribution systems (ACD) enable management to direct the speed, direction and character of the work tasks. Technical control in call centres goes further than assembly lines in assisting companies to operationalise the second dimension – monitoring and evaluating performance. The performance of individuals and teams can be compared within or across sites. In turn that information can be linked to the apparatus of reward and discipline through the formal assessment and review process. One of the weaknesses of Edwards' framework is its linear nature. If this is dispensed with, we can see that his 'next' system – bureaucratic control – is used in call centres to define skills and tasks, and specify behavioural and performance standards. In the Callaghan and Thompson case study, Telebank has 19 core standards of behaviour and a 7-point scale to measure the skills of operators during appraisal, which is used to generate high and low scores. This indicates that many controls in the modern workplace remain external. To take another example, normative rules in strong culture companies may be different from traditional task-based control, but they are still rules. There is still the question of whether such rules are internalised. Management's sources and use of information may have increased, but there is little evidence that they are unobtrusive or regarded by employees as objective and unconnected to visible authority relations. Far from supervisory power being 'rendered perfect', there is evidence that customer service representatives (CSR) strongly dislike the emphasis put on 'the stats' and the disciplinary uses made of them (Bain and P. Taylor, 2000; Callaghan and Thompson, 2001). Employees distinguish between the 'friendly' supervision of coaching to improve skills and the disciplinary use of performance data. As with manufacturing, CSRs challenge the objectivity of the data and turn it against them: 'I check everything, I take it away and check it, I don't just sign it. I go back into the system, you can actually remember a lot of things when you go back in and see the name. I know that people have had arguments with the research section' (CSR quoted in Callaghan and Thompson, 2001: 32). Though individual, technology-paced working and remote surveillance makes resistance difficult, CSRs learn informally to manipulate the codes used to claim relief from work tasks, and become skilled in setting their own pace and variation from the company scripts when talking to customers (P. Taylor and Bain, 1998; S. Taylor, 1998; Callaghan and Thompson, 2001).

None of the above observations seeking to qualify 'shifts of locus' arguments are intended to deny that changes in the nature and frontier of controls have taken place. These have been recently summarised by Thompson and Harley (2007). Many of the conceptual confusions in analysis of workplace controls would be solved if it was recognised that new forms seldom wholly displace old ones. This is what Thompson and Harley refer to as continuity, in combination. Labour process and other perspectives accept that the normative sphere has been an expanding area of managerial practice, without endorsing the view that these have replaced or even marginalised the more traditional mechanisms of bureaucratic rationalisation, work intensification, or some features of scientific management. This can be seen in both the manufacturing and service sectors. With respect to the former, Japanese-style lean production has combined work intensification and multi-tasking under modified traditional methods, described by Adler as 'democratic Taylorism'. At the same time, management focuses more on the normative sphere in order to by-pass trade union representation and secure worker identification with broader organisational norms (Danford, 1998; Delbridge *et al.*, 2000). As for services, to return to the call centre example, surveillance and monitoring is intended to create an 'assembly line in the head' (P. Taylor and Bain, 1998). Through the work is organised in many ways around very traditional methods, to gain competitive advantage from service interactions, companies frequently seek to generate high commitment and shared identity through corporate cultures or teamworking (Thompson, van den Broek and Callaghan, 2004). The outcome is a distinctive form of high-commitment, low-discretion work system (Houlihan, 2002).

More generally, the outcome in modern work settings is increased hybridity of control structures as environments and organisational structures become more complex (Alvesson and Thompson, 2005). Even in knowledge-intensive industries large companies reply on combined and integrated control structures. A good example is provided in Alvesson and Kärreman's case study of a global consulting firm. The company directs much of its control practices towards 'cultural engineering' in order to shape employee identities and identifications. However, to close any gaps and minimise uncertainties, it also creates 'a vast bureaucratic and output measuring apparatus' (2004: 441), including extensive financial controls, standardised work procedures and formal HRM systems for recruitment, promotion and evaluating performance. The lesson drawn is that:

> Socio-ideological control is thus intimately tied to bureaucracy and output control. It is not, as claimed by most of the literature on control ... an alternative to the latter two, useful in situations where complexity and uncertainty make rules for prescribing behaviour and the precise measurement of results impossible.

(Alvesson and Kärreman, 2004: 441)

Interestingly, the authors note that the combined and reinforcing nature of these controls does not guarantee their effectiveness. For example, there was 'overwhelming evidence' that time reports from employees were faked. This brings us back to an earlier theme of the chapter: the linkages between managerial controls and worker resistance.

A FURTHER REFLECTION ON RESISTANCE

In this chapter we have shown numerous examples of the persistence of worker resistance, especially to new normative forms of control that focus on worker attitudes and emotions. Though different judgements are, in part, an outcome of how case study and survey evidence about the extent of worker buy-in to managerial norms is interpreted, it is also a dispute about concepts. Categories used to describe and explain resistance have been strongly influenced by the language and experience of industrial relations with its organised collective actors – trade unions, employers and the state. As Thompson and Ackroyd (1995) and Kelly (2005) have argued, the decline of formal organised conflicts such as strikes, alongside falling trade union membership, has too often been treated as synonymous with the decline and disappearance of conflict as such.

While the concept of worker resistance was an attempt to broaden the categories of description, much of the discussion focused on organised non-compliance in large manufacturing workplaces. Something even broader was needed and eventually supplied through Ackroyd and Thompson's (1999) analysis of 'organisation misbehaviour' (see also Ackroyd and Collinson, 2005; Ackroyd, 2008). Originally directed towards a critique of mainstream and radical views that emphasised the dominance of new forms of cultural control and electronic surveillance, it also acts as an integrated 'map' of worker action and agency focused on four resource territories that both management and employees try to 'appropriate': working time, working effort, the product of work and work identities. The term misbehaviour is used ironically to draw attention to what is missed and misunderstood by orthodox accounts that assume conformity of behaviour as the norm, and to signify counter-productive behaviour – anything you do at work that you are not supposed to do.

These traditions largely focus on conflicts around the effort bargain. The mapping of organisation misbehaviour reflects changes in workplace and academic politics by including identity in the multi-dimensional framework, thus rendering 'a whole new realm of workplace practice…visible' (Fleming, 2001: 191). Put another way, the expanded categories helped us to see a new contested terrain where managerial efforts to mobilise employee emotions, commitment and personality through cultural and socio-technical practices potentially clashes with worker identities and interests. The very ambition of some companies to mould employee identity through culture change programmes and mission statements often patently at odds with day-to-day workplace experience renders them vulnerable to employee cynicism that becomes a resource for resistance (Fleming and Spicer, 2002; Fleming, 2005). A good example is provided by Taylor and Bain's (2003) graphic account of how call centre workers use humour, not only as informal dissent, but in one case as part of a campaign for union recognition.

Despite the continuity with the traditions of industrial sociology and opening up of new territories for dissent, some researchers in a labour process tradition (Martinez and Stewart, 1997) have argued that the misbehaviour categories are too individualistic and accept at face value too much from the arguments about the decline of trade unions and collectivism. But Ackroyd and Thompson's intent was to expand the scope of concepts to understand dissenting and non-compliant activities at work, rather than to argue that the conditions for broader forms of collective action and organisation have diminished.

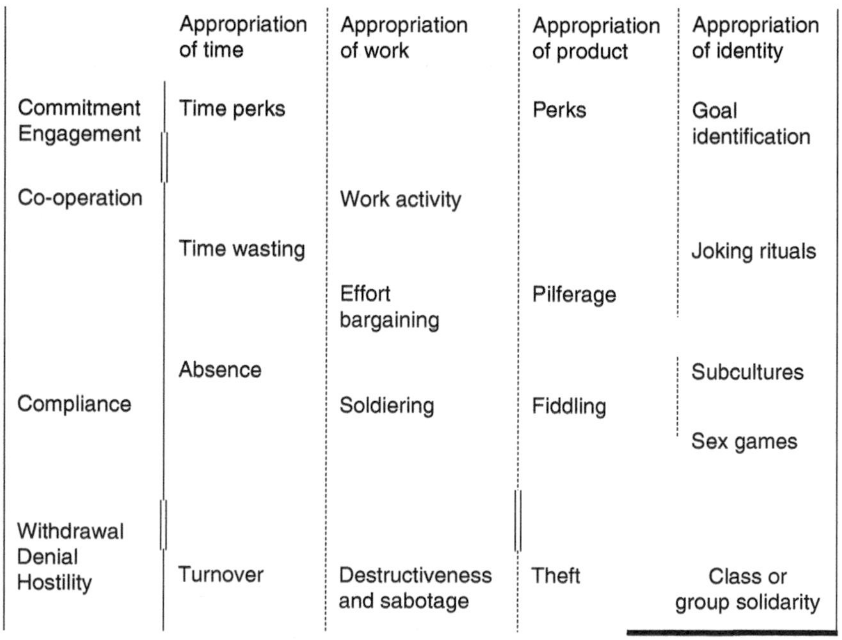

	Appropriation of time	Appropriation of work	Appropriation of product	Appropriation of identity
Commitment Engagement	Time perks		Perks	Goal identification
Co-operation		Work activity		
	Time wasting			Joking rituals
		Effort bargaining	Pilferage	
	Absence			Subcultures
Compliance		Soldiering	Fiddling	Sex games
Withdrawal Denial Hostility	Turnover	Destructiveness and sabotage	Theft	Class or group solidarity

Figure 11.1 – Mapping misbehaviour
Source: Reproduced with permission from S. Ackroyd and P. Thompson (1999) Organizational Misbehaviour, London: Sage.

SUMMARY AND KEY POINTS

In mainstream accounts, neither control nor resistance is treated as a substantial feature of organisational life, but largely as a failure of systems that are otherwise based on creativity, consensus and commitment. By analysing managerial control as a structural imperative of the capitalist labour process given that markets and formal contracts alone cannot deal with the gap between the potential of purchased labour and the desired profitable outcomes of that labour, LPT pushes the issue to centre stage. That perspective is not top down, but is a reciprocal model of control and resistance. Given both the general nature of divergent interests between capital and labour, plus the way that any control system builds up internal contradictions, the conditions for resistance are always present and tend to develop further over time. Nor is it a story solely about constraints on managers. LPT frames its accounts in terms of rival and/or changing strategies of control. Such strategies are seldom coherent in conception or content. But we can observe patterns of labour-control practices that form a significant, though far from sole, feature of the managerial repertoire. Because conditions change and employees learn to evade and exploit existing ways of doing things, control practices are inherently dynamic. In recent debates, considerable emphasis has been put on new forms based on surveillance, cultural engineering and self-discipline. The position taken in this chapter is that, though there has been some shift in the direction of policy, their intended effects – to encourage employees to internalise controls – is far from certain or complete. It is always wise not to confuse the formal capacities of technological and managerial systems with their actual usage and effectiveness. Control systems were never one-dimensional and now, given the diversity of challenges and conditions, their forms are more likely to be combined and hybrid in character. Like control, resistance also sometimes changes its form and content. We outlined some new ways of understanding such trends, drawing on Ackroyd and Thompson's mapping of organisational misbehaviour. This framework, though only part of the total picture, helps broaden our accounts of resistant and dissenting behaviours, while helping to explain their persistence in a context where others have proclaimed their demise. This is, however, not the end of some of these discussions. We shall return by a different route, to issues of culture.

FURTHER READING

The two Edwards, Richard and Paul, are a good starting point. *Contested Terrain* (R. Edwards, 1979) is probably the most influential book on control and resistance and is a very good read, while the UK-based contribution of P. K. Edwards and Scullion (1982) deserves to be better known. Hyman's (1987) journal article is still the best overview of labour process perspectives on control, an interpretation supported by the fact that it remains one of the most downloaded papers from *Work, Employment and Society* after 20+ years. Of the new Foucauldian-influenced accounts of control and surveillance, Sewell (1998) is deservedly the most influential, though you might also look at the critique by Thompson (2003b). On current debates on resistance, Ackroyd and Thompson's (and associated) various discussions of misbehaviour are a good starting point, and Taylor and Bain (2003) an excellent application to call centres. Hodson (2001) does a similar job, drawing on many of the same ethnographic labour process studies, but ties the discussion into wider issues of dignity at work. Alvesson and Kärreman's (2004) paper is a good example of a contemporary treatment of control that combines a range of concpets and theories discussed in this chapter.

Ackroyd, S. and Thompson, P. (1999) *Organizational Misbehaviour*, London: Sage.

Alvesson, M. and Kärreman, D. (2004) 'Interfaces of Control: Technocratic and Socio-ideological Control in a Global Management Consultancy Firm', *Accounting, Organizations and Society*, 29: 423–44.

Collinson, D. and Ackroyd, P. (2005) 'Resistance, Misbehaviour, Dissent', in S. Ackroyd, R. Batt, P. Thompson and P. Tolbert (eds.), *A Handbook of Work and Organization*, Oxford: Oxford University Press.

Edwards, P. K. (1986) *Conflict at Work: A Materialist Analysis of Workplace Relations*, Oxford: Blackwell.

Edwards, P. K. and Scullion, H. (1982) *The Social Organization of Industrial Conflict: Control and Resistance in the Workplace*, Oxford: Blackwell.

Hodson, R. (2001) *Dignity at Work*, Cambridge: Cambridge University Press.

Hyman, R. (1987) 'Strategy or Structure: Capital, Labour and Control', *Work, Employment and Society*, 1. 1: 25–55.

Sewell, G. (1998) 'The Discipline of Teams: The Control of Team-based Industrial Work through Electronic and Peer Surveillance', *Administrative Science Quarterly*, 43: 406–69.

Taylor, P. and Bain, P. (2003) 'Subterranean Worksick Blues: Humour as Subversion in Two Call Centres', *Organization Studies*, 24. 9: 1487–509.

Thompson, P. (2003) 'Fantasy Island: A Labour Process Critique of the "Age of Surveillance"', *Surveillance and Society*, 1. 2: 138–51.

Thompson, P. and Ackroyd, S. (1995) 'All Quiet on the Workplace Front? A Critique of Recent Trends in British Industrial Sociology', *Sociology*, 29. 4: 1–19.

REFERENCES

Ackroyd, S. (2008) 'Organisational Conflict', in Cooper, C.L. and Clegg, S.R. (eds), *Handbook of Organisational Behaviour*, London: Sage.

Ackroyd, P. and Collinson, D. (2005) 'Resistance, Misbehaviour, Dissent', in S. Ackroyd, S., R. Batt, R., P. Thompson, and P. Tolbert, P. (eds), *A Handbook of Work and Organization*, Oxford: Oxford University Press.

Ackroyd, S. and Thompson, P. (1999) *Organisational Misbehaviour*, London: Sage.

Adair, J. (1979) *Action-Centred Leadership*, London: Gower.

Alvesson, M. and Kärreman, D. (2004) 'Interfaces of Control. Technocratic and Socio-ideological Control in a Global Management Consultancy Firm', *Accounting, Organization and Society* 29: 423–44.

Alvesson, M. and Thompson, P. (2005) 'Post-Bureaucracy?', in S. Ackroyd, R. Batt, P. Thompson, and P. Tolbert, (eds) *A Handbook of Work and Organization*, Oxford: Oxford University Press.

Bain, P. and Taylor, P. (2000) 'Entrapped by the Electronic Panopticon? Worker Resistance in Call Centres', *New Technology, Work and Employment*, 15. 1: 2–18.

Barker, J. R. (1993) 'Tightening the Iron Cage: Concertive Control in Self-Managing Teams', *Administrative Science Quarterly*, 38: 408–37.

Barley, S. R. and Kunda, G. (1992) 'Design and Devotion: Surges of Rational and Normative Ideologies of Control in Managerial Discourse', *Administrative Science Quarterly*, 37: 363–99.

Berkeley Thomas, A. (1993) *Controversies in Management*, London: Routledge.

Blau, P. M. and Schoenherr, R. A. (1971) *The Structure of Organizations*, New York: Basic Books.

Boxall, P. and Purcell, J. (2003) *Strategy and Human Resource Management*, Basingstoke: Palgrave Macmillan.

Bradley, H. (1986) 'Work, Home and the Restructuring of Jobs', in K. Purcell, S. Wood, A. Watson and S. Allen (eds), *The Changing Experience of Employment, Restructuring and Recession*, London: Macmillan.

Braverman, H. (1974) *Labor and Monopoly Capital: The Degradation of Work in the Twentieth Century*, New York: Monthly Review Press.

Bryman, A. (1984) 'Organisation Studies and the Concept of Rationality', *Journal of Management Studies*, 21: 394–404.

Buchanan, D. (1986) 'Management Objectives in Technical Change', in D. Knights and H. Willmott (eds), *Managing the Labour Process*, Aldershot: Gower.

Burawoy, M. (1979) *Manufacturing Consent: Changes in the Labour Process Under Monopoly Capitalism*, Chicago: University of Chicago Press.

Callaghan, G. and Thompson, P. (2001) 'Edwards Revisited: Technical Control and Worker Agency in Call Centres', *Economic and Industrial Democracy*, 22: 13–37.

Callaghan, G. and Thompson, P. (2002) 'We Recruit Attitude: The Selection and Shaping of Call Centre Labour', *Journal of Management Studies*, 39. 2: 233–254.

Campbell, A. and Currie, B. (1987) 'Skills and Strategies in Design Engineering', paper presented to the Conference on the Labour Process, Aston-UMIST.

Carchedi, G. (1977) *On the Economic Identification of the Middle Classes*, London: Routledge & Kegan Paul.

Chandler, A. (1962) *Strategy and Structure: Chapters in the History of the Industrial Enterprise'* Cambridge, MA: MIT Press.

Child, J. (1985) 'Managerial Strategies, New Technology and the Labour Process', in D. Knights, H. Wilmott and D. Collinson (eds), *Job Redesign: Critical Perspectives on the Labour Process*, London: Gower.

Clegg, S. and Dunkerley, D. (1980) *Organisation, Class and Control*, London: Routledge & Kegan Paul.

Cockburn, C. (1983) *Brothers: Male Dominance and Technological Change*, London: Pluto.

Dandeker, C. (1990) *Surveillance, Power and Modernity: Bureaucracy and Discipline from 1700 to the Present Day*, Cambridge: Polity.

Danford, A. (1998) *Japanese Management Techniques and British Workers*, London: Mansell.

De Vroey, M. (1975) 'The Separation of Ownership and Control in Large Corporations', *Review of Radical Political Economics*, 7. 2: 1–10.

Delbridge, R., Lowe, J. and Oliver, N. (2000) 'Worker Autonomy in Lean Teams: Evidence from the World Automotive Components Industry', in S. Proctor and F. Mueller (eds), *Teamworking*, London: Macmillan.

Delbridge, R., Turnbull, P. and Wilkinson, B. (1992) 'Pushing Back the Frontiers: Management Control and Work Intensification under JIT/TQM Regimes', *New Technology, Work and Employment*, 7: 97–106.

Edwards, P. K. (1990) 'Understanding Conflict in the Labour Process: The Logic and Autonomy of Struggle', in D. Knights and H. Willmott (eds), *Labour Process Theory*, London: Macmillan.

Edwards, P. K. and Scullion, H. (1982) *The Social Organisation of Industrial Conflict: Control and Resistance in the Workplace*, Oxford: Blackwell.

Edwards, R. (1979) *Contested Terrain: The Transformation of the Workplace in the Twentieth Century*, London: Heinemann.

Edwards, R., Reich, M. and Gordon, D. M. (1975) *Labour Market Segmentation*, Lexington, MA: D. C. Heath.

Etzioni, A. (1961) *A Comparative Analysis of Complex Organizations*, New York: Free Press.

Fernie, S. and Metcalf, D. (1997) '(Not) Hanging on the Telephone: Payment Systems in the New Sweatshops', *Centre for Economic Performance*, London: London School of Economics.

Fevre, R. (1986) 'Contract Work in the Recession', in K. Purcell, S. Wood, A. Watson and S. Allen (eds), *The Changing Experience of Employment, Restructuring and Recession*, London: Macmillan.

Fligstein, N. (1990) *The Transformation of Corporate Control*, Cambridge, MA: Harvard University Press.

Fleming, P. (2001) 'Beyond the Panopticon?', *Ephemera*, 1. 2: 190–4.

Fleming, P. (2005) 'Workers Playtime: Boundaries and Cynicism in a "Culture of Fun" Program', *The Journal of Applied Behavioral Science*, 41. 3: 285–303.

Fleming, P. and Spicer, A. (2002) 'Working at a Cynical Distance: Implications for Power, Subjectivity and Resistance', *Organization*, 10: 157–79.

Frenkel, S., Korczynski, M., Donohue, L. and Shire, K. (1995) 'Re-Constituting Work', *Work, Employment and Society*, 9. 4: 773–96.

Frenkel, S., Korczynski, M., Shire, K. and Tam, M. (1999) *On the Front Line: Pattern of Work Organisation in Three Advanced Societies*, Ithaca, NY: Cornell University Press.

Friedman, A. (1977) *Industry and Labour: Class Struggle at Work Monopoly Capitalism*, London: Macmillan.

Friedman, A. (1987) 'The Means of Management Control and Labour Process Theory: A Critical Note on Storey', *Sociology*, 21. 2: 287–94.

Garrahan, P. and Stewart, P. (1992) *The Nissan Enigma: Flexibility at Work in a Local Economy*, London: Mansett.

Glenn, E. K. and Feldberg, R. L. (1979) 'Proletarianising Office Work', in A. Zimbalist (ed.), *Case Studies on the Labour Process*, New York: Monthly Review Press.

Goodrich, C. (1975) *The Frontier of Control*, London: Pluto.

Gordon, D. M., Edwards, R. and Reich, M. (1982) *Segmented Work, Divided Workers*, Cambridge: Cambridge University Press.

Grieco, M. and Whipp, R. (1985) 'Women and Control in the Workplace: Gender and Control in the Workplace', in D. Knights and H. Willmott (eds), *Job Redesign: Critical Perspectives on the Labour Process*, Aldershot: Gower.

Grimshaw, J. (1986) *Feminist Philosophers*, Brighton: Wheatsheaf.

Grint, K. (1995) *Management: A Sociological Introduction*, Oxford: Polity.

Grossman, R. (1979) 'Women's Place in the Integrated Service', *Radical America*, 14. 1: 29–48.

Hales, C. P. (1988) 'Management Processes, Management Divisions of Labour and Managerial Work: Towards a Synthesis', paper presented to the Conference on the Labour Process, Aston-UMIST.

Hales, C. (2000) 'Management and Empowerment Programmes', *Work, Employment and Society*, 14. 3: 501–19.

Harris, R. (1987) *Power and Powerlessness in Industry: An Analysis of the Social Relations of Production*, London: Tavistock.

Hodson, R. (1995) 'Worker Resistance: An Underdeveloped Concept in the Sociology of Work', *Economic and Industrial Democracy*, 16: 79–110.

Hodson, R. (2001) *Dignity at Work*, Cambridge: Cambridge University Press.

Holland, S. (1975) *The Socialist Challenge*, London: Quartet.

Huczynski, A. A. (1993) *Management Gurus*, London: Routledge.

Hyman, R. (1987) 'Strategy or Structure: Capital, Labour and Control', *Work, Employment and Society*, 1. 1: 25–55.

Johnston, L. (1986) *Marxism, Class Analysis and Socialist Pluralism*, London: Allen & Unwin.

Kamoche, K. (1994) 'A Critique and a Proposed Reformulation of Strategic Human Resource Management', *Human Resource Management Journal*, 4. 4: 29–47.

Kelly, J. E. (1985) 'Management's Redesign of Work', in D. Knights, H. Willmott and D. Collinson (eds), *Job Redesign: Critical Perspectives on the Labour Process*, Aldershot: Gower.

Kelly, J. (2005) 'Labour Movements and Mobilization', in S. Ackroyd, R. Batt, P. Thompson and Pamela Tolbert (eds), *The Oxford Handbook of Work and Organization*, Oxford, Oxford University Press.

Lawlor, E. E. (1976) 'Control Systems in Organizations', in H. D. Dunnette (ed.), *Handbook of Industrial and Organisational Psychology*, Chicago: Rand McNally.

Littler, C. R. and Salaman, G. (1982) 'Bravermania and Beyond', *Sociology*, 132: 33–47.

McKinlay, A. and Taylor, P. (1996) 'Power, Surveillance and Resistance: Inside the Factory of the Future', in P. Ackers, C. Smith and P. Smith (eds), *The New Workplace and Trade Unionism*, London: Routledge.

Maguire, M. (1986) 'Recruitment as a Means of Control', in K. Purcell, S. Wood, A. Watson and S. Allen (eds), *The Changing Experience of Employment, Restructuring and Recession*, London: Macmillan.

Martinez, Lucio, M. and Stewart, P. (1997) 'The Paradox of Contemporary Labour Process Theory: The Rediscovery of Labour and the Decline of Collectivism', *Capital and Class*, 62: 49–77.

Melling, J. (1982) 'Men in the Middle or Men on the Margin', in D. Dunkerley and G. Salaman (eds), *The International Yearbook of Organisation Studies 1981*, London: Routledge & Kegan Paul.

Miller, P. and O'Leary, T. (1987) 'The Entrepreneurial Order', paper presented to the Conference on the Labour Process, Aston-UMIST.

Morgan, G. and Hooper, D. (1987) 'Corporate Strategy, Ownership and Control', *Sociology*, 21. 4: 609–27.

Murray, P. and Wickham, J. (1985) 'Women Workers and Bureaucratic Control in Irish Electronic Factories', in H. Newby (ed.), *Restructuring Capital, Reorganisation in Industrial Society*, London: Macmillan.

O'Reilly, C. A. and Chatman, J. A. (1996) 'Culture as Social Control: Corporations, Cults and Commitment', in B. M. Staws and L. L. Cummings (eds), *Research in Organisational Behaviour*, 18: 157–200, Greenwich, Conn.: JAI.

Parker, M. and Slaughter, J. (1988b) *Choosing Sides: Unions and the Team Concept, Labor Notes*, Boston, MA: South End Press.

Pearson, R. (1986) 'Female Workers in the First and Third Worlds: The "Greening" of Women's Labour', in K. Purcell, S. Wood, A. Watson and S. Allen (eds), *The Changing Experience of Employment, Restructuring and Recession*, London: Macmillan.

Pfeffer, J. (1997) *New Directions for Organisational Theory: Problems and Practices*, Oxford: Oxford University Press.

Pollard, S. (1965) *The Genesis of Modern Management*, London: Edward Arnold.

Pollert, A. (1981) *Girls, Wives, Factory Lives*, London: Macmillan.

Porter, M. (1980) *Competitive Strategy*, New York: Free Press.

Purcell, J. and Sissons, K. (1983) 'A Strategy for Management Control in Industrial Relations', in J. Purcell and R. Smith (eds), *The Control of Work*, London: Macmillan.

Ray, C. A. (1986) 'Corporate Culture: the Last Frontier of Control?' *Journal of Management Studies*, 23. 3: 287–97.

Rose, M. (1975, 1986) *Industrial Behaviour*, Harmondsworth: Penguin.

Rose, M. and Jones, B. (1985) 'Managerial Strategy and Trade Union Responses in Work Reorganization Schemes at Establishment Level', in D. Knights, H. Wilmott and D. Collinson (eds), *Job Redesign: Critical Perspectives on the Labour Process*, London: Gower.

Schein, E. H. (1965) *Organisational Psychology*, Englewood Cliffs, N.J.: Prentice Hall (also 1980, 3rd edn.).

Scott, J. (1985) 'Ownership, Management and Strategic Control', in K. Elliot and P. Lawrence (eds), *Introducing Management*, Harmondsworth: Penguin.

Sewell, G. (1998) 'The Discipline of Teams: The Control of Team-Based Industrial Work Through Electronic and Peer Surveillance', *Administrative Science Quarterly*, 43: 406–69.

Sewell, G. and Wilkinson, B. (1992) ' "Someone to Watch over Me": Surveillance, Discipline and the Just-in-Time Labour Process', *Sociology*, 26. 2: 271–89.

Shaw, M. (1990) 'Strategy and Social Process: Military Context and Sociological Analysis', *Sociology*, 24. 3: 465–73.

Steiner, T. and Miner, B. (1978) *Management Policy and Strategy*, West Drayton: Collier-Macmillan.

Storey, J. (1985) 'The Means of Management Control', *Sociology*, 19. 2: 193–211.

Streek, W. (1987) 'The Uncertainties of Management in the Management of Uncertainty: Employers, Labour Relations and Industrial Adjustment in the 1980s', *Work, Employment and Society*, 1. 3: 281–308.

Sturdy, A. and Fineman, S. (2001) 'Struggles for the Control of Affect: Resistance as Politics of Emotion', in Sturdy, I. Grugulis and H. Willmott (eds), *Customer Service: Empowerment and Entrapment*, Basingstoke: Palgrave Macmillan.

Taylor, P. and Bain, P. (1998). 'An Assembly Line in the Head: The Call Centre Labour Process', *Industrial Relations Journal*, 30. 2: 101–17.

Taylor, P. and Bain, P. (2003) 'Subterranean Worksick Blues: Humour as Subversion in Two Call Centres', *Organization Studies*, 24. 9: 1487–1509.

Taylor, S. (1998) 'Emotional Labour and the New Workplace', in P. Thompson and C. Warhurst (eds), *Workplaces of the Future*, London: Macmillan.

Thompson, P. (1989) *The Nature of Work: An Introduction to Debates on the Labour Process*, London: Macmillan.

Thompson, P. (2003b) 'Fantasy Island: A Labour Process Critique of the "Age of Surveillance"', *Surveillance and Society*, 1. 2: 138–51.

Thompson, P. and Ackroyd, S. (1995) 'All Quiet on the Workplace Front: A Critique of Recent Trends in British Industrial Sociology', *Sociology*, 29. 4: 615–33.

Thompson, P. and Harley, B. (2007) 'HRM and the Worker: Labour Process Perspectives', in P. Boxall, J. Purcell and P. Wright (eds), *The Oxford Handbook of Human Resource Management*, Oxford: Oxford University Press.

Thompson, P., van den Broek, D. and Callaghan, G. (2004) 'Teams without Teamwork: Explaining the Call Centre Paradox', *Economic and Industrial Democracy*, 25. 2: 197–218.

Thurley, K. and Wood, S. (1983) *Industrial Relations and Management Strategy*, Cambridge: Cambridge University Press.

Tichy, N., Fombrun, C. and Devanna, M. A. (1982) 'Strategic Human Resource Management', *Sloan Management Review*: 47–61.

Tomlinson, J. (1982) *The Unequal Struggle? British Socialism and the Capitalist Enterprise*, London: Methuen.

Wallace, C. (1993) ' Reflections on the Concept of "Strategy"', in D. Morgan and L. Stanley (eds), *Debates in Sociology*, Manchester: Manchester University Press.

Walton, R. E. (1985) 'Towards a Strategy of Eliciting Employee Commitment Based on Policies of Mutuality', in R. E. Walton and P. R. Lawrence (eds), *Human Resource Management, Trends and Challenges*, Boston, MA: Harvard University School Press.

Waterman, R. H. (1988) *The Renewal Factor*, London: Bantam.

Watson, T. (1994) *In Search of Management: Culture, Chaos and Control in Managerial Work*, London: Routledge.

Westwood, S. (1984) *All Day, Every Day: Factory and Family in the Making of Women's Lives*, London: Pluto.

Whipp, R. (1996) 'Creative Deconstruction: Strategy and Organisations', in S. Clegg, C. Hardy and W. Nord (eds), *Handbook of Organisation Studies*, London: Sage.

Wilkinson, B. (1986) 'Human Resources in Singapore's Second Industrial Revolution', *Industrial Relations Journal*, 17. 2: 99–114.

Witz, A. (1986) 'Patriarchy and the Labour Market: Occupational Controls and the Medical Division of Labour', in D. Knights and H. Willmott (eds), *Managing the Labour Process*, Aldershot: Gower.

Wood, S. (ed.) (1982) *The Degradation of Work: Skill, Deskilling and the Labour Process*, London: Hutchinson.

Zeitlin, M. (1974) 'Corporate Ownership and Control: The Large Corporation and the Capitalist Class', *American Journal of Sociology*, 79. 5: 1073–119.

Zimbalist, A. (ed.) (1979) *Case Studies on the Labour Process*, New York: Monthly Review Press.

Zuboff, S. (1988) *In the Age of the Smart Machine: The Future of Work and Power*, Oxford: Heinemann.

INDEX

Printed and bound by CPI Group (UK) Ltd, Croydon, CR0 4YY